How Young Ladies Became Girls

How Young Ladies Became Girls

The Victorian Origins of American Girlhood

JANE H. HUNTER

Yale University Press/New Haven & London

Published with assistance from the Louis Stern Memorial Fund.

Designed by Mary Valencia.
Set in Adobe Garamond type by Tseng Information Systems, Inc.
Printed in the United States of America by Edwards Brothers, Inc.

Library of Congress Cataloging-in-Publication Data
Hunter, Jane (Jane H.)
How young ladies became girls : the victorian origins of American girlhood / Jane H. Hunter.
   p.   cm.
Includes bibliographical references and index.
ISBN 0-300-09263-6 (cloth : alk. paper)
1. Middle class—Northeastern States—History—19th century.   2. Women—Northeastern States—History—19th century.   3. Girls—Northeastern States—History—19th century.
4. Home economics—Northeastern States—History—19th century.   I. Title.
HT690.U6 H86   2002
305.4′09746′4—dc21   2002006675

A catalogue record for this book is available from the British Library.

The paper in this book meets the guidelines for permanence and durability of the Committee on Production Guidelines for Book Longevity of the Council on Library Resources.

10 9 8 7 6 5 4 3 2 1

To
Eliza and Sukey

Contents

CONTENTS

Endings

Illustrations

Acknowledgments

Long projects accrue especially long lists of debts. Various grants and fellowships have provided critical time in the archives, and time to write, otherwise hard to come by in the context of growing family and teaching commitments. I am happy finally to be able to note the wonderful communities nourished at the Charles A. Murray Center and the Schlesinger Library at Radcliffe, and at the Eccles Humanities Center at the University of Utah, with special thanks to the late Lowell Durham and Kasey Grier. I also express appreciation to the National Endowment of the Humanities for its support.

A number of conscientious and resourceful research assistants have furthered this project, beginning with Lisa Cody, herself now a historian. As an undergraduate, Lisa threw herself into this project, fueling it with enthusiasm and energy. She has been followed by successive generations: Deb Wood and Kimberly Matthei at Colby College, and Robin Green at Lewis and Clark. I owe great thanks to my colleagues in the History Department and Gender Studies Program at Lewis and Clark College for the quality of their fellowship, and to our departmental administrator Robbie Roy. As History Department chair for the past six years, I know the full measure of indebtedness. I'd like to especially acknowledge the support of Jane Atkinson, Dinah Dodds, David Savage, and Jean Ward, deans and friends, who provided various resources, not least among them their faith in this project and its writer.

So many others have helped this project along the way. It was a lucky moment when I ran into Paul Curran in the Milford Room at the Milford (Massachusetts) Public Library and joined the club of people who have benefited from his generosity with his sources and his passion for Milford history. A long time ago, Sally A. Adams heard me give a talk and allowed me to read the diary of her mother, Anna Stevens. The late Peter Westervelt, a former colleague at Colby College, and his son, Benjamin Westervelt, a current colleague at Lewis and Clark College, offered me a chance to read the extraordinary diary of Fredrica Ballard (Westervelt) and use her picture. Nancy McGinnis of the Hubbard Free Library in Hallowell, Maine, trusted me with one of my favorite pictures, and Cyndy Hursty, director of alumni affairs and development at Bridgton Academy, looked for and scanned several Bridgton pictures of my grandmother, Edna Hill. At the Multnomah County Library in Portland, Oregon, Cindy Winter provided critical help at the last minute. The staffs of the Schlesinger Library, the Pusey Library, the New Hampshire Historical Society, the Reed College Library (where I have often found a quiet place to work), and the Lewis and Clark Library have all provided welcome help. I'd also like to acknowledge a hardworking group of technology wizards who created a flexible database for scholars back in the dark ages, and now represent the state of the art—the makers of Nota Bene. At Yale University Press, Dan Heaton's shrewd editing saved me from myself many times over.

I thank the following archives and libraries for permission to quote from materials in their holdings: the trustees of the Rare Books Department of the Boston Public Library for the Elizabeth M. Morrissey papers; the Massachusetts Historical Society for the Robert Apthorp Boit diaries; the Sisters of Charity of Nazareth, Kentucky, for the Murphy and Sloane reminiscences; Rutgers University Libraries, Special Collections, for the Bartine, Butler, Hardenburgh, and Wendover diaries; the Hargrett Rare Book and Manuscript Library of the University of Georgia for the Mary Thomas Lumpkin diary; the Sisters of St. Joseph of Carondolet for the reminiscences of Sister Wilfrida Hogan; the New Haven Colony Historical Society for the Ida Mabel Lancraft diaries; the Manuscripts and Archives Division, New York Public Library, Astor, Lenox, and Tilden Foundations, for the Florence C. Peck diaries, 1898–1903; the Ohio Historical Society for the Hanna A. Davis diary and the Rowena P. Cooke diary; the Sophia Smith Collection of Smith College for the Kate Upson [Clark] diaries and the Agnes Garrison diaries; the Tuck Library of the New Hampshire Historical Society for the Dolloff family papers and Mrs. J. Walter Skinner's record book; the Southern Historical Collection of the Wilson Library, University of North Carolina at Chapel Hill, for the Martha Josephine Moore diaries; and the Western Historical Manuscript Collection of Columbia, Missouri, for Almyra Hubbard [Viles]'s school journal.

I would especially like to thank the Schlesinger Library for the use of a number of collections: the papers of Annie Ware Winsor [Allen], the Mary Boit [Cabot] diaries, the Dana family papers, the Browne family papers, the Ethel Sturges Dummer papers, the Charlotte Perkins Gilman papers, the Harriet Wright Burton Laidlaw papers, the Nichols-Shurtleff family papers, the Lois Wells diary, the Emily Marshall Eliot [Morison] papers, the Hamilton family papers, and the Helen Marcia Hart diary. I also thank the Library of the University of Puget Sound for the use of materials in their collections.

I especially acknowledge permissions granted by heirs and family members to quote from personal papers. Here I thank Emily Brooks Beck for the Emily Eliot [Morison] papers, John T. Edsall for the Margaret Tileston [Edsall] papers, Nora Nellis for her unpublished collection "Daughter of the Valley: The 1840s Letters of Maria Nellis," Lisa Harris for papers from the Nichols-Shurtleff collection, Rosamond W. Dana for the Dana family papers, Harriet B. Todd for the Harriet Burton Laidlaw papers, and Jeanne Godfrey Stephenson and Elizabeth Godfrey Wetherbee for the Annie Roberts Godfrey diary.

I also acknowledge permission from libraries and museums to reproduce images under their purview: Bridgton Academy; the Harvard Archives; the Museum of Fine Arts, Boston; the New Hampshire Historical Society; and the Schlesinger Library, Radcliffe Institute.

I first met Donna B. Greenberg when we were both eighteen. Since then, as we journeyed well beyond girlhood, she has offered lodging, nourishing conversation, and camaraderie over years of research and writing. Hers has been a sustaining schoolgirl friendship. There are many kinds of nourishment, and writers also need readers. I would like to thank the Feminist Research Group and the Portland Americanists for reading early bits of this book. Later, the long-haulers were Elaine Maveety and Patricia Ramsey. A fiction writer and historian herself, Elaine scarcely knew what she was getting into when she offered to do some reading, but she brought a keen editorial eye to much of this book. Patty did know, and despite a daunting schedule, she responded generously, urging me on and offering observations about the contemporary resonances of this work.

I owe a special debt to Joel Bernard. He scouted books and articles, read and wrestled with trying text, and reminded me of larger intellectual issues when I was tempted to tunnel on through. Although this book is far from his current research, he has supported me loyally in this as in all our mutual projects. From their very beginnings, two lovely and spirited girls have grown up with this book. I once worried about finishing before Eliza Jacqueline and Susannah Louise Hunter Bernard reached adolescence, but of necessity I gave that worry up several years ago. Eliza is now in college and Sukey in high school. Their energy, grace, and humor have reminded me of the reasons for this book—and of its limitations.

How Young Ladies
Became Girls

Introduction

Writing in her diary in the fall of 1901, nineteen-year-old Florence Peck considered how truthful she had been in the records she had been keeping for imaginary readers. "I wonder now if they would know how full of old 'Nick' I am," she mused. "It never occurred to me to put down the various 'stunts' I do, yet they may be a part of my life."[1] Florence Peck had been keeping her diary for three years. It represented a record of her resolutions, her relations with her parents, her school successes, her graduation from Rochester High School that June, and especially her comings and goings with a lively group of friends. With her decision that her "stunts" belonged in her diary and were part of her life, she suggested an important evolution in her thinking about who she was, and what defined her.

Middle-class male youth had enjoyed a certain liberation from Victorian rectitude for the previous quarter-century. Novelists and critics concerned about a feminized American culture welcomed their "stunts" and play as a sign of healthy growth and celebrated their rebelliousness against the proprieties of Victorian matrons. If the books of such writers as Mark Twain authorized pranks for boys, though, they did not provide the same latitude for middle-class girls, for whom "being good" remained a consistent goal, however imperfectly met. If Tom and Huck pulled antics on the river and were loved for it, even on the banks of the Mississippi in the American hinterlands Twain's Becky Thatcher remained trapped. Twain confined her to being a good girl, with clean clothes and winning ways.

Although actual girls had more latitude than Becky Thatcher as long as they were still children, parents and advisers expected teenage girls to suppress childish spontaneity and to adopt the serviceable posture of young women. The most famous girl rebel, Louisa May Alcott's Jo March, whose clothing was often awry and her temper irascible, spent much of her energy trying to overcome her hoydenish ways so that she might eventually make her father proud as a good "little woman," a virtuous odyssey suffused with loss.[2]

Even as novelists and moralists continued to celebrate propriety and virtue as the goals for teenage girls, however, and even as girls attempted to represent their successes in meeting those goals in their diaries, that Victorian domestic world was breaking down. As girls attended school, strolled the city streets, met and flirted with friends, and visited bake shops, they came to reevaluate their lives, challenging the narrow terms with which they had measured value and meaning. Girls who had been to school often joined with male classmates to bond as a generation. And they came to question, as Florence Peck did, the orthodoxies of woman's moral sphere, which located girls of the middle class apart, and above, the hurly-burly, pleasure-seeking lives of the working class.

This book is about "girls" like Florence Peck who were on the cusp of change. (I use advisedly this contemporary term to describe female youth under the age of twenty.) Her age-class—comprising middle-class adolescent females—attended schools, kept diaries, tried to be good, went shopping, flirted, and participated in a cultural revolution over the course of the late nineteenth century. In this book I explore changing ideas of the female self of the sort that Peck acknowledged. Like other girls of her class and time, Peck aspired to womanliness, purity, and virtue. But also like girls of her class and time, she inhabited a vibrant coeducational peer culture filled with antics in the city streets. Her diary came to record both sides of her life, the conscience and virtue at the core of a "good" self and the fun and play at the periphery. Initially, activities with peers suggested only who she might appear to be, not who she really was. By 1901, though, schoolgirls like Florence Peck had begun to reconsider. Peck's realization that it was important for hypothetical readers to know that she was "full of old Nick" and to hear about her high jinks and indiscretions suggests a new notion of the self which had been evolving among teenage girls for as long as they attended school.

Girls' Experience: Negotiating Family and Peers

In both its emphasis on the significance of school attendance and its focus on girls' own words, this story modifies previous portraits of middle-class, urban girls. Based on girls' writings about their lives, it is a collective self-portrait which features girls as subjects rather than objects, as agents rather than as symbols within a world whose painters, writers, and commentators often supplied them with multiple, richly encoded meanings. The prescriptive literature of Victorianism in particular often seized upon girls as the apotheosis of that search for "sweetness and light" which represented the central Victorian project. Sentimental culture presented powerful images of self-sacrificing young women, setting aside selves in service to their families or the poor. Writers from Henry James to Rudyard Kipling and painters from Mary Cassatt to John Singer Sargent complicated this portrait, lingering and puzzling over the figure of the American girl, finding in her an appealing symbol of the age.

Serious historical treatment of girls of the middle class has also tended to see adolescent girls as objects, or as dependents of their families, maybe because of the strength attributed to their mothers. Historians see middle-class daughters and mothers in Anglo-American culture sharing a porous domesticity which left girls largely their mothers' creatures. The significance of this dependence has varied. Historians of domesticity have in general taken a positive view of this mother-daughter bond, presenting a female-centered, intergenerational world of harmony, where girls grew up gently within the home. As Mary Ryan put it some years ago, "the Victorian daughter enjoyed a privileged position in a feminine universe where with relatively little trauma and at an easy pace, she learned her adult gender role from her mother." Historians of medicine have documented a negative side to this solicitude, instead stressing the costs of dependence in Victorian families and describing how constrained, inhibited lives provided the seedbed for genuine illness among an emblematic minority.[3]

Whether viewing middle-class girls' domestic dependence positively or negatively, historians have found their subjects most interesting and alive in their rich interiors. The cultural studies scholar Nancy Armstrong, writing about Britain, has suggested indeed that the modern "interior" self emerged among novel-reading women and girls. These readers, according to Armstrong, developed private and passionate sensibilities in their reading, which they kept carefully concealed from the larger world by a controlled and appropriate social demeanor.[4] This study bears out the richness and the activity of girls' interior lives, both within their hearts and within their homes.

In focusing so fully on middle-class Victorian girls' identities within the family, though, the historical literature has overlooked another arena of their lives, also revealed in their diaries. This was the peer culture of school. Middle-class, native-born girls in the urban Northeast—that group we most often identify as Victorian daughters—were exactly that same group who more and more frequently *went* to school. School attendance increased gradually during the late nineteenth century, reaching its highest ratio in northeast cities among the native-born. One set of statistics for Providence, Rhode Island, indicates that roughly a third of the daughters of native white parents (and a quarter of the sons) were enrolled in high school in 1880. That group was defined largely by class.[5] The decision to send a daughter to secondary school was born out of social aspirations for daughters, the result of a family decision to grant girls freedom from the hard work of domestic upkeep so that they might embody the gentility which signified refinement. Enrollment at rural academies and public high schools also prepared girls for respectable work as schoolteachers.

The nineteenth-century school was essentially a peer culture, like its twentieth-century successor, and presented a strong challenge to the influence of maternal domesticity. Within private, female boarding academies, duty-bound Victorian daughters learned languages of desire and emotional excess censored from other parts of their lives. They struck up relationships with peers which flowered into a full-blown sentimental culture less likely to flourish within the trying disciplines of home. In contrast, coeducational public high schools and rural academies were bracing meritocracies which stressed competition. They pitted girl students in direct competition with each other, and sometimes with boys, for grades which were often publicly posted. When classroom seats were assigned on the basis of class rank, as they often were, it became impossible for anyone to escape for a moment the competitive, hierarchical, and individualized basis for success in the nineteenth-century school.

One consequence of this empirical system of classroom grading was that girls and boys in this one arena of their lives found themselves judged on the same scale. Often girls outperformed boys, winning many of the graduation honors—a statistical likelihood given the numerical predominance of girls in public high schools. Whatever the debates about the consequences and capacities of girls for higher learning, these classroom numbers could earn girls the heady respect of boys with whom they otherwise shared little common ground. The drama of a competitive meritocracy, especially for those it rewarded, presented a forceful counter to the familial program for producing obliging daughters who had learned to subordinate individual will.

School attendance structured girls' time outside of school hours as well. Walking to and from school in company with peers, girls as well as boys inhabited the public space of cities and towns. (Remarking on this phenomenon in around 1880, Henry James commented in dismay that at some times in Boston, schoolgirls were so numerous and free as to be "in possession of the public scene."[6]) Sometimes equipped with regular allowances—like other Victorian regimens, considered valuable training in self-discipline—middle-class girls participated avidly in the late-century explosion in consumerism, visiting bake shops, soda fountains, and other commercial emporiums. Although mothers accompanied them in making larger purchases, girls' growing freedom to indulge themselves in small transactions marked a substantial break with an economy of self-denial otherwise advocated for girls' domestic lives. Freed from the constant scrutiny of adults, these girls created a culture which allowed for a greater sense of fun and play than their elders encouraged. School attendance played a large role in the emergence of a "new girl," less sober and intellectual than the New Woman, but her significant precursor.

Fears of Precocity and the Extension of Girlhood

There was an irony in this outcome. Adults concerned about girls at mid-century had hoped that school would help to counter an alarming trend, the increasing precocity of young girls. As girls matured earlier over the course of the century, their bodies came to serve as the locus for growing social anxiety about the impact of modern life. Increasingly, responsible adults began to devise strategies for protecting girls from urban ways. The historian Joseph Kett, looking back on this concern about protecting girls from adulthood, has noted that middle-class Victorian girls were "the first adolescents," the first youth granted a special status free from adult work and responsibilities.[7] Sending girls to school, initially at least, represented an effort to encourage their refinement but also to keep them from growing up too soon. From his perspective in the 1950s the psychologist Erik Erickson described an adolescent "moratorium" on the assumption of adult roles. Whether or not Victorians would have recognized his description, his terminology accords well with both girls' school experience and adult ambitions for middle-class Victorian girls.

The language of girlhood evolved over the century to reflect the significance of school in setting its parameters. Initially, at midcentury, the correct term for middle-class females after menarche was *young lady.* The term *girl* suggested the subordinate status of either a prepubescent child or a domestic laborer, or it was faintly sexualized. Over the nineteenth century, however, the term extended its reach through menarche and the years of secondary school. School attendance was a critical part of the construction of this modern version of girlhood. Our contemporary term for the stage of life beginning with puberty and ending with the departure from school—*adolescence*—did not emerge until the twentieth century, and included boys as well.[8] In defining this modern life-stage, girls led the way.

The school experience of girls in Victorian America had two plotlines and two interpretations, depending on who analyzes it. Both adults and youth saw it as a time apart from adulthood, when youths might usefully occupy themselves with activities appropriate and unique to their age group. Most adults saw schooling as simply a life-stage, however, with rules and expectations which lasted only as long as school itself. When school ended and girls went home, as one father put it to his reluctant daughter in 1859, they would need to surrender their identities as "mere school girls" and prepare to assume their status as "true women" in the "drama of life."[9] Girls themselves, however, especially graduates of the coeducational academies and high schools of the late century, could not and did not accept this life narrative. Their school experiment changed their senses of who they were. "New" girls of the late-century high school, carrying fresh memories of their right to full membership in their generation, could not go home to become "family possessions" or parlor ornaments. Many of them went out to work first, frequently as school-teachers for some years before marriage. In so doing, they changed not just themselves but American culture.

Sources

This book addresses large questions, whose answers come not primarily in aggregates but as a mosaic. Interested as I am in identity, I turn to the voices of girls themselves, drawing on diaries and letters composed by girls between the ages of ten and twenty, living primarily in the urban Northeast. These individual stories together constitute a pattern, even as they vary in nuance. Their primary principle of cohesion, however, is not geographical. Together they compose a "youth" voice within a shared Victorian culture. In the introduction to an edited volume on children's history, the historians Elliott West and Paula Petrik make the case that "children think differently from adults; they address the world around them in ways their elders find at least puzzling and sometimes impenetrable. . . . The difference between scholar and subject is not just cultural; it is also cognitive."[10] One of the goals of this book is to capture the voices of these thinking youths as they integrated parental and cultural expectations with the new possibilities of their world.

Victorian itself, of course, is a contested and complex term which in the United States has connotations of gender, class, and region. "Victorians"—those who participated in a trans-Atlantic culture of literacy and uplift—

were disproportionately white and female, clustered in the middle and upper classes and the Northeast. Yet the precepts and aspirations of Victorianism spread beyond those focal groups and influenced many of those on the frontiers, many second-generation immigrants in the cities, and a new African-American bourgeoisie pursuing a "politics of respectability." (One of that bourgeoisie recalled the formation of her "ideals" on the Victorian reading diet for girls.) Girls in the South and the West who did not attend school might still have been influenced by aspirations initially promoted in New York, London, or Boston. The girls whose voices are heard here reflect this Victorian constituency. They lived predominantly in the urban Northeast and were likely to be from comfortable, even elite, native-born families. Their diaries were primarily archived in New England. A modicum of leisure helped to define both their lives and their diaries and contributed to the formation of a "Victorian" sensibility. Although all Victorian girls had chores, those represented here were not "working," either at shops, in factories, or as mainstays of the domestic workforce. Most were attending school. Thus included here, along with the journals of members of the Boston elite, is the schoolgirl journal of Lizzie Morrissey, second-generation Irish from East Boston. Although Lizzie Morrissey's family employed no servants, Lizzie herself wrote an extensive diary in which she described watching the toils of mother and grandmother, excused from helping by her attendance at Girls' High School and by the family aspirations she embodied.[11] The Victorian ideal for girlhood—like Victorianism itself—cast its influence well beyond those whose prosperity originally occasioned it.

Some girlhood documents were particularly rich and full, of course, and I have used them proportionately. Margaret Tileston, for instance, appears frequently in this text, sometimes as the focus of an entire subsection. The daughter of well-educated but erratic Bostonians, Tileston was an unusually faithful diarist, writing daily throughout her life, beginning at the age of eleven. I do not claim that she speaks for all girls of her class and region. At the same time, she provides points of internal comparison which prove revealing of broader themes. The contrast of her experiences of girls' boarding schools and coeducational public high school, in particular, provides an especially sharp demonstration of differences which emerge elsewhere in the literature. In addition, I have used high school newspapers archived in public libraries in a number of communities in the Northeast and around the country. Written in longhand at midcentury, by the 1880s and 1890s newspapers produced by high school students were printed on the novelty presses newly affordable following the Civil War and were exchanged for common viewing.

Student-written and -edited, these papers provide invaluable windows into late-Victorian youth culture.

I have also consulted the abundant and important advice literature which has defined Victorian culture until the recent past. The Victorian prescriptive literature did not describe reality, in fact, but serves as a valuable inverse portrait of the age; its strident exhortations suggest just what was in danger of being lost. The anxieties about precocity accompanying lowering ages of menarche constitute only one such example. It would be a mistake, however, to underestimate the impact of this literature, which initially constructed the idealized Victorian girl and remained a force in the lives of many real girls. The written word packed considerable authority, and girls who read the counsel of Mary Virginia Terhune and Elizabeth Oakes Smith, or received it mediated by parents and teachers, fretted about their inadequacies. Particularly provocative were the columns of Ruth Ashmore, a pseudonym for Isabel Mallon, whose "Side Talks with Girls" were published in the *Ladies' Home Journal* in the 1880s and 1890s. Confidential and inflexible, Ashmore vigorously defended Victorian propriety before all comers, providing a rich counterpoint to the changing life experiences of many middle-class girls. Periodical fiction also struggled to hold back the erosion of traditional gender mores, as represented pointedly in a story published in a children's magazine entitled simply "She Couldn't: A Story for Big Girls." As they wrote diaries, made friends, went to school, consumed chocolates, and sparred with boys, girls of the late-Victorian middle class never entirely forgot that constraining message. This book, however, is about how girls supplemented that message with "She Could."

Work

ONE

Daughters' Lives and the Work of the Middle-Class Home

At some point in the nineteenth century, middle- and upper-middle-class daughters of the urban Northeast stopped doing substantial housework. Certainly they continued to have regular chores, to bear responsibility for tidying their rooms, picking the beans, or dusting the parlor, but girls of the new urban middle class lost the function that earlier farm girls of "the middling sort" had had as linchpins of the domestic workforce. Just as the move from the farm meant the movement of men out of the households and into urban shops or businesses, so did urbanization pull girls of a certain means away from their mothers' sides and disrupt their domestic apprenticeships. The disappearance of girls as central figures in the domestic workforce—the result of developments in the economy, public schooling, and the domestic sphere—simultaneously marginalized and liberated them. In subsequent chapters I describe and evaluate the new status that they came to occupy, both what emerged to fill time created by the loss of home work, and the consequences of that change for subsequent women's and cultural history. But first it is important to understand which girls stopped working, where and when.

The freeing of middle-class daughters was in part the continuation of the process begun in New England with the moving of much manufacturing out of the home and into factories. The opening of large cotton and woolen mills in towns such as Lowell and Waltham, Massachusetts, meant that by the 1830s fine, factory-woven cloth was beginning to make home-weaving obsolete. Cloth manufacture had traditionally been the work of unmarried daughters (as the term *spinster* suggests), and industrialists hired some of the daughters they displaced when they appropriated their work.

But there was plenty of work left behind when cloth manufacture moved from the home to the factory—the routine jobs connected with heating homes, stoking cookstoves, preparing foodstuffs, cleaning lamps, doing laundry. Historians have eloquently demonstrated the continued magnitude of women's home work well after the weaving of cloth was mechanized in factories.[1] Traditionally, all this too had been daughters' work—work done by girls assisting their mothers in maintaining a household. Families without daughters hired the extra daughters of neighbors to assist in the "daily round," such that "helping" was a traditional part of the life course for many girls. In much of rural America from the eighteenth century into the twentieth, daughters still filled these roles, growing up gently at their mothers' sides in domestic apprenticeship.

The same economy which spawned mills, though, also created a growing commercial class with new affluence and aspirations. Increasingly, daughters of this expanding capitalist elite found themselves without a job. Parents of the new bourgeoisie cultivated their daughters to embody the refinement and leisure that they were too busy to practice themselves. As they promoted higher standards for household decorum, families released their daughters from manual labor, delegating them to enhance the family's cultural and social standing, and hiring servants rather than neighbors' daughters to do the household's work. The precursor for this form of domestic labor was the "bound" service of indentured servants or slaves, who performed the menial domestic labor of the colonies, north and south, in the eighteenth century and before. Such servants occupied a distinct and inferior social position in the family and in the social order.[2] Over the course of the nineteenth century, cities on the northeast seaboard grew, as did their commercial elites, and the aristocratic practice of hiring domestic servants of a different class and status—not the sharing of daughters—came to characterize middle-class, urban life in general.

Catharine Beecher Attempts to Halt the Tide

In 1841 Catharine Beecher wrote a famous household manual entitled *A Treatise on Domestic Economy,* which was directed to that commercial elite. Intended "for the use of Young Ladies at Home, and at School," it was an attempt to reverse the trend of freeing daughters from housework, instead calling for their renewed training in housewifery. Designed to restore to all ranks of society the virtue of industrious, republican women, Beecher's treatise has been regarded by historians as an influential text in promoting a cult of domesticity, elevating the home as a source of civic significance. They may be right in assessing the broader significance of Beecher's tract, but they have generally not noted that it failed in its announced primary goal: the reformation of the education of daughters.

Beecher dedicated her treatise to elite mothers in the hopes that they would set a national example. "Whatever ladies in the wealthier classes decide shall be fashionable, will be followed by all the rest," she suggested. And she hoped that those mothers would reject ornamental education for their daughters and put them to work at home. She went so far as to enumerate chores which "should be done by the daughters of a family, and not by hired service." They included "all the sweeping, dusting, care of furniture and beds, the clear starching, and the nice cooking"—the lighter, and less arduous jobs of domestic upkeep. Despite all the merits of her arguments, she admitted that she would despair of the possibility of such a revolution in the raising of daughters, but for one fact: "the dearth of good domestics in this country." The relative attractiveness of work in the mills and in the new occupation of schoolteaching was making it difficult to find native-born farm girls to work in service. Beecher claimed that already "necessity is driving mothers to do what abstract principles of expediency never could secure," and causing them to train their own daughters to do household work.[3]

Irish Immigration and the Work of Middle-Class Girls

Even as Beecher's book began to circulate, however, environmental disaster in Ireland was preparing to spare elite women the need of putting their own daughters to work around the house. In the 1840s the potato harvest failed for several years in a row, and young unmarried Irish women flocked to the United States in search of escape and a way to assist families back home. Irish immigration brought more women than men to the United States, most of them single, helping to create new patterns of domestic servitude in the cities of the eastern seaboard. By midcentury 70 percent of domestic servants in Boston were Irish-born.[4] The Irish influx not only replaced native-born "helpers." Irish labor replaced middle-class daughters as well.

When Catharine Beecher decided it was time to put out a new edition of her manual on housework, she enlisted the coauthorship of her sister, Harriet Beecher Stowe, and reflected the new realities of domestic labor in the bourgeois home. *The American Woman's Home* (1869) was not directed to daughters nor dedicated to their mothers. The Beechers seemed to have acknowledged defeat in their efforts to transform the education of native-born

girls. Rather, in its first paragraphs, *The American Home* protested the degradation of household service, as paid work. Because of women's failure to be
trained "as men are trained for their trades and professions," "family labor is
poorly done, poorly paid, and regarded as menial and disgraceful."[5] In 1841
Catharine Beecher had pinned her hopes for the enhancement of domesticity
on educating native-born daughters; in 1869 she and her sister instead seemed
to feel the best bet lay in recruiting better paid help.

Their account included some elegiac historical analysis missing from the
1841 version about what had happened both to the notion of domestic service
and to the upbringing of daughters. Clearly the two histories had diverged.
Beecher and Stowe's *American Home* paid nostalgic tribute to the nearly lost,
and glorious, republican tradition of "helping." "In America," they wrote,
"there was a society of educated workers, where all were practically equal,
and where, if there was a deficiency in one family and an excess in another, a
helper, not a servant in the European sense, was hired." But domestic service
had not retained these republican possibilities, instead becoming tainted by
"something of the influence from feudal times, and from the near presence of
slavery in neighboring states"; the result was "a universal rejection of domestic service in all classes of American-born society." Most significant to their
story, "the well-taught, self-respecting daughters of farmers, the class most
valuable in domestic service, gradually retired from it."[6]

At the same time that "these remarkable women of old" withdrew from
paid service, daughters relinquished home labors. The Beecher sisters waxed
lyrical on the subject of "families of daughters, handsome, strong women,
rising each day to their in-door work with cheerful alertness—one to sweep
the room, another to make the fire," chatting "meanwhile of books, studies,
embroidery . . . the last new poem," spinning "with the book tied to the dis-
taff." Instead, they noted that "the race of strong, hardy, cheerful girls, that
used to grow up in country places, and made the bright, neat New-England
kitchens of old times . . . is daily lessening; and in their stead come the fragile, easily-fatigued, languid girls of a modern age, drilled in book-learning,
ignorant of common things."[7]

Both the first and the enhanced edition of Catharine Beecher's guide to
domestic life included portraits of the excessively refined daughter, ignorant
of the mundane details of home life, ill-equipped to take on the burdens of
home management. The difference was that in 1841 Beecher associated that
profile with an aristocracy, an elite she had hopes of reforming. By 1869, instead, the Beechers dropped the class reference, instead alluding simply to
"modern" girls, the girls of a new urban order. Many historians have noted

the problems in studying the rise of a class that did not name itself but instead universalized its experience. In referring to "modern" girls, Beecher and Stowe demonstrated how the habits of an aristocracy had been generalized as those of a new middle class. The "great problem of life here in America" was that "the modern girls, as they have been brought up, can not perform the labor of their own families as in those simpler, old-fashioned days." "What is worse" about the education of girls, they wrote, is that "they have no practical skill with which to instruct servants, who come to us, as a class, raw and untrained."[8] As described by Catharine Beecher and Harriet Beecher Stowe, the "American woman's home" in 1869 was not an elite but a middle-class, normative home. It relied on the work of foreign-born servants, and regrettably did not teach its daughters even enough about the running of a household to train those servants.

The Alcott Sisters

The daughters of improvident Concord philosopher Bronson Alcott and his long-suffering wife, Abigail, demonstrate the uneven course and reputation of domestic service as an occupation for native-born girls at midcentury. From the time she was seventeen, Louisa May Alcott's journals include accounts of how the family managed to get by, including her own money-making activities and those of her sisters and parents.

Louisa's sister Anna went off in 1850, at age seventeen, to be a nursemaid for a family friend. The letter of invitation to Anna's mother suggests an earlier rural model based on the paid exchange of daughters. Caroline Sturgis Tappan wrote to Abigail Alcott: "If Anna would like to come and help me take care of my baby, it would be much pleasanter for me, both for her sake and my own, than having a nursery maid, and I think Anna would find much to enjoy in Lenox." Caroline Tappan's letter declared, in fact, that if Anna would help her she would not even *be* a nursery maid, but instead a companion and friend. The next year, however, Louisa also entered service, and her experience followed another regimen—unmediated by family acquaintance, and perhaps influenced by new patterns in domestic service accompanying Irish immigration. Reports suggest that Louisa was used badly and that the entire family resented her treatment. She dug paths through the snow, fetched water from a well, split kindling, sifted ashes. She described this experience tersely in her summary notes and memoranda: "I go to Dedham as a servant and try it for a month, but get starved and frozen and give it up. $4,00." As those wages were actually for seven weeks' work, rather than the four she acknowledged in her memorandum, Louisa was badly paid. The experience clearly left a bad taste in her mouth; an Alcott biographer suggests that the Alcott family returned the wages in contempt and humiliation.⁹

Two years later, though, Louisa May again went out to service, this time "as second girl. I needed the change, could do the wash, and was glad to earn my $2 a week." Her willingness to repeat the experience so disastrous before probably resulted from a significant difference in circumstances. As when Anna had ventured out as a nursery maid, Louisa too was going into a known family—in this case a relative of her mother's who was a Unitarian minister in Leicester. By the 1850s, after the Irish potato immigration, there were two different ways to be a servant. As Louisa May Alcott's experience suggests, in the environment of Boston, the older model of egalitarian "helping" among acquaintances was giving way to a model in which relations between servant and mistress were not only hierarchical but often adversarial. By 1868 the Alcotts too had joined those dealing with the problems of hiring domestic help rather than being hired as servants. Louisa's journal noted that they were temporarily without "a girl."¹⁰

Even so, in her fiction, especially her 1873 novel *Work,* Alcott attempted to rescue the reputation of domestic service as a legitimate way for native-born girls to earn a living. In that novel, her heroine experiences both kinds of domestic labor. Alcott's idealized "situation," however, is a throwback to an earlier tradition of helping, in which her heroine not only is adopted by a Quaker woman so kindly "that mistress and maid soon felt like mother and daughter" but literally becomes a daughter, as she marries the eccentric son of the family. Her vocation is scarcely wage labor at all, a fact underlined by Christie's protestations that "she did not care for any other wages" than her place in her new family. Most significantly, Alcott felt that she could redeem domestic service only by impugning "shiftless" Irish servants.¹¹ If Alcott hoped to prettify her own bad experience with the proletarianization of domestic labor, her happy ending succeeded only in blaming the victim, as it removed her heroine from those now-degraded ranks.

Housework and Domestic Servants

Novels and household manuals written for the prosperous northeastern housewife certainly contain important clues to changing expectations for girls and for the work of the home. What can we glean from the statistical record about the prevalence of such homes? Those who have studied domestic service have confronted the difficulty in generating reliable statistics for what were frequently informal arrangements. The search for "help" of whatever kind was ongoing and erratic, and the evolution from one to another kind

1.1 Treated like "a new bonnet," 1873. In her novel *Work,* Alcott's heroine goes into service for a haughty employer who asks, "Are you an American?" Reprinted from Louisa May Alcott, *Work: A Story of Experience* (Boston: Roberts, 1873), 18.

of service uneven. Thus in 1878 one gentleman farmer's daughter described attending the wedding of two of their Irish servants at the priest's house, and later driving over with her father to a local farm "to try to get Hannah Moore to come and help us thanksgiving but she couldn't come; she gave us some nice dinner . . ."[12] Should Hannah Moore have been free, a census taker might well have discovered evidence of the persistence of the "helping" model in the 1870s within a fifty-mile radius of Boston, rather than the employ of Irish staff, which more usually characterized the running of the household.

Historians concur that live-in domestic service was primarily an urban phe-

1.2 Part of the family, 1873. Alcott can redeem domestic service only by returning her heroine to a domestic model of "helping." Reprinted from Alcott, *Work,* 4.

nomenon in the late nineteenth century. One estimate suggests that between 15 and 30 percent of northeastern city-dwellers hired live-in domestics. The historian David Katzman, who has generated the most refined statistics, demonstrates that even within relative geographical proximity, city-dwellers hired servants more often than did rural dwellers, and city-dwellers with large pools of foreign labor more than city-dwellers without. Nationwide at midcentury there was one domestic servant for every ten families, with a considerably higher ratio in large cities like Boston and New York. A greater proportion of Bostonians hired domestic servants than did residents of any other northern city, with 219 servants per thousand families. With traditions of household service born in slavery, even after the Civil War, the South led the nation in its reliance on domestic servants, with Atlanta in 1880 boasting 331 servants per thousand families. Even in the South, though, the difference between city and country was notable, with Atlanta in 1900 hiring four times as many servants per thousand families as in the rest of Georgia.[13]

Together these figures suggest the flourishing of an era in the history of

Victorianism. It was common for American bourgeois city-dwellers on the Atlantic seaboard, even ones of modest means, to rely on the labor of maids to sustain their households. Of course, the end of the story is popular cliché. With the opening of more lucrative and less degrading jobs for young women as sales clerks, "typewriters," and teachers, the "servant problem" became terminal, and by the First World War, American housewives could not depend on the hiring of live-in domestic help to assist them in their housework.[14] It is significant, though, that even when "necessity" suggested the reintegration of daughters into the domestic economy, they were gone for good. The culture had put girls to other uses, from which they would not return to their mothers' sides.

Daughters as Products

We still might ask why girls were often excused from domestic labor—especially given the compounding weight of the advice literature recommending otherwise. The answer lies in the increasing role played by daughters and servants in the bourgeois quest for refinement. Even when the gross number of live-in servants declined as production moved out of the home, the hiring of at least one domestic remained a prerequisite for middle-class status. The statistics on who hired servants bear out the middle-classness of this phenomenon, with 65 percent of servants in the Northeast in 1860 working in households with no other servants. In an increasingly mobile and prosperous society, hiring servants was one way to demonstrate standing, a concrete and conspicuous way of demonstrating what you had left behind. One historian argues that the cultural importance of servants should be measured in the amount that some less prosperous families were willing to spend to hire them—sometimes as much as one-third of family income.[15]

Clearly, the freeing of daughters from steady household work and the hiring of domestic servants of lesser, often foreign, status went in tandem with the changing purpose of the home itself. Eighteenth-century households had required helpers to assist in domestic production. The homes of the mid–nineteenth century elite instead featured housework "as the creation and maintenance of comfort and appearance," in the words of the historian Christine Stansell. As the Beecher sisters observed, families were increasing "in refinement" such that they no longer wished to live in close intimacy with "uncultured neighbors," far less daughters of foreign shores, who were working as servants. Thus one mill-owning family in rural Vermont made a point of hiring Irish help rather than the daughters of neighboring farmers, who might object to eating in the kitchen and expect to be "one of the family."[16]

Architects reflected such changes by midcentury, such that servants' quarters were designed as discrete parts of the house, with back stairs and separate entrances. Custom increasingly favored uniforms and servant dining tables in the kitchen.

At the same time that middle classes aspired to higher standards of comfort and appearance in accordance with new possibilities, women's primary responsibility shifted from the supervision of a household manufactory to family nurturance, the raising and socializing of children. Much has been written about the evolution of new ideals for motherhood following the American Revolution, as women gained responsibility for raising virtuous citizens. "Republican mothers" shaped new daughters as well as new sons. Initially considered necessary allies in the steady work of processing the stuff of survival, the daughters of middle-class families became themselves the prime products the home produced—the embodiment of the principles of sensibility and refinement.

Mothers' new responsibilities did not erase old ones. The historian Jeanne Boydston has appropriately criticized the readiness of her colleagues to mistake the ideology of domesticity for reality, arguing that by no means did the productive work of the home cease with the industrial revolution. Instead, Boydston argues, the emphasis on the emotional task of mothering tended to eclipse from view, but not eliminate, the continued real labor—the making of clothing, the putting up of preserves, the carrying of fuel—still carried on in the middle-class home. She is right in her argument that "paid domestic workers did not free the mistress of the household from labor." But even Boydston acknowledges that domestic servants instead did the work that would have been done by other females in the household—including adult female relatives and daughters.[17]

An interesting case in point is the urban family of woman's rights advocates Henry Blackwell, Lucy Stone, and their daughter Alice Stone Blackwell. As Boydston tells us, Lucy Stone, who was raised on a farm, still kept chickens, worked a garden, and tended a horse and cow, even as she lived a prosperous middle-class existence outside of Boston. Alice Blackwell later remembered that "she dried all the herbs and put up all the fruits in their season. She made her own yeast, her own bread, her own dried beef, even her own soap." In her lively diary, however, Alice Blackwell reports doing little household work. Such chores as emerge in her diary were designed to interrupt her incessant reading, which was thought to be responsible for her bad headaches. Thus her cousin, visiting the household, "had undertaken to find me something to do to stop my reading: churning; and I churned in the cellar till the butter came."[18]

In fact, advice writers who had failed in their efforts to promote domestic work for daughters on other grounds often focused on the value of domestic labor as a source of exercise. The Beecher sisters observed that if girls did strenuous housework, their parents would be spared the expense of gymnasiums. "Does it not seem poor economy to pay servants for letting our muscles grow feeble, and then to pay operators to exercise them for us?" Louisa May Alcott, whose collected opus represents a powerful gloss on the domestic debates of late-Victorianism, repeatedly suggested the healthfulness of housework, "the best sort of gymnastics for girls," according to Dr. Alec in *Eight Cousins*. Her *Old-Fashioned Girl* explicitly contrasts the healthy republican daughter skilled in domestic arts with the languid late-Victorian belle, afflicted with boredom because of her lack of home chores.[19] Mothers undoubtedly continued both to supervise and perform much household maintenance, but they did so assisted by domestics rather than their own daughters.

What did middle-class girls do instead of housework? This was a question which greatly concerned commentators, who asked, as did Mary Livermore in 1883, "What shall we do with our daughters?" Mary Virginia Terhune, too, lamented the passing of housework as girls' raison d'être and with it "that prime need of a human being—something to do." Parents found a range of things for daughters to do, including the ornamental skills of sewing, playing piano, writing and reading associated with self-culture. Increasingly, also, they sent daughters to school.[20]

Common schools designed for both sexes did not include sewing. In later years, the Beecher sisters observed, "A girl often can not keep pace with her class, if she gives any time to domestic matters." And they noted, "Accordingly she is excused from them all during the whole term of her education." Girls themselves noted the increasing power of lessons in any competition with housework. Agnes Hamilton remarked that first her French tutor and then her German homework prevented her from doing her "share of Monday's work."[21] It was not long before the work of some girls was reassigned.

Those who were serious about domestic education, such as a composer of "An Ideal Education of Girls" that appeared in an 1886 issue of *Education*, suggested, in fact, that this disjunction be acknowledged. A girl should receive the same education as a boy until the age of twelve, its author suggested. At that time a girl should drop out of school for two years and learn the complete running of a household, returning to school only with that formal apprenticeship accomplished. Only such complete separation of activities would allow the household its due.[22]

Chores and "Little Home Duties"

The marginalization of girls' domestic labor is evident in the descriptions of work that enter the records of their lives. Virtually all girls had some domestic responsibilities. (One study in 1896 found that 83 percent of high school girls said they did some "general housework" or sewing on a daily basis, taking about an hour a day.[23]) But this work was characterized by its partialness, by its incidental quality as one of many features which were intended to structure the lives and enhance the character of prospering girls. The exemplary novel of uplift and improvement for girls, Elizabeth Prentiss's *Stepping Heavenward* (1869), suggests exactly the ways in which such duties could be designed more for instructional and improving purposes for girls themselves than for actually getting the work of the household done.

In this characteristic tale of a willful heroine resisting the road to exemplary womanhood, a minister raises the question of domestic responsibilities.

> "You have some little home duties, I suppose?"
>
> "Yes; I have the care of my own room, and mother wants me to have a general oversight of the parlor. . . ."
>
> "Is that all you have to do?"
>
> "Why, my music and drawing take up a good deal of my time, and I read and study more or less, and go out some, and we have a good many visitors."

Despite the meagerness of her responsibility, it appears that the heroine, Kate, is none too diligent about keeping her room "in nice, ladylike order," and dusting the parlor every morning. She is thereby endangering her moral development. In fact, her dusting is her first step "heavenward," the heroism enhanced rather than diminished by the inability of such chores to seem, or even to be, really important. Like the "pert miss" in William Thayer's book of admonition wondering, "How can a girl like me be orderly, when I have nothing to order?" middle-class Victorian girls learned that they could practice habits of ordering on their own wardrobes and their own rooms, their labor defined by its value in building their own character.[24]

And indeed, that was often how girls' duties were defined: as the light work associated with keeping up of a private bedroom or with the genteel presentation of the household. Emily Eliot's chores, which were rarely featured in her journal, included sometimes making out a list of the soiled clothes (which were increasingly sent out to commercial laundries rather than done at home), organizing her shelves, and sometimes sewing. Martha Moore's mother often called on her to arrange flowers for the parlors before she did her school-work. Lucy Breckinridge, like Martha Moore writing in the South during the Civil War, had the lightest of household chores because of the presence of black slave labor. When she announced in her diary that she had "been a little more industrious and *housekeepy* this week," she described chores remarkable for their seeming remoteness to the real work of the household. "I have crocheted bridle reins and breakfast mats, hemmed some ruffles, and made some ice cream and custard." [25] Sewing, especially ornamental needle-work, was the prototypical girls' work, redeemed by its suggestion of industry without urgency.

The advice writer Mary Virginia Terhune, a particularly astute cultural critic, noted the consequences of the "make-work" approach to the socialization of daughters. "Our daughters fit loosely into their places in our homes," she noted. "What they do is for us, and of grace." Challenges Terhune, "Where is the mother who has the moral courage to say to the emancipated school-girl—'You begin now another and important novitiate. Under my tutelage you must study housekeeping in all departments and details.'" Such mothers were few and far between. Instead, daughters in households presided over by matrons and staffed by servants continued dusting the parlors, making cake and jelly, arranging the flowers and the fruit, all in order to oblige their mothers rather than because of any perceived responsibility to a family economy. Typical was Agnes Repplier's memory of her childhood approach to her one duty: "Once more I see the big, bare old-fashioned parlor, to dust which was my daily task, my dear mother having striven long and vainly to teach my idle little hands some useful housewifely accomplishment. In one corner stood a console table, with chilly Parian ornaments on top, and underneath a pile of heavy books, Wordsworth, Moore, the poems of Frances Sargent Osgood . . . [and] this brown bulky Byron. . . . I could not pass it by! My dusting never got beyond the table where it lay." When such household labor was in fact marginal, encouraged by advisers as "gratifying your mother in these little things," and perceived by daughters as "sacrifice of my time and pursuits," there is no wonder that girls did not take their responsibility to domestic labor entirely seriously, and sometimes chafed at or evaded those responsibilities.[26]

Especially when girls saw their house work as "helping mother," a note of wryness or rebellion crept into otherwise implacable diarists. Margaret Tile-ston, whose lifelong daily entries are notable for their flat, descriptive quality, revealed a saucy note in her contrast of her mother's activity with her own quiet reading. "In the morning, Mother was very busy getting closets in order. I helped her a little, but not much. . . . Je n'ai rien à dire." The next day, she noted that she "helped Mother somewhat by trotting up and down stairs," her duties those of an automaton rather than a coworker. An even more filial diarist, Annie Burnham Cooper, whose diary explores her sense of inadequacy in fulfilling her responsibilities to aging parents, ventured a carefree first entry to her diary describing her fifteenth summer: "I have spent my [summer] in *rowing, sailing, crabbing, fishing,* minoing, riding horseback, sewing buttons on shoes, mending stockings, gloves, and trimming *boating hats, tanning my arms and rists* as brown as a pancake, helping Mama in a few places, when I could, and not helping her in a thousand different ways when I could, and so forth."[27] As Terhune suggested, when household work was defined as "helping mama," even dutiful Victorian daughters felt infantilized and expressed rebellion.

There were other circumstances, however, when a girl described her household work with acceptance, and sometimes even pride and a sense of accomplishment. This was when her labor was in fact irreplaceable, because she herself was filling in for an absent servant or an absent mother. When the Baldwin family maid departed to nurse her sick cousin, daughter Jessie's activities took a different turn from her usual genteel schedule. She wrote to a friend, "Now I'll tell you what has been my occupation lately—Getting up at 5 A.M. cooking breakfast for H. and Papa at 7 A.M. washing the dishes at 8, dusting at 9, various odd things at 10, ditto at 11, and dinner at 12." Jessie had inherited a full-time job. For girls who already had full schedules, especially those who attended school, replacing a maid imposed real burdens. The sickness of her mother and her three brothers and the absence of a maid meant that Jessie Wendover's friend Florence "has to do all the work and is completely discouraged about her lessons, she has so little time to study." At the very least, it took a toll on a girl's leisure pursuits, so that Florence Peck could win her competition with a friend in seeing who could read *David Copperfield* fastest, "for her folks are without a girl."[28]

Daughters had a clear responsibility to replace mothers' work when mothers became ill or were away, a responsibility which they accepted and sometimes celebrated. (When mothers died or were permanently incapacitated, girlhoods summarily ended.[29]) Annie Gates's mother broke her leg when Gates was twelve, and the girl commenced her "first experience in cooking," a position which made her proud and which she "strove to prove" herself equal to, despite the disastrous results. Mary Bartine, daughter of a wealthy

New Jersey industrialist who employed several servants, noted that she had been "house keeper and sicknurse combined for the last few days," when her mother had become sick. And when Eleanor Hooper's mother was away, she wrote a friend, "I have been housekeeper and head cook and bottle-washer," a phrase which she explained by allowing, that "although we have a capital servant who has been with us almost two years, I have heaps of work to do to keep everything up to the mark." For seventeen-year-old Annie Cooper, a committed amateur artist whose family also employed servants, the managerial responsibilities of replacing her mother, away for the week in 1882, weighed less heavily. "I was housekeeper. Papa and I enjoyed it very much indeed, for I painted nearly all the time. and of course that was bliss for me."[30] The suggestion here is that for Annie, replacing her mother in her absence was less time-consuming than obliging her in her presence.

By the end of the century, cultural promoters of domesticity had almost given up on their efforts to reintroduce domestic apprenticeships among an urban elite. Instead, advice givers in periodicals found other ways to encourage girls to learn the skills of home work. The founding of clubs and the establishment of classes, like the writing of advice manuals themselves, were designed to encourage the practice of dying arts. One Hamilton cousin prepared "peach creme" "for the cooking club," in the context of a day which included reading, meeting with the Shakespeare club, a trip to town, another stint reading (this time *Knickerbocker's New York*), and some crocheting, done while listening to the reading of another story aloud. Another girl organized a cooking club for the maid's night off. A twelve-year-old wrote in to *Harper's Young People* of her desire to belong to "the Little Housekeepers," but lamented that she probably was ineligible because "I can't cook much."[31] Even promotional schemes to restore the lost art of housewifery required at least a modicum of early experience.

Allowance, Cash, and Paid Work for Daughters

Jeanne Boydston's study of housework suggests another possible explanation for the tendency of parents to withdraw their daughters from domestic employ: the devaluation of housework itself as an activity of any economic value. The introduction of a cash economy into the interstices of postrevolutionary American life meant that activities that did not customarily generate cash—including those myriad duties of domestic maintenance—became "invisible," defined as something other than work both by those who did housework and by those who did not. Women themselves increasingly devalued the importance of their own work, as evidenced by Lydia Almy of Salem, Massa-

1.3 Cooking class, 1884. A *St. Nicholas* story encourages girls to take up these lessons their mothers have neglected. Reprinted from "The Cooking Class," *St. Nicholas* 12 (November 1884): 16.

chusetts, who "wove, attended to livestock, made cider, carted wood, tanned skins, took in boarders," but nonetheless, recorded in her diary that she was disturbed to know that she was "in no way due any thing towards earning my living," unlike her mariner husband.[32] The increasing tendency to define housework as hardly work at all, because of its unwaged (or low-waged) character, influenced the calculations of parents as they made decisions about their daughters' lives.

Mary Virginia Terhune's advice explicitly attributed a cash calculation—and an invidious distinction—to the attitudes of both daughters and their fathers toward daughters' work, especially when girls had received educations. Fathers, she felt, imagined that "the labor of an educated woman,—especially if that woman is *his* child, and her scholastic education has cost him thousands of dollars—should . . . command a better market-price than that of an illiterate Celt, whose schooling cost nothing." Daughters themselves might have adopted a wage theory of value to assess the value of their own labor, Terhune speculated. A middle-class daughter's "time and strength are worth more than a seamstress's, or chambermaid's or cook's wages. The world teems with seamstresses, chambermaids, and cooks, clamoring for the very work she abhors." Frances Willard's book of advice to girls put a different spin on the situation, based on a similar hierarchy of class. She urged middle-class daughters to aspire to higher work than housekeeping, arguing that opening a place for a domestic servant in their homes created a place for a destitute young woman who otherwise "might be tempted into paths of sin." (Prostitutes themselves often compared the two vocations, to the disadvantage of housework.[33]) Writing in the 1880s, Willard and Terhune did not lament the graduation of middle-class girls from housework; they seemed to agree that middle-class girls either had priced or should price themselves out of the market for domestic labor.

That seemed to be part of the calculation made in the large family of Frederick and Ann Ware Winsor in Winchester, Massachusetts, then a semirural community. Ill-paid as a country doctor, Frederick "staggered" for his entire life under debts incurred during the Civil War, according to his daughter, Annie. In 1880, with a family of seven children between the ages of eight and twenty-two, money was particularly scarce in the Winsor household. When Ann Ware Winsor made a summer expedition to Europe—probably a gift from a friend or relative—her daughter Annie exclaimed on its anomaly: "Who'd a thought youd ever really go to Paris. . . . It's altogether too much like rich people and other folks. We poor Winsors don't go gadding to Paris. We work for our living and have to make over our cousins clothes." One of those who worked for her living was Ann Ware Winsor herself, who ran a school from their home and sought other ways to eke out the family's subsistence. In a letter to her daughter the previous summer, she informed Annie of several schemes she had for making money; for one, the boys would raise chickens. "While they make money out of hens, I expect you girls to make it out of small fruits, and I have engaged a lot of plants to be delivered here in the Spring for you to cultivate!" Ann Ware Winsor assured her daughter that not only would it provide a welcome contribution to the family coffers, but "That's the way out of head-aches and other ails. Read some books on the subject and you will grow enthusiastic."[34]

Despite the economic worries of the Winsor family, however, only one child, a middle son, actually worked at a paid job outside the home in 1880: seventeen-year-old Paul was a clerk at the railroad office. The eldest, Robert, was in college, and all the rest were in school, including nineteen-year-old Mary and fifteen-year-old Annie. Presumably the "opportunity costs" of educating the girls were low enough that it weighed against sacrificing their education. Family calculations also suggested that the daughters' extra energies would be better used in assisting in teaching in their mother's school than in doing housework. For the 1880 census indicated that the Winsor family employed three female servants. (Annie's private journal recorded cryptically, "Maids are an abomination for children.") The opening of other occupations for women did devalue housework, and those who did it. Annie's father reported on changes in the household staff in 1885, "much to our advantage, we think, getting for cook a 'Katie' who . . . was very nice in the place of a noisy, lying, dirty woman detested by the whole family." Frederick Winsor's speculation about whether "the *machinery* of life will not bye and bye be simplified" suggested an attitude toward housework at some odds from earlier domestic mystification.[35] In this debt-ridden household, it was nonetheless considered good economy to pay servants' wages in order to preserve girls' time for education and for more lucrative and respectable work in a family school.

The growth of the market economy during the course of the nineteenth century meant that girls as well as their parents felt the need of cash. Those without access to cash sought strategies to make some, whatever their attitudes toward women's wage work as a social development. Away at school in the cash-poor South, and largely abandoned as well by her father, Mary Thomas fantasized about alternative lives. In one of them she sold things, "for I mean to work a patch next year and make some money, if I don't have to come back to school; and then at Christmas, I will have a right good lot of money to do as I please with, I think I shall get a watch with it." De-spite her clear disdain elsewhere in her diary for the notion of working for a living, Mary Thomas was willing to countenance work for wages in order to be able to participate in a consumer economy. A fourteen-year-old subscriber to the youth magazine *Harper's Young People* reported that she had earned the money for her subscription herself "by sewing for the black people." She reported that she had to sew "very cheaply, because they are so poor"; pre-sumably her low wages also reflected her low level of skill. A correspondent to *St. Nicholas* also reported that she and her brother had earned the money for their subscription themselves—in this case by selling hickory nuts and onions.[36]

Elite girls came late to money earning. Mary Virginia Terhune charged late-Victorian parents with discriminating against girls in their differential train-ing in the basics of money management. "Jack raises chickens and sells the eggs and 'broilers' to Mamma. Willy splits kindling-wood for the kitchen-fire and draws his lawful wages from Papa as would any other laborer. Mamie comes down to breakfast, as gay as the morning, hair bound with a blue rib-bon that matches her eyes, waltzes up to Papa, in a gale of affectionate glee, throws her arms around his neck and begs for a kiss. She gets two and a gold dollar, fished up from the vest-pocket nearest the paternal heart—'because she looks so pretty today.'"[37] Terhune's charge that girls were not given ex-perience managing money had some basis. Women were not paid wages for housework; instead, their work was supposed to come "from the heart," and to be inspired by devotion to the family good. To the extent that girls shared in their mothers' lots, they too were encouraged to dust, to make beds, and to shell peas not as entrepreneurs but as part of their responsibilities to womanly service.

However, just as housewives made some cash through the nineteenth cen-tury for a variety of home manufactures, girls too might learn to work for profit in performing those home tasks still considered "productive." John Boise Tileston was the sponsor of his daughter's early experience in earning money in a variety of outside duties associated with their family farm. Un-like experience in the Winsor family, in which such schemes were part of a family strategy for survival, with income reverting to the household coffers, Margaret Tileston reported earning and even banking money made summers and weekends in the strawberry fields, picking grapes, rubbing shoots off of potatoes, bringing in the cows, killing rosebugs. From the age of fourteen, contrary to Terhune's accusation, Margaret managed the family chickens. Ini-tially her father paid her a quarter of a dollar per week for tending the hens, but it appears that later she was granted more responsibility, as her father passed on to her the total receipts from the sale of eggs during a period she was away from the house. That last entry also reported that her father had bought her two blank books in Boston "for which I paid 67." Presumably those two blank books would be filled with details of the chicken business.[38]

John Tileston's schooling of his daughter in the management of money owed much to new notions of a woman's responsibilities. For just as a colonial goodwife was defined by her energy and skill in a home manufactory, a provident woman of later eras knew how to keep accounts and to be a prudent shopper. Good parents saw to it that daughters had some skills in handling their own money—and because few urban girls had the money-making possibilities available to Margaret Tileston on her family's farm, some of them began to receive small sums in the form of a regular allowance. An 1897 study on "Children's Sense of Money" found that 7 percent of all girls were given a regular allowance. Jessie Wendover, the daughter of a prospering Newark grocer, was one. At the age of nine in 1881, she received ten cents a week allowance, which was raised to twenty-five cents by the time she was fourteen. She kept a careful account of every expenditure. At fourteen, her expenditures included an occasional soda water (ten cents), ice cream, Sunday school donation (five cents), a variety of school supplies, carfare, ribbons, music. Although she was not usually responsible for buying her own clothes, she also recorded paying twenty-five cents several times for a bustle, perhaps because it was not encouraged by her mother, or more likely because it was one of the few ready-made items in her wardrobe. She paid for her own magazine subscription to *St. Nicholas*, $2.75, or nearly three months' allowance. As befitted her regular habits, Jessie Wendover customarily carried a balance of $5 or so from month to month, except when depleted by the Christmas season. By 1887, when Wendover was fifteen, she was receiving fifty cents a week, and recorded paying twenty-five cents "to see picture 'Christ on Calvary.'" At sixteen, she developed a taste for milkshakes, a habit of occasionally eating lunch out, and a preference for having her bangs cut by a salon. Chewing gum, peanuts, and marshmallows made their appearance in her accounts in the summer of 1888, but so did regular contributions to the missionary box, and in the fall, a donation for yellow fever sufferers. The following year she noted frequent small outlays for hokeypoky—ice cream—and she once spent seventy-five cents to have her hair shampooed. But in October of that year she was sufficiently ahead to deposit $3.00 in the bank, and in September of 1892, her twentieth year, $20.00. Clearly Jessie Wendover's ample allowance and her own prudence allowed her early to learn not only how to spend money and account for it but also how to save it—all important lessons for bourgeois helpmates.[39]

Another pattern though seemed to be gaining currency at the same time. Increasingly, household chores began to creep in as part of the way that parents justified giving money to youth. Agnes Garrison at fourteen in 1880 reported on her moneys. She was to get fifty cents a month "allowance," but in addition two cents a day for keeping her room clean (probably excluding Sundays), adding up to a total of $1.04 a month. For purposes of comparison, a child working full-time in the textile industry in Massachusetts the same year would have made $12 a month. In 1884 an editor of *Harper's Young People* suggested to a correspondent eager to earn money that she ask for wages for housework—a radical departure from the earlier notion that housework was part of a girl's natural responsibility. "Perhaps your mother would be willing to pay you for relieving her regularly of some duty in the house," the editor suggested. But she went on to reassure her correspondent that she should not be concerned about her dependency on the allowance that came from her father. (Fathers, of course, were the sources of allowances.) "I think . . . that a daughter need not have any hesitation in considering the money given her by a dear father as her own, to spend as she pleases, just as really her own as money she earns." Occasionally, and unevenly, girls' diaries began to suggest that they themselves were beginning to expect and to receive wages for work done for their families. Marian Nichols reported receiving wages for family sewing. "Worked on some drawers for Margaret. Mamma is to pay 30 cts a pair for them." The next year she reported that she was even getting paid for exercise. "Went to school. Walked in and out by myself. Rosy doesn't like my getting money from walking out. I get 3 cts." Jane Addams's father paid her for every volume of Plutarch she read and reported on, as well as for every volume of such things as Irving's *Life of Washington*, "after the manner of Victorian fathers," according to Anne Scott.[40] The custom of paying daughters for their work in the bourgeois family suggested a new approach to girls as well as to family economics. The same study that tracked the development of the "allowance" also discovered that fully a quarter of all girls reported making money for doing housework.

It is no wonder that girls increasingly began to resist doing housework as part of their womanly lot that others were getting paid to do. Giving girls allowances was good Victorian practice—encouraging regularity of habits, responsibility, careful accounting, and prudence. Yet in its tendency to evolve into a quid pro quo for performing household and other kinds of chores it contributed to a radical new notion well expressed in the economic writings of Charlotte Perkins Gilman—the notion that daughters, if not their mothers, were autonomous economic beings in control of their own labor, and able to exchange it for currency. When Victorian fathers paid their daughters wages for housework, they were laying the seeds of turn-of-the-century rebellions against conventional notions of female self-sacrifice as woman's natural lot.

Margaret Tileston's Household Work

When girls were paid for household chores, they might well record the fact in their diaries. We might speculate that they would be less likely to note them if such chores were routine. The compulsive and complete diary of Margaret Tileston regularly recorded such routine work, however, providing additional evidence of the marginalization of middle-class girls' work in households employing servants. Her diary demonstrates the ebb and flow of domestic work, as Tileston incorporated occasional extra household need into a life centered elsewhere.

Margaret Tileston was the second daughter of a gentleman farmer, a superintendent of schools and sometime participant in the family paper business, who lived first in Concord, Massachusetts, then in Salem, and then in Brookline. Her mother was an author and an editor of anthologies of verse whose proofs Margaret occasionally read. With such literary parents, it is not surprising that she felt a certain pressure to authorship, which she filled, in part, by keeping a daily diary from her childhood virtually for the rest of her entire life. She endeavored to fill up a page of text each day and delved deep into domestic life to generate information with which to do so. From the time she started her diary until the end of her teens, she wrote about the domestic help as well as her own activities, focusing especially on her schoolwork, her reading, her exercise regimen, and her social life. She also recorded her glancing responsibilities for domestic work.

The Tileston household (excluding the farmyard) seemed to work on a quota of two servants—including a cook and a "second girl." In a period of six years during her teens, Tileston recorded the comings and goings of nineteen cooks and second girls, who were sometimes recruited from the neighborhood but more often hired in Boston by her father. In a particularly trying period for all in September 1882, the family returned early from a summer holiday when one servant gave notice. The next few weeks recorded various trips to see about "a girl," and the announcement on September 23, "Having no girls we did our own housework." On the 29th her father was successful and re-turned with a "girl to be our cook." Margaret wrote, "We are going to call her Dora, and she looks uncommonly nice." Two weeks later, however, Margaret observed, "I think that Dora feels homesick," and by early December there was no mention of Dora. Instead, on December 11 Margaret recorded that "May became half insane." The next day both of the Tileston family servants departed, Kate to take May to Worcester to the "Asylum." Margaret regretted their going, for they "have been so nice," and added "I am sorry for them and for us."[41] By December 19 John Tileston had again gone to Boston to hire for his household.

Undoubtedly the instability of domestic labor proved a substantial source of strain for Margaret's mother, Mary Foote Tileston, who had to manage a complex household with ever-changing workers, and for John Tileston, who hired new staff every several months. (Perhaps Mary Tileston, who seems to have been a demanding and undemonstrative woman, was part of the prob-lem.) Margaret's duties temporarily expanded when servants departed, as on the morning of December 5, 1885, when Margaret explained, "As Carrie was not here, I made all the beds in the morning, and washed the dishes." Washing dishes was clearly servant's work; bed making was sometimes a chore assigned to Margaret and her older sister Mary even when domestic servants were avail-able. The morning of December 8, 1885, Margaret replaced not only a servant but also her mother, who was tending a dying relative. Sick with a cold at home, it was Margaret who saw her younger sister off to school.[42] The hiring and departure of servants, like her mother's temporary absence, meant only a temporary readjustment in the duties of Margaret Tileston, however, one which she recorded in her journal with equanimity.

It was only upon her graduation from high school that Margaret Tileston noted full days of housework. At the age of twenty, in the winter of 1887, she recorded that she had swept her room for the first time—"with Carrie's assistance, or rather vice versa." At that point, as part of her preparation for a housewife's lot, she was assigned more consuming home duties, including the dusting of the parlor, and tending of her mother's new baby. (After a morn-ing of such duty, in April 1887, Margaret wrote that she "was allowed time for a walk in the afternoon.")[43] Up until that point, though, home duties played a relatively small role in the life of Margaret Tileston. She could not completely take her family's servants and the work they provided for granted; servants came and went too regularly, and chores came her way as a result. Throughout her teen years, housework, like illness, occasionally emerged to require her attention. In general, though, it remained in the background, far from the normative center of her round of concerns.

Regional Variations

In this, Margaret Tileston's experience was that of a Bostonian—a member of an urban middle class with the resources and the available labor supply to provide domestic servants for their households. As statistics on domestic service suggest, rural and frontier households were far less likely to hire domestic servants, and as a result, daughters were more likely to devote a substantial part of their day to domestic work. They were unlikely to receive an allowance or any pay for their sometimes arduous labors. Life in this traditional family economy surely characterized the experience of most girls growing up in the nineteenth century.

The farm diary of Ada Harris, from Oswego County, New York, written in 1873 when she was thirteen, provides evidence of this other model. Her diary shows her baking cookies, bread, and pies, making jellies and pickles, boiling, straining, and sugaring off maple sap, dipping candles, smoking meat, rendering soap. It shows her also gardening, picking strawberries, raking hay in the meadow, and one morning even sawing wood for three hours. Although there was a schoolhouse only a quarter of a mile from her house, she attended school sporadically, only twice during January, though school was in session. Her diary reports, "I do not go to school now, I am helping Ma get the sewing done." [44]

Between the experiences of Ada Harris and Margaret Tileston there was a complete range of variation. Myra Dolloff, who lived on a farm in the tiny farming community of Bridgewater, New Hampshire, in the 1870s, reported not only a regular course of school attendance but a good bit of domestic labor, some of it helping "the maid [probably a daytime hire] do the work." Here she used city language to describe what in other respects was likely to have been a rural pattern of helping in which she participated. Cassie Upson, whose mother died when she was an infant, alternated between the home of her aunts in rural Charlemont, Massachusetts, where she visited in the summer, and the home of her father and new stepmother in Milwaukee, staffed with two domestic servants. Nonetheless, on August 17, 1863, Cassie reported, "This afternoon washed dishes till four oclock." Several years later, she "picked over some dandelion greens for dinner and made Gusta laugh, talking Irish to her." The next day Gusta was sick, so Cassie, her stepmother, and stepgrandmother did the work, "and tired enough it has made me." A month later Augusta was gone, and Cassie reported that "'Minnie' is the euphonious cognomen of the present occupant of our kitchen." In Charlemont the next summer, where there appeared to be no hired help and school was not in session, Cassie Upson "washed and wiped dishes three times today. . . . Practiced two and ¼ hours—and wrote Aunt Abby." Even in rural Charlemont, though, there was sometimes domestic help, for in Upson's later reminiscences, she refers to the importance of Margaret, "our good Irish maid."[45] Domestic work was not strange to Cassie Upson, but just as in the diary of Margaret Tileston, who did much less of it, it was a minor theme in a diary filled with school, friends, and excursions.

Hegemony

Despite the unevenness in the evolution of patterns of domestic work among middle-class girls, there is a suggestion of a growing consensus on the subject of girls' work. The advice literature in particular notes that the desire to spare girls domestic drudgery characterized aspirants to middle-class status as well as established elites. As early as the 1830s, Lydia Maria Child recounted her visit to a family "of no fortune at all, one of those people who live 'nobody knows how'; and I found a young girl, about sixteen, practicing on the piano, while an elderly lady beside her was darning her stockings. I was told (for the mother was proud of bringing her daughter up so genteelly) that the daughter had almost forgotten how to sew, and that a woman was hired into the house to do her mending!" In an 1880 article in *St. Nicholas,* fifty years later, the social gospel minister Washington Gladden echoed Child's theme. It was not just girls from prosperous families who were "doing no work to speak of, and learning nothing about the practical duties and the serious cares of life." Even "in the families of mechanics and of people in moderate circumstances, where the mothers are compelled to work hard all the while," girls were spared. Gladden continued, "I have heard two mothers, worthy women in most respects, say, the first, that her daughter never did any sweeping. . . . The other said she would not let her daughter do anything in the kitchen. Poor deluded woman! She did it all herself, instead." As one of Gladden's correspondents summarized, "Work, which you so plainly showed to be good for our boys, is quite as necessary for our girls."[46]

Mary Virginia Terhune offered another anecdote from a visit to a farm family with two daughters. The mother was recovering from a fever and churning the butter with difficulty, without asking help from her daughters. "'I don't think such hard labor is good for growing girls,' she answered, the poor wan face softening as she went on. 'I have had to work so hard all my days that I can't bear to see them at it.'"[47] In the early century, Lydia Maria

Child suggested that social ambition encouraged mothers to give daughters a genteel rearing. By the late century, Mary Virginia Terhune alluded to medical concerns for the health of the pubescent girl, a concern which dominated middle-class debates about girls' rearing in the cities. Her story, apocryphal or not, suggested that such concerns might have reached rural New England as well. Clearly Child's, Gladden's, and Terhune's testimonies are suspect, given their role in polemics for domesticity. Nonetheless, there is every reason to grant the dominant discourse some power in influencing the aspirations of those in the rural periphery or those who were aspirants rather than arrivals to middle-class status.

The story of Mary Elizabeth Morrissey is illustrative. Lizzie Morrissey was the daughter of a deceased Canadian-born Irish "trader" in liquor and wines and a mother who worked in her home as a dressmaker. Morrissey lived in Irish East Boston and attended Girls' High School in the 1870s. Her diary mentions frequent money troubles. And yet with both mother and grandmother working around her, she, like the privileged daughters in the advice literature, appeared to do very little household work. One Sunday she reported watering the plants and picking the beans "after doing which I felt at liberty to read my book which is very nice indeed." Another day, when she was feeling lonely, she took "her little chair up in the kitchen . . . and [sat] there awhile watching ma iron." In another instance while both mother and grandmother ironed, Lizzie "employed the time by writing a letter."[48] Like Margaret Tileston, only in very different social circumstances, Morrissey commenced serious domestic work only after graduating from high school.

Living in Boston and attending high school, Lizzie Morrissey was already allying herself with a select group of privileged youths; only about 15 percent of girls in the comparable city of Providence attended high school in 1880, according to Joel Perlmann's statistics. This group was disproportionately not only native-born but the offspring of native-born parents, and of white-collar backgrounds. In her daily contact with that population at Boston's Girls' High School, she was in a position to know the life patterns and expectations of her schoolmates. It stood to reason that those patterns would exert some hold on her and on her family—which had already decided it could sacrifice her earning power temporarily in hopes of improvement. Lizzie Morrissey's case is one which suggests the power of the expectation of worklessness even in families for whom that labor was by no means gratuitous.

Clearly, expectations for daughters changed unevenly nationwide. Yet the memories of a woman who had grown up in Montana at the turn of the century suggest the means by which a distinct, minority ideology might exert influence even in the absence of the daily contact which prompted Lizzie Morrissey's home life. Dorothy Johnson remembered her response to the popular youth periodical *St. Nicholas,* which her father had ordered at the time of her birth. In a bound volume of *St. Nicholas,* she wrote, "I came upon the word allowance. The concept was attractive. I researched this pretty thoroughly. According to stories in St. Nicholas, an allowance was money your parents gave you regularly just because you were there. You didn't do anything to earn it. This struck me as an admirable idea. No child I knew in Whitefish received an allowance, not even the scions of locomotive engineers, those lords of creation who were paid a very great deal of money by the Great Northern Railroad." In the absence of allowances, youth in Whitefish were eager for any means of getting access to cash, she wrote. There was lots of work for children, she wrote, but "The trouble was that just about everything you could do was part of your normal chores and you didn't get paid for it." One way of earning money in Whitefish was in selling *Youth's Companion,* a magazine for youth that, like *St. Nicholas,* might provide more children with the opportunity to absorb eastern ways, including, perhaps, the idea that children had a right to money "just because you were there."[49]

The advice literature and the journals of girls reinforce each other in some important particulars. The advice literature argues ruefully against middle-class girls' loss of domestic function. Many girls' journals themselves document glancing, occasional involvement in the domestic work unit. Taken together with the statistics on the hire of servants in the late nineteenth century, these accounts of and by middle-class girls suggest the seeds of profound change in the domestic orientation of middle-class women. With the breakdown of the apprentice system for girls and the introduction of girls into formal education in schoolrooms of all kinds, the norms for city girls in prospering families increasingly centered not around making bread, churning butter, stoking stoves, but in writing drills, exercise regimens, reading routines, piano practice. As good Victorians, their efforts would go not so much in fashioning goods as in producing improved versions of themselves.

TWO

Writing and Self-Culture: The Contest Over the Meaning of Literacy

Middle-class girls who no longer spent their days as their mothers' apprentices in domestic maintenance and manufacture were not left to their own devices. Just as their mothers' responsibilities reoriented from home industries to the rearing of children, girls' own primary goals shifted from the manufacture of cloth and the preserving of foodstuffs to the culturing of themselves. Self-culture was a broad-based project in the nineteenth century which was central to the emergence of a middle class. In the increasingly fluid and unpredictable climate that accompanied the emergence of a market economy, young men and women were urged to form regular habits of restraint and self-control as their best protection against future disasters. A self-regulating man could chart an even course for his family; a self-cultured and refined woman could safeguard her family's standing whatever economic circumstances should befall her. Self-culture was especially critical for girls for whom freedom from domestic labor left a good bit of free time during their impressionable years. The advice writer William Thayer, who at midcentury had worried that for some girls the result might be "a study in how to kill time," offered an alternative: "What an opportunity for mental culture and religious improvement!" Thayer's proposed means to these ends was significant. He proposed that girls accomplish their goals through reading, ideally a hundred pages a day.[1] The elevation of reading to a central and defining aspect of bourgeois girls' lives helped to define a specifically Victorian adolescence.

Many girls followed Thayer's advice and read for several hours a day, often supplementing their reading with the writing of letters or the keeping of a journal and diary. Reading and writing, the twin activities of literacy, became the vehicles to self-culture and the central activities of many privileged Victorian girls' lives. They reinforced each other abundantly, as girls read and then wrote about what they read—time profitably filled twice over.[2] Although Victorians came to debate the influence of various kinds of sensational reading material and the health of the practice of writing gushing prose, the activities of literacy had much to recommend them to adults over other occupations. As pastimes which took place in the imagination, they had a provisional quality which allowed for the displacement of desires for drama. In the best of circumstances, the cautionary tales of Victorian moralists and even the passionate dramas of romance would be processed through a girl's writing and help her to grow into an understanding woman of character, restraint, and refinement.

Many middle-class girls read voraciously—their reading often limited only by supply. The diaries and journals they left contain lists of books read over the course of a year and descriptions of time spent in reading over the course of a day. The advice writer Heloise Hersey estimated in 1901 that in the years between age twelve and twenty-one, "the average young gentlewoman reads a novel more than an hour a day. Thus she gives one and one-third years of solid working days to this occupation." It was common for reading, scattered through the day, often accompanied by writing, to be the single most time-consuming activity mentioned in girls' diaries. One girl reported reading in four different books through the course of a day, and sometimes reading straight through (over the course of several days) such massive volumes as George Eliot's *Daniel Deronda,* and Dickens's *Oliver Twist.* Another noted that on July 14, 1864, "I believe that I have not read a bit today—such a singular thing that I must record it."[3] Girls read by the window, in the hammock, on the horsecars, as well as in the parlor. Not all of girls' reading was for the same purpose, of course. Some of it was dutiful and dull; some of it was romantic and dangerous; some of it was inspirational. But it is clear that in comparison both with the eighteenth and the late twentieth centuries, nineteenth-century Victorian girls of a certain class came to spend much of their lives—and perhaps also do much of their living—on and through the written word.

The dominance of the Victorian culture of reading and writing was sufficient that even girls who had other substantial chores often used their curtailed discretionary time engaged in literacy. Thus Hannah Davis, who at the age of twelve in 1851 appeared to be living out as "help" in Ohio, reported one day's activity: "I got up eat my breakfast washed the dishes and read till noon then washed the dishes after dinner and read till supper eat supper washed the dishes and went to read a while then Milton Elvira Sarah and me told some tales and went to bed."[4]

Of course, we know about these reading regimens only because they were accompanied by writing regimens. Like reading, writing was a plastic medium which filled various needs and purposes. As witnessed by numerous late-Victorian portraits, girls frequently spent hours at desks, composing poetry, writing letters, pasting scrapbooks, keeping diaries or journals. The youth magazine *St. Nicholas* received a poem from one girl not yet ten and cautioned her, "Don't write verses yet, cleverly as you do them for one of your age. There is time enough for that"—time which would come when she reached her teens. This time came not only for girls in the city, who could not "frolic" in the open air, as the little poet was advised to, but for rural girls as well. Like Mark Twain's Emmeline Grangerford, who lived on the banks of the Mississippi and wrote mournful poetry that she kept in a scrapbook, actual girls from the hinterlands, too, kept diaries and wrote poetry, and intermingled their descriptions of household chores with locks of hair, autograph albums, and florid poetry.[5]

Writing was sometimes a solitary act, as we envision it today, but it often had an important social component. Girls formed clubs to write stories together, wrote poetry for each other, and often described writing their diaries together. Writing was not simply an activity for moments of solitude and silence, but one which compelled attention even among friends and in company. This "crescendo of verbal activity"—a fascination with both the power and the possibilities of literacy—played a variety of roles for girls in the process of becoming women.[6] In particular, girls' writing was an arena of contest between parents and daughters. Girls came to use their writing, especially their writing of diaries, not as an escape from the Victorian family, but as a way of discovering self within it.

Diaries as Disciplines of the Self

Girls wrote in a variety of genres and hands, often composing notes and letters to friends within the same city. They were particularly encouraged to occupy themselves by keeping accounts of their lives in the form of diaries. Diaries filled a variety of functions for the girl diarist. Arising from an empiricist desire to record events accurately, diaries served to store a range of information, from financial accounts to observations about the wind and the weather.

Private writing had religious roots as well, in the spiritual autobiography

2.1 Journal writing, 1879. Girls learned the guidelines for keeping diaries in such periodicals as *St. Nicholas*. Reprinted from Margaret H. Eckerson, "Jottings Versus Doings," *St. Nicholas* 6 (February 1879): 282.

or conversion narrative of earlier days. Parents encouraged diary writing for their daughters as a means of spiritual reflection and to promote good charac-ter and virtue. Parents had always encouraged virtuous conduct among their offspring, of course, but in eighteenth-century New England, sustained good behavior was secondary to a conversion experience as the mark of a good Christian. Unlike tales of conversion, however, which recounted the one-time odyssey of the soul to God, the nineteenth-century diary made religious virtue a daily affair to be demonstrated through repeated good deeds and regu-lar habits. With the disestablishment of the church and the dislocations oc-casioned by urbanization and industrialization, internalized character and steady habits assumed new importance. This function of the diary is captured by the term used by the modern theorist Michel Foucault to describe the ritual practice of the Catholic confessional: parents hoped that girls' diaries would be "disciplines of the self," which would encourage them in their pursuit of a reliable and steady goodness.[7]

Parents and advice givers suggested journals for girls and boys, but the conventional wisdom was that girls took to writing and diary keeping more naturally. Agnes Repplier, who wrote a piece on "The Deathless Diary" for an 1897 issue of the *Atlantic Monthly,* repeated this common assumption: "Even little girls, as we have seen, have taken kindly enough to the daily task of translating themselves into pages of pen and ink; but little boys have been wont to consider this a lamentable waste of time. . . . As a rule, a lad commits himself to a diary, as to any other piece of work, only because it has been forced upon him by the voice of authority." Repplier had good reason to know about the affinity between girlhood and writing. As a convent schoolgirl in the 1860s, she was one of a band of friends who were "addicted" to poetry and spent long hours copying it into blank books.[8]

There were structural reasons for the popularity of diary keeping among girls, as we have seen. The affluence of middle-class urban families marginalized daughters' work within the household, yet the constraints of propriety at midcentury discouraged outside employment. Advisers encouraged girls to devote themselves to the development of order in all features of their lives. Once one's room was cleaned, there was one's own life to systematize. In 1878, when the children's magazine *St. Nicholas* published a piece on keeping a journal, it gave as the first reason that it taught habits of order and regularity.[9]

Because the purpose of a journal was to train a girl in orderliness, clearly the entries themselves ought to be orderly and reflect an ordered life. Ideally, therefore, a diarist wrote daily, and often drafted her entries first before copying them into her diary. The diary was to be a credit to a girl's accomplishments, and those included her penmanship. The diary entry, like the constitutional walk, was usually a ritualized part of the day; often the girl wrote it in the bedroom immediately before retiring. It was considered less stressful than schoolwork by both parents and their daughters.[10]

The *St. Nicholas* adviser, W. S. Jerome, suggested a routine recording of the weather, letters received or written, money paid or received, the day of beginning or leaving school, visits, books read, all set down in the correct order of time. The end result would be a useful family history. As he wrote, "Perhaps, some evening when the family are sitting and talking together, some one will ask, 'What kind of weather did we have last winter?' or 'When was the picnic you were speaking of?' and the journal is referred to."[11] Clearly, the journals Jerome had in mind were semipublic family records rather than personal confessions. They were also designed for self-grooming along prescribed lines rather than experimentation.

Closing Off Fantasy

Of course there was another, romantic use of the diary more familiar to modern Americans. Jean-Jacques Rousseau borrowed from Catholic ritual the title of his revolutionary *Confessions,* which were designed less to appease an angry God than to explore an individual life history. As such they represented less a "discipline of the self" than a "technique of the self," in Foucault's terminology. Rousseau's romantic exercise in self-construction provided one model for the nineteenth-century diary, but it was not one that most parents had in mind for their daughters. Although they often encouraged their daughters to use diaries for self-exploration, they remained ambivalent about girls' rights to a self separate from family duties and responsibilities.[12]

The advice literature describing the practice of diary keeping rushed to close off romantic possibilities. It was better for a girl to have no diary at all than to have one which encouraged fantasy and ambition and distracted a girl from her domestic priorities. Almost simultaneous with its publication of W. S. Jerome's 1878 article "How to Keep a Journal," *St. Nicholas* published two stories which represented a direct attack on the practice of girls' diary keeping. These stories especially focused on the imaginative tendencies of girl diarists and ended with girls repudiating their diaries, their fantasies, and even themselves and taking a place again within their mothers' households. Unlike Jerome's hortatory piece, which was addressed to both girls and boys, the protagonists of these didactic pieces were both girls.

"Jottings Versus Doings," by Margaret Eckerson, describes a twelve-year-old diarist who renounces and then burns her diary. The eldest of several sisters, the diarist Margy is constantly besieged by demands on her time and person—babysitting duty, loans of her new silk parasol, and so on. She escapes to her journal, where she departs from the mundane details of domestic life with musings about love, kindness, and the beauty of death. A dangerous fall down the stairs forces Margy to realize that she does not actually want to die, and she turns on her journal: "I haven't written the real truth about anything," she concludes contemptuously, and she then proceeds to make a bonfire of the offending book. Her mother regrets its loss, but her father, a minister, concludes, "Margy's burnt journal is no loss to her, dear, . . . for sometimes there is a vast difference between jottings and doings."[13] Beneath

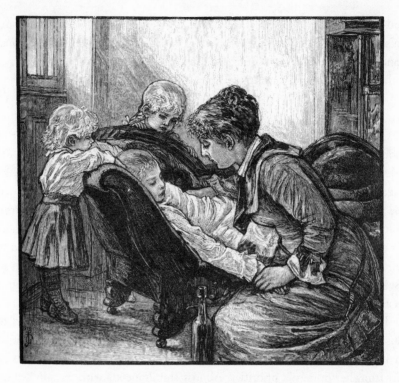

2.2 "Not in the Journal," 1879. In Margaret Eckerson's story "Jottings Versus Doings," the heroine records in her journal her dreams of greatness but not the mundane details of domestic life, like evidence of her mother's love. Reprinted from Eckerson, "Jottings Versus Doings," 283.

this mild comment lies a polemical position—a denial of Margy's right to imaginative self-definition and a reductionist insistence on appropriate role behavior as the measure of a person.

Whereas Margy's problem is silly fantasy, vain ambition is the problem for Dora, the heroine of Kate Gannett Wells's tale about diaries. Published in 1879 and described in the subtitle as a "Story for Big Girls," it is ominously titled "She Couldn't." Alienated from her mother and brothers, fourteen-year-old Dora is a "'funny girl' or a 'queer girl'" who "wrote in her journal and made up stories." What she *couldn't* do was realize her dream of being famous by the age of fifteen. She launched several schemes for greatness but failed in each, and finally resolved "to give up all idea of doing anything except school work and being good"—in itself a momentous undertaking. To commemorate this decision, she locked her door and made one last entry in her journal. Her entry took the form of two columns labeled "Wants" and

SHE ENDED IT WITH A GREAT BLOT.

2.3 "A kind of funeral over herself," 1879. In Kate Gannett Wells's story "She Couldn't: A Story for Big Girls," the heroine renounces her journal, blots her ink, and binds the book in black. Reprinted from Kate Gannett Wells, "She Couldn't: A Story for Big Girls," *St. Nicholas* 6 (May 1879): 462–68.

"Oughts." Under the first she wrote: "Want 1, to be real good; 2, to write splendid novels; 3, to be beautiful and great." Under "Oughts" she wrote: "1, to love stupid people; 2, to make 'everybody happy when I can; 3, not to think about myself, but just keep going on; 4, to talk all the time to my mother; 5, never to write another word in this journal." For Dora, writing her journal was an assertion of ambition and of self at the expense of duty to others. (Interestingly, even a desire to be "real good" seemed to be over-stepping.) Following this listing, she blotted the ink, tied her journal in black ribbon, had a good cry, ate some candy, and returned to her mother's side, saying "Mamma, I have given up all trying after what I can't be. I am just going to love you all at home with all my heart, and then you'll love me; and I wont feel badly because I can't write books or help in big ways." Wells appropriately described Dora's ritual of renunciation as "a kind of funeral over herself."[14] For it is clear that in destroying their diaries both Dora and Margy are destroying their dreams and their independent selves, and rejoining a domestic world of self-surrender.

So what do we make of Wells's and Eckerson's tales of adolescent renunciation, published in one of the major magazines for youth and children in the late nineteenth century? Together with Jerome's piece from the same decade, they set the parameters of the girl's diary. As Jerome explained, a diary should promote order and discipline, chart the writer's "progress as a thinker and writer," and record the details of family life. As Wells and Eckerson made clear, it should *not* indulge in fantasies, or entertain inappropriate ambitions. The advice givers thus agreed on the goal of promoting dutiful daughters but differed on the costs and benefits of the diary to this campaign. Jerome advocated the diary as a tool for self-discipline; Wells and Eckerson feared it as a surrogate for "splendid novels" and self-absorption. The moral for all the advice givers was the same, though (as Wells's Dora puts it): "If I try to make you all real happy in little bits of ways, I guess it will 'come out gloriously'"—a classic message of fulfillment through domestic subordination. The writing promoted by *St. Nicholas* was not meant to participate in the introspective romanticism or the self-creation which encouraged some nineteenth-century journals, but rather had earlier roots. In endorsing *writing* for self-improvement, but not for fantasizing, the latter-day Puritans who published *St. Nicholas* were echoing a frequently voiced Puritan judgment on appropriate *reading*.[15]

From Discipline to Technique of the Self

From the outset, then, diary writing was considered both, or alternately, dutiful and dangerous. Girls who received gifts of diaries from mothers and fathers on birthdays participated in the explorations of duty and pleasure anticipated and feared by adult pundits. Most began their diaries in the dogged spirit of accountants of the soul. But what began as parentally enforced "discipline" often evolved into a more self-referential "technique." This evolution sometimes involved only minute adjustments of perspective and often consisted of the internalization of strategies of self-discipline. Nonetheless, the evolution was real, and also practical. The historian Ann Fabian has cautioned us against imagining that writing about one's experience is necessarily liberating. Girls, like the dispossessed figures Fabian discusses, adopted rhetorical conventions suitable to their station. As she suggests, their efforts to write appropriately obliged them "to defer to those who claimed a right to exercise social and cultural power over them." Their diaries communicate that deference. Yet girls' diaries did not simply replicate adult teachings. The scholar of rhetoric Susan Miller tells us that everyday writing is not only where culture is made but where it is "remade, and finally ensconced in 'memory,' the miscellaneous space . . . that teaches us to ourselves."[16] The lessons girls taught themselves represented the incremental revisions of culture that occur when human agents interpret and apply social scripts.

In particular, girls' diaries offered them a conventional form within which to craft compromise. Diaries provided a way to release and contain rebellious impulses, however circumscribed, without breaking with families. Like their own rooms, girls claimed their diaries for themselves, beyond the gaze, but within the bosom, of their families. In these protected spaces, girls charted a middle way between the fiery rebel and the good daughter of advice books and fiction. Diaries offered several routes of mediation. Sometimes they served as surrogate battlefields upon which girls struggled to blend family expectation with personal impulse. Sometimes they served as parental talismans—and as security blankets—in girls' developing relations with peers. Sometimes they served to compartmentalize desire. Each of these strategies enabled Victorian girls to entertain imaginative freedom while preserving the networks of affiliation at the center of their lives.

Diary keepers agreed initially that the goal of being good required the suppression of self and the subordination of girls to their mothers. In the antebellum period, thirteen-year-old Louisa Jane Trumbull expressed a series of motivations for diary keeping which characterized later diarists as well: "In keeping a journal I at first did it because my sisters kept one—afterwards I wrote because it was the wish of my mother." Now, she wrote, "it is done not only to serve as means of being employed about something useful and proper but because it is a source of pleasure to me."[17] This sequencing suggested the role of family in sponsoring diaries and in encouraging the process of internalization by which girls defined their pleasure in the same breath as doing something useful and proper.

A prototypical model for this journey to goodness was literary—the immensely popular *Stepping Heavenward* by Elizabeth Payson Prentiss, the daughter of a Congregational minister. *Stepping Heavenward* appeared first in 1869 in fictional diary form and over the years sold 100,000 copies. It was read hopefully by farmers' daughters as well as members of a Victorian elite. Girls' multiple rereadings suggested a powerful resonance, with one reader observ-

ing that "some parts of it I almost know by heart I have read them so often."
This reader found it "more in accordance with my ideas of what such a life
should be than any I have ever read anywhere." Another rereader at the age
of twenty-one reported, "I had not read it for years and for two weeks I could
not keep it out of my mind"—a powerful tribute from a sophisticated reader,
who nonetheless was a perpetual sufferer from the Victorian urge to improvement.[18] Girls were able to reread *Stepping Heavenward,* of course, because it
was a book they were likely to have received as a Christmas or birthday gift
from an encouraging relative. The publication and reading history of *Stepping
Heavenward,* an exemplary didactic tale for girls, represented a straightforward alliance of genteel culture, concerned parents, and anxious readers who
agreed on the role that writing could play in the formulation of ideologies of
Christian domesticity.

  Stepping Heavenward documented the efforts of Kate, a willful daughter, to
grow up and be good. As with many actual diaries, *Stepping Heavenward* begins on a birthday with a series of resolutions. These resolutions are no sooner
made than broken and Kate storms off to school in defiance of her mother.
Her mother knows best, however, for upon Kate's return home, she finds a
new writing desk in her room and her mother smiling wisely. This writing
desk will allow Kate to keep the first resolution she has made—to begin her
journal. It is clear that like her other birthday resolutions, writing a journal is
a form of self-denial that will lead to self-improvement. *Stepping Heavenward*
charts Kate's progress through the loss of her father and a disappointing love
affair, and ultimately brings her to a love of God—and a simultaneous rec-
onciliation with her mother. Her minister responds to her desire for greatness
with a gentle reminder that her first act of heroism should be in "gratifying
her mother" by helping around the house.[19]

  The morality play and the plan for action embodied in *Stepping Heavenward* were models for adolescent diarists. If some of its readers "felt that they
had written *Stepping Heavenward* themselves," others attempted to use it as a
model for their own chronicles of improvement on the way to good character
and to womanhood. Georgia Mercer Boit and her daughter Mary both read
Stepping Heavenward repeatedly, identifying with its impetuous heroine and
its hopeful message of the possibility of improvement. For young Georgia,
writing at the age of eighteen in the post–Civil War South, moral improvement meant greater love for God. On her nineteenth birthday she stayed up
late to ask for spiritual aid in serving God in the coming year, and recorded
the prayer in her journal.[20]

  Georgia Mercer married a Bostonian and died young, leaving behind two daughters to a privileged existence. In 1891 her elder daughter, Mary Boit, who had remained in extended mourning, read and reread *Stepping Heavenward* three times, unaware that she was replicating the experience of her mother years before. Like her mother, Mary Boit also identified with Kate, but she focused on her efforts to be good rather than her efforts to believe. She especially identified with Kate's hot temper and her anger toward her mother, for Mary Boit had a troubled relationship with her new stepmother. "I think that Katherine in the book before she gets good is exactly like me," she wrote. "I feel the same ways. I love her and I love the book this is my third time reading it. On my birthday I am going to try to turn over a new leaf and be a better girl." Twenty years and half a continent apart, mother and daughter patterned their experience on the same template—using the occasion of a birthday to redouble their efforts for goodness, and to record these efforts in a moral account book.[21]

Funerals Over the Self

There has been much debate over the impact on actual behavior of such Victorian messages of self-chastening. Schoolgirl diaries testify to the strength of norms of denial and repression for girls in that era. The resolutions sprinkled throughout diaries suggest that exhortations to service were not simply the stuff of advice manuals but made their way into girls' own self-expectations. At the age of sixteen, Charlotte Norris made the following plans for the year 1886: "Duty shall precede pleasure. Save ten dollars by June 1st. Bathe regularly every day. Use chest weights every day until June 1st." In 1892, at nineteen, Marian Nichols offered a graver list:

Incipit hic Vita Nuova.
Resolved. not to talk about myself or feelings. To think before speaking.
To work seriously.
To be self restrained in conversation and actions.
Not to let my thoughts wander.
To be dignified.
Interest myself more in others.
Repentance is good, but it should not distract one's thoughts.

Marian Nichols's resolutions all tended to a narrowing of her possibilities—of conversation, action, thought.[22] Even feelings of guilt and repentance, those staples of the Victorian mental diet, should be spurned as indulgences, a digression from the dull business of being good.

Nichols's list of negations and self-denials recalls the adolescent negation of another member of the Boston elite of an earlier era, the self-renunciation of Alice James, the invalid sister of Henry and William James. At the age of fourteen, James wrote in a later account, she discovered "what Life meant for her." What it meant was a kind of smothering of impulse, desire, expression. "I had to peg away pretty hard between 12 and 24, 'killing myself,' as some one calls it—absorbing into the bone that the better part is to clothe one-self in neutral tints, walk by still waters, and possess one's soul in silence." By nineteen, Alice James's struggles to suppress her spirit and negate desire had led to breakdown, to "full-blown hysteria," according to her biographer Jean Strouse. Alice James's life story is a famous and extreme case of the impact of narrow parental expectations on girls' behavior and self-estimation. ("In our family group, girls seem scarcely to have had a chance," Henry James wrote of his only sister.)[23] In fact, her description of the mysterious moment of self-repression and negation which ended her autonomous life at the age of fourteen resembles the black-binding or the burning of diaries—the funerals over the selves—mentioned in *St. Nicholas* fiction.

We know about Alice James's decision of denial only because of an adult autobiography. Other girls used their teenage diaries to therapeutic effect as battlegrounds in these psychic wars. The diary of Agnes Hamilton suggests the way that testimonials of goodness might evolve into exercises in identity. This remarkable journal of life in the illustrious Hamilton family is primarily a prolonged account of Alice's struggles to be better. Within the terms of the Hamilton family (not so different from those of the James family), this meant in part becoming more accomplished. Agnes made plans not to loiter, to stop talking so much, not to speak unkindly about anyone, not to read so many novels, and "not to think of myself and how stupid I am but of other people and how bright and splendid they are."[24] Agnes Hamilton's girlhood diary is a workbook in self-discipline.

Yet it is also a confessional diary which reveals some growth in self-understanding. At the age of nineteen, after four years of making and breaking resolutions, Agnes Hamilton made an important New Year's resolution: not to make so many resolutions, "never to plan at night what I shall do the next day . . . never to plan in the summer what I shall do in the Winter or in one term what I shall do in the next." The purpose of this resolution was not to give up resolutions entirely (for it is a case in point), but to make them more realistic. Therein Agnes acquired greater tolerance of herself by virtue of a better understanding of her family. "All this planning and never carrying out," she recognized as a family characteristic. And she even went so far as to say that it might not be a fault, "for we would be pretty miserable if we had to come out of our air castles." After pages of writing in which she inveighed against her own egotism and self-preoccupation, Agnes Hamilton used her understanding of the dynamics of her family to forgive herself.[25]

In the efforts of girls to be good and repress self, diaries seem to have had a moderating effect. Certainly keeping a diary which recorded successes and failures along the road to virtue was an additional incentive to be good. A success could be recorded and celebrated. At the same time, an always-listening, never-judging diary was something of a tonic. Girls who talked enough about their efforts to be good availed themselves of a simplified version of the "talking cure" which would soon be used by Sigmund Freud and Josef Breuer with middle-class Viennese girls. (The disproportionate number of adolescent or late-adolescent females in Freud and Breuer's early work, and indeed the role of hysteria in their formulation of psychoanalysis, corroborates the special salience of language therapy for Victorian girls.)[26] Diarists *were* likely to talk themselves through some of their most censorious impulses and end up with a modicum of self-awareness. It is significant that Alice James, whose adolescent renunciation represented a victory for the dark side of genteel Victorianism, did not record her life and her thought in diary form until she was forty-one, and only then did she declare and explore the renunciation of her youth years before. Had she embarked on this venture in younger years, the creative transcendence that her biographer attributes to discovering a "voice of her own" might have modulated her earlier decision of denial.

Within their diaries, girls assiduously recorded their efforts to be better—echoing, internalizing, and ultimately softening parental imperatives. Just as diaries moderated parental dictates, they mediated parental identifications. As the critic and analyst Katherine Dalsimer suggests, diaries proved to be revisited "transitional objects" useful in the processes of adolescent separation.[27] No other metaphor quite captures the depth of attachment which girls sometimes demonstrated to their "darling" diaries than that analogy to the anthropomorphic blanket or teddy bear of early childhood. Within vessels chartered and christened by parents, Victorian girls embarked on imaginative journeys which did not threaten to take them too far from home.

Though often received from parents as gifts, diaries nonetheless granted more freedom than parents did. In diaries, girls could take on new attachments without abandoning old reliances. Thus when Margaret Tileston went away to boarding school and developed a crush on an older girl, she recorded it in her diary—as well as the news that she had just written a twelve-page letter to her mother, "the longest letter I ever wrote." And when Helen Hart fell in love with her cousin, she confessed to her diary the prolonged anguish

2.4 Girls' play, 1888. Julia Boit sent her cousin Mary surprise messages which she pasted in her diary. This pen-and-ink sketch of girls at play came in an envelope with the instructions "to be opened Easter morning 1892 at a quarter to 8 or if you forget the year after." Schlesinger Library (Cambridge: Radcliffe Institute, Harvard University), A-99-v. 17.

of one "who had never a thought, much less a sorrow" without sharing it with her mother.[28] Such confessions to diaries replaced those to parents—but with parents' informal acquiescence. The diary was thus a tool for legitimating the ongoing reorientation of girls from parents to peers.

Often the diary's role in this transition was not symbolic at all, but quite concrete. Like rolling hoops, diary keeping was a late-Victorian recreation which girls sometimes shared with friends. Mary Boit and her cousins hid secrets in each other's diaries, sometimes simply for the fun of the surprise alone. In fact, the playful fabrication of different personae in diaries was an engrossing amusement within Victorian friendships. Girls described writing diaries together in their rooms, on New Year's Eve, at boarding school, and even in the park.

Shared diary keeping, of course, carried more possibilities than rolling hoops for emotional experimentation, and diaries often became actors in the friendships themselves. Girls frequently wrote about each other, producing provocative documents that became the stuff of suspicion and intimacy. Writing diaries became a way of confessing, protecting, or creating secrets too private for speech. Mary Boit spent a delightful vacation with her cousin Manny, "a witch and a gypsy," with whom she became infatuated. The two girls did not do much at Manny's summer house on Cape Cod, Mary explained, except "write in our js [journals], bathe, read, and draw." They had a tiff, however, over Manny's request (which Mary refused) to read her cousin's journal. "Poor little witch," Mary exclaimed, repenting all the while. "I really think she will have to as I like her so much." Manny's reading of Mary's journal, of course, would let her know, as it does us, of the depth of her cousin's secret admiration.[29] Writing both privileged and protected that secret.

Without the embarrassment of spoken avowals, writing could summon a world of high seriousness distant from casual schoolgirl banter. The exchange between schoolmates and friends Mattie Walker and Mary Thomas (recorded by Walker in Thomas's diary) is a case in point. Walker had seized Thomas's diary in playful protest at being denied permission to read it. After ribbing Thomas for her appetite for peaches and then her penchant for flirtation, Mattie Walker's thoughts became more serious, as she explored the possibilities of writing for confession. "Mary Thomas if I tell you something you declare that you wont tell. Did you know that I am engaged to a fellow that I talked about so. You have been the only person that I have ever told. Dont never tell Lessie or Ida [roommates], for I would not have any bodie to know it for anything now please dont tell, I was ashamed to tell you with my mouth so I will tell you by writing it; you can judge yourself who he is, I cant tell you if I do I will have to tell a story for I promise him that I would not tell it; if you ever tell I never will forgive you. I never will speak to you. Well I must close. Please dont let any bodie see this. Good bye my *honest friend.* I remain yours until Death." Despite her conversational writing style, Mattie expressed shame at the idea of "telling with my mouth," revealing another dimension to the dynamics of the diary. In a Victorian world which celebrated civility, the diary could function as a conduit around awkwardness—even for such blithe spirits as Mattie Walker and Mary Thomas. As Ellen Rothman discovered in her study of Victorian courtship, writing allowed for intimacy which direct conversation inhibited. Written expression, of course, need never be acknowledged.[30] For the same reasons that parents might encourage their daughters to write to them—as a way of communicating without the embarrassment of face-to-face expression—girls might use their diaries among themselves. Writing channeled unseemly emotions.

Deep Ravings

That seemed sometimes to be the point of girls' diaries. Self-governance was expected in feeling no less than conduct, and the diary could prove both a convenient receptacle for—and an incitement to—emotional spillover. In addition to moderating harsh norms and mediating new allegiances, a girl's diary could inspire and then compartmentalize confusing emotions. Almost all diaries contained at least one moment of a confessional nature—sometimes crossed out, sometimes written down the spine in minute handwriting, sometimes just left dangerously on the page. For some the diary's primary purpose seemed to be to provide a safe ground for documenting, exploring, and disciplining nascent sexuality. Victorians strictly limited open expressions of sexuality, but as Michel Foucault persuasively argues, diaries dramatically encouraged discourse about sexuality. Precocious sexuality was both most censured and most discussed—an adult secret imperfectly kept from adolescents themselves.

Harriet Burton's diary, written between the ages of thirteen and seventeen, is a document "saturated" with desire. Initially, when she embarked on her diary at the age of thirteen in 1887, she was reticent: "I find it rather hard to confide all my 'inmost soul' to a journal for my 'inmost soul' is—*very inmost!*" But before long, she had discovered the purpose for which she came to rely on her diary—what she would later call her *"de-praving—deep raving."* Although she felt that her passion could not be "natural" for anyone her age and imagined "how anyone would laugh, how greatly amused they would be at the mere idea of a 'mere-child' of fourteen—*loving,*" she found her feelings "sweet" and despaired at the difficulty of doing them justice—of keeping them from seeming "small and weak." Such self-descriptions as this passage after her arrival for a summer visit in Oneonta, New York, are as of one crazed: "I am in a very hilarious frame of mind today, and can hardly curb my prancing spirits enough to 'wright' as this scrawl bears witness. My silvery voice has been heard at all hours of the day rolling forth in diabolical waves of laughter, and striking terror into the souls of the inhabitants of the house. My mind is so filled with plans which wont come true that I'm nearly crazy. My emotions for other people . . . become so conflicting that they brake from the narrow bounds of my inner man and find vent in a mad race around the house." Despite her descriptions elsewhere of complete freedom for outdoor escapades of all kinds, Harriet Burton described herself here as a *confined* hysteric, very much within the mode of the "madwoman in the attic" of gothic romances. Her confinement was clearly metaphoric, a fictive imprisonment of impulse within fragile shell. As in much of women's gothic literature, Burton saw herself as really two people—a passionate inner self and an outer mask, "a placid calm expression of contentment on my face." And she lamented "how dreadful has [providence] been in giving no times of solitude times which the soul may assert itself and the face throw off the mask, and break out and away from conformity and be *itself*." In this context, Burton equated her authentic self and her sexuality. For Harriet Burton, the only place where her passion could be confessed—with all its inadequacies—was in her diary. "It seems so ridiculous and sentimental to think of writing in a journal, and I would not for anything have *anyone* know that I keep one," she wrote. "But I will confess it to myself it *is* a sort of comfort to sit and write, although it is only talking to myself, and it is often putting down in black and white the things I most despise myself for." She explained the same day, when she was seventeen years old, what is evident from the diary itself, that her diary was for a special purpose. "I only keep this book to write in when I feel a sort of wild feeling like this." Determined not to be "such a creature of emotions and strange passions," she looked upon her diary as an "outlet."[31]

Harriet Burton's description of her crazed state of mind and her need for writing as an outlet are echoed by Charlotte Perkins Gilman's fictional heroine in her 1892 story "The Yellow Wallpaper." In Gilman's tale, a physician husband has forbidden his wife (the narrator) from writing, arguing that "with my imaginative power and habit of story-making, a nervous weakness like mine is sure to lead to all manner of excited fancies, and that I ought to use my will and good sense to check the tendency." The protagonist (a Gilman surrogate) demurs, though: "I think sometimes that if I were only well enough to write a little it would relieve the press of ideas and rest me."[32]

Burton's experience bears out both physician and protagonist. As the physician-husband argues, Burton's "nervous weakness"—or perhaps simply normal libido—did lead to "all manner of excited fancies," which were initially fueled rather than dissipated by the act of writing. But as Gilman's alter ego points out (and Gilman knew as a writer herself), the writing eventually helped to play out the fantasy and relax the writer. After a many-paged reverie of unfocused fantasy, Harriet Burton checked herself with her own "will and good sense": "The wisest thing that I can do is to go and duck my head into cold water, eat something then go downtown where I can see plenty of faces, *real* ones, then come home study my latin—*real* latin, then go to bed, a *real* bed,—to *real* sleep, get up in the morning eat a *real* breakfast, go to school make some *real* recitations, by that time I may be in the realms of *reality* and common sense!"[33]

In Gilman's story, the husband-physician was the censor of fantasy, but in Burton's diary, the writer had become her own censor; either rested or fatigued, she had orchestrated her own return to reality. As in girls' efforts to be good, the impact of the diary was a moderating one. The diary could soften behavioral commands issued by an overzealous superego; it could give rein, and then harness, the runaway fantasies of the id. As such it offered a middle way, a way of allowing momentary release without transgressing social expectations for appropriate behavior.[34]

Private writing allowed Victorian girls saving compromises, enabling the retention of familial ties without enforcing familial destinies. Of course, one could argue that this effect was primarily conservative—that writing provided a safety valve which released and contained rebellious impulses, preventing the telling break with family that might lead to "true" autonomy. But connection with family, then as now, has been important to youths seeking identities. Contemporary research on privileged girls from troubled families concludes that "even in difficult circumstances, young women may struggle to maintain connection in order to know themselves and to be known by their parents."[35] Victorian girls' diaries did not necessarily present stories of relationship with their parents, quite the contrary. Instead, they presented a sanctioned outlet for girls' autonomy within a dense familial setting. Both our understanding of domestic culture and recent work on adolescent maturation suggest the advantages of exercises in identity which allowed Victorian girls to have it both ways: to entertain imaginative freedom while preserving the networks of affiliation at the center of their lives. Victorian girls participated in the significant historical evolution of their era, sustained by, rather than isolated from, natal families.

THREE

Reading and the Development of Taste

Girls' writing was accompanied by what was often a prior activity: abundant reading in the tide of Anglo-American literature swelling in the midcentury and beyond. Girls read and wrote in tandem, often patterning their writing on their reading, and also relying on their reading experiences as the stuff of their diary writing. Restrained from having too many real experiences, they drew on their surrogate reading lives to develop the sensibility and selves they would offer to the world. Victorian girls lived in reading economies of relative abundance, certainly in comparison with those in the previous century. The dense bric-a-brac of Victorian houses was matched by a relative thickness of papers, books, and journals.

The thickness of printed materials made it important to choose among them. Although many girl diarists awaited eagerly issues of such cherished periodicals as *Godey's Ladies Book* or *St. Nicholas*, or waited several years for copies of popular books at local lending libraries, they knew to discriminate. In their judgments of their reading matter, carefully documented in diaries and journals, they developed fictive personalities, which coexisted with and sometimes trumped the dutiful daughters who lived at home.

Revolution in Reading

In part girls' extensive reading reflected new possibilities brought about by developments in the American reading public, the publishing industry, and the distribution of reading matter. Printing was one of those industries in nineteenth-century America—like the ginning and the weaving of cotton—

that was transformed by technological advances. The result was a substantial increase in the production of books and a much wider distribution of those books, helped along also by the free library movement.

High rates of literacy both encouraged and resulted from this increase in the availability of printed materials. The American Revolution itself, many historians have argued, was galvanized by a public literate enough to read and debate the pamphlets issued by politicized journeymen printers. Women were not well represented among those numbers, though probably many women who could not write could read. In the decades immediately following the Revolution, the literacy rate among women rose dramatically. A study of rural Vermont in 1800 concludes that even away from urban areas "the proportion of women engaged in lifelong reading and writing had risen to about eighty percent." With the opening of common schools in the nineteenth century, girls were educated the same ways that boys were — unevenly, sometimes at home, sometimes at school, but effectively. By 1880 reading literacy was claimed by 90 percent of the native-born American public and 80 percent of their foreign-born compatriots.[1]

The explosion of print in the nineteenth century was enabled by a variety of developments in both technology and distribution. Technological innovations in printing nourished the growth of the antebellum reading public. The innovations of stereotyping and electrotyping preserved an "impressment" of the type once it had been set so that future editions would not require expensive resetting. The result was that before the Civil War the cost of books dropped to roughly half of their cost in the late eighteenth century. Although at seventy-five cents or more such a price was still too costly for skilled male laborers who earned only a dollar a day, and although inadequacy of lighting in many working-class homes helped to limit the Victorian reading public, a substantial proportion of Americans — those who were coming to constitute the aspiring middle class — were able to gain access to books.[2] Access to books did not define an American public, but increasingly it defined a class of those who hoped to rise in station.

Improvements in printing technology fostered the growth of another literary genre, the periodical, which launched many novels in serialized form in both Britain and the United States. Periodicals in the United States and Britain budded in the early nineteenth century, and a number flowered at midcentury, feeding and fed by the literacy and leisure of Victorian readers. Included among these were a growing selection of magazines targeting special audiences, especially youth. *Youth's Companion,* founded in 1827, mustered the greatest longevity and the highest circulation, and it was joined by the influential *St. Nicholas* (1873), which amassed a distinguished group of writers. The preeminent magazine for women, *Godey's Ladies Book,* achieved a circulation of 150,000 at its prime just before the Civil War. Girls and women provided much of the readership for the general family magazine as well, including *Scribner's, Harper's Weekly, North American Review,* and *Century.*[3] Periodicals had the advantage of providing regular access to print for a reading-hungry populace and were especially cherished by those far away from lending libraries and those whose economic circumstances forced them to ration their reading.

Cassie Upson, who lived with her aunts in Charlemont, Massachusetts, during the Civil War, often experienced a shortage of reading material. At the age of eleven, she announced to her diary her anticipation, nearly a week in advance, of *Godey's.* Earlier in 1862 she had noted a period of reading famine on May 11: "I wish I could have something to read." She encouraged herself that hope was in sight, because "it is nearly the 6th of June Eddie's birthday and he will certainly have *one* book."[4] A periodical subscription could guarantee at least some relief from periods of scarcity.

The public library movement expanded access to reading material beyond the ranks of the wealthy. Along with the growth of common-school education, libraries provided the institutional underpinning of the reading revolution. As early as the eighteenth century, groups of ambitious private citizens had united to share access to precious books. Later in the century clerks, merchants, and mechanics, too, gathered to form so-called "social libraries" which could be joined by payment of a fee. It was to one of these libraries which Lois Wells, a resident of Quincy, Illinois, received a three-month subscription for her seventeenth birthday in 1886, probably because there was no public library in her town. The importance of an educated citizenry to a republic encouraged the founding of more free facilities, however. Beginning in Boston, and then expanding outward to New England and on to the Midwest, free libraries aimed to offer to all citizens the opportunity for uplift and self-culture which was previously available only to an elite. The Boston Public Library opened its doors in 1854, and other cities followed suit in increasing numbers after the Civil War. States supported local efforts by passing legislation which would allow townships to divert public funds to the support of free libraries. A massive government report in 1876 listed 3,682 public libraries, a number which would rise to at least 8,000 by 1900.[5] Access to public libraries was uneven, however, thinning out as one moved west and especially south from New England and the mid-Atlantic.

Taking up the slack between the vogue for reading and its limited supply,

Sunday schools enhanced their appeal and ensured the quality of children's reading matter by acquiring book collections and issuing weekly books to deserving students. When the American Sunday School Union and other religious publishers began issuing prepackaged "libraries" of their own publications in the midcentury (one hundred books for $10), the custom became even more prevalent—until eclipsed by the public-library movement itself. Ida B. Wells, born during the Civil War to slave parents, read all the fiction in her school and her Sunday school library to distract her from worries in the postwar years. Cassie Upson, who had felt constantly deprived of books while living with her aunts in Massachusetts, found a regular source of reading material in the Sunday school she attended in Milwaukee, where she and her siblings had joined her father and his new wife. Upson also mentioned acquiring books from the "Y.M.A.," probably a Y.M.C.A. library.[6]

Genteel Reading Protocols for Girls

The project of self-culture did not regard all reading as equal, of course. The removal of girls from their mothers' elbows as informal apprentices in housewifery meant a partial surrender of daughters to a national or transAtlantic culture. Advice givers subjected it to scrutiny, often discussing the appropriate fare for Victorian girls. In the United States, those standards became the defining standards for genteel culture as a whole. Richard Gilder, the eminent publisher of *Century*, outlined the rules for his writers. "No vulgar slang; no explicit references to sex, or, in more genteel phraseology, to the generative processes; no disrespectful treatment of Christianity; no unhappy endings for any work of fiction." Designed for reading aloud within the family circle, genteel fiction as a whole, but periodical literature in particular, had to pass what was named by poet Edmund Stedman the "virginibus" standard—whether it would be appropriate even for the unmarried daughters of a respectable bourgeois family to listen to or to read.[7]

This reading program had some general precepts. Of course, religious literature of all kinds was favored for study and improvement. The old was better than the new, a rule that encouraged history, and for younger children, myths and legends. Seventy-three years old in 1880, the writer and woman's rights advocate Elizabeth Oakes Smith suggested a conservative regimen for girls which included history, biography, constitutional and moral philosophy, geography, travel literature, science, and "the several branches of natural history which open up to the mind the wonders and mysteries of this beautiful world in which we live." An advice giver twenty-five years later explained why myths were appropriate for children's reading: they were "interpretive of the beautiful and useful in nature, of the high and noble impulses of the heart, and of the right in human intercourse."[8]

The counsel to admire the beautiful and to seek the pure and the true left advice writers conflicted about the most popular genre on the reading lists of girls: the novel. The *right* novels had power to do much good. The British advice writer Henrietta Keddie recommended "without fail [Elizabeth Gaskell's] Cranford, and Miss Austen's books, to make you a reasonable, kindly woman." The goal of such works was to discipline aspiration, however, for the exemplary woman would be "satisfied with a very limited amount of canvas on which to figure in the world's great living tapestry." Elizabeth Oakes Smith implored young girls to avoid the low road and "most of the fictions of the day," admitting only "those based on the eras of history, such as the inimitable works of Walter Scott," and the works of Dickens, which "may deepen our sympathy for the miserable and erring."[9]

Another later counselor to young girls, Harriet Paine, in *Chats with Girls on Self-Culture* (1900) also challenged the appropriateness of realism: "Girlhood is not the time for any novelist who does not believe that something besides the actual is possible and necessary." She too applauded Sir Walter Scott, who was always "to be trusted to present a natural world which is nevertheless rosy with the light of romance," and Dickens: "I never knew a girl who loved Dickens who was not large-hearted." Paine was more inclusive, though: "There are half a dozen fresh, sweet story-writers girls are always the better for reading," and then she enumerated Louisa May Alcott and a number of British writers, including Dinah Mulock-Craik, Anne Thackeray, and Charlotte Yonge.[10]

Much fiction, however, did not grow "where the rose-tree blooms" but instead led young readers "through mire and dirt," advisers cautioned. Genteel periodicals for youth contained some of the most pointed warnings to youths of both sexes about the dangers of inappropriate reading. An outburst from *St. Nicholas* in 1880 warned that a craving for sensational fiction is more insidious, but "I am not sure that it is not quite as fatal to character as the habitual use of strong drink." The reading of illicit fiction "weakens the mental grasp, destroys the love of good reading, and the power of sober and rational thinking, takes away all relish from the realities of life, breeds discontent and indolence and selfishness, and makes the one who is addicted to it a weak, frivolous, petulant, miserable being."[11] The power attributed to the vicarious excitement of the emotions remained something of a constant through the nineteenth century.

Given such acknowledged dangers, how did girls get access to such books?

The question of access played out in a debate over the holdings of public libraries. Librarians made up a new group of elite reformers who aimed to elevate the public intellect through their professional organization, the American Library Association. In 1881, the ALA attempted to impose uniform censorship on the collections formed for the public good, and got as far as surveying major public libraries and compiling a list of sixteen authors "whose works are sometimes excluded from public libraries by reason of sensational or immoral qualities." The list included twelve female domestic novelists — such popular writers as E. D. E. N. Southworth and Mary Jane Holmes.[12] It did not go farther. The library ultimately compromised its genteel ambitions with the tastes of the public, and by the turn of the century reliably stocked what its readers wanted to read.

Throughout the late century, libraries appear to have been more permissive than genteel parents. Louisa May Alcott's *Old-Fashioned Girl* satirized the silly chatter of schoolgirls, their precociousness encouraged by modern fiction available from the library. "Oh, have you read 'The Phantom Bride'? It's perfectly thrilling! There's a regular rush for it at the library; but some prefer 'Breaking a Butterfly.'" (Alcott's virtuous heroine Polly, demurs, explaining, "I haven't read anything but one of the Muhlbach novels since I came. I like those, because there is history in them.") "Regular rushes" at the library, however, could be nearly as effective as outright bans in keeping individual patrons from getting access to best-sellers. Bostonian Lizzie Morrissey waited three years to get a copy of Mary Jane Holmes's *Marian Grey* and was finally successful in 1876.[13] The book, by an author that the ALA would have hoped to "ban in Boston," told a ripe and baroque tale of a homely rich girl, a marriage of convenience, and multiple love triangles and intercepted letters, ending with a remarriage of transformed wife to unknowing husband. (A character who is in on the secret exclaims in the last lines of the book: "Ain't she pretty, though? It's curis how clothes will fix up a woman.") The flirtation of the tale with bigamy and adultery, of course, constituted its appeal — though as in most such fiction, hidden propriety undergirded sensational appearances.

The Family Circle

In theory, Victorians concerned with troublesome issues on the margins of respectable fiction for girls could deal with them within the family reading circle. Reading aloud was perhaps the most common domestic entertainment within the Victorian family, used as reward, improvement, or therapy for life's challenges. The sisters taking turns reading to accompany their needlework, the matron at the sickbed, the daughter reading to her father at the end of a business day—there were myriad arenas in which families used reading to ease, amuse, and instruct.

At its most basic, reading aloud enabled the sharing of resources (a book, or a fresh installment of a periodical) among many. But beyond that, it was a profoundly social way of responding to the lessons of history, current fiction, or poetry. The critic Andrew Blake suggests that the novel, in particular, was "a most important point of contact between the public and the private" because "it gave people a chance to discuss domestic ideology *in public* without touching on domestic secrets." The semipublic sphere that was the family circle provided an important venue for the discussion of reading. Within this context, instruction in morality could be accomplished informally, gently, impersonally, with reference to fictional characters rather than through direct criticism and rebuttal. The convention of the family reading circle generally restricted polite novels from treating illicit sexuality or immoral characters, but if any lapses occurred, the family circle could deal with them most effectively. Thus Elizabeth Gaskell said of her own novel *Ruth,* which features an orphan who has been seduced by an aristocrat: "Of course it is a prohibited book in *this,* as in many other households." The one circumstance that would change its unsuitability for young people, she opined, was if it was "read with someone older," perhaps with an older female relative within a family reading group.[14]

The kind of family conversation which could improve all who participated was explained by Sarah Browne in a private diary in 1859. "Albert brings [Harriet Beecher Stowe's] the Minister's Wooing. We sit quietly and hear how James is brought back to the living, we calmly rejoice with Mary, plan and maneuver with Miss Pressy, call Parson Hopkins in very truth a Christian and wind up the evening by wishing to see Mrs. Stowe, knowing how she would seem and if she would talk at all, like other women." Albert Browne Sr. was generally the reader in the Browne family, sometimes of "superior articles in the *Atlantic Monthly.*" In these moments of quiet, Sarah Browne most idealized her shared family life, "sitting as we do in our little western chamber, Father, Alice and I storing in the rich thoughts of others as a life element of our own."[15] Reading aloud enabled a submersion of family tensions in a focus outward on the problems of others.

The idealization of the shared reading experience suggested stylized familial communion to daughters as well as parents. During the final days of the Civil War, as she anticipated her own marriage, Helen Hart thought to memorialize the evenings reading aloud together. "I think I never enjoyed evenings more in my life. First Bertie reads, then Hady, and then Mother and I;

from History, Shakespeare, the Atlantic, and other miscellany. Such peaceful, happy winter evenings at home! Something for us to look back upon in after years when we are scattered. I have treasured up each one as it passed, as a sweet and sacred memory." The pleasure came from the contrast between "our quiet harbor" and "the world with its commotions, its struggles." Never did home seem so secure and safe as when implicitly contrasted with the adventures and misfortunes of fictional characters, warring nations, or past princes. Charlotte Perkins Gilman's biographer noted that Charlotte and her destitute and emotionally distant mother were at their best when reading aloud to each other, their fraught intimacy dissolved in their shared focus on the lives and feelings of others. Those moments of community might even be resurrected by rereading books so experienced. ("It seems as if we were gathered around the nursery fire again. I can almost hear Aunt Mary's voice.")[16] The pleasures of reading aloud were those of reading mediated—reading mediated by the fiction of shared purpose.

Reading aloud did not have a single simple meaning, however, nor did it model only one kind of power relationship. The Browne family's shared reading was patriarchal, with father reading and other family members (according to the hardly impartial mother) celebrating familial harmony. Alice Stone Blackwell, in her irreverent and spritely diary, offered another example of paternal reading aloud, lightly satirizing her father, the noted reformer and women's rights advocate Henry Blackwell: "Papa sat with his feet on the top of the stove, saturated with laziness, and rated me for enjoying stories [fiction], and formed plans to give me a taste for instructive literature, and ended by making me bring Plutarch's Lives, and beginning to read them aloud."[17] This depiction of a well-respected father indulging in playful tyranny of his only child suggests a quite different emotional shading—if a similar actual structure—to the idealized portraits of patriarchal reading circles.

Monitoring Reading

Daughters also read on their own, though, and given the risks of immoral reading and the gains from uplifting reading, good parents attempted to monitor what they read. The goal in choosing reading, as in all the lessons of character, was to instruct gently and surely so as to encourage daughters to make familial lessons their own. Advice to parents ranged from the relatively cut and dried—"Parents should choose the books that their children read until the age of 15"—to the more subtle: "Wise parents put so many good books in the way of their children that the taste for them is formed unconsciously, and there is never any feeling of restraint." (The latter piece of advice, made in 1901, was clearly advice for the book-wealthy.) Ellen Emerson's correspondence with her mother while away at boarding school suggested the appropriate supervisory relationship of parents over girls' reading. Explaining that she was reading Elizabeth Gaskell's *Cranford,* which she found "a very funny book," she went on, "I never read any that I am not sure you would be willing to have me," and recorded her assumption that Scott, Gaskell, and several others were "not forbidden." She went on to query, "May I read [Margaret Oliphant's] 'Head of the Family'?"[18] Middle-class or elite parents who participated in genteel Victorian culture assumed an important role in controlling the reading of their daughters—its quantity, its contents, and its circumstances.

In the elite midwestern Hamilton family, a family with a strong and eclectic reading tradition, novels were doled out prudently like candies during vacations from school, so as not to interfere with schoolwork. When her daughter was fifteen, Phoebe Hamilton gave her "Ivanhoe for my holiday reading, she always gives me one of Scott every vacation." The next year her mother was more liberal, providing Scott's *Quentin Durward* for a Christmas book and giving permission for the reading of Dickens's *Little Dorrit* and Jemima Tautphoeus's *The Initials.* As January arrived, Agnes lamented, "I have finished the latter but I am afraid as I go back to school next Monday I shall have to let Little Dorrit wait till summer." There was a hierarchy within Hamilton family reading, and despite her voraciousness, Agnes felt that her tastes fell short of her family's preferences. "Oh! why haven't I the love of learning of the family?" She indicated what was expected in her next breath: "Knight's England vol. III has been read all but two chapters since last fall and during two months I have read but four books of the Odyssey." She forced herself to be realistic. "During this next week [probably a school vacation] I want [to] finish half a dozen or more books which I have begun but I dare say the novels are the only ones that will be looked much in."[19]

Like the Hamilton reading regimen, other family routines, too, involved matters of both quality and quantity. There were appropriate ages for the reading of different books. At fifteen, Margaret Tileston wanted to read George Macdonald's *Alec Forbes of Howglen,* an homage to the dignity of Scots country life. The author was certainly approved, but Margaret's mother didn't want her to read the book "yet." At eighteen, Margaret was still reading under adult scrutiny. Sick at home she was "allowed" to read Charlotte Brontë's *Jane Eyre,* considered excessively charged for young girls, and polished off 340 pages on the first day. Reading was one way of being inducted

3.1 Hamilton readers, 1890s. Agnes Hamilton, left, grew up in a close-knit extended family, where she shared and competed with her cousins Alice and Allen,
together known as "the Three A's." Schlesinger Library (Cambridge: Radcliffe Institute, Harvard University), MC278-791-2.

into family ideology; when Margaret reread *Pilgrim's Progress* in 1883, she was
conscious that she was reading a book that had been important to her mother
when she was young.[20]

Family Conflict

Monitoring was in theory a matter of gentle influence. It might well emerge
as outright war, though, in efforts to regulate the subscription-driven serial
literature which arrived unannounced with the day's mail. The child-rearing

conflicts in the Blackwell family resemble modern-day struggles over access to the Web; then it was the United States mail which brought the unannounced and loosely authorized productions of a mass culture into the family circle. The focus of the struggle in the Blackwell family was the "story paper" the *New York Ledger*.

Newspapers through the first part of the nineteenth century reported commercial and political news and were of little interest to adolescent girls. Later in the century, however, hungry for expanded readership, newspapers revised their formats. In 1880 the writer and reformer Elizabeth Oakes Smith noted a change in the newspapers. In earlier times, "great crimes were infrequent and personal vices unknown; hence there was no demoralizing atmosphere in the shape of perverting advertisements or the details of moral obliquities, all being wholesome and in a manner refreshing. There were no blasphemous jokes, no irreverent handling of sacred themes, no gross allusions to corrupt and lower the sentiments of the young." In short, there was little attraction for girls. Later in the century, though, a change in format broadened the newspaper's appeal. Smith censured the tendencies of girls to read such papers as the *Ledger,* "full of mawkish sentiment and opinions counter to the true end and aim of life, which is to do good in our little sphere."[21]

When the *Ledger* became a "story paper" in 1855, it began to build toward its peak circulation of 400,000. Its success was built on its ability to pay good money to such popular authors as Sara Willis, otherwise known as Fanny Fern, to serialize their works in its pages. The *Ledger*'s publisher Robert Bonner sought out "thrillers" but intended his paper to be respectable, bragging that "there has never appeared one line which the old lady in Westchester County would not like to read to her daughters."[22] Despite its owner's proclamation, however, respectable opinion was not unanimous about the *Ledger*'s propriety.

The reading of the *New York Ledger* became a point of heated controversy in the home of Lucy Stone and Henry Blackwell. Neither parent, both outspoken orators for abolition and women's rights, would have confined women to the "little sphere" Oakes Smith advocated, but Lucy Stone in particular disapproved strenuously of the *Ledger*'s effects on her high-spirited daughter Alice. The campaign of 1872 started with rationing: "Mamma let me have a Ledger for a few minutes, and then lit the fire with it." But by May the battle was engaged in earnest. "Mama told me a Ledger had come; that she had left it behind [at the office], and never meant to let another come into the house. I said I should get it the next day when I went in; she said it had gone to be cut into wrappers. Papa said that was adding insult to injury, as indeed it was; why need she have told me? She could have kept t[w]o back and said nothing. To stop me right in the midst of 'Mark Heber's Luck!' I straightaway went off to bed mad, with tears in my eyes." Clearly her mother did not relent in her opposition to the *Ledger,* but Alice Blackwell was her mother's daughter and equally intransigent herself. By August she "eloped," as she put it, leaving home unannounced, "being bound to have my Ledger and Library books." On her way into town, however, she had the misfortune to run into her father, "who asked where I was going and if Mama knew." A month later when it appeared that her father had gone to work, taking the newspapers with him (to her "wrath and disgust"), Alice acted on her own again. "I felt that to wait till night for my Ledger meant insanity, so went to the printing office, where I found his satchel and extracted the precious document." Her last reference suggested that some kind of compromise had been reached, although likely not to Alice's satisfaction: "Glanced over a Ledger which Mama would not let me read."[23] Alice Stone Blackwell's war with her parents over the subject of her reading of the *New York Ledger* has some of the sense of a line in the sand. In denying her access to sensational fiction, Lucy Stone was determined to put some constraint on a virtually irrepressible spirit. But as in parents' efforts to assign writing for their own purposes, girls managed to appropriate reading for themselves and to use it in the process of constructing a self that was only partly their parents' creature.

Reading as Personal Community

Alice Blackwell's addiction to the *Ledger* was problematic in part because of her age. As a fourteen-year-old girl, she struggled with her parents for access to adult papers which published questionable fiction. Youth periodicals emerged in part to solve the problem the *Ledger* presented to the Blackwell family. Such periodicals reassured parents, but did not speak for them, inducting girls into membership in a trans-Atlantic youth culture which many girls experienced as their own. The arrival of periodicals in the mail had an especially magical and mysterious quality for girls and boys who had not yet grown inured to the idea of perfect strangers addressing them with intimacy and understanding. Periodical readers, at least as measured by those who wrote into *St. Nicholas*'s "The Letter-Box," asserted their strong sense of belonging to the magazine and of respect for its authority, both sentiments which the editors encouraged. Founded in 1873, with a steady peak circulation of seventy thousand, *St. Nicholas* had a remarkably long run as an elite publication for Victorian children, an age span which the journal defined as extending until the age of twenty. Circulation figures likely undercount those actually reading *St. Nicholas* because not only did one issue serve for an entire family, but evidence suggests that copies of *St. Nicholas* would circulate beyond families as well. When *St. Nicholas* ran contests of any kind it could count on several thousand responses.[24]

St. Nicholas advanced an inclusive notion of who its readers might be. In response to a letter from a nonsubscriber in 1874, the editors announced a policy of welcome to the club of *St. Nicholas* readers: "We look upon every boy and girl who can read English, or look at a picture, as belonging in some way to *St. Nicholas*." Although its readers were clearly clustered in the middle and upper middle classes and its voice was decidedly genteel, as a "commodity" sold for profit, *St. Nicholas* had only to gain from open admission to its reading community. Its reach extended into at least some households that could little afford it—such as in 1904 the desperately poor home of single mother Cora Millay, whose daughter Edna at twelve began a sustaining correspondence with the magazine that launched her career as a poet.[25]

In fact, its readers revealed more geographical than class spread. American readers from outposts around the world expressed indebtedness to the magazine for linking them to other children or youth. Both boys and girls wrote to *St. Nicholas,* too, to establish a personal connection with a distant voice and for the thrill of being legitimized on a national scale. The excitement of having one's name in print must have been a much magnified version of the thrill which one eight-year-old girl experienced when she realized that she had an identity separate from her parents—one that was even recognized by the U.S. mails: "I think the happiest day in the month is when my St. Nicholas comes, with my own name on the wrapper." Children's magazines, even more than other kinds of reading, personalized the reading process; in their special relation to children and youth they suggested, however conditionally, the intoxicating possibility of a child's independence from his or her parents, as well as separate participation on a cultural stage. The literary historian Cathy Davidson has demonstrated the importance of novels in empowering the female reader unmediated by "ministers or magistrates."[26] The children's magazine similarly came to children directly, unmediated by parents.

As a result, the child's magazine helped to lend dignity to the child. This seemed to represent at least part of *St. Nicholas*'s goal. Its editor and guiding spirit, Mary Mapes Dodge, expressed her hope that her magazine would genuinely belong to youths, rather than to their parents or their teachers. In fact, she argued for substantial autonomy for children. "Most children of the present day attend school. Their heads are strained and taxed with the day's lessons. They do not want to be bothered nor amused nor petted. They just want to have their own way over their own magazine. They want to enter one place where they can come and go as they please." For these reasons, children and youth expressed not just gratitude but affection to *St. Nicholas.* One correspondent wrote simply to tell "how I love you, — yes I believe I almost love you." Correspondents anthropomorphized magazines into particular forms as companions. One ten-year-old boy, who traveled with his mother on his father's three-masted schooner, wrote to the editors: "I am very lonely often at sea, and St. Nicholas is one of my most prized companions."[27] Because it had an address and a proper name, the magazine *St. Nicholas* was perhaps easier to anthropomorphize than other kinds of reading material, but such confessions of adoration of books were common too.

Writing in Virginia during the Civil War, Lucy Breckinridge confided in her diary appreciation for her "beloved friends, Addison, Steele, etc." She reported, "The Spectator is constantly before my eyes," and feared that without it she would die of "ennui." As girls often did, she analogized life and literature, remarking of a Confederate officer visiting her family, "Lieut. Richardson is very much like Addison." In describing books as companions, and also as pets, another conventional analogy, Victorian readers were treating books as they did their diaries — as useful transition objects into autonomy. Readers were also operating on the level of base cliché. Advice givers constantly urged such a sentiment on readers, suggesting as *Harper's Young People* did in 1884 that "every good book is a dear silent friend, always ready to give you its company, no matter whether the sun shines or the rain falls." Yet the attachments readers confess suggest more than simply convention — but instead sometimes a self-defining commitment to an author or a character. Mary Boit's response to the death of the poet James Russell Lowell did just that. On August 12, 1891, she recorded, "I feel so sad just as if I could cry. James Russell Lowell my favorite poet is dead. . . . I think his poems are beautiful. . . . Oh dear one he really is so lovely at least I think so from the way he expresses himself." Her grief was rendered a good bit more meaningful by her observation that "there is nobody here who likes him well enough to sympathize with me." Several weeks later she was imaginatively spending her anticipated birthday money. "I know just exactly what I would get for two dollars I would get J. R. Lowells complete poems for one dollar his photograph for two his life that is if Papa gave me five dollars as he did last birthday."[28] Through her admiration for James Russell Lowell, Mary Boit elevated her sense of alienation from family members into membership in a broader literary culture.

Private Reading

The plasticity of the notion of reading meant that it represented the medium through which middle-class Victorian girls passed many hours, but it did not bring a uniform message. Like their parents and advisers, adolescent girls who were writing about reading were of two minds. On the one hand, as William Thayer put it, reading could be a way of demonstrating rectitude and diligence; on the other, it could be a route to indolence and the shirking of responsibilities. Mary Thomas, away at school in Georgia in 1873, suggested these dual meanings of reading as she imagined a newly virtuous domesticity for herself upon returning home: "I will sew and read all the time, I am not going out any where, but intend to stay at home and work all the time; no matter how interesting a book may be, I will put it down and do whatever I am asked to do, they shall no longer accuse me of being lazy and good for nothing, I will work all day."[29] In its contrast to engaging in a social whirl of visiting and flirtation, reading, like sewing, represented a becoming and modest domesticity. However, reading might also subvert good intentions, and tempt a girl to inattention to, or even disobedience of, the demands of others or of household work. In any case, reading had a meaning for the self, as well as for the family and the culture.

Reading good books was of course a way of demonstrating virtue. Measured reading of improving texts was part of the regimen of many Victorian girls. As advisers suggested, the reading of history was especially praiseworthy. When Nellie Browne returned home from school in 1859, her mother noted in her diary with pride, "Nellie begins to read daily Eliot's History of the United States," a parentally encouraged discipline which would both improve and occupy Nellie now that her school days were over. Jessie Wendover, the daughter of a prosperous Newark grocer and another regular diarist, recorded a steady diet of history in her journal, justifying her summer vacation in 1888 with the reading of a two-volume *History of the Queens of England*, as well as doing a little Latin and some arithmetic. The popular British domestic novelist Charlotte Yonge wrote her *History of Germany* specifically for readers like Jessie Wendover, who began it the following year.[30] What American girl readers took from the history they read is hard to ascertain, because unlike their rapt reports on novels, they recorded their history as achievement rather than illumination. One can certainly appreciate the irony, though, in encouraging girls to read accounts of national travails, the stories of armies, wars, and dynastic succession, which were ennobled partly by their distance from girls' real lives. One of the advantages of history seemed to be that girls could be expected to have no worrisome practical interest in it—in marked contrast to the reading of romances or novels.

Victorian girls could build character through a variety of other literary projects, prime among them the memorizing of poetry. Over the course of the late nineteenth century, the publishing industry issued a number of collections of snippets of poetry known as "memory gems," designed for memorization by schoolchildren. The verse in these anthologies was to serve as "seed-thoughts" for earnest young Victorians aspiring to know the best, and these were the likely sources for many of the couplets which appear in girls' diaries and scrapbooks.[31]

Margaret Tileston's daily diary, recorded religiously for her entire life, both fed and celebrated a variety of literary disciplines, including most prominently reading and memorizing poetry. She too read histories during the summer, along with keeping up with her other studies, noting one July day following her graduation from Salem High School that she had "read my usual portions of Macaulay [a 40-page allotment] and French, but only a few pages of Spencer." Margaret Tileston also read advice literature, such as Mary Livermore's *What Shall We Do with Our Daughters?* and two books by Samuel Smiles, *Self-Help* and *Duty.* (The latter she described as looking "quite interesting and full of anecdotes.")[32] Margaret Tileston's diaries suggest a life consumed with the rewards of self-culture.

At fifteen, however, she recorded a brush with another literary genre and mode of striving—a seeking not only for mastery of the will but for beauty itself. Poetry first appeared simply as a verse of romantic poetry copied on the page: "Why thus longing thus forever sighing, for the far-off, unattained, and dim, while the beautiful, all round thee lying, offers up its low, perpetual hymn." Margaret Tileston was now away at girls' school, where she had experienced something of an emotional awakening in the intense atmosphere of schoolgirl friendships. Her turn to poetry seems to reflect the new culture in which she was briefly submerged. That summer, back with her family on vacation on the Massachusetts coast, Tileston again turned to poetry, and to beauty, in an uncharacteristic passage of effusion. "The moon was perfectly lovely in the sky and its light on the water. We quoted lines of poetry, and it was beautiful."[33]

By January of the next year, however, poetry had been incorporated into her disciplines of order and accomplishment. After returning from boarding school, she had moved with her family from the farm where she had spent her formative years to the town of Salem, where she attended the local high school. There she embarked on another campaign of self-improvement, the memorization of poetry, perhaps as a strategy to gain control of alien surroundings. Two months later she described a new discipline: the daily ritual repetition of all the poems she had learned, of which there were by then 111. On May 25 she reported that her extraordinary ability to memorize poetry was gaining her a reputation. "Miss Perry asked me if I knew about 250 poems. She said that one of the Goodhue girls had told her I did. I remarked something of the sort to Miss Perkins one day in recess, and somehow it was repeated." By the end of July she noted that she was beginning to have trouble finding new poems to learn because she knew so many already. Appreciation of the beauty of poetry had dropped out of her journal. Nor did she suggest that the poetry had any meaning to her at all. Yet she very likely gained some of the satisfactions from poetry expressed by Louisa May Alcott, some years before. After disobeying her mother, at the age of eleven, Alcott "cried, and then I felt better, and said that piece from Mrs. Sigourney, 'I must not tease my mother.'" She went on, "I get to sleep saying poetry,—I know a great deal." For those feeling guilty, sad, misunderstood, or wronged, repeating lines of elevating poetry had an effect in a secular mode analogous to the saying of ritual Hail Marys. The verses established an alliance with a higher authority and suggested personal participation in a glorious and tragic human struggle.[34]

And in fact, poetry, even more than history, was the prototypical idealist genre. In 1851 the British educational pioneers Maria Grey and Emily Shirreff proposed the reading of poetry rather than fiction, explaining the crucial distancing effect of poetic subjects. "In a poem, the wildest language of passion, though it may appeal to the feelings, is generally called forth in circumstances remote from the experience of the reader." They suggested that in poetry there was a higher truth than that of superficial realism: "The grand conceptions of the poet are true in ideal beauty." Writing fifty years later, Harriet Paine too suggested that poetry had generic qualities of elevation. "After all, in poetry itself *what* we read is not the important thing. We should read poetry to give us a certain attitude of mind, a habit of thinking of noble things, of keeping our spirit in harmony with beauty and goodness and strength and love." Earlier Paine had commended the memorization of poetry as necessary to "take in the full meaning," suggesting just such a regular regimen of repetition as Tileston had pursued. The spiritual rewards from internalizing poetry were revealed by Paine's proposal that it take place on the Sabbath:

"Surely we must give a part of every Sunday to such elevating study." Elizabeth Barrett Browning had censured poets for their historical escapism in her
1857 poem *Aurora Leigh*, arguing

> *Their sole work is to represent the age,*
> *Their age, not Charlemagne's—this live, throbbing age,*
> *That brawls, cheats, maddens, calculates, aspires.*[35]

Yet it was in just its remoteness from "this live, throbbing age," just in the "to-
gas and the picturesque" disparaged by Browning that poetry was considered
so appropriate for girl readers.

The Pursuit of Beauty

In their reading and memorizing—and in their writing—of poetry, girls
expressed their desires to reveal the heightened sensibility, the refinement of
poetic idealism. Charlotte Brontë described *Shirley*'s Caroline reciting poetry,
suggesting that "Such a face was calculated to awaken not only the calm
sentiment of esteem, the distant one of admiration; but some feeling more
tender, genial, intimate: friendship, perhaps—affection, interest." As Nancy
Armstrong suggests, Brontë's emphasis on Caroline's self-consciousness, her
calculation of the effect of her sensibility, suggested a complex of attributes
which poetry was thought to bring to those who could be moved by it.[36]
In their participation in its raptures girls were revealing their own ability to
discern and to admire beauty, and to be defined by it.

And that was one purpose of reading. Girls read in part in order to aspire
to the beautiful. Mary Boit found that "beautiful" in the *Life, Letters, and
Journals of Miss Alcott*: "I wish I could follow her life in some ways it is so
beautiful." Agnes Hamilton eloquently explained how reading could positively elevate her. Back in her family's home in Fort Wayne, Indiana, after
leaving boarding school in the East, she was beginning to feel trapped and despondent, fearing that "I should never, never leave." Her diary then changed
tone, however, as she commented on reading aloud to her brother J. H. Short-
house's *Sir Percival: A Story of the Past and the Present* (1886). "It has put me in
a different frame of mind. What could I do if I did not have books. Living in a
book for a time certainly makes one feel as if she had had a change of air. Just
the books I have lived in today were full of such splendid people that I feel as
if I had been in purer, better, higher society." Agnes Hamilton's brush with
the Middle Ages had the effect of refreshing her and also of restoring some of
the appropriate optimism to her daily surroundings. "And now it comes over
me how truly thankful I am and ought to be for the people, the real people

around me."[37] Her reading had accomplished the archetypal idealist chore: making her see her surroundings with an enhancing vision which recast the ordinary into its purified shapes and forms.

Of course, some of the aspiration reading embodied was simply the aspiration to the refinement associated with class. Frieda and Belle Fligelman, two Montana sisters, remembered their attitude toward the *Literary Digest,* a symbol of Victorian elevation. "We would read those magazines with considerable effort but with a great deal of respect for ourselves for doing it. We felt we were being quite intellectual." Less integrated into elite literary culture than Margaret Tileston or Agnes Hamilton, they associated reading with "bettering" their class standing—an aspiration to social improvement rather than individual virtue. The endemic Anglophilia of literary culture confirmed the associations of spiritual refinement with Old World aristocracy. Ellen Emerson, daughter of the prototypical voice of American idealism, in 1858 wrote to her cousin and friend with unabashed admiration for British royalism. To her friend she asked: "Are you interested in the Princess Royal of England? In this family we have a great affection for Victoria and her children, and read the Court Circular every week regularly, so for the past few weeks everything being full of her marriage we were too and we are enchanted with the descriptions of the event at last." Agnes Hamilton, writing some thirty years later shared the unashamed Anglophilia of Ellen Emerson. She read her father's Christmas annuals, which she professed to like *"very"* much. "I suppose one reason is because they are English and I like anything English."[38] Anglophilia was in part facilitated simply by the absence of international copyright protection for British authors. American markets were flooded with British reprints, which provided American readers with broad exposure to British writers. Beyond that, though, genteel idealism itself encouraged the defining of the beautiful as remote and refined—easier to imagine in the Scottish mists or in medieval tournaments than in the modern, raucous, industrial American present.

Reading as Secret Life

If reading presented an opportunity to discover national allies, to demonstrate private virtue, and to suggest the triumph of the will against ennui or boredom, it increasingly endorsed another way of defining life: the excitement and the exercise of the feelings. Girls who read their daily allowance of Macaulay or the Bible with pride and self-satisfaction upbraided themselves for their difficulties in controlling their insatiable appetites for Victorian novels of all kinds. Reading for leisure or for pleasure invariably meant reading for "sensation," reading for adventure, excitement, identification, titillation. In the process of this kind of reading, Victorian girls ministered to a complex of emotions.

Whether borrowed from public libraries, received as Christmas presents, or "approved" by careful mothers, novels were often appropriated for varied private uses by girls who read them under apple trees, in sitting rooms, or spread on the bed "with my limp collar cast aside." Eleanor Hooper located the reading that she did on the horsecars as the only moments in the day that were her own; the rest belonged to others, particularly her mother and her music teacher. Looking back upon 1865 from its last day, Cassie Upson suggested what reading meant to her. She associated leisure and her own innermost desires with literacy, during a "calm, long summer" in Milwaukee "in which I read and wrote and was lazy to my heart's content."[39] Girls chose their leisure reading for its powers to excite the imagination and for its associations with a weaker but sometimes most vivid self. For both reasons such reading was suspect.

Perhaps leisure reading can best be defined by what it was not: study, sleep, or sewing. Girls chastised themselves for imperfectly learning their lessons, and sometimes blamed the distractions of leisure reading. Martha Moore, who had just begun to attend school in occupied New Orleans during the Civil War, confessed that she found the schoolwork hard and had had two crying spells before she "picked up an interesting story and with my old habit of procrastination, thought I would read that first, and then study." She observed the inevitable consequence "that my lessons are *very* imperfectly known." And even Margaret Tileston, whose discipline seldom allowed her to swerve from duty, could be seduced by light reading. At the age of fourteen: "I scarcely studied in my history at all, because I was interested in 'Sir Gibbie,' and wanted to finish reading it." At the age of seventeen: "I undertook to spend the afternoon and evening on my Ancient History, but my thoughts wandered and I spent some time on papers and magazines." At the age of twenty: "I did not study a great deal in evening, on account of my interest in my novel, but I read over my History lesson."[40]

Girls also resolved to prevent reading from interfering with their domestic chores, usually their needlework. Treating reading as recreation, Virginian Agnes Lee observed, "I really am so idle I must be more industrious but it is so hard when one is reading or playing to stop to practice or sew." Another Virginian, Lucy Breckinridge, set up a similar opposition, noting that she and her sisters had gathered together in her room "being industrious. I am getting over my unsocial habit of sitting in my room reading all day." For Lucy

3.2 Too much reading, 1874. This illustration for a *St. Nicholas* poem suggests that the heroine lift her head up from her book, and learn from nature. Reprinted from "In the Wood," *St. Nicholas* 1 (May 1874): 425.

Breckinridge private reading not only was not industrious, it was also anti-social. Margaret Tileston offered a vain hope in late December 1885: "I mean to read little and sew much this winter." But only two days later her reading record suggested a resolution gone awry: "I finished reading 'Northanger Abbey,' and began [Thackeray's] 'Pendennis' of which I read one hundred and seventy pages. . . . I went to the Library and read 'Punch' and 'The Tuftonian.'"[41]

Sometimes sleep lost out, as girls burned late-night gas or oil (often under parental ban) in the grip of a fascinating story. Margaret Tileston was a frequent offender, and after one such late night offered a weak resolution of reform: "I intend to keep earlier hours, but it is so hard to leave my books and go to bed." Lucy Breckinridge described her frequent reading into the wee hours: "Sat up until nearly Wednesday morning to finish *Rutledge* [by Miriam Coles Harris]—it is deeply interesting. It is so singular that the heroine has no name." Resolutions about curtailing light reading were staples of plans for improvement, but they often had a half-hearted quality. Alice Stone Black-well, a serious addict, reported wryly that "yesterday or day before I made a vow not to read more than 15 min. each weekday while school lasts, out of school; not that I want to go back on that no indeed." Another such ad-dict, Agnes Hamilton, stayed up late one New Year's Eve to finish Charles Kingsley's *Westward Ho!* "for I want to leave no novel on hand till vacation," marking only a temporary lull in her heavy novel consumption.[42] Victorian girls remonstrated with themselves about their passion for novels, but even the most dutiful found it difficult to renounce them. Girls did not renounce the reading of novels, because novels provided them with an invitation to something they experienced emotionally as life itself.

Sensation Literature

Although they sometimes read books designed to help them be better, those who could get access read voraciously another kind of literature—a lit-erature which did not invite conscious emulation but instead vicarious, illicit, and guilt-ridden identification—a literature known in England as sensation literature. Written in the United States by such "questionable" authors as E. D. E. N. Southworth, Fannie Fern, and Mary Jane Holmes and in the 1860s in England by such authors as Wilkie Collins, the sensation novel introduced twisted plots, mistaken identities, brushes with adultery and bigamy, and pas-sions unrequited. A thirteen-year-old reader wrote to *St. Nicholas* about her experience of enchantment reading Augusta Jane (Evans) Wilson's *St. Elmo* (1866). "I knew all the time that 'St. Elmo' was not a good book for me; but I could not stop. It seems as though it had some strange power, which, when I commenced it, kept me from stopping, and held fast to me until I had fin-ished it."[43] Clearly the experience had left her feeling guilty, for her letter to the *St. Nicholas* editors asked them for reading suggestions.

Cassie Upson, growing up in Charlemont, Massachusetts, and then in Mil-waukee, looked to reading for just that kind of powerful involvement and ex-citement. Neither her father nor her stepmother seemed to control her choice of books, which were either preselected from a Sunday School library or ob-tained from the local Y. At any rate, in 1863, three years after the book's publication in Britain, Cassie Upson got hold of Wilkie Collins's *Woman in White,* a thriller which has been said to be the prototype for modern detective fiction. A review in *Blackwood's Edinburgh Magazine* noted the significance of such literature which must "find its inspiration in crime and . . . make the criminal its hero." Wilkie Collins appeared in several other girls' reading records, but he was clearly a controversial author for girls. Upson noted that reading Collins affected her moods. On August 12, 1863, she reported, "Am reading Wilkie Collins 'Woman in White' rather excited over it and consequently rather cross." Two days later in the morning she finished it with an effusive rhapsody. "It was splendid. I did admire count Fresco in spite of the poor fellow's vices and of course Marian Halcombe was as near perfection as is possible for any person to be without being beautiful and over Sir Percival Glyde I came very near crying for its an awful thing to be burned up, and when Lady Glyde was proved to be herself and not poor Anne Cathenick I rejoiced." Cassie Upson's effusion suggests precisely what appealed to her about *Woman in White:* that it took her on an emotional roller-coaster ride, confounding her self-expectations by encouraging her admiration for a criminal and an unconventional heroine, and ended with the relief of identities reconfirmed. A year earlier she had turned to her diary in frustration because she was out of reading materials, especially novels. "I feel so excited that I must read some exciting book or story tonight if I can find one. . . . I wish I could read all the novel I wanted to but I cant. Goodbye."[44]

For Cassie Upson, reading novels both stimulated and relieved excitement; like exercise devotees today, dependent on endorphins, the responses of a good many Victorian reading addicts to their reading matter seems to have been downright physical. One of these was Alice Stone Blackwell, who in defiance of her parents made impassioned trips across Boston to retrieve copies of the *New York Ledger* containing serialized fiction. After completing the first volume of Oliver Wendell Holmes's *Elsie Venner,* Blackwell declared that she would not begin the other that night. "Its not safe. That scene where she saves him from the rattlesnake has utterly upset me; I am so nervous I cant even write decently." Her self-description recalls the warnings of many advice writers, who feared that excessive reading of melodrama would have dangerous consequences for girls' nerves. Clearly those surrounding Alice Blackwell were sufficiently concerned about her reading to devise strategies to interrupt it, as when she was sent downstairs to churn butter as remedy for too much reading. At least once an older cousin and companion set the clock an hour forward, "thinking I was over reading myself." On hearing that, she reported she "felt very much vexed, remembering how I tore through the last part of the story without enjoying it, and lay awake afterward," perhaps a result of the early hour, perhaps simply of the adrenaline. Her father interrupted her while she was engrossed in *Les Miserables:* "Just as my favorite Enyolras had put a pistol to the head of Le Cabuc and given him one minute to say his prayers, Papa made me stop to listen to that stupid biography of Scott." She concluded: "I went to bed with the white cold face and flying hair of that young executioner before my eyes." To other reading experiences she announced similarly strong reactions: Thackeray's *Newcomes* made her "savage" and his *Pendennis* "furious"; she "raged" at the ending of Blake's *Lord and Master*. Upon reading Henry Kingsley's *Ravenshoe,* she did something less characteristic of her, though more common for other girl readers: she cried. "Made a fool of myself. It is not my habit to behave idiotically,—over a story, at least—but I did it over Ravenshoe." She retreated to her room, and there upon her bed, she lay reading, "winking away my tears when I was crying too hard to see the words."[45]

Girls Reading About Boy Heroes

Alice Stone Blackwell, and other girl readers as well, read from a varied menu, some of it designed for girls, much of it not. Mary Mapes Dodge's prospectus for *St. Nicholas* set an androgynous ideal for appropriate fare. It must not, she said "be a milk-and-water variety of the periodical for adults. In fact, it needs to be stronger, truer, bolder, more uncompromising than the other; its cheer must be the cheer of the bird-song; it must mean freshness and heartiness, life and joy." Significantly, Dodge did not distinguish girl from boy readers, offering attributes for children's literature suggestive of the sanctioned outdoor play of real boys and female tomboys. The "muscular Christianity" of Charles Kingsley's *Westward Ho* was said to appeal to boys and girls alike, and its appearance in girls' reading records bears this out. At least some girl readers preferred stories with boy heroes, who were more likely to confront grand adventure. A female writer to *St. Nicholas,* in 1875 applauded Louisa May Alcott's *Eight Cousins,* currently appearing, and lobbied its author with her hope that "most of it will be about the boys, for if I am a girl, I like stories of boys better than I do stories of girls; there is so much more excitement in boys' stories," a sentiment which Louisa May Alcott herself shared. Ida B. Wells, a schoolteacher, activist, and daughter of slaves, included the stories for boys of Oliver Optics with the writings of Alcott, Dickens, the Brontës, and A. D. T. Whitney as those who helped her to "form" her ideals. Certainly the Western pioneer experience was accessible to both sexes, with girls writing of their special appreciation for Noah Brook's tale "Boy Emigrants," in *St. Nicholas.* A small survey of girls in the West aged fourteen to eighteen revealed that the solid majority preferred adventure stories to "anything about girls." (Girls in the South apparently asked for "straight" love stories.)[46]

In general, though, girl readers read omnivorously—reading both adventure stories and romance. One Victorian critic suggested that romantic sensation literature represented the translation of boys' adventure stories into

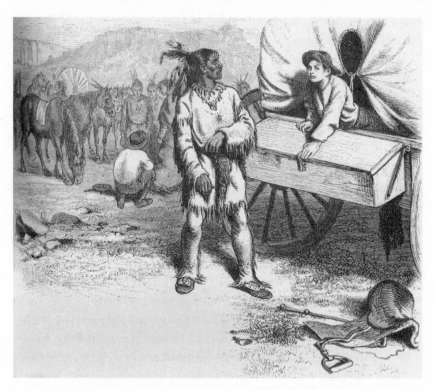

3.3 "So much more excitement," 1876. In the androgynous world of childhood launched in *St. Nicholas,* girls read and exulted over stories with boy heroes. Reprinted from Noah Brooks, "Boy Emigrants," *St. Nicholas* 3 (April 1876): 369.

the female vernacular, that women and girls read of female romantic heroines "as boys read of Captain Kidd, forgetting criminality of the deed in the excitement of the danger." However, evidence would suggest that girls read of Captain Kidd too—at least that Alice Stone Blackwell and her cousin Catherine Barry (Kitty) did, for they used "Captain Kidd" as Kitty's nom de plume in a spirited and playful correspondence. Female readers identified variously in their wide foraging for reading matter. Agnes Lee read Washington Irving's three-volume history of Columbus's voyages and imagined herself befriending the explorer in his later years. "His last days were the saddest of all Ferdinand's treatment was unbearable, I felt—I hardly know how—but only wished I had been a *man* then! Columbus should have found out he had *one* friend in the world. But 'tis all past now." [47] Lee's reading of Columbus elicited a feminine response of comfort, friendship, and support, but significantly Lee phrased that support in the form in which Columbus needed it: as the sponsorship which only a man, with his standing in the public world, could provide. Hence her imagined gift to Columbus came in the form of masculine identification.

Was there a cost in girls' mediated access to boys' adventure tales? Was there a cost to girls of identifying with a protagonist through adopting a male persona? Judith Fetterley has argued famously that women have on some level been "resisting" readers of fiction written from the male point of view. While identifying as male, female readers are constantly reminded "that to be male—to be universal—is to be *not female*." Fetterley concludes that this sub-text leads to an "endless division of self against self." There is scant evidence in reading journals to resolve this debate. One boys' text that a substantial number of girl readers mention reading is Thomas Hughes's *Tom Brown at Rugby* (as well as its sequel, *Tom Brown at Oxford*). There seems little in these rough-and-tumble stories of British public school life for boys that addresses the qualities of a separate girls' sphere. Alice Blackwell, again, supplied an especially full account of her response: "Read Tom Brown at Oxford in the morning, and felt so delighted I squirmed all over, and laughed, and would have liked to hug Tom Hughes. . . . What he says meets my views just—especially what he says about wild oats—and all sorts of things too. What he says is good and true and brave, and he says it so well and bravely and truly that I feel braver and better for it." Blackwell's hearty response suggests a relatively simple if androgynous identification with energetic youth—of whatever sex. However, Blackwell's final clause lends some support to Fetterley's analysis. "I feel braver and better for it," Blackwell ends, "even when it does not especially apply to me." It was not a boy student that moved Frances Willard, the inspired leader of the Women's Christian Temperance Union, but she too was inspired by a figure from the same boys' preparatory school in Britain. She remembered the impact of reading *The Life and Correspondence of Thomas Arnold* (1844), headmaster at Rugby School, in redirecting her life from the aimless "drift" of a girl's life toward a teaching career.[48] Perhaps self was divided against self when Victorian girls read books designed for boys. But the same was true of most Victorian reading. Victorian girls read with many selves—dutiful daughter, passionate rebel, noble hero—which were often in opposition. Identifying with male heroes may have created dissonance, but it also expanded girls' imaginative repertoires—as the lives and careers of both Willard and Blackwell suggest. Gender difference encouraged internal contradictions—but it was far from the only way in which self was divided against self for Victorian girl readers.

The question is how to interpret these powerful reading experiences. Did

Victorian girls read more deeply and differently from other readers in other times? And if so, how? And to what end? One simple answer is that they read differently because there were different books to read. Most historians agree that the evolution and the triumph of the novel went in tandem with the growth of a new reading public which was dominated by leisured women and girls. Emotion-wrenching novels engendered emotional responses no matter the reader. In an essay on an early blockbuster, Susan Warner's *Wide, Wide World* (1851), the nineteenth-century American writer Caroline Kirkland suggested that it had similar impacts on whoever read it. Originally "bought to be presented to nice little girls, by parents and friends who desired to set a pleasant example of docility and self-command before those happy beginners," the book gradually engaged elder sisters, and then mothers, for "it was very natural that mothers next should try the spell which could so enchain the more volatile spirits of the household. After this, papas were not very difficult to convert, for papas like to feel their eyes moisten, sometimes, with emotions more generous than those usually excited at the stock exchange or the counting house." The only holdouts Kirkland would allow were the elder brothers of the family, "for that class proverbially despises any thing so 'slow' as pictures of domestic life."[49] Victorian girls read novels differently because everyone read them differently, because novels offered a privatized reading experience which fostered emotions. Novel reading differed markedly from the public, political, and commercial discourse of the republican era.

Yet Victorians agreed that girls were arguably more at risk from novels than their parents, because they had both more time to read them and, lacking knowledge of the world, more incentive. Novels seemed dangerous to Victorians, the cultural historian Peter Gay suggests, exactly because they suggested action. "Notoriously uneasy about their own hidden impulses, [Victorians] could only conjecture that suggestive fiction must invite imitation—and most fiction struck them as suggestive." Action, of course, was exactly what Victorian girls' reading was supposed to displace. Gay dismisses these pre-Freudian Victorian fears of reading as naive, but there is some evidence that romantic fiction did indeed pattern girls' expectations—or construct their desires. Lucy Breckinridge's observation about her cousin was a common one: "All of the girls are desperately in love with Cousin Watts—say he is like a novel hero. I like him so much." As the historian Barbara Sicherman shows in her reading of the Hamilton family papers, Agnes Hamilton and her cousins saw and interpreted the world—and even chose marital mates—under the influence of fictive prototypes. (The thirteen-year-old Agnes and her cousin Alice wrote off to their cousin, "Do you find boarding school as nice as it was in 'Gypsy's Year at the Golden Crescent,' or in 'What Katy Did at School'? or are you homesick like the story Mrs. Stanton told in one of the Bessie's?") Breckinridge's reading of De Quincey's *Confessions of an English Opium Eater* caused her to long, with what degree of commitment it is hard to tell, "for a dose of laudanum."[50]

Gay takes Freud's lead in his interpretation of Victorian reading. He argues that reading was essentially harmless, to be described as "playful regression—regression as it awakens and enlists memories, playful because the reader well knows, even as he is absorbed in his story that it is not real somehow and that he can withdraw from its spell." Gay concludes that reading is "in the psychoanalytic sense of the term, an economic activity: it rehearses, at a smaller expenditure of energy than action in reality would require, splendid adventures and forbidden pleasures, and all with little risk to the consumer."[51] There is certainly some basis for this perspective in the ultimate life histories of these middle-class teenage Victorian readers—who in the main did not bear children out of wedlock, elope with dark-eyed counts, and surrender prudence for passion. Yet Gay's dismissal of reading's harmfulness also robs it of impact—an impact which is so forcefully described and dramatized in girls' own descriptions of their reading experiences.[52]

At the opposite extreme from Gay's and Freud's psychoanalytic perspective are the powerful analyses of contemporary cultural critics—many from literature departments—who invest novels and periodical fiction with preeminent power in their ability to construct gender, social ideology, and ideas of the self. Writing on British Victorianism, the critics Andrew Blake and Nancy Armstrong suggest the essential social meaning and function of private reading in the construction of the ideology of both class and gender. Yet in the process, such critics end by flattening and oversimplifying the impact of reading. The variousness of the Victorian reading diet—and its complex legacy for girl readers—becomes lost.

Blake is especially interested in how Victorian reading contributed to the maintenance and the enlargement of the middle class. Drawing on writings in diaries and letters as well as published literature, he suggests a continuous loop of reading, writing, and interpretation in which individuals make and remake a bourgeois social ideology—an ideology which, for instance, suggests appropriate marriage partners, agrees on what is vulgar and what genteel, and censures immorality.[53] In American girls' reading, *Stepping Heavenward* was one of many books that was important in exactly the terms that Blake sug-

gests—a book that was simultaneously polemical, absorbing, and provocative, that confronted girls exactly where they lived in their efforts to adjudicate their desire to be good and their knowledge of their own resistances.
Girls loved *Stepping Heavenward* both because they could identify with its
stubborn heroine and because they could draw hope from her.

Yet other items in the American Victorian reading diet worked to somewhat different ends. Girls who read Wilkie Collins's *Woman in White* or even
Charlotte Brontë and the American domestic novelists Fannie Fern and
E. D. E. N. Southworth were reading novels laden with sentiment and over-
wrought female emotion. Armstrong's reading of Charlotte Brontë is important to her argument that nineteenth-century domestic fiction constructed
a privatized female self who defined herself by her "sensibility," her interiority, her "feelingness." But Armstrong reads Brontë out of context. To the
extent that such works stood on their own, they did indeed contribute to
a construction of gender which defined womanliness as a product of emotions and deep feeling. However, in Victorian terms *Jane Eyre* flirted with
sin and deviance, and critics worried greatly over the "lessons" it might be
teaching. Writing in the *London Quarterly Review* in 1848, Elizabeth Rigby
deemed Jane Eyre herself "the personification of an unregenerate and undisci-
plined spirit" and the book "pre-eminently an anti-Christian composition."
William Dean Howells, writing what was intended as a rehabilitative essay
in 1900, still found it very easy to understand why "the young author should
have been attainted of immorality and infidelity, not to name that blacker
crime, impropriety. In fact it must be allowed that 'Jane Eyre' does go rather
far in a region where women's imaginations are politely supposed not to wander." Charlotte Brontë was controversial, prohibited, for instance, to Margaret
Tileston until the age of eighteen. Girls loved such novels, and they gloried
in the sensations such reading often unlocked, just as Armstrong posits. But
at the same time, in more sober moments they were suspicious of those feelings. Frances Willard, who gained encouragement from the life and letters
of Thomas Arnold at Rugby, recalled that her father had successfully protected his children from novels, such that she did not see one until the age
of fifteen, when a "seamstress" brought *Jane Eyre* into her house. From her
maturity, Willard recalled that "the glamor of these highly seasoned pages was
unhealthful," a feeling she likened to "spiritual hasheesh-eating." In just the
ways Willard experienced, parents and critics encouraged girls to feel guilty
about the passions and the obsessions that their reading invoked. One could
easily argue that the net result of the debate over the novel was to teach girls

to distrust rather than to honor their feelings and emotions. Novel reading caused many girls to feel ashamed of their own fascinations.[54]

Taste and Individuality

If novels did not construct one prototypical heroine for girls to emulate, however, the process of reading and writing about it did encourage something else—the cultivation of personal taste. The literary historian Michael Warner has described how Bible reading of the Puritan era functioned as a "technology of the self" which produced "an individual printed from an authoritative stamp." Readers attempted to absorb and to become one with the text, obliterating any sense of self.[55] Fiction reading by Victorians was also a "technology of the self," but a self formed not by "imprinting" texts but by responding to them—raging at them, adoring them, rejecting them, disapproving of them. In one way of considering it, abundant and sometimes promiscuous Victorian reading was a process of mental consumerism, in which the self was formed not by what one bought or ate or selected, but by what one preferred, or found tedious, or identified with.

The most restrained Victorian journal writer felt entitled to—indeed obliged to—express opinions about reading. Emily Eliot, writing at the age of fourteen in 1871, in general simply recorded the accomplishments, the comings and goings, of the day. However, when she read *Papers for Thoughtful Girls,* by Henrietta Keddie (who also wrote *Sweet Counsel*), she ventured an opinion: "It is too priggy, and not *nearly* so nice as *Citoyenne Jacqueline.*" Mary Boit, who often felt inadequate and angry, felt no compunction about comparing her feelings about Sir Walter Scott with her friend Bessie's. "She has read five of Scotts novels and I have only read Ivanhoe and hardly remember what it is about. I *hate* Scott's works as I think they are so hard to get into." Cassie Upson religiously recorded her responses to reading. Epes Sargent's *Peculiar* she found "quite exciting. I really most fell in love with Vance. I had wanted Clara to marry him, but still it was better to have him true to his first love." The next year she observed, "I cant say I particularly admire [Hawthorne's] 'Marble Faun' though the style is very easy and pleasant." Other entries were more telegraphic: Scott's *Anne of Geierstein:* "very good indeed"; E. D. E. N. Southworth's *Lucia:* "splendid"; Fannie Forester's *Alderbrook:* "perfectly delightful"; Jane Austen's *Mansfield Park:* "Do not like it at all."[56] (Undoubtedly too subdued for a reader used to more sensational fiction.)

These assessments did not necessarily reveal the adoption of particular traits of personality or character. But together they suggest the validation of the notion of individuality—the notion that when you were talking about fiction, as contemporary students will say to this day, "everyone *is* entitled to her opinion." There was only one book mentioned in Cassie Upson's reading diary, on April 24, 1864, for which she recorded no opinion: "Finished my Bible today I commenced it a year ago last New Year's." The omission suggests a world of difference between old and newer modes—and purposes— for girls' reading. Reading once was a strategy for imprinting wisdom; the Victorian age transformed reading to a strategy for defining a self grounded in taste.

Parents encouraged girls to express opinions about reading. The point was that you *have* opinions, not what they are. However, responses to reading could take a more pointed form when girls used them in skirmishes with real-life adversaries. Books sometimes provided the vehicles for challenges of those most difficult to challenge: parents themselves. In the case of such periodicals as *St. Nicholas,* with its "Letter-Box," a reader could hope for direct assistance. One eight-year-old boy took his mother up on a challenge and wrote to *St. Nicholas* directly: "Mamma says to ask you if you think it wise for me, a boy eight years old, to begin to read the St. Nicholas as soon as I rise, and during all my play-hours? I am so fond of it, and find so much of interest in it, that I think it is the best kind of play for me—don't you?" Put on the spot, the editors demurred, and left the two to their own resolution. Mary Boit, in constant trouble with her stepmother, seemed to gain some sense not only of reassurance but of superiority from her counsel with *The Children's Saviour* on Easter Sunday. She described it as "a perfectly beautiful book" and went on, "Often when I feel trouble or have had a fuss with Mamma and read that book it always makes me feel better for it." Margaret Tileston, whose multiple journals were often extremely circumspect on matters of any controversy, placed one such reading comment in the margins of her diary, even going to the trouble of (imperfectly) inking out the last phrase. "In the evening before supper, I read in 'Aids to Family Government' according to Froebel by Bertha Meyer, which set me to thinking deeply."[57] This enigmatic comment, with its revelation of "deep thinking," clearly suggests a critical observation about her own parents, one which Tileston preferred not to reveal but was daring enough to intimate, if only deep in the spine of her diary.

In the less abashed Blackwell family, such controversies could more readily surface. Alice's cousin Florence boldly brooked family heresy, inspired by a reactionary novel. Florence was the eldest daughter of the feminist Antoinette

Brown Blackwell, the first woman ordained as a minister in the Congregational Church and, like Alice's parents, a lifelong and outspoken women's rights advocate. Alice reported:

> While F. and I sat over the fire, she said, after we had confabbed awhile, that she knew it was very dreadful, but she didn't believe in women's rights! I saw she expected me to be horrified and explode, so I asked coolly why. She said she didn't want to vote. I asked her if that was any reason why I shouldn't, and she said that it wasn't the voting she minded so much, but that she thought married women oughtn't to have professions, etc.; went over the usual rigmarole in fact, and said that the sentiments expressed in Only a Girl a most aggravating book which Aunt N. [Nettie—Antoinette Brown Blackwell] and I had joined in abusing, were hers exactly. I didn't take the trouble to argue much with her, but told her she would come around when women's rights became fashionable; which remark she took with great good humor.[58]

The women in the extended Blackwell family were formidable, and Florence undoubtedly felt the fresh air of freedom open above her head after announcing her heresy—a heresy that Wilhelmin von Hillern's bizarre novel of domesticity and surrender had helped foment.

It would be inaccurate, however, to suggest that reading simply validated the expression of girls' own selves, because of course it also set up competing selves among which girls had to adjudicate. Alice Blackwell described one such conflicted reading encounter. She began with a common enough observation: "Read Real Folks. Desire Ledwith seems to me like myself, something like." As if to gloss the previous observation, she went on, "I have got into a very bad habit of trying to sift myself out, and find what there is of me." (It is somewhat disingenuous that she describes this as "a bad habit," for of course self-inventory was a staple of any plan for self-culture.) She went on to suggest, however, what it was that she found: "It is unpleasantly plain that there is a great deal of selfishness; an awful deal; also laziness." And she then suggested the multifaceted self which often emerged from such inquiries. The selfishness would have "to be punched out of me; and I've got to punch it!"[59] In this inquiry into self-consciousness, the will to virtue was transformed into the self (the "I"), and the feeling—in this case selfishness—was interpreted as nothing more essential than an unwelcome parasite.

Lucy Breckinridge demonstrated a similar sense of divided self over her reading of Michelet's *Woman*. She concluded: "I do not like that kind of reading. It scares me of myself, and makes me rebel against my lot."[60] Even more than Alice Blackwell, Lucy Breckinridge could not keep her pronouns under control. Clearly her initial subject was her self-image as a good daughter with an assigned gender and "lot" in the world. It was this good daughter who was scared by another self—an impassioned champion of fair play, a rebel lurking beneath a willed exterior. Unlike Alice Blackwell, Lucy Breckinridge did not presume to root out that terrifying imp—though she did not intend in the future to indulge it, for she did not "like" it. In Lucy Breckinridge the will to be a good girl was pitted against the maverick feelings of a rebel, resulting in a new set of feelings—discomfort, fear, unease. It was those feelings, in alliance with her strong sense of propriety, that won the day.

Did girls' reading "construct" them? The Victorian reading menu at the birth of mass culture was too various to present a unitary prototype, though it certainly set parameters. The reading of novels, rather, validated the notion of taste, and with it the responsibility and the right of individual girls to have likes and dislikes in literature. The arcane and even arbitrary discriminations of girl readers may well have helped to make them high-strung and over-refined—a notion famously presented by Jane Addams as she contrasted the fastidious daughters of the American elite with their large-hearted and generous mothers on the American tour of Europe.[61] But at the same time, it did teach them to develop ideas, opinions, a sense of themselves *as* selves. For some girls, responses to reading may well have felt like discovery: it is hard to read the impassioned responses of readers like Alice Blackwell and feel that her reactions were entirely patterned, though the expression of strong reaction was likely a response to parental models. For others, those who commenced journals with confessions of diffidence, responding to reading was a learned exercise.

And it *was* often an exercise. In promoting reading for the American common person in *Democratic Vistas* (1871), Walt Whitman proposed it as a process of self-construction very similar to bodybuilding or calisthenics. He called for books for both men and women "on the assumption that the process of reading is not a half-sleep, but, in the highest sense, an exercise, a gymnast's struggle; that the reader is to do something for himself, must be on the alert, must himself or herself construct indeed the poem, argument, history, metaphysical essay—the text furnishing the hints, the clue, the start or frame-work. Not the book needs so much to be the complete thing, but the reader of the book does."[62] In idealized form, American girls, like self-improving mechanics, used books to refine, complete, construct selves, not to put them to half-sleep. But not all girls wrestled with their reading and subordinated it to their purposes in the industrious manner Whitman suggested. To a far less exalted degree, however, they did come to acknowledge their right and even their responsibility to like or to dislike books, a different kind of reading from the reading of "sacred" texts. This legitimating of taste brought with it a formally self-conscious sense of individuality. In this way, as in others, Victorian reading helped to construct the modern self.

❦

Geographies

FOUR

Houses, Families, Rooms of One's Own

Jane Addams's 1902 description of the middle-class daughter "as a family possession" summarized the status of girls as property and ornament of the bourgeois family. Well through the Victorian period and beyond, mothers and fathers valued daughters as both the "charm and grace of the household" and its finest product. Girls responded by using their regular regimens of reading and writing as devices for moral and spiritual self-grooming. In the past two chapters I have discussed these verbal disciplines as conflicted mediums of self-construction. Now I turn to three emotional geographies of the self: the home, the school, and the city streets beyond.

City-dwellers who left home for the counting house, market, shop, or factory floor had long learned to adjust their behavior to the different settings of their lives. But it was a late-century philosopher who considered what it might mean to a person's identity to live in the complex and anonymous Victorian city. Writing in 1890, William James commented on the "division of the man into several selves": "We do not show ourselves to our children as to our club-companions, to our customers as to the laborers we employ, to our own masters and employers as to our intimate friends." James especially noted the several roles inhabited by youth: "Many a youth who is demure enough before his parents and teachers, swears and swaggers like a pirate among his 'tough' young friends."[1] It should not be surprising to discover that Victorian girls, like boys and adults, reserved disparate selves for parents, teachers, and peers. Negotiation of the fragmented and even conflicting identities appropriate for home, school, and the streets helped to define their modernity.

The girl's sense of self began at home, in her relations with parents, in the transformations of puberty, and in her exploration of domestic and personal interiors. At home, girls absorbed, confronted, distilled, and interpreted parental expectations. Sometimes in rooms of their own, girls worked on not just managing unruly emotions but transforming them, often trying to describe their struggles as crises of religious faith. Whether religion helped or failed them, however, they learned that trouble was best managed in their hearts. When matched with appropriate conduct, it might evidence maturity, depth, and womanliness. More so than for her mother, as one commentator put it, for the daughter, the home, her room, and certainly her soul was "her battleground . . . life militant."[2]

Middle-class teenage girls spent more time at home than did their brothers in the urban Northeast and throughout the country. Whereas at age eleven most boys and girls were out of the home in Providence, Rhode Island, in 1880, by the age of fifteen many of the girls had returned, with twice as many girls as boys at home. As they matured, boys were less and less likely, girls more and more likely, to be at home, so that at the age of seventeen, nearly a quarter of all girls were at home, compared with well under 3 percent for boys, most of whom were working. The daughters of native-born, "white-collar" fathers were especially likely to be at home, with more than half of that group neither at school nor at work.[3]

These statistics must be read with some care. The substantial majority of teenage girls were either at work or at school. In theory, older daughters were kept at home to help with the housework, which was often the case among the laboring classes. But many of the daughters of the middle and upper middle class were at home with less-defined purpose. It was this sense of purposelessness that prompted the turn-of-the-century critique of such writers as Charlotte Perkins Gilman. In her 1903 book *The Home,* she observed tartly: "To find an able-bodied intelligent boy in a home between breakfast and supper would argue a broken leg. But girls we find by thousands and thousands; 'helping mother,' if mother does the work; and if there are servants to do the work, the girl does—what?"[4] As we have seen, girls often read and wrote, sometimes discovering reservoirs of "self" in their projects of self-culture. These discoveries were eked out at the interstices of a prior project, a parent's project of rearing a graceful daughter who would fulfill the needs for nurture at the center of the domestic sphere.

The Victorian House and a Room of One's Own

In their idealized version, the projects of domesticity took place within a house which was evolving in design to represent its new ambitions to mediate between private and public worlds. The complex design of the Victorian house signified the changing ratio between the cultural and physical work situated there. With its twin parlors, one for formal, the other for intimate exchange, and its separate stairs and entrances for servants, the Victorian house embodied cultural preoccupations with specialized functions, particularly distinguishing between public and private worlds. American Victorians maintained an expectation of sexualized and intimate romanticism in private at the same time that they sustained increasingly "proper" expectations for conduct in public.[5] The design of the house helped to facilitate the expression of both tendencies, with a formal front parlor designed to stage proper interactions with appropriate callers, and the nooks, crannies, and substantial private bedrooms designed for more intimate exchange or for private rumination itself.

Just as different areas of the house allowed for different gradations of intimacy, so did the house offer rooms designed for different users. The ideal home offered a lady's boudoir, a gentleman's library, and of course a children's nursery. This ideal was realized in the home of Elizabeth E. Dana, daughter of Richard Henry Dana, who described her family members situated throughout the house in customary and specialized space in one winter's late afternoon in 1865. Several of her siblings were in the nursery watching a sunset, "Father is in his study as usual, mother is taking her nap, and Charlotte is lying down and Sally reading in her room." In theory, conduct in the bowels of the house was more spontaneous than conduct in the parlor. This was partly by design, in the case of adults, but by nature in the case of children. If adults were encouraged to discover a true, natural self within the inner chambers of the house, children—and especially girls—were encouraged to learn how to shape their unruly natural selves there so that they would be presentable in company.[6] The nursery for small children acknowledged that childish behavior was not well-suited for "society" and served as a school for appropriate conduct, especially in Britain, where children were taught by governesses in the nursery, and often ate there as well. In the United States children usually went to school and dined with their parents. As the age of marriage increased, the length of domestic residence for some girls extended to twenty years and more.

The lessons of the nursery became more indirect as children grew up. Privacy for children was not designed simply to segregate them from adults but was also a staging arena for their own calisthenics of self-discipline. A room of one's own was the perfect arena for such exercises in responsibility. As the historian Steven Mintz observes, such midcentury advisers as Harriet Martineau and Orson Fowler "viewed the provision of children with privacy as an instrument for instilling self-discipline. Fowler, for example, regarded private bedrooms for children as an extension of the principle of specialization of space that had been discovered by merchants. If two or three children occupied the same room, none felt any responsibility to keep it in order." Although the room of one's own was beyond the reach of most families, novelists, advice writers, and architects promoted the concept starting at midcentury. Its significance was suggested in an epistolary novel by Mrs. Amelia Opie, *Madeline's Journal*. First published in London, republished in Boston in 1827, and read repeatedly by Robert E. Lee's daughter Agnes in the 1850s, *Madeline's Journal* told the story of a Scottish cottager reared by a wealthy gentlewoman but returned, upon her benefactress's death, to her own humble family. Upon her return she discovers that her family has constructed a new addition to their cottage to accommodate her. She is at first chagrined at their exertions on her behalf, but then decides, "This can only be a temporary feeling; for, if I have not a sitting room to myself, all my studies must be given up, and everything I now know be neglected and forgotten. A bed to myself is equally desirable."[7] In this British context, space of one's own was needed to preserve the ornamental accomplishments which marked genteel girlhood. Within American evangelical culture, a room of one's own gained a moral function. It allowed one to take one's self seriously.

This at least was the connotation conveyed by Annie Cooper in her 1885 diary. In one of many characteristic rhapsodies, she noted the significance of her room in allowing her to surrender reserve enough to genuinely experience virtue. "Oh! How I love my room, this room in which I am now writing, it is a great comfort and a great blessing. If it were not for the refuge of my room, I fear I should not ever be able to be good, or think of serious things, if Celia [her sister] was here, it would seal my lips, and actions, as much as I love her."[8] What Annie Cooper was inhibited from saying or doing in public— or even in the company of her sister—is not quite clear. Her further reverie suggests, though, that like many girls she was having difficulty navigating the conflicting expectations of Victorianism for both virtue and candor. A room of her own allowed her to ponder the contradictions in an atmosphere of uncompromised moral seriousness.

Earlier in the century, in the 1840s, Louisa May Alcott wrote to her mother about her hopes for contentment and for a room of her own. "Dearest Mother, I have tried to be more contented and I think I have been more so. I have been thinking about my little room which I suppose I never shall have. I should want to be there about all the time and I should go there and sing and think." Alcott sought privacy for expressiveness, so that she could sing freely, and perhaps think freely, and perhaps also so that she could write freely. As we know, though, what Alcott wrote often represented her internalization of the rules she rehearsed so regularly with her parents. The next year, when the Alcott family came into some money, the family bought a new house, and Louisa at the age of thirteen finally got the "little room" she had hoped for. She described herself as "very happy about it" and noted, "It does me good to be alone."[9]

The argument for the girl's room of her own rested on the perfect opportunity it provided for practicing for a role as a mistress of household. As such, it came naturally with early adolescence. The author Mary Virginia Terhune's advice to daughters and their mothers presupposed a room of one's own on which to practice the housewife's art. Of her teenage protagonist Mamie, Terhune announced: "Mamie must be encouraged to make her room first clean, then pretty, as a natural following of plan and improvement. . . . Make over the domain to her, to have and to hold, as completely as the rest of the house belongs to you. So long as it is clean and orderly, neither housemaid nor elder sister should interfere with her sovereignty." Writing in 1882, Mary Virginia Terhune favored the gradual granting of autonomy to girls as a natural part of their training for later responsibilities.[10]

In the accounting of both girls and their parents, the room of one's own served as a metaphor for a developing self. Several years after she had actually received a room of her own, Alcott explained its importance to her investment in self-discipline. She needed privacy, she explained, because "in the quiet I see my faults, and try to mend them; but deary me, I don't get on at all. I used to imagine my mind a room in confusion, and I was to put it in order; so I swept out useless thoughts and dusted foolish fancies away, and furnished it with good resolutions and began again. But cobwebs got it. I'm not a good housekeeper, and never get my room in nice order. I once wrote a poem about it when I was fourteen, and called it 'My Little Kingdom.' It is still hard to rule it, and always will be I think."[11] Alcott's reflections suggest the matter-of-fact psychology which governed a Victorian's approach to the self. Her mind was no more complicated than a room, and its governance simply a housekeeping chore. But at the same time, it was a kingdom, subject

to her own commands. And as befit their sovereignty, girls could rule well or
poorly.

The Emotional Work of Being Good

Victorian parents convinced their daughters that the secret to a successful life was strict and conscientious self-rule. The central administrative principle was carried forth from childhood: the responsibility to "be good." The
phrase conveyed the prosecution of moralist projects and routines, and perhaps equally significant, the avoidance or suppression of temper and temp-
tation. Being good extended beyond behavior and into the realm of feeling
itself. Being good meant what it said—actually transfiguring negative feelings,
including desire and anger, so that they ceased to become a part of experience. Historians of emotion have argued that culture can shape temperament
and experience; the historian Peter Stearns, for one, argues that "culture often
influences reality" and that "historians have already established some connections between Victorian culture and nineteenth-century emotional reality."
More recently, the essays in Joel Pfister and Nancy Schnog's *Inventing the
Psychological* share the assumption that the emotions are "historically contingent, socially specific, and politically situated."[12] The Victorians themselves
also believed in the power of context to transform feeling.

The transformation of feeling was the end product of being good. Early
lessons were easier. Part of being good was simply doing chores and other
tasks regularly, as Alcott's writings suggest. One day in 1872 Alice Blackwell
practiced the piano "and was good," and another day she went for a long walk
"for exercise," made two beds, set the table, "and felt virtuous." Josephine
Brown's New Year's resolutions suggested such a regimen of virtue—sanctioned both by the inherent benefits of the plan and by its regularity. As part
of her plan to "make this a better year," she resolved to read three chapters of
the Bible every day (and five on Sunday) and to "study hard and understand-
ingly in school as I never have." At the same time, Brown realized that doing
a virtuous act was never simply a question of mustering the positive energy
to accomplish a job. It also required mastering the disinclination to drudge.
She therefore also resolved, "If I do feel disinclined, I will make up my mind
and do it."[13]

The emphasis on forming steady habits brought together themes in religion and industrial culture. The historian Richard Rabinowitz has explained
how nineteenth-century evangelicalism encouraged a moralism which rejected the introspective soul-searching of Calvinism, instead "turning toward
usefulness in Christian service as a personal goal." This pragmatic spiritu-

ality valued "habits and routines rather than events," including such habits as daily diary writing and other regular demonstrations of Christian conduct. Such moralism blended seamlessly with the needs of industrial capitalism—as Max Weber and others have persuasively argued. Even the domestic world, in some ways justified by its distance from the marketplace, valued the order and serenity of steady habits. Such was the message communicated by early promoters of sewing machines, for instance, one of whom offered the use of the sewing machine as "excellent training . . . because it so insists on having everything perfectly adjusted, your mind calm, and your foot and hand steady and quiet and regular in their motions." The relation between the market place and the home was symbiotic. Just as the home helped to produce the habits of living valued by prudent employers, so, as the historian Jeanne Boydston explains, the regularity of machinery "was the perfect regimen for developing the placid and demure qualities required by the domestic female ideal."[14]

Despite its positive formulation, "being good" often took a negative form—focusing on first suppressing or mastering "temper" or anger. The major target was "willfulness." An adviser participating in *Chats with Girls* proposed the cultivation of "a perfectly disciplined will," which would never "yield to wrong" but instantly yield to right. Such a will, too, could teach a girl to curb her unruly feelings. The *Ladies' Home Journal* columnist Ruth Ashmore (a pseudonym for Isabel Mallon) more crudely warned readers "that the woman who allows her temper to control her will not retain one single physical charm." As a young teacher, Louisa May Alcott wrestled with this most common vice. Of her struggles for self-control, she recognized that "this is the teaching I need; for as a *school-marm* I must behave myself and guard my tongue and temper carefully, and set an example of sweet manners."[15] Alcott, of course, made a successful career out of her efforts to master her maverick temper. The autobiographical heroine of her most successful novel, *Little Women*, who has spoken to successive generations of readers as they endured female socialization, was modeled on her own struggles to bring her spirited temperament in accord with feminine ideals.

So in practice being good first meant not being bad. Indeed, it was sometimes better not to "be" much at all. Girls sometimes worked to suppress liveliness of all kinds. Agnes Hamilton resolved at the beginning of 1884 that she would "study very hard this year and not have any spare time," and also that she would try to stop talking, a weakness she had identified as her principle fault. When Lizzie Morrissey got angry she didn't speak for the rest of the evening, certainly preferable to impassioned speech. Charlotte Perkins Gilman, who later critiqued many aspects of Victorian repression, at the advanced age of twenty-one at New Year's made her second resolution: "*Correct and necessary* speech only." Mary Boit, too, measured her goodness in terms of actions uncommitted. "I was good and did not do much of anything," she recorded ambiguously at the age of ten. It is perhaps this reservation that provoked the reflection of southerner Lucy Breckinridge, who anticipated with excitement the return of her sister from a long trip. "Eliza will be here tomorrow. She has been away so long that I do not know what I shall do to repress my joy when she comes. I don't like to be so glad when anybody comes." Breckinridge clearly interpreted being good as in practice an exercise in suppression. This was just the lesson of self-censoring that Alice James had starkly described as "'killing myself,' as some one calls it."[16]

This emphasis on repressing emotion became especially problematic for girls in light of another and contradictory principle connected with being good. A "good" girl was happy, and this positive emotion she should express in moderation. Explaining the duties of a girl of sixteen, an adviser writing in the *Ladies' Home Journal* noted that she should learn "that her part is to make the sunshine of the home, to bring cheer and joyousness into it." At the same time that a girl must suppress selfishness and temper, she must also project contentment and love. Advisers simply suggested that a girl employ a steely resolve to substitute one for the other. "Every one of my girls can be a sunshiny girl if she will," an adviser remonstrated. "Let every failure act as an incentive to greater success."[17]

This message could be concentrated into an incitement not to glory and ethereal virtue but simply to a kind of obliging "niceness." This was the moral of a tale published in *The Youth's Companion* in 1880. A traveler in Norway arrives in a village which is closed up at midday in mourning for a recent death. The traveler imagines that the deceased must have been a magnate or a personage of wealth and power. He inquires, only to be told, "It is only a young maiden who is dead. She was not beautiful nor rich. But oh, such a pleasant girl."[18] "Pleasantness" was the blandest possible expression of the combined mandate to repress and ultimately destroy anger and to project and ultimately feel love and concern.

Yet it was a logical blending of the religious messages of the day as well. Richard Rabinowitz's work on the history of spirituality notes a new later-century current which blended with the earlier emphasis on virtuous routines. The earlier moralist discipline urged the establishment of regular habits and the steady attention to duty. Later in the century, religion gained a more experiential and private dimension, expressed in devotionalism. Both of these demands—for regular virtue and the experience and expression of religious joy—could provide a loftier argument for the more mundane "pleasant." These dual expectations emerged in an uncomfortable correspondence between mother and daughter about faith. Annie Winsor's mother hoped that her daughter would be redeemed "if only you translate feeling into action, and unite a stern moral integrity and conscientious sense of duty, with the enthusiastic glow of devotion to the higher life."[19] For Annie, this religious admonition took its place as part of a personal project to unite her strong sense of obligation with a sunnier and more buoyant personality—a project to be good through being happy.

The challenges of this project were particularly bracing given the acute sensitivity of the age to hypocrisy. One must not only appear happy to meet social expectations: one must feel the happiness. The origins of this insistence came not only from a demanding evangelical culture but also from a fluid social world in which con artists lurked in parlors as well as on riverboats. A young woman must be completely sincere both in her happiness and in her manners if she was not to be guilty of the corruptions of the age. One adviser noted the dilemma: "'Mamma says I must be sincere,' said a fine young girl, 'and when I ask her whether I shall say to certain people, "Good morning, I am not very glad to see you," she says, "My dear, you must be glad to see them, and then there will be no trouble."'" This, then, was the project of female adolescence—the obliteration of one kind of self and the assumption of another. Girls naturally experienced it as trying. Annie Winsor's efforts at personal reconstruction revealed the tensions inherent in her project. She reported with pride at age nineteen that she seemed to be succeeding in her efforts to make her personality more engaging—that more people were finding her "an essentially cheerful person. I know I ought to seem so and I knew I tried but I didn't know I seemed really cheerful. . . . I am apt to feel so solemn that—well, you know just what I mean I think." What Annie was undoubtedly referring to was her mother's previously expressed fear that her once "sunny" daughter was becoming "sulky and heavy" as she moved through adolescence.[20] But who the "real" Annie Winsor was remained a matter of uncertainty to Annie, who knew that she often felt solemn, whatever her success at pretending otherwise.

No wonder that girls filled their journals with mantras of reassurance as they attempted to square the circle of Victorian emotional expectation. Anna Stevens included a separate list stuck between the pages of her diary. "Everything is for the best, and all things work together for good. . . . Be good and you will be happy. . . . Think twice before you speak."[21] We look upon these aphorisms as throwaways—platitudes which scarcely deserve to be pre-

4.1 "An essentially cheerful person," 1895. In response to her mother's fears that adolescence had made her "sunny" daughter "sulky and heavy," Annie Winsor worked on seeming cheerful. Here she smiles for the camera, well before convention demanded it. Schlesinger Library (Cambridge: Radcliffe Institute, Harvard University), MC322-671-8.

served along with more "authentic" manuscript material. Yet these mottoes, preserved and written in most careful handwriting in copy books and journals, represent the straws available to girls attempting to grasp the complex and ultimately unreconcilable projects of Victorian emotional etiquette and expectation.

Such aphorisms copied among earnest descriptions of emotional striving represent girls' efforts to internalize and adopt the moral perspective of an era. In the copybook such aphorisms simply stood on the page, still undigested and lumpy. In the diary, though, they often represented exercises being worked out and worked in to a virtuous self. Margaret Tileston quoted Ruskin: "'Wisdom never forgives. Whatever resistance we may have offered to her, she avenges forever. The lost hour can never be redeemed, and the accomplished wrong never atoned for.'" Her aesthetic in some part entwined with the moralism of Victorianism, Tileston proclaimed the selection "beautiful." Her collected opus, a complete set of diaries written fervently, even obsessively, through her entire lifetime, testifies to the extent to which she adapted a harsh Calvinist pronouncement of everlasting sin to a Victorian work ethic. When such a demanding conscience took over, there was little need of much remonstrance on the part of parents urging daughters on to higher standards of energy and productivity. In their denial of indulgence, such strategies of self-control among adolescent girls might lead on the one hand to the enormous accomplishments of disciplined Victorians, on the other to a range of maladies, from hysteria to *anorexia nervosa,* as argued from different vantages by Nancy Armstrong and Joan Brumberg.[22]

Present Mothers, Absent Mothers

Relations with real parents, of course, provided the context and often times much of the subterranean content of girls' socialization. As the age of marriage increased, middle-class daughters resided for a longer and longer time with their parents. The historical literature has appropriately stressed the dependence of Victorian daughters, yet it has disagreed on how to interpret it. Historians of medicine and of the prescriptive literature have tended to stress the costs of such training in self-discipline, seeing girls' exercises in self-suppression as the origins of a range of psychosomatic ailments. With a more positive emphasis, historians of domesticity have emphasized the health of girls' gradual socialization into the world of their mothers and grandmothers, depicting daughters and mothers "lolling [together] in placid domesticity."[23] The legacy of the Victorian home was more variegated than either vision allows, though, with maternal dependence often suppressed in accounts of actual lives.

In some sense, the object relations theory of gender socialization was designed for the Victorian family. Nancy Chodorow's argument about the "reproduction of mothering" assumes an asymmetrical family structure with mother at home and father at work. Unlike her brother, the theory goes, the girl learns gender behavior through imitating her mother, often blurring her own sense of self with her mother's. In this environment, affiliation and nurturance emerge naturally at the center of her identity. (Her brother needs to learn masculinity from a largely absent father and must therefore break abruptly from his nearest love object, his mother, in order to assume an abstract masculinity.)[24] This insight about the blendedness of female identity in late-Victorian America helps to explain the anomalous position of mothers in many of the documents of girlhood.

Frequently mothers simply did not appear in their daughters' daily accounts of their lives. The absence of a mother in a diary often did not reflect her real-life absence. Instead, it was likely to suggest that she was omnipresent, part of the assumed background of her daughter's life rather than its figure or pattern. Even fictional accounts of girls and their journals acknowledged this absence. Mothers frequently emerged in diary accounts only to depart or to return or to get sick. In diaries from three different years in the 1880s, Mabel Lancraft, daughter of an oyster grower in Fair Haven, Connecticut, mentioned her mother scarcely at all. Her mother took an active role only in regard to three separate events: a contentious shopping trip, a trip to school as her daughter's advocate, and her rare absence from home, which required that Mabel herself prepare dinner. It is in such moments as the last that daughters paid tribute to mothers and to their particular and often archetypal qualities. When Bostonian Agnes Garrison was in New York and got an earache, she realized how much she counted on her mother in the normal run of things: "I don't know when I have had such a hard time or when I have missed my dear Mamma so much. Cried as much for her as for earache. . . . There is nobody like Mamma when one is sick." Southerner Lucy Breckinridge "spent the day" watching for her mother to return, and noted that when she finally arrived, "The house is much brighter now."[25]

Literary critics have often noted the propensity of nineteenth-century female authors to "express hostility toward their mothers by eliminating them from the narrative," in contrast to twentieth-century authors, who dramatized the conflict. One such contemporary observer was Florence Nightingale, who during her own crisis over her life purpose commented on how the novels of her age featured a heroine who "has generally no family ties (almost invariably no mother), or, if she has, they do not interfere with her entire independence."[26] According to the critic Carolyn Heilbrun, the removal of familial impediments represented wish fulfillment—a magical, fictive freeing from real-life constraints, especially those imposed by families. Girls' diaries seem to have shared in both the plotting templates and the psychological bedrock which underlay such portrayals of familial displacement and liberation.

Agnes Lee's experience of reading and rereading *Madeline's Journal* reveals one such resemblance between fiction and self-construction. After pouring over *Madeline's Journal* yet again, to distract herself from a painful finger, Lee reflected on her own identification with the semiautonomous heroine. "I wish Madeline was a real character I am sure I should have loved her. I have never read a book which has taken such hold of my heart and imagination before." The fictional Madeline's autonomy was the result of successive maternal separations; Agnes Lee knew no such displacement, yet her mother figured virtually not at all in her description of her adolescent experiences, first when her father was superintendent of West Point and later when Agnes was a student at a female seminary. Only one expression of surprise—at finding "my darling Mamma sick upstairs with *rheumatism!*"—revealed that her mother was indeed usually present, and usually healthy.[27] The life Agnes scripted for herself in her journal suggested otherwise.

So what do we make of girls' frequent decisions to leave their mothers out of the record? We might conclude that a mother's absence from journals and diaries represented the same thing as a mother's absence from novels—an easy resolution to the need for imaginative space, without yet the daring demonstrated by such writers as Virginia Woolf, who confronted and considered killing the smothering, maternal "angel in the house."[28]

The potency of the maternal ideal became especially apparent when mothers had died. Indeed, the death of a mother might be the initial inspiration for a daughter to write. Grief over a loss that often seemed equal to a loss of self found a ready outlet in one strand of girls' autobiographical writing in which the spirit of the "angel of the house" was described, memorialized, and apotheosized. The critic Elaine Showalter has observed that many Victorian women writers had lost, or were alienated from, their mothers. Showalter concludes that the resulting male-identification contributed to their careers. The diary evidence from the United States suggests another possibility—that the loss of a mother may have encouraged writing which was initially a form of communication with an absent or imagined "other" from beyond the grave. In such journals, the palpable agenda of the journal writer was to apply a salve of words and an illusion of communication to the intense aloneness of the orphaned or the motherless. When Helen Ward Brandreth began her journal, at the age of thirteen, she described herself ("a low forehead, light hair and eyes"), noted her age, and then recorded the next significant information about herself: "My Mama is dead, she died March 5, 1871, so my eldest sister May takes care of me."[29] The death of a mother during a girl's childhood or youth distilled and romanticized maternal imagery. In their depictions of their dead mothers, girls concocted a powerful maternal essence which inhibited and censured with far greater impact than could any living representative.

As such, dead mothers came to stand in for a potent superego—an angel in fact rather than simply in allusion. In Victorian America, the association of mothers with religious virtue, as a "channel of God's grace" (according to Jane Tompkins), was a commonplace. For girls whose mothers had died, the association was fixed: mothers, feminine virtue, and an idealized but elusive better self. Mary Boit's mother, who had died at the birth of another daughter when Mary was only one year old, existed for her daughter only in archetype. Nonetheless, Boit's mother was never far from her thoughts, particularly as

4.2 "Angel Mamma," 1870. Mary Boit's mother, Georgia Mercer Boit, had died when Mary was one year old, yet she figured centrally in her daughter's emotional life as a perfect source of guidance and love. Schlesinger Library (Cambridge: Radcliffe Institute, Harvard University), A99-23av-40.

she wrestled with her demanding stepmother. In one extended reverie, Boit imagined her mother as a perfect source of guidance and love: "If I only had someone who would explain religious things to me and tell me how wicked it is to do some of the things I do and would encourage me and help me to be good. O my darling Mamma if you were only here to guide me and help me to do right I think I could do it better. . . . I do not feel that I really love any human being I do not feel I love anybody except you O mother." A few days earlier she had dreamed of "my own darling sweet Mamma" and experienced her death anew. That memory and association were intensely private, and close to her core of self. "I wouldn't let anybody see what I write for anything." Her thoughts of her mother were especially fresh because her mother's brother had come visiting from Georgia dressed in his military uniform. And as befit an emissary bearing intimate knowledge of another world, he had seemed both familiar and strange. "He said Yes'm to Mamma [Mary's stepmother] which sounded very queer. He said I look something like my angel Mamma which made me feel very happy but I know I shall never be quarter so nice looking."[30] Idealized heavenly mothers embodied the perfected features of womanhood — and served as icons impossible for mortal girls to approach.

In some sense, idealizing mothers, especially dead ones, bespoke a universal urge for the perfect unity of the womb or before. In that sense, the strong identification and attachment between mothers and daughters argued by Nancy Chodorow and others was intensified by its arbitrary dissolution through death. Testimonials in diaries about lost mothers provide the words to suggest the bonds which often remained unvoiced in the diaries of the daughters of living mothers.

Girls' Secrets

Mothers were often absent from the record when present in fact, and most clearly articulated in the fabric and manuscript of self when they were in fact dead, sick, or away. Whichever the case, the writings of Victorian daughters confirm the prolonged attachment of daughters to mothers with whom they shared a largely domestic sphere. Yet that primal bond of identification, encouraged by the Victorian separation of male and female spheres, was also subject to countercurrents from the culture of selfhood itself. As adults claimed a private self removed by propriety from public view or discourse, they taught those same values to growing girls. In theory, a girl told her mother all, and had no secrets. In practice, daughters, like their mothers, resisted expressing or confessing controversial emotions. In rooms and journals provided by their parents but taken for their own, girls, too, elaborated a layered culture of private secrets which sometimes pitted them against their mothers.

This was less true earlier in the nineteenth century. Parents claimed privacy for themselves but resisted giving it to children. Parents who had scrutinized their children's writings for signs of grace earlier in the century were not indulging idle curiosity but fulfilling their highest parental responsibility to see to the spiritual salvation of their children. The substitution of character building for salvation seeking as the goal of adolescent socialization was a change in vocabulary rather than a revolution in parent-child relations. Adults' increasing rights to privacy within their homes meant greater parental obligation to monitor children, rather than less. When parents took their children inside and closed the door, they gained sole responsibility for their upbringing.

The private writings of Louisa May Alcott in 1845 enacted the transparent and complete linkage of mother and daughter. Written when Louisa was twelve, her journal contained "this note from dear mother": "My Dearest Louy,—I often peep into your diary, hoping to see some record of more happy days. 'Hope, and keep busy,' dear daughter, and in all perplexity or trouble come freely to your Mother." Louisa responded: "Dear Mother,—You *shall* see more happy days, and I *will* come to you with my worries, for you are the best woman in the world. L.M.A." Louisa May Alcott's journal was to be a workbook which she shared with her mother who was both her prime ally and her prime role model in her efforts to conquer her "moods" and to be good and be happy.[31] When Alcott turned thirteen, she announced a plan for her life, "as I am in my teens, and no more a child." (Her plan: "I'm going to *be* good.") Alcott declared that she had told no one about her plan, but inscribed in her permeable diary, it represented a secret with her mother, an effort on the part of pure will to accomplish what myriad strategies of virtue had failed at.

Yet the idea that "a secret is not a good thing for a girl to have" became harder to defend as Victorianism evolved to encourage the privacy of the individual. The surreptitious surveillance which we associate with Victorianism was the result of the twin beliefs in the abstract value of privacy and the responsibility of parents to monitor children. Motivated perhaps by the greater actual autonomy of their daughters, who were no longer constantly at their mothers' elbows, and also by their own increasing responsibility for girls' upbringing, parents were often interested in the contents of daughters' diaries and journals. Although we think of the Victorians as inappropriately intrusive, their recourse to indirection was a sign of their deference to the *idea* of privacy. Earlier generations would have had fewer scruples about direct intervention.[32]

As youths made the transition to adulthood, they at first felt guilty about secrets they kept from parents. Lucy Breckinridge neglected to tell her father about her engagement, and remonstrated with herself for the omission: "I am afraid it is deception, and yet, I cannot make up my mind to do it. I am a coward! I try to reconcile myself to it by arguing that if I am silent now, there may something occur to make Pa favor my plan and if I told him now, it would distress and anger him. . . . And then, all girls do it. Sallie Grattan did not even tell her mother! But that's small comfort. I'll think of it and try to make up my mind."[33] Lucy Breckinridge's defenses of her secrecy in the 1860s lacked conviction. In resorting simply to fashion—"And then, all girls do it"—she was leaning on a reed so weak as to offend even her own sense of righteousness.

Yet at the same time, Breckinridge was offended at an incursion on her own sense of privacy. When a letter came into the house from Captain H., the man to whom she was engaged, "Pa got hold of the letter and read it and then sent for me to get it, a very bad thing in Papa." When Lucy decided to break off with her Captain H., largely because of her parents' disapproval, Lucy referred again to her father's intrusion on her privacy: "Pa opens all my letters since Eliza's alluding to Capt. H., and I have not a doubt was very much interested in the Capt.'s letter today." [34] It was wrong for her to with-hold important information about her engagement from her father, Breckin-ridge seemed to feel. It was perhaps even worse for her father to pry into her mail, without her express permission, "a very bad thing." The certainty of that last judgment suggests that girls were increasingly claiming a right to their own privacy.

As might have been expected between such a fiery duo, the etiquette and the morality of privacy also figured in the relationship between the feminist orator Lucy Stone and her diary-keeping daughter Alice Stone Blackwell. Per-haps not surprisingly, as in her campaign to restrict her daughter's reading, Lucy Stone upheld woman's self-sovereignty—as long as it did not extend to her daughter. In February 1872, when Blackwell was fourteen, her mother scolded her sharply for reading someone else's letter. "Mama told me I had never done so naughty a thing since I was borne." This strong rebuke upset Alice "utterly," and she described herself going off to school "in a very low state of mind." [35] Several months later, though, the tables were turned. Alice recorded: "I accused Mama of scratching out something in my diary, and she confessed to having done so. We had a conversation which nearly resulted in my giving up keeping a diary and burning the old ones, but the affair ended satisfactorily." Coming from the champion of women's rights, Lucy Stone's act of willful intrusion on her daughter is shocking. Not only had she read her daughter's journal, but she had been unable to resist obliterating contents which displeased her. The conversation between mother and daughter nearly ended in a dramatic scene of destruction, with the daughter threatening to break off the edifying practice of journal writing and to burn the old ones if her mother couldn't guarantee their privacy. Clearly, Alice had learned the les-sons about the sanctity of privacy which her mother had been trying to teach her. Equally clearly, Lucy Stone was still participating in a nineteenth-century culture which exempted relations between mothers and daughters from the strict code of privacy which characterized relations between adults. As late as the 1890s, *Ladies' Home Journal* was still declaring the rights of parents to open letters addressed to a daughter, but even this conservative publication suggested, "This is seldom done where the confidence between the parents and child exists."[36] The controversy in the spring of 1872 between the women of the Blackwell family, like those of myriad other families throughout Victorian America, were skirmishes in a prolonged cultural conflict over the rights of daughters to identities separate from their mothers'.

Having It Both Ways

Such skirmishes did not usually end in familial rupture. Rather, they represented daughters' often successful efforts to discover arenas of privacy within an overarching loyalty to families, especially mothers. Revealed in an unusually rich paper collection, Annie Winsor's struggles with an overbearing mother demonstrate the way that a girl might claim privacy for exploration and release without rejecting the family claim. In addition to her private journal, Winsor wrote numerous letters to various family members and kept a diary for her parents to read. Annie Winsor's journal allowed her private space within the heart of her close and intrusive family, while her diary was the work of a dutiful daughter. In combination, Annie Winsor's writings allowed her to express her grievances and affirm her separate opinions without threatening her familial lifeline. The resulting compromise between parental domination and personal rebellion helped Annie Winsor to go on to a notable career as a progressive educator while continuing to be sustained by her natal family. Annie Winsor's characteristic Victorian diary was a sometime partner in her transformation into a New Woman of the turn of the century.

Annie Winsor grew up in Winchester, Massachusetts, the daughter of a normal-school graduate and a Harvard-educated physician. Ann Ware Winsor was a powerful presence, both inspiring and overbearing. She took seriously her responsibilities for supervising the moral development of her seven children, and to this end, she expected access to their thoughts. When Annie was in college in the 1880s, she kept a diary "For My Mother dear, and because *it* is for her, For My beloved Father," and when another daughter mentioned a journal she was keeping, her mother requested to see it. Ann Winsor also insisted upon reading her daughters' letters to other family members. When Annie was traveling in England at the age of twenty, for instance, her mother confessed that her feelings were hurt at not being the recipient of confidences exchanged among the sisters. "Mary does not show me your private letters to her; which makes me sorry. . . . I don't love to think that my children say things and feel things that they are absolutely unwilling that I should know, even though I can understand their not wanting to say them at first hand."

She had no choice but to conclude, somewhat contrary to the evidence, that "Still, I can trust my children, and I do trust them." [37]

Her daughters, on their part, despaired of ever pleasing her, and alternately retreated from and resisted her intrusiveness. At the age of twenty-one Annie wrote a revealing letter to her mother. "I know very well—and I know it much to my mortification that I seem sort of sneaking and evasive when I am with you (and indifferent too). I have worried about it and even cried over it, mother. The conclusion I've come to is this. I am so afraid of the criticism, correction or dissatisfaction that may be in your face and eyes that I do not dare to look up." She concluded with insight, "You see I care more than anything else at home to be a daughter who shall repay all the worry and care that have been expended on her." [38]

Especially on the matter of reading personal letters, though, the eldest sisters attempted to take a stand in defense of their privacy. The elder, Mary, in a letter addressed to Annie at the age of fourteen, asked that her mother be instructed to wait her turn "and that meantime she must possess her soul in patience and not be fired with jealousy." It was easier when the sisters grew older and had left home, Mary thought, "so that my letters to you won't either be shown round or make the family jealous by being kept for yourself." Using incantations more often used to defend diaries, Annie at age twenty began a personal letter to her sister with a series of warnings: "Pedlars and mothers ragmen and sisters warned off the premises. Private. No Admission Except on Business! All rights reserved." And the next year, she addressed a curt reprimand to her mother for her snooping: "How did it happen, I wonder, that the letter you forwarded was opened. Can you explain the principle if you please?" [39]

In the face of this intrusiveness, Annie Winsor kept a private journal to help her think about the rights of young people. Begun when she was sixteen and a student at Winchester High School and continued through the age of twenty-one, her journal consisted of high-minded reflections on the appropriate relations between the generations, a forum which allowed her obliquely to vent her frustrations with her own upbringing. In contrast with the direct language she used in defending her privacy, the private journal itself used the language of high Victorian rationalism and abstraction (and the obfuscation of either the third-person "one" or the first-person plural). Through these means, Annie Winsor began to express a rebellion against her mother which she could not admit to more personally. She started her journal with an epigraph: "What youth saw plainly manhood loses sight of," and went on

to explain her goals: "To help me to remember my faults, and my convictions as relate to the behaviour of older people toward younger." (She later
referred simply to "O.P.s" and "Y.P.s.") She also voiced her hopes that her
journal would remind her in later years "to try to keep up with the fashions
and with the new manners and customs which are continually coming and
going, so that when I have young people in my charge I may be in sympathy
with them, and not restrain them with my 'old fashioned ideas.' "[40]

She embarked on a program of reflection ("Must we girls never think of
the questions of love and marriage?"), self-admonition ("I incline to be too
heavy and serious"), and resolve ("Perfect goodness is the only thing worth
aiming at"). Her journal tentatively voiced complaints about her censorious
home environment. "I can't see why a person who is evidently trying to do
right as hard as she can, should ever be blamed as harshly as though she meant
to do wrong," she wrote, and then pondered "why any person should ever
be blamed harshly at all." She explored her claims to privacy, a right she had
declared on the cover of this "Private" journal. "I have a hatred of showing
letters which come to myself," she wrote. Parents had a responsibility to make
sure the letters were suitable, she agreed, and she even agreed that "in the case
of letters of general interest this feeling should be overcome." But at eighteen
she protested having "one's faults, failings or anything of that personal kind
talked of before a whole family."[41]

Before she was done, Annie Winsor had offered the skeleton for a generational rebellion against parental authority. She observed that little children
often expect "to love without liking" because adults make themselves so disagreeable. She defended peer culture, arguing that "the way for people to have
a really delightful time is to be with their equals." She supported the custom
of going out to commercial establishments—presumably soda fountains or
fairs—with young men, "since young men have no way of returning the hos-
pitalities shown them by ladies except by taking the ladies to places of amusement, etc." And she even defended, and participated in, sexual high jinks.
"To me there is an exquisite thrilling pleasure in real, hand to hand, private
'fooling' with a boy that I like. . . . And yet I can easily see that an older person ought not to openly countenance it. I don't think it does me harm, but—
positive good—it sort of ennobles me."[42] Her vocabulary was high-minded,
but with it Annie Winsor was defending the "ennobling" qualities of sexual
pleasure and the rights of youth to defy parental dictates.

Annie Winsor's journal from her sixteenth year was written in 1881, when
she was a student at coeducational Winchester High School. She went on
to attend the Harvard Annex (later Radcliffe), to teach and participate in

social reform, and then to found her own school, the progressive, coeducational Roger Ascham School. Under a pseudonym, she wrote frequent columns of advice on women's subjects. Annie Winsor became an archetypal New Woman, attending college, marrying late, developing a career, and campaigning for sex education—however euphemistically she delivered her advice. Her private journal was an important part of that development. In the measured voice of a true Victorian, she used that protected space to chip away at the fetters of obligation and guilt which still constrained her. Her critique declared a generational revolt.

Annie Winsor's bid for personal autonomy within her family was always muted by family claims, though, and it is for this reason that her journal needed to be private: she was in no way eager to sever family bonds—in fact, quite the contrary. "It is my duty to confide in my mother, even though it be most difficult for me," she wrote after a declaration of her need for privacy. And that same year, she observed in her journal that journal writing did not always satisfy her, that it seemed a little abstract and remote. "I want something more substantial. So I write to my mother. I can put my love in as much as I like." Annie Winsor might rail in her journal against the way Old People misunderstood Young People, yet she remained too dependent on her parents' moral and emotional universe to break away from home completely. Ultimately Annie Winsor wanted to be good, and depicted her life as an independent woman with the moral earnestness of a good daughter. In this need for parental connection, she shared emotional bedrock with Dora, the heroine of the *St. Nicholas* story "She Couldn't." Dora had finally set aside her ambitions, bound her private journal in black and resolved "to talk all the time to my mother," and "to love you all at home so you'll love me."[43]

But unlike Dora, Annie Winsor did not forswear her ambitions—or her journal. Rather, she protected her conflicted self within its private pages. This claim for privacy allowed Victorian girls to assert new selves without rejecting their domestic identities. They thereby could sustain, without being oppressed by, the maternal bonds which many historians see as the heart of the nineteenth-century women's world.[44] For Victorian girls, a blend of private experiment with public loyalty made sense.

Fathers and Daughters

Daughters' skirmishes with mothers cut close to the bone, working the borders of identity often blurred by shared location within the home. With their responsibility for the reproduction of domestic roles, mothers lay centrally in the line of command over the lives of their daughters. Of course

4.3 "A duty to confide," 1880. Annie Winsor, front row, left, felt a duty to confide in her forceful mother, Ann Ware Winsor, top row, but also kept a private journal to allow her to explore the rights of Young People. Schlesinger Library (Cambridge: Radcliffe Institute, Harvard University), MC 322-687-14.

their authority was shared power—power that originated with wages earned by husbands and fathers. Traditional patriarchy had been in decline for some time in the late nineteenth century. Without land to disperse, fathers had been losing their authority over their sons' destinies, and as they moved to cities and took up work outside of the home, fathers were less and less involved in the delegation of work within the home. But in fundamental and important ways, they still ruled. Those responsible for advising girls on their role in life reminded them of their continuing need to curry favor with fathers—and with reason. The Victorian patriarch could appear unexpectedly, thwarting plans, making pronouncements, breathing moral fire. Yet he was not always successful in these less and less common rulings. When opinion at home had congealed elsewhere—particularly when mothers and daughters agreed—the Victorian patriarch could find his authority hollow. Especially as daughters matured from childhood and found their lives inscribed with the expectations of gender, fathers receded from the line of command, expecting of their daughters, as they did of their wives, not obedience but domestic ministration.

Fathers' familial responsibility for daughters translated into responsibility for guidance in two particular arenas beyond the walls of the home. Men were responsible for supervising their daughters' academic education and for assisting them in their studies in religion. This responsibility is well communicated in the kinds of gifts bestowed by fathers on daughters on birthdays—prayer books, writing books, pens, dictionaries, atlases, library subscriptions.[45]

Fathers' responsibilities for higher duties were reflected in their stern communications with daughters at midcentury. Agnes Lee received letters reinforcing the importance of studies from her father, Robert E. Lee, in the 1850s when she was away at a female seminary. He took issue with a bit of exuberant homesickness: "I must take you to task for some expressions in your letter. You say, 'our only thought, our only talk, is entirely about our going home.' How can you reconcile that with the object of your sojourn at Staunton! Unless your thoughts are sometimes devoted to your studies, I do not see the use of your being there." It was often fathers to whom daughters recited lessons, and whose words of commendation were particularly meaningful.[46] Fathers' responsibilities for their daughters' educations represented a vestigial authority for a family's competency in the world—and continued when responsibility for other aspects of daughters' lives had receded.

The same was true, though to a lesser degree, for fathers' responsibilities for daughters' souls. Kathryn Kish Sklar has written powerfully about the intertwining strands of patriarchy and evangelical culture which bedeviled Catharine Beecher's quest for a conversion experience early in the nineteenth century. As mothers took up their newly won roles as moral exemplars, they supplemented but did not replace fathers as the guardians of familial faith. Robert E. Lee encouraged his daughter's relationship with God as well as her studies, and his daughter wrote back a shy profession of faith, offered to her father as to one to whom it was owed: "I have something to tell you which I know will make you very happy. It is, I believe both of your daughters are Christians. I am sure Annie is, and O Papa I am resolved to doubt no longer that there has been a great and blessed change wrought in my wicked heart." Though absent from the day-to-day dealings of the household, fathers' interest in the state of their offsprings' souls extended to the their moral training as well. Margaret Tileston's diary, which included financial accounts, also included a moral accounting with her father. "I told Papa of a lie I told him about a week ago, last Tuesday or Wednesday." It was in such a grave consciousness of his paternal responsibility for the character of his daughter that Albert Browne wrote a long letter to his daughter Nellie as she was preparing to leave school, ending with the admonishment that "a true christian woman, should make it a *religious* duty, to blend gentleness and dignity, as to *win* love, and *command* respect." [47] Albert Browne had no doubt of his authority over his daughters' transition to womanhood, just as over other family matters.

Patriarchy Challenged

Yet gradually, daughters began to question paternal dictates of all kinds, with particular vigor when encouraged by dissension between parents. It is a cliché that the Civil War divided families, pitting brother against brother in this internecine conflict. The power inversion also crossed gender lines, as wives and daughters secretly questioned the authority of fathers making unusual demands in trying times. Eliza Frances Andrews, writing in the plantation South, drew some comfort from her hopes that her mother might have been secretly on her side when the Civil War divided her Georgia family. Although her father owned two hundred slaves, he remained a staunch Unionist, even as his three sons enlisted with the Confederacy. His daughter professed pity ("Poor father") and personal shame ("I know I deserve to have my head cracked") even as she cooperated in the stitching of Georgia's secession flag. "What would father have done if he had known that that secession flag was made in his house?" she wondered subversively. She gained some support from what she imagined was her mother's ambivalence: "Father sticks to the Union through thick and thin, and mother sticks to father, though I believe she is more than half a rebel at heart on account of the boys."[48] Clearly paternal dictate did not rule unquestioned.

The Civil War also revealed fissures in the confident authority of Albert Browne, who had written his daughter with ponderous advice about her role in life. Doing his part for the cause even in his maturity, Albert Browne enlisted in the Union Army in the quartermaster corps. He was stationed in Beaufort, South Carolina, in 1863 and appears to have summoned his two daughters to come keep him company. Nellie's younger sister Alice conveyed the family's astonished response: "Last night we were in a state of utter amazement on the arrival of your letters, at your dispatching matters in such an expeditious manner. You must have had a very strange idea of your two daughters to have thought, that in a fortnight they could bid good-bye to Mother and Eddie and all our friends, and get ready for a stay of several months at Beaufort. No. Father if we go, Mother and Eddie go too, and on no account could we consent to start till after Thanksgiving." Alice concluded in advising her father not to be disappointed at finding his daughters in rebellion. "Bear it meekly and hope for better success in the future." Alice's tone, bordering on defiance, clearly gained support from her mother's concurrence. Her brother Eddie confirmed that one of Albert Browne's problems in receiving familial compliance was his wife. "Mother thinks that Nelly and Alice won't go down to Beaufort until Mother goes and I go to [sic] and that may never be." We do not have Albert Browne's retort, but a letter of Nellie's from a later month suggests that he renewed his beseechment, and raised the stakes. "We laughed heartily over the last few lines of your letter, where you threaten to *disinherit* your daughters, if they do not come to Beaufort. Do you still hold to the threat?" Perhaps Nellie was correct in thus adopting a light tone with which to parry her father's petition. Nonetheless, it seems unlikely that her father was completely in jest in soliciting the ministrations of his daughters, thrust as he was in middle age to the edge of a war zone. The teasing continued, as Alice wrote again to her father about her mother's independence since his departure. "Don't you think that your wife has grown very smart, during your absence? Isn't your curiosity fully aroused to know what is going on? Well, you must remain in suspense, for I shall not tell you in this letter."[49] The tweaking, if not defiance, of Albert Browne's family presents something of a puzzle. Did Albert wear his authority lightly at home, and invite the kind of ribbing which he received? (Both of Nellie Browne's parents, Albert and Sarah, were given to writing her letters laden—and leaden— with parental admonition.) Or was the family staging a coup, finally liberated from the weight of his overbearing administration? Whether the Browne family correspondence represented good humor in a family already conscious of power inequities or a rapid redressing of previous abuses, it is clear that even as early as the 1860s, Albert Browne had tested his power and found it wanting—at least for the moment. By the next year, his wife and daughters had joined him in South Carolina.

Though Albert Browne eventually prevailed in this long battle, he did not win the war. The conservative *Ladies' Home Journal* in 1895 attempted to re-affirm masculine authority in what must be seen as a reactionary challenge to feminized domesticity. In reasserting "The Father's Domestic Headship," the Reverend Charles H. Parkhurst, D.D., acknowledged a "great deal of domestic reciprocity" but pronounced that "the husband and father is the point of final determination." He sought an analogy for the moral authority of husband and wife in anatomy: "The bone and sinew of character will probably be a quotation from the father, and the delicate tissue with which it is over-laid will as likely be a bequest from the mother."[50] This late-century contrast between the strong force of paternal dictum with the more diffuse "tissue" of the maternal presence acknowledged a long-standing reality—that absent fathers would need to make their authority felt concisely in worded dictates, rather than through the steady example of a more present maternity.

By 1895, however, when Parkhurst was writing, he was in many ways too late. His assertion of masculine hegemony in the household was regressive—and claimed an authority for fathers in their daughters' lives that they could not count on. Those girls in the postwar years most likely to reveal their dependency on paternal dictates—for instance, the reformer Jane Addams growing up in the late 1860s and Mary Thomas away at school in Georgia in the 1870s—used their fathers as live models of correct conduct with good reason, for both their mothers were dead.[51]

If daughters empowered by the increasing moral authority of their mothers were beginning to feel free to challenge paternal prerogative, fathers them-selves showed, over the nineteenth century, a diminishing sense of identifi-cation with their daughters. Fathers like Robert E. Lee and Albert Browne took seriously their paternal responsibility for providing guidance to their maturing daughters, but that guidance often required setting a new form of reference—the inscribing of gender on girls defined previously by their status as children. Albert Browne's advice to Nellie intended to prepare her for that new station. He reminded her that leaving school would require that she end her time as a "mere" schoolgirl to take her part "in the drama of life" as "a *true* woman." Doing so would mean surrendering part of her genetic inheritance, and becoming only part of who she had been. For Browne admonished his daughter to emulate her mother's qualities of "mildness and amenity, love and kindness," so "as to temper and subdue any unruly and unamiable tendencies which may have come to you from your Father."[52] This gendered lesson, of course, was a distancing one which signaled the attenuation of a relationship as well as a stage of life.

Girls who had been accorded the freedom of childhood by fond fathers found this withdrawal of paternal identification to be painful. Writing in the late century, Mary Virginia Terhune recounted such a moment: "I have now before me the picture of myself at ten years of age, looking up from the back of my pony into my father's face, as in the course of the morning ride we daily enjoyed together." They had been conversing about politics, and the child had offered an apt analysis. "My comments called up a smile and a sigh. "'Ah, my daughter! If you had been born a boy you would be invaluable to me!'" Terhune recalled the sense of destiny. "I hung my head, mute and crushed by a calamity past human remedy or prevention. There is a pain at my heart in the telling that renews the real grief of the moment." Terhune had been taking advantage of a latitude granted to Victorian children of both sexes; she observed that some of "the finest women, physically and mentally," were "famous romps in their youth." Such girls, she noted, "during the tom-boy stage lamented secretly or loudly that they were not their own brothers; regrets which were heartily seconded by much-enduring mothers and disappointed fathers." Literary historians have observed that the 1860s saw the emergence of a new literary type—tomboys—who, as Barbara Sicherman has observed, were "not only tolerated but even admired—up to a point, the point at which they were expected to become women."[53] The extension of the rights to romp and play to girls confirmed their identity as children, a state that often ended surprisingly and arbitrarily, with fathers' rejections.

Terhune's memory of paternal humiliation recalls from earlier in the century young Elizabeth Cady [Stanton]'s realization that she could not remain the confidante and paternal protégé she had been as a child. In her perhaps mythic retelling of the tale, that youthful epiphany produced a sense of injury and injustice which would help to fuel the woman's rights movement itself. Both Stanton and Terhune gained their sense of betrayal from the contrast between their spirited childhoods and their sense of gendered destiny descending to restrict them in their teens. Mary Virginia Terhune concluded with an admonition to fathers which gave them responsibility for this curtailment of aspiration in the world: "Your girl wants to help *her* father and to be of use in the world. Make her feel that a woman's life is worth living, and that she has begun it. Do not brand her from the cradle, '*Exempt from field duty on account of physical disability.'*"[54] For both Stanton and Terhune, it was a shock to discover that life "as a romp," "as a half-boy," in fact as a Victorian child, was only temporary, conditional. Their fathers, who often had invited their daughters along in their common round, withdrew that invitation as they approached maturity.

By later in the century, urban fathers were often absent from the beginning of their daughters' lives, working in shops and offices away from home. When Louisa May Alcott commented on this new order, as she did most pointedly in *An Old-Fashioned Girl,* she depicted the father of her modern family as absent, "a busy man, so intent on getting rich that he had no time to enjoy what he already possessed." In a later passage, he "had been so busy getting rich, that he had not found time to teach his children to love him," neglecting both sons and daughters. His son he ordered "about as if he was a born rebel," and was always "lecturing him." His daughters, however, he let "do just as they liked."[55] By today's accounting, the Victorian father was notable for the extent to which he assumed and discharged a role as paterfamilias. However, that brief moment (if there ever was one) when fathers presided supremely over a small, nurturant family was in decline as soon as it was constituted. The movement of men's labor outside of the home also removed them from their role as the preeminent guide and adjudicator of their daughters' conduct. As women challenged men's domestic authority, so did men increasingly abdicate, letting go of prerogatives they were not in place to oversee.

Girls remained dependent on fathers, however, a condition that their increasing participation in the labor force would diminish but never erase. Conservative advice givers made it their business to remind girls of this status. Multiple authors in the *Ladies' Home Journal,* starting with the *Journal*'s editor, Edward Bok, urged on girls their responsibilities to practice as apprentice wives in their ministrations to their fathers. "Helping her father to remember his daily engagements, seeing that his accounts are properly balanced, following his personal matters—all these things enter into the life of a girl when she becomes a wife," Bok wrote. A girl should not imagine "that her father represented a money-making machine, bound to take care of her and give her a good time," the *Journal*'s columnist Rush Ashmore added. It was the daughter who owed her father a good time. She should remember that it is "her honor to be his daughter" and greet him with a smile. "He who is out in the busy world earning the bread and butter doesn't want to be met with complaints and cross looks; he wants to be greeted with a kiss, to be entertained by the mind which he has really formed by earning the money to pay the teachers to broaden and round it, and to be able to look at the bright, cheery girl, neat in her dress, sweet in her manner and ever ready to make merry those who are sad." Abba Goold Woolson, writing critically about the place of *Woman in American Society,* specified how she might demonstrate this gratitude. "Duty to papa consists in putting his slippers near the grate before he comes home; in laying his evening paper where he will see it; and in reading to him the price of stocks." Another *Journal* commentator summed up the message: "'Petting' comes with charming grace from an affectionate daughter." [56]

Increasingly teenage daughters' approaches to fathers, like those of their mothers, focused on the interaction of two separate worlds. Advisers' exhortations that daughters should be affectionate and "pet" their fathers rather than "obey" them suggested the ways in which the family had become an arena of intimate exchange rather than hierarchical responsibility. Increasingly fathers did not induct their growing daughters into adulthood but instead looked to their daughters to offer them an escape from that world.

The "othering" of daughters to some degree began earlier in the nineteenth century, with the romanticization of childhood for boys and girls. Once selfish sinners, children were now considered to possess natural qualities of innocence in comparison with their elders. As girls became female adolescents, children's culture and domestic culture intermingled. Growing girls continued to inhabit a magical child's world but also began to join a mystified domesticity. Separate children's fairy lands were enhanced to become enchanted castles, sexualized by Victorian gender imagery. Emily Eliot's descriptions of her relationship with her fond and nurturant father suggest some of the dimensions of this world. Samuel Eliot was at various times headmaster of Boston's Girls' High School, superintendent of Boston public schools, and president of Trinity College. From the time she was twelve, Emily had been providing her father with the attentions appropriate from a good daughter. Emily's vocabulary in her diary was telling. On December 14, 1869, for instance, when the family was abroad in England, Emily described her activities: a music lesson and a walk with her father. "When we came home I dressed for dinner and after dinner I read and recited my lessons to Papa, and cosseted him, and read in my Bible and wrote in my journal, also in this diary, and read in 'Hitherto' which I got from Croydons." Over the next year or so, Emily often used the verb *cosset* to describe her daughterly displays of affection, including several weeks later when, after Sunday lessons, "I cosseted papa, and wrote a note to Edith Beach." "Cosseting" often took place in the evening after dinner in the library and likely meant the same thing as petting,

4.4 "Playing house," 1898. Advisers encouraged older daughters to practice the role of wife with their fathers, as modeled here in this story of a father visiting the world of childhood with his daughter. Reprinted from Albert Bigelow Paine, "Playing House," *St. Nicholas* 25 (August 1898): 871.

a verb Emily Eliot used the next October. Cosseting and petting probably included "sitting in Papa's lap" (which Emily also mentions) and maybe, in a different mood, "scuffling." (After tea one day, Emily "'scuffled'" with Papa, a new word to her that she enclosed in quotation marks.) Cosseting also included reading aloud to her father. (Emily read the newspaper, Longfellow's "Evangeline," Alcott's *Little Men*, Austen's *Northanger Abbey* and *Persuasion;* one evening when her father was ill in bed, she mentioned reading a book called simply *Marriage*.) In Mary Boit's household, cosseting included "tickling papa's head so to put him to sleep."[57]

What to make of these ministrations? Emily Eliot considered them worthy of reporting in her diary, perhaps in part because they constituted one of a number of dutiful actions performed by a good girl. (Others included reading, writing, studying, and walking.) Annie Cooper, who at age twenty-one was considerably older than Emily Eliot, defined her vocation as the youngest daughter in similar terms. Attending to her father's spiritual and emotional needs came hard to the reserved young woman, but she felt that serving God through serving her father "is my calling for the present." As she put it, she wanted to be "a sweet, affectionate, fascinating, entertaining daughter," the list suggesting the subordination of self which defined a good daughter in preparation for being a dutiful wife.[58]

The identification of daughters with a mystique that was one part childhood and the other mystified domesticity charmed but also distanced fathers, who increasingly felt that they lacked knowledge and understanding of daughters. In lacking understanding, they also could feel that they lacked responsibility. From all evidence, Frederick Winsor was a kind and loving father to his several daughters. (Indeed, he wrote to his daughter Annie that he felt sorry for fathers who had no daughters.) He was also impecunious, a result of lingering debts accrued during the Civil War. The family's lack of resources, especially in comparison with their friends and relations, conditioned the lives of his daughters, who worked in a variety of capacities to support the family and themselves. Yet his tone toward his daughters belied the shared knowledge that they must work. A letter written to his daughter Annie at the mature age of twenty-three suggested the way that mystifying rhetoric could obscure those practical realities. Annie was living with her sister Mary in Bar Harbor, Maine, where the two seem to have been conducting a scientific school in hired rooms over the summer. Frederick Winsor wrote, "We like to think of [you] in your tower—like enchanted princesses—with the instruments of your mystic art laid out on your table." The language of enchanted princesses and mystic art was, of course, the language of a romanticized childhood, not a metaphor for single women's work in the late nineteenth century. That a father could confuse one with the other suggests the salience of Mary Virginia Terhune's observation about the relation of nineteenth-century fathers and daughters: "To the wisest fathers daughters are forever children, without responsibilities and futureless."[59] This had not always been the case. The separation of spheres reinforced the romanticization of childhood to constitute a new category for girls—a category doubly distanced from the control, responsibility, and identification of fathers.

The Daughters of Edward D. Boit

One result of this distance and "othering" of daughters was a potential for sexualizing girls, in part the result of power inequities. As Lenore David-off and Catharine Hall have written about English families in the nineteenth century, erotic associations were "found wherever there was the constellation of male power through age, experience, material and cultural resources."[60] Victorian and Edwardean scholars have long observed the particular intensity of the father-daughter relationship, perhaps best embodied by Freud's pre-eminently Victorian theorizing of its erotic potential. Mary Boit, daughter of the Boston businessman Robert Boit, found herself uncomfortably confronting the implications of that connection when she was traveling in Europe during her nineteenth summer. In Paris in 1896 she visited her uncle Edward Darley Boit, an expatriate artist and recently widowed father of four daughters. Fourteen years earlier, her Boit cousins had been the subject of one of John Singer Sargent's most famous paintings, *The Daughters of Edward D. Boit* (1882), which depicts four girls of varying ages in a richly detailed interior. Although it is an ensemble portrait, three of the Boit sisters look out at the observer with direct gazes, each adopting a singular, autonomous pose. (The eldest reclines against a wall, less engaged than her sisters.) The family portrait in fact suggests the potential for individuality within the confines of high-Victorian domesticity. Generations of viewers have seen in *The Daughters of Edward D. Boit,* a popular attraction in Boston's Museum of Fine Arts, the innocence, composure, and sheer prettiness of Victorian girlhood.

Mary Boit's visit to her cousins in Paris at the age of nineteen brought adult interest in viewing girls, and specifically Edward Boit's relationship with his daughters, into disconcerting focus. Mary began by confessing her discomfort with her uncle: "Uncle Ned quite scares me. I stand very much in awe of him." She went on to suggest what distressed her: "I think he seems quite preoccupied and now we are over here Uncle Ned says he is going to marry Florence Little next month. Well it is a very strange thing and I am more sorry for the girls than anything. Poor dears and it seems so queer to look at Uncle Ned and then think he is in love with some one my age. . . . Well goodnight I'm very blue and long for my own Dad." Clearly, Mary Boit's unease was rooted in the incestuous implications of a father falling in love with and planning to marry one of his younger daughter's "special and intimate" friends, "some one my age." (Edward Boit's eldest daughter was twenty-seven

4.5 "The Daughters of Edward Darley Boit," 1882. Mary Boit visited her cousins
in Paris in 1896, shortly after their father had decided to marry the "special and
intimate" friend of his young daughter following the death of their mother. John
Singer Sargent had painted the girls fourteen years earlier. Courtesy of Museum of
Fine Arts, Boston. Reproduced with permission. © Museum of Fine Arts, Boston.
All rights reserved.

at the time, and his intended bride, Florence Little, was twenty, just older
than his niece Mary.) His preoccupation or aloofness suggested his remoteness from ordinary familial exchanges with his family, the kinds of interactions which inscribe the incest taboo. As a result, he seemed dangerous to
Mary Boit on her own behalf and behalf of her cousins. (He "quite scares
me.") To those who follow late-Victorian elite culture, the culture which produced Alice in Wonderland and her child-loving creator, Charles Lutwidge
Dodgson, it should be no surprise that the images of girlhood embodied in

Sargent's painting of the Boit girls might also provoke an adult love affair. As Mary Boit astutely observed, such a marriage could have the effect of alienating permanently Edward Boit's own daughters, for whom she was "more sorry than anything." Still in mourning for their mother, they might well have felt that they had lost a father, too, when the person who filled that role chose to marry one of their own.[61] Post-Freudians all, we nod knowingly when Victorian girls describe "cosseting" and "petting" their fathers. The Victorian bourgeois family was born in part from the breakdown of authority and responsibility that impelled Robert E. Lee and Albert Browne to pontificate to their daughters about their roles in the world. Granting children—and especially daughters—a separate, mystified world also meant "othering" them—looking at them across a divide which had the potential to be eroticized.

Fathers: Escorts to Urban Culture

If girls' attentions to fathers at home represented the enactment of domestic nurture, fathers sometimes reciprocated with excursions into a suspect public world that was rarely condoned by mothers. Alluring and dangerous, the world of popular culture—of races, popular celebrations, alcohol, arcades—was off-limits to middle-class girls, unless escorted by fathers themselves brooking the confines of genteel Victorianism.[62] Victorian culture itself contained some of the seeds of this rebellion—and associated them with fathers. One St. Nicholas story described a thirteen-year-old girl whose mother had ambitions to foster a perfectly accomplished young woman. Her regimen never allowed for a holiday, however, so her father arranged for a visit to his sister's family in the country. On their journey, the young Edith confesses that though she likes to be shown off, "it's nice to have no lessons, and to be with you, papa." When Edith spies a fruit seller, she lowers her voice to a confidential whisper and asks "'Papa, did you ever suck an orange?' . . . Papa tried to look shocked and solemn, and said in a stern voice, 'Did you?'" So the happy couple commenced a restorative vacation sucking oranges together, away from Victorian overcivilization.[63]

In the actual documents of girlhood, fathers similarly offered excursions away from Victorian domesticity, sometimes on the sly, sometimes in open challenge to its narrower confines. Thus when the Fair Haven schoolgirl Mabel Lancraft got off the cars after school one September day in 1889, whom should she meet there but her father, with a subversive offer: "If I would ride right home with him he would take me to the horse trot." When Emily Eliot's mother was away in Newport, she met her father in Pemberton Square in Boston, bought an arithmetic book, "and then we went to a place, where we had some oysters, and ale and then I walked part way across the common with him and part way by myself."[64] It is significant that Emily did not have the vocabulary to name the alehouse they visited in 1870, because it was undoubtedly expected to be well beyond her ken.

The relationship of Mary Boit with her parents—an indulgent father and a withholding stepmother—suggests the important role fathers sometimes played in providing alternative scripts to an overbearing domesticity. In some sense the deck was stacked in the Boit family, as stepmother struggled ineptly to retain control of daughters not her own. Yet each parent drew lines provided them by the culture, as they faced off in domestic disputes over child rearing. The dynamics especially emerged in a series of diary entries in June and July of 1891, when Mary was fourteen years old. Mary had long been in conflict with her stepmother, an overstressed woman who was raising two stepchildren as well as two of her own. Mary's depiction of her stepmother's expectations revealed a classic struggle between boisterous children and a mother seeking propriety. One day, Mary wrote in protest at her stepmother's refusal to permit roughhousing and play. "We can not do anything in this house as soon as we start to have any fun we are stopped. . . . It seems as though we were kept in a glass case and everything else in this house. I am sure I never seem to be able to do anything to suit Mamma." A week later the two clashed over how long Mary should practice the piano. "Georgia [Mary's younger sister] tried to defend me in something I said and M. said well you usually do right but Mary I can't do anything with her. Mamma told me a few days ago that she had given up trying to make a lady of me long ago."[65] In the case of Mary Boit and her stepmother, the rhetoric of Victorian domestic refinement provided the vocabulary and the manifestation of power struggles that were embedded in the structure of the Victorian family itself.

Robert Boit himself offered his daughter an escape from "the glass case" of young ladyhood. During these difficult weeks with her stepmother, Mary's father provided excursions outside and beyond the boundaries of domestic propriety. One such excursion was simply a trip to see her cousins, the family of her father's sister. "I nearly danced out of my shoes I felt so **happy** I think I should have shouted **Hurrah** if Mamma had let me."[66] Whether her stepmother actually forbade these hurrahs is doubtful; at least in the home, though, Mary had learned to censor her expressiveness herself.

Another outing brought the Boit family into the increasingly elaborate world of consumer choices. It started with a trip to have tintypes taken, "but when we got there the cupboard was bare as the store was closed. We went in to Pierces where papa lighted his cigarette and we were weighed. . . . He was going to take us to the Public Gardens to see the beautiful new plants just put out but we stopped first to get some soda water and then it was too late to go. Papa got ginger, G. lemon and it was very hard to decide but at last took Coffee. I now have made up my mind that whenever I take a soda [at] Kelley and Durkey I will take each kind in the order they are arranged and so not waste so much time."[67] In Mary Boit's family, a consumer world of rich variety administered by her father counterpointed a home world of studied discipline and self-denial administered by her stepmother.

It was Robert Boit, too, who introduced his family to the new working-class celebration of Independence Day known as the horribles. In place of plumed and ornate militias, such as the Ancient and Honorable Artillery Company, antic groups from the working class formed "Antique and Hor-rible" companies of crusaders or pirates to mock their betters. Robert Boit elected, against his wife's better judgment, to take his family. The day of the trip, Mary captured the sense of danger the controversy had excited: "Today is the fourth Hurrah Hurray I am going with papa to Wellesley today I ex-pect I shall be killed before I come home or thrown out of the carriage but if I am not why my wonderful adventures will be related tomorrow there are so many accidents I am quaking with fear." United with her father, Mary could take her stepmother's disapproval of the horribles with equanimity: "We teased Mamma and she said they were common and vulgar." On the day itself, Robert Boit kept his daughters out late, catching the train back to Brookline only at 10:25, with his daughters getting to bed after midnight. His wife disapproved, and his daughter took sides: "Mama did not like it at all because papa kept us out so late. She thought it was outrageous. I should not think she would mind for almost once a year." It was clear that the ex-pedition had not delivered the anticipated dollop of danger, but nonetheless Mary announced, "I had a perfectly beautiful time."[68] Robert and Lillian Boit represented polarized opinion on this custom, and on many others as well. In other marriages less fraught than the Boits', however, fathers' rebellions against domesticity's confining dictates cut daughters some slack as well.

Alice Blackwell described a journey with her father outside of her pro-tected home world which left her feeling less kinship with her father. The two were walking with her uncles in patrician New York at dusk discussing the architecture. They "told which we liked and should like to live in, and which we disliked, and argued and disputed and disagreed with each other, and finally we stopped before one most beautiful large brown stone front, and burst out into unanimous exclamations of rapture. The lights were just begin-ning to be lighted, and shone faintly through the curtains—real starry lace—

that hung in the tall, clear windows. It was beautiful." Their euphoria was short-lived, however, interrupted when one uncle "quietly remarked, 'That's Madam Restelle's.'" Though only fourteen years old, Alice Blackwell was old enough to know who Madam Restelle was—an infamous abortionist who advertised her "little pills" in newspapers throughout the country. Alice wrote, "We went on, quenched most effectually, I feeling queerer and queerer." This abrupt initiation into the deceptiveness of beautiful exteriors was followed by another. "There were flocks of little beggar children with whining voices, who sallied out upon us; and a little boy sat by the railing, with a fiddle laid across his knees, crying." To this latter scene, a classic one from Victorian sentimental literature, Henry Blackwell was unsympathetic. "Papa made some remarks about his doing it for pretense (not to him of course) and joked about it." Alice Blackwell herself, though, as befit her sex and status, was less callous. She noted, "I felt more like crying than laughing. It was such a contrast somehow."[69] If fathers transported their daughters into the teeming social world of the late–nineteenth century city, their daughters sometimes viewed it through identities already formed by domestic culture.

Whether daughters demurred from father's judgments or endorsed them, fathers' representation of an outside world to their daughters signified divided authority. They allowed the challenge of domestic and feminized dictates with the liberalizing impact of a still suspect, and perhaps vulgar, consumer society of choice and possibility. It was the novelty of fathers which earned them mention in daughters' diaries. Mothers constituted the backdrop of daughters' lives, often most integrated into their lives when most taken for granted in daughters' accounts. When trouble erupted, it was often over the porous boundary between mother and daughter in a world which did not grant daughters rights to privacy or even to selves of their own. For daughters, therefore, divided authority between mother and father meant divided inheritance—a freedom within the family itself to venture beyond domesticity's confines.

FIVE

Interiors:
Bodies, Souls, Moods

If girls had fathers and mothers to play off each other, there was much that they did not have under control. In activist modes, they could practice the myriad disciplines imposed on them—piano playing, constitutionals, room tidying—but those routines often seemed a substitute for action rather than action itself. Most girls found it difficult to sustain the cheerful demeanor expected of them, especially as they experienced a series of baffling changes in their bodies, often with minimal preparation. Nearly as surprising as new bodily imperatives were the restrictions of adults, sometimes accompanying a birthday, arbitrarily denying familiar freedoms. Girls occasionally rebelled, but more often they tried to adapt, often in confusion. If the diaries they wrote had any purpose at all, it was to absorb and process this confusion, to provide on a personal scale the mechanism of adjustment to the new order that awaited them whenever it was that they were grown.

Victorian parents and advisers did not agree on when that was. Certainly the arrival of menarche was one such marker, yet the normative age of menarche in the late nineteenth century was not a matter of scientific record, and many adults anticipated their daughters' menarche later than it actually occurred. In any case, Victorian reticence did not encourage the open acknowledgment of such private bodily functions. Instead, parents introduced adult responsibilities and new standards for conduct and fashion gradually as girls moved through the teen years. Various in timing and family-specific in application, together these moments came to define a continuum which only later would be considered a distinct stage of life.

Age at Menarche and Fears of Precociousness

Much of Victorian girlhood can be explained in the context of a lowering age of menarche among daughters of the urban bourgeoisie. Adults often denied the earlier maturing of their daughters, or worried about it and attempted to fend it off obliquely with a prolonged campaign against precociousness, leaving girls ignorant and alarmed at the arrival of menarche. The pioneer woman physician Elizabeth Blackwell in 1852 was an early and unusually outspoken observer of the trend toward the earlier maturing of girls. In the middle of a long tract advocating more vigorous physical education for girls, Blackwell buried an empirical observation about the different ages at which menarche was occurring: "The growth of the generative organs is greatly influenced by the place of residence, whether town or country, and by the habits of different classes of society." She noted the earliest arrival of menarche "in the wealthy classes," followed by those "amongst the laboring population of towns," with the lowest rate of all to be found "amongst the inhabitants of the mountain districts." Blackwell's demographic observation came to a point: "It was observed in the same city, that in the children of the wealthy classes, this period was more than a year in advance of the lower classes."[1] Blackwell's impressionistic observation that wealthy girls were menstruating as much as a year before the working class remained just that for much of the rest of the century. Her insight was reflected in oblique debates about precociousness as a defining and disturbing trait of the modern girl.

Nearly a half-century later, Helen P. Kennedy interviewed 125 high school girls as part of a study of the effects of education on reproductive health, providing some data to substantiate Blackwell's hunch. In asking her sample about their menstrual histories, she discovered a discrepancy between her findings and medical wisdom. She noted that among her population of high school girls (then seventeen years old) the average age of first menstruation was 13.72 years of age. She observed, "This is nearly a year younger than the age given by Playfair, Lusk and other obstetricians," which was closer to fifteen. Late-century physicians did not have the empirical evidence to keep up with the declining age of menarche resulting from improved standards of living. When they did offer advice they were off by at least a year. Historians have estimated that age at menarche declined at the rapid rate of one year every thirty years over the late nineteenth century, a trend which would accord with Blackwell's observation and Kennedy's findings. Extrapolating back from trends in the United States, one might conjecture that just past the age of fifteen was normative for 1850, fourteen for 1880, and thirteen for 1910.

(Despite recent attention in the press, the trend has virtually stopped over the past few decades as prosperity is distributed more broadly through all socio-economic groups.)[2] Some parents maintained an ideal of sixteen for the age of puberty through the late nineteenth century, however, while physicians announced a mean of fifteen. In fact, the daughters of the bourgeoisie were likely to reach menarche at the age of fourteen and younger—and to confront that fact with little preparation.

This scientific confusion about the age of menarche both reflected and fed an anxiety about what it might mean that girls were maturing earlier, and especially that urban girls with advantages were growing up fastest of all. Elizabeth Blackwell decried the declining age of menarche, arguing that it was a "premature development" resulting from "rich food, luxurious habits, mental stimulus, novel reading, late hours, and over-heated apartments." She urged families to throw their influence against the tide of precociousness, a phenomenon that Blackwell felt was reversible. Her proposed solution was exercise, in which she early elaborated an insight known today to athletes around the world: "The physical education of the body, its perfectly healthy development, *delays the period of puberty,* and . . . a true education in which all the *bodily powers* were strengthened as well as the mental and moral ones, would be the most effectual means of outrooting this evil." She argued that the evil of early menarche resulted from "a diseased mind in a diseased body." When Helen Kennedy discovered that girls were maturing a year earlier than the doctors were predicting, she too knew just what had to be responsible: city life. She noted that "the mode of life" brought about early menstruation "appearing earlier in girls living in cities than those living in the country."[3] Commentators observed that modernity was responsible for the moral crisis represented by early menstruation.

Fears of precocious sexuality in girls often made parents and advisers reluctant to broach the subject of menarche until it was too late. When they did get around to discussing reproductive physiology, they presented the subject in the rhetoric of romantic mystification. As scientific moderns, we blame Victorian mothers and advice givers for their failure to provide straight talk to girls. Yet the Victorian romanticization of the female body conveyed significantly more respect, if not more information, than often misogynist pre-modern visions of the female body. Especially in contrast to earlier notions of the differences between women and men, which saw women as inferior and imperfectly developed men, the nineteenth-century's romantic explanations of female physiology had much to recommend them.

As the historian Thomas Laqueur argued several years ago, before the Enlightenment, scientific and popular thought in western Europe agreed that men and women represented different stages in development along a similar trajectory. Female reproductive anatomy, with organs inside the pelvic area, were simply less advanced than male reproductive organs, which had descended outside. The difference between the two sexes was a difference not in kind but in evolution. (Indeed, medical drawings of the different sexes virtually mirror each other.) In this "one-sex" model, women and men shared sexual appetite, and the sexual climax of both was necessary for conception to take place.[4] As befit the more primitive sex, women lacked reason, strength, and self-control. In this premodern vision, women's sexual anatomy and reproductive function marked their incompleteness. Menstruation was a shameful marker of that imperfection.

The empiricism of the Enlightenment broke down cosmic and scientific typologies of all kinds, including the notion of men and women's reproductive similarity. Revolutionary thinking of the late eighteenth century introduced a new model of sex difference which argued "incommensurability" — that men and women were fundamentally different, that there were not only two sexes but two different orders of being. Women's greater attendance at church and special responsibility for family life allowed for a new understanding of sex differences which celebrated not only differences of physiology but differences of temperament and morality. Women's moral superiority came coupled with new ideas about female sexuality. Women were no longer defined by their carnality, their inability to control their passions, but rather by their relative "passionlessness." The discovery that female orgasm was not necessary for conception meant that women might be different beings than men, less subject to impulse and desire rather than more so. Under this new two-sex model, women were men's equals but occupied a separate sphere, defined by their moral and spiritual superiority, though not their intellectual preeminence. The language with which advisers attempted to explain puberty to American girls adopted a reverence deriving from this relatively new notion of the sacredness of female reproduction.

The tendency to romanticize menarche conflicted with another simultaneous tendency in culture, a "civilizing process," first defined by the cultural historian Norbert Elias. If the doctrine of the separate spheres dignified menarche, the civilizing process attempted to prettify it. In the relatively stable Middle Ages, Elias argues, people did not worry about cleanliness because it made no difference to their circumstances. Status was inherited. With the breaking down of this stable order, however, competition for status and power contributed to rising standards for personal hygiene and refinement.[5]

Throughout the modern centuries, men and women jostling for standing increasingly hid their animal functions—defecation, urination, sex, and, for women and girls, menstruation. At the same time that some writers and advisers were inclined to revere the feminine essence at the heart of woman's sphere, they also shared a reticence and shame about animal processes.

These tendencies together reinforced the fears of precociousness to explain the shadowy presence of the subject of menstruation in the diary literature, nearly an absent core to the relationship between mothers and daughters. In a maternalist culture, which raised daughters to be wives and mothers, there seems to have been considerable silence and indirection between mothers and daughters on the central facts of puberty. Such anecdotal and social science evidence as we have documents that ignorance. The British physician Edward Tilt, writing of the late nineteenth century, noted that a quarter of his female patients had been left totally ignorant of the menstrual cycle so that "when their first menstruation occurred, many were frightened, screamed, or even went into fits. Some thought themselves wounded and frantically tried to wash the blood away." The statistics of Kennedy's interviews suggest that a similar percentage of American girls confronted menstruation with no preparation. Kennedy was shocked at the ignorance which she discovered, a finding she expressed in the language of Victorianism. Thirty-six of her population she said "had passed into womanhood with no knowledge whatever, from a proper source, of all that makes them women." This group had received no instruction from their mothers at all, and another thirty-nine indicated they had not "talked fully." Fewer than half of her sample had talked "freely," a finding which Kennedy described as "criminal ignorance." (About a half had fully discussed the issue, and another quarter had "talked in a constrained way.") Looking at this same period, the historian Joan Jacobs Brumberg has concluded that girls' knowledge about menstruation declined in the late nineteenth century before going up again in the twentieth century in response to new mandates to scientific mothering.[6]

This is not to say that girls were well instructed in less-privileged circumstances with less domestic privacy. There's evidence that in rural America and on the frontier, too, in the nineteenth century, parents went to some lengths to conceal the details of childbirth, for one, from daughters. Robert Clark's depiction of farm girl Ada Harris's 1873 diary when she was thirteen records her responses to her mother's morning sickness before the birth of her last child. "We were all scart," Ada's diary reported. Clark observes: "The part of her that was still a child did not know, and none of the grown-ups told her, that her mother was pregnant with the last of her babies, who would be born in July." Similarly, Mabel Barbee Lee's account of growing up on the frontier includes a wrenching banishment from home upon her mother's mysterious "sickness"; only after the fact did she discover that her departure had allowed for the birth of her brother.[7] Farm life likely did not make parents more communicative and direct with children. Yet it may well have allowed for the kind of informal education by observation that over the centuries has inculcated children into "the way things are."

In the bourgeois home of the city, animal functions moved behind doors in conjunction with a new imperative to communicate within the Enlightenment family. The need to talk in an uplifting manner about a shameful subject produced a rhetoric of excruciating indirection on the "facts of life." Elias notes the increasing intensity of familial relations themselves as both incentive and impediment to open communication. Increasing social constraints on discussions of sexuality in the public world (as represented by the passage in 1873 of the Comstock laws barring "obscenity" in the U.S. mails) made it the parents' responsibility to provide sex education; yet in Elias's words, "the manifold love relationships between mother, father and child tend to increase resistance to speaking about these questions."[8]

The indirection began with the advice writers. Marion Harland (aka Mary Virginia Terhune) endorsed the reverential language which contributed to the mystification of the subject. She sensibly urged mothers to teach their daughters not to hate their sex, "but to reverence 'The Temple of the Body,'" and offered her book as a remedy for all women, whom she described as "a mighty class of human beings." She urged them not to consider "the holiest mysteries of their natures an unclean thing," nor to hold "carelessly the sublimest possibilities of their kind." Yet when it came right down to it, she could do scarcely better than anyone else. "When Mamie approaches you with the inevitable—and, I submit, perfectly natural and proper—questionings about the Unknown Country peopled by unborn infants, tell her that God sends them to the earth in charge of His holy angels; that since babies must have fathers to work for them abroad, and mothers to tend them at home, He waits until after marriage before He gives them." Perhaps realizing how unsatisfactory an explanation this might seem, she suggested a posture of finality so as to discourage further questions: "Say it so simply and solemnly as to calm curiosity." A few pages on, she returned to the "facts of life," this time providing a more biological accounting with medical terminology. She suggested that parents literally begin with a treatise on botany—"I know of none better than Gray's 'How Plants Grow,'—and read with her of the beautiful laws of fructification and reproduction."[9] She then recommended a fairly straightforward accounting of ovarian function, with reference to "periodical flow," and so on.

Even Mary Virginia Terhune balked at the next step, though. After urging her pupils not to be afraid to thus label ova or eggs, she proceeded to reveal her own sticking point. How did this explain life? "From these, by some mysterious law of the loving oneness of the married state, are evolved the germs of living human beings." After this brave foray, she proceeded to congratulate herself—and her class of maternal tutees. "That is the plain truth—and all of it! What a thing of purity is it beside the trickeries of ribald-mongers, the meretricious maunderings of sensational fiction; the phantoms created in the imaginations of timid school-children by hints and *double-entendre,* and midnight confabulation upon themes which any girl who cherishes a spark of moral decency would blush to speak of by daylight!"[10] This bravest of declarations left "mysterious law" and "loving oneness" at the heart of the matter.

The teenage diarist Annie Winsor later in life wrote a memoir of her father and mother in which she recalled her mother's inability to explain female physiology to her. "The facts of life were hidden away, as too sacred or too ugly for her view. . . . These natural reticences were only enhanced by the spirit of the Romantic Age, so that her daughters had to wait for the Age of Science to give them the key to physical life as it really is." Yet in her own life, when at the age of forty-two in 1907 she wrote for *Ladies' Home Journal,* Annie Winsor too seemed overcome with the need to mystify. Her response to a questioner about what to tell daughters of the facts of life led to reference to "virginal delicacy," resistance to speaking "graphically and explicitly to any girl," and eventually to an analogy with plant life. Writing under the pseudonym Marian Sprague, Annie Winsor bettered Mary Virginia Terhune in her reference to "organs of sex" (whatever the accuracy of her account); otherwise, though, she shared her mother's tendency to confuse the "sacred" with the "ugly" as she perpetuated the Victorian mystification of sexuality.[11]

"Monthlies" and Regularity

If Victorians were loath to anticipate and educate girls about the particulars of sexuality and reproduction, they were not so hesitant to spell out the appropriate conduct for a girl once her "monthlies" had begun. Good health demanded regular exercise before and after—though not during—menstrual periods. It was Annie Winsor's father, a country physician, to whom she addressed her questions about menstrual health in writing when she was away from home. (Presumably her father represented "the age of science" she would refer to in contrast to her mystifying mother.) Earlier, such knowledge would undoubtedly have been the province of women rather than doctors.

Frederick Winsor's instructions to "My Nannie girl" included reassurance about sleeping posture ("suit yourself") and washing. (In suggesting sponging during the menses itself, he was modifying—slightly—a myth that girls should not bathe during their periods.) Following the concerns of the time about prolapsed uterus, he instructed his daughter that if she jumped from a fence with knees bent "so that they may 'give' a little and not [inflict] a shock stiffly to the trunk, [it] will do the pelvic organs no harm," while cautioning, "Of course at the time of monthly illness . . . you will not be climbing fences etc." Annie wrote to her father again, perhaps the next year, about mountain climbing (protecting her letter from her home family's reading with the heading "Professional private"). She had hiked up "Mt. Willard on the fifth day of my monthly turn when I generally do as I like." She noted that the flow picked up a bit but assured him, "I felt all the better for my walk." She then asked for advice on her plan to climb the more demanding Mount Lafayette. This seemed extreme to her father, who advised against the climb "unless you are assured that it is not severe for a woman."[12] Frederick Winsor, like the other physicians of the era, assumed authority over the subject of girls' menstruation, and counseled in particular against jarring, sudden motion as threatening to the organs' delicate maturation.

Thus Sally Dana reported having been told by a doctor that "I must not run up stairs fast because . . . it was bad for girls of my age but that I might run *down* stairs as fast as I wanted to." Ohio school boards too worried about sending high school girls up and down stairs "as a menace to normal functional development" and proposed installing elevators or building schools no more than two stories high. Girls were warned off tennis but encouraged to play "baddledore" (akin to badminton), "a very nice game for girls." The protective sentiments of Victorian experts were perhaps best embodied in the publication in 1904 of G. Stanley Hall's magnum opus *Adolescence,* in which this important psychologist and theorist extended Victorian thinking about the needs of the maturing girl. Hall imagined an ideal calendar in which maturing girls would follow their own biological clock, ideally "lying fallow" for about a quarter of the time. In urging girls to regard their fecundity with reverence, he commended the practice of isolation during menarche, as practiced by other cultures in the tepee or the grot. His corollary for Western society was the Sabbath. "The time may come when we must even change the divisions of Sabbaths per year for woman, leaving to man his week and giving to her the same number of Sabbaths per year, but in groups of four successive days per month." This plan he promoted as a strategy for helping menstrual cycles to be "well established and normal."[13]

Regularity, in fact, was a watchword for the moral and physical health of adolescent girls, and was attested to by the diary record. Girls usually kept such records themselves, but one extraordinary document from the 1870s suggests the significance which Victorian mothers attributed to the regular functions of the female reproductive system. In a telegraphic summary of "days of importance" in the life of her daughter, "Baby Maud," Mrs. J. Walter Spooner of New Hampshire fixed her sight on the age of sixteen as the appropriate age for her daughter's first menstruation. After recording the first day of music lessons (at the age of fourteen) and other notable firsts, Spooner noted that "July 7th 1876 is a day worthy of record, and will not be forgotten by Maud or her Mamma. Maud will be sixteen Oct. 25th—" In September the periods regularized. "Her record continued by noting that "Sept 25 1876 is the second memorable day—Maud will be sixteen in one month," and then October 22, "the third memorable day. Maud will be sixteen in three days." Mrs. Spooner's frequent references to the age of sixteen suggest that at least for this mother, that represented a modal age for menarche. Certainly few would argue with this mother's claim that the onset of the menses was indeed a "day of importance" in the life of a girl. Her ongoing interest in its timing, though, suggests the era's focus on the regularity of hormonal clocks as an indication that all was right with the world. Spooner's book continued with a careful notation of the date of onset of each of her daughter's menstrual periods until 1891— when her daughter was thirty-one years old. Her record represents an extreme example of the era's obsessions with menstrual regularity in its simultaneously vague and cloying solicitude.[14]

Diaries clearly had as one of their functions the accounting and predicting of menstrual periods. Then, as today, such record keeping attempted to remove the element of surprise and to protect privacy. Like their elders, girls used mystification or indirection—an *x,* a star—and the language of illness. Catherine Hardenbergh, seventeen years old in 1869, marked the first day of her periods with an *x* and often described herself as sick: "Was quite sick all day." Hardenbergh's entries suggest that such language was not euphemistic. For instance, on June 8, "Was quite sick all day. Went out with all the family to take a ride to see if it would make me feel better." On Thanksgiving Day, "Felt very sick at dinner time, so could not eat any turkey." The next year she was luckier, however. Twice Catherine Hardenbergh's menstrual periods commenced on the same days as scheduled concerts. She reported in the first case that the concert was "perfectly lovely" and in the second that it "passed off very nicely."[15] In both cases, Catherine Hardenbergh seems to have felt fine and was in attendance. Perhaps the eighteen-year-old Catherine was adjudged beyond the age when special monitoring was necessary to assure a girl's safe passage through the treacherous straits of puberty.

The same did not seem to be true for Margaret Tileston. In 1883 she too marked the first day of her "monthlies," beginning several months before her sixteenth birthday, and regularly indicated subsequent periods. She made no direct mention at all of this proscribed subject, but descriptions of subsequent days showed a marked decline in activity. She described a mixed group going off to play tennis while she "stayed at home with the baby." The next day, while others went on a sailing expedition, she "stayed at home and read some of the time." She skipped her long constitutional walks and often her studying while menstruating: "I sat out on the piazza some times, but did not walk or study." Seldom did she go out of the house on the first day of her period. On days when she planned to go out, she prepared by extra lounging in the morning. "It was a dismal day, and rained. I didn't get up until after ten, to rest myself before going to the theatre." She skipped her dancing class, too, staying home to write a letter to a friend "instead of sitting to watch the dancing as I should have done if I'd gone to Papantis." Clearly the Tileston regimen for girls during their monthlies represented not just a cessation of physical activity but also a temporary reprieve from the earnest disciplines which otherwise structured the lives of Victorian girls. (In this, Victorian practice may owe something to one line of anthropological writing which argues that menstrual taboos interrupting women's work represented a needed break from otherwise relentless responsibilities.)[16]

Perhaps Margaret Tileston was not consciously "lying fallow," but she was following medical protocols for late Victorianism which argued that girls needed to conserve energy in other areas of their lives to supply it to their maturing reproductive systems. Critics of education for girls had argued that too much honing of the mind might deplete limited reserves needed by the body. Most days Margaret Tileston worked hard at her schoolwork, supported by her parents. During her menstrual periods, however, she paid tribute to such critics of female activity as Edward Clarke by lounging and indulging, virtually the only such occasions in this dutiful diary.

When Helen Kennedy interviewed students in 1896, there seemed to be less "lying fallow," at least among eighteen-year-olds. About two-thirds of the students she interviewed "made no change in their habits," with the remaining third keeping "quieter, avoiding all violent exercise, and taking rest the first day or two if it were possible." Going to high school sometimes made such rest impossible, but Kennedy was pleased to report the general health of her cohort. Kennedy did raise one cause for concern. She observed disapprovingly that one-half of her sample recklessly took "violent exercise" during menstruation—dancing, riding horseback, or skating, "as if nothing unusual were the matter."[17]

Rites of Passage

For whatever reasons—the difficulty of predicting the moving target that was age at menarche, the reluctance to discuss it, the desire to fend off precociousness, the unwillingness to lower the boom on free-spirited daughters—parents and advisers did not agree on when girls were grown, and marked the coming-to-womanhood at a range of different ages, through different social rites of passage. The English writer Charlotte Yonge marked one end of the continuum. In 1876 she encouraged great freedom for young girls—"a wholesome delight in rushing about at full speed, playing at active games, climbing trees, rowing boats, making dirt-pies and the like"—which she declared must end at age twelve. Most parents granted girls status as children for considerably longer. The literary figure of the tomboy, which some scholars have seen as "disruptive to rigid taxonomies of gender identity," in fact reflected a reality in Victorian child rearing, freedoms granted to girls whose parents had yet to rein them in.[18] The end of youth arrived conclusively with the leaving of school, mandating a new way of allocating girls' time. Between twelve and twenty, there were harbingers ranging from putting up hair and lengthening dresses on one hand to the prodding toward religious commitment on the other. Different families chose different ages to signify maturity, suggesting a continuum which would not be named until G. Stanley Hall published his stage-constructing treatise *Adolescence* in 1904. At the time, contemporaries vacillated between the languages of childhood and adulthood to define the teenage years. The elite children's magazine *St. Nicholas* claimed readers up until the age of twenty, and conventional wisdom encouraged the consignment of youth to childhood as long as possible. At the same time, Louisa May Alcott's famous girls' book *Little Women* advanced the premise repeated in endless moralist literature that girls should learn early the self-discipline and control demanded of adult women. Small wonder that actual girls were confused.

The markers of impending adulthood arrived unheralded in the surprising denials or demands of adults. At the age of eleven, Mary Boit, as she always had, wrote to Santa Claus. "Papa thinks I am too old but I do not," she reported. The next day she repeated the exercise. "I had supper and wrote a letter to Santa Clause as papa burned up the other." The strength of her father's denial was matched only by the daring insistence of Mary Boit on her rights to childhood. Two years later, however, the generational roles in the Boit family were reversed. It was thirteen-year-old Mary who was insisting on the marks of adulthood and her stepmother who was holding her back. "I think it is just as mean as it can be that I can not have my dresses longer as they are nearly up to my knees and all the girls of my age wear there dresses longer."[19] The gradual transition to adulthood was marked by these regular games of tug-of-war.

Dress length was an interesting issue both for advisers and the mothers who attempted to comply with them. On the one hand, long dresses signified adult status and therefore should be resisted as long as possible. On the other hand, long dresses covered girls' legs and therefore should be adopted as soon as such legs might invite unseemly attention. Lillian Boit took the former position, the writers of *Ladies' Home Journal* the latter. Isabel Mallon, writing under her own name rather than her famous pseudonym Ruth Ashmore, noted that she could "hear the dress reformers objecting to this" but declared that "keeping our girls modest is of very much more importance." Emma Hooper's descriptions of "A Schoolgirl's Outfit" in 1894 recommended that skirts hit the leg halfway between knee and ankle at age ten. At age eight, they should be from one to two inches shorter. Several advisers agreed that at age thirteen a girl's skirts should reach her ankles, while at fourteen through sixteen they should go just below her ankles. Seventeen marked full adulthood for purposes of dress length, for a girl should wear her dresses "the length that any lady does."[20] In essence, fashion advisers on hem length were gradualists, suggesting that hems travel steadily down a girl's leg in accord with her increasing years.

According to the *Ladies' Home Journal,* hair had its own separate clock; with no implications for modesty, hair should be kept off the top of the head throughout most of the teen years, the *Journal* urged. At separate times advisers staved off readers' suggestions that fourteen, fifteen, and sixteen might be appropriate times for a girl to begin wearing her hair up. At fifteen, it might be worn "braided, looped and tied with black ribbon" for novelty, one writer suggested. Only at nineteen might a girl earn the right to arrange her hair "in any way she wished."[21]

As in the *Journal*'s recommendations for other kinds of conduct, though, it seems likely that few readers actually complied. Margaret Tileston, who was brought up conservatively, noted her gradual adaptations to more adult presentation, beginning in 1881, when she was thirteen, with the decision that

GOWNS FOR GIRLS OF TWELVE, FOURTEEN AND SIXTEEN

5.1 Gradations of girlhood, 1893. *Ladies' Home Journal* suggested gradual adjustments of dress length and hairstyle on the way to adulthood. Dresses should move
gradually down the leg, reaching full length by sixteen, while hair should go gradually up, first worn loose, then back, then off the neck, and only fully up at age
eighteen (not pictured). Reprinted from Isabel Mallon, "Dressing a Growing Girl,"
Ladies' Home Journal, August 1893, 21.

she and her older sister would begin to wear "corset waists." (The same year,
Agnes Garrison at fifteen noted her astonishment that a new acquaintance
wore *"corsets."*) The next year, at the age of fourteen, Tileston noted, "I did my
hair up myself behind for the first time." A month later, wearing her hair up
and behind had evolved from noteworthy event to planned habit. "I intend
to generally now," she reported. At the age of seventeen, after her graduation from high school, she began wearing a bustle, another contested arena of
maturity. As with dress length, bustles came calibrated for age and sophistica-
tion, with the progression left to family decision. "Misses" bustles had two or

three coils, while those allowed to older girls had four, and bustles for fancy wear sometimes had six.[22]

In the incremental adoption of the marks of adulthood, some ages were more resonant than others. In Louisa May Alcott's novels the age when childish high spirits must be put aside for young adulthood was fifteen. On the eve of Julia Newberry's sixteenth birthday, she imagined herself saying farewell to childhood, for "when once a person is sixteen, though they are still very young, they can never be called, 'child.'" Fond parents might grant girls freedom to "run wild" longer. Frances Willard's parents chose her seventeenth birthday as "the day of her martyrdom," as she recorded it in her diary. "My 'back' hair is twisted up like a corkscrew; I carry eighteen hair-pins; my head aches miserably; my feet are entangled in the skirt of my hateful new gown. As for chasing sheep . . . it's out of the question." Altogether, Willard felt she had lost her "occupation" as a free-spirited and adventurous child. Emily Eliot was allowed to hold on longer, announcing on her nineteenth birthday, "It is so horrid to get out of your teens and when you are 20 you must leave girl-hood behind you and become a woman. I like *teens* ever so much."[23]

The age of eighteen seems to have borne the most cultural freight, though, indicating the time when a girl simultaneously came into possession of herself and became eligible for possession by someone else. If her parents martyred her at seventeen, at eighteen Frances Willard claimed her own destiny, if only in choosing her reading material, declaring: "I am eighteen—I am of age— I am now to do what *I* think is right." In elite society, as well, eighteen was a common age for a girl to "come out" into society, and become eligible for courtship and marriage. Birthday gifts of money to serve as a dowry and of tokens befitting young ladyhood suggested these implications. A Paterson, New Jersey, manufacturer gave his daughter yellow roses and pinks "36 in all," and Lucy Breckinridge's father gave her $200. Margaret Tileston received a $1,000 savings bond from her grandfather, as well as the news that she would have a regular allowance, a privilege enjoyed earlier by some of her class.[24] The age of eighteen in fact was often thought to be the conclusion of a process of growing up which had commenced years earlier.

Some fond—or negligent—parents demonstrated little relish even then for moving girls from carefree childhood to responsible adulthood. Such girls were lucky. Annie Cooper grew up the youngest daughter of a retired boat builder in what she described as a near-idyllic rural setting in eastern Long Island. When she turned eighteen in 1882, she still found herself enjoying exuberant girlhood. "I am still spared, well and happy, no care yet hath been

5.2 Liking "*teens* ever so much," 1876. Emily Eliot's parents granted her a prolonged girlhood, leaving her in school until the age of nineteen. After leaving school
at midyear, Eliot, left, visited a friend in Buffalo. Emily M. Eliot, "Journal of the
XIX Year of My Life." HUG(FP) 33.6, Samuel Eliot Morison papers, Harvard University Archives (Cambridge: Pusey Library), February 14, 1876.

put upon me, I am still a happy, joyous, merry, hearty, and healthy, school
girl, girl of 16 in feeling, but eighteen in years." In reflection, she imagined
the consequences of her new age. "I can't bear to think how fast my happy
youth and childhood is slipping from me, that I soon will be too big to climb
trees and ride horse back straddling, etc. yes, that in fact I am too big already,
it makes me feel badly, for although I love the deeper and more sound stuff,
yet too I love nature, in all its phases, I love the woods the air, the birds, the
storms, the water, the animals of every description, and I love nature's sports,
and I feel that in advancing age I am getting too big to do with propriety all
the sports which belong to nature." Her concerns for propriety encouraged
her to imagine cutting back her activity, but she felt reassured that some activities were still left to her. "Thank God who has given them to me, that I
still can ride horse back and go boating as much as I please, with propriety,

if I can not climb trees (in the front yard.)" Of course there was always the back yard, where it was clear that Annie Cooper would continue to retain the entitlements of a girlhood that she remembered in later days as being "full and rich and innocent and happy."[25]

Yet for every such memory of girlhood seized and held, there were other memories of entrapment, of moments when the meaning of maturing was frozen in claustrophobic anxiety. One such memory was recorded by Elizabeth Coffin, writing about her girlhood in Germantown, Pennsylvania, in the 1890s:

> I can never forget my first long dress. It had an overskirt, too, which was insult added to injury. I felt 'tied and bound' with it, and it seemed as if, on account of it, my old life with its care-free associations had come to an end. . . . When I found myself robed in it, with my pet dog Koko I went to the garden and told my story of woe to the great cornstalks, who I felt understood me as nothing else in nature did. It seemed to me that the cornstalks waved and bowed their heads in sympathy. . . . There would be no more boiling of corn in the old kettle, climbing trees, coasting with other girls and boys, hitching my sled to the backs of sleighs or romping with the dogs. I was grown up now and serious duties were expected of me.[26]

The donning of a long dress was only the beginning of more profound changes accompanying the arrival of adulthood.

Religious Quest

Girls used available explanatory systems to describe and acknowledge their metamorphosis into adulthood, often slipping into alternating romantic, social, familial, and spiritual narratives. In the early and midcentury, girls' diaries strove for an appropriately spiritual analysis for such changes. Later in the century, girls were less reliably successful in finding religious justification for their states of mind in an environment of increasing religious skepticism. Whether successful or failed, however, girls' spiritual quests encouraged them to scrutinize their emotional lives and provided them with the vocabulary to do so. Unlike the keeping of diaries, however, religious commitment often required a public profession, which brought private feeling into public display.

Agnes Lee's 1850s journal described an intense malaise which evolved through several rhetorics of understanding until resting in a religious crisis. She first considered the possibility that she was homesick, and then wondered whether her longing was "to be loved, to be worshipped by something or some one?" Once out, this thought provided the occasion for a final resting point for the evening's reveries. "No—that is *sinful,* silly and impossible. I hope, I pray my *yearnings* . . . may be for something holier higher than I have yet felt. . . . I am told and I know I can, I must find it in the bosom of my Saviour and only there. I have tried, but my heart seems shut up, it is so hard! . . . Sometimes the awful thought comes to me, I am one of those who are never to be good—one of the doomed."[27] Agnes Lee's progression, all documented in the pages of her journal, ended by dropping her in the center of a traditional and appropriate script for a girl her age, especially in the early to midcentury: the quest for a conversion experience.

By midcentury and beyond, the expectation of a moment of sudden epiphany had been muted a bit; it was no longer necessary to have a moment of mystical communion to signify an indwelling Christ. Nonetheless, the anticipation of a mature coming-to-God pervaded and sometimes shaped the experience of youth. Sometimes the signs were overt. Emma Hidden got a severe case of chicken pox during her teenage years and nearly died. On January 28, 1869, she noted the anniversary of her illness. "One year ago today I was taken sick with chicken-pox—What changes has that year brought to me. One year ago I was so silly and thoughtless—and now I have a sweet hope of a change." Several weeks later she gave thanks to God "that he has made me pass thro' the fire to purify me."[28] The loss of "silly" girlhood through spiritual "change" was a clear formula which was applied in anticipation and description of religious commitment.

Ideally, a religious quest had institutional consequences. A religious experience was formalized by joining a church. Parents were centrally involved in encouraging, promoting, and celebrating this process as a critical part of their responsibilities. Sally Dana's letters from seminary in the late 1850s made it clear that under her father's oversight she was to have established a connection with a local minister, an acquaintance of her father's, to facilitate her confirmation. She wrote, "Has Mr. Wilmer said anything about me, I have not seen him to talk to for two weeks and that on Sunday a little while after church (he has been here to see me two or three times, since I have been here) but I feel as if I wanted to see him, or his wife more but, perhaps I expect too much of a minister." Dana went on to ask "God my Father, Friend" "to give me strength that I may continue my efforts and not disappoint my very dear parent and friends."[29] Obligation and succor were reciprocal, with Sally Dana asking God for help so as not to disappoint her father, just as her father asked her to seek help from her local minister so as not to disappoint her God.

Perhaps as early as several weeks later (the year of this letter is not noted), Dana wrote about greater resolution to this crisis. Her letter commenced with a description of a calm joy and serenity. "Father, I cannot tell you what a pleasant day last Sunday was to me, particularly after church, and after talking with Mr. Wilmer a little while. I felt so quiet and calm and peaceful, I had my Bible lesson early and I had time to read a little and then. I really loved that Sunday I wish I could have others like it." Dana's description of her state of mind had particular significance, because it accompanied a moment of commitment: "I am so glad I can be confirmed, I look forward to it with pleasure, I think of it (if I can express my self right) as being a kind of shield and defense from the world and its lusts, as if I should *be nearer my Saviour friend.*"[30] Sally Dana's confession of religious calm and commitment to her father represented her fulfillment of youthful obligation to both earthly and heavenly father, even without a moment of spiritual epiphany.

If girls sought commitment at parental directive, they often experienced conversion within a youth cohort. Agnes Lee wrote lengthy journal entries about her personal and spiritual journey to God, seemingly an individual internal odyssey out from under "an angry black cloud that [was] ever over *me,*" which left her feeling and acting "*so* strange." This intensely spiritual experience did not happen in isolation, however, for "Annie, Mary, Ada and Annette took the same step." Individual quests under parental guidance often took place in company—sometimes of family members, sometimes of schoolmates, even sometimes in classes. When Sally Dana was attempting to process her confirmation, she noted that she "was not in any class yet," an acknowledgment by the churches themselves that routes to salvation might run through education and preparation, rather than through the spontaneity of random epiphany.[31]

The religious quest of late Victorianism was a responsibility of the teen years, increasing in intensity as girls approached the age of twenty. At the age of seventeen in 1882, Annie Cooper worried about her spiritual immaturity, for she was not yet a church member, but still a silly girl. "Weighing the subject of religion and dancing in my mind" had taught her that she was "a sinner Oh! how great a sinner." While still in her teens, she delayed a commitment, however, because "I don't want to join the church and be a stumbling block to others." Annie Cooper's quest took three more years. On December 7, 1884, she announced: "Today I have taken the boldest and best step of my life. I have *joined the church,* and am happier and feel freer than I ever did in my life before." Her conversion and confirmation were not of the ecstatic variety but reflected "a peaceful joy." She included the key language of change. "I have felt no great change, sudden and terrible, but I *do* feel changed." And she also acknowledged the critical role played by her age in bringing this quest for religious legitimacy to conclusion. "I shall be 20 this week. I am so glad I have taken this step while I can say I am in my teens."[32] Annie Cooper's diary suggests that by the 1880s a search for religious commitment was ideally consummated while still a youth, defined by Cooper as the teen years. No longer the primary object of life and work, as it was in seventeenth-century New England, religion by the late nineteenth century was foundational, necessary to resolve before one made other commitments.

Professing faith, like being good, was emotional work which required the acquisition of appropriate feelings. Unlike the quiet display of pleasantness, though, loving God required girls to verbalize their feelings to parents, ministers, and congregations. Evangelical culture encouraged a language of feeling often embarrassing to girls still trying to get their emotional bearings. Annie Cooper had delayed until what she seemed to think was the last acceptable moment—the week of her twentieth birthday—perhaps partly because she found public acknowledgment of her faith to be excruciating. When a minister asked Annie Cooper to help with a female prayer meeting, she was thrown into a panic. "*Oh! my God! how can I?* I do wish I could but have not the gift of 'gab,' *I don't see how I can.* I, who can not even, to save my life, say a single word at home, how can I brake through the barriers of timidity and natural diffidence to *such an extent as that?*"[33] Annie Cooper's worries about her ability to articulate religious feeling came allied with worries of all kinds about her emotional depth, especially her ability to be the kind of understanding, helpful daughter who could assist her parents in their old age. Speaking about religion meant speaking sincerely about feelings; speaking about either constituted a substantial challenge to late-Victorian girls still trying to manage complex emotional protocols.

The prospects of professing faith, receiving baptism, or joining a church often intimidated girls who were not used to appearing in public. Floride Clemson, a southern girl traveling away from home during the Civil War, took advantage of her visit to her uncle, who was a minister, to dispatch the worrisome matter. In a letter which she marked "Private," she suggested to her "darling mother" her serious thoughts about joining the Episcopal Church. She could not pretend that she had become a better person or "that I have very strong faith, yet I want to believe, and have been convinced of the truth of most of the important points for some time." Her faith came not from iron conviction but instead from earnest desire—and from an opportune moment. She relinquished final judgment to her mother, but her main reason for seeking confirmation on her travels was that away from home, "it can be done quieter." [34]

Her mother clearly acquiesced. Nonetheless, the actual baptism, which was performed by her uncle, was traumatic. Clemson confessed that she had hoped the ceremony could take place in the evening, with fewer in the congregation, but was told it wasn't customary, "so I had to go up right after the second lesson." She felt "very badly" when the time came, "but I thought it was my duty so I did it." She reported that "it nearly made me sick and I cried like a baby," but she was helped along by her cousins and uncle, "who were very kind." Nonetheless, "I had to go to bed with a headache as soon as I got home." When she had gotten through this ceremony, Floride Clemson's dominant mood was relief. "I am very glad it is over, and I am equally glad to have done it, for it has worried me for a long time." Clearly what upset Floride Clemson about her confirmation was its requirement of public profession. Not only did she mark her letter to her mother "Private," but she cautioned at the bottom, "Don't show this." And the only consolation after her appalling experience of crying in front of a church congregation was that the church "is a very small one, and the congregation still smaller, and as few knew me, I did not mind it so much." [35] If one important part of the work of youth was religious profession, with its public display of private feelings, perhaps the sooner done with it the better.

In the context of lives defined by duty and subordination of self, it is not surprising that girls like Floride Clemson found the self-revelation of religious confirmation to be difficult. By its very nature, the experience of religious conversion, or even the reconfirming of religious commitment, depended on private, personal feeling. What was at issue was not what or how much you knew, or how you acted, but instead what you felt. However, unlike most other circumstances, in which private feeling was appropriately closeted in one's heart, religious profession meant speaking of that feeling in a compelling way. Just when girlhood's lessons had been learned, religious profession required that they be overturned in a potentially embarrassing confession of religious enthusiasm. Coming in the context of a life defined by being good and subordinating selfish desires, such public self-revelation was anathema.

Once unleashed, however, the discovery of religious feeling often came allied with a distinctly earthly romanticism in the lives of Victorian girl diarists, a linkage which both inspired and scared parental observers. When Alice Stone Blackwell came under the sway of a charismatic minister, she forswore her parents' rationalist religion and took on a defining religious identity of her own, blending romantic sensibilities with religious ones. A "crush" on a minister encouraged Alice Stone Blackwell's quest for religious consolation and a spiritual identity. The daughter of late-Victorian skeptics and staunch theological liberals Alice Stone Blackwell drew from her parents a tradition of independent thinking which caused her to strike her own religious course at the age of fourteen.

Blackwell used her journal as a sounding board in her religious quest: "Am feeling unhappy; I don't know exactly what the matter is; I think—I want—God." She was clear about what she didn't want—such Unitarian notions as dominated her parents' world: "Not the 'Spiritual Consciousness' or 'Pervading Power,' that one supposes about. . . . Mama believes in a Guiding Influence, and gets along somehow; but I shouldn't wonder if her blues came somewhat from the want of—something in that direction. As for Papa, I don't know what he does believe; I think he supposes that creation is a sort of machine, set going once for all." She was also clear why she didn't want her parents' religion: "Religious talk with Mama. Set spinning and let go is her theory. I'd rather be blue Orthodox and believe in Hell than believe what she does. She'll have a pleasant surprise when she dies." Instead, Blackwell wanted a God "to love, to really believe in and trust utterly. . . . And being a Blackwell, I keep all the worry to myself; there really seems no one I could tell." That night, though, as if on command, she went to hear the evangelist Robert Collyer speak. During the prayer, Collyer seemed to be speaking just to her. The best part, though, was his appearance: "He has such a pleasant, hearty, cheery, ruddy, jolly, good face, strong and pleasant at once." When she was introduced to him afterward, "He shook hands with me, and put his head down and said, 'Kiss me.' I was taken by surprise, but gave him a real smack in the face of 600 people—who weren't looking at us, though. He said 'Oh you little darling!' and went on talking to my folks, and I listened, till Mama began to take him up on the subject of Woman's Rights, and then I cleared after the girls." Blackwell was sufficiently fastidious that when she received a kiss from a female visitor several months later, she "slipped away to the pump" and washed her face. But despite her certainty that Mr. Collyer had been smoking, which she disapproved of, she reported "I could just have hugged him. I love him!"[36]

It took a while for her private personality cult to develop. A week later, once again, she noted in her journal, "Am feeling very unhappy because I cant love God." In another day or two, she "worried about that idea Mr. Collyer put into my head, as to whether I had just to try my best to 'do my duty in that station of life unto which I am called' or whether it is no use unless I love God; which I don't." Given that she couldn't help herself with the loving, she decided she had no choice but to be dutiful in her station, a dreary conclusion to her quest. But she continued her discipleship with Robert Collyer. "Down in the Slough of Despond again. I did think I was through that. Mr. Collyer pretty effectually pulled me out before, and I went and read The Life that Now Is, and was pulled out again for the time being. But for Mr. Collyer and those two books of his, I don't know what I should do. I really felt as if I was praying that night when I said God bless him." The next day she was back in despair: "It appears that last nights pull out was only for the time being. I felt dreadfully; went into the parlor in the evening, and down on my knees in the dark, praying and crying for help, with a dreadful feeling that after all I might be praying and crying to nothing, and no one any where to hear me." Alice Blackwell's prolonged crisis of unbelief, so characteristic of her class and region, was mediated by her infatuation with a charismatic minister. Robert Collyer gave God a face, and the face was his. When her cousins were plaguing her, she thought of Mr. Collyer and "blushed so furiously as to astonish both them and myself," and stole up to the pulpit and kissed the Bible he had read from. Later in the spring she made a personal icon. "Have crocheted a circlet of blue worsted, sewed a bit of black silk (on which I had worked Mr. Collyer's initials) into it, and wear it around my arm for love of him." She wore her circlet in honor of Collyer, "who once and again pulled me out of the slough of despond." It is not surprising that the next day she concluded that if she were to be anything but a Unitarian (a step to which her religious crisis had not yet brought her), "I should have to be an Episcopalian or Catholic; I don't think I could stop at any of the intermediate stations."[37] Her private rituals of adoration accorded more fully with an ornate religious tradition.

Assisted by her infatuation with Collyer, Alice Blackwell seems to have come to some personal resolution. She noted and recorded the anniversary of her hearing of the evangelist, and when a friend wrote her a religious letter, she "answered it immediately, in excitement, stating my views. I stated them in rather strong language I believe, but I felt them strongly."[38] Eager to discover a different way than that offered by her parents' pale Unitarianism, Alice Blackwell had followed the route laid out by a seductive minister, acted upon her feelings, and discovered a religious identity she could vigorously defend. Luckily for her, she had survived the process with her self-respect intact and even enhanced.

The experience of Alice Stone Blackwell with Robert Collyer revealed the close link between spirituality and sensuality in the lives of teenage girls, a linkage which cut both ways. To the extent that Victorian parents and advisers demanded religious profession, they were asking that girls look deep inside themselves and come up with something profound, sincere, pure, and winning. This, of course, was what girls brought to romantic relationships as well, an alliance that brought possibility as well as danger. One mother explained to her constrained daughter the relationship between religious and romantic spontaneity, suggesting that the expression of religious feeling might itself lead to more genuine communion with those around—perhaps even a more direct route into the hearts of men. Though they may be "apparently thoughtless young men," Ella Lyman wrote, a woman's "carrying into life the life-giving idea" might lead men to "show their best deepest side and one immediately establishes real trust and friendship." With a young woman's expression of religious sensibility might come the realization of oneness, "that we are God's own children with one aim one hope one aspiration."[39]

But this experience of spiritual and romantic oneness was just what Annie Winsor's mother feared. Ann Winsor put off the matter of her daughter's soul until just a few weeks before Annie's twentieth birthday. At that point she sent a letter of gentle inquiry to her daughter at college, revealing her sticking point: a need to reassure herself about the role of feeling in her daughter's life. Although she urged Annie to express religious enthusiasm, she feared feelings of other kinds, warning about the lamentable career of George Eliot, another intellectual daughter. George Eliot's extramarital affair with George Lewes gave Ann pause. Without "clear sight to guide it, and strict 'puritan' principle to strengthen it," such feeling could lead a girl directly into the biggest kind of moral trouble.[40] The cultural critic Nancy Armstrong has argued that the development of a specifically feminine identity in nineteenth-century England rested on the construction of a psychologized, feminine protagonist in the romantic novel. According to Armstrong, the drama of the domestic heroine lay in the richness and the interest of her feelings and her sensibility, not in the interplay of bold actions on a large stage. What Armstrong's theory overlooks, which was especially significant in the United States, is the central role that the search for a religious self played in the development of a feeling and romantic self of any kind.

Not all advisers agreed about the need for girls to demonstrate engaged spirituality. Some moralists feared excessive piety in the same way that they feared sensational fiction: it might divert girls from their little duties at home. Writing for *Ladies' Home Journal* in the 1890s, after the flowering of a religious culture of personal pietism, Ruth Ashmore attempted to correct some of the excesses which could result from too much passion and too little sense of duty. Upon describing one especially enraptured young Christian, Ashmore

5.3 "Carrying into life the life-giving idea," 1889. Ella Lyman's mother had encouraged her to look to religious enthusiasm as she attempted to build relationships with young men. Lyman later married Richard Cabot, with whom she appears here. Reprinted from Schlesinger Library (Cambridge: Radcliffe Institute, Harvard University), A99-149-8.

launched a critique of the "ecstasy of religion," arguing that "it is almost worse than no religion at all." She explained, "Wrapped up in prayer you find your daily duty troublesome, uplifted by heavenly words the ordinary speech of life seems coarse, thinking of the lives of saints and martyrs you seem wicked, and there is an absolute pleasure in reminding yourself of that fact. Now, my dear girl, this is only an evidence of vanity."[41] Ashmore correctly judged the potential of deep religious feeling to contribute to a heightened sense of self and of vanity, and to lead girls to neglect the "littleness of life." Ashmore was writing against a powerful current of religious experientialism which, in anxiously inquiring after a girl's feelings about God, encouraged her belief in her private soul.

The expectation that girls speak about religion, like the expectation that girls like or dislike books, was a cultural demand that girls have and then be able to communicate an interior, private being. When girls like Ellen Regal, daughter of an itinerant minister in Michigan added "secret divotion" to her attendance at family worship and her memorizing of the Bible, she was exercising a private, personalized religion which would pay dividends in the development of an enriched sense of self.[42] Girls' reservations in speaking about such a private subject as religion revealed their discomfort in speaking about, or perhaps even in having, feelings they could trust and report on. Once mastered, though, religious profession might lead to emotional assertions of other kinds.

Moods: Depression

Throughout much of the nineteenth century, the language of belief and disbelief was the appropriate language in which to cast emotional distress of all kinds. "The Slough of Despond" Alice Blackwell referred to was a temporary trial in a Christian pilgrim's progress toward spiritual peace. Pilgrims all, young girls understood that they should engage in a ceaseless quest for the ultimate trust a good Christian put in God's love. Girls of such different family and religious backgrounds as Virginian Agnes Lee in the 1850s and Bostonian Alice Stone Blackwell in the 1870s settled on their lack of faith as the most useful way to understand the dark moods that they sometimes experienced.

A girl's conviction that her unhappiness was a result of spiritual failure, of course, was a cultural script. A religious vocabulary in theory could handle any emotional crises. In this scenario, disbelief was itself the problem, and could be worked on by earnest pilgrims eager to transcend and traverse despondency to emerge on the other side restored. Religion provided a gratifyingly activist program for girls like Floride Clemson, Annie Cooper, or Agnes Lee. It offered hope: the solution to despondency lay within you.

By the latter decades of the century, however, some girls did not and perhaps could not revert to a Christian paradigm to explain both the generalized ups and downs of mortal existence and the more specific challenges of puberty. In an environment of religious skepticism, disbelief too could trump. By its very definition, depression constituted a worldview, one which emphasized girls' inability to effect change which was happening *to* rather than through them. Increasingly, later in the century, girls confronted challenges of self-management which did not resolve into religious crisis.

Margaret Tileston was subject to periodic depression, which she seemed unable finally to envision as a religious quest. The family of John and Mary Foote Tileston practiced an eclectic, liberal Protestantism which usually brought them to church, but not always to the same church, and which sometimes was characterized by religious conversation at home. "Mamma read to us in Sunday Chats for Sensible Children," Margaret wrote about one Sunday on which she did not attend church. She was the only one in the family to attend church on a number of occasions. In the course of her diary, Margaret mentioned different family members attending the Unitarian Church, the Orthodox (Congregational) Church, the Barton Square Church, the North Church, the Baptist Church, the Church of the Advent, and "Uncle Henry's church." In her sixteenth year Margaret Tileston announced that she planned to attend various churches that summer because her own Unitarian church would be closed; presumably its well-heeled parishioners had other summer plans.[43]

During her fourteenth year Margaret Tileston was away at a girls' boarding school for the first time. In this supercharged atmosphere of sentiment and intimacy she learned the language of feeling, which had largely been absent from her dutiful diary. From a special friend, Nellie Taft, Margaret learned to exclaim over high points. But Margaret Tileston also began to comment on dark moods. One passage, entered down the spine of her diary and partially obliterated, suggested such a moment: "I didn't feel very well nor happy in the a.m. I consecrated myself to God and Jesus hereafter. After dinner I was alone a little while." Margaret Tileston's first impulse was appropriately spiritual. Entrusting herself to God and Jesus was in part an acknowledgment that she had nowhere else to turn. A few weeks later she again confessed malaise in the spine of her diary. "I felt unhappy after dinner, cast down, and discouraged because I am not as other girls. I wandered off, read Fenelon and felt somewhat comforted." Margaret's reading of the seventeenth-century French theologian François Fénélon would have encouraged a passivity of her soul before God, the complete suppression of desire and even of herself, an eradication of the impulse to wallow in self-pity.[44] Yet she could not contain her misery so conveniently.

The next month she reiterated it in starker terms. "I felt miserable in the a.m. I wished that I were dead. Feel unhappy still." A week or two later was her last Sunday of Prospect Hill School. "I spent some time in N.'s room in the evening. it was dark and there were several girls in there." In the spine of her diary for that day, Margaret again voiced supplication—tinged with the melodrama of imminent departures: "O Sanctisissima! Ora pro nobis. Thou who hast looked on death, help us when death is nigh. Thine too hath bled." Tileston's invocation of a death wish remained a minor refrain through the next several years:

> [2 December 1883] I have come to the conclusion that life is not worth living and I should be glad to have my inevitable existence put an end to.
> [14 December 1883] Dismal as usual. Should like to be extinguished forever like a candle.
> [11 April 1884] Easy ways to die. Let's do it after the high Roman fashion.

Tileston's beseechments were interrupted, though not checked, by one effort at a more conventional resolution, perhaps encouraged by her father. "I am beginning to . . . be good and to love God," she reported in February 1883. By the end of that year, though, Margaret no longer identified her demoralization with her Christian failing. Her appeals were sometimes terse: "I took a bath last night. Life is not worth living." They were sometimes Shakespearean: "'Oh, that this too, too solid flesh would melt, thaw, and resolve itself into a dew, Or that the Everlasting had not fixed his canon against self-slaughter, Oh God, Oh God! how weary stale, pale, unprofitable seem to me all the uses of this world.'"[45] Together these entries represented a countertext to her other entries' upbeat accounts of poems memorized, birthdays celebrated. What is significant about such entries is their open-endedness. There was no comforting moral—no religious awakening or confirmation ritual. Instead, they took their place with the despair of other late-Victorian skeptics for whom life itself was the question—and had to be validated or rejected on its own terms without recourse to hopes for an afterlife.

Margaret Tileston was not the only diarist for whom discussions of suicide, however melodramatic, accompanied depressions. The spirited diary of Cassie Upson, who was being raised by her aunts, blended descriptions of urban escapades with occasional moments of despair. For instance, one April day when Upson was fifteen, she declared herself "perfectly sick of life," continuing, "I have been debating whether or not to poison myself. I would if it were not for auntie. I do believe. I wish I might have the cholera or anything to take me away from this wretched world. . . . If I had a cup of poison I would drink it so heartily wearied am I of this useless erring unsuccessful life." Having thoroughly documented that emotion, she briefly moved on to the other event of the day: "Lou Hood took me to ride this afternoon. I enjoyed it very much. Wrote a letter to Lou." Her concluding sentiment reverted: "Oh how perfectly wretched I feel I wish I were dead." A devoted and passionate reader of sensation literature, Cassie Upson certainly had imbibed the high-contrast, emotional texture of its plotting. Several weeks later she once again demonstrated her emotional range in one day (and several entries), at first declaring herself "wretched, wretched, wretched" and repeating her wish for cholera. Later in the same day's entry, however, after a "splendid boat ride tonight on the lake" with her brother, her mood evened out. "My despairing mood has quite passed away and I haven't the least desire for the cholera just now."[46] Ups and downs have often been associated with adolescence, but their particular plotting requires historical speculation.

In particular, the "schoolgirl" rhetoric of such entries poses a problem of interpretation, of authenticity. How should we regard such morbid, melo-dramatic thoughts, recorded in private diaries by readers of romance? Were these adolescents in any concrete sense "suicidal"? Were Victorian girls more troubled, or differently troubled, than youth today? Louisa May Alcott, who also suffered from depression as a girl, suggested one such burden in the con-flict over the self. Part of her problem, as she saw it, was excessive self-love, less likely to be considered a problem today in a culture which promotes self-esteem: "If I look in my glass, I try to keep down vanity about my long hair, my well-shaped head, and my good nose. In the street, I try not to covet fine things." Part of it was excessive emotion. "My quick tongue is always getting me into trouble, and my moodiness makes it hard to be cheerful when I think how poor we are, how much worry it is to live, and how many things I long to do I never can." The energy involved in trying to be good, Alcott suggested, was part of what exhausted her. "So every day is a battle, and I'm so tired I don't want to live." Yet the very moral scruples which exhausted her also shut off her escape. "Only it's cowardly to die till you have done something." When part of the challenge involved taming and humbling one's "odious self-esteem," as Cassie Upson put it, girls could err both coming and going, with their joy as well as their despair.[47] Surely adolescence has always offered an especially intense mixture of both dreams and doubts; the Victorians offered a narrow channel in which either could be acceptable.

Such musings about suicide as engaged Louisa May Alcott and Cassie Upson and others revealed then, as they do today, the limited range within which youths, especially girls, felt that they had agency. At some surprising moments it was easier to imagine poisoning yourself, as Cassie Upson did, than it was to imagine otherwise adjusting the circumstances of your existence. It is common wisdom today that perfectionism contributes to the kind of binary thinking that can lead to suicidal impulses. (One commentator observes that it is "evidence of the dark side of unrelenting standards for achievement.") Certainly Victorian morality and child-rearing regimens provided just such a perfectionist culture which might encourage the dark fantasies of girls.[48]

Moods: Boredom

At the opposite pole from such heroic action, though drawing on a similar narrowness of options, was a more common lament in schoolgirl diaries from urban areas—the expression of boredom. Of course, girls who no longer played a crucial role in the domestic workforce did have more leisure time at their disposal. But that was only part of the problem. In a more global sense, they had "nothing to do," no indispensable work through which to secure a sense of self-worth.

That was the subject of a poem submitted by a reader to *St. Nicholas* in 1876. Entitled "Nothing to Do," the poem is a robin's song of commiseration addressed to an idle and bored young girl.

> *"Oh, maiden fair,*
> > *I'm glad I ain't you;*
> *I am glad, I am glad,*
> > *For you've nothing to do.*
>
> *"The leaves they do grow,*
> > *And the grass grows too,*
> *And the apple-tree blooms,*
> > *But you've nothing to do."*

The poem continues through several species of birds and such inanimate objects as smoke and clouds, all of which, according to the poem's author, "Crocus," have more to do than a young girl. The poem ends with the poem's object, a "maiden fair," discovering a voice:

> *I rose from the grass,*
> > *And the long hours did rue*
> *Which I'd spent lying there*
> > *With nothing to do.*

On my chair were the socks
Full of holes it is true;
But I said to myself,
"Here is something to do!"

Crocus appears to be mocking the summer lethargy of a girl shirking her household duties. Certainly conventional moralism supported the value of such household chores in promoting mental health and combating boredom. Louisa May Alcott's novel *An Old-Fashioned Girl* argued the emotional as well as the physical benefits of housework. When Fanny, the urban belle, reports that she is "so tired of everybody and everything, it seems sometimes as if I should die of ennui," the wholesome heroine, Polly, explains how she licks anxiety. Polly explains: "Things worry me sometimes, but I just catch up a broom and sweep, or wash hard, or walk, or go at something with all my might, and I usually find that by the time I get through the worry is gone, or I've got courage enough to bear it without grumbling. . . . A little poverty would do you good, Fan; just enough necessity to keep you busy till you find how good work is; and when you once learn that, you won't complain of ennui any more."[49] Alcott's prescription for boredom was just that— a palliative, designed to assist girls in "bear[ing] without grumbling" whatever is bothering them. In these instances, neither Polly nor the protagonist of "Nothing to Do" pretends that darning socks or sweeping is itself a rewarding activity. Instead, such activities fill time, and absorb nervous energy. Both serve as a "good enough" solution to the problem of adolescent underemployment.

Charlotte Perkins Gilman's discussion of adolescent work acknowledged as much. "Yes, there is occupation enough as far as filling time goes." But Gilman went on to suggest the limitations of the domestic duties assigned to girls: "But how if it does not satisfy? How if the girl wants something else to do—something definite, something developing? This is deprecated by the family. 'Work' is held by all to be a thing no mortal soul should do unless compelled by want. . . . What the girl, as a normal human being, wants is full exercise in large social relation; things to think about, feel, and do, which do not in any way concern the home."[50] With this language of need, Gilman attempted to suggest the inadequacies of the girl's lot in the family, filled as it was with vague, repetitive, cramped, domestic duties. For Gilman, the "ennui" described by Alcott's Fanny or the idleness described by Crocus suggested a concrete remedy in the form of women's work for society outside the home.

Gilman was writing as a realized adult, however, who in two revolutionary breaks with conventional domesticity had extricated herself from a failed marriage and the responsibilities of motherhood. Her perspective, earned through hard experience, was not available to contemporary girls, who saw both the problem and most nonreligious solutions as well beyond their control. Even Jane Addams, in a letter written to her Rockford seminary friend Ellen Starr at the mature age of twenty-six, took responsibility for her malaise but felt powerless to transcend it. Writing in 1886, she described herself as "filled with shame that with all my apparent leisure I do nothing."[51] Her "leisure," by definition discretionary time to be filled according to her own desires, was only apparent; like younger girls in other places and circumstances, Addams seemed to feel that she lacked the wherewithal to make something happen on her own.

Complaints about ennui or boredom had only a loose relationship to actual unstructured or free time, however. When Margaret Tileston wrote in December 1882, "My diary gets very same and tiresome now, for nothing happens, but Christmas will soon enliven the monotony," readers might be misled.[52] In fact, within the past month, Margaret and her family had moved from the farm home where Tileston had always lived to the town of Salem, where Margaret and her sister Mary had recently begun to attend coeducational public high school. Certainly part of the boredom which Tileston felt might have resulted from the family's departure from a working farm—where her father employed several hired hands, planted and harvested crops, and raised animals—to an urban household, which purchased rather than raised food, and which her father left daily to go into Boston to work. On the farm, Margaret's diary entries recorded the number of eggs laid, the strawberries picked, the roosters slain. In Salem, the refrain "nothing happens," was perhaps a commentary on the contraction of the household, and hence the narrowing of the world of those confined to it.

But Margaret Tileston was not confined to the home, instead embarking on a brave new high school course that was ultimately to provide the greatest excitement in her exhaustive diary. Initially, though, school itself contributed the substance of her complaints. After Christmas in 1882, Tileston reported: "Mary and I went to school as usual in the morning, and recited Latin. 'Forenoon and afternoon and night,' the same dull round. The trivial round, the common task Would furnish all we ought to ask." Several days later she noted that she and her sister "went to the High School as usual in the morning to our one session. Nothing whatever happens nowadays." Implicit in Margaret Tileston's sense of boredom, it seems, was a sense of comparison. On the one hand, nothing happened in Salem in comparison with her former life on the farm in Concord. Nothing happened at Salem High School in comparison with her intense and intimate personal life when she was away at Prospect Hill School the previous year. Boredom is a "longing for lost satisfactions as in depression and a feeling of emptiness as in apathy," according to one psychiatric writer.[53] Margaret Tileston's expressed boredom conveys this sense both of a lost past and of emptiness in the present.

According to this definition, boredom was comparative, a dimension which emerged in Mabel Lancraft's laments of boredom within a vibrant social life. As with Tileston's experience, wails of boredom suggested not absolute inactivity—far from it—but a discrepancy between what might have happened and what did, perhaps inevitably the anticipatory experience of youth. As she began public high school in New Haven in 1889 at the age of sixteen, Lancraft interspersed descriptions of gay social activity with expressions of boredom. "Nothing particular happened in school. . . . I walked down at noon with Charlie Walker so Kit was introduced to that wonderful piece of humanity." (In a marginal comment she exclaimed, "I wish something exciting would happen.") Several weeks later, Lancraft noted, "I walked up with the girls but C.P.W. did not wait for me to walk down." This unfulfilled expectation led Lancraft to conclude, "I didn't do anything of any importance today. Went through the same old routine got up, went to school, came home and ate my dinner, looked at my lessons, played states, practiced a little, went to bed." Once again she implored "I wish somebody would do some[thing] for excitement." Mabel Lancraft's wish that "somebody would do something for excitement," even "something rash," came in the context of a flirtation in which she was far from passive. "The emptiness in boredom," holds psychiatrist Ralph Greenson "is due to the repression of forbidden instinctual aims and objects along with inhibition in imagination."[54] In the case of Mabel Lancraft, "instinctual aims" may have been forbidden but certainly lay only slightly below the surface of her impatient waiting.

The experience of boredom was at heart an expression of lack of agency. Girls had traditionally been socialized to wait for "something to happen," rather than to make it happen. Indeed, female adolescence itself has often been characterized by this passivity, with scholars today debating whether or not it is still so. (Heralding a new era in the history of girls, the psychologist Janet Mendelsohn claims that contemporary elite girls do feel able to influence their destinies themselves—in contrast with girls in the past who held identity "in abeyance," waiting "for something to happen," waiting to be rescued and sealed in identity.) This sense of impotence was precisely the malaise experienced and expressed by Victorian girls attempting to learn to endure the frustrations of their suspended state. One could argue, as does the critic Jane Tompkins, that some of the novels girls read gained their force from "their dramatization of the heroine's suffering as she struggles to control each new resurgence of passion and to abase herself before God." As we have seen, writing in a diary was a limited form of agency which provided an exercise book for girls attempting "*not* to do anything" and to "make the best of [their] situation." [55]

Moods: Daydreams

Expressions of boredom were a form of suspended agency, a station on the way to the goal of completely controlling desire so that it would not erupt in active rebellion or even impatience with the way things were. Another such way station lay in daydreams, a kind of swooning of the intellect, in which fantasy substituted for ambition. Daydreaming was a common enough experience, and for those keeping reflective journals, it was an appropriate subject about which to write. If boredom represented suspended agency, daydreaming represented displaced agency, the movement into the imagination of the subject self.

Nineteenth-century critics preferred boredom to fantasy, "inhibiting" rather than "unfettering" girls' imaginations. But the program of reading and writing urged as part of the program of self-culture brought with it an irresistible invitation to daydreaming, which sometimes doubly filled time, first in the dreaming itself, and then in the writing about it. Lucy Breckinridge, writing in a southern home with African-American "servants" during the Civil War, gave herself an advanced education through her wide reading which was reflected in her literate diary. Her brother Johnny had been killed in the war. Breckinridge proposed her diary as a way to keep herself occupied during the trying days that remained— "when we have no visitors to receive and no visits to pay, no materials to work upon and no inclination to read anything but the Bible and the newspapers." [56] Aside from telling "all the events of the day," she explained she planned to tell "my thoughts, feelings, etc."

The context for Lucy Breckinridge's daydreaming was mental but not manual idleness. In particular, she often noted that the mechanical exercise of knitting unloosed what Freud called the "private theater" of her imaginary life. "Knitting will make anyone think so fast and such silly things," she commented, referring back to a conversation with her beloved sister-in-law. "Fan says she's glad she lives in war times, that it makes her feel like a heroine." This recollection of the past then propelled her into the future and a fantasy of herself as a heroine talking to her future children. Freud's essay on creativity and daydreaming suggested that fantasies drew together three times, a past memory of primal fulfillment, a present stimulus to that memory, and an imagined future when that wish might be filled again.[57] The substance of Breckinridge's daydream lay in the contrast between her mundane, "mindless" present activity, and the aspiration to heroism, shared with a dear confidante and then projected into the future.

Girlish daydreams, of course, stereotypically dealt with dreams of future romance, which Breckinridge acknowledged when she found herself stripped of material for fantasies following the break-off of her engagement. "I feel so alone," she wrote. "I can't people the room with sweet fancies and imaginations now. When I was in love, some four or five months ago, I always had something interesting to think of." In fact, though, Breckinridge's imaginings stopped with marriage, which she dreaded as much as she relished romance. Her most romantic daydreams remained displaced outside of historical time, focused not on any magical future nor on an actual present but most commonly on an imagined past. She saw her maturation as decline and loss, as she moved from girlhood into the bad choices that constituted her view of adult womanhood. If she was sad at the age of nineteen, how much more cause for sadness she would have later, she imagined. "The mountain is not *blue* enough yet for me to be thinking so sadly. What will my reflections be 10 years hence if I begin so early to moralize, then I'll have cause . . . for mournfulness, being quite a desolate old maid or still worse a married woman with ever so many crying babies and a cross, horrid husband as all husbands are. Oh, dear! Oh, dear! How gloomy the prospect."[58] If some of Lucy Breckinridge's daydreams represented erotic fantasy, as indeed seems to have been the case, they didn't linger long before being accompanied with a reality check which virtually cut her off from any positive expectations for the future. Instead, Breckinridge's daydreams were suspended outside of time, reaching, if anywhere, back into a lost past rather than toward a hopeful future.

The same was true for Lizzie Morrissey, whose daydreams about the past underscored the emptiness of her constrained and proper present. Morrissey kept her diary during 1876, the spring of her eighteenth year and her final year as a student in the normal track at Girls' High School in Boston. She lived with her widowed mother and her grandparents in straitened financial circumstances which represented one part of her loss. (On her nineteenth birthday she wrote that she expected no presents "as money is very scarce.")[59]

The other part of her loss involved the shrinking of her social world as she struggled to sustain the expectations for propriety assumed as a maturing young lady.

Lizzie Morrissey's diary documents her time as a spectator watching vibrant urban life pass her by outside her parlor window. Sometimes she actively enjoyed the show: "In the evening sat by the parlor window which was open gazing at the passers-by. It is quite amusing to sit thus listening to all the different scraps of conversation; I should like to write it down for the fun of it." Sometimes her interest bordered on the voyeuristic: "After supper watch some fellows in the next yard exercise their muscles." Sometimes she was simply bored: "Sat by the window in the evening and watched the clouds and the people passing. I wish something would occur to raise some fun." Often though she thought about her merry freedom as a child: "I sat upstairs by the window thinking of old friends and old times when, after school we enjoyed ourselves on the sidewalk in the games of hide-and-seek, puss in the corner, etc. . . . I heard the boys outside playing bar-up and among them were several with whom we used to play." She concluded, "It hardly seems possible now, our relations are so changed." At heart of the change was an evolution in the sense of appropriate conduct from being "a set of noisy young ones" to being "young ladies"—and a shrinkage of her physical world from her neighborhood, often simply to her house. Sadly she noted, "I begin to realize that those times can never come again."[60] For Lizzie Morrissey, becoming a young lady in Irish East Boston meant casting off old friends as well as changing clothes to sit in the parlor. What she often daydreamed about in her parlor (for visitors seldom came) were days gone by. These daydreams dramatized the multiple losses—of freedom, of friendships, of fun—which growing up might mean.

Daydreams of course, like night dreams, are not commonly considered to be historical phenomena. Yet in contrast with night dreams, daydreaming is possible only when the mind is loosely engaged by the immediate environment. To the extent that girls' labor was mechanical or marginalized, to the extent that, like Lizzie Morrissey, they observed the world from the sidelines, to the extent that they had time on their hands for looking out the window or writing in diaries, middle-class girls had more opportunity for daydreaming than either their mothers or their more wide-ranging brothers—or maybe even than their rural sisters.

Indeed, adolescent girlhood came to be defined by its "dreaminess," both in the advice literature about girlhood and in its iconographic representations. When elite painters depicted Victorian girls, their subjects were either engaged in reading or focused in a dreamy distance, their expressions suggesting their absence from the immediate scene, their penchant for daydreams. When fiction writers depicted adolescent odysseys in the early twentieth century, as Anne MacLeod writes, they too celebrated a transformed personality. The personalities of such heroines as Anne of Green Gables and Rebecca of Sunnybrook Farm evolved as they hit their teenage years. "Their colorful (and undeniably intrusive) qualities of mind and imagination dim to 'dreaminess' in their mid-teens." The dreaminess of teenage girls was part of their allure but also a sign of danger. F. M. Edselas, writing in *Catholic World,* expressed more broadly applicable views in an article entitled "What Shall We Do with Our Girls?" The reason for the concern had to do with girls' daydreaming. "Hopes and fears, plans and purposes, flimsy and illusive in themselves perhaps, but none the less important to our young maiden, come in turn like so many air-castles, taking a hundred different shapes, ever tumbling down only to be rebuilt under other forms: these fill the new world before her, as Miss Marguerite sits by her moon-lit window. There, imagining herself a Juliet, Desdemona, or some other romantic damsel, she passes through the greatest of all crises."[61] The crisis was her concrete vulnerability to the scent of actual romance.

Another contemporary, writing about bourgeois girls in Vienna, shared Edselas's sense of the danger of daydreams, not from their susceptibility to enactment but from the distance they could establish from the real world. Sigmund Freud's writing about daydreams noted their healthy derivation — "a continuation of, and a substitute for, what was once the play of childhood." Problems arose however, when distinctions between reality and daydream broke down. "If phantasies become over-luxuriant and over-powerful, the conditions are laid for an onset of neurosis or psychosis."[62] In particular, among the daughters of educated bourgeois, the "private theatre" of daydreams could lead to hysteria.

Indeed, Freud and his colleague Josef Breuer seem remarkably modern in their interpretation of what was ailing "Anna O.," their code name for the young Jewish woman Bertha Pappenheim who figured in their explorations of hysteria. They described Pappenheim "bubbling over with intellectual vitality" yet confined to "an extremely monotonous existence in her puritanically-minded family," with her daydreaming a natural, though dangerous, response to her constrained existence. As they put it in their famous article,

1) Her monotonous family life and the absence of adequate intellectual occupation left her with an unemployed surplus of mental liveliness and energy, and this found an outlet in the constant activity of her imagination. *2)* This led to a habit of daydreaming (her "private theatre") which laid the foundations for a dissociation of her mental personality.[63]

Breuer's subsequent analysis of Bertha Pappenheim led to her "talking cure" and the invention of psychoanalysis.

Modern feminist scholars have largely embraced Freud and Breuer's analysis of the malaise that led to Pappenheim's breakdown. To contemporary feminists, the daydreaming of girls and women has marked their lack of access to more direct forms of agency. Elaine Showalter agrees that daydreaming or fantasy was the "product of repressed sexuality, boredom and vacuity." Pointing out that "it was Pappenheim's transition from daydreaming to speech that marked her cure," Carolyn Heilbrun sees the daydreaming of such women as Florence Nightingale and Beatrice Webb as "a sign of their meaningless lives." Girls' inability to base their visions of the future on reality and the resulting need to root them in fantasy have been appropriately seen as indications of their powerlessness.[64]

At the same time, it is important to consider what daydreaming *cons*tructed as well as what it obstructed. Surely girls' indulgent reveries and "air castles" contributed to a particular view of adolescence, as itself a time in which dreams were appropriate. Writing at the turn of the century, the moral reformer Jane Addams was one who defended the role of romance and daydream in the lives of youth. She made her case for theater at Hull House on the basis of youth's need for romance and dreams to stretch the narrow limits of their lives. "A child whose imagination has been cultivated is able to do this for himself through reading and reverie, but for the overworked city youth of meager education, perhaps nothing but the theater is able to perform this important office."[65] Late-Victorian idealists, if not contemporary feminists, might well acknowledge a place for nonproductive dreaming in the context of cramped lives.

The diarist Agnes Lee confirmed just this power. Her prolonged reverie in the 1850s commenced with her identification with the epistolary romance *Madeline's Journal* and developed into a concern for her soul. Agnes Lee ended her long soliloquy with a Victorian's worry about its effects on her. "I *won't* write this way any longer, I fear this must be daydreaming which if longer indulged in will do me harm." In particular, she railed in frustration with her own leisure—with the extra moments in her school day and night which allowed her to react with such excruciating sensitivity to the slights of every-day existence. "Then I wish I couldn't think," she wrote, "[I wish] that I was plunged from day to day in something that would absorb me entirely."[66]

Such an absorbing struggle for existence or for survival certainly ordered the lives of much of the world in the mid–nineteenth century, as it does now. Agnes Lee, however, couldn't leave her thoughts there. She could not wish herself so totally occupied that she did not have time to reflect. "If I couldn't *think* a second life would be taken from me," she mused.[67] Over the course of the nineteenth century, with the apotheosis of the bourgeois culture of the self in the lives of idle schoolgirls, "second lives"—devoted to reflection and self-scrutiny—were awarded to or claimed by a growing proportion of the population, becoming a defining feature of modern personality itself.

These blended practices of self-culture celebrated a particular kind of self, a complex, intricate, and unique package of sensibilities located well beneath the placid exterior of the good Victorian girl. Girls both carefully nurtured and carefully concealed this romantic self. A girl's serenity masked a soul deeply engaged in the struggle between desire and virtue. In her analysis of Victorian fiction, Nancy Armstrong suggests that it is perhaps mistaken to look for the origins of the modern psychological self among impoverished artists, burdened as they were by the kinds of struggle for survival which we imagine might have dispatched Agnes Lee's romantic angst. Writes Arm-strong, "the heightened state of mind in which pleasure and torment are blended is not that of a professional poet. It is the mental state of a schoolgirl who finds herself with 'nothing else to do.'"[68] Leisured schoolgirls like Agnes Lee used diaries and letters to demonstrate that whatever the superficial evi-dence of composure, they did have inner "qualities of mind" which secured their identity as romantic individuals and true women.

This was especially important for apparently silly girls. After many years keeping a full diary of her flirtations and her shames, Annie Cooper began to worry about the revelations she had committed to paper. "I would not like to die before these books go out of existence," she worried. They "would be shocking revelations of my inner self, which I never wish to be revealed." In the next sentence, though, she acknowledged the true purpose of the diary: "I know that Papa thinks I am light and *frivorless* to a shameful degree, with never a thought deeper than *fun and going,* but he's mistaken!"[69] What this passage reveals is both that young women ought to have inner depths be-yond frivolous comings and goings, and also that they must remain secret. For all its embarrassments, Annie Cooper's diary, and many like it, did "cultural work" by reassuring Annie Cooper that she did indeed have psychological complexity, that she was not just a silly girl but a "true woman" of whom her father could be proud. The diaries of Annie Cooper and Agnes Lee fulfilled a cultural prescription which constituted female identity in a dutiful and compliant appearance covering a profound, and richly textured "interior."

SIX

Competitive Practices: Sentiment and Scholarship in Secondary Schools

Girls' moods and reveries emerged in the interstices of what increasingly became a major device to structure and improve middle-class girls' time before marriage: attendance at school. Attending school was more encompassing than piano lessons, reading programs, or the writing of diaries, and it answered a number of cultural needs, among them the training of future guardians of the home in the best and most elevating knowledge, and the occupation of daughters who were both maturing earlier and marrying later than had their mothers and grandmothers. Schooling also offered important routes into respectability for newly consolidating ethnic and religious elites. Girls who went to school earned entry to worthy vocations, too, preparing themselves for self-sufficiency whatever their marital lot.

The experience of school, though, often belied sober parental intent. Instead of facilitating the production of compliant and graceful matrons, school was primarily an institution of peers, then as now. Well before the 1920s, when historians often identify the emergence of a high school culture, students attending schools of all kinds created there a youth culture which featured their own language and practices. Attending school challenged maternal domesticity, and for girls, who constituted the majority in secondary schools in the United States, it also laid down self-expectations and experiences which would profoundly unfit them for domestic subordination. Both in girls' schools, which cultivated intense peer bonds, and in coeducational schools, in which girls often dominated the scholastic rankings, girl students discovered alternative sources of identity which subverted and helped to transform middle-class female culture. One can understand the emergence of New Women at the turn of the century and after only by understanding the "new" girlhoods which brought them into being.

Who Went to Secondary School?

Throughout the nineteenth century and into the twentieth, more girls than boys went to secondary school in an increasing ratio in all parts of the country. Girls represented 53 percent of all students in 1872 and 57 percent in 1900. They were especially overrepresented in public schools. Although private schools had equal percentages of male and female attendees, by 1900 about 60 percent of the students in public high schools were girls. In the West girls attended high schools at an especially high rate in relation to the attendance of boys, whose labor was generally too valuable for families to forgo.[1] Most students in secondary schools lived in the Northeast, however. The educational historian Joel Perlmann's rich statistics from Providence, Rhode Island, allow us to consider the role of class and parentage in determining girls' high school attendance.

In 1880 about 14 percent of all teenage girls were enrolled in high schools in Providence, compared with perhaps 2–3 percent nationally. Although high schools were supported by public funds, those who sent their children needed to be able to do without their labor. Native whites in Providence sent a third of their teenage daughters to high school and nearly a quarter of their sons. White-collar workers (whether immigrant or native) also sent a third of their teenage daughters and just over a quarter of their teenage sons to high school. (The elite were more likely to send their children to private schools.) Where class and native-born parentage overlapped, as it often did, secondary school attendance was especially high. Yankee, white-collar parents sent the highest proportion of both daughters (46 percent) and sons (36 percent) to secondary school. Though a significant majority of teenage American girls could not afford to go to school, those who did represented a growing and influential segment of the youth population.[2]

These carefully compiled statistics raise some important questions. Why did girls go to secondary school in higher numbers than boys? How might one explain a family's decisions to allow a girl to remain in school while sending her brother out to work? Conventional wisdom cites the lower "opportunity costs" of educating girls. Girls' work was sufficiently devalued in the urban labor market that families would consider forgoing the potential income for other desired ends.[3]

One such end, as we have seen, was the goal of refinement, that eighteenth-

and nineteenth-century project designed to demonstrate the genteel sensibilities of aristocracy as a means of securing middle-class respectability. The historian Richard Bushman has pointed out the numerous contradictions of this aristocratic aesthetic which coexisted both with a capitalist culture based on labor and a republican tradition that dignified it. He has also argued, however, that the strongest constraints on conduct in the name of gentility were levied on young women, who from the eighteenth century forward were expected to demonstrate reserve and grace to establish their family's standing.[4]

In the late eighteenth century, this quest for refinement fostered a gendered, ornamental female education. Eliza Southgate, attending school in Boston, responded to her brother's compliments on her letter writing with thanks and her "hope I shall make a great progress in my other studies and be an 'Accomplished Miss.'" What that might mean was fleshed out a bit by Rachel Mordecai's report for her mother of her younger sister's progress. She noted that her young charge read well, knew several pages of French nouns, added and multiplied, knew first principles in geography, knew parts of speech and conjugated verbs in grammar, played a number of songs. Mordecai concluded: "She sews plain work tolerably well, and has marked the large and small alphabet on a sampler."[5] The seamless blending of parts of speech and piano, sums and sampler, characterized an era in female education in which accomplishments were equally academic and ornamental. An educated and accomplished miss was expected to call a certain attention to herself.

The common-school movement of the early nineteenth century educated boys and girls together, and with the republican and Jacksonian revolution in culture, commentators grew less comfortable with the ornament of aristocratic accomplishment. Instead they praised the restraint, reserve, and womanliness of well-educated girls. Refinement in lessons as in life might be measured less by conspicuous self-display and more by selflessness, by learning what not to do, and how not to be. *Youth's Companion* expressed these lessons in an 1868 story of an exemplary schoolgirl: "She was quiet, almost to reserve, though her dimpling smiles were prettier than any language; but when she did speak, her words were well chosen, though few." She had applied the same lesson to her music. Though she played the piano well, "Jenny made rare use of her accomplishment. She never bored anybody, as the best players do at times."[6] All in all, Jenny had grasped the true restraint which represented a gendered lesson well learned. Whatever it actually delivered (and I shall argue that it largely delivered something else), school *seemed* to be the best strategy for ensuring that at least one member of the family—the one whose wages could most easily be forgone—might embody the class aspirations of the rest.

Vocational Insurance

To demonstrate class standing, increasingly, young women did not work for wages. The irony was that attending school equipped young women for work—especially for one of the few semirespectable jobs available to them. Accompanying the message that education was refining and improving was a parallel rationale that was often hidden: in the unstable economy of the nineteenth century, education provided an entrée to the job of schoolteaching, a tolerable means of wage-earning for young women in need. With the expansion of school systems in the nineteenth century and the growth in the national economy opening more lucrative opportunities for men, low-paid women increasingly replaced men as the nation's teachers. By 1870 about two-thirds of the nation's teachers were women, a proportion that increased to nearly three-quarters in 1900. In the major cities of the Northeast, more than four-fifths of the teaching profession was female.[7]

Undoubtedly, girls filled high schools in part because high schools prepared them for teaching jobs. Much has been made of the low wages paid female teachers, and that was certainly part of their appeal to cash-poor local school districts. Yet girls had fewer occupational options than boys, and schoolteaching paid better than those other options. As two economic historians put it, "Access to good jobs for men was acquired through on-the-job training, while access to the good jobs for women was acquired in schools." A contemporary report on the public high school in Chicago in 1899 reported an especially skewed ratio of girls to boys because of this fact. Describing Chicago's public high school as "almost entirely a professional one," a reporter noted that 70 percent of the student body was female, with 60 percent of them seeking admission to normal school, the training ground for teachers.[8]

The statistical correlation between girls' attendance at high school and the feminization of teaching suggests a powerful economic undercurrent to girls' high school attendance. Yet especially at midcentury, few parents, commentators, or girls themselves would confess to such vocational thinking. Teaching was to be either a temporary expedient or an insurance plan for daughters who would find their highest destiny within the domestic sphere. Writing in the 1840s, Jason Whitman, in his *Young Lady's Aid to Usefulness and Happiness,* had cautioned girls concerned about self-support against learning a trade, instead suggesting inculcation of "the whole round of ordinary, domestic, female duties and labors." Such training would allow a girl to dismiss her father's servants, or to take their place in someone else's house. As a last resort only Whitman recommended paying attention in school, so that a girl could become qualified to teach. A fictional heroine too suggested that in genteel circles, teaching was the dirty secret, rather than the noble end, of school attendance. In Anna White's novel *Kate Callender,* subtitled *School-Girls of '54,* the heroine's impoverished parents consider teaching as an option for a daughter they can scarcely support. "But would she accept it? Ah! there was a doubt. He had heard her say more than once that she would pull weeds, rake and pitch hay, even; but she would not sink into the insignificance of a 'schoolma'am.'" Writing in the South following the Civil War, one diarist expressed sympathy for a classmate confronting the need to make her own living. After describing her as "well educated," "a strong, intellectual woman," with "open candid eyes," she acknowledged, "It is a pity anyone like her should have to teach, while a great many, worthless, stupid girls seem to be the favorites of fortune."[9] Few families seemed to want to admit to the increasing likelihood that their daughters would teach.

The ability to teach then was a subtext rather than the professed rationale for school attendance for many girls in the second half of the nineteenth century. Even historians looking back at the evidence have hedged their bets. Catherine Kelly notes the "haphazard approach" of families and daughters who "agreed on the value of an education" yet were "uncertain as to how the particulars of that education might be turned to the service of kin and community." Kelly concludes that secondary education was "not a necessity, part of a rational plan to prepare their daughters for careers in teaching." John Rury found no statistical evidence to argue that girls attended high school in order to teach, although that was often the outcome of their educations. Instead, girls' school attendance was inspired by several complementary but not equally acknowledged motives. Privileged parents might send their daughters to school to occupy and improve them during years they might otherwise be underoccupied, before anticipated marriage. (They might send their sons to high school, too—on their way to college.) Striving lower-middle-class parents might send their daughters to high schools with similar aspirations, while sending their sons directly onto the job. This difference in plans for sons would account for the greater numbers of girls in schools.[10] Both sets of parents would likely agree on the preferred outcome for their daughters: comfortable, refined homes with good providers. Both sets of parents, however, would welcome the insurance plan provided by schooling for girls. Being a "schoolma'am" was not a glamorous or an attractive option within the context of genteel Victorian culture. Aside, perhaps, from pseudonymous writing, there was no attractive vocation in those terms. Schoolteaching, however, was the better option among degraded alternatives, including domestic service and factory work, and that was good enough.

Kinds of Schools

The reason that public secondary schools could seem a route to class mobility was that education had long been a critical marker of class. In the early republic, only daughters of men of wealth and standing could secure an education at young ladies' seminaries, institutions opened following the Revolution as a means of securing "republican mothers" for a new citizenry. Beginning in the Northeast and spreading west and south in the nineteenth century, the common-school movement offered free primary education to all children. Often set in a rural one-room school with students ranging in age from six to twenty, the nineteenth-century common school attempted to fulfill the democratic promise of the republic by educating an intelligent citizenry.

At the secondary level, though, until the 1850s and thereafter students would need to pay, either at young ladies' seminaries, Catholic convent schools, or at the privately funded "academies," many of them coeducational, that were scattered throughout the Northeast. Catholic convent schools and young ladies' Protestant seminaries both offered religious programs taught by staffs of mostly unmarried women. That the two venues shared many fundamental principles emerges in the enthusiasm with which Protestant men of property, especially in the West, supported "the Sisters" in their project of supplying schools for their daughters. In fact, the efforts of Catharine Beecher, an early–nineteenth century advocate for female education, were in part competitive, as the Catholic orders began to build a significant network of secondary girls' schools, numbering 202 in 1860. Some convent schools in the West educated more non-Catholics than Catholics and advertised their openness to Jews as well.[11]

The founding of the public high school was an outgrowth of the same Jacksonian, democratic principles which promoted elementary, common schools. The first "free" high schools opened in the 1820s, and indeed Massachusetts directed its towns of more than five hundred families to build high schools in 1827. Many of the early high schools subsequently closed, though, and the public high school movement in Massachusetts languished until the 1850s. (One early high school, Boston's Girls' High School, apparently closed shortly after it opened in 1826 because it was besieged with applications from more than three times the number of girls that it could accept.) It was only in the

1880s, according to one historian, that public high schools nationwide educated more students than private secondary schools.[12]

It would be easy, though, to overestimate the distinctions between these high schools and one class of precursors, the private academies that preceded and coexisted with high schools scattered through the Northeast. Academies often drew on a diverse rural population, including farmers' sons and daughters, and were not primarily designed to prepare students for colleges or more advanced learning.[13] The tributes accorded rural academies mirror twentieth-century tributes to the urban high school as the source of encouragement and social mobility for hardworking and able youths of humble background. Often early so-called public high schools were not in fact free, and equally often, local townships bore some of the costs of supporting local academies.

One other way in which public high schools resembled academies was that they were sometimes coeducational and sometimes single sex. Given the gendered divisions within nineteenth-century society, it made sense that citizens who proposed public secondary schools for youth initially imagined separate academies for girls and boys. The city of Boston, which opened the first publicly funded secondary schools, reflected that predisposition in its separate girls' and boys' high schools. Based on that prototype, Boston and a number of other northeastern urban school systems retained separate boys' and girls' high schools well into the twentieth century. (New York City's famous all-girls' high school, Hunter College, still reflects that heritage.)

The fact was, though, that the economics of school funding militated against sexually segregated schools. As it was, it was a hard sell to persuade taxpayers to support another tier of schooling on top of the commitment to primary grades. School districts founding high schools in the latter half of the nineteenth century concluded that there were neither the money nor the students to maintain two separate secondary systems. In debating the merits of coeducation, the nation's magazines—and especially a new journal, *Education*—vigorously debated what was largely a fait accompli by the late century. By 1890 a national advisory board announced: "The question in its practical aspect, is settled. . . . The public mind is made up." Five years later, 94 percent of American cities provided only coeducational public high schools.[14]

The debates about the relative merits of same-sex and coeducational learning for girls have been reignited in recent years, though, so it is of interest to consider the nineteenth-century evidence. How did girls' descriptions of coeducational academies and public high schools compare with all-female seminaries and private girls' day schools in curriculum, culture, and expectations? And how did both compare with the home environment and its domestic culture? Given the heterogeneity of nineteenth-century schooling, it is difficult to make useful generalizations. It is clear, though, that for different reasons but with similar impact, girls' schools and coeducational high schools challenged the dominance of domesticity in defining girls' lives and their expectations.

Girls' Boarding Schools and Girls' Culture

Girls' schools promoted an intense female peer culture which contrasted with the disciplines of moralistic home environments. Evidence from the accounts of girls attending the myriad female seminaries and girls' boarding schools throughout the Northeast suggests that their academic programs were relatively gentle, and that their peer culture was powerful and often fun. Despite the best efforts of outnumbered teachers, relations with friends tended to overshadow lessons learned. Overwhelmingly when girls wrote home to their parents, they described the girls they had met, and the antics they had shared; in diaries they noted the romantic intimacies they had formed, with academic work generating only occasional mention. Girls' peer life at school was high-spirited, collective, and ritualized all at once.

Teachers themselves often participated. At Miss Porter's in Farmington, Connecticut, in 1860, teachers organized a costume party, suggested characters for everyone, and helped sew costumes—perhaps in part a sewing lesson. (For Lily Dana, suggestions included an elf, Mischief, or a witch.) At a Prospect Hill School party in 1882, townspeople came, the girls wore flowers and white dresses, and Margaret Tileston reported that she had done the quadrille with Miss Clarke and the gallop with Miss Tuxbury—concluding that she had had "a very nice time."[15]

Girls remembering their days at convent schools report similar good times. Julia Sloane Spalding recalled elegiacally her years at Nazareth Academy, a school run by the Sisters of Charity in Louisville, Kentucky, in the 1850s. "The sisters allowed us to romp and play, dance and sing as we pleased and our stage performances were amusing, if they had no greater merit. Musical soirees, concerts, serenades and minstrelsy kept our spirits attuned to gladness. Varied by picnics, lawn parties, hayrides, phantom parties, nutting parties in summer and candy pullings and fancy balls with Nazareth's colored band to fiddle." Exclaimed Spalding, "O what fun!" in fond reflection on the good times among the sisters who served "good substantial sandwiches, cakes and fruit" from "great big baskets." She concluded, "and so, the spice of life conduced to our health and happiness." Mary Anne Murphy arrived at Nazareth Academy with her sister in 1859 during a quadrille, the slave musicians

6.1 Girls' school, 1887. Female academies nourished a spontaneous and intimate school culture, as captured in this portrait of the St. Agnes Class of 1887. Schlesinger Library (Cambridge: Radcliffe Institute, Harvard University), WRC-Pa2-9).

calling out the figures. She and her sister stood in "wonderment that such fun was tolerated in a convent."[16] Whatever the nostalgia of middle age, certainly these reflections suggest that elite Catholic and Protestant girls' academies left some of their richest memories in collective fun.

If teachers sponsored some activities, they implicitly sanctioned many more. Wilfrida Hogan attended the Sisters of St. Joseph convent school in St. Paul in the 1870s and remembers fondly her class, which was known for its lively irreverence: "Each girl seemed to view the other as to who could play the biggest pranks, or have the most fun." Ellen Emerson overflowed with delight in a letter to her mother (significantly, not her father) while at Miss Sedgwick's School in Lenox, Massachusetts: "Every night we do things which it seems to me I can never remember without laughing if I should live to be a hundred. The most absurd concerts, ludicrous charades, peculiar battles etc. etc. Then the wildest frolics, the loudest shrieks, the most boisterous rolling and tumbling that eye ever saw, ear ever heard or heart ever imagined. I consider myself greatly privileged that every night I can see and join such delightful romps." When teachers were around, the pranks were more likely to occur upstairs in student bedrooms. Lily Dana and friends joined together to victimize two other girls by putting crumbs in their bed, and cutting off

candle wicks. Another evening Dana noted that she "Had some fun throw-
ing pillows and nightgowns," and though Miss Porter caught her, it did not
seem to dampen much her spirits. Teachers at girls' schools were occasionally disciplinarians, clearly. One teacher told Lily Dana that "she supposed
my mother let me do everything," and the sisters at St. Mary's Academy in
South Bend, Indiana, turned the piano to the wall in order to keep girls from
waltzing with each other. Yet students often emerged victorious; at St. Mary's
they played combs for dance music instead. (One participant reported that
"the Sisters had to give up, for they knew not what to do.")[17] The ideology
of nurture combined with the shared exuberance of age mates overpowered
much teacherly remonstrance.

It is sometimes hard to read such tales of schoolgirl exuberance without
wondering whether the inmates had taken over the asylum, however, so a
corrective is in order. One such account which requires a second look is the
spirited account of Agnes Repplier, *In Our Convent Days* (1906), about her
time in the late 1860s at a Pennsylvania school run by the Sisters of the Sacred
Heart. Repplier writes of the pranks and passions of her band of seven partners in crime, in an ebullient account designed to appeal to a readership newly
attracted to childhood naughtiness in revolt against Victorian propriety. It is
clear in retrospect, though, that she must have concealed or minimized another side to her experiences. For the denouement of her story is her expulsion
and removal from a school she adored.[18]

Peer cultures could also be cruel and hurtful beyond the control of evangelical teachers, as the practices of hazing in British public schools testify.
Some of the most painful memories of inclusion and exclusion in girls' schools
centered around that most primal of media, the sharing of food. Food boxes,
customarily sent from home, were the occasion for impromptu parties, a demonstration of wealth and taste, or an opportunity to play favorites. The elation
which greeted such arrivals might well prove a commentary on the regular fare
at boarding schools, which sometimes undoubtedly was very poor. (The advice giver Mary Virginia Terhune's critique of girls' boarding schools included
the accusation that they fed their students from a "common vat" which supplied breakfast, dinner, and supper all together, a practice partially confirmed
by one account of eating the same stew at least twice a day at an Ursuline
academy in San Antonio in the 1890s.) At any rate, the arrival of food from
home occasioned select gatherings and provided opportunities for discrimination among friends. When one friend's mother brought good things to eat,
Josie Tilton noted that "we" had a feast tonight, explaining for the future who
she would always mean when she said "we" — "Lizzie, Emma, May and I" —

the groupness secured by inclusion in this select group of diners. Lily Dana suspected a friend of being miserly and so snuck into her room to inspect. "There was a box which had been filled with cake, part of a pie and several other things filling her trunk nearly half full. . . . If I had a box sent to me I think I should give my friend more than 'five or six cookies.'"[19] If girls could feel short-changed by each other, relations with parents could also strain over the sending of food boxes, which represented extremely conspicuous consumption for girls attempting to "belong."

In an unusually direct letter home in the 1840s, Maria Nellis passed on to her parents her unmediated hurt and sense of disadvantage in the competition for food—and the status that came with it.

> Elizabeth got her box yesterday and was favoured with six times more things than I was. Her box was so large and heavy the master found it his match to carry it upstairs. She has 4 kinds of cake, nuts, apples, candy, clothing and every thing else, but after all, Dear Poppy, I am not jealous. . . . When you sent that box you did not send half what I asked. I was very disappointed. You said it would be eatables, but it wasn't. You sent only a few apples, one cake and some clothes. Why didn't you send me some nuts? I haven't had a nut yet this winter, and indeed I expected nuts above all things. E. Fox had a box worth speaking of. Now that shows that you don't care enough for me to even send me a few nuts.

Intermittently, Nellis regained control, but her grievance was palpable. Finally at the end, she acknowledged to her parents that she might be hurting their feelings, reassured them that she loved them all with "a deep and fervent love," and promised better behavior in the future.[20] Clearly at stake for her was both status in the school world and a primitive sense of deprivation in her own family.

Female World of Love and Ritual

As the correspondence suggests, the emotional atmosphere in girls' boarding schools was not only intense but more expressive and enacted than that within moralistic, Victorian households. Within private, female, boarding academies, duty-bound Victorian daughters learned languages of sentiment, desire, and emotional excess censored from other parts of their lives. The elaborate conventions accompanying the expression and affirmation of affection among boarding-school girls, sometimes involving teachers as well, was indeed a separate "female world of love and ritual," as Carroll Smith-Rosenberg affirmed in a classic article about nineteenth-century women's culture. In recent years, Smith-Rosenberg's "Female World of Love and Ritual" has been attacked for its overgeneralizing characterization of an exclusively female emotional sphere in the nineteenth century, but her strongest evidence confirms the significance, the power, and the longevity of girls' boarding school friendships, which were enacted through elaborate rituals in a range of schools.[21]

The rituals of boarding school life centered around the making and breaking of special friendships, known variously as "affinities," "specials," or "darlings" and increasingly as either "smashes" or "crushes." One way of expressing interest was to "filipine" with someone, to leave her a surprise gift outside her door. (When Lily Dana was caught, she needed to give her gift, a large apple, outright.)[22] Such relationships played out in diaries, letters, and the poetry of autograph books.

Girls expected to pair up for many school activities and entertained a variety of "dates" with different girls for walking, going to church, and sleeping. Sally Dana wrote home to her mother explaining that she was following her father's advice not to form special friendships too soon, and so had "slept in eight different beds." During these private moments, girls would share secrets about their own likes and dislikes, each other, their teachers, families, and their school lives. The intricacy of such social calendars opened ample opportunities for misunderstanding and frayed feelings.[23]

These peer relationships characterized elite female seminaries in the Northeast, but they also appeared in a range of schools, including the African American Scotia Seminary, founded by the American Missionary Association in Concord, North Carolina, following the Civil War. Scotia had northern roots, which may have influenced its student culture. Glenda Gilmore tells us it was modeled on Mount Holyoke, and was "calculated to give students the knowledge, social consciousness, and sensibilities of New England ladies, with a strong dose of Boston egalitarianism sprinkled in." Roberta Fitzgerald went to Scotia in the early twentieth century and kept a composition book, likely in 1902, which was filled with the talismans of schoolgirl crushes. A note inside addressed to "Dear Roberta" asked, "Will you please exchang rings with me to-day and you may ware mine again," and Roberta herself wrote a sad poem to a friend "Lu" who had thrown her over.

> And so you see as I am deemed
> Most silently to wait
> I cannot but be womanlike
> And meekly await my fate.

6.2 *The Morning Walk: Young Ladies' School Promenading the Avenue*, 1868. Winslow Homer captured the demure composure expected of young ladies walking in couples rather than the heated negotiations behind them. Schlesinger Library (Cambridge: Radcliffe Institute, Harvard University), Gr10-17+ 166.

> *Ah! sweet it is to love a girl*
> *But truly oh! how bitter*
> *To love a girl with all your heart*
> *And then to hear "Cant get her."*
>
> *And Lulu dear as I must here*
> *Relinquish with a moan*
> *May your joys be as deep as the ocean*
> *And your sorrow as light as its foam.*

On the back of the notebook, which also contained class assignments, was a confidence exchanged with a seatmate. "I was teasing Bess Hoover about you and she told me she loved you dearly."[24]

For those much in demand, this charged atmosphere of flirtation and intimacy in the North and South represented an exhilarating round of fun and sport. For those less secure, diaries and letters presented an obvious outlet for the anguish of the neglected. Agnes Hamilton, a member of a Fort Wayne clan which sent several daughters to boarding school on their way to prominent careers in progressive America, experienced some of both. Sometimes she basked in the glow of family reputation; often she worried over her own inability to keep up with her illustrious cousins. Her unusually detailed accounts document an entire school culture rather than just an individual emotional life.

Hamilton's first impressions of school social life at Miss Porter's School were favorable, but even these revealed insecurities to come. In an entry from November 1886, when she was seventeen, Hamilton noted that "Farmington is just as perfect as they all said it would be, the girls, Miss Porter, and all." Her reservation had to do with her own imperfections: "But I don't think I am the right sort of a Farmington girl." Even so, Agnes was in demand, describing a flurry of close attentions from numerous girls. A week later, in her cousin's absence, she received displaced attentions:

> Yesterday Mannie was very nice to me. I suppose she thinks I am lonely without Alice. We walked past the fill around by the river to the graveyard. Then she came in and we talked for an hour. All evening we were together. This afternoon we walked together too for Tuesday is her day with Alice. We went down to the green house where Mannie gave me some lovely roses. I would give anything to know what she thinks of me. . . . Will I ever be able to talk and be jolly as other girls? Some girls are frightfully stupid and yet they can make themselves somewhat agreeable. I have struck up

6.3 "The right sort of Farmington girl?" 1888. Agnes Hamilton, left, was alternately exhilarated and insecure in the swirl of friends surrounding her beautiful
and accomplished cousin Alice at Miss Porter's School in Farmington, Connecticut. Schlesinger Library (Cambridge: Radcliffe Institute, Harvard University), MC
278-791-3.

> a sudden friendship with Lena Farnam. We were together Saturday after-
> noon and evening and Sunday I asked her to be my church girl in Alice's
> place.

Agnes was still in a position to be picky, noting one drawback: Lena "seems
very nice indeed but I wish she were not only fifteen." Lena was far from
the only prospect. Agnes noted another new friend: "I have seen a great deal
lately of Edith Trowbridge too. When she overcomes her shyness she will be
exceedingly nice." Not surprisingly, with all the intensity of the socializing,
Agnes mentioned with no comment that only three out of thirteen in the
class were prepared for their lessons that Tuesday.[25]

In those early weeks, Agnes Hamilton's enthusiasm for this exciting life of emotional intrigue was palpable. The next week (she seems to have written on Tuesdays), Agnes announced to her diary "the jolliest crush in school" involving one of her very own intimates of the week before. "I walked with Edith Trowbridge this afternoon, on purpose to have her tell me about Lena. I hinted and hinted in vain. I told her about every other crush in school but she never said a word about Lena's, so at last I told her that I knew all about it but even then she would not say a word about the subject. I hope she will tell Lena so that she will speak to me about it next Saturday when we are driving." The triangulation of such relationships increased the possibilities for intrigue. Agnes wearied a bit of the uncooperative Edith, though, observing that though "very nice . . . she did not get over her stiffness."[26]

Agnes Hamilton seemed to be trying to do her schoolwork, but her roller-coaster social life intervened. One day when she was preparing for class, a friend came by to teach her a dance step, from which she was interrupted by the arrival of a buggy she had rented to take another friend for a ride, the same girl whose "jolly" crush had amused her the week before. ("The more I see of her the better I like," she now reported. "Her face is rather attractive at first and then it grows on one.") When she returned, she found another visitor who stayed till it was time for tea. The result: "I have not looked at my Mental since Thursday." By the end of the same day, yet a new "crush" had taken over when Agnes got word of someone's interest in her, and Agnes wondered "if I have ever been as actively happy." The frenzy had settled down a week later, when Agnes announced that she had all her walking days "just as I want them." Each day of the week was assigned a different companion, with whom Agnes would exchange intimacies and gossip, using the rituals of girls' school life to structure its emotional extravagance.[27]

Such excesses could include lows as well as highs. Her final year at Farmington, Agnes Hamilton found herself wishing for the friends she had taken for granted the year before. "Then they were much more forlorn than we were and seemed to like me quite well but I did not care at all for them." She ended her lament, "Our tea set this year is a vile affair," and "my walking girls are not much better." During the winter, she was morose enough to wish that she had never come to Farmington, in the shadow of her cousins. "I do so hate to be considered the weed of the family."[28] Diaries suggest the centrality of social life at schools specifically for young ladies.

One diarist who suggested otherwise was Agnes Lee, who had been the belle of West Point her thirteenth year in the 1850s, when her father, Robert E. Lee, was commandant of the military academy. She found it hard to settle into the Staunton Female Seminary, where she and her cousins had enrolled, writing far less than other correspondents about the other girls. Her studied nonchalance revealed that social life in the girls' schools of the South resembled that in the North, though. Writing to her family, she apologized, "It seems to me I say very little of my schoolmates, but there is not much of interest to say. Some are pretty, some are sweet, some are je ne sais quoi. My partner for breakfast and dinner is Mary Pendleton. Lizzie W____ is my sweet little beau for tea."[29] World-weary Lee might regret the days gone by at West Point, but she was sufficiently attuned to the protocol of girls' school social life that she had arranged to fill the formalities by engaging dates and expressing "affinities."

Perhaps as a result of her schooling at West Point, Agnes Lee "read" these schoolgirl relations in language borrowed from the world of heterosexual flirtation rather than from sentimental domesticity. Analogizing one schoolgirl "idol" with an acquaintance who "found her victims among the young men," she noted that Sue "is now compelled to enchant only schoolgirls." She went on to "pity the girl who blindly loves her and tells her so," for "in a short time the once devoted Sue quarrels and casts her off for some new worshiper." At a fancy dress ball, in which a number of girls came in drag, Lee recorded that she "quite lost [her] heart" to another schoolmate who came as a "romantic young highlander. Before going up stairs I threw my arms round her and said I must have a kiss for she had fascinated me so I could not keep my eyes off her[.] As she bent her head in ready assent her romantic face and dreamy eyes were a picture to gaze upon." Lee was unusual in providing her own heterosexual correction on her fantasy. She went on to suggest that such a face would have been a picture "to *think* upon," but only "if really of the other sex."[30] Lee's language of description and also of admiration might have fueled the writings of later physicians who censured such same-sex boarding-school infatuation.

One must conclude that the intensity of the social life was seen to serve some purpose, for evidence suggests that it was allowed to flourish until the turn of the century. (Lily Dana noted that Miss Porter's permission had been sought for at least one and probably more sleeping dates.[31]) At that time, new sexualized interpretations of girls' and women's friendships brought a crackdown on such friendships. At the time, though, they appear to have received official sanction.

In fact, one of the first of *Ladies' Home Journal*'s "Side Talks with Girls" took up the question of "School Girl Friendships." The *Journal* endorsed such girlish relationships for their innocence and energy and their precious brevity, saluting "the giddy, gushing period" as one which "never comes to some and to most it soon passes." In particular, it contrasted this girlish spontaneity with the superficiality of the jaded young lady. Its contrast of "young girls, lively, radiant, energetic, spirited, loving girls" with "young ladies who talk of their beaux, dresses and the surface shows of society" represented another version of a conventional warning against precociousness. Girls' crushes on other girls were still perceived as innocent and healthy—and would be well after doctors first began to cast suspicion over such relationships in the 1880s and 1890s.[32]

A *St. Nicholas* story suggests another powerful interpretation of those friendships: in the process of competing for one another's affections, girls were learning how to present themselves in the more unforgiving marriage market. "Wild Becky" by Emma Plimpton tells the story of a local farmer who has "taken it into his dear old head" to make a lady of his rustic granddaughter and takes her to the local boarding school, "the pride of the village." The refined girls snub the awkward and unfashionable girl, and when they pair off for their walking dates, she reflects: "'Nobody isn't anybody here unless they are a couple, and I aint!'" The plucky girl invites the scholars home for some country play in the fields, though, and begins to make friends. This is at the core of the school experience. As author Plimpton explains: "She began to truly like the girls; then she loved one or two dearly in true school-girl fashion, and to be worthy of their love, she tried to improve her manners. Ultimately she became a lady "in every sense of that much misused term."[33] The process of loving in true schoolgirl fashion was critical to this outcome. Such love was probably far more effective than formal lessons in encouraging girls from all backgrounds to aspire to improve their manners and to compete successfully for walking partners. The explanation that these friendships were both "true" and "school-girl" suggested the contradictory qualities which they embodied. They were "true" because they were characterized by intense emotions and rich sentiment. They were "school-girl" in fashion, because they were experimental and contingent, as befit lovers-in-training.

The power of special friendships to transform the junior partner undoubtedly also explains another kind of friendship that appeared to flourish in girls' schools—the idolizing hero worship of younger girls for special teachers. Ellen Emerson was enraptured by the young teachers who taught her first at the Sedgwick and then the Agassiz School. After confessing that she felt as if she *"must **must must**"* see her old school, she fixated on Miss Bessie Sedgwick: "I don't know what I should do if I saw *her*, it seems as if it would make me wild." Emerson was similarly infatuated with the beautiful Ida Agassiz,

6.4 Not a lady yet, 1878. In this *St. Nicholas* story, Wild Becky's farming grandfather drops his rustic granddaughter off at the local female seminary in order to make her a lady. Reprinted from Emma Plimpton, "Wild Becky," *St. Nicholas* 6 (December 1878): 75.

who taught at the Agassiz School, reporting her euphoria at seeing her again several years later: "I couldn't see her enough she was so beautiful I couldn't have enough of her she was so good, and there she always was, and I might always sit by her and talk with her just as much as I chose. And when I came home Father was so good, he said 'And have you been to see the Lady Ida?'" Though Ida's brother Alexander also occasionally taught at Agassiz School, he did not invest himself in the project the way his sister did. (Emerson commented: "The son is handsome and I believe a fine young man, but he doesn't love teaching much and so is not very popular at school.") By later in the century, custom had become culture. Writing of her time in an Ursuline convent school in San Antonio in the 1890s, Emily Edwards reported that "it was the fashion among the younger girls to have 'darlings.' Perhaps one would have several, a choir sister, a lay sister, and a big girl. Usually the chosen one would be unaware of being one's darling or most admired. Madam Mary was my darling! She called me her 'little Emmy' and I never doubted that she loved me. Ma'am Mary was Irish with warm brown eyes, strong teeth, and a flash-

ing smile. She was smart and kind and full of fun, and I loved her." The power
of such emotional bonds between student and teacher at many girls' schools
suggests the profound challenge which schools might offer to familial identification. At Protestant schools, girls graduated and often went sadly home.
At Catholic schools there was an option. Wilfrida Hogan so loved her school
experience at the Sisters of St. Joseph convent school that she was not allowed
to return for a second year, her mother "fearing lest I should join the Sister-
hood."[34] Her mother's fears proved justified, for several years later Wilfrida
returned to preserve her school days, to cement a spiritual identity, and take
up her life as a member of the order.

Spontaneity and Sentiment at Home and at School

This school world of spontaneity and sentiment often represented a contrast with home life, circumscribed as it was with parental expectations. The
peer culture in girls' boarding schools differed substantially from the conventions which characterized girls' relationships with their mothers and other
family members within the domestic sphere. This seems obvious, but it runs
contrary to Caroll Smith-Rosenberg's important argument about nineteenth-
century women's culture. She presents strong evidence, confirmed by my findings, of the significance, the power, and the longevity of some girls' boarding school friendships, but she is less successful in demonstrating that this
kind of "giddy, gushing" world also characterized intergenerational familial
culture. Contrary to Smith-Rosenberg's thesis, these school friendships were
essentially peer and extrafamilial bonds that united girls with special friends
in some tension with family bonds (mothers included) rather than in an un-
differentiated continuum with them. Indeed, girls' boarding schools often
taught duty-bound Victorian daughters languages of sentiment, desire, and
emotional excess rare in other parts of their lives.

The aggrieved schoolgirl Maria Nellis, who found her parents' box of food
inadequate, suggested another component to her complaints about home.
Nellis's parents were members of a German Calvinist denomination, the Pala-
tines, and had probably sent her away to Pittsfield Young Ladies' Institute
in hopes of improving her health. Boarding school did not improve Nellis's
health (in fact, she died the following year), but it did introduce the young
girl to a social life and a culture at clear odds with what she had left behind.
She wrote home to her family that her community of twenty boarders "enjoy
ourselves greatly." And she contrasted her school life with the life she would
be living with her peers back at Palatine Church. She asked her parents: "How
are the young ladies at Palatine? Are they enjoying themselves or are they as

usual the same stiff girls who think it rude to play or have fun?" At boarding school, considerations of propriety frequently gave way to spontaneity and play: "The young ladies and even the teachers, Mr. and Mrs. Tyler, join with us in our sports. We play such things as to catch each other and run around chairs—all kinds of such play which the Ladies at Palatine would think un-ladylike and would not do it for anything."[35] Nellis's contrasts on one level are the contrasts between two kinds of religious culture: the strict Calvinism of her home faith community and the "born again" enthusiasm of the Second Great Awakening likely to have characterized her young ladies' seminary. They also suggest, though, the contrast between a peer community of schoolgirls, who could draw their teachers into their play, and a group of dutiful daughters tending to maternal admonition and attempting to absorb the lessons of female propriety of a new American culture.

There's some evidence that convent schools, too, despite their stricter discipline, allowed for a similar flowering of peer culture. Girls who were educated by the sisters in the nineteenth century were often educated in cloister, with strict restrictions on contact with the outside world, with parents, and even among themselves, for silence was often expected during meals. (Emily Edwards noted of the Ursuline school she attended in the 1890s that on Sunday "we could talk quietly, but on weekdays meals were in silence.") It seems indubitable, as historians have recently allowed, "that convent academies had more student supervision and regulations compared to other secondary educational settings." Nevertheless, life among the nuns with other children and peers often competed favorably with the disciplines of home. Agnes Repplier's biographer makes this point explicitly. "Although the girls at the convent were governed with what passed for an iron hand, Minnie [Repplier's childhood nickname] found the discipline at Eden Hall far less stringent than at 2005 Chestnut Street. Because the rules at the convent were common to all, which was not entirely the case at home, they seemed fair. And as the essayist would blithely point out, even though you followed them, which, she added, she did not always do—you had a good time." Repplier herself made the contrast between her own mother and the Virgin Mary, the embodiment of maternal love within convent walls. She felt sure of the Virgin Mary's love. Her own mother, whom her daughter remembered as thwarted and unhappy, stood for authority: "Indeed she represented the supreme, infallible authority, from which there was no appeal."[36] Repplier preferred to take her chances with the forgiving Virgin Mary.

The diaries of Margaret Tileston, too, suggest the development of expressive emotion away from home within the context of boarding school culture. Tileston's diaries, nearly unique because of their faithfulness, provide evidence of the evolution of a sensibility over the course of an adolescence, and indeed a lifetime. They include several different kinds of school experience—a primary school, a girls' boarding school, and a public high school—and therefore provide a valuable opportunity to assess and compare different school cultures.

Margaret Tileston was the second daughter of a gentleman-farmer who lived in Concord, Massachusetts, and lived a life governed by regular habits. The diary she kept every day revealed not only that regular discipline but other chores, reading, and schoolwork that she did on a regular basis. In the fall before her fifteenth birthday, she and her sister were sent off to the Prospect Hill School, a girls' boarding school in Greenfield, Massachusetts, where she met an older girl who completely swept her away. Margaret Tileston had had special friends before in her grammar school in Concord. Several years earlier she had mentioned that one had given her a Baldwin apple in recess. Apparently the feeling was reciprocated. "I like Alice very much, better than any other in my class," she reported. The next year, when Margaret was in a shoe store with her mother, the same friend Alice came in and Margaret noted that "she kissed me when she came in," sufficiently noteworthy for recording in her diary.[37] But in general Margaret Tileston's diary from her years at home was characterized by its laconic understatement.

All that changed, though, with her introduction to Nellie Taft while away at boarding school. When the former student Taft arrived on the train after missing the first semester of the school year, several girls went to greet her, and Margaret Tileston's attention was caught. "She kissed the girls when she arrived," she reported, a simple enough description, but then came the unexpected: "She's a daisy!" A few days later, she demonstrated a similar emotional quickening, revealed in part by her writing of the longest letter she ever wrote (twelve pages) to her mother. The cause of the effusion was clear: her decision that "Nellie Taft is the sweetest girl that ever was,—too sweetly sweet." Tileston concluded, "I love her very much," probably the first use of the word *love* in her multivolume diary. Later she tried out superlatives, not only repeating that Nellie Taft was "too 'sweetly sweet'" and "a daisy" but calling her "a poem," and "quite too consummately utter." When Nellie (perhaps for effect) announced that she was not coming back in the fall, Margaret expressed her first regrets of her long diaries: "That will be dreadful." Over the next few weeks, Margaret's involvement deepened as the two played cards until ten, exchanged good-night kisses, and looked at photographs, having "well, a very interesting talk." Margaret Tileston gave her bunches of hepati-cas—four bunches by April 21.[38]

By May there were signs that perhaps Nellie Taft was tiring of her young conquest. When Tileston was feeling sad at bedtime, at first Nellie would come and comfort her, and call her "Honey." Sometimes they would talk about the world of courtship, Tileston's shorthand suggested. "Talk about dresses parties, this gentleman and that." And there were new endearments, "Baby dear." By the end of the first week of June, though, Nellie Taft was in short supply. Tileston mentioned sobbing miserably after she was in bed. "Nellie didn't come to me or speak to me all day, only kissed me good-night. I don't believe she loves me much. She doesn't take much interest in me, or hardly ever comes to see me in my room." And later, she and her sister were excluded while "all the girls but Mary and I" were feasting and having "a good time in Nellie's room." The morose Tileston lamented, "I never am in things."[39]

Contrary to such harbingers, however, the romantic friendship did not die when both Nellie Taft and Margaret Tileston failed to return to the Prospect Hill School the following year. As they parted they exchanged mementos, and they corresponded over the summer, Margaret topping her record of twelve pages to her mother with sixteen regular pages to Nellie Taft. She mentioned the romantic weather on one day: "weird, wild, wet weather," raining "ram-pagiously much of the day." As Margaret Tileston passed through Lynn on the train headed for the North Shore of Boston that summer, Nellie Taft met her along the route and "gave me some roses." They talked until the train started again. Margaret's sister Mary had also made a special friend at board-ing school, and the sisters shared each other's letters, some acknowledgment of participation in a common culture of romantic friendships. For the next several years, Margaret faithfully remembered Nellie Taft's birthday, a tribute to the emotional reverberation of this schoolgirl "crush."[40]

It is hard to discern the ultimate impact of this intensely emotional and romantic schoolgirl friendship within the life record of a dutiful and other-wise understated young woman. Margaret Tileston largely left this world be-hind when she returned home, and then moved with her family to the town of Salem, where the girls attended Salem High School. With her enrollment at Salem High School, the action of Tileston's journal changed completely, from the intense emotionalism of those months to a competitive academic program, in which Tileston bore down with increasing intensity as she dis-covered her capacity for accomplishment.

It is significant to Smith-Rosenberg's argument, though, that Tileston's relationship with Nellie Taft was a thing quite apart from her life at home with a mother who often seemed hard to please. This clear disjunction within Margaret Tileston's life is particularly noteworthy, because in fact Tileston's mother was, more than most mothers, involved in the propagation of the "cult of domesticity" which Smith-Rosenberg and others see emotionally sustained by a female world inspired by boarding school friendships. Mary Wilder Tileston compiled anthologies of devotional and inspirational poetry and thereby played a key role in describing and honoring what then and now has been known as "woman's sphere." Named and described by ministers and by women writers such as Mary Tileston herself in their writings, that sphere provided the context in which Smith-Rosenberg saw the development of a gendered emotional world.

Despite the claims of literary theorists in past years, however, the power of discourse went only so far. It was not her mother's demands or her mother's language which seemed to open Margaret Tileston to a newly emotive self. Instead, the world of intense schoolgirl friendships supplied a clear counterpoint to the days of obligation she described at home. There were worlds of difference between her own role as a dutiful daughter and the intensely romantic world she briefly inhabited in a ritualized world of love and friendship at school. That the two were not entirely divorced in the mind of the daughter, though, emerges from a surprising juxtaposition. When Margaret Tileston parted with her special friend Nellie Taft, she sought a gift that would be appropriate for the occasion. What she chose was an anthology *Tender and True: Poems of Love,* a gift book designed to be full of feeling. (Nellie responded with three silver pins in a little box.)[41] The editor of this anthology was Margaret's own mother. One might argue that this gift made Smith-Rosenberg's point—that domestic circle and schoolgirl friendship were two halves of one sphere. Evidence in the diary suggests otherwise, though. It suggests a radical transformation in emotional life within the context of an eroticized girls' world. That a mother's book played a role in the confirmation of those relationships might best be noted as provocative irony.

The Curriculum of Female Seminaries and Convent Schools

The intense social connectedness of girls' school life coexisted with a curriculum which was broader than it was deep. The curriculum of most separate female seminaries, boarding schools, and convent schools for girls reflected their ambitions to provide improving education and appropriate ornamentation for young women destined for genteel domestic life. Protestant ladies' seminaries were often run by a minister's wife and her sisters, or by unmarried women of respectable background who formed part of the superfluous population of women in the Northeast in the mid- to late nineteenth century. Girls at such schools as Miss Porter's in Farmington, Connecticut, or the Prospect Hill School in Greenfield, Massachusetts, studied English, Latin, French, history, literature, mathematics, and botany. They also studied music and needlework and often took drawing lessons. (Lily Dana reported back from Farmington that she was learning to darn at Miss Porter's School.[42]) Evenings were often occupied sitting together in the parlor sewing and playing piano for each other.

Convent schools added religious lessons to the curriculum, such that the course of study for St. Joseph's Academy in St. Paul in the 1870s included in its extensive list "religious instruction, orthography, reading, writing, grammar, geography, mathematics, use of globe, prose and poetical composition, sacred and profane history, astronomy, rhetoric, botany, intellectual and natural philosophy, chemistry, bookkeeping, French, German and Latin language; music on pianoforte, melodeon and guitar; vocal music, drawing and painting in oil, water colors and pastille, Plain and Ornamental needlework, tapestry, embroidery, hair and lace work; and the making of artificial fruit and flowers." Historians of Catholic education concur that the lessons of Catholic womanhood in the nineteenth century shared much with the notion of woman's separate and special sphere.[43]

As befit this primary goal, girls' accounts of their days in female seminaries suggest only modest academic pressure with little competition, a deliberate strategy by educators anxious to avoid overtaxing delicate young women. Although competitive practices characterized most schools in the early nineteenth century, teachers in female seminaries appear to have modified this program in deference to concerns about their impact on young women. The historian Nancy Green has documented a lively debate among educators in the 1830s and 1840s about the dangers of "emulation," the competitive practices by which a student was motivated to learn by comparing her performance with that of her fellows. Those teaching girls were some of the earliest critics of such standard educational practices as public recitation, the arrangement of seats according to class rank, and the awarding of prizes to the best students. Writing in 1833, Catharine Beecher proclaimed that such practices might be "good for intellectual development, but bad for moral development," a special concern in educating women. The problem seemed particularly acute in the context of the evolving ideology of spheres, in which girls and women were being encouraged to be everything that boys and men were not. The educator George Emerson, for instance, asked whether teachers really wanted to reward the most aggressive girls with prizes, a practice which "tended to repress the gentle and retiring qualities which are the most beautiful in the female character." He asked rhetorically, "Would the desire of distinction, of surpassing her friends, be the most sure to suggest to a wife the numberless little kindness and attentions so essential to the happiness of a husband?" The debate appears to have had a lasting impact on female seminaries. Catharine Beecher and Emma Willard gave no awards at their seminaries, and many schools for girls deemphasized competition among their scholars through much of the nineteenth century.[44]

Certainly evidence from girls' own records of their seminary experiences suggests a relatively gentle academic regimen without many of the competitive practices which characterized boys' and coeducational grammar and secondary schools. The goal instead seemed to be the teaching of high ideals and steady habits. Agnes Hamilton, distracted from her studies by her social life, reported on one lesson she had learned from a German teacher. "What you wish to be, you are," he told her, and though she initially resisted, she reported that she had later found out "how true it is." This Victorian project of keeping eyes trained on the ideal suggested the methodology and the pedagogy of seminary education. Other parts of the informal curricula had to do with religious observance, appropriate manners, emotional etiquette, and even hairstyles. The example chosen by one teacher in instructing Sally Dana suggests the stress placed on the cultivation of gracious manners. Writing home to her mother, Dana repeated the example that her teacher had used to instruct her. "Last week my fault was rather hard to put on paper but Mrs. G. said that I had improved, this week she gave me as an illustration of what she meant that if one day I should kiss her to[o] hard the next day I would kiss her so that she would hardly know whether I kissed her or not, that I must try to practice moderation."[45] Practicing moderation in kissing suggested exactly the lessons in graceful and winning conduct that the traditional female seminary aspired to for its students.

Occasional parents, with more academic aspirations for their daughters, resisted the relative laxness of academic programs at girls' seminaries. The correspondence of Ralph Waldo Emerson with his daughter Ellen while she was a student at Sedgwick School in the 1850s suggests his interest in her substantive education and his reservations about the sociability of her school companions. He told Ellen of seeing a girl examined who won thirty-seven approbations and urged her on to excellence in her work, setting her the same task. And he instructed her to "find or make an occasion to tell Miss Grace

[Sedgwick] that it is a principal point with you to learn to speak French; and, at all events . . . papa, who knows that no French man or woman ever set foot in Concord, was on the verge of sending you to a convent in Montreal for no other purpose." In particular, Ellen Emerson's august father urged her against too much frivolity, encouraging her to find time and space in her overfull social world for solitary reading and reflection. One letter suggested that he had heard much about school social life: "I am glad you find so much to enjoy in your schoolmates, but you must insist on a fair share of work every day. One good scholar who tasks herself—only for the love and beauty of the thing— with a daily solitude such as a book can make in the thickest crowd, for a measured hour or hours will have followers in a few days, and in a fortnight a fashion." Ellen's dry response to her father's pronouncement suggested the realities of her school life. She noted that there was only one other girl who read substantially and that that girl was "the least liked and followed in the school." After that tart response, she hastened to reassure her father of her respect for him and for learning: "I don't mean to speak against it for I am going to do it and it certainly isn't the reading that makes the girl disliked." Especially when one contrasts with school letters the extensive reading records of girls living at home, however, it is clear that female seminaries more resembled thick crowds than opportunities for the solitude Emerson famously claimed for the true American scholar.[46]

It is true that certain female seminaries set out to provide rigorous training and to correct the deserved reputation set by others of not providing a strenuous or demanding academic curriculum. Catharine Beecher's Hartford Female Seminary opened in 1823 and provided four hours of classes every day and two weeks of exams at the end of term. Yet Beecher aimed to train women for their own sphere and was an early opponent of excessive competition. The efforts of Emma Willard to ensure that her seminary in Troy, New York, offered a serious education in science are legendary. Willard was a compelling educator and inspired her students to take themselves seriously. Yet Willard clothed her ambitions for her students in the language of the spheres, and according to one biographer "closed her mind" to political rights and "did not believe in the same education for boys and girls."[47]

Even a school with perhaps the most luminous faculty in the country produced scarcely different letters home from its young students. Like many educated women in need of money, Elizabeth Cary Agassiz in the 1850s decided to open a school for girls to supplement the family finances. Her husband grew interested in his wife's project and volunteered as a teacher. Louis Agassiz, Harvard's illustrious naturalist, enlisted some of his friends on the Har-

vard faculty to teach as well, long before the opening of Harvard's women's
college. If this brought a sense of intellectual engagement to the school,
though, one would not know it from reading the letters of Nellie Browne
home to her mother in Salem. Ellen Emerson, too, was a student at Agassiz School after her fun-filled years with the Sedgwick mother and sisters
in Lenox, Massachusetts. Although she praised Agassiz's lectures as "invaluable," a "most marked feature," she emphasized other features characteristic of girls' seminaries: "There was a feeling of home which I never had in
any other school—the carpeted rooms and open fires and the being in a private house. Then the crowds of girls, the very best of Boston, so many beau-
ties, so many bright and interesting ones. Then Miss Ida." At girls' seminaries, the refining nurturance of domestic influence and the elevating company
of "the very best" girls and teachers were critical parts of the curriculum.
When the Englishwoman Sara Burstall visited the United States in the 1890s
to report on girls' education, she observed that the rise of social class owed
much to the development of private secondary schools for girls, which she
considered to resemble women's colleges "in their social life, in their atmosphere of culture and refinement, and in the freedom of their discipline." [48]

Elite parents and daughters seemed to share this sense of the greater rigor
but lesser status accompanying public secondary education. Emily Eliot attended Girls' High School in the 1870s while her father was its headmaster.
Writing in her fourth year, she remembered that people thought it "an extraordinary thing" that one from her social background should go to *"Public"*
school. Yet she considered it worthwhile. "They little know what advantages
it has over a private school," she observed, "where the parents rule the teachers and make them do what they want." Despite receiving a "condition" in
astronomy, she announced herself "very sorry to leave school," which she did
at the advanced age of nineteen. [49]

Fifteen years later, public secondary schools had not completely closed the
gap in respectability. Robert Boit was a cash-poor member of the Boston elite,
who left a series of rich and candid diaries about his inner life—including his
marriage and children. In 1891 he commented on his eldest daughter: "Mary
is now 14 and continues to go to the public school in Longwood where she
has continually done well and learned a great deal. Next year I shall feel it
necessary to send her to a good school in town where she will probably learn
less in three years than in one of public school tuition but where on the other
hand she will make friends among her own class with whom she should associate." [50] Here Boit confirms what the diary evidence seems to communicate.
Private boarding schools served social ends, in particular the perpetuation of

class. Public schools, usually coeducational, were more demanding academically than private girls' schools, at least until the turn of the century.

Robert Boit therefore made other plans for his younger daughter, based on his sense of the rigors of public schooling. "She is of a more delicate and sensitive nature than Mary, so I was unwilling to subject her to the difficulties and severe discipline of a public school." Private girls' schools were better choices for "delicate" girls, or girls with health problems. Similar concerns encouraged John Tileston to withdraw his daughters from the local public school to send them to boarding school. In the summer of 1881 John Tileston was debating what to do for the education of his thirteen- and fourteen-year-old daughters. His eldest daughter had been sickly and had missed a good bit of school the previous year in family efforts to bring her back to health. He first announced that he would keep his girls home from school in the afternoon, but three weeks later he changed plans, announcing instead his decision for boarding school.[51] In Tileston's case, boarding school represented a compromise similar to the compromise of sending his daughters to school for half-days. Perhaps the wholesome and gentle environment of a boarding school might restore his daughter to health.

Coeducation and Competition

If girls' private schools encouraged an intimate atmosphere of nurture, sociability, and fun, much coeducational public schooling retained its competitive practices and was more challenging. Opponents of coeducation argued that the presence of girls feminized and compromised the secondary curriculum. But evidence suggests the contrary: that expectations of male achievement raised the stakes and the competition for girls. As it was put in an 1841 article in *Ladies' Repository,* in many young ladies' seminaries "the girl is excused of strict scholarship. . . . She works to disadvantage. The mind *itself* has not been educated." In contrast to girls educated at such "finishing schools," the author argued, "see here and there is one who, we *may* say, *has been educated*—who has *studied* like a boy" and you will see "equality of attainment with any male youth of like years and pursuit." Encouraging a girl to study "like a boy" was seldom the goal of the citizens who sponsored secondary schools; coeducational secondary schools which taught ostensibly parallel classes for boys and girls did not always deliver classes of like intensity to both. And sometimes, especially in the earlier days, there were different requirements for girls and boys. (A letter from one rural Massachusetts girl to a friend at midcentury reported, "We have to write compositions every other week but the boys have to write Compositions one week and Declaim the next so you see they have a pretty hard task to accomplish to what the girls do.")[52] Public schools sometimes attempted to soften lessons for girls so as to address the concerns raised by the debate over emulation. Nonetheless, in comparison, the point seems indisputable. Girls studying in coeducational secondary schools were more likely to participate in a competitive and meritocratic form of schooling which rewarded and encouraged individual achievement among both girls and boys. Such schools published class rank and scheduled public exhibitions. Evidence from the few coeducational private boarding schools suggests that this might have been the case for both public and private, day and boarding schools.

Coeducation in practice in the nineteenth century included various arrangements governing the schooling of girls and boys together and apart. The word itself was of American origin and set up an implicit contrast with the tradition of same-sex schooling in Great Britain and in many parts of the American Northeast and South. Common grammar schools united boys and girls in the same classes under the same roofs, and many secondary schools adopted a similar model. Yet the "coeducating" of boys and girls in secondary schools, and sometimes even in grammar schools, generally involved some separation of boys and girls, by administrative order. As we have seen, some high schools, particularly in the Northeast, went so far as to conduct parallel classes for girls and boys, using gender as a principle for dividing students into different sections for as long as they could. Gradually, however, throughout the country, school districts bowed to economic realities and chose to educate their boys and girls together, offering a common curriculum and a common standard for success.

For those attending the new public high schools, which became increasingly common in the Northeast at midcentury, coeducational schooling meant attending schools which enrolled more girls than boys. The actual ratio varied from school to school. Where the public high school served as a college preparatory school for the affluent native-born, the numbers of boys tended to increase. In less affluent or immigrant communities, boys instead would leave school to take jobs, and high schools would sometimes graduate two or even three girls for every boy. The underattendance of boys at high schools was a cause of regular lament by all, including girl students who were left without escorts after school social functions. Yet it presents the historian of gender with some interesting questions. Some of them are simply statistical. Did girls excel and win honors proportionate to their greater attendance at high school? Did they excel at greater rates than the statistics might predict? And if so, why?

Girls and boys attending public high schools shared a liberal curriculum, competition, and grades. Unlike female seminaries and convent schools, which taught ornamental and domestic arts alongside more traditional liberal studies, the public high school at midcentury and after did not offer a gendered curriculum. Instead, it taught a classical or liberal curriculum, rich in history, moral philosophy, mathematics, Latin, Greek, and French. Botany, chemistry, and physical sciences were also often taught. Girls and boys took these classes either together or in separate tracks, a significant commonality in a world otherwise stratified by gender.[53]

Increasingly toward the end of the century, citizens and educators came to question the usefulness of this classical learning to boys and girls attempting to make their way in the working world. And when high schools responded, they brought the gender segmentation of the workforce into school. Commercial subjects supplemented liberal studies, and educators provided manual training and home economics to prepare boys and girls for the future. Even then, though, high schools retained an important core of liberal studies, which established common ground between boys and girls, as well as across classes. In high schools, girls and boys studied together and competed to master abstract subject matter which neither sex could lay special claim to. In studying North Carolina's African-American community in the 1890s, Glenda Gilmore has noted the significance of its leaders' dissent from the Tuskegee program of agricultural education and manual training advanced by Booker T. Washington. She sees their defense of a classical curriculum for the children and grandchildren of slaves as significant resistance to attempts to create a separate caste in this country under Jim Crow. Classical education was similarly important for girls, for it offered a common ground on which to compete and succeed beyond the hierarchy of gender.[54]

The practice of recitation, saying one's lessons orally, was not initially designed as a competitive practice. It was simply the most convenient way to test rote memory, the common style of teaching and learning in most grammar schools in the nineteenth century. Yet recitation meant that all would know when a student succeeded, and when one failed. More deliberate was the spelling bee, a competition that was both a game and a pedagogy. Some schools held public examinations, which elevated the pressure to "know one's lessons" to a higher degree. Almost all schools scheduled exhibition days in which students read or recited pieces to the general public and received awards. (In fact, the decision of the cloistered convent schools to bar the public from the awarding of prizes in the mid–nineteenth century was a cause of conflict with parents.)[55]

6.5 Latin class, 1900. Girls and boys competed together in coeducational classrooms, as in this Latin class taught by Miss Edith Walker at Concord (New Hampshire) High School. (The Greek was left on the board from a previous class.) New Hampshire Historical Society.

The consequences of such a system for teenage girl students, as for boy students, were that strong students thrived while weak ones foundered. This is an obvious result, of course. Yet in the world of Victorian gender relations, what is significant is that girls and boys were playing fundamentally the same game, both competing in the rough meritocracy that such competition encouraged. At least initially and sometimes later as well, they were not equally comfortable with that competition: domestic culture discouraged self-promotion in girls, and successful girls were sometimes abashed and embarrassed. Sometimes, too, parents did not notice, honor, or encourage girls' school accomplishments. (Elizabeth Cady's memory of her father's failure to celebrate her Greek prize is only one example.) But within the universe of the schoolroom and at schoolwide ceremonies (neither insignificant for a peer-based social world), girl scholars were encouraged and rewarded for achievement—for scoring high, for spelling well, for accomplishments of both mind and habit. They felt the sweet rewards of victory in conquering rivals, earning respect, and taking as prizes a seat at the front of the room. These school rules made the institution unique within a woman's life as it extended from cradle to grave. Not in the family or the workplace or the halls of government did females and males share so similar an experience. Even within the church, where souls were ungendered, women did not preach, sit as deacons, or otherwise live out their identities as equal competitors for eternity. Co-educational grammar and secondary schools made all kinds of distinctions, and even those who encouraged girls to compete might in the same breath warn against it. Yet medals were awarded and reputations made in coeducational high schools. Of all the unequal institutions, such schools were the least unequal, and thus must stand as both an important harbinger of the future and a transformer, gradually, of their present.[56]

Academics and Deportment

Girls outnumbered boys in school. Barring other factors skewing accomplishments, girls could thus be expected to outnumber boys on the honor rolls. All things being equal, girls should have been salutatorians and valedictorians and honor-roll students in percentages similar to their representation in the class. In fact, though, girls tended to do better proportionately than boys. Statistics on one school, the high school of Milford, Massachusetts, reveal that between 1884 and 1900 girls represented 64 percent of graduates, a ratio of nearly two to one. But girls accounted for nearly three-quarters of those graduating in the top ten places during the late century. When valedictorians and salutatorians were designated, beginning in 1889, 86 percent of those so honored through the next decade were girls.[57]

Girls' tendency to dominate the academic ratings was an accepted part of the school's culture and can undoubtedly be explained in part by Milford's policy, probably followed by many other schools as well, of granting honors on the basis of scholarship and deportment together. Deportment grades measured decorum and tractability; both by socialization and reputation, girls could be counted on to turn in higher performances. Usually there were a few male standouts, but sometimes it was a clean sweep. In the class of 1887 at Milford, for example, boys were completely eclipsed. The class began with an equal number of boys and girls, thirty-one each. By the end of the four-year span, though, the numbers had been dramatically reduced to twelve girls and five boys. The student newspaper announced: "The girls claim the first ten in scholarship *and* deportment. In attendance three girls are perfect and in deportment eight; of these, two have the honor of being perfect in both." The article ended by noting, "These are facts of which they may well feel proud."[58] The reference here is a bit unclear. Perhaps it was referring to the individual girls who had triumphed, each of whom should feel proud. But a more plausible reference is to girls of the class as a group, all of whom, the article suggests, might take pride in their sex's collective sweep of graduation honors.

How much of girls' success can be attributed to their greater skill at achieving perfect conduct? For girls, for whom "being good" was a high priority, school offered any number of ways to fulfill that mandate. If being "perfect" simply required getting to school every day, or behaving once in school, it was certainly doable—a gratifyingly concrete measure for an otherwise elusive moral status.

Almyra Hubbard, a schoolgirl diarist in Hayesville, New Hampshire, wrote in 1859 of her discovery of this back door to school achievement. She knew that she worked hard; her journal, a school assignment itself written faithfully in a careful hand, indicates as much. Yet she did not get top grades and did not seem to be one of the handful of students she mentioned in February who would need to draw to see who got the first seat in the class. She could, however, make sure she got to class—a trip that took her an hour and a half when she walked it—and she seized upon this route to class honor. One day, she wrote in her journal, "There are but few scholars here this afternoon. The room is quite still." The quietness was not just a result of how many were there, but who was there: "As a general thing the noisy ones do not venture out in unpleasant weather." Almyra Hubbard was both quiet and present, even when her classmates were fair-weather scholars. When she attended her great-uncle's funeral in April, it was the first time she had missed school in a year and a half. In May the school principal adopted a new rule which advantaged Hubbard, "by which any one who is absent cannot make up her lessons." She imagined, "It will cause some of the girls to be a little more regular in their attendance at school." One key component of school success, as Almyra Hubbard had discovered early, was simply the ability to meet school demands for the regular habits of industrial discipline. Girls outdid boys in this arena so regularly that when the Milford paper in 1890 reported on two students with perfect attendance throughout their high school careers, it featured what was newsworthy: "Wonderful to relate, one is a boy!"[59]

Not all girls had stellar grades in deportment. A consistent problem for boy and girl students both was "communication." Students in many schools were forbidden to talk among themselves between classes and expected to be quiet most other times, an expectation which few could meet. The entire first-year class at Milford High School in 1865 was called to the teacher's desk and scolded so that they nearly all cried, Annie Roberts Godfrey reported. Godfrey was in the second-year class, and was also called up, where she "acknowledged that I had communicated but would try to improve. I did not cry." The next year, though, Godfrey's problems with communication meant that her deportment grade was very low—"only 78, lowest in school, I fear." We have no records for how Godfrey fared at graduation, but clearly convent schools were not alone in attempting to impose serious constraints on student sociability during school itself. It was an innovation in 1894 when Salem High School instituted a "whispering recess," which allowed students to talk softly between classes.[60]

Boys were initially more comfortable with certain kinds of head-on competition, which gave them one kind of advantage within the nineteenth-century high school. But girls tended to have better "school skills," especially when deportment and attendance were factored into class rank. Rapidly, success at school turned girls into ardent and delighted competitors who were engaged and then transformed by the process. The diaries of winners in the competition of school suggest the power of that experience.

Competition and the Thrill of Winning

Competition was built into the pedagogy and the most gripping practices of nineteenth-century schools. Cassie Upson's diary is especially valuable in documenting classroom life, because she brought the book to school daily and seems to have amused herself writing in it when she had free time (and

even when she didn't) during the school day. While living first in the rural
community of Charlemont, Massachusetts, and then in Milwaukee in the
1860s, Cassie Upson described a variety of school experiences in which students demonstrated their learning through public display. "Today we choose
up sides and speak pieces," she wrote about one day in Charlemont. "I should
like to stand up the longest but don't know as I can." The next year in Milwaukee she mentioned three separate exercises in one day in which she could
show off her knowledge. "Spoke pieces and read compositions my composition was 'History of a pin' we spelled down and of course I stood up longest
Its my private opinion that there are not more than ten decent spellers in
Milwaukee." On another occasion, she expressed her contempt for the performance of other scholars. "I never shall forget how they spelled danger darn-
jur. picture picksure. and city sytie. One of them compared good. good . . .
gooder, goodest." Under such circumstances, it was not surprising that Cassie
Upson, champion speller (if indifferent master of punctuation), "Had a good
time." Examinations, too, were sometimes public and provided entertainment
in rural communities. In July, Upson reported, "Went to the examination of
the upper school this afternoon very good." She was less sanguine, however,
when the examination was her own. Writing clandestinely in school (as she
often did), she gave an up-to-the-minute report on public examinations in
her Milwaukee school when she was fifteen: "Three hours more and I shall
be up on the stage on which are now mounted the sub-juniors in arithmetic
doing horridly too, failing downright. I expect I shall do just so. I am sorry
for Lou. Jeannie is at the board. . . . How I *dread* this afternoon. I know I
shall fail."[61] Generally, though, Cassie Upson did not fail, and loved school
because of the chances it gave her triumphantly and publicly to vanquish the
opposition.

Of course, school competition was exciting and dramatic for strong students precisely because they could imagine failing. In a rural school in Iowa
in the 1860s, sixteen-year-old Sarah Jane Kimball was drafted to bring down a
cocky classmate. Kimball didn't expect to better John Niles, the "brag speller,"
she confessed to her diary, but "as luck would have it," she spelled him down
twice. "Our crowd cheered for me," she reported, admitting only that "I
felt pretty well." Despite the confidence of her classmates, Kimball had self-
doubts, which might loom especially large when confirmed by friends or parents. On the first day of school when she was fourteen, Mary Boit confessed
herself "dreadfully scared as I know I will get about 0 in my studies they
will be so hard and so much home work to do." Later in the month her class
started English history "and I cant stuff it into my head. . . . I have read

a chapter in two books over and over again and I cant get it through my stupid brain." In another entry, Mary Boit revealed part of what upset her about the competition of school. After lamenting the Latin that she could "never stuff . . . into my brain," she noted "I hope I will be decent and good this year in school. I do hope I will get a good seat in the other building." Robert Boit did not always respect his daughter's intellect, penning colorful doggerel which might encourage her self-doubts. ("So what is the use of her trying to learn/ Better put her to wash or to cook or to churn.") Yet public coeducational school gave his daughter an opportunity to prove him wrong. When she began in public school, he reported to his "surprise and pleasure" that Mary was at the top of her class of "40 boys and girls." [62] Coeducational competition seemed to be good for his daughter, who "for the first time," he reported, "seems to have had her ambition aroused." With her own self-doubts reinforced by the bantering of her father, it is no wonder that Mary invested the energy in a competition she could win for a seat at the top of the class.

Some girls' diaries report on grades and class rank with the same kind of thoroughness which farm diarists might give to the weather, or business diaries to accounts. Jessie Wendover was one such grade accountant. Her first year of school, when she was twelve, she listed her grades, the mediocre marks of a child behind her classmates (76 percent in history, 86 percent in grammar, 67 percent in arithmetic). Jessie Wendover dropped out the following spring after an illness and repeated the year in 1886. Her natural abilities were enhanced by the gain in repeating her studies, and she began to report the grades of a contender for top seat. At the end of the first month back, she reported that seats had been changed, and the class was reseated according to averages in scholarship and deportment. "Mine was 97 1/4, which gave me the third seat with Florence whose average was 95. I like her for a seat mate very much and like the place where my seat is also." Two months later, she could report another change in seats. "My average was 99 3/25, and I am number one. I sit with Maggie Nichols again, only of course she has the second seat now." [63] Jessie Wendover and three or four other girls traded top seats over the next several years based on differences of half a point or so in their grade-point averages. A late arrival in school due to her frailty, Jessie Wendover was hooked by the gratification of grades as rewards and became a zealous and devoted competitor.

Competition among students for grades and prizes became especially significant in coeducational classes. With girls constituting the clear majority in almost all public high schools, it stood to reason that they would capture the lion's share of end-of-term prizes. The historian John Rury, who has studied a number of high schools in the Midwest and West, where classrooms were coeducational from the beginning, found evidence of just such a pattern. In Denver in the mid-1880s, boys won the prize for the best essay in history for the first two years it was awarded, and girls won the next six years. In Cincinnati during six years in the 1870s, girls won the prize for excellence in mathematics four times, while boys won twice. Shortly thereafter, Cincinnati instituted separate prizes for boys and girls.[64] The awarding of separate prizes to boys and girls represented one of the ways that the schools responded to the embarrassment that such lopsided achievement might bring.

Margaret Tileston and Competition

The diaries of Margaret Tileston, who had been swept into the vortex of sentiment circulating through a Massachusetts girls' school, suggest some of the ways that the competition of coeducational high schools might reorient a talented girl scholar. At the girls' boarding school Tileston attended with her sister, her diary had scarcely mentioned studies at all, instead documenting an intensely emotional world of smashes and intimacies. The Tileston girls spent only one year at Prospect Hill School; their family had moved to Salem in the interim so their children could avail themselves of better public educational opportunities there. In November 1882 Margaret and Mary Tileston began to take classes at Salem High School. There Margaret Tileston metamorphosed into an ambitious, competitive, and triumphant scholar.

As befit its early founding, Salem High School aspired to educate its boy and girl students separately. When the Tileston girls attended Salem in 1882, in theory they were initially enrolled in all-female classes. At the beginning, presumably ill-prepared by Prospect Hill, Margaret Tileston foundered even in the girls' classes, reporting frequent discouragement with her studies. "I dont' learn Greek very well, nor do anything well," she reported a month later. She had reported grades of 100 percent on her Latin at Prospect Hill, but at Salem High, she appeared to be struggling in Latin, too. Gradually, though, Tileston rose to the challenge. Five months into her high school career, she was chafing at the reduced expectations of the girls' classes. "Miss Gray said that the boys were ahead of us girls in Caesar," she reported. "I should like to go as fast as the boys do, and I think I could."[65]

Increasingly Margaret Tileston gained the opportunity to test that presumption. As a college-bound young woman, Tileston occasionally found herself in classes with the boys. She and her sister took geometry and had something in common that summer with a boy they met while getting ready to go out for a boat ride. "He asked Mary what she had in Geometry," she noted, a classic exchange in the high school dialogue across gender lines. Another boy pushed the boat off.[66]

There were only three girls in the geometry class, presumably too few to run a separate class. But the next year the high school principal drew Tileston and another girl aside to tell them "that if [they] had any thought of going to college," they should join the boys in sight-translation in Latin. Tileston at first received separate treatment in her classes with the boys. Her first class she sat by herself, and the teacher didn't call on her. The next class, he called on her, but she did not know all her words, while "some of the boys translated very well." She noted in her diary, "I studied quite a while in the evening. I always do now."[67] Her studying began to pay off, and Tileston began a surge which would carry her through commencement.

Although the principal encouraged her in her course selection, the head teacher of the young ladies, Susan Osgood, was not so enthusiastic. As the head of the Girl's Hall, as it was then called, Susan Osgood had on the first day of school the previous fall instructed her scholars about "what we came to school for, manners, morals, and other subjects," a vestige of the ideology of separate girls' education in the high school. That day also, Tileston learned that the girls would have the second-best Latin teacher. "Of course the boys, particularly the college boys must have everything of the best." When Tileston asked about taking ancient history, "Miss O. talked to me . . . about how it was especially for the college boys etc, though she didn't doubt I should be an ornament to the class."[68] The use of the stereotypical language of femininity to refer to Tileston's role in class suggested at least some ambivalence on Susan Osgood's part about Tileston's trajectory. The reservations of Osgood, though, were a minor theme in Tileston's snowballing successes.

Initially inhibited in her coeducational classes, Tileston began to enjoy them—and her competitive advantages over male classmates. On one disastrous day for the rest of the class, Tileston noted that everyone else was failing. As for Tileston, "It really amused me to see 3 or 4 boys in succession shake their heads when called on," she reported. The next month, when her class was scolded for doing badly, Tileston checked in with the principal, who said that his remarks applied only to the young gentlemen, not to the young ladies, "who, he heard, had done excellently well." She reported one sight translation in Latin class. "'The girls of this school have become learned.' Filiae!" and true it was.[69] After a difficult beginning at high school, Margaret Tileston was feeling better.

Despite her accomplishments, Margaret Tileston did not lose her gendered identity in the high school. When she arrived in July to hear about classes for the next year and found no girls there, she retreated to the girls' dressing room. And the next year, when the Latin prose class started, she didn't hear about it until a day later: "Miss Porter and I, being only *girls,* were forgotten." She still sometimes got excused from coming after school when her classmates were unruly, and one time when she and another girl arrived at class, the door was locked, and "the boys all laughed when we came in."[70]

But the teasing accompanied a growing respect. Although one Latin teacher forgot her and spared her detention, another began to give her the same rough treatment he accorded the boys. ("Mr. Goodrich made the girls change their seats, and spoke very roughly.") And the boys she shared classes with themselves began to acknowledge her preeminence. They asked to know her year's average, and they surreptitiously checked out her grade on a Greek test. (After getting 100, Tileston reported, "Some of the boys saw my mark.") When she found that she had made an error on a test her final year of high school, one boy seemed happy to remind her that she wouldn't have a perfect score this time. Sometimes, though, the acclaim was more positive. When she jotted a verse on the blackboard for her friend's eye, a male classmate complimented her by saying "that he thought I could write a poem, or essay."[71] Margaret Tileston's public high school experience demonstrated the kind of meritocracy which might give a talented and ambitious girl a chance to work hard and triumph even within a highly gendered universe. For strong girl students like her, high school offered a chance to take oneself seriously. Although always aware that she was a girl, as a girl she dominated the competition, and enjoyed the rewards of the victor.

Of course, the reservations of the head of the Girls' Hall and the conditional support of the principal, who encouraged Tileston's course selection of ancient history "if I did well in it!" remind us that Tileston was going against the grain. For Tileston, though, the glass was half-full, full enough so that the school responded to her ambition by giving her a chance to demonstrate her talents. A student who had to push harder was Anna Julia Haywood [Cooper], a black girl studying in the South in a coeducational freedman's school, St. Augustine's Normal and Collegiate Institute. She wrote eloquently about her sense of injustice at the differential encouragement given to boys and the forsaking of talented girls like herself, who felt "(as I suppose many an ambitious girl has felt) a thumping from within unanswered by any beckoning from without." In contrast, "A boy, however meager his equipment and shallow his pretensions, had only to declare a floating intention to study theology and he could get all the support, encouragement and stimulus he needed. . . .

A self-supporting girl had to struggle . . . against positive encouragements." Even so, the historian Glenda Gilmore argues, coeducational St. Augustine must get some credit for Anna Julia Haywood Cooper's awakening, and for finally allowing her into the Greek class to which she sought entrance. As Gilmore puts it, the concept of gender equality was "a visionary proposition that Cooper could articulate only because she had caught a glimpse of men's opportunities. Coeducation gave her a chance to peek into their lives."[72] If the glass was nearly half-full for Haywood, then, it was easily half-full for girls like Margaret Tileston in the coeducational high schools of the late century, where girls' talent encouraged the rewriting of premises about what girls could and should study.

Katharine Busbey, a commentator writing in 1910, observed the consequences of this public coeducation. It did not necessarily produce the most poised young woman, as did the female seminary, with its emphasis on appropriate manners. However, "in the classroom the average American girl is serious; and here the really good features of co-education are demonstrated in the sex-rivalry and sex-pride as spurs to excellence. It is not what might be called 'polite' education, an education that is available for social parade; but the American girl is obliged, by the very processes of our universal public education, to be more thoroughly grounded than she likes to appear."[73] Coeducation did indeed seem to have inspired girls to compete and to have grounded them in knowledge and competence. In the nineteenth century, too, before the backlash against girls' dominance of the high schools, girls such as Margaret Tileston even seemed to enjoy their preeminence.

Failure

Of course if some students jockeyed for top seat in the classroom, others struggled to avoid the last seat, a palpable and permanent humiliation in the meritocratic classroom.[74] Jessie Wendover, who lingered so lovingly over the grade-point averages of herself and her competitors, also provided indirect evidence of the experience at the back of the class. That same successful fall, when Wendover came into her own as a standout student, she reported one day that the teacher had asked her to explain an algebra problem to a weak student, "and to go and sit with her in the back seat to do it. I did not want to go a bit and the girls had lots of fun over it."[75] Jessie Wendover's resistance to leaving her seat in the front to help a confused student at the bottom of the class suggested the strength of some of the distinctions peers made among themselves. The "lots of fun" was clearly meant to be at Wendover's expense; such humor for Wendover meant humiliation for the needy student, though, and likely added insult to the omnipresent sense of injury that must have resulted from a regular seat in the back of the room. The system of inscribing academic rank in the very layout of the classroom, no matter how slight the variation in grade point, communicated a hierarchy of merit which characterized and pressured most schoolrooms in coeducational schools in nineteenth-century America and created clear winners and losers.

Humiliation was an everyday possibility, but there were greater consequences at some moments which determined whether students could go on to the next grade or enter high school. Out and out failure was of course the ultimate penalty which reminded students of the stakes in their school work. Lily Dana reported the anxious atmosphere which characterized entrance examinations to the public high school in Cambridge in 1862. Lily herself was a high school student when her younger sister Rosa took the entrance examination. "She burst into tears as soon as she saw mother, so we knew that she had failed on her examination for entering. She cried the whole evening and shut herself up in the bath room, but at last she ate some supper and went to bed. She was quite sick in the night." The atmosphere at Rosa's grammar school was fraught, with teachers as well as students succumbing to the pressure. One teacher, who had been feverish the night before, fainted in school, Rosa reported, because she "had done too much." Another teacher "cried when she heard that two of her scholars had failed, the first two she had ever had rejected." Just before her graduation from high school, Jessie Wendover described the dolorous atmosphere among her classmates who had not done well. "It is quite an ordinary thing to see a senior weeping with a crowd of the other seniors about her."[76] In fact, the emotion which girls expressed over failure in school helped to fuel the argument that advanced academic programs were too stressful for female constitutions.

Health

Both winners and losers felt the stress of a system which operated at such odds with more conventional domestic ideologies of gender. One way that these conflicts were expressed was internally, within the body, as challenges to girls' health. In these days before antibiotics and the passage of compulsory education laws, school attendance was always conditional. Decisions to send girls to school might have had much to recommend them; school structured girls' time and promised to improve it. But embedded within the orderly discipline of school attendance was a maverick element which could arise at any time to subvert such plans. Sickness, either the kind that could strike anyone in the bacterial-infested world of the nineteenth century or the chronic

"unwellness" which was thought to make adolescent girls especially susceptible to the stresses and strains of modern life, could cause girls to leave school
and go home. Such fears kept some girls from coming to school in the first
place. And they caused some girls to doubt their abilities to succeed at the demanding schedule of a secondary course. A girl's health hovered as a perpetual
question mark bracketing her studies.

The most common source of remonstrance was a concern about eyes and
eyesight. Girls often complained of pained eyes, and parents cautioned against
overstraining them. In an age of proliferating print and only gradual improvements in lighting, eyestrain could strike anyone. Alcott's *Eight Cousins* gave
the problem to an incautious boy whose studies would be interrupted for several years because of his bad habits. Her heroine, a sickly girl, scolds Mac:
"'Now, Mac, listen to me. . . . You know you have hurt your eyes reading by
firelight and in the dusk, and sitting up late, and now you'll have to pay for
it; the doctor said so. You must be careful, and do as he tells you, or you will
be—blind.'" The nonfictional high school student Annie Roberts Godfrey
dropped out of school for several weeks on account of her eyes in the 1860s,
returning in part because of her terrible boredom. Youth magazines reinforced
parental dictates to encourage students to protect their eyes. One concerned
father, Ralph Waldo Emerson, who at other times urged his daughter on in
her studies, struck a common note of alarm when he heard that her eyes were
troubling her, commanding her not to "read, or, much less, write a line, in the
evening" and to "strike off all your letters." Diary writers gave every indication that they had heard parental admonitions, either by their compliance—
"I should have been reading if my eyes hadn't ached so"—or by their rebellion—"being a sinner I calmly disobey my absent parents and sit and write
when my eyes are hurting like fun."[77]

The route from aching eyes to an aching head was direct. Girls who suffered from red and watery eyes almost always also suffered from pounding
heads. Annie Winsor, for instance, whose writings document problems with
chronic headache, gained some relief when a doctor prescribed glasses. She
wrote to her mother: "My spectacles are a great relief to my eyes. Isn't that
good. They particularly make a difference when my eyes grow a little tired—
just as Dr. J. said they would. My eyes have been used in the evening steadily,
but they haven't ached or looked red in the morning at all." She fell short
of pronouncing a complete cure, however, noting only that "my head isn't
better but it is prevented from getting worse at times." The incompleteness
of Winsor's cure was the result of the numerous other causes of headache.[78]
Girls and their parents both recognized that girls were prone to get headaches

just from the stress and strain of their lives. In popular accounting, this stress included a number of components: the natural pressures of modern, urban life; the physical challenge of schoolwork; and finally, the demands of maturing bodies as they passed through puberty on their way to adult womanhood. It was not clear to everyone at this time that maturing girls could withstand a challenging and competitive academic program.

Elite commentators agreed that modern life could be overstimulating and draining on anyone's system, but especially on the lives of the overprivileged, whether adults or children. Headaches appeared in a *St. Nicholas* story about a children's party, where "there is to be a fine supper set out, and a great deal of gas lighted, and a great deal of heat. The children are to stay late, and one of you will be needed to go home with every child, and remain with it all day tomorrow." An 1896 article in *Ladies' Home Journal* on "Headaches: Causes and Cures" applied the analysis to the overcivilized adult. Headache was "a state of general debility or nervousness, brought about by overwork, over study, carelessness or a sedentary life." The *Journal* noted a range of specific precipitating factors: strained vision, the abuse of tea or coffee, heavy hair, too many hairpins, cold or overheated rooms, bad posture, "poor blood and unsteady circulation; sleeplessness, and general dullness from lack of an object in life."[79] Many of these causes echo the list of precipitating causes for the adult malady of "neurasthenia." The richness of modern life itself could bring on chronic headache in overindulged children and in overcivilized adults, many of whom were women.

For schoolgirls the cause could be more immediate; sometimes schoolwork was hard and kept girls up late. The southern diarist Martha Moore, starting at a girl's school in occupied New Orleans during the Civil War, found her course extremely challenging and complained of frequent headaches as a result. One day she had a rhetoric assignment of nineteen pages to learn, as well as work in French and a writing assignment. After working late into the night, she rose early to complete her work. "But when morning came and I awoke I had such a headache that I could hardly see, and it was so painful by schooltime that I thought I had better not attempt to go to school, as I knew from experience, that studying would only make it a great deal worse."[80] Martha Moore's headache was exactly the kind of complaint that confirmed critics in their convictions that girls could not and should not endure demanding academic programs.

But it was not just the duress of hours of evening lessons which could set a girl's head to throbbing. Like neurasthenia, headaches had a psychosomatic component. Headaches could result not just from straining the eyes but from

worrying the entire system. Girls were especially susceptible to headache—
and to a range of other maladies—as a result of both their sex and their age.
Girls were taught, and many of them believed, that their ailments were the
result of a special sex-linked propensity to "nerves." The diagnosis of "nerves"
had been common for women throughout much of the nineteenth century.
In 1873, when Georgia Mercer was twenty, her family called a doctor, fearful
that she had heart trouble. She was greatly relieved when the doctor listened
to her heartbeat and proclaimed it "perfectly healthy and regular" and her
malady "nothing serious." He left her with a prescription "to strengthen my
nerves which he says have been too much taxed and which cause me all my
trouble."[81] As more and more girls went to school, doctors, educators, and
parents—and as a result girls themselves—worried more and more about the
ability of their nerves to withstand the pressures.

Throughout the late nineteenth century, professional concerns mounted.
A succession of articles in both professional journals and the popular press
raised questions about the demands of modern life, particularly as they were
imposed on schoolgirls. Elizabeth Blackwell had broached the topic at midcentury, arguing the injurious impact of excessive mindwork on young, maturing female bodies, exacerbated by the "emulation" of a large school. For
the rest of the century, a succession of commentators took up the question.
Addressing "Needs in American Education" for the professional journal *Education,* Eva Kellogg asked, "Is the hurried, anxious look upon the faces of our
school-girls, the easy exhaustion, frequent school absences from illness, but
the visitation of past excesses in nervous expenditure 'upon the third or fourth
generation.'" Observing girls in the Boston system between the ages of twelve
and sixteen, another educator observed that just as they hit a growth spurt,
"their studies are increased in amount, and they cease to romp freely. They
grow up slim, round-shouldered, and occasionally twisted." E. H. Clarke's
Sex in Education (1874), which achieved near notoriety within second-wave
feminism for its attack on collegiate education for young women, was quite in
keeping with much contemporary thinking when it raised questions about the
healthfulness of a further intensification of the academic program for women
in college courses.[82]

For at the root of such concern was a conviction that the demands of reproduction on a woman's body were such that as a girl entered menarche she
could not expect to do much more than let her body mature—certainly not
as much as boys. The advice giver Mary Virginia Terhune, who in many ways
championed female capability, nonetheless adopted this perspective when she
quoted the writer Mary E. Beedy on "Girls and Women in England and

America": "So long as girls require from one hour and a half to three hours a day to be, or to develop themselves into the conventional girl, and boys require only about one-third of that time to get themselves up into the conventional pattern for a boy, girls must either be superior to boys to begin with, or they must economize their power better if they are able to do as much school-work in a year as boys." Where this timetable came from is difficult to conjure. Nonetheless, with the female chauvinist Terhune acknowledging that girls would need to be more efficient than boys if they were to accomplish as much, it is not surprising to see G. Stanley Hall in *Adolescence* later explaining that girls could learn as much as boys only at a risk too great to take. Hall only followed several generations of medical opinion in encouraging teachers and others to take the initiative in excusing girls from their tasks, even urging them to "command it without request." When the Englishwoman Sara Burstall visited the United States late in the century, she was struck by the special solicitude of American teachers for their girl students.[83]

Many scholars have commented on the extent to which Victorians seemed to identify illness with an idealized femininity. (The literary historian Anne MacLeod, for instance, notes that in Alcott's *Jack and Jill* "the message is unmistakable; the characteristics of a permanent invalid making the best of her lot are a useful example for all women.") Writing about girlhood at the end of the Victorian era, Hall summed up that line of thinking when he noted that because "reproduction, the deepest secret of animate nature," plays such a large role in the life of a woman, illness too characterizes her life.[84] Ample medical opinion encouraged girls to doubt their own strength and capability and to imagine that puberty in fact introduced them to a regimen of illness.

Their language would suggest as much. As we have seen, girls used the language of sickness throughout the nineteenth century to describe their menstrual periods. Thus when Sally Dana in 1857 wrote to her mother about a sprained foot, she explained her general health in this way: "My health is very good better than it has been for some time I don't have so many little pains, — short breath and if it was not for one thing I should think that I was wholly well (that is being unwell) I went to the doctors two weeks ago and he gave me some medicine but it has not taken effect yet — I do feel very well — and I love to study now I think."[85] That one thing — "that is being unwell" — which kept Dana from being "wholly" well was probably her menstrual period; she had presumably requested some medicine for cramps or irregularity, which when taken might adjust how she felt — "generally very well" — without changing her regular condition occasionally "of being unwell."

Girls might pick up the language of strength and frailty to refer not to routine "unwellness" but to particular assaults on their nerves. Agnes Garrison during summer vacation used this language to describe her fatigue after a fun-filled few days at a seaside resort with friends. She concluded, "I have been doing too much lately I fear, for this morning I collapsed utterly and spent the whole day on the bed. I was so sorry to miss the church, but had to give it up." If high-spirited play could bring about collapse and get one excused from church, so, certainly, could hard work. Girls picked up the message about the dangers of overstudy from stories in youth magazines with titles like "Precocious Girls," in which overstudious girls were depicted with wasting diseases, without husbands, with incurable coughs, dying at nineteen. When actually back at school in the fall, Garrison, who had collapsed after too much play, reported one of her "spells" which brought her a "miserable headache," so she had to leave her "lessons in the lurch again." When Marian Nichols announced her first day at a new school, at the age of eleven, she might well have been surprised to discover, as she did, that she had "stood it pretty well."[86]

Jessie Wendover: Sickness and Schooling

With the uncertainty surrounding girls' ability to withstand the challenges of schooling, it is not surprising to find illness a significant theme in some schoolgirl diaries. The language of health and sickness covered a spectrum of conditions, ranging from life-threatening infections and viruses to fatigue and anxiety. The daily diary of Jessie Wendover, star student and daughter of a New Jersey grocer, has already appeared as the record of an eager competitor and sometime champion within the nineteenth-century high school. Wendover began her school days inauspiciously, however, as a chronic invalid. Her diary provides an opportunity to consider the ways in which sickness could set the parameters, and sometimes permanently interrupt a girl's school life.

Jessie Wendover's only sibling, an older sister, was no longer living at home when Jessie embarked upon her lifelong diary. The diary was probably a Christmas present from her parents when she was eight, the first entry written by her mother. "I am sick. bad sore throat so Mama is writing for me." Eight-year-old Jessie Wendover did not go to school, and was not to go for the next several years. In September, after she had turned nine, Wendover no sooner announced that she was starting school than an entry by her mother noted that she was sick again. Over the next few weeks, we learn that the doctor had diagnosed malaria, and that though she was recovering, she was still too sick for lessons. There is no mention of school for the rest of that entire academic year, and for the next year as well, when she was ten years old. In the spring when she turned eleven, her diary noted that her aunt had given her a book in which to write her "imaginary people," a good activity for an invalid. That August, when a friend came over to play and Wendover had a cold, "Ma was afraid that I might get a fever if I played around very much, so [the friend] had to go home."[87] It seems likely that Wendover's parents considered her frail and were unwilling to add the stress of school to a weak constitution.

The fall of her twelfth year, Jessie Wendover tried school again, and for the first time was able to follow through. She enrolled in a grammar school class taught by her aunt, and she announced with some surprise that she thought she would continue at school. "I get along very well almost better than I expected to." Wendover progressed rapidly in her studies and the next year was ready to start at the high school, where she prospered through the first term. At the end of January, though, she got sick again, and did not fully recover until early April. At that point, she noted that she was too far behind to pass the end-of-year exams and that "it would only be a waste of time and strength" to return to school that year. She began to study Latin, French, and physiology on her own, enrolling the next fall to repeat her first year of high school.[88] Due to a fragile condition, Wendover had sat out at least three years of school that her parents had planned for her to attend. By the age of fourteen, the schoolgirl Jessie Wendover had completed only one and a half years of school and might well have been launched on a career as an invalid.

After embarking for the second time on her first year of high school, Jessie Wendover was through with her bouts of illness; thereafter, she established an exemplary attendance record. Perhaps because of her own history, though, she made a regular part of her diary the school careers and history of illness within her circle of friends. For instance, in her first year of high school, she announced that Cora was "blubbering" to a teacher one day, and the next that Cora had left school. "Cora has not liked it up at [the] H.S. and as she is not very well her doctor said she must leave." It is hard to know whether Cora's doctor was providing cover for a girl's failure at high school or whether the student's illness might have contributed to her difficulties at school. In any case, it is significant that Wendover mentioned in the same breath both illness and unhappiness, which together made an invincible case for leaving school. The same month, though, when Wendover's friend Carrie was having health problems that threatened her studies, Wendover noted, "Carrie does not want to leave and so tries to be as well as possible." Clearly, leaving school was one of the first directives for girls with health concerns; Wendover commented that her friend's doctor "has been wanting her to leave school for some time." Within the month, Carrie departed from school under doctor's order; five months later, she stopped by school to say she was still "not at all well" and had to stay home "and give herself up to the Dr.'s care."[89]

The nature of these illnesses is impossible to know. Sometimes the language suggests a clear crisis, as when one student left with rheumatic fever. At other times the language is more ambiguous, as when one teacher got "quite sick" and Wendover explained, "She is all run down and worn out and will not be back till she gets well again." In the absence of a clear alternative diagnosis, school itself might help a physician to arrive at a diagnosis of "nerves," a convenient and undoubtedly sometimes accurate reflection of the particular challenges of a competitive public school environment. Jessie Wendover made the diagnosis herself when she reported that a friend "says she has one of her nervous headaches again and is quite sick," reflecting, "It is too bad she is always sick at examinations." Less clear, though, was the acute sickness of Flora Vliet, who Wendover reported one February to be "seriously sick with nervous prostration," with some danger of "brain fever." A later report suggested that Vliet's head was somewhat better, "but she has pain around her heart now, and has had to be under the influence of morphine most of yesterday and to-day." After Flora's recovery, her parents might well have been forgiven for keeping her home for the rest of the year, although Flora herself demonstrated her resolve by keeping up with her lessons at home and coming into school to take the examinations. (Wendover stopped by to tell her her grade on a Latin exam—72—and reported that "Flora was tickled over it as she hopes she may now be able to pass.")[90]

Jessie Wendover took illness seriously, as might be expected of one who had known much of it, but she took school perhaps even more seriously. She reported one December the absence of a friend because she "was not very well," observing acerbically, "she seemed lively enough this afternoon."[91] Jessie Wendover's was a school success story—a story of a sickly child who was kept from school but who recovered and discovered that school was just the structure that she needed to feel accomplishment in her life. Her evident zeal must have reassured her skittish parents; they did not insist that Wendover remain the fragile female that she had begun, and even acquiesced when her high school teachers insisted later that Wendover should go to college.

Wendover's diary suggests, though, the multiple levels which could inform assumptions about the sickness and health of schoolgirls. Sometimes girls got sick and nearly died, and after such grave illness they were likely to remain at home during a prolonged convalescence. Sometimes they had a chronic complaint, like migraine headaches or an uncorrected astigmatism or low blood sugar. Though unlikely to have been sanctioned in boys, these conditions might well serve as an explanation why a middle-class girl should not go to school. And sometimes girls got cases of nerves in school, which might be reified into actual nervous conditions. All these possibilities together might explain some of the early statistics which the historian Reed Ueda found in the Somerville High School students that he studied. Ueda found that among the students who left Somerville Free High School before graduation in the late 1850s, by far the single largest category for girls was "personal illness or infirmity," which accounted for eleven departures. Only one boy during this period departed for health reasons, although ten left high school to take up jobs in business.[92] More girls than boys went to secondary or high schools in the first place, but that number was undoubtedly kept lower than it might have been by a tendency not to enroll girls, or to withdraw them, as the first response to infirmity of any kind.

Fredrica Ballard and Frailty

If the story of Jessie Wendover was one of surmounting invalidism to prosper in school, the story of Fredrica Ballard was of an extraordinary girl who became cocooned within a familial model of female frailty. Like Jessie Wendover, Fredrica Ballard was the youngest daughter in a small and solicitous family. She remembered that her mother was "delicate" and often spent "weeks" in bed with an unspecified illness. As a child living in Philadelphia, Ballard attended "a well-established school for girls from primary grade to 'finishing school.'" It was badly heated, however, and when she caught a cold, she was withdrawn from this school, though she continued with her studies reading and rereading Shakespeare on her own.[93]

In her next school, a Friends' School, Ballard suffered her defining illness, which consolidated an identity perhaps already in embryo. She at first showed signs of "nervous exhaustion," which developed quickly into a full-blown case of diphtheria, a disease which afflicted roughly one-tenth of all children in this country in the nineteenth century, killing as many as one-tenth of those. Her convalescence involved hot salt baths and rubs in Atlantic City and a mandate to play outdoors. An imaginative child, she was prohibited from a favorite fantasy play, undoubtedly judged to be unhealthy for her nerves. Like Jessie Wendover, Fredrica Ballard remained out of school for the entire academic year, returning in September to repeat the grade "so that the first months should not be a strain." She received other instructions designed to preserve her health, however, which distinguished her story from Wendover's. The previous year, she recalled retrospectively, she had had the "almost embarrassing experience of being read out as the head of the class." In later life,

Ballard denied any responsibility for her success, recalling that she had self-consciously gathered her books and walked to the first seat in the classroom. That later judgment suggested the lesson that diphtheria taught her: the possible costs of ambition. She returned to school with instructions not to "try for first place," an instruction she complied with. Although her pride kept her among the first two or three, she had learned that she was too fragile to go all out, to compete vigorously.[94]

This self-image undoubtedly influenced another moment of decision. As a student enrolled at Drexel Institute, an art institute in Philadelphia, Ballard was required to take classes in physical education at a gymnasium. Mandatory physical training, especially for girls, was the response of many schools and colleges to critics who claimed that study damaged girls' health. Ballard's father felt that such classes might be good for her. Ballard remembered, however, that "the gymnasium didn't agree with me." She convinced her mother, who in turn convinced the doctor "that it was doing me harm," and she was excused. Her memoir is no more specific than that, though she had earlier referred to an injury to her knee.[95]

Fredrica Ballard's subsequent schooling was as scattered as it had been in her earlier years. She left a secondary school when her mother got the flu. "I was needed at home and had lost too much at school to carry on that grade." She never went back, and she later remarked wistfully about her failure to graduate, "I have never had any sort of document to display to attest to any goal in my studies." She manifested the same regret about her failure to go to college. Her brother, a successful businessman, offered to send her to Bryn Mawr, and she remembered that she "truly wanted to go." She was held back by her parents' need for her—an invalid mother's need of companionship, and her father's need of a "domestic atmosphere." She also mentioned her frailty: "I was not strong—my nervous energy exhausted my physical strength every day." In retrospect, she wrote, "I have often wondered what my life would have been had I gone to Bryn Mawr. I had a mind, not brilliant, but quick and pliable, retentive and intelligent. I could have done the work I am sure if I had first been properly prepared for it and if my health had steadied up under the routine of college life as it might have done. But any sort of study or worthwhile reading was such an exciting thing to me that I wore myself out with the very joy of it. It is entirely possible I might have broken down."[96] Her fear of her own excitement, of the "very joy of it" betrayed a common notion that women's nerves were not up to intense emotion or experience, that excessive imaginative stimulation might well undo them. In Ballard's case, this was an idea that Fredrica had about herself, perhaps first

6.6 Fearful of the "very joy" of intense study, [1890?]. Fredrica Ballard was an avid intellect, yet a case of diphtheria, an invalid mother, and her physician convinced her that her nerves could not withstand the excitement of serious study. Courtesy of Peter, Nancy, and Benjamin Westervelt.

planted by the model of female invalidism lived by her mother, but reinforced by doctors who had discouraged her imaginative play and academic ambition after diphtheria. The men in her family spoke with mixed voices. Her father needed her at home to provide "a domestic atmosphere" but also encouraged her at the gymnasium. She felt that her brother never really understood her decision to pass up a college education and judged her lazy-minded for it.

As college became a more conventional goal for women of her class, subsequent women's history reinforced Ballard's regrets. When she wrote her memoirs, she voiced her own suspicion that perhaps the "routine of college life," the dailiness of school, the expectation that she would finish an educational program might have "steadied up" her health. Fredrica Ballard's memoirs themselves are a tribute to her wit, creativity, and tenacity. But they also betray a sense of her own fragility, her awareness that at any moment she might break down, an attribute inherited from her childhood sickness but also from her invalid mother. They suggest the ways that a gendered inheritance could encourage female resignation and dependence, a kind of self-limiting that might avoid a rigorous academic program out of fear for the stress it would impose on a weak constitution. Alice James's biographer, Jean Strouse, has suggested the costs of women's failure to get an education earlier in the century, arguing that "if early-nineteenth-century society assumed women were not worth education, that assumption profoundly influenced most women's attitudes towards themselves."[97] In the next century, Ballard's memoirs reveal a sense of personal failure in her wistful reflection on a risk not taken.

The story of secondary schooling for girls in the nineteenth century presents the historian with something of a puzzle. On the one hand, as Fredrica Ballard and countless others testify, parents feared the impact of intense study on delicate girls. Health concerns ranged over a wide spectrum, from life-threatening bouts with diphtheria to the effect of the overheated pace of urban life on girls' nerves and their reproductive systems. Those who succumbed to such fears might find themselves stuck not only within a domestic space but within a static "daughter's" role for much of their lives.

With only a peripheral role to play in the bourgeois household, however, girls increasingly went to school and stayed—both to the female seminaries and to the new high schools opening in the Northeast at midcentury. School changed many things. Girls who went to female boarding seminaries found themselves in a dense and sociable world which challenged home obediences and loosened emotional moorings. Girls at coeducational high schools were likely to be swept up in a contentious world of peers. In either case, the tempo of school had a compelling momentum of its own. Despite cultural cautions against overexertion, many girls attended school regularly, winning awards for perfect attendance and exemplary deportment. Others threw themselves into the academic competition, often thrilling at their advance through the meritocratic classroom. Girls' discovery that they could compete and win contributed to a new attitude toward themselves and their lives.

SEVEN

High School Culture: Gender and Generation

Success at school could make an enormous difference in girls' lives. Girls who were healthy enough to go to school, and successful enough to stay, brought from their accomplishments a new perspective on their ability to compete and perform in life. But of course graduation and end-of-term honors are only one way to measure success in the nineteenth-century high school. Those markers, conveyed by adults at the end of the year, do not let us know much about the student power structure within the high school. In order to understand the full impact of the high school experience on girls' expectations, we need to know about the gender politics within the student population. Who did students listen to? Were girls and boys equally or differentially represented in student offices? To what extent did girls occupy positions of authority and influence comparable to their numbers and academic accomplishments? Within the girl-dominated high school, who was the normative student?

These are difficult questions to answer. Girls' diaries and letters provide some help, but they also leave much out. We are helped in understanding the complex student culture of the 1880s and 1890s by the increasing publication of a raft of student newspapers, some of which have been preserved in town historical societies and public libraries throughout the Northeast. In the early 1870s the manufacture of inexpensive "novelty" printing presses unleashed a flood of amateur publications, many published by youths but by other hobbyists as well, throughout the country. By the 1880s fledgling high schools and their students had begun to take advantage of this new technology to put out school newspapers. These student-written newspapers were nourished by a practice of national "exchange," a tradition borrowed from the hobbyists: student editors from Boston, Concord, and Milford exchanged their newspapers in the 1880s and 1890s with editors of high school newspapers in Denver, Tulsa, and Portland, Oregon, as well as those of neighboring communities.[1] (It was customary to offer comments on the papers received in a separate column of one's paper for that purpose.) One might argue with cause, as does Reed Ueda in his *Avenue to Adulthood,* that these eagerly awaited and devoured papers from all over the country contributed to the formation of a national youth culture well before it is usually described in the 1920s.[2]

These student newspapers provide rich evidence of the gender politics of coeducational high schools in the nineteenth century. In their leadership and their reporting, they testify to the persistence of traditional gender relations in the adolescent culture of the high schools. But they also offer evidence of another sort, evidence suggesting the impact of liberal education in redressing gender inequities, especially when helped along by numerical imbalances. It took especially lopsided imbalances to bring administrators and male and female students to new understandings of old social truisms, but with those imbalances, the world changed. It changed for individual students, but it also contributed to a larger social transformation. Victorian girls who went to high school learned to vote in class meetings. They learned to give as good as they got in the gender sparring that was a constant in the late-century high school. With male classmates they participated in class governance and published student newspapers. These social experiences accompanied girls' academic dominance. This shared participation helped male and female classmates to a different understanding of what the "rules" for each sex were.

Coeducation in Practice

The gender segregation of nineteenth-century society reached deep into coeducational high schools. Students may have shared classes and competed for awards, but they were slow to lose their consciousness (if they ever did) that they belonged to two opposing corporate bodies, distinguished by culture and loyalty: the boys and the girls. Such distinctions were often made by teachers and administrators even in grammar schools. One female letter writer to *St. Nicholas* noted a divided playground. ("The cherry-trees are on our side, and I like it the best.") At Alice Blackwell's neighborhood grammar school, girls and boys used different staircases (with demerits administered to violators). Jessie Wendover's grammar school teacher "sent the girls

7.1 Newspaper staff, 1896. By the 1880s and 1890s, many secondary school students published school newspapers, notable for their independence from school administrators. This is the staff of the *Stranger* from Bridgton Academy, North Bridgton, Maine. Courtesy of Bridgton Academy.

down in the court to eat their dinner and gave the boys permission to talk and eat for twenty minutes." The same kinds of arrangements in secondary schools allowed for separate girls' and boys' floors. In the early days of Bridgton Academy in North Bridgton, Maine—and surely in many other schools as well—boys and girls sat on opposite sides of the room.[3]

Even where girls and boys intermingled freely in the classroom, though, they tended to be segregated in the free parts of the school day. The British observer Sara Burstall, who came to the United States in the 1890s to investigate the American education of girls, observed "no difference" between boys' and girls' conduct and freedom in the classroom. But she noted, "out of class there seemed to be very little general intercourse—girls speaking to girls, and boys to boys. At recess the sexes are generally separated, the boys occupying the basement, and the girls the upper part of the buildings." The Somerville, Massachusetts, student newspaper, observed, probably caustically, "We think that rail between the boys' and girls' side of the lunch room is quite an institution." Where there were no such administrative separations, girls and boys often segregated themselves and participated in separate activities. Ellen Emerson loved the extraordinary Sanborn School, which she attended following Agassiz School in the late 1850s, in part because "boys and girls go together which I think is essential to a good school." However, she went on, "They do not play together. I don't think that could be done in this generation, but it will in the next, but the girls have at least the recreation of seeing the boys play, and it is a great one." This wistful vision of girls watching boys play, sometimes football, sometimes leapfrog, suggests the distances which separated boys and girls even in this progressive midcentury private school run by the radical abolitionist Franklin Sanborn. And as Burstall reported, such separation did not end in the next generation. When a male classmate died in Jessie Wendover's school in 1885, girls and boys separately sent flowers, the girls "in the form of a pillow," the boys, "a broken pillar of flowers." The same sense of distance between girls and boys was evident in Margaret Tileston's discussion of interactions between the girls and boys in Salem High School, which still maintained separate classes for boys and girls. Tileston had several brothers, but within the context of her school experience, boys existed in Margaret Tileston's diary (and in her view of the universe) as alien creatures. She noted a rare encounter that spring: "A boy sat in the room finishing his examination while we had our French. The girls stared at him as he came in as if he had been some strange animal."[4] Initially, even in coeducational schools, much divided girls and boys, who approached each other warily.

In completely coeducational schools, the tone changed, though some divisions between the boys and girls seemed to hold up. A boy's description of corridor life in the Brookline, Massachusetts, *Sagamore* in 1896 noted an innovation in their new school building: "a roomy, pleasant, well-lighted gathering-place, where the whole school may meet on equal terms at recess." The scene was raucous. The writer turned "his head just in time to escape a flying waste-basket, used as a foot-ball by some would-be members of next year's team." Boys with buns in their mouths and cups of chocolate in their hands from the lunch counter were playing leap-frog. A curtain was lifted at the end of the hall, and a girls' calisthenics class in "dainty slippered feet and bloomers" ran "the gauntlet, one after another, not altogether unwillingly," the author concluded, encouraged by boys' cheers. There was clearly a "boys' side" and a "girls' side." "Teachers and girls, all eating their lunch and all talking at once, occupy the settees along the wall." There was some fraternizing. "Several gallant fellows were entertaining groups of girls," the author noted.[5] But it took "gallantry" for boys to cross the line to the girls' side, so clear, still, was the gender divide.

Gender Sparring

In fact, gender relations in the Victorian high school often crossed a highly charged field separating two opposing camps. Although a Victorian chivalry might govern official relations between "the young ladies" and other scholars, the open columns of school newspapers, bearing such titles as "Shavings" and "Scintillations," allowed for ample sparring in an ongoing battle of the sexes. The intensity of that sparring suggests the extent to which coeducational high schools by their nature ended by challenging orthodoxies. Insults appeared in the earliest journals. The handwritten Winchester, Massachusetts, *High School Offering* of 1861, issued by two female editors, asked, "Why are the young gentlemen of this school like vessels plying between Boston and New York?" The answer: "Because they are *coasters*." In 1879 the *High School News* of Great Falls, New Hampshire, published in two sections, with a "Supplement" from "The Young Ladies' Department." As befit their divided school and polarized presentation, the two sides found their best copy in each other. In their fifth issue in May 1879, "Vox Puellarum" (the voice of the girls) rallied her readers: "Girls, here it is again, a fling at us! can't we retaliate? I propose 'diamond cut diamond' with such editors as ours!" Previously, she implied, the boys had made some cracks about the weaknesses of young ladies' "anatomical construction." "The following month . . . we present to them a Hero; again they retort with 'Our Model Girl' as if we (the H.S. girls) thought of nothing but promenades and spring styles."[6] Although the boys signed their pieces, such daring talk from young ladies required a pseudonym, and was signed with one. It was not until the 1890s that girls' full and correct names accompanied their pieces.

Behind the reciprocal digs were some truths. Discipline fell most strenuously on male heads. ("Poor young ladies! Too insignificant to be noticed!" commented one columnist on the apparent immunity of girls from punishment.) And boys often had to answer for girls' relative accomplishments. An 1883 letter from a "former classmate" to the male editor of the Concord, New

Hampshire, *Comet* observed, "Your success seems to be due in a great part to the literary ability of the fairer sex." The letter writer went on: "It seems to be a peculiar fact . . . that women are born to rule, and, as in this case, to be among the first to start a paper which is open to the general criticism of the people."[7]

The result was that some parries had undeniably violent subtexts. In 1884, the year after the *Comet* editor heard of the accomplishments of "the fairer sex," his successor ran an exchange item. Untitled, it was a first-person poem about the modern schoolgirl. The *Comet* ran it on the back page as filler. It bragged about schoolgirls' appearance as "the handsomest girls of our race/ Superb in form and of exquisite face," who "dress with perfect, consummate grace." It then referred to their accomplishments, suggesting a critical lack:

> *We know many tongues of living and dead,*
> *In science and fiction we're very well read:*
> *But we cannot cook meat and cannot make bread,*
> *And we've wished many times that we were all dead.*[8]

This verse took the common form of the assault on the New Woman, an attack on her lack of domestic accomplishments, managing to avoid fictive murder only by putting the action in the first person and arranging instead for a suicide wish.

The compliment was returned in a poem published by the *Comet*'s successor, the *Volunteer,* in 1887. Under the title "Boys! Don't Read This!" came an attack on the cigarette-smoking dandy. Appealing to the nonreading boy with its sensational title, the poet asked

> *To you who smoke the cigarette*
> *(I wonder if you've thought it)*
> *Who made this little cigarette?*
> *You only know you bought it.*
>
> *Perhaps some dark Italian,*
> *Or Jew from foreign land,*
> *Rolled up that little cigarette*
> *With greasy, dirty hand.*

This nativist jab from the hinterlands on the new immigrant workforce was not the point of the poem, however, but only the vehicle to its ultimate pronouncement.

But if boys will smoke cigarettes
Although the smoke may choke them,
One consolation still remains—
They kill the boys that smoke them.[9]

Seeping through Victorian niceties, these death wishes illuminate only the obvious: that the gender challenges occurring in the nineteenth-century high school did not come without unleashing considerable unease as well as possibility. To understand the dynamics of this change, it makes sense to trace the action in a number of arenas. As we have seen, girls dominated the academic rankings in most high schools. They made slower inroads in extracurricular activities, especially in the important male-gendered activities, debate, athletics, and military drill. The awarding of direct political power, in the election of class officers, remained surprisingly uncontested, with boys seemingly the only possibility for class president. The more substantial role of girls in student newspapers, however, was particularly important by virtue of the power this bestowed to influence school opinion.

Politics and Debating

In the election of class officers, high school classes demonstrated a penchant for patriarchy. Despite skewed gender ratios, and even in years when academic honors went overwhelmingly to girls, students meeting together to elect class officers for their senior years elected boys as presidents of their class. The other positions were up for grabs, though most classes usually elected at least one girl in a subordinate position as either vice president or secretary-treasurer. No rule was as constant, though, as the tendency to install male leadership at the top, which senior classes did again and again.

The uniformity of male class presidency from school to school across entirely different administrations of coeducation, however, suggests that it did not require administrative dictum to enforce that "natural" hierarchy. Any political culture the students had been exposed to would have encouraged them to assume that political leadership should be male. High school classes remained faithful to this sense of how matters should be even when tradition or logic suggested otherwise. The Star and Crescent Society was a literary society at Los Angeles High School, and from its founding in 1879 until 1895 the president of the society was a girl. In the 1890s, though, the school principal gave the society governance responsibilities, converting it from a cultural to a political institution. Thereafter, the historian Victoria Bissell Brown re-

7.2 Gender skirmishes, 1896. Girls dominated the academic ranks in high schools, and that was enough for boys to feel besieged. The competition was usually verbal, but vigorous. This Charles Dana Gibson drawing, *The Coming Conflict*, captures the mood. Reprinted from Charles Dana Gibson, *Pictures of People* (New York: Russell, 1896).

ports, the president was male. The Concord, New Hampshire, *Volunteer* of 1897 noted the insistence of the class of 1898 on having a male president, an attitude the paper's editor termed "a bit risky." The reason: "Three boys stole away, one after the other, and brought upon us the name of a 'class without a president.'"[10] The tendency of boys to leave school to go to work was wreaking havoc with class solidarity. The female editor of the *Volunteer* insinuated that the class might have done well to elect female leadership. Her own position as editor of the newspaper may have allowed her thinking to outstrip that of her classmates and her fellow girl students in high schools around the region. Again and again, they cooperated with the male minority to elect boys president of coeducational senior classes.

In the fall of 1883 the *Comet* introduced a subject which brought the issue of gender to the foreground of student discussion both at Concord and at high schools around the region. On October 15, 1883, the *Comet* reported a meeting sponsored by the YMCA "composed largely of High School boys" for the purpose of establishing a debating society. The *Comet's* editors were enthusiastic. They exhorted: "Boys, this is what you want, and what you need, and now is your opportunity to obtain it."[11] Debating, allied as it was with political discourse in a public world, was gendered male, and nearly always began as an activity thought appropriate for boys alone. Yet the fundamental premises of liberal high school education—and indeed of debate itself—encouraged both boys and girls to challenge the notion of boys-only debating societies. The irony, though, is that once the doors were open, it was difficult, in Concord anyway, to find any girls who wanted to join this exclusive club.

The Concord High School Lyceum, as the debating society was informally named, met throughout the 1880s to debate a range of issues. Its membership overlapped with the male leadership of the newspaper and the senior class to constitute a high school elite. The supposed cachet of debaters with girls was revealed in the account of a girl student who "thus interprets CHSDS: 'Charmingly Handsome, So Distractingly Sweet.'" The columnist summarized: "Surely the young men of this society ought to feel complimented." The topics chosen for debate generally revolved around current events. In 1887 the Lyceum debated the resolution "That the Chicago Anarchists [judged guilty in the Haymarket riot] should be granted a new trial," a question so well-argued by the affirmative that only three members of the audience voted for the opposition.[12]

The question of girls' participation in the debating society arose with a suggestion in 1887 in the Concord paper for a parallel girls' organization. The first suggestion was glib: "Why don't the girls form a debating society? The boys would be on hand to tell them when to adjourn." The second mention was earnest. "We learn from our exchanges that in many of the schools literary societies are organized and successfully carried on by the young ladies. We think the plan a good one, and we have no doubt that an organization of this kind would prove a source of interest and profit to the girls of the Concord High School." No sooner had the suggestion been made than the *Volunteer* reported that the Young Ladies' Literary Union had conducted its first meeting, in which they discussed the work of "Josiah Allen's wife."[13] The elevating discussion of literature was deemed more appropriate for girls than the direct combat of adversarial debate.

Clearly, though, from the beginning, the formation of the Young Ladies' Literary Union was meant to initiate cooperation with the debating society. Members discussed a "union" meeting with the boys' lyceum at the YLLU's first meeting, and by the second meeting, the *Volunteer* was questioning the appropriateness of a separate agenda for the girls' society: "Although, as yet, there has been no debating, doubtless the young ladies could spend a part of their time in this department with benefit and credit to themselves. The time is coming when it will be as necessary for the ladies to be able to speak in public as the gentlemen." Breaking out of the distanced references to "young ladies" and adopting the first-person plural, the partisan female reporter (probably Grace Seccomb, an editor of the *Volunteer*) suggested an expanded agenda for the YLLU: "We hope that the members of this organization will overcome their timidity and that some evening in the near future we may hold a meeting with the Lyceum and discuss the subject of Woman Suffrage."[14]

An item in the same *Volunteer* provided additional context for the formation of a separate society for girls in Concord. In reporting on a coeducational society in a neighboring city, the paper's reporter observed that the Concord Board of Education had objected to the formation of a lyceum comprising both boys and girls. The example of Keene, New Hampshire, however, revealed that its coeducational "society is in a prosperous condition, and no harm as been discovered arising from the mingling of the two sexes." Even better, "the fact that the girls are not regarded as inferior members was demonstrated recently in the election of a young lady as president." The article ended with a head-on challenge: "We think that the objections of the board were unwarranted, as in nearly all schools the lyceums contain both young ladies and gentlemen, and nothing but good results have followed."[15]

The dispute with the local board of education over students' rights to a coeducational lyceum seems to have translated into a heightened awareness among both girl and boy students of the issues of women's rights. A brief mention in the same issue of the *Volunteer* noted that "the members of the [boys'] Lyceum seem to advocate Woman's Rights."

As proposed, the YLLU and the Lyceum met together at the end of April 1888 to debate women's suffrage. The results were not exactly as anticipated. The boys were urged to "bring your Miltons and bibles and demonstrate to the young ladies that they should not take an active part in the affairs of Government." Yet the report on the debate suggested the more significant opposition of some of the girls to extension of the franchise to their sex. "The large number of young ladies opposing woman suffrage at the recent debate was a good index of the general opinion of the female sex upon this question. When women as a whole desire to vote, in all probability the right will be extended them; but they never have, and do not at the present day, wish for it in the least." This critique of the suffrage case was tempered by several items in the "Personal" section of the *Volunteer,* one of which noted that the affirmative speaker Miss Gutterson "made one of the best arguments we have heard this year."[16]

A "School-Boy's Dream," a poem written the following fall, suggested that at least some boys, whatever their feelings on women's suffrage, continued to smart at the school committee's refusal to allow a coeducational debating society. In a poem which predicted brilliant futures for three male friends, a Harvard presidency for the respected high school principal, and a beautiful new building for the high school, the poet "M" recorded his imagined pleasure at the correction of a keenly felt injustice:

> *The Lyceum and Y.L.U.*
> *Had long since been united.*
> *And thus the wrong of my school life*
> *By later hands was righted.*

The reference to the separation of these two societies as *the* wrong of the poet's school years suggests that the issue had come to represent a good bit to the boys of the Lyceum. Students at public Concord High School did not have the option taken by the college class at Bridgton Academy of dropping out over this infringement of their "manly" access to female students. (Apparently this was the result of a new ruling in 1869 barring boys from walking girls home after evening lectures.)[17] Nonetheless, the boys seemed to recognize that their autonomy as well as the girls' was being limited when the school committee forbade admission of female members.

Through the 1880s the Lyceum and the YLLU continued to meet separately with frequent joint meetings, moot courts, and sociables. Debating societies, with their parliamentary procedures and abstract subjects, fell onto hard times in the 1890s in Concord and at other high schools around the region, however. In the mid-1890s, the principal proposed a change in the society's constitution. Perhaps by this time, the school board had come to regard a coeducational debating society as a positive way to structure extra-curricular mingling. A *Volunteer* editorial writer wrote: "The amendment of Mr. Page to change the article on membership from boys to pupils is in the opinion of the majority of the members of the Lyceum a step in the right direction. If this amendment is passed and there is little doubt it will be, it will admit any pupil of the School, either boy or girl, to the Lyceum, and it is hoped the girls will avail themselves of the opportunity to join." Poised to work this change in their bylaws, in April of 1896 the society pulled back. The *Volunteer* insinuated that the problem might have been with the interest of the girls rather than the inclinations of the boys. Noting that "it is rather late to accomplish anything in the matter this year," the writer ventured to "hope that another year the boys will begin early and arouse the girls to take a more active interest in debating than they have heretofore shown."[18] The same issue of the *Volunteer* reported the formation of a bicycle club with all female officers. Just as the school committee was coming to see the relative advantage of such a therapeutic coeducational regimen as debate, the girls had moved on to more active interests.

Reports of future Lyceum meetings did not again raise the possibility of adding female members. A little less than a year after the members of the Lyceum thought better of an invitation that might be spurned, however, they were presented with another opportunity to show their eagerness for coeducational debate. While negotiating a debate with Manchester High School, the Concord representative learned that Manchester had a girl on its team. Concord's response was unequivocal: "Mr. Joslin then told them we would not debate on any such terms. . . . The lyceum confirmed Mr. Joslin and instructed him to notify the other delegates of their decision not to compete with girls." The decision of the Concord debaters to make a virtue of the necessity of their all-male debating team was its last official act. In March, the *Volunteer* announced that the debating society had voted to disband. The reason: "There was not enough interest to keep the Lyceum going." The Lyceum's reactionary refusal to debate with girls represented the sour grapes of an organization that had failed to adapt to the times. A decade earlier, girls' equal membership was a cause célèbre with the boys' debating society, the fulcrum of a power struggle between school youth and school administration. Under these circumstances, the members of the boys' Lyceum did seem to advocate women's rights in protest, as the *Volunteer* suggested in 1888.[19] The long-term result of administrative fiat, though, was that Concord did not have a tradition of co-educational debate to encourage "young ladies" to participate. In mandating separate societies for girls and boys, the Concord school committee turned what was a despised ruling into a besieged aspect of group identity.

This trajectory of debate was not unique to Concord High School. Debating was earnestly encouraged by high school principals—and sometimes even mandated by them. But even with administrative support, debating clubs struggled to survive. In many cases it was not until the mid-1890s that high school principals acquiesced or encouraged the opening of membership to girls in order to try to resuscitate struggling organizations. The Brookline, Massachusetts, *Sagamore* reported of its all-male lyceum in April 1895 that "two of the meetings have been complete fizzles." The following January the principal announced that "he had received a petition from twenty-one of the young ladies of the school, requesting that they be admitted to the Club on an equality with the young gentlemen." Whether the principal inspired or simply responded to the petition, he rushed to endorse it, saying: "I cordially recommend that the petition be granted." It was in order to facilitate the integration of the girls to the society that he saw to it that "provision was made that the vice-president and the secretary should always be girls."[20]

In May 1897 a frank-talking editor at Salem High School discussed the difficulties of forming a debate society: "We do not urge you to form one. The reason for their failure is obvious—they admit no girls to membership; therefore if you do form such a society by all means remember the young ladies, for nothing seems to go without them." By the late 1890s it was beginning to be common wisdom that you needed girls for edifying extracurricular projects to succeed. Perhaps that was why Los Angeles High admitted girls to its debating society in 1902.[21] By the time many debating societies got around to getting girls on board, though, debate had lost its central position in the extracurricular calendar. With high school athletes competing on rivals' fields, and with American troops fighting on the shores of Cuba and the Philippines, debate had come to seem abstract and impractically academic. More activist high school programs had taken its place at the center of high school life.

Athletics

When the members of the Lyceum of Concord High School voted to disband because of lack of student interest, they made a telling allocation of the society's funds. They voted that "the funds in the hands of the treasurer be given to the Athletic Association."[22] The Lyceum was a traditional boys' activity which foundered in part because it failed to accommodate girls until it was too late. Athletics was a new center of high school life which, like debate, was gendered masculine despite the scarcity of actual boys in some high schools. In fact, one could argue that the enthusiasm for athletics in the late nineteenth century was part of a process which ended by remasculinizing the high school. However the enthusiasm for male athletics began and ended, though, in the 1890s girls too claimed sports as part of their self-definition as "new girls."

Student newspapers promoted athletics just as they promoted debate as a way to build school spirit and prestige. From the beginning, boys and girls (or, more commonly, "young ladies") had distinct relationships to school sports. Boys played and girls cheered. The Concord *Comet*'s editor in 1884 offered "a word to the boys of the school" about his hopes that they could form a good baseball team. And in 1891 editor William Pond addressed his school with a proposal to initiate a new sport for Milford High School: "This is the season when all the high schools and colleges of the country are playing football. . . . Why not organize a football team and practice according to the rules, and then play some of the neighboring school elevens." He knew he was really talking to only part of the school though, as he ended, "Boys, let us talk this up and try and do something about it." Funding for sports teams was raised through the formation of athletics associations, sometimes initiated by high school principals; boys, too, bore primary responsibility for membership. On discovering that many boys were not members, the Milford paper expressed censure: "This is not as it should be. Every boy in school ought to be a member of the association, and to aid it in every possible manner." By the following year, Milford's student newspaper, *Oak, Lily, and Ivy*, had apparently succeeded in rallying membership from among the boys and now was trying to marshal greater attendance at games. The editor urged Milford students to "cultivate a spirit of love toward our school and display it." And a later editor allied boosting at high school with manhood, encouraging boys to "stand by the institution where you are being trained to be men, and support your school as you will in future years your town."[23] The alliance of school spirit with civic virtue suggested that cheering at high school games was a pathway to manly citizenship.

If that was true, however, most student editors were women's rights advocates, for they quickly realized that the largest potential pool of cheerleaders were girls. The sometimes explicit presumption behind such bids for female boosters was that "a girl would not care to go on the track or field as her boy friend does," yet "she is of great assistance in the grand stand." Appeals to the young ladies into the late 1890s sometimes presumed that "they may not take an active part in the sports" but that they were uniquely suited to "spur on the boys to victory by their kindly feelings." Noting that "nothing helps a team to win away from home as much as a good crowd, especially young ladies, to cheer them on," the editor of the Milford paper outlined a strategy for effective support: "A good plan is for each one to carry a scarlet flag with M.H.S. inscribed thereon, as was done to some extent last year; or at all events to wear the school colors." [24]

High school athletic associations had other uses for girls as well. They needed their dues as members in order to sustain perpetually cash-starved teams. Usually girls' loyalty to boy athletes was considered enough of a reason for them to turn out and cheer, but when it came to joining the athletic association and paying dues, advocates knew they needed to go farther. To those who would say that girls did not care about baseball, Milford Athletic Association advocates responded, "'Tis false!" Arguing that to know baseball was to love it, they proposed an education campaign. "During practice games on the park, let the young ladies be asked to act as spectators, and let all the boys who are not playing constitute a committee to instruct the ignorant and bring them into the fold." Such recruiting efforts, however, continued to appeal to girls through encouraging their support for boys' athletics. As boys' interscholastic competition took up more and more of the space in student newspapers, girls were asked to watch, to cheer, and to raise money, but in support of boys' athleticism and their agendas. All were urged to support "our national game" so that society will "have manlier boys to deal with, who are self-reliant and honorable." [25]

Such articles as touched on girls' physical activity focused on calisthenics and "physical culture" in the schools. Exercise regimens were deemed especially important for girls, who lacked "those vigorous and enjoyable outdoor exercises" available to boys. (Calisthenics and "Swedish" gymnastics were two common programs.) An article on "Physical Exercise" in the Milford paper also promoted lawn tennis and skating for young ladies. When Sara Burstall visited the United States in the 1890s, she found in American schools "the comparative absence of free games," arguing that "no formal method can do as much for physical health and development as games in the open air, pursued freely, and not as a task." [26]

Evidence suggests, though, that the strategy of luring girls into athletic associations as boosters was not successful. Gradually, and somewhat grudgingly, suggestions emerged in high school papers that girls join athletics associations for themselves, so that they might be able to play and therefore would be willing to pay. A history of coeducational Bridgton Academy in North Bridgton, Maine, suggested that it happened naturally in this small community; in 1884 the boys had five baseball nines, the girls two. Another early mention occurred in the Concord *Volunteer* in 1888: "The girls should organize a ball nine and play the boys. Some of the young ladies are quite expert in the national game." In 1895, finally, the Milford paper suggested the obvious: "Why not start a department for the girls? Surely the girls have as much need of sports as boys."[27] Girls played baseball in informal family games during the late century, but organized team competition was less common. Women's colleges provided some important precedents for high school programs. Immediately following the Civil War, students at Vassar College had organized baseball clubs, and shortly after basketball was "invented" in Springfield, Massachusetts, in 1891, the Smith College athletic director incorporated it into that school's program.

Male athletic editors at the Milford newspaper — who were also players — began to supplement their pitch for cheerleaders with this angle. Not very far below the surface of such pitches, however, was the fear that girls' sports meant that girls would be competing with boys in athletics as in other arenas. In December 1898 one editor noted sardonically: "The girls are contemplating the forming of a basketball team. We would be greatly pleased to have them run opposition to the boys, but first of all we would like to have them join the A" — the athletic association. The editor used the same tone in the spring, chastising his female classmates, "Now don't cry any more for 'Woman's rights' when you have the chance to display your ability in that line. So girls, 'Please join the A.'"[28] Male high school students were not necessarily convinced that girls belonged on the baseball field or at the basketball hoop. Rather they were bowing to the realities of female high school attendance to broaden the base of financial support for boys' high school sports.

During the 1897–98 school year at Milford High School, J. F. McDonnough was athletics editor of the *Oak, Lily, and Ivy* and wrote copious stories documenting boys' sports. His only mention of girls was his appeal for girls to attend basketball games, to cheer on the boys. Certainly a reader of the paper would conclude that Milford girls had not followed through in forming teams. In April 1898, however, the "Locals" column, edited by two girls, told a different story. "What would the athletic association be if it wasn't for the girls?" the editors asked. "We come pretty near paying all their bills." Another item noted, "The girls' basketball teams have disbanded. It was getting too warm to play, and some of the girls were tired of it. The last game was played in Town Hall, April 7, when the Blues won over the Reds 10 to 8."[29]

Taking up girls' basketball in her lead editorial in fall 1898, Lillian E. Fales referred back to the success of girls' basketball the previous year. "The teams were not formed until late in the season, and therefore only a few games were played. The girls took up the game quickly and did fine work for such a short time, and all felt sorry when the play was dropped on account of the warm weather. There is plenty of material in the school for two good teams, and we think that if they were formed now creditable games could be played at the height of the season."[30] Intramural basketball for girls involved several teams and at least several games. The male athletic editors' neglect, though, suggests the level of resistance which accompanied girls' movement at Milford into an arena assumed to be the boys' sphere. It took female editors to move female athletics into view.

Drill and Nationalism

Today we recognize the origins of a familiar culture in the emergence in the 1890s of athletics as a central high school activity which solidified school and class spirit. Equally important to the emerging high school in the 1890s, though, was a somewhat less universal institution, paramilitary drill, which organized large companies of boys and sometimes girls into military companies which marched in formation carrying simulated weapons. Lillian Fales endorsed girls' basketball as her second idea for girls' activity during a time when the boys were drilling. Her first suggestion was the formation of a girls' battalion, which would also use the time for drill and exercise.[31]

Military drill had been an activity for youth since the revolutionary era. However, it had fallen on hard times, perhaps in the aftermath of the devastating losses of the Civil War. In the early 1890s, as the sustained drumroll leading to war again began to build, student writers reinscribed military drill as a feature of a modern high school. Drill, like both debate and athletics, was an activity favored by newspaper editors and school principals as a way to build school spirit and to produce manly men. The editor of the *Oak, Lily, and Ivy* in 1889 noted the "round shoulders and weak bodies" which were "too conspicuous" among Milford scholars. "How can we remedy this defect? We notice that a majority of our exchanges have considerable space devoted to military drill and athletic games." The editor concluded, "If we could have a military drill we might have a stronger looking set of boys." Just as with athletics, mounting a drill team served to enhance prestige within a competitive regional and national context. Milford editor Frank Holbrook reported in 1890 on the first field day of the "newly organized" Second Massachusetts School Regiment, which made him "long for the time" when Milford would be represented. He proposed to "agitate the matter" in order to promote scholarship and deportment and "give the boys a more manly bearing."[32] Within a year the paper reported the first drill of the male High School Cadets, with forty-six responding to the roll call.

The exercises of the Second Massachusetts School Regiment inspired Salem High School editors, too. Salem's battalion had been disbanded "owing to the ungentlemanly behavior of a few unruly members." The editors asked for reinstatement, charging the town elders with cosseting its boys. "Many careful parents think that the strain and discipline of the necessary drilling will be too much for the constitutions of our younger and more delicate boys. Others look at the expense, and no doubt, some mothers shrink with horror at the idea of beholding their sons decked and equipped, as it were, for stern and bloody battle." The clincher for the Salem *Advance* was that Salem's unwillingness to fund a school battalion was making it hopelessly out-of-date.[33] Despite the long history of military drill as an activity for youth, in the nationalist climate of the early 1890s, drill had been reinterpreted as an essential element of a modern high school.

With the actual outbreak of war in 1898, however, the abstract encouragement of manliness became suddenly concrete. The Concord *Volunteer* wondered, "What war news is there left for a school paper to tell that would stand any chance besides the enormous headlines of the world's daily press?" and answered the question in the only possible way: "Only what changes the war is making in our school." The staff documented more overt patriotism at Concord High School. The singing of "America" "does not drag as it often did 'before the war.'" Yet the editors also challenged the student body to demonstrate even more patriotic ardor. Earlier they had asked, "Why does everybody look bored Monday morning, when the flag comes in? It is a fact. Don't try to get out of it." Now it proposed more demonstrative and rapt attention. "We have noticed that the school, as a whole, seat themselves every Monday morning immediately after the singing of 'America.' We believe it would be more patriotic to stand until 'Old Glory' has retired from the hall. At the same time it would seem more spontaneous for the school to rise instantly when the doors are swung open, and the 'color' and its guard revealed to our sight."[34] The paper was filled with the indirect impact of the war.

One reason for such intense interest was revealed in the issue of May 1898: "Several say the war seems like a dream or like the reading of some story, and not actual fact; but it seems all too real now some of our C.H.S. cadets have 'enlisted.'" In this war, as in most others, boys enlisted and girls did not. Well before the outbreak of hostilities, in November 1896, the *Volun-*

teer had begun listing the rosters of the two male companies of the Concord battalion in a position of honor below the staff of the newspaper. After the fighting began, Concord High School graduates who had volunteered were featured. The June 1898 paper contained a report from a Captain Hammond, who had trained the high school battalion and now was overseas, as well as an account of a female student's revealing dream: "One of the girls enlisted the other night in her sleep. She went on to dream that her father didn't approve of her going to war and gave her seventy-five cents to go and get an honorable discharge from Captain Hammond."[35] That dream suggests one clear lesson of the Spanish-American War to girl students in Concord High School: they and their activities were marginalized. A girl could dream that she was part of the action, a natural impulse in the relatively egalitarian world of the high school. Even in a dream, though, a high school girl understood that her choices were constrained by fathers.

Such a dream did succeed in getting a girl in the newspaper. The next year at Concord High School few girls made it into the news at all. The November 1898 issue of the *Volunteer* contained an article about the New Hampshire Volunteers, another about the Concord High School Cadets, a sports story about football, and notes from a meeting of the all-male Lyceum. If not for one article with a female byline (an article about a naval show which re-created famed battles from the war), the girls at Concord High School would have been completely eclipsed.[36]

The war filled the paper at Salem High School, too. In September 1898, the *High School Advance,* published under a brilliant cover in red, white, and blue, noted that "Salem, we are proud to say, furnished her full quota and even more, for the war just ended." In addition to one schoolmate who had enlisted, the *Advance* editors noted the deaths of two alumni, one with Roosevelt's Rough Riders and another with Torrey's Rough Riders.[37] At the time of the war, Salem High School had not yet become "modern," though, for it did not have a battalion within the high school. Perhaps Salem's mothers had been right to fear the consequences of paramilitary companies in the schools (if indeed they had, as the *Advance* editor conjectured). But perhaps, too, like their hero Theodore Roosevelt, some of the well-mothered sons of Salem might have felt that they had something to prove when war broke out. Several generations of scholars have noted the appeal of that "splendid little war" to a male elite increasingly feminized by the loss of the frontier and the overcivilization of bourgeois culture. Certainly the outnumbered boys of the modern high school saw their collective status rise as they demonstrated their claim to manly militarism.

Milford High School, too, featured the Spanish-American War. It sent one member of the class of 1898. The class historian, Lillian P. Swasey, noted its pride "that one of their classmates has answered the call of his country and bravely gone to the front, willing if need be to give up his life for his beloved country and the dear old flag which floats over the heads of its people." In November 1898 the school paper reported the triumphant return of Company M of Milford from Puerto Rico; they were greeted by the High School Cadets and escorted to a feast at the armory.[38]

By the following March, the *Oak, Lily, and Ivy* reported that the girls at last had formed a military company of forty members, with a full retinue of officers. The paper's editor, Lillian Fales, commended the battalion for its prowess, citing "the quick execution of the orders, the perfect alignment of the columns, the excellent marching." By 1899 high school girls were drilling in Concord as well.[39] It is not hard to understand why girls were finally marching. The high school which they thought they knew well had been awash in a militarist zeal which might have left them behind. Girls could support naval expansion and write editorials about the Philippines; they could imagine the sanctity of their vote and extend the influence of democracy into the granting of academic honors; they could feel their equality in myriad ways. But with the outbreak of fighting, they could also feel their sure footing erode with the surging tides of nationalism and war.

Newspapers and Voice

The management and voice of student newspapers provide another way to chart the gender politics of the 1890s high school. Newspapers, of course, both represented student opinion and formed it. The students who edited the paper were elected to their positions, but they also earned those positions. Unlike class officers, who had limited and discrete tasks to perform, usually beginning and ending with presiding over class meetings, student editors had substantial ongoing duties which required stamina, initiative, and responsibility. Student editors needed to persuade other students to write articles, and they needed to write articles themselves on deadlines. Their business editors needed to cajole local merchants to advertise, despite testimony frequently conveyed in their pages that advertisements brought few new customers. Student newspapers both created and reported the big stories of the 1880s and 1890s: the coalescing of school spirit around senior class identity, the rise of athletics, the receding of the lyceum, and the emergence of a vigorous nationalism surrounding the build-up to the Spanish-American War. School newspapers documented the masculinization of the high school in the 1890s.

7.3 Girls' battalion at Concord High School, 1899. Girls of all philosophies united in the cadet corps, including self-declared New Woman Sarah Woodward, second row, left, editor of the Concord (New Hampshire) High School newspaper. Vinnie Boutwell, front row, foreground, author of a prize-winning essay excoriating the New Woman, is captain. New Hampshire Historical Society.

Yet those are by no means the only stories the newspapers tell. The sparring in newspaper columns between boys and girls suggests profound movement in concepts of gender. Both boys and girls took note of girls' academic prowess and paid it respect. The numerical predominance of girls in some high schools, too, brought with it a surprising (and temporary) normalization of femininity, such that students and teachers sometimes assumed, and usually at least acknowledged, the feminine application of advice and insight. The eventual emergence of "new girls" as editors and actors accompanied an egalitarian approach to gender roles that would not characterize the society beyond school walls for several more generations, and then only temporarily. Within these generalizations, though, there was enormous variety from school to school, and we now turn to two of these individual stories.

Concord High School in New Hampshire had a rich newspaper tradition, with six papers opening and closing in the last third of the nineteenth century. Concord's early papers were created and managed by boy editors. Its earliest printed paper, the *High School Mite,* appeared in 1880 and was the brainchild of a committed amateur high school journalist, W. J. Drew, and his friends. Published as the "official organ" of a mysterious organization, the "G.C.A.P.A.," the *Mite* measured 2½ by 3 inches and was designed as a novelty entry in the swelling world of amateur journalism that followed the production of the new presses. Drew's irreverent voice is unmistakable during the year of the *Mite*'s existence, his senior year of high school. After graduation, when he could no longer claim to be writing as a high school student, he conveyed high school news in a column of his new publication. The *Mite* and its successor publication communicated Drew's desire to speak for an authentic "boy culture" in competition both with the slick New York papers and with the Victorian voice of mainstream culture.

The *Mite* was gently subversive. It carried a woodcut of a "High School lad, in his favorite position—asleep," and a piece by "Ike the dog" offering to "tell you more about dogvanes, doggerel, sad dogs, and merry dogs; but you would think me dogmatical." It observed that "all young men dream of becoming professional base ballists." In the fourth issue, April 1881, the *Mite* announced that a "large majority" of the members had met and decided "to admit as members young ladies interested in this work." The "young ladies" never got a chance to make many contributions, though, and it is unclear whether any joined the *Mite*'s staff before Drew graduated several months later and the paper ceased publication. The *Mite*'s final issue covered Concord High School graduation, indicating that attendants heard boys give the valedictory and orations, including one entitled "Every man is the architect of his own Fortune." A girl gave the salutatory, and another read an essay (girls usually did not orate), "How Shall We Dress?"[40]

The last issue of the *Mite* announced that it would cease publication, and that Drew would publish a paper under the masculine and somewhat daring name *Amateur Sportsman*. Drew made sure to distance himself from the disreputable associations of "sporting" culture, though, promising, "We shall publish no slang." The first issue came out the month after graduation and included a poem about an old drunkard and a story about hunting for woodcock. It also included a column, "High School Notes," in which Drew and his editors reported on graduation for the second time. *Amateur Sportsman*'s version noted that graduation was "largely attended, the ladies predominating as usual," commented on the excellence of the floral display, and noted the sex of the graduates: ten boys and "9 gi—young ladies."[41] Drew's play with the terminology for his female classmates suggested his ambivalent posture toward them. The charting of the construction of the term *girl* in Concord High School newspapers and the nation at large—along with its replacement of *young lady* as the preferred term for respectable middle-class females in their teen years—is one way of charting significant historical changes in the history of female adolescence.

Amateur Sportsman lasted only two issues before Drew folded it into the *Granite Echo,* which he coedited with a kindred spirit, Herbert D. Smart. No longer students themselves (Smart, too, had graduated from Concord High School), they turned over the column "High School Notes" to "a competent student, who would be glad to receive items relating to his department." Significantly, the editors continued to see the paper as a vehicle for the voice of irreverent youth, which was in theory coeducational. The editors announced themselves "Devoted to the Interests of Boys and Girls of the Present Generation," adopting parallel rather than chivalrous language. They were most interested in representing an inclusive youth cohort, the next month describing themselves as representatives of the "rising" generation. Still without female staffers, however, they spoke primarily for boys' culture. Their high school columnist favored jokes about boys' facial hair, teacher-student poker games, and bad behavior. When President Garfield was assassinated, Drew and Smart fantasized devilish punishments for the killer, appealing to—and reflecting—a juvenile, masculine imagination.[42]

The activities of girls (though this time "young ladies") received scant, even generic treatment. Another column (now known as the "High School Mirror") noted,

Hall has gone to Warner, farming.

Conn to West Concord, ditto.

Some good drawings in crayon were done this term.

Some of '82s young ladies are engaged. Who'd a thunk it?

Fuller reports on the activities of girls were either strained or naive, as revealed in two items from the issue of November 1880. One used a rhetoric derived from big-city society pages to report on the "very brilliant" party given for one girl's fifteenth birthday. ("The toilettes of the young ladies were exceedingly handsome, and indeed, some were very elaborate.") Another item from the same issue revealed a naive perspective on female classmates: "For some weeks, the boys of the High School have been busy balloting for the prettiest girl in school. The result as announced a few days ago, showed that Miss Kate Jones was the lucky candidate, she having received 16 votes." The winner over eleven other candidates, the lucky Miss Jones received "a solid silver medal beautifully engraved as follows: 'Awarded to Miss Kate M. Jones, the prettiest girl in the High School, Concord, N.H., Nov. 1880,'" and on the reverse "Compliments of the boys of the Concord High School." There is no evidence of how this early beauty contest played with Miss Jones and the others, but its frank mention of "girls," along with its familiar presumption of the right to rate them on their looks, was in keeping with Drew's attack on Victorian niceties. Drew and Smart continued their attack on chivalric forms, dropping the honorific "Miss" when referring to high school girls in 1882. The coeditors' fresh and saucy voices suggest that it was probably the pair of them that their high school column was referring to when it noted that the younger high school classes regarded the alumni "as seditious demagogues."[43]

Concord High School's next student newspaper, the *Comet,* appeared in November 1882, after Drew announced his retirement from amateur journalism. Edited and published by the senior class, the *Comet* pronounced itself "devoted to the welfare of Concord High School and to the educational interests of the city." But beyond this stolid mission statement, the *Comet,* like the *Echo,* saw itself as a reporter on youth culture. It recorded high school fads, noting, for instance, that "nicknames are somewhat scarcer than they were two or three years ago in our school."[44] Its inaugural issue had a male editor and two female "associate" editors, a pattern that once established lasted through the *Comet*'s tenure and into that of its successor, the *Volunteer.* Although the editor was a boy, girls were well represented on the *Comet*'s staff, and together they advanced a generational perspective, seeking to present a student voice.

The *Comet* documented changing gender patterns and markers on the road to maturity. As might befit an editorial staff reporting in part on itself, the editors alternated between first and third person. In January 1884 the editors noted the introduction of some high school girls into adult society: "Several of the young ladies of the School received [callers] on New Year's." (The practice of remaining at home to receive visitors meant that girls were now part of society and might allow or invite gentlemen to pay visits.) That year it was decided that girls, too, would need to declaim their pieces at Concord High School graduation, rather than hiding behind written texts. The boys offered their condolences: "It is rather rough we will admit, but you have our warmest sympathies." The editors noted girls' advances elsewhere, too. At an exchange newspaper, "The young ladies seem to be at the head of the editorial board, a fact which certainly speaks well for them."[45] Whether the item was inserted by girls, admiring others' successes, or by boys, condescending to them, we cannot know.

The parallel structure of the language sometimes led to surprising equalities. When editor James Halloran in 1888 began a postelection editorial in the *Volunteer,* he emphasized shared experiences: "Boys! the campaign is over. Girls! Torchlight processions and paying off election bets are things of the past and distant future. So now we have no excuse for poor lessons." Whether or not girls had marched or wagered or been distracted, or whether boys had, for that matter, Halloran chose to generalize a common election experience.[46]

In 1889 another newspaper project united student leaders of both sexes in the "bad boy" posture advanced by W. J. Drew. The project was a one-issue newspaper entitled the *Bombshell,* which was designed to "make a loud explosion." Bearing the epigram "Let not your angry passions rise," printed backward, the paper professed to hope that "no stray fragment will wound a passing friend." Nonetheless, the editors announced, "We make no apologies, but in brusque boy (and girl) like fashion, with our little air gun 'shoot folly as it flies.'" The *Bombshell* was clearly designed to stir up some controversy at Concord High, to be "full of life and interest." A daring send-up of school authorities, the paper began by taking on the board of education, then went after the high school principal and the teachers. The editors noted that a good deal had been said in the newspapers about displaying the flag in the schools. "We guess the board thought it said flog." They ridiculed the principal as "a rather nondescript personage," of gangly limbs and humorous physiognomy, and described a new young teacher as "plump as a partridge, ripe and melting and rosy-cheeked as one of her father's peaches." As to the students' posture toward this new teacher: "No, we did not try to initiate her. We dreaded the consequences." The paper mentioned one student who "had the misfortune to experience such a catastrophe. After the ordeal was past he could not be recognized." Years later, a former student penciled in the reason in her copy of the paper: "Holden got slapped in the face."[47]

The publication did indeed cause an explosion—from the superintendent's office, in a letter published in the *Volunteer*. The letter writer, "One Interested in the School," purported to have been looking forward to the publication of the *Bombshell*, "knowing that if it at all resembled the 'Volunteer' it would be well worth the reading." However, the interested party continued, "I was greatly shocked . . . when I saw the nature of its contents. A chapter of slander and misrepresentation, clothed with a ludicrous attempt at sarcasm, is directed not only against the pupils, but the corps of teachers and the board of education. It suffices to say that serious results might ensue to the publishers, if the matter were pushed." The superintendent and principal's offices, however, did not elect to push the matter. Instead, they let the *Bombshell*'s editors off with a warning: "School journalism is a good thing, if not carried beyond the bounds of decency. The managers and editors of this paper are worthy members of the school, as far as I know, and it is to be earnestly hoped that this will be their last attempt at hurling a 'bombshell' which may have the qualities of a boomerang."[48]

The "worthy" names on the *Bombshell*'s masthead included much of the student leadership of Concord High School. Although the editors' introduction spoke for both male and female students, the dedication to the High School principal, John F. Kent, was more specific, inscribed as it was to "A man who once was a boy . . . by boys who hope to become as genuine men." (Evidence suggests that Kent was indeed an inspired and dedicated educator—as perhaps the derring-do of the students might confirm.) It seems likely that the point man was publisher S. E. Burroughs, also the publisher and business manager for the *Volunteer*, who cut something of a swath through the school. The entire editorial staff was female, however, including Emma E. Jones, president of the Young Ladies' Literary Union, and Edith Ayling and Minnie Day, writers for the *Volunteer*. What is significant here is that girls active in the life of Concord High School seem to have gone along with Burroughs in his bold tweaking of institutional authority. Their status as otherwise exemplary young ladies might well have provided useful cover for Burroughs. The instance of the Concord *Bombshell* suggests the ways that adolescent solidarity between boys and girls may have helped to provide some of the meaning of the late-century high school and the emotional coloring of the fin-de-siècle "girl."

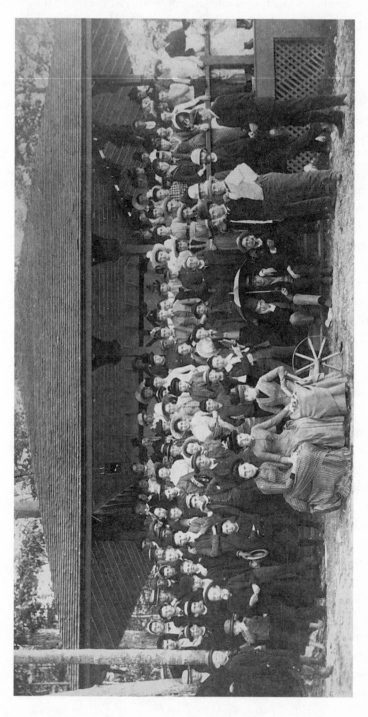

7.4 A generation "full of life and interest," 1888. Concord High School celebrated the end of school by a picnic to Penacook Lake in June. Included in this group shot are Sherman Burroughs, responsible for the *Bombshell* caper, Emma Jones, president of the Young Ladies' Literary Union, and Lena George, the class's valedictorian and "a powerful advocate of the cause of Woman's Rights." New Hampshire Historical Society.

The Concord *Volunteer* went into hibernation during the early 1890s. Whether the controversy over the *Bombshell* was a factor is unclear. The *Volunteer*'s publication of the superintendent's letter of rebuke seems to have sowed some discord between Burroughs and *Volunteer* editor James Halloran. Given the heavy hand of the school board in barring girls from the Lyceum, it is conceivable that the board discouraged the continued publication of student newspapers in the wake of the *Bombshell* caper. The *Volunteer* made only a brief resurgence in 1892 under the leadership of a male editor in chief.

When it reemerged for the long haul in 1895, though, it was under the auspices of the entire student body, not just the senior class, and the editorial board included one male and one female representative from each class. The leadership had been refigured as well, with a female editor in chief and a male business manager sharing top billing. The use of the designation "editor in chief" to refer to a girl editor was especially significant given the reluctance of class organizations to elect girls as class presidents. (It was during this landmark school year of 1895–96 at Concord High School that the debate society, presumably with the principal's acquiescence, took up the question of opening the club to girls, voting against the proposal largely because there seemed to be no girls interested in joining.)

For the next two years, the paper had a female editor in chief and a male business manager. During 1896–97, in particular, the *Volunteer* noted the significance of girls in many departments at Concord High. It commented on the girls' dominance in the prize speaking competition, an important annual event. Concluding that this demonstrated a new balance of power, the *Volunteer* observed, "The girls seem to be taking the lead in the school this year." The paper itself was an important indicator of this leadership. That year the editors ventured into gender politics when they took on "the boys" on the sincerity of their opposition to smoking. Noting that most of the boys had signed a declaration from the Anti-Cigarette League opposed to the manufacture of cigarettes, the editors commented tartly, "We think that the idea is laudable, but would it not serve a better purpose if it stated that the 'undersigned will not smoke cigarettes?'" Perhaps it was this "chilly climate" for boys that caused the Lyceum that same January to refuse to debate another school because there were girls on the team.[49]

In the fall of 1897 Elmira Lamprey was appointed editor in chief and Lawrence Hill treasurer of the *Volunteer*. Lamprey and Hill's *Volunteer* challenged the habits of both the school's girls and its boys. One column observed dryly, "It is fin de siecle for girls to giggle spasmodically, especially in public places. More should cultivate this charming habit."[50] And, more substantively, the

Volunteer ran an editorial which took on schoolgirl excesses of language and emotion. Although the editorial was not signed, the "voice" seems to have been female, and chances are that it came from Lamprey herself.

The editorial described a young man in Washington, D.C., taking a girl-friend through the new Congressional Library, "the grandest building in the country, a building that one wants to look at and take in silence." The "gush-ing young woman," however, thought the library was *"pretty!"* "Pretty dresses, pretty pins, pretty pictures, a pretty day, a pretty girl, a pretty sky—is there anything we don't call pretty in these days when we exclaim over everything and anything we see? What is a little more than *pretty* is *lovely;* and what is a little more than lovely is so *lovely* or JUST *lovely;* and what is too utterly utter of description is 'JUST PERFECTLY LOVELY,' with three nods of the head to make it just perfectly *lovelier!*" The student editor went on to describe a mountain-ous scene, with "snow-tipped Cardigan, and way back in the distance the still whiter Lafayette. . . . The view would be more *heavenly* than lovely, were it not that *heavenly* at once calls up 'those *heavenly* pickles' and that '*heavenly* dancer' and the 'perfectly *heavenly* time' of some enthusiastic schoolgirl." Nor were boys immune: "If girls talk 'just perfectly lovely,' boys have an 'awfully stunning' and 'mighty neat' way of saying things, too. It is only the careless, every-day use of all these 'lovely' words that makes them sound so ridiculous when they are applied to what is truly beautiful and heavenly and entranc-ing." The *Volunteer*'s editor urged her readers to go cold turkey. "So don't call everything *pretty* from a sunset to a string of beads, and don't call Huyler's bonbons *heavenly* and the latest game perfectly *entrancing.* Just put 'pretty' and 'lovely' away in a drawer until you learn to do without them." The au-thor knew that there might well be consequences for those who forswore such conventional markings of femininity as the gushing language of schoolgirls. But she urged them on "even if it does give you the reputation of being 'so stiff and cold.'"[51] In encouraging her fellow students to forgo the hyperbolic language of sentimental schoolgirls, she was urging them to adopt the cooler and more deliberate stance toward life favored by the New Woman. Lamprey seemed to appreciate that new language might be appropriate for a new girl's anticipated role as full partner in the coeducational high school.

At the same time that Lamprey was exercising still-new authority as edi-tor in chief and proposing new models for femininity, however, the center of gravity at Concord High, at least among some boys, was clearly elsewhere. Even under Lamprey's editorship, the outbreak of hostilities in Cuba sug-gested what stories would be run. War news took up many of the spring issues. The class historian of Lamprey's class of 1898 published a piece in the commencement issue of the *Volunteer,* the last issue under Lamprey's editorship, and managed to avoid nearly any mention of her or of any other girl at all. (His piece, which according to convention mentioned as many classmates as possible, saw fit to refer to only two "young ladies," one who was noteworthy because she died, the other because she was a champion speller.) Instead, the historian, who signed himself "an ordinary member," recalled his class as the class "for Athletics." He celebrated and named three class presidents who had left, the three members of the Lyceum, two star athletes, two classmates who had played a role in a town "carnival," an expert punner (known as the "Funny Man of the Senior Class"), a male two-time champion speller, and one brilliant classmate who "must do nothing except study dictionary and encyclopedia." He mentioned without naming the class's contributions to the high school battalion (a captain, a lieutenant, two sergeants, and a corporal). All in all, one might have imagined that all the noteworthy students in this class were male. In fact, however, the "ordinary member" noted that nine members of the class had college plans, four men and five women.[52]

Perhaps at Concord High School the turf was divided. Certain kinds of activities were performed by boys. The class historian's vision embraced such activities as these—the informal antics which centered around athletics and the bantering exchanges of class meetings. In part, this vision suggests the kinds of divisions suggested in the historian Laurel Ulrich's image for the economy of rural Maine in the early century. Boys and girls simply saw different things, noticed different people, wrote different narratives, even though their activities took place side by side, or, as in Ulrich's image, were interwoven, just like the contrasting threads in a gingham check pattern.[53] Girls clearly were everywhere in Concord High in the 1890s, but despite their numerical majority, it was possible for some sets of eyes to look and simply not see them.

Whatever currents were sweeping up "the ordinary member" of the class of 1898 took over the *Volunteer* and seemingly the entire high school the following year. During the fall of 1898 the *Volunteer* broke its recent tradition of dividing responsibilities equally between boys and girls and named a boy editor in chief, who was given dominant mention on the roster, and a girl "literary editor," the title recalling the formation of a girls' literary union as an appropriately genteel counterpoint to the debating society. Girls virtually disappeared from the *Volunteer* as its editor urged Concord students on to greater patriotism and school spirit. Concord High School had been successful at coeducating its student elite for a time in the mid-1890s, often by bringing successful female students into newspaper work. But during the year

1898–99, it looked as if that power sharing had come to a halt. The impact of the war, the linkage of nationalism and school spirit, and the increasing centrality of boys' sports seem to have succeeded in canceling the impact of girls' numbers and their scholarly accomplishments as routes to public power and influence.

A particular marker of that change was the publication in April 1899 of an essay which had gained Vinnie M. Boutwell first prize in that year's essay contest. The daughter of an employee of American Express, Boutwell contrasted "The Girl of Yesterday and the Girl of To-day"—the home-centered, self-denying girl of the past with the selfish, disrespectful girl of the present. She commended the dignity of "our old-fashioned girl," the "gentle bearing that came of good breeding and careful home influence." In contrast with the "arrogance of self-assertion" that characterized the modern girl, the old-fashioned girl "did not scorn parental advice" but took as the keynote of her life "not only to be happy but to make others happy." The essay derided the girl of today, "who lives in the so-called 'woman's century'" and "often unsexes herself by donning hideous and unhealthy styles of garments. . . . Many of us turn our heads with shame and disgust as we notice the selfishness and worldliness that exist where formerly dwelt true womanhood and sweet, ladylike manners." To clinch its carefully constructed critique of the modern girl, Boutwell put her to the ultimate test: who "would a thoughtful man choose for a helpmate?"[54] One might imagine that the "new girl" was already obsolete.

The following year, though, she was back at Concord High School, at least temporarily. Sarah J. Woodward was the editor in chief, and she brought with her a still jaunty voice as she took on squarely the claims to masculine authority made possible by the Spanish-American War. "Why these canes, why these arms in slings, these black eyes, these broken ribs?" the *Volunteer* asked in December of 1899. "Are they the results of the war in Manila?" The answer was negative. "No, they are simply caused by a little pleasant recreation and gentle exercise indulged in by the boys. To one who does not understand foot ball, its only aim seems to be for the players to knock each other over and fall in a heap."[55] The insouciance with which Woodward made fun of boys' athletics suggested a high school atmosphere far away from what would come in the next century—and also perhaps a debt to her uncle, Will Drew, the irreverent founder of the *High School Mite* twenty years earlier.

Under Woodward's editorship, the *Volunteer* offered mixed coverage and continuing evidence of the health of the high school's "new girl." Particularly noteworthy was a story proposing winter recreations for the Christmas break.

To its female readers, in particular, the paper suggested forgoing the traditional, passive, indoor pursuits: "Now, girls, instead of sitting in the house reading stories, why not get some snow-shoes and, when the snow is hard packed and dry, make trial of them?" Anticipating objections, the editors urged self-reliance: "Do not say that you can not do it because you have no one to show you, but start out alone and, if you do not try to run at first, and are careful, you will get along very well and have a merry time." Perhaps not the cry of a revolution, its support of female autonomy was direct and no-nonsense. The same year, the *Volunteer* announced the formation of a Girls' Basketball Association, and acknowledged the continued life, despite earlier reports to the contrary, of the Lyceum, to which two girls were elected as "honorary members." [56]

The Spanish-American War had reinforced Concord's discovery of the excitement of interscholastic athletics to marginalize temporarily the activities of girl students, despite their academic success and their substantial numbers. The birth of "school spirit" was an energizing source of collective fun, but it centered around boys' sports and the boys' cadet corps and often left girls in auxiliary positions as chief cheerleaders or as members of the girls' cadet corps. (Both Vinnie Boutwell and Sarah Woodward joined the girls' cadet corps, Boutwell in a leadership position.) The student newspaper was a critical part of this complex of generational solidarity, and as such it often contributed to the coalescence of student identity around the competition of boys' athletic teams. During 1896, when Concord had a championship football team, one journalist wrote, "How distressing it would have been if we had been without a paper this year to chronicle the accounts of the boy's great athletic victories!" [57] The heralding of the accomplishments of boy athletes and boy soldiers, though, was tempered by the spirited ribbing awarded "the lords of creation" in the columns of the *Volunteer* by their female classmates. Not a completely gender-balanced utopia, the Concord *Volunteer* revealed a nineteenth-century high school world in which the competitive claims of the sexes were vigorously aired by girl editors who had imbibed the high school's egalitarian implications.

There were more girls than boys at Concord High right through the late nineteenth century, with girls making up about 60 percent of the typical graduating class. Even with that lopsided ratio, it was still possible for some boys not to notice the girls, as witnessed by the 1898 class historian's odd history of his class stripped of its female majority. Girls were unlikely to return the compliment; they certainly knew their male classmates and recognized them. But at the same time, their numerical dominance in the coeducational

classroom encouraged a lively sense of self-respect which emerged in the humor, the program, and the language of their student newspaper.

Where the numbers were even more dramatic, the acknowledgment of
gender issues might emerge not only in the writings of girl editors and journalists but in the culture of the school itself, among administrators and male
students as well as among the female majority. In the case of the high school of
Milford, Massachusetts, where only one-third of the graduates were boys, one
could argue that the high school was to some degree feminized. The protagonists of high school stories, and indeed the normative students, were often
female.

In the 1880s and 1890s, Milford was a town with a large first- and second-
generation Irish population and increasing numbers of Italian workers coming to work in the quarries and foundries, as well as the city's straw factories
and millinery business. As was often the case in second-generation immigrant communities, most sons and daughters went to work in their teen years.
If there was any income to spare, though, "lace curtain" Irish might send a
daughter to school in preparation for teaching, or enroll a son to prepare him
for the priesthood. (The athletics editor at Milford, J. F. McDonnough, was
so destined.) The expectation of girls' eventual work, along with their significant numerical preponderance in the high schools, made for a uniquely
sensitized culture of gender at Milford High School.

From the inception in 1884 of the school's newspaper published by the
senior class, girls and boys shared leadership, a pattern that would characterize the paper for much of the rest of the century. The *Oak, Lily, and Ivy* was
led by two general editors, one male, one female. Its title was meant to embody "Strength, Purity and Tenacity," its editors imagining that they would
need strength to withstand an anticipated "storm of criticism" and hoping
that their readers might resemble "the ivy, clinging to us through fair weather
and foul." The lily, of course, signaled the cultivation of purity of action and
thought. The editors eschewed politics but hoped to give the greater community, especially the alumni, "some idea of what we are doing." They also
hoped to obtain practical experience for later life.[58]

The pattern of appointing one boy and one girl to each editorial office
established a tradition of gender balancing which characterized few other student institutions, or indeed newspapers at other schools.[59] At Milford, of
course, such a practice wasn't truly representative, for there were substantially
more girls than boys at the high school. Nonetheless, it set a pattern for shared
leadership which would color the stories the *Oak, Lily, and Ivy* published and
the perspective that it adopted. As the student voice of Milford High School,

too, the *Oak, Lily, and Ivy* contributed to the making of a student culture which sometimes advanced a distinctly female point of view.

Milford's student newspaper published many stories with young female protagonists and also published stories that addressed gender as a concept. An 1886 graduation number published "Extracts from the Diary of a High School Girl," a concept that was sufficiently popular that a year later the paper featured "Leaves from a Trojan Girl's Diary." The November 1885 issue included one story on "The Kitchen of the Future," another on Framingham Normal School, largely attended in the mid-1880s by girls. The paper took up gender as a category, reflecting on "'father-land' but 'mother-tongue.' How suggestive are these compounds!"[60]

It also took on gender roles, as a subject both for fun and for reflection. A standard—and brutal—feature of the gender sparring of the late nineteenth century was the attack on the effeminacy of the fin de siècle dandy, with his flannel waist, soft tie, crimped mustache, and pompadour. "Our young man also affects a certain air, which he fondly hopes to be 'killing'; it is killing, but in a way he does not intend. And as he struts along perfumed, befrizzled, satisfied with himself and the whole world, he really does look 'just too lovely for anything.' If he only would put on petticoats, what a charming girl he would make!" Accompanying such gloves-off assaults were more modest reflections, such as one about a show featuring manual arts, many of them domestic. One female editor reflected that "the boys also ought to know something about plain cooking and sewing," noting that "those boys who intend going away to school will find it very convenient to know how to sew on a button or mend a tear." Such skills might have come into use more immediately, as revealed by a schoolwide trend of beautifying the schoolroom with desk covers, which the "young ladies" appear to have made both for themselves and for their less needleworthy male classmates.[61]

If girls promoted sewing for boys, they appear to have been willing to lean into school jobs gendered male. In May 1887 the paper reported the annual reappearance of the "rake brigade," celebrating the sure arrival of spring. The editors noted, "This year the troop has not been limited to one gender, but the girls, too, have done nobly, and now the yard presents a creditable appearance to the passers-by."[62] More pointedly, the *Oak, Lily, and Ivy* reported on what seemed to be a nearly inevitable assumption of women's rights to political participation. The mood of the nineteenth-century high school seemed to suggest that women's suffrage was preordained, and indeed imminent.

The language of the women's rights controversy was high school vernacular. One article about teachers' meetings began, "It has been publicly acknowledged in the Milford high school that woman should have her rights." Whether by earning them or by natural inheritance was a matter of debate. One editorialist observed that many of those buying newspapers on a recent train ride were women. The conclusion: "What a striking commentary of the times! Surely, if woman shows such interest in the welfare of the country, the time is not far distant when she will stand in places of trust and honor, before judge and jury, and at the polls equal to man." A less sanguine girl journalist begged to differ on the facts, observing that high school girls "do not and will not" read the newspapers. Noted Rena Matthewson in 1889, "The boys all read the papers. They are interested, for before long they will have a share in making their country's history. If the girls expect to live to have the same privilege, why are they not willing to do all they can to become worthy of it?" To the end of making women worthy, in 1892 senior M. Bessie Gates introduced a new column entitled "Current Events," which reported on the Homestead arrests and the Populist Party. That year the paper reported that many college girls had participated in mock presidential primaries "just for the purpose of finding out what 'might have been' if women were allowed the right of suffrage."[63]

Of course, not everyone at Milford High School was of a mind about woman suffrage. One male editorialist suggested in 1893 that the question "Should Women Register" provoked lively debate that year, and he went on to spoof, "It is reported that one or more of our most stylish young ladies were so enthusiastic in regard to this matter that, forgetful of their age, they presented themselves to be registered. Out of respect to our Civil Government teachers, however, we are inclined to believe that this story is the invention of a malicious slanderer of the school." Malicious slanderer or not, women's rights were the talk of male editors as well as female editors. John McNamara told his readers about women's rights in England, noting "that woman has far more privileges in England than in the United States." And when a writer took up the critique offered by Henry Ward Beecher of the working woman's "double shift" (a problem described by Beecher as the problem of the "eight-hour man with a fourteen-hour wife"), it was accompanied with the acknowledgment that "the most of us think that there will be a time, we cannot tell how near, when the women will have their rights and honors, too, long since due to them."[64] The culture of Milford High School, with its preponderance of high-achieving female students, could not help but promote such a view.

The result was that female writers for the *Oak, Lily, and Ivy* evidenced a complicated relation to gender. Sometimes, from their positions of leadership, they adopted the "male gaze," briefly surrendering their own sense of gendered limitations and speaking with a universal masculinity. At other times they inadvertently seemed to naturalize their female identity, assuming it as their high school norm, and therefore the norm of their world. These practices were by no means consistent or dominant, but in the few places they emerged, they are noteworthy. The nineteenth-century high school, Milford High School more than most, communicated to its female students that they might temporarily forget gender—or fundamentally reinterpret it—as they thought about their possibilities.

Numbers were part of the story. One could argue that it took not just numerical superiority but overwhelming numerical superiority for girls to accomplish this divorce from such a fundamental parameter of nineteenth-century life. Conjoined with their numerical superiority, of course, was the impact of academic superiority, as demonstrated in Milford by the tendency of girl students to dominate the honor rolls and to claim the top spots again and again. One anonymous editorialist acknowledged this trend when she or he suggested that one should look to the girls to see the stress and drama of impending graduation exercises. Noting that "it is the boys who are weak just now," the editor offered visitors help in interpreting what might be perplexing behavior: "If you see a stout hearted young miss . . . with an anxious face and a heavy sigh draw a note-book from her pocket, jot down a brilliant idea before it escapes, slip the note-book back in place, then hear a sigh of relief coming from her troubled heart, don't think she is a juvenile reporter, oh, no, she is only an innocent school-girl preparing her essay for graduation."[65] The reference to "an innocent school-girl" suggests that the visitor might be surprised to see girls in such roles; in the context of Milford High School in the 1880s, however, schoolgirls might easily be stout-hearted.

Female editors sometimes found themselves providing leadership to both male and female classmates in their editorials, in the process confusing their own points of identification. In 1888 a female editor wrote to encourage "Ambition in Life." Warming to her subject, she encouraged all her classmates to think about their responsibilities to their country: "You all, I doubt not, will soon have the privilege of suffrage. Will your influence always be for the right?" There was a problem with her analysis, though, which she moved to correct: "Think not that I exclude the young ladies, for even if we are now denied the right of voting, it will not be so long." Whether referring to her sex in the third person or moving to join it in the first, she felt that the civics lessons that were good for her male classmates were equally appropriate for her female classmates—destined to wait thirty-some years before actually reaping the results of her optimism.[66]

An inspired spokesperson for woman's voice in the early 1890s, Luella Ballou demonstrated similar leadership and a similar universalizing of her gender. Her comments were New Year's thoughts, which she offered as inspiration to all of her classmates: "If you wish to do some good deed, do not wait until the next New Year comes but go about it at once. Do not sit with folded hands because you think you have no bad habits to break, but stretch out a helping hand to poor humanity struggling at your feet." Certain examples leaped to mind. "Think of the Kings' Daughters [a religious benevolent organization] and the noble work in which they are engaged. They comprise ladies of all classes all over the United States. They go into the haunts of poverty, the homes of the sick, and with a few cheering words and such help as their means will admit, leave sunshine behind them and go home happier in the consciousness of one good deed done. If you should spend this year in lightening a few of the cares of those who have cause to be despondent, instead of making mountains out of the small mole-hills of your own cares, do you not think you would look back upon it as the happiest year spent?"[67] What is significant about Lulu Ballou's reminder is its unself-conscious generalizing. At Milford High School, Lulu Ballou did not need to—nor did she think to—direct her advice to "the young ladies" to follow in the highest traditions of women's benevolent work. To her, either the advice was equally relevant to her male classmates, or she had come to naturalize femininity as she thought about the people in her immediate universe. Either response was significant within Victorian America.

In another editorial Lulu Ballou adopted a different solution—in this case the use of universal "man"—as she urged her classmates on to higher ambition. Addressing her exhortation to "boys and girls," she asked her classmates to "fix some point for which to strive and work hard to gain it, and when you have reached it fix another one farther ahead and strive for that. Let there be no limit to your ambition." Her conclusion: "It is the best mascot a man can have."[68] The use of universal masculine nouns and pronouns, of course, was common until the recent past, however dissonant it has become. Current practice has rejected such usage for its disregard of the possibility of a gendered "difference." Such language from the pen of Luella Ballou, however, was significant in just the way it rejected the gender differences which characterized nineteenth-century culture, instead entertaining shared ambitions for all her classmates.

Milford's principal, too, came to apply these ambitions to all his students —and to reveal the inadequacy of his language to express those thoughts. In a similar exhortation two years after Lulu Ballou's essay, he belatedly and humorously learned that he needed to address and include his majority-girl student body when he offered advice and admonition to his students. Admittedly, he started off inauspiciously, as he addressed the Milford student body: "Aim at something; don't shoot at random boys! You who are familiar with such sports as base-ball and foot-ball, are well aware of the inestimable advantage of what is termed 'team work.'" He went on, though, to include and to specifically describe challenges for both sexes. "No person who is in the habit of dealing with young people of both sexes, whether in the schoolroom or at the fireside, can fail to have observed what a wonderful transformation it will effect in a young lad or lass, when once he gets something to work for. When once Mollie has decided to fit for college, or Jack for a technical school . . . they seem to blossom out like new things. They are like a football eleven with a clear-headed captain. . . . . They are like a ship with a rudder: they steer straight for the port. They are rifles with a bead-sight and wind-gauge: they aim square at the bulls-eye." Metaphors from male culture streaming behind, Milford's principal launched full-speed ahead into a progressive program for women. That program encouraged girls to avoid drift, and to take charge of their destinies. "When the world is full of positions for bright young men and women who are not afraid to work and do not know too much to be taught, the listless, purposeless boy who wants nothing more than a seat at his father's table and a bed in his father's house, or the insipid young girl who has nothing in view but to slide through school and wait around for someone to come and marry her, is indeed an anomaly which smart, energetic people cannot understand."[69] Clearly, not only had the gender politics of Milford High School influenced female and male students; the principal as well had received a political education. In presiding over the students who came to his high school, he learned that he would need to take his female students seriously. They dominated the academic rankings and were critical to the success of most endeavors at Milford High School, including its illustrious newspaper. As befit someone backing into new insight, Milford's principal, just like his students, stumbled to find the words to speak to both "listless, purposeless boy" and "insipid young girl." What emerged was awkward and disjointed, indeed humorous to modern ears.

It is exactly that language, though, that suggests the significance of the transformations in late-century high schools. It was language on the cusp of change, not yet smoothed out with a new set of conventions, still struggling to keep up with emerging understandings. When Milford's principal reached for the available language for student exhortation, he emerged with gendered sports metaphors. It may not have occurred to him to reject them, but he did understand that he could not simply universalize the high school boy but needed to speak explicitly to his female students as well. At high schools around the region, girl editors also sought the language and the voice which could speak both to and for all their classmates, and they too came up with strained and awkward locutions. It was that language of strain, though, which told the story. Girl editors, and surely many girl students as well, were coming to think of themselves as full players in the world of the nineteenth-century high school, and they needed new language and new voices to communicate that fresh understanding.

Certainly, the coeducational high school was no gender-free utopia. School newspapers and girls' diaries suggest that it was an arena of contest and intermittent blindness. Feminist scholars and theorists in the 1980s have had cause to challenge any "myths of coeducation" which suggested that equal access meant equal outcome. Even those who point out the inadequacies of nineteenth-century coeducation, however, acknowledge its contributions.[70] Girls who had been trained to doubt their intelligence in the nineteenth century discovered their academic competence in coeducational high schools. In the lopsided awarding of academic honors to girls, too, they discovered the general aptitude of their sex. This represented an incremental addition to the moral authority women were accustomed to claim as the attribute of their "separate" sphere. In discovering their brains, they also discovered their full humanity, coming to claim with male classmates a sense of generational identity and common citizenship which brought them into the new century prepared to join the public world. They discovered in high schools a spirit of parity and partnership, which encouraged them in forging new lives for themselves and new options for other women.

EIGHT

Friendship, Fun, and the City Streets

Going to school did more than enhance girls' senses of competence. It also pulled them out of their mothers' houses into the town and city streets, introducing them to one another and to the shops, squares, and sidewalks of urban life. In their walks to and from school, in their constitutionals, their flirtations, and their trips to bake shops, middle-class girls participated fully in the culture of their time. The pronouncements of Victorian morality, so widely and explicitly disseminated, gained their urgency from the strength of the opposition—the flowering of a consumer culture of goods, the growth of peer-based institutions, the expansion of heterogeneous cities; all were seriously threatening to notions of a uniform and genteel moral righteousness. In recent years, historians have paid increasing attention to the presence of shopgirls and factory workers promenading in the city streets. It is clear that as middle-class girls withdrew from the domestic workforce and attended schools, they too filled the city streets. Like their working-class sisters, they found a new kind of peer culture which challenged patriarchal and domestic authority. This new culture of friends celebrated fun and challenged rectitude. It ultimately contributed to the modification of the program of Victorian self-culture to create a prototype for a different kind of girl—less sober and purposeful than the New Woman but nonetheless her linear progenitor.

Outdoor Play and Childhood

The nineteenth century is often known among historians as the century of the child, when children were first accorded what is to us a natural quality of precious innocence and spontaneity which adults aspired to preserve. In some sense, the freedom of teenage girls in the streets was a prolonging of a sanctioned childhood status. Before they reached puberty, girls as well as boys of the middle classes were urged outside to play robust, healthy games and to savor the once-only experience of childhood. Children undoubtedly have always played in the bits of time left over from the subsistence chores assigned them. But it was only in the nineteenth century that a class of adults, and their children, too, came to consider playing the appropriate occupation of children, whether male or female. Nineteenth-century children who worked might even deny their status as children. The children of the middle classes played, and they played most healthfully and most picturesquely out of doors. The editors of the children's periodical *Harper's Young People,* in response to a reader, put it narrowly: "I think it is very proper for girls to coast, skate, and amuse themselves in healthful ways out-of-doors."[1] Others offered more expansive endorsements for the health of outdoor play.

Growing up in rural Concord, Massachusetts, at the age of eleven Louisa May Alcott narrated the prototypical child's experience. She complained about her piano lesson: "I hate [Miss P.], she is so fussy." She described a romp outside with her sisters: "I ran in the wind and played be a horse, and had a lovely time in the woods with Anna and Lizzie. We were fairies, and made gown and paper wings." With allusions to nature and fantasy, Alcott, already a serious reader, was living out a romantic vision of childish play. Two years later, in 1845, the thirteen-year-old Alcott could still savor the freedom of a child's life in the country. In a letter she told a friend of a walk with a teacher which found them all wading across a big pond: "We went splashing along making the fishes run like mad before our big claws, when we got to the other side we had a funny time getting on our shoes and unmentionables, and we came tumbling home all wet and muddy, but we were happy enough, for we came through the woods bawling and singing like crazy folks. . . . We are dreadful wild people here in Concord, we do all the sinful things you can think of."[2] Louisa May Alcott's letter to a friend in Boston implicitly contrasted the abandon possible in the natural world of Concord with the constraints on life in the city.

But even for children growing up in the city in the mid-nineteenth century—the children of the rich as well as of the poor—play took place outdoors. The Bostonian Emily Eliot kept a diary which suggests the freedom in public that even the maturing daughters of the elite could experience as late as the 1860s. The Eliot family lived near Boston Common, and Emily's father, Samuel, a Brahmin educator, occupied a series of prestigious positions, serving as a lecturer at Harvard and superintendent of Boston schools. (Emily Eliot went on to marry John Holmes Morrison and to mother Samuel Eliot Morrison, one of the preeminent representatives of Yankee aristocracy.) Eliot's diaries, kept after the age of eleven, describe her attendance at school and at parties, her intense family life, and her far-ranging unsupervised play in the city streets.

One March day in 1869 after school, for instance, Eliot stayed in the schoolyard for a while to play "poison," went home for a music lesson, and then swung by to pick up four friends; together the friends went down to the Berkeley Street bridge "to watch the cars," a classic urban activity for children of all classes. The next year, when Eliot was twelve, she and a friend walked downtown to get a soda, and "then we played on the State house steps, but a man set us off." The friends then played in Hancock Avenue and went back for another soda. At different times Eliot mentioned rolling her hoop on the parade ground, playing by herself in the public gardens, and playing "in" Commonwealth Avenue, Chestnut Street, and Arlington Street. When her music teacher had a recital at her rooms across town, Eliot and a group of playmates walked over on their own and "the boys" hitched rides for them on their way back. Even Emily's description of a mobbed St. Patrick's Day parade in 1869 suggested a fundamental sense of comfort in public Boston. At the age of twelve, she and her friend Gracie set out to watch the parade "where the crowd was very great and all of a sudden, Gracie disappeared." Eliot did not panic but found a sheltered corner to protect her. After the crowd dispersed, Emily remained unfazed, reporting that she "got out and met Grafton Abbot and walked with him as far as Arlington Street where I saw Mamie Perkins and rolled hoop with her." Well after the 1840s Irish potato famine spurred massive immigrations into the eastern seaboard—a time that most historians see as the beginning of the withdrawal of genteel women from the streets—Emily and her friends seemed to regard the city landscape surrounding them (or at least its downtown center) as no more threatening, and perhaps equivalent to, their own back yards.[3]

Discipline of Walking

Even beyond the age when girls might be encouraged to play in the city streets, their presence was sanctioned by another activity: the healthful walking between home and school, and the long constitutionals judged critical to a maturing girl's health. If the lives of Victorian girls were defined by disciplines, one of those disciplines was daily exercise, most commonly long walks, sometimes of several hours' duration, from one side of town to the other.

Good daughters embraced a walking regimen as religiously as they did a regimen of diary keeping. Like writing, though, walking suggested form rather than content. In their long rambles from one side of town to the other or into the country, or their promenades back and forth along Main Street, girls achieved a level of social freedom which ran against the grain of chaperoned domestic propriety.

Most physicians and advisers agreed about the benefits of walking. Writing in the 1890s, the *Ladies' Home Journal* quoted "a celebrated physician" when it endorsed walking as the preferred form of exercise. "Tennis, he believes, is too violent; cycling renders women awkward in their walk; cricket is also an uneven exercise; at golfing the strokes made are not conducive to the cultivation of physical beauty. . . . Riding is one-sided, and croquet is not exercise at all. Walking, however, may be fast or slow, according to the desire or health of the individual. Walking is probably the only exercise which calls every part of the body into active and healthy motion." Earlier, a writer for the same magazine instructed American girls how to walk: "Let the arms swing free; throw the shoulders back, the chest forward and the head high." Another columnist recommended other sports for girls, including tennis, bicycling, rowing, and any men's sport "with but one exception, foot-ball." But she fell back on walking as both the simplest and "perhaps the best," suggesting that girls build up to six miles per day.[4] Walking was an approved form of exercise for a range of Victorians, but it was clearly girls who had both the most time and the most need for its healthful effects. G. Stanley Hall, in his opus *Adolescence,* suggested the special role which walking filled in the lives of unmarried women, who "are, and ought to be, great walkers." Walking, Hall implied, might tap energies otherwise likely to go to unhealthy activities, such as "estheticism" or the solitary vice of "self-abuse." He explained, "Dr. Taylor thinks . . . that the difference between boys and girls in learning self-abuse on account of the more obvious anatomy of the former is overestimated, and that the latter, more commonly than is thought, not only find their organs and use them improperly, but are more difficult to cure of this vice." A healthy alternative for unmarried women was to spend that excess energy in walking which married women and mothers might spend "normally in other ways—" an allusion both to the demands of raising children and to coitus itself.[5]

Walking was exercise, therapy, and ideology all in one. Sarah Browne, a married woman writing at midcentury, explained her walking in language appropriate to her region and class: "I walk again this forenoon in search of health—my walk is a principle, a religious duty, so the time is not lost."[6] Time

8.1 "Serene enjoyment and blistered feet," 1894. As part of their "constitutional" responsibility for their health, girls and young women routinely walked for several hours and substantial distances—up to twelve miles. These fashionable young walkers leave the city receding behind them. Reprinted from *Ladies' Home Journal,* August 1894, cover.

spent walking was time invested rather than squandered. Less intense than modern jogging, aerobics, or weight regimens, the walking of nineteenth-century girls nonetheless could compete in seriousness; what it lacked in strenuousness was compensated for in its duration, sometimes occupying two or three hours of the day.

Margaret Tileston's sister Mary was afflicted with health problems throughout her adolescence in the 1880s. Undoubtedly Margaret's regular walking, on the streets of Salem, Massachusetts, at first in her sister's company, was in part a response to Mary's "search for health." Beginning at the age of thirteen, Margaret worked up to two hours per day as the time she was expected to walk. Even when it was bitterly cold outside, Margaret walked. Even when she had no company, she walked, "simply for the sake of taking a walk." Some of her walking took place at school recess, but that still left an hour and a half of walking to do either before or after school. When she missed an hour of exercise, she recorded it in her diary. She sometimes walked early in the morning before the sun came up. (One May morning she got up at 4:20 and walked an hour before breakfast.) She often did not return home until after dark, one winter night not making it back until 7:00 P.M. After one day of walking, during which she had "thought a good deal," she still found herself short of the required two hours, so she and her sister walked up and down in front of the house before going to bed. Only once did she confess to her diary that walking two hours was "a tiresome thing to do daily." As befit her self-improving temperament, she instead used this bodily discipline as the occasion for a mental one, explaining that during one long walk she had "got some more ideas about walking."[7]

Seldom do we have witnesses—or walkers—quite as disciplined as Margaret Tileston, but documents of other teenage girls suggest that walking was considered both a preventative and a palliative. When Alice Stone Blackwell's head "felt as though I had been hung up by the heels and all the blood had run into it, filling it almost to bursting," her cousin Emma "prescribed a walk, and we found our way to the chocolate factory." When she took a long circle route home from school— "about 7 miles I should think"—she relayed her sense of accomplishment: "Am at present in serene enjoyment of a good conscience and blistered feet." Growing up in Fort Wayne, Indiana, Agnes Hamilton, too, reported frequently on walks of ten to fourteen miles. When she missed her walk one day while she was away at school, she reported her regret to her diary: "I do not like to spend a day without any exercise." Annie Winsor, writing to her parents while away at school, described one day's activities: "Not much walking here you see," but she reassured them that the day was unusual, and that "besides I have my early morning walk of half an hour."[8]

In addition to being a discipline, however, walking was a necessity for most maturing girls. Going to school in the nineteenth century usually meant walking to school, often in company with friends and classmates. Between discipline and necessity, there were enough agemates walking in the streets that urban girls rarely needed to walk alone. Indeed, the hours spent walking became opportunities for sociability, for making and broadening acquaintances, for flirtation. The walking that began as a discipline or an expedient eventually turned into an occupation in its own right, which gained its meaning from the opportunities it offered for peer relations beyond adult authority.

Walking to school in itself could become a highly choreographed peer ritual. Jessie Wendover attended public high school in Newark, New Jersey, in the 1880s and 1890s, and in her diary she enumerated her walking companions. When she was fifteen, Wendover often collected friends as she went so that "we eight went down together." Sometimes, however, they would break into pairs or regroup, as when one friend "got one of her amusing cranky spells on and tried to make herself believe she was mad at me, and said she would not walk with me." The foursome broke into pairs then, with one pair removing their hats as they puffed up the hill, and the other sitting on the stoop and laughing at them. For Wendover the significance was that "we four have gay times going to and from school now-a-days." In Shelby, Iowa, a few years later, two friends ducked out on fourteen-year-old Josephine Brown, leaving her to walk to school with a boy. Brown noted, "They thought they had a good joke on me but I didn't care." Later, on the way back from a trip downtown, the arrangement that had begun as a prank was formalized. The girls stood out of sight on the depot platform to pull up their stockings, "and Daisy made the arrangements that she was to walk to school with Ed Schmidt and Mary and I might walk with Lew Benham. When those two gentlemen came along they were notified of the arrangements. They complied with them and all was so."[9] Trips to and from school brought school cohorts out into the unsupervised "public" world, where youth could devise their own rules and practices.

The forthright "Daisy" took matters into her own hands. For the more reserved Margaret Tileston, walking in the Salem streets only gradually expanded her social world and encouraged her to take initiatives within it. After a slow beginning in coeducational Salem High School, Tileston gradually discovered connections to her community. "I can scarcely take a walk without meeting one of my school-mates or at least some one that I know," she observed in the spring, after beginning classes the previous December. She soon began to walk with some of these schoolmates, noting the next fall, "I begin to feel better acquainted with the girls in my class." The next winter she noted the company of a boy: "Dick Manning walked along with me for a part of the way." By the following month, she confessed in the spine of her diary, she felt bold enough to initiate relations: "I bowed to Master Smith on my way to school." The next week, the group of girls she was walking with actually invited some boys to "turn round with us, but they could not." The confidence Tileston was gradually accruing allowed her on her own to overtake a boy that month and accompany him to school. Margaret Tileston did not record the ensuing conversation, but she did note some of the subjects she touched on in her long walks with other friends. On one three-hour walk, she and her companions talked of friends, boys, teachers, and dancing. In different walks that summer of her sixteenth year, Tileston mentioned conversations "about calling boys by their first names." Margaret Tileston was a purposeful young woman, as her extraordinary diaries make clear. Yet even for Tileston, the meaning of walking gradually incorporated its sociability. For many girls less focused than she, walking up and down city streets—or "promenading" as detractors would describe it—nearly lost its function as exercise in its fostering of peer intimacies.[10]

Ruth Ashmore, the *Ladies' Home Journal* columnist championing restrictive morality, cautioned that if there was a possibility that a girl might be joined by boyfriends on a walk, she should be accompanied by a chaperon. (And in any case, a girl of eighteen should not go out without a chaperon.) This was only one of a long collection of warnings—observed mostly in the breach—offered by advisers anxious about the freedoms of girls in the city.

Ruth Ashmore's advice ran at cross purposes with other, older codes of courtliness which made men responsible for the safe passage of women through city streets. In reflection of this chivalric remnant, it was customary for boys to escort girls during and after evening events, dances, or parties. Often these escorts seem to have been assigned by the hostess. In a later interview, Etta Crawford recalled her life as a girl in frontier Portland, Oregon, in the 1860s and 1870s. Customarily, she would receive written invitations to dancing parties in homes, which specified the name of the escort who would be responsible for getting her to and from the event and for seeing "that you were properly escorted all evening." She was careful to distinguish this constant attendance from the practice of "dating" popular in the 1930s at the time of her interview: "We really didn't have dates. Mother considered we were too young. . . . I don't approve of this present-day manner of traipsing around half the night. None of the boys that attended me to the dances were on calling acquaintance."[11] This imposed arrangement was reflected in other girls' accounts of such evenings.

At the age of twelve in Milwaukee in the 1860s, Cassie Upson wore her white dress and pink sash to a "sociable," returning home at 11:30. She declared that she had enjoyed herself "only *pretty* well," perhaps because of her partner: "I think my escort's name was Clark. Oh! he *was* a gawky." When Jessie Wendover attended a boy's birthday party in 1885 at the age of thirteen, she noted that there were about a dozen "couples there." She arrived at about 8:00 P.M., she said, and returned home at the extraordinary hour of 3:00 A.M., noting that "Harry Mccarthy saw me down to supper and home."[12] Wendover led a protected life and was most often accompanied by her parents to and from social affairs and when she went downtown in the evening. It appears, though, that her parents on the Atlantic seaboard shared with Etta Crawford's on the Pacific Coast a parental protocol which sanctioned the assignment of "escorts" for girls as young as twelve and thirteen.

Whether assigned or not, though, it was incumbent on boys or men not to leave girls unescorted in the evenings—especially as those girls became young ladies. (This chivalric convention put a strain on outnumbered high school boys, who nonetheless remained responsible for their female classmates after evening events.) While a student at the Harvard Annex, Annie Winsor recorded an embarrassment in the diary written for her parents. She had attended an evening party in Cambridge which her attractive Latin instructor was also attending. She and a fellow female student had agreed to go home together. (She reported that her friend "trots to and fro from Miss Smith's at all hours and did not a bit mind going from here alone.") The two young women timed their departure carefully: "We waited till Mr. Preble [their teacher] and two girls had got safely out the door and away, and then started downstairs, and with averted eyes 'thro' the entry, opened the front door, and there stood Mr. Preble leisurely fixing his neckhandkerchief—evidently waiting for some one." The friends "felt like two children caught at the jam-pot and no way of escape." The consequences were preordained. Mr. Preble would be obliged to walk everyone home, which was indeed what happened. In a letter to her brother, Ellen Emerson, daughter of Ralph Waldo Emerson, described her discomfort with such genteel expectations when she returned from a party. Her escort, she explained, was a Mr. Soule, "who— I can imagine your exultation—made me take his arm. But the experiment confirmed me in my old opinion. It is easier and pleasanter to walk alone and be able to keep one's dress out of the dust. There!"[13] Like other chivalric practices, being escorted was a ritual meant to convey obligation as well as protection.

Girls' presumed need of escorts provided access to welcome and unwelcome suitors alike. Cassie Upson noted in 1866 that "that abominable little nip of a Perkins" had walked her home from church and had discerned only that "I wasn't quite as talkative as usual." A reprinted item from a student newspaper in Kingston, New York, in the 1880s suggested that girls reject the terms, replying, "'I would rather be excused,' when asked by young gentlemen for the privilege of escorting them home from church at night. The practice may be hard on the 'boys,' but it is one which every self-respecting girl will adopt and adhere to. For a young lady to be asked on coming out of church, . . . to surrender herself to the society of some young hoodlum who has been waiting outside while she was decorously attending divine worship, is an insult which would justify a kick from father or big brother." Rather than seeking contact in "this sneaking, unmanly, vagabondish way," an interested suitor should "call upon her at home, and take pains to ascertain whether his society is agreeable to her parents as well as herself."[14] This item suggested the dilemma embedded in the system of boys escorting girls: sometimes the solution was worse than the problem it was meant to address.

The practice of escorting equally opened possibilities for flirtation, of course. The Milford student newspaper slyly noted that the "girls of '88 all believe in 'protection'—after class parties." Lily Dana noted one such arrangement: "Of course Brinckerhoff went with Edith Barry and I saw them turning up one of those lonely streets by the Catholic church, in just the opposite direction from her house. Mother says she does not think it was proper." Whether proper or not, it was clear that intimacies contracted within approved contexts of school or church would have ample room to flourish even within genteel practices coming and going in the city streets. The historian Beth Bailey has found radical changes in courting practices in the 1920s resulting from the movement from the maternally supervised "front porch" of home to the "back seat" of male-owned cars.[15] The fact was, though, that many middle-class girls in the nineteenth century were not at home but at church or at school, and in the evening they were presumed to need male escort well beyond the surveillance of their mothers.

During the day, girls had more freedom to walk on their own. These less-formal walking arrangements—ostensibly undertaken to run errands, to get to or from school, or for exercise—provided ample opportunity, too, for flirtation. Alice Blackwell and Lizzie Morrissey, both writing in Boston in the 1870s, though from different class perspectives—found themselves unwitting walking partners in such scenarios. When Alice Blackwell, nearly phobic about encounters with boys, went to meet two schoolmates, the pair was otherwise occupied, talking loudly and waving handkerchiefs to attract the attention of two boys. Alice was so mortified that she hid behind a hedge and finally strode home by herself, "descended to the cellar, groped my way to the milkroom, and soothed my irritated feelings by drinking an enormous quantity of milk." When Lizzie Morrissey walked to a nearby square to hear a public band concert with two friends, she reported that the walk down was nice, "but when we got there Ida soon left me for Art Woodride and didn't come back again; I felt provoked. Then Hattie left me for two fellows, but she came back and introduced them." After this bad experience, Morrissey concluded that she would "never go to the square again when anything is up with either of them."[16] Part of her subsequent isolation within her house might have been a response to discovering herself abandoned by her best friends in favor of flirtatious promenading.

A more willing participant was Mabel Lancraft, a high school student and spirited daughter of a Fair Haven, Connecticut, oyster grower, whose 1880s diaries cover her fourteenth through seventeenth years. Lancraft spent much of her time in her early teens promenading and flirting outdoors. One summer day of her fourteenth year, for instance, after a trip to the ocean, she and her friends were playing house—"I was the mamma and they were the children"—when a neighborhood boy came along and suggested they go to the park. "So we went and we met Mr. Hovey down there though he didn't approve of us going." The group of friends continued to play, though, picking up others. "Sadie and I had our arms around each other and Sadie was my beau." The boys accompanied the girls nearly home and exchanged compliments. "Sadie said I was awfully pretty and if she was a boy she would be in love with me. And he [Ed Dupee] said what pretty eyes that Miss Lancraft has got and he agreed with Sadie." Mabel Lancraft later drew a line through the above, an early—and ineffective—moment of reserve; Lancraft grew more daring as time went on. By the end of the summer, she announced boldly that she and a friend met two boys of their acquaintance "and we raised ____ and we promenaded up and down with them in front of Mr. H. Olds."[17] At the beginning of the summer, Lancraft simply disregarded the advice of a neighboring adult; by the end of the summer, the opportunity to flout respectable opinion was part of her pleasure.

Mabel Lancraft's early teenage flirtations were generally confined to friends and schoolmates, whom she met and bowed to in their mutual walks around her Fair Haven neighborhood, to the station, and also sometimes through downtown New Haven. When she was seventeen, though, Mabel Lancraft confessed a modest initiative with a stranger. "Coming out in the car a young fellow stood up in front of me and I am afraid I flirted a little." At the age of nineteen in Providence in 1879, Charlotte Perkins recorded more daring ventures into the public world in the context of her busy social, school, and work life. Perkins's own air of gay abandon during these years becomes particularly intriguing given her later persona as Charlotte Perkins Gilman, perhaps the most searing critic of the constraints of late-Victorian womanhood. When she was a teenage girl, however, Perkins's life was active, independent, and dense with friends and acquaintances. One January day in 1879 she recorded going skating with a friend: "See many fair damsels and noble youths. Skate with a noble youth by the name of Mathewson." In all she summed up her time out of the house at the end of her diary entry: "Walk 3 m. Skate 2 h." Other days produced other walking companions to evaluate. One day she left her studies at the Rhode Island School of Design with "ye gentle Douglas. Lo he dwindleth into insignificance on acquaintance. Pah!" A trip to Boston occasioned several dates. After a trip to the theater, Perkins reported on a "very pleasant walk home. Rather prolonged beyond the strict bounds of necessity, thus"—and here she diagramed a detour around the block. Her verdict: "Nice boy, Walter, but young." Despite her worldly tone, though, it was not until the end of the summer that one of her walking companions took her up on her flirtatious gambits. She reported a walk with a Robert Brown, not one of her favorites: "Go to walk with him. Pitch dark Grove. Attempts a mild embrace. First time from *any* man! . . . Quench his advances with much coolness. Becomes respectful, even awestruck."[18] Though not as grave as her later persona, clearly, even in girlhood Charlotte Perkins was formidable.

Much of Perkins's skating, walking, and flirting took place unchaperoned in public spaces. It probably involved her with a fairly narrow range of middle-class, Yankee young men, many of whose attendance at nearby Brown University suggested their "respectable" origins. Clearly they were not all prior acquaintances. For instance, after one day's skating, she reported, "Wandered home from park alone." She noted a new acquaintance made along the way: "Befriended by youth whose name I have forgotten." On the train returning from Boston, though, she made a mistake: "Mildly attempt to flirt with gorgeous neighbor in cars," she wrote in 1879. However, this "youth" responded with unease and stiffness and the deferential comment, "Yes, Miss." At this point Perkins reported, "[I] congeal." Clearly she had misjudged the social circumstances of this handsome stranger and concluded that he would recognize her as a peer, but he did not. What is significant here is Perkins's comfort and confidence. Far from regarding her public world with caution (if her journal is a reliable guide), she seemed to come alive in it, take risks in it, and to rejoice in her freedom to go where and how she pleased. From the later author of "The Yellow Wallpaper," one of the most powerful fables of the domestic

8.2 Freedom in public, 1883. As a teenage girl, Charlotte Perkins came and went freely in the streets around her home in Providence, Rhode Island, frequently meeting and flirting with nearby college students and other young men. Perkins here is in her early twenties. Schlesinger Library (Cambridge: Radcliffe Institute, Harvard University).

imprisonment of Victorian wives, this record of the public freedom of Victorian daughters is striking. In a recent book, Sarah Deutsch has argued that only in the 1890s did bold New Women begin to appear unescorted in Boston streets, using big vocabularies to defend themselves from forward strangers. The journals of Charlotte Perkins, among others, however, suggest that Victorian girls in previous decades led lives far less cloistered than advisers would have wished.[19]

Shopping

If sometimes it seemed as if girls walked in order to flirt, it was equally true that middle-class girls' walking increasingly was tied up with shopping. Aside from going to school, the most common destination for a walking girl was "downtown," where girls got drinks at soda fountains, bought treats at a bake shop, and did errands for themselves and their mothers. Usually mothers accompanied teenage daughters for major purchases—of coats, for instance—and in those cases shopping was often characterized as work. But the multiple small trips girls reported—for a bit of lace, a bag of candy, or some coffee for their mothers—initiated girls into the world of discretionary shopping beyond parental supervision in the city streets.

The northeastern seaboard had participated in a market economy since it was settled in the seventeenth century, but following the Civil War, which dramatically expanded transportation networks and industrial capacity, Americans saw an increase in the kinds of goods now widely available. In the early nineteenth century, stores sold staples which home manufacturing could transform into appealing apparel. Good taste was demonstrated by the skill and ingenuity with which a home seamstress could transform standard stock into original creations. By the late-Victorian era, it began to be possible for consumers to satisfy themselves at the store rather than in domestic workrooms. Shopping was transformed from arduous work to good fun. Middle-class girls, who were leaning to discriminate in what they read, found shopping as well to be an arena in which they could demonstrate taste and through taste, *self.*

Sarah Browne, a Salem housewife and mother of schoolgirl Nellie Browne, went out to buy provisions for her family in 1859 and recorded the event that evening: "I go through an ordeal of shopping in the morning." Sarah's correspondence with her daughter over her wardrobe suggests that for both Brownes outfitting Nellie was indeed something of an ordeal, requiring multiple calculations to determine whether to buy ready-made, to have made, or to make oneself. Nellie wrote in some detail about a quest for a summer bonnet. "If I cannot get one with white ribbon on the outside, may I get what Miss Mary thinks pretty for me. I may not see one I like ready-made, then I should buy the straw, buy the white ribbon, and have it trimmed at the store you spoke about." The shopping expedition, accompanied by "Miss Mary," a teacher at the Agassiz School, ended with a bargaining session in which Remick's store was persuaded to make a bonnet for Nellie for the sum of $7, bargained down from the $8 originally asked. Unsure of herself as a shopper, Nellie requested affirmation from her mother. "Do you think I have done wrong, to get such an expensive bonnet? We tried, but could not get one for less."[20] The mails documented negotiations that otherwise took place on the spot.

When Alice Stone Blackwell and Lucy Stone went out shopping together in 1873, Alice reported the discord in her diary:

> We mutually begged each other to put on our tombstones
> "Died of shopping with an unreasonable mother"
> "Died of shopping with an impracticable daughter."

Mabel Lancraft, too, was an exuberant explorer of her urban landscape, but she "just hated" going shopping with her mother. "After hunting around all the afternoon," the pair finally found a blue flannel bathing costume for Mabel to wear to the shore.[21] The problem was undoubtedly the question of authority. Victorian mothers had not yet learned to defer to daughters' tastes, yet daughters were modern enough to feel the significance of the statement of fashion.

Margaret Tileston rarely expressed open displeasure, but the language with which she came to describe shopping trips with her mother suggested her sense of her own marginality. When she was fourteen and fifteen, the pair went to Boston and her mother bought her a Dolman Cloak, a sacque, material for a spring dress, summer balmoral skirts, yellow gloves, and so on. She "tried to get me a made sailor suit in Boston, but did not succeed." By the ages of sixteen and seventeen, Tileston used the passive voice for their joint shopping trips. "Boots were bought for me." "A new brown jersey was bought for me." It is true that her syntax robbed her mother of responsibility for the purchases, but it also served to underscore her own remoteness from purchase decisions. Tileston's use of the passive voice for shopping decisions resembles other moments in her journal when she chooses to blame a vague fate for what happened to her rather than confronting her feelings about her controlling mother. When away at school when she was fourteen, Margaret went shopping alone with her sister. Her language marked the difference. "Among other things we got 21 yards of red picture-cord to hang up our pictures with." She reported, "We had a very funny time."[22] For Margaret Tileston, it was far easier to have a funny—or even a fun—time when she could avoid the sticking point at the moment of purchase when her mother affirmed her ultimate authority over her daughter's desires.

It was therefore a noteworthy event when girls made serious purchases on their own. Margaret Tileston's full maturity as an independent shopper did not come until she was nineteen. She announced that she parted from her father at 3:20 and "went to do some shopping—about the first time I ever went alone." As befit her new sense of responsibility, she carefully documented her purchases: "a pair of boots at Tuttle's for $3.00, a plaid waterproof for $3.00, a pair of dog-skin gloves for $1.25 and a pair of fleece-lined for .88, a night-gown for .75, 2 corset-covers for .75 a table-cover for $1.00 and a veil for .37." Margaret Tileston's independent shopping coincided with her graduation from high school and her initiation into the multiple roles of womanhood. Lily Dana and her sister Rosa got a brief taste of this serious responsibility when their mother went off to the mountains in the summer and the two girls were boarded out for a few weeks. "About ten o'clock we went down town and felt quite independent, buying our own things," reported sixteen-year-old Lizzie.[23] Serious, deliberate shopping was one marker of adulthood.

Most girls had some discretionary moneys, though, and began to record shopping trips very different from the purposeful and responsible "ordeals" shared by mothers and daughters. Girls who had allowances or were given pocket money by parents began to shop for fun and seemed to regard shopping as more akin to recreation than to work. Cassie Upson, who was raised by her aunts in the 1860s following her mother's death, routinely made small purchases when she visited her father and his new wife in Milwaukee. In sociable trips downtown she bought birthday presents, food treats, and items for her own use. For her friend Ida's twelfth birthday, for instance, Upson bought a picture of Tom Thumb and his wife, and for other friends at different times she bought a little doll and a pewter tea set. She also bought treats for the moment, sometimes more than once a day. For instance, on Friday, September 4, 1863, she went downtown in the morning with two friends to get some plums and a blank book. In the afternoon, she went downtown again, this time getting more plums and some peanuts. (She also got some calling cards, "for Lizzie and I are going calling soon.") On other trips downtown with friends, Cassie bought a bottle of "New Mown Hay" (perhaps a fragrance) and "got me some gaiters." Several decades later in Salem, Massachusetts, Margaret Tileston and her friends bought food to eat on their walks around town. After one long May walk with friends, she wrote, "we hungered after buns, and after Sally G. had plunged into one or 2 shops, she bought a dozen buns and we ate 3 apiece. She also bought some pickled limes. We felt mashed on buns all the way home."[24] The buying of peanuts or plums to eat on the spot, or even a fragrance, could not themselves have justified Cassie Upson's trips downtown. As a schoolgirl, though, Cassie did not have other strenuous demands on her time. The same leisure which allowed her time to read and write in her journal and to play with friends also left her time to go downtown and go shopping.

And indeed groups of schoolgirls, either before or after school, on the weekends, or during the summer were early recreational shoppers. Their journals describe leisurely trips inspecting wares, admiring shop windows, and purchasing sodas or incidentals. At the age of fourteen in 1871, Emily Eliot went off shopping as well as playing alone, noting a trip "to Young's bookstore, where I bought the Gypsy Books, and also to a dollar store where I bought a pair of imitation gold earrings." At the age of sixteen, Margaret Tileston may not have gone shopping alone, but once when out walking she met a friend and tagged along with her when she "stopped quite a while at Shaw's picture store." As often as not, girls were "window shopping" rather than engaged in serious searches for needed objects. Jessie Wendover and friends went downtown one November day on an errand, but when they got there, they discovered that Haines's store had been redone, so they went all the way through it, noting that "it has been much enlarged lately and they keep all most all kinds of fancy articles now." Another time Wendover resisted her friends' pleas that she accompany them to Ruckleshaus's in Newark. The goal was "a music-box chair which when one sits in it plays till they get up, and they wanted me to sit down without knowing about it."[25] Not yet serious consumers for such luxury goods, Jessie Wendover and her friends were beginning to experience the fun and the frivolity which might lead to more spontaneous buying as adults.

Mabel Lancraft in 1889 only occasionally noted idle visits to stores as part of her promenading pattern. One summer day, though, she reported that "Maude and I went up town and went through Cutler's Art Store," on the way to meet a friend. In another remarkable passage, she described an aimless trip after school meandering and shopping up and down New Haven's main street in a reverie, oblivious to other demands. "After school I promenaded Chapel St. for the brief space of two hours and then I took my wandering foot steps to W. B. Ferris's Shoe Store and then proceeded to encircle my fairy shadowy foot. . . . 'How funny' is that most useful of useful articles nameless [sic] a pair of shoes. Then I betook myself to the Paris Kid Glove store and perceeded without hesitation or delaying as I had hitherto afore. . . . About this time appeared to be a strong censation coming over me as if I had lost something or not had something! Imagine my surprise when I discovered upon further investigation that I had *not* had my dinner!"[26] What's extraordinary about Lancraft's reverie is her total surrender to the tempo of promenading and shopping—and the freedom which allowed her to become so lost to domestic obligation that she overlooked such an elementary piece of daily scaffolding as the noontime meal.

Shopping and Self

Generally girls walked, shopped, and promenaded with peers. Excursions with mothers signified serious business and were sober affairs. One family which did not fit this pattern was the family of Jessie Wendover. Jessie and her parents often went to downtown Newark in the evening in the '80s "to do a little shopping," stopping and having soda water on the way home. After one such recreational evening trip, Jessie reported that her mother and grandmother had accompanied her; "had a nice time. There were *lots* of people out." Some of the Wendovers' shopping excursions were farther ranging but still intent on pleasure. On one April day when Jessie was sixteen, she reported "Mamma and I went over to N.Y. this afternoon, just on a 'lark.' We walked up 14th St., 6th Ave. and 28th St., and had a good time doing a little shopping and looking in the windows, etc." Mother and daughter returned to New York to inaugurate the Christmas season, as they had before. By the late century, Christmas emerged in a number of diaries as an occasion for shopping. Wendover reported: "Mamma and I spent the day from about 11 A.M. till nearly 6 P.M. in N.Y. shopping for Christmas. I never saw anything like the number of people that were out; the stores were one perfect jam, and it was almost impossible to get near the counters, and still more so to purchase anything." Nonetheless the pair managed to buy "quite a number of things," and once more the daughter reported they "had a 'lark.'"[27] The Wendover women's association of pleasure with shopping represented a victory for the new department store barons of the late century, who were increasingly successful in encouraging shopping as a pastime for affluent women of all generations. What distinguished Caroline Wendover from other mothers was her leisure. Jessie was her only daughter at home (another had married and moved away), and she no longer bore the relentless burdens which characterized the Victorian matron's life. Her daughter remained her boon companion for life, never marrying and continuing to live at home after her mother was widowed.

Mother and daughter shared a pleasure in shopping born of a common pickiness. One characteristic of Jessie Wendover's consumer odyssey was her increasing willingness to discriminate as a consumer within the context of an otherwise extremely obliging life. Like Margaret Tileston, Jessie Wendover was a faithful diary keeper, a diligent student, and a loyal daughter. In her diary she kept account of moneys received and spent, friends received and visited, and schoolwork completed, and she ventured few negative comments at all. However, as a shopper, Wendover discovered something of a voice. When she was still twelve, she and her mother went shopping for an autograph album, but "could not find any to suit me." Two days later, her mother came to pick her up at school and repeated the trip, but they still could not find any "to suit" her. After the pair had bought a rubber stamp with a *W* on it, a few years later, they decided it was unsatisfactory and went out the next evening in search of a smaller *W*.[28] It is clear that Jessie Wendover's mother facilitated her daughter's fastidiousness; she may well have encouraged it.

In any case, it was after another mother-daughter shopping trip to New York at Christmas time that Wendover recorded one of the starkest negative comments in her diary. Jessie reported on the crowds and the window of Macy's department store, which was "decorated with a moving panorama representing certain events in the history of the U.S." In 1874 Macy's had begun its custom of elaborately dressing its windows for Christmas, and by the time the Wendovers visited thirteen years later, Macy's window had assumed its status as the symbol of the Christmas shopping season. Wendover was not impressed with the panorama, however, concluding, "I do not like it very well." In itself a fairly mild judgment, Wendover's pronouncement gains its significance from its surroundings. In the prolonged diary of her adolescence, Jessie Wendover never second-guessed her parents, despite their extreme protectiveness. She expressed only the mildest of disappointments when she did not receive the teacher of her choice, or the grade she aspired to. Yet when it came to her status as a shopper, Wendover felt that she had particular standing. Affluent and leisured, she recognized that in the increasingly overstocked marketplace of the late century she had choices that she did not feel in other more personalized areas of her life. These choices included a right to an aesthetic—and negative—judgment on perhaps the most ambitious production yet of the embryonic dream industry of salesmanship— Macy's Christmas window: "I do not like it very well."[29] In this statement, Jessie Wendover asserted her authority as a person and a self. This selfhood evolved through her membership in a discriminating class of consumers.

Girls begin to assert their selfhood through the choices they made as shoppers, just as they had through the stories they liked. These were, of course, limited choices made within a narrow range, choices which in Wendover's case did not threaten her extremely close relationship with her parents or her status as an exemplary student. And in the late nineteenth century they were also choices born of privilege. (Resisting the allure of Macy's Christmas window might have earned Jessie Wendover, demure schoolgirl, the status of being one of the toughest customers in the nation.) Increasingly, though, girls, women, and men of all classes came to be persuaded that shopping was one good way to assert and define a self—a way that, as in the Wendover family, was redeemed by its failure to challenge fundamental power relations.

Schoolgirls and Public Space

Between their walking for exercise, their walking to school, their flirting, their shopping, and their playing, adolescent girls were often outside in the squares and the streets. They were likely to seize any opportunity to get outside, to run errands, to go "down town." Cassie Upson commonly walked the few blocks from her house on the bluff to Milwaukee's business district along the river several times a day. At other times she walked a few blocks in the other direction to the shore of Lake Michigan to play or read with friends. One October day when she was twelve, she reported that it had been unpleasant and damp, "but notwithstanding have been down town three times." On many other occasions, it was true, as Upson put it for one August day in 1863, that going downtown was her "business."[30] Girls' lives in the late Victorian era consisted of reading, writing, school, and chores. Clearly though, a substantial other part was walking—running errands, taking constitutionals, and keeping company.

The same remained true in villages and towns late in the nineteenth century. Anna Stevens was fifteen in 1895 in the mill town of Guilford, Maine. Her diary describes a virtually wall-less public and social life, in which she and her friends moved as easily in and out of each other's houses, up and down the town's streets, as some might move from room to room. Her father was an engineer at Stearns, a local mill, and the Stevenses lived on Water Street, perhaps renting from the same mill. After school, Anna Stevens mentioned repeated visits of the same friend, and an incessant stream of moments of sociability. Particularly on warm weekends and during the summertime, when she was not in school and was not curtailed by inclement weather, Anna and her friends seemed to operate as free agents in their communal world. One April weekend, she explained that she "walked the streets" most of the time on both days. One summer's day she reported going over to the mill in the morning and "up to the P.O. two or three times." On another summer day, "over to Bessie's this P.M. Florence in three times." On yet another, three friends came to visit for a few minutes at different times; Anna Stevens reported that she herself "vibrated" between two other friends' houses for

8.3 Sociable youth, 1898. Anna Stevens grew up in the milltown of Guilford, Maine, where she graduated from high school in 1898. The diary from her fifteenth year records a busy social life in a virtually wall-less downtown. Courtesy of Sally Adams.

most of the day.[31] For such girls as Anna Stevens in small town Maine, Cassie Upson in frontier Milwaukee, and even Emily Eliot in downtown Boston, the late-Victorian distinction between private home and public thoroughfare virtually did not exist during their teenage years. Their time excused by their status as schoolgirls, they romped through their neighborhoods with abandon and what certainly seems to have been freedom.

Of course, in the late–nineteenth century city, as in cities and indeed in rural villages throughout time, there were real dangers to young girls — thieves, kidnappers, and rapists, at one extreme, rakes and mashers at the other. Precautions, protections, and outright restrictions on the conduct of girls undoubtedly bore some relation to actual incidents of crime. More important than actual statistics, however, were relative thresholds for the dangers and discomforts associated with public life — the extent to which families and girls themselves accepted innuendoes and impertinence, and sometimes even more, as urban facts, which were sometimes worthy of remark but little more. The dominant theme of girls' urban diaries was their movement, often free, often unescorted, through a public world. Yet at the same time, girls occasionally reported moments of discomfort inspired by looks or comments from strangers that at least briefly challenged their sense of security in the late-century city. When and for whom did these discomforts translate into curtailed movements, restricted behavior?

When Emily Eliot's companion was swept away by Boston's St. Patrick's Day parade in 1869, Eliot waited until the crowds dispersed, then went off to roll hoops with another friend she encountered by chance. Also in the 1860s, when Cassie Upson was visiting in the rural town of Rockville, Connecticut, one May day, she reported, "We saw a drunken man — oh horrors! He could only just totter along — He went into the hotel saloon." Her exclamation of discomfort nearly immediately subsumed by self-mockery, Cassie Upson clearly had learned to endure, if not completely ignore, the sight of drunken men in frontier Milwaukee, even then a major brewery city, where she lived before returning to New England. Trips through public life often included such isolated moments of excitement.[32]

Of course there were some general principles undergirding the movements of middle-class girls through city streets. When girls traveled by themselves from city to city, they were often put in the care of conductors or chaperons. (Emily Eliot and Lily Dana, who walked unimpeded through Boston's streets, both were put under the protection of conductors when they traveled by train.) And the onset of darkness required precautions not taken during daylight. (Both Jessie Wendover's and Marian Nichols's fathers demonstrated concern when rainstorms darkened the city prematurely and their daughters were still not home.) Even Cassie Upson, who was unusual in the uninhibited way she moved through Milwaukee, mentioned one evening in which she felt stranded because she was downtown alone. She had gone to church with a friend but on the way down had been distracted by a fire, "so I staid at a Mrs. Starr's on Milwaukee St. watching the fire and waiting for Lou. But instead of coming around and stopping for me she went off home. It was at least very unkind in her." Upson had probably chosen to stay by herself on this street of respectable houses and had been offered a harbor by a stranger whom she accepted as benevolent, of her own kind. Having been deserted by one friend, she could report a fortunate outcome: "Happily one of Eddie's [her brother's] friends . . . came along and offered to take me home so I got home safely."[33] It is unclear why in this one instance Upson felt there was a question as to whether she would get home safely. Presumably her friend Lou, like Emily Eliot when she lost her friend in the St. Patrick's Day parade, had taken up and walked with other friends when one disappeared. Certainly a fire at night was unnerving in itself, and for once, Cassie Upson was left at a loss, dependent first on the kindness of strangers, and then on serendipity which sent an acquaintance in her direction.

Cassie Upson's experience with the fire suggests the parameters of her comfort. Victoria Bissell Brown's important work on girls in turn-of-the-century Los Angeles observes that girls did not have the same freedoms as boys to cruise the late-century city. This was undoubtedly the case in mid–nineteenth century Milwaukee as well. After dark, by herself, Upson felt vulnerable, and she was glad to be "taken home" by a male friend. Still, her account demonstrates that girls had substantial freedom to come and go at a time often thought to be characterized by its constraints.[34]

Some girls were routinely more fearful than Upson. Alice Stone Blackwell, who took long walks to and from her Dorchester home, often reported fears for her safety. Without streetlights and relatively unsettled in the 1870s, her Dorchester neighborhood featured scattered prosperous houses in a rural setting. Lacking the dense population of the city, Dorchester was linked to Boston by rail and horse cars; Alice's knowledge of city vices without the protection of busy urban streets might have encouraged her to imagine danger whether or not it existed. On one March day, she didn't return until "it was quite dark . . . and I was horribly scared on the way home by a boy sitting on a fence and hooting, whom my fancy magnified into three drunken men." Her romantic reading habits fanned an already ardent imagination which was sometimes reinforced by the warnings of her mother, the feminist Lucy Stone, who the next week forbade her daughter to go out in the evening "and gave me a lecture on drunken men." Blackwell's mother proposed buying a large dog to escort her daughter through the city streets in the evening. Another winter evening when Blackwell was returning alone, she held a penknife open in her hand "in expectation of robbers and murderers, scared at every sound." Lucy Stone tried not to overindulge Alice's fears. The next year Alice reported that her mother sent her and her cousin Edith down to "Mrs. Sullivan's [the laundress] to pay her some money that is owing her, quite late in the evening, and it was very weird and windy and ghostly, especially where we came out upon the marshes. . . . When I left I whispered to Mamma that if I was assassinated she was to give my love to Papa and Mr. Collyer [the charismatic minister on whom Alice had a schoolgirl crush], which she promised to do."[35] A trip to Mrs. Sullivan's was likely to play to urban fears of new ethnic neighborhoods, as well as the "ghostly" fears of the supernatural.

Public Space and Girls' Reputations

If parents and commentators were sometimes concerned about the safety of middle-class girls in city streets, however, they were increasingly concerned about the moral implications of "good" girls taking to walking the streets in such numbers. Fears of precociousness not only encouraged parents to pospone discussions of menarche, they also created a reactionary challenge—too late—to girls' social freedoms. European observers had commented on the relative freedom of American girls from the routine restraints imposed on European girls for much of the century. In his 1840 opus *Democracy in America,* Alexis de Tocqueville noted the early emancipation of the American young woman from maternal control. "She has scarcely ceased to be a child when she already thinks for herself, speaks with freedom, and acts on her own impulse. . . . The vices and dangers of society are early revealed to her; as she sees them clearly, she views them without illusion and braves them without fear, for she is full of reliance on her own strength, and her confidence seems to be shared by all around her."[36] With the expansion of northeastern cities following the Civil War, and the increasing presence of middle-class girls unregulated in the streets, a range of commentators began publicly to reconsider that confidence.

One of the first broadsides in a newly intensified public debate about the character of "the girl" came from Britain and the pen of a journalist and clergyman's daughter. Eliza Lynn Linton's essay was notable in part because of its description of a modern type, not limited to one class. "The Girl of the Period" was published as a pamphlet in Britain in 1868, sold forty thousand copies from a single publisher, and first ignited a controversy there. Linton's British "girl"—in future debates known simply as the "G.O.P."—was loud, brassy, and disrespectful. She had traded in purity and "delicacy of perception" for the slang and the conspicuousness of the demimonde. Linton went on: "The Girl of the Period is a creature who dyes her hair and paints her face, as the first article of her personal religion—a creature whose sole idea of life is fun; whose sole aim is unbounded luxury; and whose dress is the chief object of such thought and intellect as she possesses." Linton's "G.O.P." was "far too fast and flourishing" to listen to her parents, "indifferent" to duty, "useless" at home, and dedicated to the pursuit of money.[37]

Henry James, who later made the character of the American girl a subject of his fiction, reviewed Linton's pamphlet in the *Nation*. He began by denying its relevance to the United States. "The American reader will be struck by the remoteness and strangeness of the writer's tone and allusions. He will see that the society which makes these papers even hypothetically—hyperbolically—possible is quite another society from that of New York and Boston. American life, whatever may be said, is still a far simpler process than the domestic system of England." In contrast to Linton's portrait "of youthful Jezebels with plastered faces and lascivious eyes," James offered the "large number of very pretty and, on the whole, very fresh-looking girls" of Boston or New York, "dressed in various degrees of the prevailing fashion."[38] James's use of the term *girl* to refer to wholesome and respectable teenage females was an early instance of its contemporary usage.

No sooner had James denied any comparison, though, than he began to warm to the task of finding similarities. He found American girls excessively devoted to the idea of being well dressed, which had "a sacred and absolute meaning." A girl of fashion "is undeniably a very artificial and composite creature, and doubtless not an especially edifying spectacle. . . . She has, moreover, great composure and impenetrability of aspect. She practices a sort of half-cynical indifference to the beholder (we speak of the extreme cases). Accustomed to walk alone in the streets of a great city, and to be looked at by all sorts of people, she has acquired an unshrinking directness of gaze. She is the least bit *hard*."[39] James's novel *The Awkward Age* (1899) took up the consequences of the "exposure" in public of British girls for their marriage prospects. As much as James admired the independence of "the American girl" (always to be considered as part of American elite), his hypersensitive self was shocked by the toughness of her exterior.

Several years later another literary figure entered the debate over the impact of modernity on middle-class American girls. Louisa May Alcott acknowledged Linton's influence in the preface to her book *An Old-Fashioned Girl* (1872), a tale of a simple, affectionate country girl of fourteen who goes to live with a sophisticated and unhappy friend, a fashionable girl of the city. "The 'Old-Fashioned Girl' is not intended as a perfect model, but as a possible improvement upon the Girl of the Period, who seems sorrowfully ignorant or ashamed of the good old fashions which made woman truly beautiful and honored, and through her, render home what it should be,—a happy place, where parents and children, brothers and sisters, learn to love and know and help one another." Readers first meet Alcott's heroine Polly when Tom, the brother of the family, arrives at the train station to pick up his sister's friend and lights in error on a passenger who might pass for a G.O.P. She is in gorgeous array, with "a flapping of sashes, scallops, ruffles, curls, and feathers." The passenger, "a breezy stranger," eyes Tom with a "cool stare that utterly quenched him." Just as he is gathering his forces to initiate conversation, up runs our heroine, "a fresh-faced little girl, . . . with her hand out, and a half-shy, half-merry look in her blue eyes."[40]

Like *Little Women,* published several years before, *An Old-Fashioned Girl* celebrates the beauty of girls' devotion to home and family and their rejection of the material, selfish world of the modern city. A comparison of titles, however, suggests an important difference in the implications of the two books for female adolescence. In contrast to *Little Women, An Old-Fashioned Girl* encourages girls to hold on to their status as children, rather than embracing too early the roles and manners of women.

The problem of the urban sisters Fanny and little Maud in Alcott's novel is their precociousness. Fanny explains to Polly, "You are fourteen; and we consider ourselves young ladies at that age." Alcott, in contrast, describes Polly as a "fresh-faced little girl." In fact, the family's grandmother suggests that her own granddaughters scarcely were ever children. "'You mustn't mind my staring, dear,' said Madam, softly pinching her rosy cheek. 'I haven't seen a little girl for so long, it does my old eyes good to look at you.'" Her own granddaughters, she explains, are "not what you call little girls. Fan has been a young lady this two years, and Maud is a spoiled baby." Even Maud, at the age of six, has the accoutrements of maturity in the form of calling cards, crimping pins, and a "box of dainty gloves." Alcott explains that Maud "belonged to a 'set' also; and these mites of five and six had 'their' parties, receptions, and promenades, as well as their elders, and the chief idea of their little lives seemed to be to ape the fashionable follies they should have been too innocent to understand." Alcott is so concerned with demonstrating the folly of

8.4 Old-Fashioned Girl, 1886. Alcott's novel suggests the appeals of simple "fresh-faced Polly, an old-fashioned girl" with a "half-shy, half-merry look in her blue eyes," who knows the value of work and remains loyal to those at home. Reprinted from Louisa May Alcott, *Old-Fashioned Girl* (Boston: Roberts, 1886), frontispiece.

precociousness that she turns fifteen- or sixteen-year-old Polly's interest in the attractive son of the family into an object lesson. "Polly shut her door hard, and felt ready to cry with vexation, that her pleasure should be spoilt by such a silly idea; for, of all the silly freaks of this fast age, that of little people playing at love is about the silliest."[41] Alcott's fear of precociousness cuts such a wide swathe that she admits little distinction between the pairing off of six-year-olds and the infatuation of teenagers.

The explanation for the precociousness of girls is their involvement in a new peer culture, facilitated and expanded by attending school. When Polly

8.5 Girl of the Period, 1886. Alcott contrasts her wholesome Polly, the "old-fashioned girl," with the fashion-conscious and vapid "Girl of the Period." Here Polly has yielded to "forbidden fruit," in attending the theater, and is experiencing the compromises of modern urban culture. Reprinted from Alcott, *Old-Fashioned Girl*, 244.

asks Fanny why she spends so much time getting dressed just to go to school, Fanny responds, "All the girls do; and it's proper, for you never know who you may meet. I'm going to walk, after my lessons, so I wish you'd wear your best hat and sack." In Alcott's novel the custom of walking, encouraged to provide girls with appropriate exercise, appears as a vapid excuse for socializing, especially in contrast with the health of children's play. Polly scorns it. "To dress up and parade certain streets for an hour every day, to stand talking in doorways, or drive out in a fine carriage, was not the sort of exercise she liked. . . . At home, Polly ran and rode, coasted and skated, jumped rope and raked hay, worked in her garden and rowed her boat; so no wonder she longed for something more lively than a daily promenade with a flock of giddy girls."[42] It is the strength of urban peer culture which leads to the unhealthiness and unhappiness—and the unlovableness—of the bored and fashionable Fanny.

Other commentators as well attacked the danger of precociousness in the rearing of girls. Washington Gladden, liberal clergyman and promoter of the social gospel, was persuaded in 1880 to provide advice for girls in *St. Nicholas* to complement an earlier article for boys. He censured "a too early initiation into the excitements and frivolities of what is called society. It was formerly the rule for girls to wait until their school-days were over before they made their appearance in fashionable society. At what age, let us inquire, does the average young lady of our cities now make her debut?" Like Alcott, Gladden dipped down into the early years to see the onset of preciousness. "From my observations, I should answer at about the age of three. They are not older than that when they begin to go to children's parties, for which they are dressed as elaborately as they would be for a fancy ball." If Gladden focused on the social folly of children forced into early maturity, for Mary Virginia Terhune the practice was evil: "We *sin* in allowing the fears, hopes and flutters of nubility to obtrude, even in imagination, upon this most susceptible stage of the formative period. There is vulgar violence in the excitation of coy tremors and coquettish projects in the mind of one who is as yet incapable of comprehending the meaning or tendency of the novel emotions." Employing the earthy, agrarian metaphors which were one way of objectifying girls' maturation, Terhune expounded, "Premature bloom is imperfection, too often deformity. Forced fruits lack the flavor of the summer's prime, the beauty and richness of *seasonableness*."[43] If Henry James felt that girls were becoming hard from their exposure in the city streets, Terhune and others feared that they were becoming blemished or prematurely soft—a different kind of distortion of the "girl crop" that was everyone's property.

"*Our Lost Girls*"

The allure of city streets was only part of the story, though. Critics cautioned that weakening family ties helped to push girls into the streets. In Alcott's accounting, and in the ongoing debate over the Girl of the Period, the declining authority of parents played an important role in the dissipation of girls. Alcott's fashionable fictional family is headed by an absent father and an invalid mother. Mr. Shaw is "a busy man, so intent on getting rich that he had no time to enjoy what he already possessed." He has a habit of lecturing his son "and letting the girls do just as they like[]." Mrs. Shaw is "a pale, nervous women," an invalid, defined by needs rather than by her ability to give. The family might meet for dinner, but after eating "they all [go] about their own affairs."[44]

Whatever else was to blame, there was no question that the "girl problem" was in part the problem of urban parents losing control over their daughters. When Washington Gladden addressed the problem of girls, he titled his article "A Talk with Girls and Their Mothers" because he felt the problem lay with both. The commandment that children should obey their parents, he asserted, was disregarded by both mothers and teenage daughters. "The girl of thirteen regards herself as her own mistress; she is already a woman in her own estimation, and has a right to do as she pleases." Despite his strenuous support elsewhere for longer and more vigorous walking for girls, Gladden could not countenance the freedom of girls in the city streets. "This habit of running loose, of constantly seeking the street for amusement, and even of making chance acquaintances there, is practiced by some of the girls of our good families, and it is not at all pleasant to see them on the public thoroughfares, and to witness their hoydenish ways. . . . The delicate bloom of maiden modesty is soiled by too much familiarity with the public streets of a city, and a kind of boldness is acquired which is not becoming in a woman."[45] Gladden's worry for the "delicate bloom of maiden modesty" reflected a legitimate concern for how girls' culture was being influenced by urban freedom.

An article published in *Ladies' Home Journal* in 1884 took a different tone in reporting on "an epidemic" of disappearances of girls: "One doesn't bring up a chubby baby girl to bang upon a grand piano, outdress other girls and graduate with nuns' veiling and sixteen hired bouquets, to have some dark night bring a rascal and a rope-ladder to steal her away just when she is getting big enough to do the marketing and darn her father's socks. . . . The sympathy of the entire world goes out to the bereaved owners of these pretty girls, spirited away." Despite its glib and knowing tone, itself a radical break from the earnest, idealist rhetoric which usually accompanied such discussions, the article had a strong message for mothers: "The fact is, the mothers of to-day do not exercise enough maternal authority and vigilance over their daughters. . . . Female chums call for them to spend the night, and who they meet while absent from the home circle mothers never know."[46] The pull of "chums" drawing girls away from their mothers' households was a far cry from the idealized intergenerational domestic world promoted by advisers.

A signed article republished from the *Congregationalist* in 1889 explored the distance between domestic ideal and urban reality. Mrs. J. G. Fraser titled her piece "Our Lost Girls" and subtitled it "A Mother Sadly Regrets That She Can Not Have the Training of Her Daughter." Fraser exclaimed, "Alas! just as our daughters are entering their teens, or before, we discover that we have lost them. Where have they gone?" Her answer was clear. "It is a fact that the average girl is restless unless she can visit or receive visits from some young lady friend most of the time." Such chores as a daughter might have "are hurried through with unseemly haste, to the end that she may leave home as soon as possible." Informed by the dictates of domesticity, Fraser knew what her maternal role should be: "Sympathetic companionship, little seeds of counsel dropped wisely here and there, a knowledge of what the girls are thinking about and what they are interested in; a wise ignoring of some girlish follies — all these are needed." But there was one problem in applying techniques of domestic influence. If they could help it, girls were probably not at home to listen to their mothers' advice. Fraser uttered a complaint with a contemporary ring. "Our homes should not be simply boarding houses where our children eat and sleep, but dwelling places where they are to spend most of their time out of school hours."[47] If they were to sustain the culture of the "old-fashioned girl," mothers must take their daughters back from the streets and from the friends they promenaded with there.

Girls and Class

Girls who appeared in public and walked the streets were historically "public women," prostitutes. What distinguished the debates of the 1870s and 1880s was that they were not about prostitutes but instead about a more broadly defined and owned group of daughters. Not distinguished by class or profession, the G.O.P. was not a fallen "other" but instead a creature of modernity, created by the industrial city. When Henry James, Louisa May Alcott, *Ladies' Home Journal,* and *St. Nicholas* wrote about girls, they were talking about their own daughters, or nieces, or grandchildren, or the daughters of their friends and colleagues. Mrs. J. G. Fraser, of course, most literally seems to have been writing about her daughter. In contrast with later discussions about "the girl problem," these late-Victorian debates were explicitly not focused on working or shopgirls. Instead, such discussions hit closer to home, often debating the impact of modern culture on *Our Girls,* as an advice book published in 1871 was entitled.[48]

These girls might even be considered to belong to an urban elite. Louisa May Alcott's Fanny differs from her country friend because she is a girl of fashion, whose parents can afford to buy her the new offerings of urban dry goods stores. When Kate Tannatt Woods excoriated the rude and showy "Manners in Public" of a certain young concertgoer, she characterized her explicitly: "Sallie Ducats, whose father is a celebrated statesman, and whose mother bore a grand old name prior to her marriage." The conduct of Sallie (spelled in the French fashion) and her friends sets a bad standard for other girls: "Their heavy steps and bustling noise disturbed the entire [concert] audience. . . . This was not all. They removed their wraps with much parade and noise, raised their seats and let them fall again, and then, after some further maneuvers, produced some bon-bons which they proceeded to eat with evident relish. During the entire concert they whispered, giggled, looked about, and made comments on people about them." Woods concluded by asking: "What is to be done when young women belonging to our so-called 'best families' are guilty of such conduct?"[49]

This was the tack taken by Henry James in two pieces published in 1906–7 by *Harper's Bazar* on the manners and speech of American women. Here James recalled a scene he had experienced twenty-five years earlier in Boston at about the time the controversy over the "Girl of the Period" had first erupted. What he had then remarked at—and was largely appalled at—was the free conduct of schoolgirls taking their recess in the streets of Boston. A nearby "seminary for young ladies" had been released and their noise was filling the neighborhood as James had walked to breakfast. As James put it, the girls were in full "possession of the public scene."

> Nobody else, no doubt, during that part of the morning, was much in possession—so that the vociferous pupils . . . had the case all in their hands. My point is simply that, being fashionable, they yet were vociferous, and in conditions that, as they ingenuously shrieked and bawled to each other across the street and from its top to its bottom, gave the candid observer much to think of. They were freely and happily at play, they had been turned out for it to the pavements of the town, and with this large scale of space about them for intercourse they could scarce do other than hoot

and howl. They romped, they conversed, at the top of their lungs from one side of the ample avenue to the other; they sat on doorsteps and partook of scraps of luncheon, they hunted each other to and fro and indulged in innocent mirth quite as if they had been in private gardens or a play-room.[50]

James's curiosity was especially piqued by his knowledge that this particular seminary was "'the most fashionable school in Boston,' as I heard their establishment described." And he was surprised at the laxness of school authorities. "The supremely interesting thing was that, even at the fountain-head of our native culture, nobody, and least of all their remunerated instructors, seemed to doubt for a moment that these were good formative conditions." As did others in different ways, Henry James commented in surprise at the comparative freedom experienced by these schoolgirls, not only in comparison with those he had recently observed in Europe, but perhaps also in contrast with the upbringing of his sister, the confined and miserable Alice James. Indeed, the biographer of James's younger sister notes a critical moment when her nearest brother went out to play, and Alice was left behind in the nursery, "at first because she was the youngest and then, apparently for ever, because she was a girl."[51]

In describing elite schoolgirls, James was simply emphasizing a status which to some degree was shared by other schoolgirls. In the late nineteenth century only a small proportion of teenage girls went to school. As we have seen, schoolgirls were most likely to be white, native-born daughters of white-collar workers.[52] They therefore represented something of a de facto elite. But their status was normative if not statistically dominant. When pundits debated the status of the American girl, they were not likely to be referring to domestic servants or factory operatives; they were more likely to be referring to American schoolgirls, despite their distinct minority status. The debate over the conduct of the American girl gained an edge of urgency because of the class standing of the girls now out in public. At the same time, that urgency helped to create a more broadly defined and collectively owned group of girls.

If advice givers needed to vouch for the respectability of schoolgirls, however, they could still remain disturbed by some of the after-hour implications of school attendance, especially at the more suspect public schools. The *Ladies' Home Journal*'s glib answer to the question "Why Girls Disappear" blamed mothers but indirectly it blamed school, too. "School-girls here have been seen year in and year out being joined on a certain corner by rakish-looking boys who carried their books." Another article in the same magazine the next

year lambasted the dangerous influence of the roller-skating rink on schoolgirls as well. Under the title "Flirting Girls," the writer noted that "school
girls in great numbers frequent these pleasure resorts and emulate each other
in picking up the greatest number of gentlemen acquaintances. So large is
this class of chance acquaintances, that the girls in our public schools already
recognize these men by a slang term, a humorous but pitiful term, when one
thinks of the underlying fact. These 'pick-ups' are not obtained in the skating
rink alone but are made on the sidewalk with a bow, a smile, a word, or in
a horse car or at a base ball match or at the theatre."[53] The outcry of concern over the modern girl focused on middle-class girls, and the impact of
a range of social developments—school among them—which were breaking
down the authority of parents, the strength of the home, and the domination
of traditional morality.

Ruth Ashmore and "Side Talks with Girls"

The result was the creation of an intensified moral improvement campaign for girls which we today confuse with Victorianism itself. This campaign aimed to undo the damage being done by urbanization, schooling, and
the liberation of middle-class girls from domestic labor. The advice given to
young girls in the 1880s and 1890s is noteworthy for its distance from the
actual conduct of girls. It represented polarized reaction in force, often seeming to respond point for point to the lives and the feelings that girls experienced and then described in their writings.

Emblematic of this campaign was a column initiated in the *Ladies' Home
Journal* in 1890. It debuted with some fanfare. The magazine advertised that
the column would "be made the brightest department for girls ever sustained
by a magazine." Acknowledging the special needs of such readers, the editors
proposed to enlist "a corps of the most clever writers who fully understand
the needs of young women." A month later, however, the column revealed a
more conventional prototype. Writing under the guise of an advice column in
response to girls' queries, a fictional "Ruth Ashmore" (in reality, writer Isabel
Mallon) adopted the intimate tone of a confidante chatting companionably
"about the doings of the day" before a bright fire. A daughter of Maryland
society, Mallon was married at sixteen and widowed at twenty; she wrote
the column as one means to livelihood in her late twenties and thirties.[54] As
Ruth Ashmore, Mallon became something of an American institution, and
was said to have received 158,000 pleas for advice over the life of her column.
Although relatively young herself, her tone belied her youth; she wrote in the
voice of an older aunt. The title, "Side Talks with Girls," suggested an effort to

exert influence gently from the "side." But Ashmore/Mallon could not help herself. From the beginning she delivered a barrage of heavy-handed moral pronouncements especially targeting girls' social freedoms.

The key to Ashmore's campaign was the reinstatement of the mother. In choice of companions, "the first person for you to consider is your mother and her wishes." In listening to "a piquant story think for a minute if you would like to write it down and submit it to your mother." In speech, "my dear girl, make up your mind that . . . you are not going to say one word that you cannot repeat to your mother." And in conclusion, "Never say that you don't expect a man to marry your whole family. It's vulgar. You do." (In response to imagined critics, Ashmore concluded that the truly worthy boy would appreciate this loyalty to mother in a girl.)[55]

In fact, though, Ashmore took a dim view of boys altogether. Her accumulated advice seemed to add up to a suggested boy-cott. She disliked the messiness of coeducation, thinking it unnecessary "for you to speak to the young men with whom you are not acquainted simply because they are in your class at school." At dances, she suggested that girls "anxious to gain the respect of the people in your own set" dance only with their brothers. Fourteen-year-olds should not "go out to places of amusement or to evening parties with young men." Fifteen-year-olds should not be allowed to fraternize, "as both of them should be thinking of their school-books." A sixteen-year-old could not "comprehend where she felt a real love or not." Girls of seventeen were "too young to receive men visitors." The foolish girl (or the proxy Ashmore set up) who asked, "Is it wrong to flirt?" was answered in venom: "Maud— You ask 'Is it wrong to flirt?' and I answer you in this way. Unless you knew it was wrong you would not have asked me the question: and it is more than wrong—it is vulgar and under-bred." Of course she disapproved of cosmetics, chewing gum, or eating in the streets. Her ideal girl could be identified "at the first glance, whether she is walking, shopping, in an omnibus, or whatever she may be about on the street. She goes along quietly, intent on her affairs, without thought as to the rest of the world." The combined impact of Ruth Ashmore's advice to girls was extraordinary for its systematic repudiation of an entire range of contemporary conduct.[56] Not only did her advice counter the habits of daring iconoclasts like Charlotte Perkins, socialites like Marian Nichols and Emily Eliot, and giddy free spirits like Mabel Lancraft and Cassie Upson. It also challenged and censured the habits of such dutiful daughters as Jessie Wendover and Margaret Tileston.

In fact, Ruth Ashmore seems to have been on the defensive because of the extent to which her advice seemed beyond the pale. In one column only two years after she began writing, she had to defend herself from the legitimate suspicion that she did not approve of romance at all. "I DO believe in sweethearts, I do believe in the right of every girl to have one." Acknowledging the tone of her jeremiads, she subtitled the concluding section of more than one column "The End of the Sermon." Perhaps fed by growing public incredulity at the opinions she expressed, Ashmore's columns reveal a growing curiosity about who exactly she was. She kept it secret, announcing it as one of her "own little fancies." She refused requests for photographs, coyly affirmed her unmarried status, and several times expressed outrage (feigned or otherwise) at a rumor, perhaps fed by Bok's writing of the pilot column, that she was a man. Ruth Ashmore remained in place for the decade of the 1890s, a decade singled out by cultural historians for the pluralization and broadening of a Victorian consensus. Opportunely, it would seem, Isabel Mallon died in 1898. Bok did not find a replacement. By the end of the decade even the *Ladies' Home Journal* seems to have had enough of Ruth Ashmore. In the last month of the century, a new column appeared. Written by Margaret E. Sangster and adopting the still-proprietary title "My Girls," it nonetheless adopted a new tone, opening a wider umbrella. It welcomed those with "brown skins and with blond, with black eyes and gray eyes and with eyes of blue. . . . You may come in, every one of you; there is plenty of room." The more there are, Sangster wrote, "the more real love, sympathy and friendliness there are uniting our different groups in one great family." Complementing this progressive message of different groups united in one family was a chatty column stripped of moral commentary initiated in May of that year. Entitled "The Gossip of a New York Girl," this column by Edith Lawrence suggested that Ruth Ashmore's moral pronouncements from the parlor hearth were dated— and might be replaced instead by chatter about fashions and parties.[57]

Incorporating Victorianism

However out-of-step with actual conduct such columns as Ruth Ashmore's might have been, there clearly was a market for her wisdom. Perhaps it was the market which Edward Bok, *Ladies' Home Journal* editor, had originally targeted with the popular column. He had intuited that "in thousands of cases the American mother was not the confidante of her daughter" and had offered his Ruth Ashmore as a surrogate.[58] The weight of her wisdom, its definitiveness, was restrictive, but perhaps its actual impersonality, circulated in a mass-market magazine (despite the intimacy of the tone) made it more palatable than the polemics of actual mothers. The dicta of Ruth Ashmore might well have represented an effort to consolidate some social rules with which to structure urban possibilities truly boundless in their potential.

From the early days of the debates over the "Girl of the Period," some girls gave evidence that they had read the advice literature and absorbed its wisdom. In 1875 a letter writer from New York named Cora wrote to *St. Nicholas*'s "Letter-Box" to ask for the magazine's help in finding a wholesome summer place for girls away from "crowded watering-places and fashionable Summer hotels." Her specification of what she sought was modeled closely on Alcott's "old-fashioned girl." "A few weeks in some nice, old, quiet farm-house, for instance, where they could go berrying, boating, and perhaps fishing, wear cool calico dresses all the time without fear of being wondered at, and live on real, plain, good old-fashioned food, and in fact, be real country girls for a while, until they lost their pale cheeks and headaches." Nineteen-year-old Ethel Sturges, daughter of a wealthy Chicago businessman, in 1883 wrote a school composition which showed that she too had learned the rules of public decorum raised by critics of the G.O.P. In her piece titled "Street Scenes," she described herself observing a busy thoroughfare from a carriage. The scene is an urban medley, with "people of different nations, people of different classes, some in gay colors and some in dark." As she watches from her protected perch, she notices "a group of young girls. They had just met and their greeting seemed to me rather too affectionate for the street. Their voices were raised to such a high pitch that several people turned to look at them. Their dresses were very showy. I noticed also that they were eating candy." With this depiction, Sturges caught the negative image of the Girl of the Period—exhibitionist, loud, eating in public. She then presented her counterpoint: "My eyes fell with pleasure upon two others who came behind them. These were dressed simply as school-girls should be. They looked as if they were enjoying themselves, talking in a quiet way; but not one word did either say, nor one movement did either make which would have attracted the attention of any one." Sturges did not attribute venality or even ill-breeding to the first group, but simply carelessness. She concluded in good essay form with a moral: "Always behave in the street so that you will not attract the slightest attention." Unfortunately Ethel Surges did not leave a diary which gives us any way of determining whether or how she applied the lesson she had learned.[59] But the admonition to deflect public attention was the equivalent of domestic admonitions to suppress self—an apt lesson for girls to develop in lessons written for school.

Another girl who took to heart the concerns for girls' propriety expressed by advice writers was Lizzie Morrissey, the second-generation Irish schoolgirl who watched life go by her East Boston window as she waited in her parlor for callers who never came. Lizzie Morrissey's diary of her nineteenth year in 1876, the year she graduated from the normal department of Girls' High School, is an extraordinary document of the incorporation of a restrictive program of Victorianism. It is clear that Morrissey was avidly attentive to the lessons of respectability that Ruth Ashmore later retailed. Morrissey's diary documents multiple losses—of youthful freedom and of prosperity—following the death of her father, a liquor trader, when Lizzie was six. It is also an account, however, of Lizzie's movement back and forth between two worlds, one represented by her "lace-curtain" existence in urban Boston, the other by several visits to rural Quincy and the young family of a woman she called Sis. For Lizzie Morrissey, life with Sis in Quincy embodied what historians would call a preindustrial, rural world of expressiveness without social inhibition, a world of fun. Unlike many teenage girls of the middle class, Lizzie Morrissey felt she must repudiate that world as part of her efforts to better her station in urban Boston. The moroseness of her Boston entries measures the cost.

Sis's identity and relationship to Lizzie Morrissey are not clear. Census records from 1860 do not indicate any siblings older than the three-year-old Lizzie in the Thomas Morrissey household. The census does report one unattached female, though, an Ellen with an obscured surname which might well be Morrissey. Ellen Morrissey—if that indeed was her name—was sixteen in 1860, and unlike Lizzie's father, Thomas, who was born in Canada, Ellen Morrissey was born in Ireland. Ellen Morrissey is certainly a plausible candidate for "Sis"—an Irish relative sent to live in Boston with a cousin as help. Sis first appeared in Lizzie's diary when she and her baby Georgie visited East Boston, a visit Lizzie had been eagerly anticipating. Sis brought candy and joined Lizzie and her mother at the window, "eating chocs and laughing; we were telling many old stories of the past." Sis had lived as a domestic servant before her marriage, and she represented a different social world from the one Lizzie was joining. She and her husband made "all manner of fun" of Lizzie's diary, for instance, which for them must have represented putting on airs. When Sis and Georgie returned to Quincy, Lizzie reported herself "as lonesome as I can be—I miss Georgie and Sis dreadfully and have got a fit of the blues." She turned to one of her usual, genteel recourses, reading a book, but after the lively time she had enjoyed, "I didn't care much about it I felt so lonesome."[60]

Lizzie's return visit to Quincy in the summertime was a trip into another way of life, and indeed into another personality. In contrast with the life of malaise and propriety Lizzie expressed in Boston, her visit to Sis represented a hilarious and pastoral round of fun, foolery, and flirtation in the pastures and roadways of the town. She and Sis (and Sis's baby) were frequently outside, waving to strangers on the train and sitting on the grass eating apples. On one walk to town, they ran ahead of a passing teamster, hid in the bushes, and joined in with him as he sang "Little Brown Jug." ("He looked all round and we had fun.") Another day, Lizzie reported, en route to the horsecars they encountered a neighbor's boarders. "We had lots of kisses thrown us and then had a dance down in the field. . . . I did my hair up in a new style and they said it looked real good." Other days brought similar high jinks. "We had our arms round each other and hop-skipped all the way singing at the tops of our voices." Later in the day, Morrissey reported, "we went out and sat on the banking near the road and sang and spoke to everyone going by on the road; we had splendid fun." On a Sunday, "when we went into church they all began staring at us and we were on a broad giggle. . . . Coming home we met 'shoot the hat' in the church door and he bowed and laughed; we had fun on the road—looked into a church window, spoke to fellows sitting on [a] stone-wall, sang, pounded the back of a milk cart and raised cain generally." The next day, Lizzie Morrissey finished up her report on Sunday's fun with Sis's friend: "Sis and Ma spoke to lots in teams too but Annie and I behaved ourselves then." Her final comment, anticipating her return to another reality: "I can't help laughing to think how such actions would look in East Boston."[61]

For Lizzie Morrissey, some of Boston's control seemed to be externally imposed. Exchanges with strange men in urban Boston felt more sinister than Quincy antics. One such exchange used the language employed by Cassie Upson and others for such one-time events. Earlier in the summer of her Quincy playfulness, Morrissey reported an "adventure" while out walking with her friend Ida in Boston: "Two fellows came up, one on each side of us and stared into our faces; we looked astonished and they went on." Later that fall, though, any notion of adventure had fallen out of a description of a wait for the horsecars with a friend: "We went into an apothecary's to wait for an E.B. car and while there a dark complected man kept passing the door and staring at us but we took no notice of him." In the interim Lizzie had reported on a disturbing event: the disappearance of an East Boston girl who, like Lizzie, attended Girls' High School. The first mention in Lizzie's diary indicated that the police had been at school asking about Mary Harrington; Lizzie cryptically reported that she didn't think that Mary would be found. The newspapers picked up the story, and several days later, the *Herald* published a letter purporting to be from Mary saying that she was never coming back. A few days later, a friend of Lizzie's went over to visit the Harrington household, and Lizzie reported, "Mrs. Harrington don't believe that letter came from Mary." Beyond her early fears of the worst, Lizzie confessed her own confusion about the troubling episode: "I'm sure I don't know what to think of it."[62] Whatever the circumstances, though, the case of Mary Harrington could not help but cast a sobering light on the advisability of free exchanges in the streets of urban Boston.

Even before Mary Harrington disappeared, though, Lizzie Morrissey saw things very differently in Boston than she did in Quincy. On one trip home from school early in 1876, she observed her classmates disapprovingly: "Some of the girls acted horrid in the car." As a consequence, "everybody was talking of them." In the fall she adopted a more cautious standard than one friend, who called to ask her to go to the library in a nearby square one evening. She was glad that she could not go, "for I don't care about going down to the square at that time." The problem may have been the company as much as the destination and the hour. By November she had decided to break with the same friend based on her free manners in public. "I don't like the way Blanche appears in the street and I don't care to go out with her again." The next day she amplified. "I think she has changed wonderfully, and appears in my opinion very fast on the street; she was singing and laughing all the way to and from the library."[63] What was hilarious and fun in the summer in the country with a surrogate sister was in bad taste for a young lady in training for the respectable job of schoolteaching in the city. Certainly the city was a more threatening environment. Strangers really were strangers, rather than faces from church. But more important than actual danger seemed to be Lizzie Morrissey's efforts to defy an image and fill a role. Unlike the schoolgirls from the "best schools" witnessed by Henry James or other commentators, Lizzie Morrissey was second-generation American, the daughter of a seamstress and a deceased liquor trader. She felt confident of little, least of all her ability to retain her precarious standing at the same time that she traveled freely in the city streets. The result was her assumption of an exaggerated Victorianism of excessive propriety which revealed itself in a painful self-censoring and a severing of social connections.

The striking contrast of Lizzie Morrissey's Quincy and Boston existences recalls a comparison made by the patrician intellectual Henry Adams, who grew up in Quincy and Boston in the 1840s. Adams aligned his life according to two polarities, "Winter and summer, cold and heat, town and country, force and freedom. . . . Town was winter confinement, school, rule, discipline; . . . society of uncles, aunts, and cousins who expected children to behave themselves, and who were not always gratified. . . . Country, only seven miles away, was liberty, diversity, outlawry, the endless delight of mere sense impressions given by nature for nothing, and breathed by boys without knowing it."[64] Lizzie Morrissey's descriptions lack Adams's literary invocation of smells, tastes, and colors. Yet in her accounts of picking fruit from the trees and sitting right there to eat it, of banging on milk trucks, and of sassing men in the street, she captures much of the sensuality that Adams associated with Quincy license. For Lizzie Morrissey, as for Henry Adams, Boston represented a world of straitened expectations—for Adams living up to family expectations, for Morrissey transcending them. The gray of Lizzie Morrissey's Boston, like Henry Adams's, was the gray of restraint, respectability, and control, which for all the myriad differences in class and family background seemed conveniently exemplified in the "double nature" of city and country.

Lizzie Morrissey's "hyper-Victorianism," her concern about what was proper and what not, helps to explain other groups and audiences for Ruth Ashmore's column, and indeed for a restrictive plan for the rearing of respectable young women. One such group was the black bourgeoisie, which after the nation turned away from radical republicanism was reduced to making its case through self-improvement and self-culture. It was along the lower boundary of the middle class that the maintenance of propriety and refinement was most critical. Particularly within economically disadvantaged communities, behavior was all. Exercising a wistful "politics of respectability," the black "better classes" attempted to distance themselves from negative social stereotypes by imposing on their daughters restrictive codes of behavior. This politics "equated public behavior with individual self-respect" and provided the black bourgeoisie with moral superiority over at least some whites in one arena over which they had some control.[65]

Perhaps, then, the demand for codified programs of propriety arose from the aspirations of families and their daughters who were strangers to the luxury of Victorian leisure. One story of the origins of "Ruth Ashmore" suggests such a scenario. Edward Bok, the editor of *Ladies' Home Journal,* explained that the idea of a column of advice for girls had been his. In his frustrated efforts to communicate his vision to prospective authors of the column, he had drafted a sample column himself. His essay mistakenly found its way to the composing room, where the workforce consisted of young women. The earliest response to the column came from that workforce. Bok relayed the report of the superintendent of the composition room: "'My girls all hope this is going into the magazine. . . . Well, they say it's the best stuff for girls they have ever read. They'd love to know Miss Ashmead [*sic*] better.'"[66] Leaving aside the real possibility of self-interested flattery of "the boss," the prime market for Ruth Ashmore, and for Victorian etiquette manuals as a group, might well have been girls such as *Ladies' Home Journal*'s typesetters and Lizzie Morrissey herself—girls for whom refinement seemed an elusive key to standing. For girls from the working classes, propriety needed to be learned and practiced, not just assumed. Just as religious converts often seemed the most zealous, converts to Victorian propriety were allowed, and could allow themselves, fewer mistakes than those who imagined themselves born to it.

Contested Spaces

If certain girls were especially concerned about appearances in the street, there were also daring occasions or destinations, newly open to women, which provoked special concern and excitement for most middle-class girls. One was the theater. In the early nineteenth century, American theater audiences were boisterous and disorderly, and most respectable women stayed home. In the latter part of the century, a more centralized theatrical industry began to offer more polished traveling performances which appealed to a more refined middle-class audience, including women and children. The theater retained its mixed reputation, however. As a result, when middle-class women and their daughters ventured into theaters, they kept on their guard. Sometimes just getting tickets required steeled nerves. Annie Winsor bought tickets for her parents to a production at the Globe Theatre. She described the purchase for them as a minor drama requiring a measure of resolve. "I just skipped up from Park Sq. to the Globe Theatre, stepped demurely in,—nothing but one or two men waiting for tickets, took my stares for a couple of minutes, then stepped up, stated my wants . . ." Unlike polite, periodical literature, the theater did not abide by the "viriginibus" standard. Agnes Hamilton, going to see *Maggie the Midget* with her mother, knew to hold her approval in abeyance. "She isn't much but still there was nothing vulgar or disagreeable in the play so it was quite fun." Hamilton's equation of "fun" and "respectable" suggests a certain minimalism in her expectations. Margaret Tileston was another playgoer who kept a careful eye on respectability. When she and her cousins attended a comedy entitled *The Ladies' Battle* in Roxbury when she was fourteen and found it "rather vulgar," they left before it was over. Several years later she and her sister went to another play and "fell among dreadful young men, who talked and laughed the whole time in the most vulgar way."

She expressed her displeasure by changing her seat, however, not by exiting the theater.[67]

Margaret Tileston was not always frozen in fastidious reserve, however. Later that year, she went back to the theater with a friend to see a production of *A Scrap of Paper*. Among the familiar faces she saw on the stage was "the Spaniard, Mr. ____, with whom I fell in love. He is perfectly fascinating and such hair! such eyes! The acting was perfection and I never enjoyed an evening more. It is impossible to give any idea of it. Mamie and I raved about him all the way home." The next day she was still in the same state: "Martha H., Mamie Lord and I are all 'gone' over the Spaniard. '20 lovesick maidens.'" Ten years earlier, Emily Eliot entertained a prolonged infatuation with actor George Reynolds, whose portrayal of Henry V she witnessed three times. First with opera glasses from the back, and then from prized second-row seats, she admired his beautiful eyes, his gray silk doublet with cherry tights, and his ardor. During her third viewing, she could not contain herself: "He looked so lovely—I think it was after the battle—the end of that act when he kneels down (while the monks are chanting) and then rising stretches out his arms that I could not help giving a kind of groaning sigh which meant 'You are *too* lovely' and a lady next me turned around and looked at me in utter astonishment! Oh! I enjoyed it *so* much!" Eliot bought pictures of Reynolds, and she and her school friends wrote adoring poetry.[68] As her response suggests, those who feared the impact of the stage might well have had reason. If "sensation" literature had the potential to excite feverish fancies, how much more so the stage, where clusters of girl viewers could fan each other's fervor and where romantic heroes were embodied. When combined with audiences of mixed propriety, the theater was especially threatening—and especially attractive—to middle-class girls with time on their hands.

Similarly attractive—and similarly threatening—was another venue of popular culture increasingly commercialized over the course of the late nineteenth century, the beachfront arcade or boardwalk. It was surely to such a destination that Lizzie Morrissey went on one of her rare good times in the restrictive context of her Boston life. Morrissey's friend Ida persuaded her to join "a party" going to the beach at Oak Island in the summer of 1876. Once there, they hired a grove with a picnic table and were joined by a similar party from another Boston suburb. The two groups of picnickers hit it off, and Lizzie Morrissey and Ida made a new and fast friend. "Her name is Lizzie Day and she is just as pretty as she can be. Her, Ida and I were together all day with our arms round one another, Lizzie being in the middle." The circumstances of the summer day conspired to rapid intimacy. "I think I really

8.6 "Too lovely," 1875. Emily Eliot developed a crush on the actor George Reynolds, collecting different copies of his picture, like this one stored in her diary. Emily M. Eliot, "Journal of a Boston Girl of 18 Years," HUG(FP) 33.6, Samuel Eliot Morison papers, Harvard University Archives (Cambridge: Pusey Library), December 30, 1875.

love her. We were all a jolly party indeed," Morrissey reported of Lizzie Day. The recreation of the day included watching an Indian who "dressed up fancy for the picnickers," and admiring the dancing from the sidelines. "We felt highly honored for we had 20 invitations to dance and accepted none." At eight o'clock the girls kissed their new friend good-bye, exacted a promise that she would come visit them sometime in East Boston, and started for their homes. The three girls also promised each other to keep always as a souvenir of their marvelous day the "small green tickets" they bought to take them through the picnic grove. Unlike other girls described in the literature of the "Girls of the Period," Lizzie and Ida were not looking to "pick up" boys. After all they turned down many invitations to dance. Yet the anonymity of the commercial circumstances, and the pleasure-seeking indolence of a day at the beach, enabled an intense crush on a stranger—an indication of the dangers and possibilities of letting parties of "youth" go to dance halls at the beach on their own.[69]

New Girls and the Celebration of Fun

Ultimately, the fledgling peer culture discovered and encouraged by attendance at school, the custom of walking, and girls' participation in consumer culture encouraged middle-class girls to think of themselves in different terms than were encouraged by ministers, advice writers, and probably by their parents as well. Late-Victorian pundits had affirmed and reaffirmed the particular responsibilities of daughters to subordinate their own impulses to the needs of the family. But girls who were no longer defined by domestic work, and who spent much of their time outside of the home, either at school, or in public thoroughfares walking to and from school, began to think of themselves in different terms. Girls began to define themselves by their capacity for fun, and by the figure they cut stepping out in public, rather than simply by their domestic virtue.

As in all kinds of cultural change, the process was gradual and uneven, with overlapping and contradictory sentiments expressed throughout the northeastern middle class, and even within the same girls' diaries. It was more likely to be expressed later in the century, in late rather than early adolescence, and among daughters of businessmen rather than within an intellectual elite. The culture of the "new girl" gained strength from numbers and was often affirmed and expressed in the form of peer solidarity in public. In those terms, it represented a substantial challenge to established Victorian propriety.

The culture of the "new girl" is captured in a poem copied in 1897 by the diarist Mary Bartine, who celebrated the culture of fun shared in her informal club of "frolicing, rolicing, daring six young maids." Entitled "Our Jolly S.F.J.," the poem celebrated the antics of this group of friends in public, their flirtatiousness, freedom from domestic constraint, irreverence, and above all, their peer solidarity:

> *There is a merry six in town that's called the S.F.J.*
> *And they are known for tricks and pranks only they can play.*

They are as wise as Solomon and they're sure to find a way
Out of all the mischief, pranks and jokes that cause so much dismay.

And this same crowd to picnics go, and to dances now and then
And they know how to act in such a way to please the men.
And if you'll kindly listen, we will tell some escapades
That have happened to these frolicing, rolicing, daring, six young maids.

One summer day this jolly six to Rocky Hill repaired,
There came along a thunder storm and this is how they fared
They slept the night (t'was Saturday night) and in the morning clear
Just as the churches were letting out in Somerville did appear.[70]

The poem deliberately defies a succession of expectations of "good" daughters. Not only were the S.F.J. known for their naughtiness, they were also adept at getting away with their pranks, showing no remorse, and paying no price. They prized themselves on their flirtatiousness, and didn't fear for their reputations. In fact, they sought to be as offensive as possible, managing to time their return from their overnight escapade just in time to flaunt their conduct in front of the churchgoing community.

The poem was undoubtedly circulated among the membership and advanced an exaggerated and daring chronicle of bravado and camaraderie. Bartine inserted it in her diary, a document which itself might have been expected to be less daring. Bartine's diary recounted one such appearance of her group of friends in public—and recanted only a bit from the daring generational statement of the poem: "This afternoon six of us girls walked abrest on Main Street," she reported. Swept up in the giddy joy of the moment, the six undoubtedly monopolized the sidewalk and called significant attention to themselves. In comment, she added, "We ought to have been ashamed," leaving ambiguous the extent of her regret.[71]

The diary of Florence Peck, who attended high school in Rochester, New York, in the 1890s, suggests a gradual process of evolution to a new girlhood. Like most middle-class girls, Peck participated in a Victorian culture of uplift and idealism. While in high school, she reported attending a lecture by a speaker on "purity" who was "pure as gold and pearl and spoke beautifully." Her conclusion: "I guess I won't sip wine or dance with young men, or wear unwomanly dresses for I *do* want to be pure and womanly, God helping me." Her efforts to conform to a standard of elevated womanhood emerged when she thought about her diary itself, which she judged critically for its haphazard, scribbled quality and resolved to do better or give it up. "So now if I don't feel like writing carefully and nicely, I won't write at all." As an afterthought to this self-chastisement on the proper subjects and treatments for a diary, she remembered an appropriate entry. "Of all nice things that have happened to me, and ought to be put down in here, and which I shamefully neglected to was my going to hear the Thomas Orchestra. . . . I shall never forget it." Attending the symphony had come to be an expression of gentility, making it an exemplary subject to record as part of the presentation of a refined and womanly self.[72]

There were powerful crosscurrents, however, challenging Peck's "nice" notions of what was important material for a diary—and perhaps a self, too. Following her triumphant graduation from Rochester High School several years later, she spent part of a summer at the beach resort of Dunkirk, New York, on the shores of Lake Erie, where, as she put it, "All the boys work here so they will not be around except at night." She suggested the consequences for the girls: "The mornings go somehow—we sleep and read in the afternoons and at night we *live*." Ten days later, she explained what she meant in a rhapsodic entry that did not obey her expectations for careful—or probably by her definitions, of "nice" either. "Hoorah for this day forever more—I shall only write a few words but I'll never forget this day." She began just with names:

> Jerome and I
> Agatha and Henry Weeks

To any who want to know what happened to those couples, she provided an answer, easily misread by modern readers: "We *did it*!" What "it" was is unclear, but it may well have meant getting "pinned," a reference to the fraternity version of "going steady." In any case, that event, and its attendant emotions—"Happy!"—found a featured role in Florence Peck's diary. In the fall, after recounting her pranks with friends at an extracurricular French class, she reconsidered the proper material for a diary, deciding that readers needed to know "the various stunts" she did, and "how full of old 'Nick'" she was.[73] Serious romance, whether or not "careful and nice," had always been the appropriate material for a girl's diary. The admission to her diary of simple fun, of jokes and frivolity, was more significant. Peck's belated acknowledgment, at the age of nineteen, of the significance of "stunts"—both to her diary and to her life—represented a changing notion of self characteristic of a "new girl."

Mabel Lancraft, daughter of a prosperous oyster grower in Fair Haven, Connecticut, left a considerably fuller set of papers than either Florence Peck or Mary Bartine, conveying a number of traits which together made her nearly a prototype for a "new girl." Lancraft attended Hillhouse High School in New Haven in the 1880s and conducted a vibrant extracurricular life in the streets and parks beyond. The language, content, and emotion of her diary suggests a thoroughly "modern" identity which was spread more diffusely through the documents of others. Like Bartine, Lancraft dared to act out in public, though without Bartine's apology, and she too defied her mother's authority in the name of fun.

Most distinctive about Lancraft's diary was her language. Over the course of several years, Lancraft seasoned her high-minded tone with a mannered and airy irony which would become more common in the next century. Lancraft was in decided contrast with Annie Winsor, who wrote her prescription for generational revolt in the earnest and heavy language of a Victorian. Lancraft did not philosophize rebellion; she simply rebelled. "Excused from two recitations today but I wasn't too sick to go skating in the afternoon. Oh! no!!" she exclaimed after her evasion of the sick room for winter skating. After one summer's day with her cousin, she laid the rhetoric of Victorian affectation on thick: "Clara and I adorned ourselfs in our simple but becoming costumes and preceded without hindrances and encumbrances to call on Miss Emery of #135 Blatchley Ave. Arriving at the abode of the above young lady we were delighted to find that she ('whose name shall be nameless') was home. We made a very fashionable call, there staying only about two hours more or less and then amid many lamentations and expressions of regret we preceded to hasten our wandering footsteps homeward."[74] Like her "vulgar" walking with Sadie, Lancraft's excessive language was the conspicuous if playful subversion of high-minded conventions.

Such language—and subversion—became most pointed when Lancraft was describing her own "spooney" behavior, during two separate visits to her cousin in Bridgeport. Over the summer, a game of hide-and-seek left Mabel and "Fred H." hiding in the shop. Lancraft began with direct exuberance: "Oh! in all my life I never acted so soft—but I never had such a lovely time. Then we came up on the piazza and Alice and Will spooned in the hammock while Fred and I sat in one of their big chairs!!!" At the end, she became arch, speaking to a hypothetical (and indulgent) reader: "Oh! the pathetic parting. Forgive me?" She used the same tone to report on a Christmas reunion of the foursome after an evening concert. "In front came of course Alice Hall and Will Paul, next in order was my adorable self and Freddie Bishop. . . . Did I enjoy that walk? Did I tell something I oughtn't to? Were my hands cold?"[75] The exuberance which Lancraft communicated with her hyperbolic (and hypothetical) questions did indeed make her feel "adorable," however ironic her usage—surely not the first time that being admired has had that heady effect. What's significant here, though, is that Mabel Lancraft felt free to use her diary, by tradition her highest and best form of self, to express that sentiment of conspicuous self-approbation, unaccompanied by qualification.

This point is critical. High-spirited quests for self-expression have frequently characterized the life stage of youth, in the late nineteenth century no less than any other. Victorian, moralistic fiction was filled with bold and gay girls seeking fun and pleasure. But such daring assertiveness needed to be costly. As Alcott put it in a description of her Old-Fashioned Girl's one burst of flirtatious gaiety, "having nibbled at forbidden fruit, she had to pay the penalty." Victorians knew—and writers saw to it—that bold girls who said and did what they pleased, who indulged their desire for fun, and who attracted attention by their conspicuous self-display would pay. In the case of Alcott's virtuous Polly, it was by realizing the hurt she had caused. For more hardened rebels it was by marrying drunkards, or being seduced, or otherwise coming to a bad end. What made a "new girl" was her claim to public space and public attention without paying a price—her claim of the right to walk up and down with a boy in front of Mr. H. Olds as Mabel Lancraft did, or to walk six abreast down Main Street as Mary Bartine did, or simply to wear a white rose, as Florence Peck did. ("I love to wear flowers," she reported of herself at age sixteen.)[76]

Thorstein Veblen allied a conspicuous consumption with the rise of the haute-bourgeoisie in the Gilded Age—in which the acquisition of goods allowed would-be burghers to demonstrate their claim to social respectability. For girls of the middle classes, like those among the working class, that which they were displaying was themselves—their newly adorned bodies—and in so doing they were challenging rather than affirming a traditional Victorian gender ideology of self-abnegation. Unlike other forms of display, critics would argue that such display declassed them. Two unlikely allies, however, defended this more assertive and pleasure-oriented culture of girlhood. The British chronicler Rudyard Kipling joined the debate with an article in *Ladies' Home Journal* in 1899 in which he argued the superiority of new American girls. His analysis, told through the objectifying male gaze, nonetheless endorsed the propriety and essential innocence of American girls' self-assertion in public: "They are original, and look you between the brows with unabashed eyes as a sister might look at her brother. . . . They possess, moreover, a life among themselves, independent of masculine associations. . . . They are self-possessed without parting with any tenderness that is their sex-right; they

understand; they can take care of themselves; they are superbly independent.
. . . Yes, they have good times, their freedom is large, and they do not abuse
it. They can go driving with young men, and receive visits from young men to
an extent that would make an English mother wink with horror."[77] Kipling's
American girl was one version of the brave and forthright Anglo-Saxon
woman of the empire that perhaps found its American embodiment in the
"Gibson girl."

From a much different perspective, the social reformer Jane Addams, in
The Spirit of Youth and the City Streets (1909), offered a defense of the impulse
of "new girls" which represented a powerful gloss on the meaning of girls'
camaraderie and culture in the streets. Her subject was the working girl and
not the middle-class schoolgirl, yet her analysis represents one of the few—
and certainly one of the best—efforts to understand, as experienced from the
inside, the meaning of youthful promenades. "The rest of us see only the
self-conscious walk, the giggling speech, the preposterous clothing. And yet
through the huge hat, with its wilderness of bedraggled feathers, the girl an-
nounces to the world that she is here. She demands attention to the fact of
her existence, she states that she is ready to live, to take her place in the world.
The most precious moment in human development is the young creature's
assertion that she is unlike any other human being." The assertion of individuality, as Jane Addams saw it, was dependent on that dramatic "demand"
of attention, and attention in public. The critics Carolyn Heilbrun and Myra
Jehlen have challenged the tendency of historians to find power and authority
within women's domestic sphere, arguing (in Heilbrun's gloss of Jehlen) "that
women's selfhood, the right to her own story, depends upon her 'ability to act
in the public domain.'"[78] When Heilbrun and Jehlen talk about such action,
they likely have in mind such activists as Jane Addams herself. Along with
other New Women, Addams brought an ideology of woman's moral authority
into the public sphere and converted a "family claim" on woman's service into
a "social claim." When writing about girls, though, Addams talked not about
society's claim on the girl but instead about the girl's claim on society, a claim
of the right to a life and self.

Such a defense of girls' "rights to life" could by no means be assumed
in these days before the passage of women's suffrage. G. Stanley Hall, who
described and named the stage of life adolescence, would have agreed with
Addams about what such girlish promenading meant, but would have condemned rather than defended its legitimacy. Writing in 1904, he worried
about girls' attention to "good looks" and their "activity of mind and body,"
which like Addams he saw as "augmentations of [girls'] individuality." He

worried that "energy spent on self" would overdraw girls' "reproductive power" and leave girls without the "energy meant for the altruism of home and of posterity."[79] Hall's defense of a generic femininity, confined to home and defined by family service, was just what "new girls" were defying. In their promenading with peers and their quick senses of fun, new girls of the middle class, like those of the working class, simultaneously asserted their right to act in public and their right to the experience of a subject self temporarily freed from any claim but that of a moment's pleasure.

Endings

NINE

Commencement:
Leaving School, Going Home,
Growing Up

Going to school authorized girls' participation in a youth culture of "mere" schoolgirls, protected from arduous domestic chores by their youth and their studies, which also freed them to fun and frivolity in the streets. Many girls in the new public high schools of the mid–nineteenth century stopped attending school before graduation. They went home to assist in family emergencies, followed physician's orders to recuperate from a range of ailments at home, or increasingly, over the course of the century, went out to work as sales clerks, office assistants, or teachers. Some also failed to be promoted and left school in tears and disgrace. By late in the century, however, more and more girls stayed in school through the course, attending school more frequently than boys and graduating from public high school in even greater proportions.[1] Graduation from high school certified academic accomplishment but increasingly also bore symbolic significance as the celebration of middle-class girls' coming of age, the end of a girlhood moratorium on woman's role, and the "commencement" of a life defined by bifurcated gender expectations. Virtually overnight, with little preparation, many girls who had been granted reprieves during their days as schoolgirls finally were expected to assume the status of grown women. High school graduation celebrated the "coming out" of girls from a status as near-equals to boys into an officially sexualized world. High-performing girls felt fresh status at their recognition at graduation, but for most girls and their audiences, the meaning of graduation was best understood as a rite of passage—from girlhood to the responsibilities and restrictions of womanhood.

Graduation and Public Display: Recitation and Ritual

Graduation ceremonies bridged the significant divide between youth and adulthood for both boys and girls, but they bore special freight for girls, who constituted the clear majority of those graduating. Girls dressed in white and stood on stages covered with flowers. They often read essays to crowded halls of parents and other members of the community, worrying about what they were going to say in their graduation essays and how they were going to look in the gowns sewn for the occasion. It was perhaps the most public moment of their lives, and they prepared for it accordingly. A student preparing to graduate from Concord (N.H.) High School in 1875 broadcast her worries in a humorous "Song of the Graduation Gown" in a hand-copied student newspaper. She described herself sitting up all night, "With fingers inky and black/With eyelids heavy and red," writing her essay:

> *Write! write! write!*
> *In head-ache and desperation,*
> *   And still, with feelings blacker than pitch,*
> *She sang of her graduation.*

Equally stressful were the sewing of her dress and the uncertainty the moment heralded:

> *And what's the result? A diploma,*
> *   A graduation gown,*
> *An afternoon's display, bouquets and other fuss,*
> *   And brains so full with the studies of school,*
> *What will become of us?*

Yet there was really no time to think of the future, given the demands of the moment:

> *Think-think-think,*
> *   How we shall our hair arrange,*
> *And what attitude we shall strike*
> *   When we have our pictures taken,*
> *Till our face is flushed and our locks uncurled,*
> *   And our faith in our looks is shaken.*[2]

In theory, of course, graduation exercises recognized all graduates for their academic accomplishment, but often it was simply the graduates' presence that girls worried about and audiences remarked upon.

The public display of girls' scholarly accomplishment was initially controversial on grounds of propriety. It was this exhibition of girls' education that
the Rev. R. W. Bailey responded to in an article published in *The Patriarch,
or Family Library Magazine* in 1841. To an opponent who argued that it was
"indelicate and unnatural" for young ladies to appear before mixed audiences
at celebratory recitations, he drew the contrast with the appearance of young
ladies at balls and dancing parties. "You object to have your daughter rise . . .
to speak her mind and exhibit the results of study, in presence of her particular friends, while you encourage her to stay at her toilet, and appear . . .
in a public attitude purposely arranged to display her person." This scruple
about women's appearance before public audiences meant that Oberlin valedictorian Lucy Stone in 1847 could not present her commencement speech
herself, for convention deemed that it be "read by a man!" (Stone, who would
go on to a career as a pioneering feminist orator, refused to write a speech
under those conditions.)[3]

By the 1860s and 1870s, the remnant of that reservation about girls' appearance in public was a distinction between boys' and girls' presentations.
Girls generally held a script and read their essays; boys memorized their parts
and declaimed. The difference reflected the uncertainty of elders about the
propriety of direct eye contact between respectable girls and strangers in the
audience. Lily Dana's report of her high school exhibition in Cambridge,
Massachusetts, in 1862 observed that the young ladies buried their heads in
their texts and did not talk loud enough to be heard. When girls were reading
essays in whispers, appearance was all. It could scarcely be otherwise. Such was
the stuff of the Dana family's observations: Her sister "thought that Miss P.
appeared better than she had ever seen her and made quite graceful curtsies,
but she wore leaves on the top of her head which I did not think at all becoming." Dana's mother "thought that Miss Cutler was pretty and acted the
best." In contrast, the boys were performers. Dana noted two who presented
a costumed Latin dialogue, and the impact of another who was admired by
many. (Dana herself demurred: "I must say I think he acts like a regular rowdy
and looks very conceited.")[4]

With distinct guidelines for boys and girls, both participants and observers
viewed high school graduation as a celebration of the persons of girl graduates—their appearance, their modesty, and above all their status on the cusp
of two worlds. Schools had held girls in a state of nonadulthood for several
years after menarche. High school graduation released both boys and girls in a
ceremony which represented simultaneously the culmination and the ending
of their youth. The anthropologist Barbara Myerhoff notes that "the interplay

of biology and culture is the subtext of all rites of passage, and often the play is fast and loose." Coming as it did well after the onset of puberty, high school graduation was just such a "fast and loose" coming-of-age ceremony. (Myer-hoff herself argues otherwise, concluding that "the overwhelming emphasis at the graduation ceremony is on academic achievement," while other factors, "such as a sense of separation and transition," are alluded to in passing if at all.[5]) To the contrary, my evidence suggests the attenuation of an emphasis on academics over the nineteenth century. The experience of separation and transition suffused responses to graduation exercises.

Graduation presents, and especially the gift of flowers, spoke to that trans-formation. The graduation presents Lois Wells received in the 1880s when she graduated from high school in Quincy, Illinois, represented both the ac-complishments of book learning and an imagined future as a young lady. The thirty-one "tokens" she received included four volumes of poetry, a finger bowl, a napkin ring, a fan, gloves, a handkerchief, and, of course, flowers.[6] The gift of poetry was especially intended to locate a young girl's future life in a young lady's world of romantic idealism—suggestive of passions con-trolled. The other emblems of refinement, too, sought to encourage a life of domestic influence. They offered no encouragement for the continuation of the schoolgirl's life of freedom and exploration within the public sphere.

At the turn of the century, as the number of graduates picked up, dem-onstrations of student learning took up less of the program. The gradual dis-appearance of graduation recitations affected both male and female gradu-ates and may have signaled the collective triumph of a succession of bored audiences, as well as the increasing size of graduation classes. A piece pub-lished in *Ladies' Home Journal* in 1896 explicitly advocated this evolution in girls' school graduations. It described such ceremonies as "a succession of the most beautifully suggestive events which it is possible to have fall under human eyes." Beyond simply the appreciation of girlhood, "always beauti-ful to a healthy mind," it especially celebrated the piquancy of graduation ceremonies marking the end of girlhood and the commencement of adult womanhood. "The girl feels the thrill of the moment, and to the auditor the importance of it all comes strangely home. It is alike an epoch in the life of the girl and in that of her parents and friends. The time of the year is in full sympathy with these events, and everything about the commencement exercises of a girl's school, college or seminary is thrilling to the pulses. To be present at such exercises is one of the most exhilarating experiences that can come to either man or woman." The rhetoric of the thrilled auditor reso-nates with Myerhoff's anthropological analysis of the significance of "rites of passage" to those watching, for whom "the initiate is thought to embody messages about the cosmos, is considered a microcosm or miniature version of the largest concerns of the natural and the supernatural order."[7]

After applauding what was "so fresh, dainty and beautiful" about such exercises, the *Journal* author came to the point: "I want to quarrel with the principals of these institutions for allowing one part of the exercises to be entirely incongruous with the other portions." This portion? The essays read on topics "that are nearly always far beyond the ken or conception of girlhood," such topics as "A History of Civilization," "Republic Vs. Monarchy," "Trades' Unions and Monopoly of Labor," "The Negro and His Right to Vote," "Some Factors of the Labor Problem." "Surely, questions of politics, labor, government or race have no proper place at girls' commencement exercises." *Ladies' Home Journal* was no more enthusiastic about essays on issues more central to woman's sphere, such as "Is Love Worth Striving For?" Instead, it protested the association of high school graduation with girls' intellectual development. Ultimately, it argued, "Parents and friends journey to commencement exercises to see their daughters, or the girls in whom they are interested, look their prettiest and seem their best. . . . It is not a time for mental calisthenics."[8] This description of school graduation exercises as a pageant for girls' "looking" or "seeming" their "prettiest" and "best" and its rejection of "mental calisthenics" reflected a hopeful attitude about secondary education for girls; many adults hoped it would define a period of girlhood rather than intellectual development, and close conclusively a chapter in the female life course.

For many girls then as now it appeared to mean just that. When Florence Peck graduated from high school in Rochester, New York, in 1901, she focused her excitement on the dress which seemed to summarize the occasion. She pronounced it "perfectly lovely," and described it as "a creation, an event" in itself. Peck granted even more significance to the dance in the evening which represented a high point in her diary. "Never in the history of events did I have a better time." She danced until 2 A.M. and received numerous presents. Among those, the best was "a *ruby* ring from *father*!!" Even more than an eighteenth birthday, graduation from high school signified a functional change—an official entrance into maturity appropriately marked by such gifts of acknowledgment and farewell from fond fathers.[9]

It did not mean the same thing to many girls or to all adults, however. A high school graduation presented a few girls—valedictorians and salutatorians—with an opportunity. One writer recalled "fine young girls in fresh white dresses," especially remembering a speaker "whose eyes were clear and whose voice was earnest." "After all these years I remember her dignity of bear-

9.1 "Fine young girls in fresh white dresses," 1898. The graduates of the class of 1898 from Hallowell (Maine) High School wear virtually identical dresses, except for the lone male. Courtesy of Hubbard Free Library, Hallowell.

ing, and the impression of her motto has never been lost." She had chosen as her topic, "I have made of myself all that could be made of the stuff."[10] Girls graduating from high school knew that this was the moment unique in their lifetimes to call attention to themselves and their "stuff" of self.

Margaret Tileston: Graduation and the Class of 1885

The diaries of Margaret Tileston suggest the significance of high school graduation for some girls. Tileston's graduation from the Salem High School class of 1885 brought about the flowering of a positive identity as "young lady" scholar and also solidified her membership in a cohort of peers. The growing solidarity of the boys and girls of the graduating class presented a prototype for a community of equals unique in their life experiences.

Graduation often served as the capstone to a prolonged flurry of collective activities of the senior class, bringing together boys and girls in numerous common meetings. Just before their dispersal, graduating girls and boys discovered an intense communalism linking them in shared purpose. They appointed representatives, planned gifts, adopted mottoes or colors, and selected class flowers in an ongoing series of class meetings which united them in fiercely if briefly shared citizenship. Well before the passage of women's suffrage—which in any case her mother actively opposed—Margaret Tileston depicted the boys and girls of the senior class negotiating and voting in a spirit of high seriousness and fun.

On a committee to select a motto for the class of 1885, she initially took a traditional, "girl's" role: "After some talk I wrote seven mottoes on the board, as John R. said I wrote the best, and we finally decided on, 'Vincit qui se vincit' [He conquers who conquers himself], which was the one he wanted." The ground had been laid for conversation, though, and Tileston reported that after the meeting "John R. and Frank Fabens walked along home with Mabelle and me." Four days later, the class met as a whole. "We discussed about colors a long time, the whole class being made a committee. Light blue was finally adopted. Mouse-color, deep green, crushed strawberry, and pale pink-blue were jocosely proposed. We voted also to have a Greek motto instead of a Latin one." Perhaps in disappointment at affairs being dispatched so rapidly—vitiating the need for further meetings—a week later the class opened everything up for reconsideration. Some girls favored lavender for a class color, other students proposed gray, and the class ended by reaffirming its commitment to light blue. The proposal for a Greek motto was reopened, and a Latin motto—"Fasta quam verba," Deeds rather than words—was adopted temporarily pending research on past class mottoes. Procedural matters pre-occupied some. A senior boy brought a note in to Tileston in her class for young ladies. "It said that he had heard that I desired to have a committee meeting but that the committee had been dissolved by action of the class." As a serious scholar, Margaret Tileston took some classes with boys preparing for college, which made her influential with both male and female students. After school one day, Margaret Tileston ran into another male classmate and "walked along with him, talking about mottoes and colors." Apparently, the class was still meeting regularly, because another meeting yielded a new set of decisions, however tentative. "After much indecision, a shade of cherry was adopted as the class color, the Greek motto restored, maintaining the same committee and we decided to have the class meeting at the houses of the members, though many were not in favor of it." Several weeks later, the first class meeting met at Margaret Tileston's house. She described the meeting as a "good deal of fun," and announced another decision: "We decided to have 'Learners, not learned' in Greek for our motto." This time, though, the class meeting moved beyond its strict business agenda, and various class members played on the piano or sang. The meeting ended with a classmate's sugges-tion that they keep early hours and with a vote of thanks to Margaret for her hospitality.[11]

The class meeting schedule intensified as graduation approached. The next issue was a class gift, to be presented to the principal at an evening party at his house to which he had invited the senior class. ("He warned us not to eat too hearty a supper beforehand.") At one meeting the subject was discussed. Three days later, in another meeting, the class resolved that the gift would be a steel engraving, and then set about the difficult business of finding a representative to present it. Tileston distanced herself from this negotiation. "Smith, Sargeant, Harris and Lefavour were proposed and resigned and then they chose me and I tried to resign, but they didn't take notice of it. Some of us talked about it afterwards. I intend to get off." The next day the class met again as time was running out before the principal's party. This time Tile-ston took control. "I was made chair-man. We voted to have Richard Dodge present our gift. Some more money was collected. I gave 25 [cents] besides the 50 I had given before." Margaret Tileston clearly had contended for and won leadership in her own right, and as "chair-man."[12]

Another far less routine matter occupied the class's attention—a tragedy, in fact. Tileston's diary recorded a class meeting in early May at the house of Jimmy Harris, one of those who had evaded responsibility for presenting the class gift to the principal. This occasion was more notable for its sociability than the business transacted. One girl talked constantly, a boy sang some solos, and they played conundrums. The host, Jimmy H., amused them with an unspecified "funny thing." Jimmy H. was not to graduate with his class, however. Six weeks later, Margaret reported his sudden, severe illness just before he was to take his college entrance exams; he was not expected to live through the day. As was appropriate for such occasions, Margaret's comment in her diary was a quotation of verse. "'Our common grave, whither all footsteps tend, whence none depart.'" When his death was announced the next day, the class appears to have acted spontaneously, collectively deciding to call off graduation exercises in his memory. Tileston was part of this shared reaction of shock. She reported paralysis. "Mabelle feels dreadfully, and so do we all. . . . I didn't feel like doing anything."[13]

The solidarity that the students of the senior class forged during class meetings after school still did not extend to structures within the school. For in the same passage in which she expressed her participation in collective mourning, Tileston used the distancing third person to explain that when the senior class was allowed to go home at recess, "some of them stayed." Once again a committee was appointed (probably by the principal) to act on the matter, although this time Tileston was not included, nor did she describe the committee's membership. Probably, as before, "the young ladies" were represented on the committee that went out at noon to select a floral offering, on the theme of *The Gates Ajar,* a popular work of inspirational religious literature.[14]

Several days later, Margaret Tileston and her classmates attended Jimmy Harris's funeral. "We were in a room at the Harris house, while the services were going on. Some of the girls cried. I'm sure I did. Afterward, we all passed through the room where he lay in his coffin, and looked at him. He was terribly changed and looked much older. We went to the grave in Harmony Grove Cemetery, the girls in carriages."[15] Although the girls cried and rode in carriages while the boys stifled tears and walked to the cemetery, the Salem High School class of 1885 clearly shared in the sobering odyssey of their friend and classmate from jovial host to aged corpse buried in Harmony Grove Cemetery. In the 1880s at Salem High School, the "young ladies" were an influential but separate block. As they participated in decision-making class meetings, however, they grew to think of themselves as full partners in a community defined by class color and class motto, as well as by shared sorrow at the untimely death of one of their own.

Jimmy Harris's death could not permanently suppress the spirit of the Salem High School graduating class. After mourning his death and without Margaret Tileston's comment, the classmates seem to have overlooked their earlier resolution to cancel commencement in his memory. Even between the death of Jimmy Harris and his funeral, the class attended a convivial class meeting in which birthday books and photographs "were the rages." Tileston's modern usage, new to her and awkwardly pluralized, suggested the reserved Tileston's surrender to the generational solidarity of the moment. Boys and girls wrote in each other's books, exchanged lists of class birth dates, and discovered new friendships. Meeting a casual acquaintance out walking, Tileston was inspired to invite her home, where they looked at photos and wrote in each other's albums. Margaret volunteered an advance look at her commencement essay.[16]

Margaret Tileston's exhilaration at the time of her graduation was enhanced by this special role in the ceremony. As the girl with the highest grades, she was to read an essay she had written. It was this luster which drew special attention to Tileston the weeks before graduation, fueling her good spirits. After Tileston had begun work on her graduation essay, but several months before the actual date, she was forced to acknowledge her growing reputation as a scholar. "As we were coming out of the Greek recitation, Richard Wentworth asked me if I would give him a complimentary copy of my memoirs," she reported one March day. The next month, she observed that a male acquaintance had begun bowing to her in the streets. "He never did before and I don't know why he does."[17] Margaret Tileston was beginning to discover the status a competitive boys' culture could confer on a winner.

Her new position could even translate into a new standing as a "young lady" within the coeducational social world of the class of 1885. At an evening garden party, Tileston had the unprecedented experience of being attended by a boy. "Everyone" had come to this party at the tennis club, to which Margaret belonged. "There was tennis-playing and the Japanese lanterns were perfectly lovely. Sally Goodhue and I talked a great deal with Dick Manning and Frank F., who was very attentive in getting us things to eat. I had 3 helpings of ice-cream and 2 cups of lemonade. Frank and I were together a great part of the evening. After the rest had gone, the workers [members and co-hosts] sat on the piazza and talked and drank coffee. . . . Then he went home with me. It was nearly midnight when I reached the house. Everybody of the Tennis Club wore yellow ribbons, the club color. Neddie P. and Miss P. played banjos and sang college songs."[18] For this one evening, Frank Fabens, Tileston's partner in academic excellence, was filling the accepted role of escort, fetching food and accompanying her home. The extent of her departure from her role as class grind was revealed the next week, when she reported that a friend had accused her of flirting with "F.F." Far from being dissuaded by such a charge, Tileston set out on class business to find Fabens and ended up with classmates at his house, cutting out letters for their motto.

She won other chivalries for boys' interest in her academic prowess. "Sam G. went up to the top of the tree and got me some cherries on condition that I would tell him the subject of my essay," she reported after one class meeting.[19] In a competitive school culture, Margaret Tileston's triumphs had earned her the respect and the recognition of male classmates, from whom she had no other particular claims to attention.

Tileston's sense of belonging was exhilarating. A later class meeting at a friend's house, this time entirely stripped of business agenda, featured ice cream and games and produced "a noisy time." Another day she and classmates "stayed at the school-house, having a good time." Frank Fabens gave her "a slice of bread and butter and half a hard-boiled egg," and she went home to finish her supper, remaining there only briefly before returning to the school house. Even the acknowledgment left until the end of her entry that "Frank Fabens is smitten with Annie Hansen" didn't seem to dampen her radiant good spirits.[20]

Graduation day itself lived up to anticipation. Margaret Tileston's mother bought her a bouquet of "lovely roses." "After prayer and the opening chorus, came my essay. I felt funny when I got up, but got through all right. . . . Frank Fabens was requested to turn around to face the audience when his splendid record of 'no conditions' and 'Honors in Classics' was mentioned. . . . When my turn came, Dr. Atwood [perhaps the superintendent] spoke of 'Sartor Resartus' (one of my [prize] books) and threw in a compliment about my scholarly ability, and said that I was the first young lady . . . and then everybody clapped. . . . The mayor made a long speech to us."[21] For Margaret Tileston, who had excelled in her academic program, graduation from high school represented a translation of scholarly expertise into a valued and honored social identity within a newly close circle of male and female peers. The graduation exercises of the Salem High School class of 1885 confirmed this new identity. Just as contemporary college football players peak at the Rose Bowl, or high school players at the state tournament, Margaret Tileston's life, in terms of her sense of recognition from a community of her peers, was at its zenith. Never again, in a life carefully documented throughout, would she feel the same sense of unequivocal social endorsement as a scholar. The coeducational public high school, for all its encoding of gender roles along the way, at graduation ultimately paid homage to female intel-

lect and accomplishment in its awards and in the diversely freighted gifts of
books and flowers with which it honored girl graduates.

Solidarity and Flirtation

Other depictions of school leave taking expressed a shared generational
solidarity less evident in day-to-day school relations. Although the girls and
boys did not associate extensively at Franklin Sanborn's school in Concord,
Massachusetts, the end of school brought them into close relations. Ellen
Emerson exclaimed over the fraught emotions on the last day of school. "Oh
how sad that was! . . . Then when we were going some of those who were not
coming back cried, and the lamps got very dim, and it seemed melancholy,
and the next day to find the school all gone, and hear the songs of yesterday all
the time in your ears and think of this wonderful lovely year being all gone."
Boy and girl graduates would clearly be parting company in the future, many
of the boys destined for Civil War battlefields, but in 1859 the schoolmates
still perceived themselves to be fellows, with Emerson referring to the boys
in the first-person plural and possessive. Emerson continued: "Then the next
days were so anxious while our boys were being examined to enter college and
finally the getting them back for one last day to tell us how they got in and
have a rejoicing with us was so exciting and delightful."[22] The girls' vicarious
excitement over the boys' college entrance examinations was the harbinger of
inequalities to come, but their solidarity as classmates still ruled that "one last
day."

Perhaps not surprisingly, other accounts worked the ground between class
solidarity and individual flirtation. At Lily Dana's graduation, as at Margaret
Tileston's several generations later, class meetings brought together in common cause sets of boys and girls previously somewhat uncomfortable in one
another's presence. Lily Dana picked up a friend on her way to one meeting "because I was afraid of being the first at Slaters and I am glad I did, for
I found I should have been the first girl among a whole lot of boys." However, when a week later two male classmates paid a call at Dana's house to
solicit money for a class gift, Dana reported on her increasing comfort in
doing business with boys. "I had to go down alone to see them. I expected
to be frightened out of my wits, but I wasn't; I am not half so bashful as I
used to be."[23] The camaraderie of graduation festivities modulated customary
reserves between the sexes.

For Lily Dana, however, romantic excitement sparked the more diffuse
sense of solidarity at the time of her graduation from Cambridge High School

in the 1860s. Dana's account of the Exhibition Day dance in particular represented the peak of the diary records of her youth. She wore a low-necked dress, with her hair in Grecian braids and decked with flowers. Her class ribbon, "white with 62 on it in gilt," was crossed over the waist of her dress in the front. She especially described the attention of one "Dodge," who brought her strawberries and an armchair, and with her observed the "toasts for the different teachers, the class and the country," and joined in the singing of "patriotic, funny and class songs." He confided his future plans to her: "He told me that he is not going to college for a year, as he thinks he is too young (only just fifteen), to enter yet and I told him I thought so too, but he is not any too small, for he is one of the tallest boys in the class." Likely Dana could not respond in kind, for her plans did not have such definition, and would not throughout her life. Nonetheless, Dana's account stands out in her diary for her unbridled excitement. She acknowledged as much in her eight-page account. "I suppose I am rather foolish to write so much about today but I can't help it I had such a nice time and I stayed up ever so long telling father and mother all about it." Others seemed to share Dana's excitement, for during the dance the classmates threw a spontaneous class meeting in the cloak room to strategize about how to meet again soon. "We decided to give Mr. Williston a present and to meet at Slater's tomorrow night to see about it." Lest there be doubt about Dana's motivation for attending that meeting the next day, upon her return she reflected her disappointment in her diary. "As I told father after I got home, nobody was at the Class meeting. that is to say Dodge wasn't there." Dodge thereafter seemed to elude Dana, though she enlisted her sisters' help in tracking him, listened for him, and saw him looking up at her house. The word was out that maybe his mother was responsible for his absence at one meeting. "Some of the girls said that he always did just what his mother told him to and as she was rather particular, perhaps she hadn't let him come."[24]

At the last class meeting recorded in Dana's diary, the presentation of the gift to the principal six days after the official celebration of Exhibition Day, Dana recorded a missed communication between the two excruciating to Dana. Perhaps fifteen-year-old Dodge was unprepared for the weight of their sudden intimacy. In any case, Dodge didn't hear Dana's whispered greeting, Dana was too embarrassed to repeat it, and Dodge departed early. The other classmates lingered on, singing songs on the principal's front steps. For Lily Dana and for others, the reluctance to go seemed to be informed by their awareness that they had run out of excuses for meeting. For the girls, the departure from Mr. Williston's front steps meant more—that never again would they meet as "young ladies" with "young men" on a basis of such mutuality.[25]

Ethnic and Religious Division

High school graduations were richly significant to entire communities as well as to the graduates themselves. For minority ethnic communities, high school graduations could be especially important moments of collective pride. Sarah Rice, an African American who gave a valedictory oration at her high school graduation in Eufala, Alabama, in the early twentieth century, remembered what it meant to her personally: "People gave me gifts! . . . I thought I was the smartest person, knew everything. . . . I knew that I was going to be somebody, because I always felt that way. It didn't matter when we didn't have food or clothes like other people." This community recognition was mutually enriching. "Graduation was a great time in Eufala for black people; everybody tried . . . to go, and the church was packed full of people," she recalled.[26] Community investment in high school graduations might become problematic, however, in divided communities. Such was the situation in 1892 in Milford, Massachusetts, when two-thirds of the class, including its valedictorian, Mary McDermott, were not able to participate in their long-awaited graduation exercises because of ethnic and religious dissension among adults.

A significant proportion of the high school population of Milford in the 1880s and 1890s was second- and third-generation Irish Catholic. Irish had first arrived in Milford in the late 1840s to escape the potato famine and work on the railroad. By the 1880s and 1890s, Protestant and Catholic students appeared to share the high school in harmony. Beginning as early as 1865, the school committee regularly granted student petitions for a holiday on St. Patrick's Day. In 1892 the non-Catholic student editor of the *Oak, Lily, and Ivy* editorialized favorably on the "Irishman's custom of consecrating one day in each year to the memory of the mother country," commenting, "Yes, let each St. Patrick's Day see Erin's and America's flags float together in the breeze; but, with the Boston Post, we say, 'Every true Irish-American will always place the glorious starry flag above the green of the Oak.'"[27]

Catholic and Protestant students worked together on the student newspaper, on the sports teams, and in the athletic association. The student body was clearly divided into boys and girls, but ethnic divisions were muted. At Milford, as at Salem, Concord, and many other high schools around the region, senior classes bonded, raised money together for graduation and for class gifts, staged a sequence of class parties, and selected flowers, mottoes, and class colors (one year "rose pink and Nile green," another lavender and pink). The closeness of Milford senior classes is revealed in a story that the class of 1884, which consisted of equal numbers of boys and girls, told about itself. One member proposed that a marriage of the fifteen couples was in order—only prevented, the class reporter remembered, by the plans for the priesthood of one class member. The class of 1889, "being as sound in mind as we can be on the eve of graduation," bequeathed to the following class "our gum, our seats in the rear of the room, our special privileges of the little room, our valuable notes on 'Town Government' and our part of the deportment board."[28] Classes with such strong fellow feeling appeared to forget other divisions as they looked forward to graduation itself.

Thus the class of 1890 was distressed when the school committee abruptly canceled its graduation exercises. The local paper noted that the school committee simply appeared in school on a Wednesday morning and presented diplomas to the eighteen graduates in a "most unsatisfactory" ceremony which bitterly disappointed not only the class itself but also "the many people who enjoy attending public graduation exercises." It is true that schools had not always had graduation exercises. Bridgton Academy in North Bridgton, Maine, for instance, introduced the "novelty of graduation" only in 1880. (Previously, its historian reports, a student came, "stayed as long as necessary for his purpose or until his money was exhausted. Then he left without ceremony.") When the students of the Milford Class of 1890 looked behind them, however, they saw a steady stream of graduation ceremonies.[29]

Students dismissed financial considerations, pointing to their own fundraising efforts, yet concerns about the expense of graduation for families may well have figured into the thinking of school officials. Over the late century, girls increasingly wore similar graduation attire, white, and ornate, taxing both family seamstresses and budgets. The 1875 graduates of Boston's Girls' High School, for instance, were under orders from the school committee to dress "as simply as possible," Emily Eliot reported, "and Papa (who is the Head Master of the school) wished *me* to be the most simply dressed girl there, and he wanted me to wear a dress without a speck of trimming on it." Adult efforts to stem fashion expectations seem to have made little headway, though. ("I told him human nature could not stand *that* and that I must have some trimming on my dress," Eliot responded, compromising with flounces, but no ribbons, and a blush rose in her hair.) The Milford student paper of 1886 simply noted that "in dress, simplicity is the first step to elegance," an insight "for the benefit of the young ladies on June 25." Two years later, the graduating class voted "not to receive bouquets upon the stage," thus nulli-

9.2 "Dainty commencement gown," 1895. Over the course of the late nineteenth century, elaborate commencement attire excited girl graduates but burdened home economies. Wrote Isabel Mallon in *Ladies' Home Journal,* "I can always understand why the girl who is just about to graduate, as well as the one who is just about to be married, wants to wear pure white." Reprinted from Isabel Mallon, "Dainty Commencement Gowns," *Ladies' Home Journal,* May 1895, 21.

fying a highly public way of distinguishing students' relative popularity and affluence.[30] A working-class community might well have worried about increasing financial pressures on overstressed family economies.

Many of the members of the Class of 1890, however, felt victimized. Rena Matthewson, who was to have shared the spotlight with co-valedictorian

Susan Frances O'Sullivan, wrote as much at the end of school. "The class of '90 feel aggrieved. They feel that in some way or other a wrong has been done them. . . . Why they are to have no public recognition they have not been able to discover. They only know that the thing has been decided by higher powers than they. . . . However it is, dear friends, you cannot go to Music Hall to see the graduating class in holiday attire and to hear their essays. Do not expect to see or hear anything of them unless you happen to be on School Street the last day just as school is dismissed. Even then you will not recognize them from the other pupils, unless, perhaps, by faces a little more sad." The specter of a canceled graduation loomed over subsequent classes. By September of the next year, the incoming seniors had already selected their class colors and had begun their "fervent prayer" for a graduation ceremony. In the spring, the school committee complied, and tickets disappeared early. The town newspaper reported on the lovely event: "The stage was beautifully decorated with various kinds of flowers, and the motto 'Sapeintia nobis est praeceptor, virtus dux' [Wisdom is our teacher, virtue is our leader] was arranged on the curtain in letters made of daisies. The graduating class, consisting of 26 young ladies and gentlemen, made a very pretty appearance as they were arranged on the platform, and it is difficult to say who looked the best. Each of the graduates wore their class colors, old gold and white, and a small bouquet of the same color."[31]

Taking nothing for granted the next year, however, "A Senior" wrote again to the school committee about "the all-absorbing topic" of graduation for the class of 1892. The class representative insisted on the class's "educational rights" to a formal graduation. The student also made a programming suggestion: wouldn't parents prefer to see their children performing, rather than listening to an outside speaker? The school committee granted one request and scheduled graduation exercises. It also announced a valedictorian, Mary McDermott, third-generation Irish, one of five living siblings, and daughter of a prosperous painter and paper hanger. Mary McDermott (signing herself Mami at one instance) wrote occasionally for the school newspaper, including a light piece entitled "Fashionable Follies" about the feminine dandy and the "masculine girl of to-day." After announcing the student speakers, the school committee disregarded the student suggestion to forgo an outside speaker and turned to procuring a speaker from the community, first inviting a leading educator to speak to the class. When rebuffed, the superintendent proposed "as a solution of the difficulty" the invitation of a new spellbinding, Methodist minister in town, the Rev. Luther Freeman; his acceptance was announced thirteen days before the ceremony. In a longish story, the *Milford Gazette* told of "The High School Graduation Matter," which had already been picked up by the *Boston Globe*. Accounts differ about whether the two Catholics on the school committee were overruled or acquiesced in the invitation of the Reverend Freeman.[32] In any case, arrangements were proceeding until the powerful priest of St. Mary's Parish, the Rev. Patrick Joseph Cuddihy, issued a dictum to his congregation on Sunday, June 19, four days before graduation.

The *Boston Globe* published extracts from Father Cuddihy's remarks. Citing twenty-five years of "amicable relations," Father Cuddihy nonetheless protested vigorously against the selection of a Protestant minister for this secular occasion, accusing the committee of being "Free Masons" deliberately out to "insult the priest and Catholics of this town." Then he lowered the boom on his parishioners in the class of 1892: "I positively forbid the members of this congregation from attending and the graduates from going or accepting their diplomas from his hands." After accusing the school committee of "trying to rear a prejudiced feeling between the Catholics and Protestants of this town," he repeated his warning "not to have any of my congregation attend the graduation exercises at Music Hall next Thursday evening if the Rev. Mr. Freeman delivers the oration."[33]

Father Cuddihy's fourteen graduating parishioners, who constituted two-thirds of the senior class, must have been stunned. They organized quickly and drafted a protest to the members of the school committee, which met in special session to hear the petitioners in person the next night. They requested that the orator be replaced, as his appointment gave "rise to a feeling of religious disquisition" and created controversy. The school committee apparently listened and merely filed the Catholic students' request, tantamount to a pocket veto. Their options running out, "ten to twelve" courageous members of the senior class went back to Father Cuddihy the night before graduation to try to persuade him to relent. Not only did the formidable priest hold his ground, but he upped the ante. The *Gazette* reported: "He flatly refused to [reconsider] in remarks more forcible than complimentary to those present, and threatened to excommunicate them if they dared to disobey him in the matter." The graduates of the class of 1892 were caught. Graduation proceeded without two-thirds of the class, including its valedictorian, Mary McDermott, who did not have the opportunity to deliver the address she had prepared. Perhaps most painful for the Catholic students was the warm reception accorded the controversial speaker, who "was welcomed with a burst of applause which lasted fully five minutes. This hearty greeting given to a comparative stranger seemed to fill the young orator with enthusiasm and inspiration," the local paper reported; he held his audience rapt, pausing only for more spontaneous clapping.[34]

There is too much we don't know about the meaning of this sad event for the community, the high school, and especially the Milford class of 1892. The *Milford Gazette* expressed great sympathy for the students, implicit criticism of Father Cuddihy, but no censure of the school committee. Were the graduating minority applauding as strenuously as the rest of the Protestant community for a speaker who had broken their class apart? The *Gazette* noted that "the unfortunate affair is regretted by none more sincerely than by most of the members of the class, who are, after all, the real sufferers in the case, by being deprived of the privilege of participating in the crowning event of the long years of study." This statement does not indicate whether or how far the rest of the class stood by their Catholic classmates as they were caught in the crossfire of adult jealousies.[35] (We do know that none joined the Catholic students petitioning the school committee.) We can imagine, though, that the community's warm reception for a speaker that had cost the Catholic students their role in the graduation ceremony must have unsettled many of the Catholic students reading about it in the Milford papers.

We also don't know the impact of this loss on Mary McDermott, primed for and then denied a significant triumph at the dawn of her adult life. The testimony of other girl valedictorians, such as Rena Matthewson, Sarah Rice, and Margaret Tileston, gives some sense of what she lost. Instead of community affirmation, she received a double repudiation, first from an authoritarian priest and the school committee careless of her needs, and then from a broader community apparently endorsing her exclusion. Mary McDermott herself went on to teach school following her graduation, remaining single and living near home for the rest of her life. (When the census taker came around in 1900, Mary's seventeen-year-old sister Elizabeth was "at home," not in high school.) The class of 1892 had selected "Ad Astra"—To the stars—as its class motto. Chances are that all the members of the class, but especially the Catholic members of the class who were unable to celebrate, felt distinctly earthbound after the sorry dissolution of their commencement ceremony and division of their community.

Going Home

Life after graduation was challenging for many students. In 1886 the Milford student paper anticipated the "metamorphosis" of graduation day: "A Senior, for whom the day was made, will then fall from his dizzy height to the plebeian level of a common citizen of Milford and 'will be lost to sight.'" For most girls, scarcely full citizens, leaving school meant trading in the activism of school life for the relative passivity of supervised domesticity. After they left school, girls went home. Their diaries report the letdown. Lily Dana wrote in mid-July that she "felt sort of dull and had a kind of homesick feeling I suppose because I have had so much excitement the last two or three weeks and now there is nothing going on." Lizzie Morrissey dozed off while sitting reading. "I have felt heavy and dull all day," she wrote, "and this afternoon as I was sitting in the chair I actually fell asleep and I can hardly ever sleep in the daytime." At first Florence Peck found it "very nice" to sleep late in the morning, and ten days after graduation she was still "rather enjoying life." But a week later malaise set in. On one day, all she reported was "nothing doing," several days later, simply "living." A month later, after a nice week, she reported, "I want a vacation, vacation, vacation. I want to go off somewhere!! I shall go crazy pretty soon."[36]

Girls' lives had been structured by school for many years. School not only accounted for their time for seven to eight hours a day, but it also structured their out-of-school time. It provided the staging area for sociability with friends and the justification for the recreation of the weekend. The end of school left an enormous gap in girls' lives. They filled it, at least initially, with a long-delayed education in sewing and housework. After Nellie Brown graduated from the Agassiz School and came "home to stay" in 1859, her mother reported that she was being "domesticated," as they worked together through the day. The next fall, Nellie and her sister made quince jam. "They have a long lesson to learn from the cookery book, in order to move freely in life," her mother observed, the language suggesting an earlier era's instinctive association of domestic skill with female fulfillment. Ellen Emerson, in her description of the closing of Sanborn's school in Concord several weeks later, noted that after the flurry of activities at the end of school, girls and boys parted company. After the boys went, "we settled back into thoroughly domestic life, for the first time for a long while." Her editorial comment, "and I find it very charming," echoed Sarah Browne's idyllic portrait of Nellie Browne's domesticity from the same year.[37]

Later accounts also described girls' postgraduate absorption in domestic pursuits, though with less romanticism. In the 1870s Lizzie Morrissey, whose mother had protected her from household labor while she attended Girls' High School, found that the very day that school began in her absence was the day of her initiation into household chores. "It was my first attempt for

I never swept before," she reported, "but I am now going to learn how to do housework." When she spent another afternoon sewing with her mother, instead of reading or writing as had been her custom while a student, she congratulated herself. "I think I'm quite industrious," she wrote. In 1901 Florence Peck announced that she and a friend were taking a sewing class the summer after her graduation from high school. She admitted to resistance, however: "It seems funny that I should go—now am just using a thimble. How I used to hate a thimble." As with other girls, on some level she seemed to be resigned to her new activity. "Well now shall make shirtwaist galore."[38]

The Ideology: Leaving School and the End of Girlhood

The assumption of domestic roles should not have been a complete surprise to girl graduates. Parents sometimes tried to prepare daughters for the difficult transition from school life to home life. Correspondence between two fathers and daughters in the late 1850s suggests agreement about the symbolic significance of leaving school. Robert E. Lee wrote to his daughter Agnes in March 1857 about her impending departure from Staunton Female Seminary. He cautioned her that as she prepared to leave school "for good to enter upon a new course of life[,] I hope you will find yourself prepared for it, and be ready to meet all its necessities." Agnes reflected upon her departure from school at the end of the year, announcing herself "no longer a free thoughtless child" but instead "at sixteen too truly commencing the *battle of life.*" She anticipated the loss of the "joys" of school days: "When careless girls together we gave our whole time to our studies, enjoying the pleasure of gaining knowledge, while our *hard* lessons, our momentary annoyances were the subject of many a laugh and threat of vengeance." Particularly sweet were her last two months of school, which represented the "mingling of hard study" with "expectation, trepidation, speculation, animation and ambition," crowned by "our merry ride home young *graduates.*"[39] The adjectives with which Agnes Lee described her days as a schoolgirl or recent graduate—*careless, thoughtless, merry*—suggested her sense of freedom from real responsibility when consigned to the company of her peers.

When Nellie Browne was approaching graduation from the Agassiz School two years later, her father too wrote her a letter of admonition and preparation. After she came out from the company of "mere school girls" that June, he wrote, she should be prepared to acquit herself as a "true woman" in the "drama of life." Nellie responded to her father's admonition with earnest resolve and then mounting anxiety. "*I will* try to improve," she wrote. "I know

I am careless and thoughtless at times, but I mean well." When she contemplated how soon this transition would take place, though, she confessed herself "unfit for the task" and a few sentences later wrote, "I am completely lost, when I think of being *a woman,* of playing *my part,* in the drama of life." In the middle of May, with only five weeks to go, Nellie Browne dug in her heels. "Five weeks from today, I shall no longer be a school-girl. I cannot realize it. I shall not go to school again. But I intend to be a school-girl, for certainly two years if not longer. . . . *I will* be called a school-girl, if other people won't call me one, I will call my-self one." Nellie's insistence on preserving the label *schoolgirl* represented her resistance to the assumption of adult roles. As the time approached, Nellie also anticipated and mourned the loss of her school friends. "What shall I do? . . . It will be *very hard* for me to part from all the girls. I have formed many strong friendships that will last through life." She had heard that leaving school was "the first *great event* in a young lady's life," and she mused, "It is true."[40] As a great event, however, it seemed to promise mostly loss.

Once out of school, young women similarly mused on the import of their new role in life. A graduate's letter from her new home in Mobile, Alabama, to an old friend still in the North reflected on the anomalousness of losing her status as a schoolgirl: "I am out of school now, and as most persons style me, 'a young lady'! I assure you, Emma, that I am not more a young lady than I always was. In fact, I feel more like a *child,* than ever; . . . I sometimes feel like laughing at the idea of *my* being out of school. . . . I try now, but in vain, to be *dignified.* There is not a bit of *dignity* in me." Rhetoric and self-image adjusted slowly to acknowledge the abrupt change in status following the departure from school. In the postwar South, Georgia Mercer hoped that a planned picnic, which she regarded as a "frolic," would not get converted to a more adult evening party. "I sometimes like to forget that I really am grown, and to go back to the freeness and easiness of a school girl." A half-century later, some of the meaning of school had not changed. As Florence Peck anticipated her graduation from Rochester (New York) High School, she mused, "One almost hates to leave we have had such good times but we can't always be children."[41] Graduation from high school or seminary, more than passing through puberty or turning eighteen, seemed to be the point above others which meant that childhood had definitively been left behind. There were good pragmatic reasons for this to be true. Unlike either a birthday or the arrival of menarche, school was an activity, a program which ordered the days of girls. Once that program had been completed, it was time for girls to get on with their lives. The problem came in knowing what that meant.

Learning to Subordinate Self to Service

What it came to mean was managing morale. Advice givers acknowledged the difficulty of the years between school and marriage. Writing in 1888 in *Ladies' Home Journal,* one author contrasted the lives of girls with those of boys after school. "The boy, . . . having finished his school course, enters at once upon some chosen pursuit, as a matter of course, and quickly finds his proper level. Not so fortunate his sister. When not actually driven by necessity to become a bread-winner, there are few young girls who have the spirit to choose an active life rather than aimless dependence upon an indulgent father." Elaborating on the experience of "aimless indulgence," the author predicted the results of "life without an object": "The human mind is not so constituted that it can subsist upon husks, without rebellion." Later commentators like Jane Addams and Charlotte Perkins Gilman used this argument to advocate meaningful work for middle-class women—indeed a line of argument implied by the reference to "spirited girls" who "choose an active life" instead of depending on their fathers. In this piece, entitled "The True Relationship of Mother and Daughter," however, the writer fell back on an appeal to the fostering of intimate mother-daughter relations, urging the mother on in "daily, anxious, but tactful observation." Another adviser from the same year, taking up the challenge of "Our Girls—After School Days," also advocated "an object in life—some 'art, craft, or trade,' which would occupy her leisure hours, if not all her time." In fact, though, the regimen recommended for girls substituted structure for substance, enumerating a litany of small chores as the key to the "occupation" which would be the "secret of true happiness." Even the proposed "object" was in fact marginal: "an hour devoted to solid reading, to art, work, to music, or to the real business of life or hobby she may have chosen." In addition to this hour for the "real business of life," this adviser recommended confidential chatter between mother and daughter. "Anything a girl cannot discuss with her mother in an afternoon over their fancy work or the family mending basket, is something that means danger to the peace of all concerned."[42] Beyond instruction in the small skills of domesticity, these maternal chats were clearly critical in reconciling a young woman flushed with the heady excitement of school years to the vulnerabilities and responsibilities of woman's lot.

The messages were clear. Girls accustomed to the gratifications of personal accomplishment and the careless pleasures of school must learn to serve. To the "Elder Sister in the Home," newly out of school, Ruth Ashmore (aka Isabel Mallon) suggested that God meant for her to give herself to her family, especially to helping her mother. God had meant, too, that she "be merry and wise, happy and considerate, counting it no trouble to do a service for those you love." In particular, Ashmore brought up the case of a grandparent, "one who is queer, possibly tiresome and yet who has the claim that blood and poverty always have on kindred and kindness. . . . She exacts from the daughter of forty-five what she had from the daughter of fifteen—that is, continual consideration and obedience." For the granddaughter who might resist the burden of relieving her mother, Ashmore rephrased the challenge: "Here comes one of your opportunities. You have left school; you have a good bit of time on your hands; devote as much of that as you can to grandmamma; make the hours that you spend with her pleasant to her, and when you grow weary . . . remember that some day you will be as old as she is."[43]

Perhaps unlike her own mother at fifteen, though, the graduate of the late century at fifteen had not granted to her own mother "continual consideration and obedience"; on leaving school, she would need to learn to provide that service afresh.

Despite Nellie Browne's own resistance to becoming a "true woman," on Nellie's birthday following her graduation from Agassiz School, her mother mused that her daughter was ready. As she embarked on the "marked period of eighteen," her mother observed that she lacked selfishness and that already "the crown of self-sacrifice sits gracefully on her brow." She hoped that God would spare her daughter from "the harrowing trials of life," and that she would always be "as dutiful, affectionate, and lovely" as she was then.[44] Leaving school meant leaving friends and freedom. It also meant leaving "self" and learning sacrifice.

Emily Dickinson Leaves School and Goes Home

Midcentury girls like Nellie Browne and Ellen Emerson attempted to do just that. They may have experienced momentary rebellion against their new mission of service and self-denial, but they recognized that they had few choices. The duties of true womanhood were as inexorable as the calendar. One can understand the subsequent careers of some remarkable women, though, including the poet Emily Dickinson, as a prolonged campaign of passive resistance to the changing of the rules for girls upon the departure from school. Dickinson was a serious though sometimes sickly student when she attended first Amherst Academy and then Mount Holyoke Female Seminary in the 1840s. She then returned to her father's house in Amherst, Massachusetts. One way of understanding her later life of social withdrawal and private creativity is as a quietly defiant response to that moment when the rules changed.

Like many fathers of high-achieving daughters, Edward Dickinson had provided his daughter with an excellent education, which he did not intend to allow to interfere in any way with her future obligations to home and family. He did not approve of intellectual women and did not acknowledge his daughter's talents. Emily Dickinson's letters from her young womanhood had a savage tone as she confronted the precise limitations on her existence, especially in comparison with—and in longing for—her absent elder brother.

Aside from her impressive intellect, her biographer Cynthia Griffin Wolff concludes, in many ways Dickinson had been "a typical teen-aged girl." She developed crushes on teachers and gossiped, flirted, and joked with an informal club of spirited friends known as "the five." She briefly spelled her name Emilie after the Francophile fashion of the day (a custom excoriated by critics of schoolgirl fancies), and revealed the mood of her school days in a playful (and famous) letter written at the age of fifteen about teachers, studies, and her changing body. "I am growing handsome very fast indeed! I expect I shall be the belle of Amherst when I reach my 17th year. I don't doubt that I shall have perfect crowds of admirers at that age. Then how I shall delight to make them await my bidding, and with what delight shall I witness their suspense while I make my final decision. But away with my nonsense." Upon Dickinson's return home at the age of seventeen, however, her father joined other parents in expecting his daughter to set aside her delight in her looks, her desires, and her aspirations, and with her sister to become domesticated, keeping his house in place of her invalided mother. A letter to a dear friend at the age of twenty suggests her rebellion: "So *many* wants— and me so *very* handy—and my time of so *little* account—and my writing so *very* needless—and really I came to the conclusion that I should be a villain unparalleled if I took but an inch of time for so unholy a purpose as writing a friendly letter—for what need *I* of sympathy—or very much less of affection—or less than they all—of friends—mind the house—and the food." Like other girls returning from school, she was encouraged to use housework as solace for ennui or sadness: "*Sweep* if the spirits were low—nothing like exercise to strengthen—and invigorate—and help away such foolishness— work makes one strong, and cheerful—and as for society what neighborhood so full as my own."[45] Unlike most other girls, though, she did not accept the terms she was offered.

Dickinson had already revealed what she was made of. Her last year of school, during a powerful, schoolwide revival presided over by evangelical Mary Lyon herself, Dickinson had refused to succumb to the conversion experience which was nearly obligatory for girls of her background. This was a costly and willful act which brought social consequences. When she resisted godliness itself, she shut herself off from a major source of power and sociability for women in her circumstances, the female religious auxiliaries which provided assistance for the needy. Dickinson did not participate. At the age of twenty she wrote, "The Sewing Society has commenced again and held its first meeting last week—now all the poor will be helped—the cold warmed—the warm cooled—the hungry fed—the thirsty attended to—the ragged clothed—and this suffering—tumbled down world will be helped to its feet again—which will be quite pleasant to all. I dont attend—notwithstanding my high approbation—which must puzzle the public exceedingly. I am already set down as one of those brands almost consumed—and my hardheartedness gets me many prayers."[46] Though Dickinson complained about her isolation, she considered the charitable work of woman's sphere yet another burden, another reminder that she was now to surrender the vocabulary of self entirely.

Dickinson's problem in accepting her lot was undoubtedly exacerbated by comparisons with her brother Austin, who without her extraordinary skills was her father's pride and joy. A letter to her brother that year suggests her outrage at her brother's neglectful failure to write: "Permit me to tie your shoe, to run like a dog behind you. I can bark, see here! Bow wow! Now if that isn't fine I don't know! . . . Permit me to be a fowl, which Bettie [a servant] shall dress for dinner, a bantam, a fine, fat hen. . . . Herein I 'deign to condescend to stoop so low,' what a high hill between me, and thee, a *hill,* upon my word it is a *mountain,* I dare not climb." Warming to her subject, Dickinson here seems to have come a little unhinged at her perceived lack of power, marked by her inability even to elicit a letter from a beloved brother. Dickinson's problem seems to have been her unbending spirit. In her earlier letter of rebellion, she noted, "The path of duty looks very ugly indeed— and the place where *I* want to go more amiable—a great deal—it is so much easier to do wrong than right—so much pleasanter to be evil than good." Emily Dickinson was unusual in resisting the twin demands of evangelical Christianity and female socialization in the late 1840s. Dickinson could not and did not surrender the *I* which had been nurtured during her youth to follow the ugly "path of duty." She turned to her writing to rescue her. In her vexation upon understanding that the worlds opened to her during her education were only temporary, to be renounced at eighteen, Dickinson shared intellectual and emotional ground with a range of feminist intellectuals. For Elizabeth Cady Stanton and Jane Addams, as well, that moment of epiphany fueled and shaped a life's work. But it was not just brilliant young women who found it difficult to leave school and go home. In her 1870 novel Anna L. White titled the chapter following her heroine's return from school simply "Depression."[47]

Learning to Wait: The Crisis of Eligibility

Learning to subordinate self, whether for the first time or yet again, was one of the lessons of the return home. Perhaps even more challenging was another lesson of the return home: learning to wait. It was no secret to girls or families what it meant to leave girlhood behind. Being a "school girl" (the two words reinforced each other) meant to be too young to entertain marriage proposals. The "suggestive" drama of the graduation ceremony, its exhilarating influence on observers, surely lay in its enactment of a significant rite of passage in which girls became "young ladies" eligible for matrimony. Whatever the flirtations of earlier years, they had a provisional, playful quality, protected by the temporary status of girlhood. The stakes increased dramatically once a girl had left school and returned home.

Yet girls had little control—and felt less—over the event of all events in their lives which would determine all others: marriage. Who, when, and whether a young woman married were questions, unlike school problems, that did not necessarily repay concentrated effort. Indeed, some said that those most successful were those who worked at it least. Such, anyway, was the advice doled out by *Ladies' Home Journal*'s Ruth Ashmore. In making the case for the role of "Elder Sister in the House," Ashmore suggested that older girls devote themselves to a life of selfless familial service and let magic, or fate, take care of the rest. ("When Prince Charming comes he will be made the happiest man in the world, because all of the family will say, 'What will we do without sister?'") To twenty-year-old girls who were beginning to worry because "no gallant has come a-courting" Ashmore counseled patience rather than action. "The man and the hour will come, and surely you do not wish for some one who will have to be forced from the highway." In an astonishing assembly of truisms, she offered, "The old French proverb that 'All things come to him who knoweth how to wait,' is a true and good one, and a bone worth having is worth waiting for, believe me." Writing after the turn of the century, G. Stanley Hall used the language of Darwinism to explain the conundrum which ensnared girls who would take control of this as other aspects of their lives. It was men's choice, and men chose women who didn't take control. Invoking the laws of natural selection, Hall wrote, "Men's right to decide what women should be like is 'inalienable and eternal.' Men will continue to make women what they want them to be by marrying those who correspond to their ideals; thus real womanly women are not doomed."[48] To be a "real womanly woman" you did not force men from the highway. Instead, you waited for the right one to find his way to your door.

The problem was, as Hall himself admitted, that waiting aimlessly was not healthy. Along with those who sponsored elite social rituals of "coming out," Hall granted girls only one or two seasons of availability before the psychic costs of their situation caught up with them. A girl was at her most perfect and most beautiful, he claimed, at the ages between eighteen and twenty. But then, "in our environment . . . there is a little danger that . . . there will slowly arise a slight sense of aimlessness or lassitude, unrest, uneasiness, as if one were almost unconsciously feeling along the wall for a door to which the key was not at hand. Thus some lose their bloom and, yielding to the great danger of young womanhood, slowly lapse to an anxious state of expectancy, or they desire something not within their reach, and so the diathesis of restlessness slowly supervenes."[49] Unconsciously feeling along the wall for a door which you're powerless to open—Hall's metaphor nicely captured the diffuse anxiety of "our environment," the sex-gender system of the late-Victorian middle class, which consigned previously resourceful and vital schoolgirls to the passive pageant of eligibility expected of young ladies.

Waiting for What? Ambivalence About Marriage

Complicating this crisis of suspended agency was a profound ambivalence among many such young women about the status ostensibly being sought: marriage itself. Schoolgirls were reluctant to surrender their youthful freedom for the status of "young lady," but they were even more ambivalent about trading in the known experience and freedoms of home for a hazardous dependency upon a man likely to be at least part alien. Girls who had known the excitement and rewards of success at school saw the life of a married woman as a comedown. Fictional schoolgirl Kate Callendar, one of the "School-Girls of '54," spoke for a growing group of girls when she declared herself unwilling "to dwindle into the insignificance of a married woman."[50]

The centrality of the marriage question was revealed in the folklore of girls' prophecy, circulating to this day among girls who still envisage marriage as a powerful game of chance. At the beginning of the journal she entitled the "Literary and Artistic Vurks of the Princess Charlotte" (written when she was ten years old), Charlotte Perkins [Gilman] composed—or repeated—a game she entitled "the Book of Fate," which itemized a series of questions on the subject of "Who will you marry?" The answers copied out in her collected "Vurks" ranged from "a big dunce" to a murderer, a prince, a "dirty swell boy," or an organ grinder. The rest of the questions in this "Book of Fate" elaborated: "How much is he worth?" (answers from nothing to one hundred billion dollars); "What will you live in?" ("a hole in the ground," "a white marble palace"); "What is his business? (the traditional professions, or "to beg"); and perhaps most important, "What is his disposition?" (with eight options, two of which were "pleasant" or "perfect," and the rest negative—"cross," "quick-tempered," "uneven," and so on).[51] Charlotte Perkins was in a good position to know the extent to which a woman's fate depended on the character of the man she married. Her father, a cultured member of the Beecher family, had abandoned her mother and his children to a life of poverty and instability from which none of them entirely recovered. Indeed, the child's play which entertained Perkins as a ten-year-old represented the searing, central insight of the adult Gilman.

Children might confront the centrality of marriage head-on and devise games of chance to predict their fortunes. The folklore of marriage lay close to the surface for other ages as well. Nighttime dreams sometimes provided the occasion for the expression of anxieties about marriage. During her senior year of high school, Margaret Tileston had such a dream about "being half-engaged" to a second cousin, a dream she pronounced "queer." For girls like Tileston and Lizzie Morrissey, who also dreamed of being married in her last year of high school, such dreams were disconcerting in their focus on anxieties banished to just beyond the periphery of daylight consciousness. At the age of thirteen Mary Boit reported her sister's dream about a marriage proposal from an acquaintance, which Mary greeted with hearty laughter. "Is that not silly I laughed so when she told me her *silly, silly* dream it seems so absurd."[52] Later that year, she inserted in her diary a commercially printed arcade fortune, "For a Young Lady," which warned against a deceitful lover and promised eventual marital happiness with four children ("One of them will be a doctor, and will make your happiness"). At the beginning of her teens, Mary Boit could collect penny fortunes and guffaw, if a little too emphatically, at a subject which by the end of her teens would be no laughing matter.

However decentered during the schoolgirl moratorium, the marriage plot was the central conventional drama of a girl's life. Not only did marriage determine status and position, but for Victorian girls, it was expected to be the apotheosis of romantic love—a newfound mystery thought to be the most

Planet of the Fortune

FOR A YOUNG LADY.

My dear girl your tendency is to be merry and prudent ; you will not be very lucky in love, but in the flower of your life a young man will show himself to be your lover, you will nevertheless take no notice of him, because he would deceive you, now that you are warned think of it ; before long you will undertake a long voyage, for a strange combination ; you will be married to a rich gentleman, and you will be happy ; you will be mother of four children, and one of them will be a doctor, and will make your happiness ; you and your husband will live to the age of about 70 years.

Meanwhile you will play at the Lottery

1, 45, 71.

Await for the drawing, and you will be sure to win.

9.3 "A Young Lady's Fortune," 1891. Mary Boit probably purchased this fortune at the beach in Cotuit, Massachusetts, where she was vacationing with her cousins at the age of thirteen. This fortune, like most for girls, attempted to predict a girl's luck in love. Schlesinger Library (Cambridge: Radcliffe Institute, Harvard University), A-99-v. 17.

profound expression of inner self. Girls who read romantic novels participated in the celebration of love and marriage as one of the defining characteristics of schoolgirl culture. (Lucy Breckinridge suggested as much when she noted that "Sometimes I am wild and school-girlish enough to dream of connubial bliss.") Engagements were exciting. When Mary Winsor learned of her brother's engagement, she wrote to her sister to express her exhilaration: "I have been wild all the morning to scream very loud, or run very hard or squeeze somebody very tight." Proposals of marriage and engagements were scripted in girls' accounts along the lines of romantic fiction. Nineteen-year-old Ella Lyman's description of an engagement among her friends suggested the script. The announcement followed a season of partnering at Boston parties, Lyman reported, and "was no surprise to anyone, for the admiration on both sides was very apparent." At the same time, the proposal itself was said to have surprised her friend, as befit a feminine modesty. "He came to call and she had no idea it was coming till he got to the very words. It was in the little red room! Edith is wildly excited and happy, very sweet and rejoicing in the knowledge of his love." Edith offered reassurance on one issue: "that she never thought one could know whether one were in love or not but now she knows." As befit the transforming power of romantic love, Edith seemed visibly affected by her new estate: "She can hardly keep quiet but clasps her hands tremulously, breathes deep and smiles continually with little murmured ejaculations." As Karen Lystra has argued, over the course of the nineteenth century, the experience of romantic love began to emerge as the defining moment for the individual self, by the late century replacing the religious conversion experience as the marker of a fully realized adult.[53] The need for a spiritual conversion experience as a rite of passage had provoked great anxiety among youth unsure about how to accomplish such a moment of spiritual awakening. Yet the conversion experience required a meeting of only one soul with spirit. The experience of romantic love culminating in an engagement required the commitment, the negotiation, and the mutual surrender of two bodies and souls entrapped in a gender system which did not grant them equal access to initiative.

If the ineffableness of romantic love seemed to reinforce girls' mandated responsibility to wait for it to happen, their search was complicated by what girls knew (and mostly did not know) about sexuality, which remained at the heart of love's mystery. As we have seen, Victorian mothers were reluctant to address the subject of sexuality directly, in part because of the "civilizing impulse" which cast a screen of modesty over bodily processes of all kinds. As Lystra demonstrates, however, such resistance to a materialist interpretation of sexuality was also the result of the triumph of romanticism. Sex was itself seen symbolically as the crowning moment of the meeting of souls which defined romantic love. "Properly sanctioned by love, sexual expressions were read as symbolic communications of one's real and truest self, part of the hidden essence of the individual."[54] This was the theoretical center of the mystique of Victorian sexuality.

One disadvantage of Victorians' focus on the mystique of sexuality, rather than on its mechanics, was that little pragmatic counsel was provided on the nitty-gritty of sexual desire. The few mothers who aspired to do so remained bound in available language. Thus Lucy Stone took up the subject of male desire with her daughter Alice Stone Blackwell, and her daughter recorded her interpretation of the conversation in her diary: "We drove into Boston to take the train, and in the carriage Mamma told me all sorts of queer things about boys—how if you show them any attention they immediately think you want to marry them, and that they would like to marry you." This conflation of sexuality and marriage led to a confusion of meaning which Blackwell responded to in baffled understatement: "How very inconvenient."[55]

As for female desire, it too was rewritten to accord with cultural prototypes. One such rewriting emerged in a fantasy scripting of Lily Dana's "crush" on fifteen-year-old Frederic Dodge, which emerged at the time of her graduation from high school. Their actual relationship seems to have been born and then died in an intimate conversation about future plans on July 11, 1862, the night of Exhibition Day at Cambridge High School. Several weeks later, Dana reported that she, her sister, and some school friends had played "Consequences," a midcentury parlor game whose object was the spinning out of a fanciful narrative of romance. The game Dana played offered a collective and lurid rewriting of the Dana-Dodge relationship which located Dana's desire in Dodge, and removed her from any responsibility for this much-desired union. In this rewritten version "the very handsome Frederic Dodge met the beautiful but bad-tempered Lily Dana in Fayette St. He gave her a bunch of flowers and she put it in her pocket. He said 'May I have the pleasure of walking home with you?' and she told him to mind his business. The consequence was a rope ladder on a dark night, suspended from a back window, and the world said 'Just what I prophesied.'" In this sensationalized version, Dodge was transformed from reluctant suitor to dashing Romeo, and Lily Dana from timid initiator to proud beauty. The rejection was rewritten as well: Dana was described as rebuffing Dodge's polite gambit rather than vice versa, with a primal consequence: "a rope ladder on a dark night," sensation literature's equivalent of rape. In this scenario, we might assume that hereby Lily Dana was being teased, but with a narrative which represented a fictive recasting of her youthful longing to fit the contours of contemporary romance. Contrary to Dana's own account of the saga, in which she offered ineffectual encouragement, the game scripted the affair along conventional lines in which the male Dodge initiated, the female Dana's "no" really meant "yes," and the affair ended in passion and scandal. Social acknowledgment of Dana's crush involved the suppression of her own initiatives and their projection onto a dashing and potentially violent male actor.[56] Small wonder that girls might be afraid of their own desires when allied with such "consequences."

With all that needed to come together to bring about the flowering of mutual love and desire in appropriate marriage, girls sometimes talked about that state as if it were another country and those who lived there strangers. At midcentury, at the advanced age of twenty-one, Ellen Emerson felt so shy when contemplating the change worked by marriage that she found herself avoiding former friends who were engaged. When she realized that she would need to encounter one after church, she reported, "I was frightened and got behind Mother who advanced upon Sophy with all her heart and shook hands with her and rejoiced. Then I emerged and Sophy shook hands with me and said she was sorry not to see me yesterday and I said I was sorry but I felt as I was very cold." She wrote to another engaged friend of her sense of alienation from her upon hearing the news. "I am almost afraid to ask you to come and see me, because now we are more than ever different, yet I want to see you." Several years later, she relaxed a bit, reporting that she was happy to say of a Miss Leavitt that she didn't seem "altered by her engagement as we used to say people were. She is natural as ever." Ellen Emerson had an extreme reaction to the marital divide, across which she never seems to have considered journeying. Yet her genuine fear only exaggerated a common notion that marriage fundamentally transformed and distanced young women from their former selves. When Louisa May Alcott's elder sister became engaged at the time of their sister Lizzie's death, Alcott felt that she was losing two sisters and is said to have contemplated suicide.[57] (Her depiction of Jo's horror at Mr. Brooks's courtship of Meg in *Little Women* captures that mentality well for modern readers.)

Even those who were engaged seemed to find it hard to imagine themselves actually married. Lucy Breckinridge, who was engaged to be married several different times, distinguished sharply between the two estates. "Though I am engaged to Captain Houston, I have no idea that we shall ever be married. I never have been able to imagine myself Mrs. H. How ridiculous it sounds. God bless him!" Several engagements later, she suggested the risks of engagement—yet its advantage over the alternative. "Engagements lead too certainly to matrimony. It is happy to be 'in maiden expectation fancy free.' I envy girls who are free—they cannot realize the blessedness of it. I hate the idea of marrying. I saw a quotation tonight that expressed my ideas exactly, 'the hour of marriage ends the female reign! And we give all we have to buy a chain.'" Her preference for being engaged over being married characterized many young women who found their ability to set the time for their wedding to be a power worth holding on to as long as possible.[58]

For as much as marriage was the overwhelming paradigm for women's lives in late-century Victorianism, it increasingly seemed to present uncertain prospects for women's happiness. Even the writers of advice literature wrote guardedly about the rewards and responsibilities of marriage. In an article published in the *Ladies' Home Journal,* Mrs. A. D. T. Whitney revealed to her readers "The Truth About Marriage," that it was work and discipline. "I suppose it amounts to this: 'Take hold of hands, children, and go along together to school.' Just when they thought vacation was to begin, and school never to keep any more." Mrs. Whitney's interlocutor disputed the analogy: "'I could understand it better if they went together, and were dismissed together,' the girl said slowly. 'And if all the lessons were given out beforehand, so that they both knew just what they had to learn, and when to recite, and all the questions that would be asked of them. But things come so haphazard, and take us so by continual surprise.'" The girl student, of course, recognized a critical distinction between school and marriage. Unlike the coeducational high school, anyway, not only did husband and wife not perform the same roles in marriage, but the lessons for each were different. Ruth Ashmore underscored the point in her heavy-handed advice for young wives in their first year of marriage (perhaps a sad commentary on her own marriage at the age of sixteen). "No matter how much a wife may suffer (and she certainly will) she must learn to control herself, and to bear as much as possible with her husband's weaknesses." If a husband were to throw his linen around, "Pick it up! Otherwise you might quarrel." If a quarrel should develop, "No matter if you are in the right," you must "say that you are sorry and you hope that it will never happen again." She realized that to the "advanced woman," this advice might seem weak, but concluded ambiguously (and weakly), "It is the only way that one can become a good wife, and a happy one." For girls who read such advice, or who leafed through books like one that Margaret Tileston found, entitled *How to Be Happy—Though Married,* it might well seem as if the culmination of the plot of their lives—marriage—was best postponed indefinitely.[59]

Girls' observations of marriages around them did not necessarily encourage them to a more positive view. All tended to agree that marriage brought burdens and sorrow. "A woman's life after she is married, unless there is an immense amount of love, is nothing but suffering and hard work," Lucy Breckinridge concluded, observing that she "never saw a wife and mother who could spend a day of unalloyed happiness and ease." Some of the suffering was the consequence of childbirth. Girls who witnessed the multiple births of mothers or aunts in the home had ample opportunity to judge the results of the curse of Eve. A year or so after the marriage of a dear friend from boarding school, Helen Ward Brandreth began to have dreams about her. "Thursday night, the 10th, I dreamed that she was sick in bed. I thought I was sitting near her kissing her hand. All of a sudden she started up and began to *shriek* and *shriek* with *horrible* pain! With those terrible cries ringing in my ears I fled from the room to call the nurse, but while I was in the hall I heard Susie scream so loud that I woke and started up cold with terror; somehow I had a presentiment that my darling was suffering, but all I could do was to pray for her. I could not sleep for almost two hours. I could only lay there and think of her!" Instead, though, Brandreth reported the referent: "Early Saturday morning I got a letter saying that Susie's little girl was born the *very night* I had that *dream*!!" Reflecting changing standards for family size, Georgia Mercer in 1871 pitied a friend who was, "Poor child," having another baby, "the mother of two children before she is twenty-five."[60]

Lucy Breckinridge's dark view of marriage was a commentary on the pain of childbirth, which unfairly afflicted women, but on something more as well. "Poor women! Why did God curse them so much harder than men," she wondered. When her aunt died following a stillbirth, Breckinridge found it a "happy release for her, for her married life has been a long term of suffering. She has been married about seven years and had five children. I never heard of anyone who suffered as much." The details of her death added a poignant note to Breckinridge's description. "They all thought she was doing well after the birth of a dead child, and Uncle Wilmer went to the bed and felt her hand and brow and finding they were very cold, he called the Doctor; they found she had died without anyone's knowing it." Such circumstances implied that her aunt had died at least in part from neglect, slipping away without anyone knowing she was at risk. But for Breckinridge an even darker, more actively sinister image of her aunt's death presented itself: "I cannot help thinking that Uncle Wilmer is a Bluebeard."[61] This final judgment laid at man's door the responsibility for the suffering, and in this case early death, he brought to woman through childbirth.

Breckinridge's dread of marriage was based on a real tension in a woman's life course. As an unmarried woman, she was accorded great liberty of movement and freedom from housework. Yet within marriage she would experience onerous, endless, narrowly prescribed duties. If an unmarried woman might organize her life around a quest for romantic experience, a married woman must organize hers around the fulfillment of familial obligations. As Karen Lystra puts it, "Victorians conceived of marriage in terms of love and personal choice. Yet spousal roles were largely defined as compulsory social obligations. An act of self-determined choice, Victorian marriage nonetheless imposed a set of mandatory sex role–specific duties upon husband and wife. The contradiction was at the heart of the nineteenth-century middle-to upper-middle-class conception of marriage."[62] Alexis de Tocqueville had commented on this disjunction in the 1840s, when he observed unusually spirited and free young women choosing the circumscribed role of wife. Tocqueville suggested that this tension had been absorbed in a smoothly functioning social order. The testimony of young women such as Lucy Breckinridge suggests otherwise; as girls participated in a culture of romantic love which celebrated mutual discovery and shared fulfillment, the unequal constraints and burdens of Victorian marriage began to look less and less attractive—or even palatable.

Coming Out

After leaving school and entering a world governed by women's roles, young women (no longer girls) found themselves learning some hard lessons. First, girls who had done only token service in housework received their first serious educations in housewifery. Many learned for the first time what it really meant to subordinate self and serve. And they learned, or tried to, how to wait with composure while trusting in fate to supply them a suitable mate. Complicating this process of waiting was a creeping ambivalence about the object of all this waiting: Victorian marriage. No wonder that young women waxed nostalgic for their days as schoolgirls. In 1873 a critic and a graduate of Portland (Maine) High School for Girls described the state of eligibility as "that purgatory between school and marriage, that death in life which our social arrangements doom all women to pass through." What a recent graduate might not understand, Abba Woolson wrote, was "that all she is living for is to secure a husband . . . and that to do this she must pretend all the while to be doing something else."[63]

For a select group of young women, however, the enactment of eligibility was moved to the foreground in a series of rituals which could confuse no one about their ultimate purposes. The social ritual of "coming out" arose as part of an effort by prosperous parents to exercise some control over their children's choice of spouses. In seventeenth-century New England, youth needed parental and even community approval to guarantee the economic wherewithal to consummate a match. In the aftermath of the revolutionary eighteenth century, however, youth expected to contract their own engagements, asking parental blessing only after the fact. Parents who could no longer select a mate for their children instead worked on controlling the pool of possible choices by a round of private parties in which young women and young men of respectable origins might intermingle.[64]

After the economic and social fluctuations of the late nineteenth century, the introduction of daughters to society came to have a broader social function for older elites attempting to secure their status against new arrivals. Mary Boit's father Robert described the evolution of these rituals of inclusion and exclusion over the course of the nineteenth century, noting that the earlier "assemblies" were now called "cotillions" and were the "Balls of Society to which four hundred or so go. . . . Those people who wish to go and cannot get invitations cannot be said to be in Society, or at least fashionable society. It in a way marks the limits of Society, while within it are cliques and still more exclusive sets." Less affluent than many of his relatives, Robert Boit sent his elder daughter Mary to public school, but also to the dancing lessons which would prepare her to come out, so that she might "know the boys and girls of her class." Boit especially troubled himself with these rituals because his second wife, his daughter's stepmother, would not. Generally the rituals connected with social debuts, which often consisted of an afternoon tea hosted at the girl's home, in conjunction with a first appearance at the subscription cotillions, were women's territory. (After the 1880s, teas were the preferred form as both less formal and more economical than dinners or evening parties.)[65] In their control over these important affairs, elite matrons exercised considerable influence over the construction of class in the late-century cities. The practice of announcing a coming out into society also allowed elite parents some control over the age at which their daughters might entertain men, one part of an effort to forestall precociousness.

Whether or not connected with a separate individualized party, girls customarily first attended "assemblies" at the age of eighteen in an occasion rich with meaning. Nellie Browne, at the Agassiz School in Cambridge, Massachusetts, in 1859 referred disparagingly to one such party, remarking, "I think it very foolish for Kitty Hodges to have a 'coming out' party." The following fall, however, after Browne left school, her mother recorded that Nellie and her brothers were taking dancing lessons at their aunt's house in preparation for a "Cotillion Party." On December 22, 1859, Sarah Browne reported Nellie's first appearance at the Salem Assembly. The significance of the occasion was marked by the visits of family members. "Coz Sarah brings Nellie a beautiful Bertha [a shawl] and Wreath for tonight," Sarah Browne wrote. The occasion prompted a mother's reflection: "Nellie's best adornment is her own unselfish heart. Dear child may she ever be as artless as now! The morning of a new life is hers, may no shadow fall upon its evening."[66] Nellie's appearance at the Salem Assembly was another step in the process that had begun with her departure from school, when she resisted so articulately the loss of her status as "school-girl." However she felt about the holding of individual coming out parties, Nellie Browne now was officially "out" and eligible for marriage, a status confirmed by her engagement several years later.

Such a season of parties and frivolity with such explicit intent offered fun as well as stress. Susan Coolidge's "A Coming Out," a story in *Ladies' Home Journal* in 1889, commented on the "bliss" of a sequestered girl's formal admission to the pleasures of society. "There can scarcely ever be in the experience of a human being, a time of such care-free and entire abandonment to pleasure as comes to a modern girl of eighteen, when after long restraint and seclusion, she is at last suffered, and not only suffered, but encouraged to drain to the very bottom the long deferred cup of enjoyment; the very abstinence which has preceded the draught makes it doubly delicious."[67] For the true belle, the attention gained in this unbridled celebration of allure could be intoxicating.

Emily Eliot had been in training for her arrival in polite society for some time. In the back of her 1871 journal, kept when she was fourteen, she stored illustrations of flirtatious dialogue doodled during school at Miss Foote's by her friend Nellie Eldridge. These dialogues, which Eliot may have helped script, suggested Eliot and Eldridge's shared interest in the language and strategies of female seduction and conquest. Indeed, they resemble truncated versions of the game of Consequences—the drafting of dialogues of chance encounters—which Lily Dana had played with school friends. Unlike Lily Dana's displacement of actual desire onto the handsome Dodge, however, the younger girls imagined female agency, projecting a pattern of female initiative, male response, and immediate female surrender which might well have been based on the reading of romances:

SHE: Oh dear I dont know where to walk
HE: come with me I know a nice one
SHE: oh thank you.

SHE: I love dancing don't you?
HE: Yes it is splendid will you dance with me?
SHE: Yes, with pleasure.

SHE [man is handing over horse to woman]: Oh I am afraid to go alone
      he is so wild
HE: If you wish I'll go with you
SHE: oh do!

In any case, by the time Emily Eliot had reached the age of twenty, she had developed considerable skill in charm and flirtation and recorded her conquests in her social diary. During one January week in 1878 she recorded a dinner party at her house—"(uproarious laughter 3 on a sofa!)"—a german dance party at Papanti's dancing school, a talking party at which she entertained twelve beaux "from 10 to 11:15," and an enumeration of how many invitations she had received for two weeks running (eighteen invitations in one week, fifteen in another, during which she expected to accept seven).[68] Whatever the desirable combination of charm, money, and status, Emily Eliot clearly had it, and from all appearances greatly enjoyed the seasons in which she was featured.

Other girls fresh from the activism and autonomy of their days at school found the rituals of their arrival in society more trying. Adopting the voice of a recent schoolgirl, the critic Abba Woolson asked: "Since intellect goes for nothing, and externals for everything, why then . . . was not small talk, coquetry, and unabashed assurance under all compliments taught us at school? Why did we not write notes of invitation, instead of compositions; and practice bows and hand-shakings, instead of flinging bean-bags at each other's heads to develop our muscles? This is the knowledge that would have fitted us for the new sphere to which we are called." Not only were girls poorly prepared by school for the rituals of society; they were also ill-prepared for their own objectification. Due to concerns about her health, the author Edith Wharton, who grew up in a wealthy New York family in the 1870s, had not been to school as a girl, instead devouring her father's library on her own. When she reached the age of seventeen, she reported in a later memoir, "my parents decided that I spent too much time in reading, and that I was to come out a year before the accepted age." Her mother elected to forgo "advertising" her daughter with a tea, choosing instead to launch her more informally, by simply escorting her to a ball. Even so, Wharton recorded the passive misery of the evening, "put" into "a low-necked bodice of pale green brocade," with her hair "piled up on top of my head." Some friends of the family sent her "a large bouquet of lilies-of-the-valley," and she was off. "To me the evening was a long cold agony of shyness. All my brother's friends asked me to dance, but I was too much frightened to accept, and cowered beside my mother in speechless misery, unable even to exchange a word with the friendly young men whom I regarded as elder brothers when they lunched and dined at our house."[69] The anguish, of course, came from her abrupt change in status, from agent to "goods" on display. Whether or not her mother had elected to advertise her with a special tea or reception, it was clear that she was now on the marriage market, eligible for bids from appropriate suitors.

Coming out itself only initiated social obligations, many of them less painful but more wearisome than such display. In smaller towns and cities without such elaborate rituals, a girl's maturity might be signaled by her participation in the system of calling, which connected leisured women with each other. Under this system, a woman (and by extension her daughter) might designate a particular afternoon every week in which they would receive desired guests for tea and conversation. (When undesired callers submitted their cards to the requisite maid, they would discover their hostess mysteriously indisposed.) Thus in 1884 the Concord, New Hampshire, student newspaper noted that, even before their graduation, "several young ladies of the School received on New Year's." It was customary for girls new to society to accompany their mothers on calls to her friends—a practice which one girl described as an agonizing trip up and down the columns in her mother's address book. The party would await the mistress in the parlor, engage in a round of predictable small talk, then move on. The same diarist reported of one round of calls in New York in 1891: "This afternoon Mother took Louise [her cousin] and me on our stupid old visits—we made 14 and 10 were out—it is terrible—Louise and I sit and grin and say nothing."[70]

Despite the palpable anguish of the social debut for at least some girls, relatively few seem to have challenged the system head-on. Indeed, one might ask why not. One clue comes from one who did successfully challenge the social system of the debut. Elizabeth Coffin, who grew up in Germantown, Pennsylvania, in her 1916 memoir recalled her sister's feeling that "a reception should be given for me to mark my *debut*." (Coffin's mother was dead.) Coffin remembered: "I flatly refused to have it. I *naively* told my family that I did not like the idea of standing up with a placard round my neck announcing that I was in the marriage market and was willing to accept any kind man who would propose. . . . I also recalled to my father's mind the fact that he had always said that he would shoot the man that married me, and that it did not seem fair to advertise for a husband who, when he appeared, was to be shot. My last argument settled the matter in my favor, and I am glad to say I never had to wear the placard."[71] Perhaps Elizabeth Coffin was able to prevail because she was challenging a sister rather than a mother and could successfully rally her father to her side. Perhaps she was dramatizing her own role from a later vantage point. Evidence suggests that most girls whose parents expected them to "come out" did so.

Indeed, such was the dominance of elite forms that parents from certain

9.4 "Had expected to come out," 1896. Instead, Mary Boit went to Germany with her sister Georgia to study music, where the girls were visited by their father Robert. Schlesinger Library (Cambridge: Radcliffe Institute, Harvard University), A99-149-4.

classes who could not present their daughters at teas or receptions felt neglectful. Throughout his daughter's youth, Robert Boit was anxious about his inability to launch her appropriately in society because of his troubled home life. Instead, he arranged to send his daughter to Germany to study language and music and to get her out of the way during her eighteenth year. Reported Boit, "This was a great disappointment to Mary who had expected to come out this winter," but she "agreed with me it was the best that could be done." Mary Boit never did come out, but when she was twenty-two, her father insisted on taking her to three cotillions, enlisting her aunts' help in providing for her "a really handsome dress for the first ball." (Money seemed to be part of the problem in the Boit family, for his wife Lillian "was indignant that Mary was permitted to go to the Assemblies when she herself could not because she had no suitable dresses.") Boit's concern, of course, was his daughters' ability to negotiate appropriate matches, given that "they do not command the attention in Boston society which their position entitles them to," a fear that must have been assuaged when Mary married the influential physician Hugh Cabot in 1902.[72]

For all its pain, coming out represented privilege within a social elite, and girls whose family circumstances denied it to them might feel short-changed. Fredrica Ballard's account of her upbringing observed a bit sadly that with an invalid mother, she never officially entered society as "noone concerned themselves about my social life." And Charlotte Perkins herself, who later said that she "despised the whole business," at twenty had clear regrets about her failure to come out. In April 1880 she announced a surprise: "*Red letter day.* . . . Am presented with an 'at home' from Mrs. Burney! Ah-ha! Ah-ha! Of a truth I am coming out. They are going to the J.X. [probably a dance or cotillion] and will take me. (As I privily desired.) And, furthermore, as the crowning glory of all my desires, I—Am—to—be—Invited to Oak Woods [a resort community] this summer!!!! At the same time as May! 'Joy Joy! my task is done! The gates are passed and heaven is won!'"[73] Clearly among girls from certain social backgrounds, the only thing worse than the social ritual of coming out was *not* coming out.

The historian Leonore Davidoff in her study of Victorian Britain discovered a bemused viscountess reflecting later on her compliant youth in the season she was presented to society: "I do not remember that I consciously criticized a system which . . . hypnotized a perfectly intelligent, though perhaps rather naive young woman, already anxious to investigate most accepted notions impersonally and dispassionately, into acceding without question to indulgence in this odd form of occupation, which in fact she was hating so much."[74] Anthropologists tell us that rituals help people move from one stage in life to another, and that suffering can enhance the value and the effectiveness of such rituals in easing the transition. Clearly the journey from free and autonomous girlhood to responsible and obliging womanhood could be abrupt and traumatic. Perhaps girls accepted the humiliations of coming out because this social practice was doing significant "cultural work" in helping them to adjust to circumstances they saw as akin to their destiny.

If young women did not outwardly repudiate the humiliations and the objectifying process of the elite marriage market, their letters and papers suggest their discomfiture with one aspect of it: its brevity. When Ella Lyman breathlessly announced the engagement of Edith Paine, who murmured expressions of intense happiness, she ended with one reservation. "Oh! dear she is the first of our 'old maid' clique to go. The remaining 'maiden ladies' must stick fast to their colours." At the age of nineteen herself, Ella Lyman was hardly over the hill. But like all young women who had appeared in society, she knew that the clock was ticking through the short time for which a debutante (sometimes known as a "bud"), would remain fresh. A year and a half later, Lyman herself was engaged—in time, but just in the nick of time. One objection to college for young women was that it released them too late for the marriage market.[75]

A letter written by a mother to her daughter suggested the invidiousness and also the relentlessness of the public and formalized ritual of coming out. Elizabeth Fisher Nichols's response to a tea she attended in 1893 noted both her participation in and her discomfort with the system of debuts. "Certainly two thirds of the crowd must have long since left the days of buds far behind them," she commented acerbly. When she got down to particulars, she seemed to regret her snideness. "There isn't room at parties for a third year girl it seems there are forty-four buds this season so they crowd out the others, perfectly absurd isn't it to make such distinctions."[76] The precise number of eligible young ladies suggests how perfectly closed was the Boston upper class in the 1890s. Elite young women who announced their new status by coming out into society were both the luckiest and the most objectified young women. The formal social system of debuts exposed girls to marriage opportunities and a plan of action in the face of the challenge of the years after school. But it also displayed them in a crass marriage market, which quickly detected the scent of stale goods. The shelf life of a debutante was short indeed.

Margaret Tileston: Eligibility

Coming-out rituals provided an activist program for a girl growing up but they did not necessarily solve the problem of a girl's destiny. In her essay "Rites of Passage: Process and Paradox," the anthropologist Barbara Myerhoff urges scholars to undertake a "psychological anthropology" which asks what it feels like to go through such a rite of passage, raising the question "How is culture communicated, not simply as an external, neutral set of principles, but as a motivational, internalized system, so that one's duty, as [Victor] Turner puts it, becomes one's desire?"[77] The detail of Margaret Tileston's diary allows for a close look at just this process of internalization, the sequence of a triumphant high school graduation, and then the voluntary return home, deferral of aspiration, and social debut of one high-achieving late-century Bostonian. Margaret Tileston chose her destiny along lines prescribed by society, but her choice did not necessarily make her happy.

Margaret Tileston's graduation from high school took its triumphant quality from its context. Tileston had often been miserable throughout her youth, more than once suggesting sufficient despair to her diary that she had contemplated suicide. In December 1883, for instance, she recorded that she was "dismal as usual. Should like to be extinguished forever like a candle." Her scholastic success at high school had given her a brief stature which at gradua-

tion seemed to light up an otherwise morose youth. An important component of Margaret Tileston's misery was her growing awareness that maturity
was not making her pretty. Her own perception of her looks gained unwelcome reinforcement from her peers. When Tileston was seventeen at Salem
High School, a classmate circulated a description of Tileston walking with
two friends. She confided to her diary, "I was described as 'tall, stout, and
Homely.'" At the time she tried to make light of it: "'That 'tis true, 'tis pity;
and pity 'tis, 'tis true.'" That it wounded her more deeply was confirmed by
her mother's efforts at reassurance the next day. "Mother had a long talk with
me after I went to bed, which decided me not to be discontented anymore,
but to try to get out of self."[78]

It was not so easy to get out of self, however, and the next month Tileston confided, "My hair is growing thin, which distresses me greatly." Four
months later the problem had not been solved, Tileston noting, "My hair is
the mere ghost of its former self." The day before she had commented simply,
"I should be happier if I were not as ugly as sin." In the spine of her diary,
where she kept especially private thoughts, she could be forgiven for confessing her feeling that "Beauty the greatest gift a woman can possess."[79]

Tileston's ongoing misery about her looks coincided with a series of discussions within her family which touched on her future. She, her aunt, her
sister, and her mother sat on the steps in the full moonlight for one such discussion, talking about marriage and beauty. In another discussion with her
mother alone, Margaret heard about a married couple who had separated. Her
mother reported that the wife had "the fatal gift of beauty," and then went
on to talk with Margaret about "earning my living, good looks, friends, etc."
By the end of the summer before her final year at Salem High School, the direction of the family discussions became clear. Tileston reported an evening
conversation with both parents about "school, college, my future etc. I now
expect to study Greek this year." The Tileston family decision that Margaret
should study Greek meant that she would prepare for college. Clearly Tileston's parents, themselves well educated, had decided that Margaret might
need to provide her own livelihood; they probably also had concluded that her
marriage prospects were uncertain. The drift was not lost on Margaret. Following the conversation about Greek, she reported, "I felt quite melancholy
in the evening, and lay awake for some time."[80]

As Tileston approached graduation from Salem High School as the top
"young lady" in her class, she prepared for the entrance examinations for
the Harvard Annex, which she took at the same time as her male classmates
took the examinations for Harvard. When she received the certificate attest-

ing that she had passed in ten subjects, she reported, "I showed Mr. Goodrich my paper from Harvard, and he shook hands with me."[81] Margaret Tileston seemed to be prepared by talent, inclination, and training to proceed directly on to college with her male classmates. Her studies had taken clear priority over other pursuits during high school, which seemed to indicate a familial commitment to their continuation. Her graduation essay, entitled "Success," seemed as much a forecast of her immediate future as a summary of her high school career. Such was not the case, however.

Following Tileston's triumphant graduation from Salem High School, she, like less proficient scholars, went home and embarked on the tedious and menial projects of domestic life. Her diary from the month after she graduated suggested the lethargy that accompanied "helping Mother." She assumed a daily regimen of sewing, mentioning on August 29, "I sewed twenty-five minutes in the early morning, and completed my hour in the evening." She began darning socks. In December she resolved "to read little and sew much this winter."[82]

In fact, Margaret Tileston's education did not end with her graduation from Salem High School. In October of that year, she enrolled at "Miss Ireland's," a Boston finishing school for young ladies, which she attended sporadically for two years. She later attended a school to prepare kindergarten teachers. But neither school filled the role in her life that public high school had. Although she retained her preeminence among her peers, she herself seemed to stop trying. She reported a conversation with Miss Ireland over a conflict between two classes. The consequence of the conversation: "I decided not to prepare for the Harvard examinations, if Papa did not object." John Tileston apparently acquiesced in this plan, and Tileston studied French rather than physics, attending school half-heartedly. The next month she reported that school was "getting somewhat played out." A few months later, in the spring, she even stopped preparing, noting one day, "I was idle, instead of studying," and several days later, "I went to school again, but I did not know my lessons, not having had my books at home." Her routine seemed increasingly dull, and Tileston even had trouble filling her diary, reporting "There is nothing under the sun to say. I never was stuck so far up [the page] before."[83]

Part of Tileston's diminished investment in school was the result of increased expectations for her help at home. Her mother occasionally kept her there, as in one day the next year, when Tileston reported, "Mamma did not feel very well, and so she kept me at home from school to help her. I had not studied my History recitation. . . . As I was kept at home to help, I suppose that I took care of the baby and read to Roger [her ailing brother] part of the time, though I cannot remember anything about it." Other days she seemed to have made the decision for domestic tasks herself, as in one day when she "read over my History notes, but decided not to go to school. I collected a great many old gloves and sewed on all the missing buttons. I cleared up in the house to some extent." As befit one who was taking more responsibility for housework, Margaret Tileston could appreciate its monotony, as on another January day when she confessed to her diary, "It is discouraging to try to clear up the house." If she could feel oppressed by the repetitiveness of keeping house, she could also feel restricted by the relentlessness of child care. The birth of a new baby in her mother's forties meant that Margaret sometimes had charge of her sister, a task she occasionally resented. Despite her attendance at several schools, Margaret Tileston was officially at home — and often depressed—following her departure from high school. The fall after her graduation from high school, she once again mentioned her dismay about her looks. "My face is perfectly horrid," she wrote. Ten days before Christmas that year, she wrote, "Life looks very dark," and the next day, "I tried to study in the evening, but failed. I hate to live."[84] With study robbed of its purpose and her life measured in domestic duties in her parents' house, Tileston found little to live for.

Perhaps even more than increasing expectations for work at home, however, the launching of Margaret Tileston's social life diminished the importance of school in her life. Tileston and her parents seemed to regard the Greek courses Tileston took at Salem High School and her academic prowess as an insurance policy. The central plan for Margaret's life, which she sometimes seemed to be initiating, however miserably, lay within the domestic world of genteel society. Even from the dark years of puberty, when Margaret was coming to terms with her new body, her mother and female relatives aimed to bolster Margaret's confidence for the challenge ahead. When Margaret confessed her fears, her mother offered reassurance, which Tileston copied in tiny letters in the spine of her diary. "You're not handsome but you're sufficiently good-looking. you have a pleasing face." At a reunion of Tileston's classmates from the Prospect Hill School, Margaret Tileston heard the kind words of her aunt, which she stored for future reference: "M. told me that Aunt M. had said that I had improved greatly in looks and she thought I should make a fine-looking woman." Most significant was the endorsement of Tileston's cousin Eliza, who as a single woman of nearly thirty years herself was free to provide counsel and the wisdom of recent experience for her younger cousin. After Tileston's graduation from high school, she often saw her cousin, who told her that she liked her and thought her pretty. One day in the summer of 1885, they discussed "young men, marriage and kindred topics," and the next year, under a spreading apple tree, after reading Charlotte Brontë's *Shirley*, they talked of "love and marriage, men and women and a novel that Eliza has projected." Later that month they discussed "girls, and stylishness, and spending much time and thought on dressing, and later on young men, and inviting them to call."[85]

It was Eliza who broached the subject of Margaret Tileston's attendance at Papanti's dancing school the fall of Margaret's eighteenth year. The Italian immigrant Lorenzo Papanti had opened a ballroom in antebellum Boston, and the classes there were patronized by youths of the Boston elite into the twentieth century. Tileston reported that her cousin Eliza was in favor of her going to Papanti's and would chaperone her part of the time. Tileston's mother apparently agreed with this social initiative, and perhaps had even first broached the subject with Eliza. A spot was secured in a Saturday evening class, and in preparation for Papanti's the Tilestons contracted for some preliminary tutoring in dancing. At first Margaret's teacher had thought that "it was absurd for me to take private dancing lessons," Tileston reported, "but she found plenty to teach me. I have always waltzed the wrong way—Miss Post's, not Papanti's." As for Papanti's class, Tileston received some welcome intelligence: a dozen girls had backed out of the class, "and consequently there would be 42 girls and 65 men—fine for me." Finally "the fatal Saturday" came around, and under her mother's escort Tileston attended her first dance class at Papanti's, which was so exciting that she had difficulty falling asleep that night. Other lessons were less smooth. After the next class, she reported, "This time Mr. Papanti had to provide me with a partner for the german, and Prescott Hall was the victim. . . . Mrs. Lowell brought up Robbie Atkinson, and introduced him. . . . I sat alone part of the evening." The next day, she visited some friends and "poured out my woes about dancing to them." The lessons had high points. After one January class, she reported that she had had "a very good time, though there were a few blots on it"; at another she had "long and deep discussions on social and philosophical questions" with two young men.[86]

Dancing lessons were only part of Margaret Tileston's debut, however. In the winter of her nineteenth year, she reported another conversation with an aunt and her cousin Eliza: "They talked about the importance of my having a tea this spring. The thought makes my heart heavy." Having a tea would launch Tileston definitively, and would inspire obligatory calls and reciprocal invitations—and it would represent another concerted offensive in her effort to secure a conventional match. Her heavy-heartedness lingered as she considered the prospect. Two weeks later, she read two installments in *Littel's Living Age* on "The Land of Darkness," "which I seem fast approaching," she wrote, confessing in the spine of her diary, "I spent half an hour in the p.m. in having a good cry."[87]

In the fall, the idea of a reception was still in the air. As with the dancing class, Tileston carried the idea from Eliza to her mother, picking up support from various other friends and relatives. As the plans progressed, Tileston seemed to feel better. She wrote down the names of "persons that I know." Her mother engaged a Salem caterer; they addressed invitations. On the day itself, four days after Tileston turned twenty years old, November 5, 1887, the younger children were sent away and "Cassell and his two colored men came at one and arranged the dining-room." Her aunt brought her white roses, and she wore a new silk and cashmere dress. "We were 'at home' from 4–7," Tileston reported, and more than two hundred people came, including family friends and girlfriends from Salem. Her baby sister later celebrated the occasion by standing alone on her feet for the first time. Margaret's sister and brother stayed up late with her to make a list of all those who came. After all the fuss, the significance of having a tea seemed to be largely its activism. It was one way for an elite young woman and a family of means to command attention. And to that extent it worked, intensifying invitations and bringing young men calling. One young man paid "a long party call"; another "stayed some time." Tileston received invitations to winter parties at Eliot Hall at Harvard.[88] For a time that activist agenda seemed to bring its own rewards. But for all its politeness and gentility, it did not yield a courtship, which was the ultimate goal. For that reason Tileston's social debut, her declaration of eligibility, was a failure, and interrupted her malaise only temporarily.

Margaret Tileston's malaise was the result of the coexistence of her conventional expectations and her uncommon talents—and maybe her lack of qualifications for her designated role. And its seeds were present even at the moment of her great triumph, her graduation from Salem High School. She did not leave a copy of her graduation essay, but she did note its length, eighteen pages, and its title, "Success." She also indicated one source. As she did some preliminary thinking in January of her final year at Salem High School, she recorded, "I think of taking 'Success' as my subject. . . . I read in 'The Gentle Life,' with a mental eye on my future essay." Tileston's reading in James Hain Friswell, *The Gentle Life: Essays in the Formation of Character*, published in London in 1866, would not have encouraged her in a scholarly or bluestocking career. Friswell would have told her that the world had decided to agree with Tennyson that "Woman is the lesser man." He celebrated the balance of "A Certain Noble Animal" paired with "The Weaker Vessel," and would have told Tileston that "the weaker sex must fail in competition with that which has a stronger physique, larger bones, and more powerful brain." Whether her mother agreed with this depiction of the absolute superiority of men over women, we do not know. More likely she would have supported the concept of spheres—that women were destined to rule and prosper at home, and men in the world. We do know that Margaret Tileston joined her mother in her opposition to one claim for equality, the claim for women's right to political voice. ("A petition against woman suffrage was brought in, and I signed it, as well as Aunt Fanny," she reported the spring before her tea.)[89] It is therefore no wonder, in the milieu in which she lived, that whatever her talents, Margaret Tileston would have first turned her energies following graduation toward a conventional career for a woman of her background: a respectable marriage. It is telling that at her moment of triumph as a scholar she should define "Success" in terms which obliged her to forgo the college study for which she had qualified and instead to turn her hand to the needle and her mind to society and courtship.

Brothers and Sisters: Margaret Tileston and Anna O.

Margaret Tileston's story is especially important because of what she did not push to do in her early twenties, because of what she set aside, because of the decisions she appears to have made about her future. Tileston's account of the end of her girlhood, her departure from school, and her young ladyhood is the account of a young woman who was living out, not testing her fate. Sometimes she was miserable, because she did not feel naturally advantaged. But she did not change direction and push to play to her strength. Instead, assisted by her cousin Eliza (perhaps at her mother's behest), she participated in decisions to privilege domesticity over studies, to forgo college, to begin dancing lessons, and to have a tea.

Margaret Tileston had a brother two years younger than she, and his career, recorded in her diary, offers a valuable opportunity to compare the expectations and attitudes shared by this Boston family, and by Margaret Tileston herself, about a son's and a daughter's role. Like Margaret, Roger was a star student, at the top of his class. When Roger turned sixteen, his father took him to Germany to study for the year. Like Margaret's study of Greek, Roger's study in Germany was an indication of the scholarly ambition of John and Mary Foote Tileston for their children. At Roger's departure for Germany he received five dollars from one uncle, and his sisters each received fifty cents, the first time in Margaret Tileston's copious records that a younger brother had been privileged with a greater monetary gift.[90]

Roger returned from Germany, with voice and manner changed, the month before Margaret's high school graduation. He brought cologne for his sisters, and Margaret was glad to have him home again. That summer, the two often played tennis together, and when Roger was sick, Margaret read, sang, and played the piano to him, a sister's ministrations. In conjunction with her family's move from Salem to Brookline, a Boston neighborhood, Margaret Tileston no longer went walking in the evening unescorted, and sometimes Roger was called on to accompany her, a brother's attention which he may or may not have given willingly. As deliberations about Margaret's entry into society were beginning, however, Roger's entry seemed simply to happen: he was invited to "fortnightly sociables" given by a mother for her daughter and was fitted for a cutaway (which his sister pronounced "very becoming"); he was off at the age of sixteen. (In New York, too, a society matron commented, "The gentleman somehow slips into society without formality.") On July 10, 1886, the summer before Margaret's nineteenth year, she reported that Roger was going off on a ten-day bicycle trip and that she had worked "three little fishes and the outline of a bird on my splasher [a linen fastened to the wall behind a washstand]." For his seventeenth birthday, Roger received a subscription to *Scientific American* and a cyclometer for his bicycle from Margaret.[91] For Margaret and Roger Tileston, the years of 1884–87 represented a gradual parting of ways which had previously been remarkably similar. With Margaret's graduation from high school as a woman and Roger's return from Germany as a man, his world seemed to open steadily before him, just as hers was gradually closing in.

In the spring of 1887, when Margaret was nineteen and Roger seventeen, several weeks before Eliza broached the idea of a tea for her reluctant cousin, Margaret advanced her own idea for her beloved brother. She suggested to him that he shorten his course at Roxbury Latin School and go directly to college (which in the Tileston family meant Harvard), the following year. She reported, "He became eager to do so and Papa also desired it, so that matters seem tending to that end." To assist her brother, she offered the fruits of her experience: "I showed Roger some of my Harvard examination papers." Roger's enrollment the fall of his eighteenth year yielded a present for his sister's twentieth birthday, four days before her coming out "reception": a book, *Songs of Harvard*.[92]

Margaret's support for her younger brother's education seemed to make perfect sense within Tileston's worldview. For the moment, she had freely chosen a destiny which, while it did not make her happy, did seem appropriate to her on her own terms. From the age of eleven, when she started keeping her daily diary, Margaret had always been a "good" girl, eager to determine the correct course and to follow it. Being good at first had meant paying attention at school and succeeding in her lessons. At nineteen and twenty, it meant helping at home and becoming a young lady. (It also meant participating in an archetypal Victorian good work, a "flower mission," bringing bouquets of flowers to the sick and to workers in sweatshops—and, when there were extra, simply going to "scatter flowers through the poorer streets.")[93]

There was little intellectual stimulation to challenge Tileston in her life at home, and her circumstance brought a certain monotony. Sewing on buttons, tending her new baby sister, sometimes attending a school for young ladies, awaiting a courtship which did not materialize, ambivalent about whether to look forward to such a courtship, it was no wonder that she sometimes became depressed. She shared this plight with other young women from her class and background who left an active school life for passive waiting at home. It might be too extreme to describe this period as Woolson's "death in life," but it certainly was a kind of "purgatory between school and marriage" which asked young women to forget what they had learned about action and agency as they quietly awaited their destiny.

Ethel Spencer, who grew up in Pittsburgh in a large family at the turn of the century, credited her mother for realizing that not all girls would "finish school, 'come out,' get married and live happily ever after." But for herself, she remembered that "it took seven unhappy years of doing nothing more interesting than making clothes and teaching a Sunday School class to make me realize that I wanted a college education." Agnes Hamilton acknowledged her unhappiness earlier. After her exciting life at Miss Porter's School for Girls in Farmington, Connecticut, she too went home—but found it hard to accept the tedium of her days. When one plan for a school reunion was given up, Hamilton expressed her desperation: "I do so want to go. I want to go somewhere, anywhere. I am getting into the same state I was before I went to school. Then I had that to look forward to, now it seems as if I should never, never leave." Like Ethel Spencer and Margaret Tileston, Agnes Hamilton had an especially encouraging family and extraordinary intellect to make her unfit for the common round of domestic life. Unlike Tileston and Spencer, however, Hamilton was early in direct contact with her resistance.[94]

Margaret Tileston's apparent acceptance of the conventional plan for her life, and her efforts to contain her intellect within the humiliations of feminine eligibility, rendered her more at risk from depression than Hamilton,

with her more articulate rebellion. Indeed, there are some resemblances between the story of Margaret Tileston and that of Bertha Pappenheim, better
known as Anna O., the collaborator with Josef Breuer and Sigmund Freud
in the invention of psychoanalysis. Pappenheim finished the schooling available to her as the daughter of a wealthy Jewish family in Vienna at the age of
sixteen, and, like Tileston, she went home. She too had a younger brother, in
her case without her talents, who went to university and then to law school
while his sister led "an extremely monotonous existence" at home, pursuing embroidery and other refined, domestic pastimes. She too probably sang,
played, and read to her father, invalided at home, whom she nursed until his
death of consumption in 1880. Freud and Breuer attributed the origins of
Pappenheim's subsequent hysteria at the age of twenty-one to the discrepancy between her "powerful intellect" and "penetrating intuition" and the
circumscribed life allowed her.[95]

"The Daughter's Disease," a contemporary term for hysteria, was most
likely to occur in just such situations. It was more likely to afflict a "good"
girl, who internalized narrow social expectations for appropriate behavior and
overruled renegade feelings. (Alice James characterized her predicament as
having "not only all the horrors and suffering of insanity but the duties of doctor, nurse, and strait-jacket imposed upon me, too.")[96] In hysteria, such feelings retaliated against the body. In the case of Margaret Tileston and others
like her, such feelings emerged as the sorrow and despair—the depression—
that were occasionally concealed in the spine of the most private diaries.

For many young women of the middle class as well as the elite, the departure from school set the stage for subsequent crisis. Active, energized, self-
respecting girls asked themselves to suppress their girlish spirits and adopt
the demure, patient, and diffident posture of the eligible young lady. It is
no wonder that young women had trouble integrating those two stages and
experiences. Young women looking back at their school experience sometimes remembered their school years as "dreams" in the context of their imagined futures. Recalling her years at Staunton from the end of her graduation
year, Agnes Lee reflected, "It all seems a dream of fairyland now," and Nellie
Browne, too, looking back on her school years mused, "When I look back,
and think I have been here three years, it seems like *a dream*."[97] In choosing
the language of dreams, Browne and Lee suggest the fantastic otherness of
their school associations, bearing as they did little relation to their imagined
futures.

For young women who had experienced a true moratorium from traditional gender expectations, it was sometimes hard to determine which stage

was real, which fantasy. Those who had wandered freely through city streets suddenly found themselves needed at home to share some of the household's work, caring for the sick or younger siblings. Those who had competed successfully at school for academic standing found themselves attempting to suppress self in service to domestic routines. Abba Woolson regretted "that law of growth which renders it necessary that kittens should spoil into demure cats, and bright, joyous school-girls develop into the spiritless, crystallized beings denominated young ladies."[98] The production of such young ladies took enormous energies and produced abundant anguish, as the programs of young women like Margaret Tileston suggest. It is true that some had more fun along the way. Flirtation and merriment accompanied courtship for many; one cannot read the diaries of Lucy Breckinridge, Emily Eliot, or Helen Hart without appreciating the high spirits soaring there. But even for such belles, the subtext was sober. Within a few years, destiny would be met, either with scripted moments of ecstatic excitement or in the nearly audible tick of time passing beyond marriageability. And either way, young women acknowledged, the freedom and equality of the schoolgirl years would yield to the narrow obligations of service and selflessness expected of true and mature women.

School graduations and social debuts both served to mark this transition.[99] They both constituted clear "rites of passage" across a liminal space which separated two radically different sets of rules and expectations. Anthropologists tell us that such collective and shared "rites" are the means by which societies encourage individuals to buy in to a changing order. According to this model, shared rituals help girls rewrite their scripts of self, regretting but accepting the new rules which require them to set aside the freedom and pleasure of youth in order to assume the sober, gendered lot of womanhood. Upon leaving school, schoolgirls at midcentury usually did just that, saying good-bye forever to their school selves as they wistfully took up new responsibilities.[100] Later in the century, though, educators and parents did not resolve things as neatly as anthropology's "rites of passage" might suggest. The process of attending school and bonding as a graduation class had its own momentum which changed the outcome, as history tells us. Girls may have looked back on their school experience with bemusement as though it was a dream, but they did not forget it. And increasing numbers of girls came to draw on those formative years as they attempted to chart a new path for themselves in a new century.

TEN

New Girls, New Women

A wide cross-section of girls recorded domestic malaise following their departures from school. After the whirl of examinations, class meetings, and exhibitions, returning home to household chores and selfless service was a significant comedown. At midcentury most girls came home to stay, stung by the dawning realization that now that their schooling was done, the rules had changed, and they were now expected to forgo girlish pastimes and take their place as "true women" within the home. Increasingly, over the subsequent decades, though, departure from school and a return to mother's household was temporary. The trajectory of the girl graduate often led into the work world for a sojourn before marriage. By the late decades of the century, clerical work had supplemented teaching as a respectable paid occupation for a middle-class daughter and had widened her opportunities.

Women had always worked, of course, most often within subsistence households, but also, with the advent of the market, in the interstices of the cash economy. What was notable about the work of former schoolgirls in the late century was the spirit attached to it. School attendance involved girls in a complex of cultures which challenged and ultimately overturned the meaning they attached to their work, and indeed to themselves. Parents who sent their daughters off to school in the hopes that they would be more serviceable to the family found that the competition, the success, and the high-spirited peer culture made them into "new girls" en route to becoming the New Women of the new century. These "new girls" sometimes shared moral earnestness with women reformers of earlier eras but brought to their lives also the spirit of high school culture. They came to maturity willing to validate their pleasure, as well as their worth, and to claim rights to selves of their own.

Middle-Class Girls and Paid Work

Going to school helped to create this culture. The pursuit of secondary education, either in private girls' seminaries or in new public high schools, was one track followed by increasing numbers of middle-class girls in the late nineteenth century. It accompanied two other tracks for teenage girls: staying at home or going out to work. The preponderance of girls in the northeastern immigrant cities were working: 42 percent of all fourteen- to fifteen-year-old girls in Providence, Rhode Island, in 1880, according to one researcher.[1] Yet that work was far from liberating—often long hours drudging as "wage-slaves" in textile factories or as domestic servants in private households. Although girls' work represented a substantial revision in the shape of nineteenth-century society, it empowered girls only obliquely. Earning wages did not by itself bring the sense of civic entitlement that resulted from schooling.

As we have seen, girls' attendance at school in the first place was the result of a reordering of production such that homes were no longer the prime site for the manufacture of domestic goods. Native-born farm girls had initially followed that manufacturing process into New England mills, but as competition increased and working conditions deteriorated, farm girls went on strike or went home; mill owners increasingly came to rely on captive, landless labor, especially waves of desperate immigrants arriving from Ireland and then from eastern and southern Europe. With an influx of foreign workers, mill owners no longer needed to reassure anxious farm families about the safety and security of working conditions. Girls working alone outside the home were vulnerable to every kind of exploitation. At the least, their reputations were at risk. For families attempting to secure their status within the refined ranks of elevated Victorian society, sending a daughter out to work with strangers (in contrast to the rural "helping" pattern) chanced ruin for both daughter and family.

The degradation of paid work for girls extended from factories into other spheres. Victorian literature at midcentury helped to construct that critical distinction between the degrading specter of work outside the home and the worthy work of the home, which built character, however dull it was. The negative reputation of earning one's keep extended even to include such "respectable" work as teaching in some circles. *Harper's Young People* recounted, though without endorsing, such an attitude in one of its characters. An impoverished young orphan is ill treated by her relatives. As one child reports, "'Mamma says that she is sure Nan will have to teach or do something for her living as soon as she is old enough, and so it won't do for us to make too much of her now, as we might not wish to know her at all when I am a young lady.'" Louisa May Alcott, one such intellectual young woman who needed to work, acknowledged in her fiction the social rejection which could befall working women. Her "old-fashioned girl," the wholesome Polly, is wounded by the discovery "that working for a living shuts a good many doors in one's face even in democratic America. As Fanny's guest she had been, in spite of poverty, kindly received wherever her friend took her, both as child and woman. Now, things were changed; the kindly people patronized, the careless forgot all about her, and even Fanny, with all her affection, felt that Polly the music teacher would not be welcome in many places where Polly the young lady had been accepted as 'Miss Shaw's friend.'"[2] To be poor was clearly a fate that might befall anyone; for a girl to go out to work to remedy the situation contributed to a change in class status.

Later in the century, however, the opening of new kinds of jobs challenged the notion that native-born girls could not work. In 1860 immigrants had dominated the female labor force in Boston, constituting nearly two-thirds of all the women working. By 1900 there were nearly twice as many women at work as had been in 1870, increasing numbers of them native born. They were unmarried, as well, with fewer than 5 percent of married white and foreign-born women working during the 1890s.[3] The industrial explosion following the Civil War not only lured immigrant populations from throughout the world into the American labor force. It also created thousands of jobs in offices and sales rooms which were increasingly filled by young, single, native-born women.

Ruth Ashmore and the "Womanly" Worker

Conservative advisers were slow to catch up with this reality. Writing well after many middle-class girls had gone to work, *Ladies' Home Journal*'s Ruth Ashmore, in her "Side Talks with Girls," tried to persuade girls to stay home and resist the bright lights. Her regular and famous column represented one of the most consistent, and most read, sources of advice for girls of all kinds attempting to maintain status and respectability in a modern world. In March 1890 Ashmore commented on "the great fault of the girl of today": "She wants to go out into the world and work." Ashmore tried to persuade her otherwise: "Now, my dear girls, if she will only stay at home, she will find work and womanly work waiting for her pretty white hands. There is too much of a desire to do unnecessary work. . . . Don't you chicks who are in a soft, downy nest be too anxious to tumble out of it to see what is going on in the world." Ashmore offered the inducements of an easier life at home, but she also tried to humble those who dreamed of "the big gay world, where each is for herself and only God for all."[4] Even Ashmore realized, though, that not every chick had a downy nest to snuggle in. She began to acknowledge that many girls would need to come up with cash to feather those nests themselves.

Other writers at *Ladies' Home Journal* were ahead of her. An 1886 article entitled "Woman's Sphere" considerably expanded its definition of what was acceptable for women. Acknowledging that woman's sphere was "once considered to be bounded on all sides by the circle drawn round the domestic hearth," it offered a new definition. Eschewing even the conventional modification that "woman's sphere" was wherever women exercised their maternal qualities, the *Journal* here allowed, "we think 'woman's sphere' is the same as that of man, i.e., to do cheerfully and well the work that comes to her hand, whether it be with a pen, a surgeon's knife, a dentist's drill, a pair of scissors or a broom." As part of this new initiative, the *Journal* began to publish articles about different vocations for women. (For girls "who have any intention of making public singing their profession," a first piece of advice: "Be Sure You Have a Voice.") The *Journal* even endorsed vocations for girls as a necessity, recommending especially typewriting and the taking of shorthand.[5] What was critical was the justification. Girls needed an insurance policy, not a redirection of their life energies.

The *Journal*'s sometime acquiescence in the reality of girls' work outside the home did not mean that it endorsed autonomy and individual fulfillment for daughters. Even as Ruth Ashmore acknowledged the increasing pressures on girls to make money, she threw her energies into preserving rural life and protective, patriarchal families. To stem the tide of farm girls leaving home in search of wage work in the cities, Ashmore tried to be especially helpful when rural girls wrote asking for ideas about how to make money. She was eager to suggest ways for a girl to make money in her hometown and avoid such fates as befell Dreiser's Sister Carrie: "You go over to your grandmother's every Friday, straighten up and trim her lamps for a week. . . . Then find others who are unable to get their lamps to burn as brightly as they wish." She also suggested hair dressing ("You needn't look so disgusted at the idea of dressing hair") and gave examples of other bits of rural ingenuity: a girl who shipped ivy to city florists, another who took orders in her town for bread and biscuits, another who grew vegetables.[6] What finally succeeded in justifying girls' work for critics like Ashmore was the end. Prescriptive fiction honored heroines who managed to rescue their families by whatever means it took.

As the nineteenth century progressed, writers for the genteel youth press could no longer consider the working girl an unfortunate "other." She was "us," a potential reader, one whose moral development might depend on the words of wise counselors. Ruth Ashmore, in particular, but others as well, struggled to save the working girl for a culture which promoted womanliness, refinement, and the pursuit of the beautiful. In a piece entitled "How Girls May Succeed," Ashmore acknowledged that some of her readers might be out in the world earning their own living. ("You have had to do it to help somebody at home as well as to take care of yourself.") To such workers, though, Ashmore urged high standards: "Make the drudgery divine, but don't call it drudgery." Girls needed to transcend the work world, or they needed to compartmentalize it. She urged the working girl to establish a domestic enclave in the evening which would allow her to preserve her virtue and distance herself from the compromises of the day. Ashmore's message was mixed. On the one hand she seemed to encourage girls to take pride in their work, urging them to consider "how good work can be," telling them they need not "shrink, hesitate, stammer and blush" when someone discovers they work for their living. At the same time, she urged girls not to talk of their work (just as men were not to), and to find for themselves good society. The working girl who could not find decent society to join outside of work should keep a nice room herself and take pride in her isolation. She might need to distance herself from the very identity of working girl. ("When you come home at night put on another gown and seem to become another girl for a little while.") As construed by Ruth Ashmore and other advice writers, a good working girl might work for wages to support herself and her family, but she should not leave behind the ideology of home and sphere. Work, as Ashmore theorized it anyway, should not lead to individuality or autonomy; instead, it represented another way that a good girl might help her family and demonstrate selfless service.[7]

There is some evidence to suggest that women's wage work over the late nineteenth century was increasingly functioning just as Ashmore would have wanted it, at least in industrializing Massachusetts. As factories moved into urban areas and employed immigrant daughters, workers were increasingly girls living at home, their wages contributing to family upkeep. The historian Thomas Dublin's study of women's wage work in Massachusetts finds that over the course of the nineteenth century, women's work was increasingly integrated within a family wage economy. Thirty-two percent of all of Boston's working women in 1900 were daughters living at home, in contrast to 14.1 percent in 1860. By 1900 much of women's work, including the work of girls, served to support families rather than to enhance female autonomy.[8] As theorized by Ashmore and other advisers and described by Dublin, the work of girls did not itself create the conditions for the New Woman, or the girl who preceded her.

High Schools and New Women

Education did. Scholars looking for the origins of the image of the New Woman in the popular press in the late nineteenth century have often looked to the graduates of women's colleges following the Civil War. Although the number of women attending and graduating from college was tiny, there were certainly enough graduates to provide models for illustrator Charles Dana Gibson's strong-minded and independent young women and for the figures both celebrated and criticized in the *North American Review* and other magazines of the era.

But a logical place to look for the New Woman and her admirers is neither in the workplace nor in the tiny population of college graduates, but instead in the schoolgirl, especially in the increasing numbers of high school girls who had experienced the spirited jousting which took place within coeducational high schools and academies in the late nineteenth century. Throughout the nineteenth century, girls graduated from high school more frequently than boys, but went to college far less frequently. Between 1879 and 1889 roughly 13–14 percent of girls who graduated from high school went to college, in comparison with 60 percent or more of boy graduates. Fifteen percent of white girls born in 1870 went on to graduate from high school, but only 3 percent graduated from college. Five percent of nonwhite girls graduated from high school and fewer than 1 percent from college.[9] High school girls, more than college girls, constituted a large enough cohort to lay claim to changing a culture. Though still a small proportion of the teenage population as a whole, girls attending school were a significant part of the middle-class, native-born population. Influenced by their numerical predominance in public high schools, girl students realized their academic and intellectual capabilities, and wondered what it meant that they were dominating the competition. Although they sometimes went home following their graduation from seminary or high school, they were ill-suited for the confinement of home. After sharing in school's high ideals, and the experience of freedom in the city streets, they took themselves seriously as intellects and actors. Within coeducational high schools and rural academies, girl students became "new girls" and helped to create a new women's culture which challenged the gender polarities of the earlier nineteenth century. Critical to these life outcomes were the plans they ventured while still in school, plans which often included work, but as a means to fame and significance, not simply a livelihood.

Ambition

Given the uniform outcome of most girls' lives as wives and mothers in the mid–nineteenth century, their aspiration to accomplish something noble and noteworthy is striking. Equally striking is the language of outright ambition which they dared to embrace. To confidential diaries, they expressed hopes both that they might be good and that they might "be somebody," a suggestive phrase. Writing in 1855 in the South, with few concrete options available, Agnes Lee too felt a longing within her "to *do* something to *be* something." She asked for God's help in achieving this end, which we might imagine to be a cry for recognition, for notice from the rest of the world. To be somebody, of course, was to be a person of consequence and respect, to have power and to cut a swathe. Julia Newberry, daughter of a Chicago merchant, remembered that her father had told her to be somebody, and, she insisted, "'be somebody,' I WILL. — I've always been told I had plenty of brains, and every natural advantage; so why shouldn't I be somebody??? Laziness is the bane of my existence." Writing at the age of sixteen in 1869, Newberry had only vague ambition, as befit her status as a daughter of privilege before the legitimation of professional aspiration for women.[10]

Later diarists' visions of accomplishment were more concrete. They frequently considered the arts as a vehicle for a girl to show herself off in an appropriate way. Harriet Paine in *Chats with Girls on Self-Culture* concluded that girls want to make "something of a figure in the world," but also to add "to the beauty of life," a suggestion of the kind of figure they'd like to cut. Authorship was a frequent ambition, well modeled by the prominence of women novelists generating sentimental literature at midcentury. New Yorker Eleanor Hooper confessed "something egoish, perhaps conceited" to her friend Annie Winsor in 1881, and gave her permission to lecture her on it afterward: "I have often felt that perhaps I might be able to write something worth reading when I was old enough to have had some experience and knowledge. . . . During the past year five stories almost entirely different from each other have grown in my mind at odd moments." Confessions to such ambition were often couched in apology, but like other kinds of fantasies, they required an outlet — as much as would "an explosive gas bottled up in one's brain."[11] Girls' reading nourished the imagination, and the dream of writing yielded a double return on energy invested—both the gratification of the story itself and the dream of its explosive success.

These "girlish" ambitions represented a compelling version of the future. Mary Thomas, who at one point envisaged herself as a calisthenics teacher, also tried on the idea of becoming a serious musician, modeling herself on her dead mother. "I wish I could sing and play like Mamma did, then I would devote all my time to my music, I wonder if Papa will be willing for me to take music lessons after I am grown, from some noted musician. . . . If I found I had anything of a voice, I would be willing to go to school all my life in order to practice to see what I could do; I wonder, if I was to practice for years, by the time I am thirty-five, if I will be as good a musician as Miss Kate Milledge."[12] What's distinctive here is that Mary Thomas was not at this point a musician, inspired by her craft to understand her potential. Even so, she considered expertise and accomplishment to be a critical part of her gendered future.

Such aspiration was more credible when there was something to back it up. Florence Peck was an accomplished orator, a skill she'd had a chance to demonstrate in exhibitions as a high school student in Rochester, New York. At a presentation at the Lyceum, in which she represented her high school, she stood before a full house and recited a poem, "the only funny selection on the program." People told her that she "spoke the best of all in fact was queen of the day. I was not nervous not one bit." Peck in fact confessed, "I *like* it and if the stage was the place for a woman I'd go on mostly for the excitement and the pleasure." The stage was not the place for a woman, and by June of that year, after graduation from high school, Peck had resolved to be a teacher. The next month she accompanied her father to Boston and announced "I am nineteen. Am at home with father in Boston. . . . Nineteen and what have I done to help the world to be better for my presence?"[13] Girls who had experienced Victorian schooling could not help but see themselves trailing clouds of glory in their later lives—clouds which needed to be seen to be meaningful.

It is clear what school did and did not do. Just as it did not particularly prepare girls for futures as housewives, it did not prepare them to think of themselves as housewives. When they thought of their idealized future selves, as they were prepared to do by the culture of schooling, they thought of themselves as aspiring souls, desirous of making a mark on the world. This is not to say that they did not expect to marry and mother; they clearly did. But they carried with them a parallel and even contradictory vision of themselves which answered to another set of prerogatives. At midcentury and beyond, that vision was often an airy vision of artistic accomplishment. By the end of the century it was focused on more concrete vocational options. For the daughters of the extraordinary Hamilton family, by 1889 it included debate about becoming a physician or an architect. For more ordinary children, surveyed in 1898 for the periodical *Education,* it included a range of pedestrian possibilities. This survey, completed by nearly two thousand school children in Massachusetts, was distinctive in that none of the girls said that they expected to marry rather than follow a vocation. Teaching headed the list and was mentioned by more than half of the nine-year-old girls, but by fewer than a third of the sixteen-year-old girls. A third of the boys and a fifth of the girls were interested in the trades, with the girls mentioning stenography, bookkeeping, and typewriting. More than a quarter of the girls wanted to be dressmakers or milliners. A fifth of the boys (but only 8 percent of the girls) chose the professions, excluding teaching. When asked why they made the choices they did, 44 percent of the girls cited personal preference, compared with 30 percent of the boys. Roughly a reverse ratio mentioned money as determinative.[14] Going to school with peers, itself a venture into a world beyond the home, set a trajectory which girls imagined pursuing on into the world beyond their parents' houses. Vocational commitment was one part of this resolution. Significantly, girls even more than boys phrased this preference as a matter not of service to family or society but instead of personal *liking.* Clearly, by the turn of the century, school culture encouraged at least some girls at some ages to think that they had the right to make decisions based on their own individual proclivities.

Class Prophecies

If expressed ambitions offer one way of tracking individual girls' plans for the future, a convention of school graduation offers a collective alternative. As we have seen, the year of graduation from high school and academy brought an often loosely affiliated group of boy and girl scholars into a sometimes-frenzied series of class meetings and other activities which united them into a cohort. Encouraged by news of like activities carried in exchange newspapers around the country, classes beginning in the 1880s chose officers, a color, and a motto and also produced a class history and a class prophecy. The class prophet's assignment was to look into the future, ten years or so hence, and devise destinies for his or her classmates. Speaking either as an imp, the Sibyl of Cumae, or whatever, class prophets borrowed heavily from each other as they drew their fictive portraits. These prophecies provide one way of deter-

mining just what students themselves, as organized bodies, considered to be
a collective legacy of their school years. Class prophecies, of course, were not
reasoned documents. They were meant to be fanciful and funny. At the same
time, prophets needed to speak for a collective body, to represent a common
culture. As such, class prophecies are valuable indications of what graduating seniors were bringing with them—silly and sober—as they faced their
futures.

Class prophecies were collective, but they were made up of individual portraits. A good prophet captured something unique about each member of
the graduating class so that her classmates could recognize her; prophecies—
and destinies—needed to be varied and entertaining. Yet the range of the
variation helps to suggest some of the parameters the students imagined for
themselves. An early prophecy, published in the *North Granville Quarterly*
of North Granville (New York) Ladies' Seminary in July 1866 provides one
set of such parameters well before the rituals of the senior year became stan-
dardized. This document from a midcentury female seminary presents some
illustrative contrasts to the prophecies of coeducational high schools of the
1880s and especially the 1890s.

The conceit of the piece, "Our Class Meeting, 1885," was a reunion nineteen years hence. It revealed the still-powerful midcentury notion of woman's
sphere—that women belonged within a domestic orbit. As the alumnae arrive for the meeting, they are described as looking "old and care-worn." ("I
suppose it must be family cares," notes one). One by one they tell the stories
of their marriages and the work of their husbands in far parts of the globe.
One, who had been "so sure she would never marry," appears "dignified and
matronly." In fact, she has married a missionary and lives in Australia in a
log house, "but the vines and roses climbing over the verandah about it make
it a beautiful home." Another, after teaching in the West, lives "in the City
of Mexico" where her husband is the governor of this new American possession (a commentary on the imperial reach of midcentury fantasy). Yet another has traveled through Europe during her husband's term as minister to
France but has returned to Washington since her husband's appointment as
secretary of state. Trigonometry allowed one graduate to help pilot her sea
captain–husband's boat in a storm, and so on.[15]

This harmonious reunion is marred with one moment of dissonance
though. When Lizzie Gardner is asked about her husband, she responds that
he is at home taking care of the children in her absence, "and from here I
go to keep an important engagement." To the question "How can you leave
him so?" Lizzie responds breezily: "Oh, he don't mind it much. Besides, what

are a man's feeling? My influence is great, and my time is of too much importance to be wasted at home, when he can better attend to the housekeeping arrangements." Lizzie goes on to reveal that she is an advocate of women's rights and has recently published "a long essay on Woman's Superiority." Her classmates rush to censure her. One unmarried classmate, a "maiden aunt," acknowledges her own singlehood but defends her status: "I will not speak of blighted prospects and buried hopes, I have at least kept within woman's sphere." The moral of the tale: "In the exerting of pure home influence is woman's truest work. No, Lizzie, you have mistaken your 'sphere.' If we are Christian women we need not fear for rights."[16] The students at North Granville Academy imagined adventure-filled lives for themselves, but located their work within the context of woman's sphere, as wives and mothers or as single women still loyal to their womanly mission. The one women's rights advocate, Lizzie Gardner, is depicted as a pariah. The extent of Lizzie's outcast status is revealed in the same issue of the *North Granville Quarterly,* published in 1866 at the end of the Civil War. Included is an article by her, a favorable portrait of "Jefferson Davis, C.S.A."

At least as described in their prophecy, the female graduates of Granville seemed to be looking for ways to reshuffle their affiliations, but within the confines of woman's sphere. By later in the century, girl students had modified that stance, adopting images of their future which suggested less nurture and more competition in a big and dangerous world analogous to the one imagined by their male peers. Whereas Granville graduates of the class of 1865 looked to unite themselves by their shared loyalty to a common ideology of "woman's sphere," girl graduates from the 1880s and 1890s instead appeared in class prophecies as individuals, with unique pasts and futures. Sometimes these destinies followed conventional gender patterns, but as often, prophets ascribed great professional accomplishment or bizarre destinies to their classmates. The actual destinies—whether as doctor, lawyer, or Indian chief—were less significant than the range of individual differences designated within each graduating class. The point came to be, and it was an important one, that each classmate have a unique destiny and identity which would extend to particularities of personality. Graduation portraits had celebrated this uniqueness. In an era in which girls had often been expected to suppress self, this celebration of individual futures for girls in parity with male classmates was significant.

A feature published in Milford High School's *Oak, Lily, and Ivy* in 1886, a year after the fictive reunion described in the *North Granville Quarterly,* suggested this different world. "Extracts from the Diary of a High School Girl of '86" began with the author wishing always to be a schoolgirl, "eating

10.1 "The stuff of self," 1876. High school graduates worried over their senior pictures, which celebrated their uniqueness as they "prepared and packed" for their future lives. Here is the class of 1876 grouped around Concord (New Hampshire) High School. Courtesy of the New Hampshire Historical Society.

pickled-limes at recess, conning French and Latin conjugations, and learning multitudes of things which are soon forgotten." After considering that care-free existence, though, the unnamed schoolgirl wonders "should I be happy?" On second thought, she seems to think, perhaps she would tire of the regulations and slow pace. Instead, she abandons womanly conventions to observe that she longs to "join the ranks of the many who are pushing and struggling for preeminence." A more conventional phrasing from a female editor of the same Milford paper five years later described school days as the "preparing and the packing before we start out for ourselves." As graduation approaches "the last trunk is nearly packed, and we can almost hear the whistle of the incoming train which is to bear us to trials and disappointments, or to pleasures and happiness."[17] As the train comes barreling down the tracks, it is clear that the voyager is approaching a grand and personalized adventure, taking her, at least in imagination, far away from home.

There was one significant exception to the tendency of school newspapers to project futures for girls as professionally varied and glamorous as those for boys. The few extant issues of the *Living-Stone*, a student newspaper published at African-American Livingstone College in Salisbury, North Carolina, in the 1890s suggest a different climate from the contentious gender competitions at northern high schools. Two women and one man founded the campus newspaper at this coeducational African Methodist Episcopal-Zion institution in 1890. Yet its student writers propounded "their own" models of manhood and womanhood focused on marital harmony, according to the historian Glenda Gilmore. The vocational consequence? A female student proposed that women wield influence through their menfolk, pronouncing it "unseemly" for women to become lawyers, doctors, or lecturers.[18] Students fantasized about that which was most elusive and novel—for white students, the assumption of a full range of exciting vocations for girls; for black students, access to the wherewithal to launch compatible unions with full male partners.

It was particularly challenging for high school students in northern high schools to imagine destinies for girls which were as diverse and individualized as destinies for boys. Whereas boys in theory had available to them the full gamut of occupations, girls might work in one of the occupations designated as "women's occupations": teacher, seamstress, and increasingly "typewriter," telephone operator, or clerk. (Domestic service and factory work would have been considered beneath the aspirations of a girl who was graduating from high school.) Some girls would marry soon, many of the rest of them later. The male authors of the prophecies for the Milford Class of 1892 stretched within conventional gender vocations to suggest a range of possibilities for women. Males were assigned twelve different occupational statuses, ranging from baseball player to clothing manufacturer. There was less variety for the women: a dressmaker, an actress, a shorthand teacher, and a typist. The female valedictorian of their class, Mary McDermott, was made a professor at Wellesley. To provide another woman wealth they made her a "teacher of high rank": "Her salary was good, and in a few years Mamie will become a wealthy lady and occupy one of the finest residences in the state." What is significant is what the class prophets elected not to do: they did not have Mamie marry wealth, in fact her best chance at it. Nor in fact did they ascribe marital status to anyone, male or female.[19]

Class prophets increasingly granted women access to the professions, and to a palette of futures nearly as richly colored for girls as it was for boys. Along with more conventional female futures, the Salem *High School Advance* predicted futures as "one of our best doctors" and "the great American novelist." One destiny appeared so frequently as to be a stock figure: that of women's rights activist. The *North Granville Quarterly* had presented such a figure in order to lambaste it. During the 1880s and 1890s, the role of political woman merged with regularity and complexity in class prophecies. The Concord, New Hampshire, *Volunteer* printed a prophecy for the class of 1888 which led with the prediction that the class's valedictorian, Lena V. George, "will become a powerful advocate of the cause of Woman's Rights. From Maine to California her voice shall be heard, sounding through every state and territory in the Union, strengthening and encouraging the heart of the persecuted female to rise against the tyranny of man and fight for liberty." The prediction, written by a male student, pictured George teamed with another female student, an "able lieutenant." The two together would found a new political party, the "Independent Females," and run as its presidential ticket in 1899.[20]

Many high school students of the 1890s seemed to consider the prospect of the female politician to be an idea for the near future, an idea they associated with their own educational odyssey. They were not necessarily comfortable with it, and there was often a hint of derision in the portrait, but it seemed a logical extrapolation of their school trajectory. The Salem *High School Advance* ran this thread through a number of prophecies. An 1896 forecast featured a dialogue between two male graduates meeting in the West. (The West represented the land of the future for many northeastern high school graduates.) One sees a campaign button on the other's coat. "'I am for Lovett. Are you?' 'What! Miss Lovett of our class?' 'O yes! that is a button we used in old Mass, during the last gubernatorial campaign, which I forgot to take out of my coat.'" The conversation moves on, enough said. In this brave new world, it will not be a subject to dwell on, a woman running for governor. The same issue of the *Advance* ran a "A Letter to Our Future Governor," dated 1906, which provided congratulations to the first woman governor of the state of New York, and referred to the female governor of Massachusetts. We learn that "She is highly in favor of our new aerial navy," and also favors the maintenance of the gold standard. So by 1906 there are *two* women governors, and they can handle military technology and the economy. The next year's prophecies offered a woman on the Massachusetts Board of Education and a female candidate for mayor. In 1897 congratulations were tendered to Mabel for getting elected governor of California. The convention emerged in Milford High School too, where Bessie Gates, who had written a current events column in the newspaper, was described as a women's rights advocate and the governor of "Dakota."[21]

Given the inability of any actual high school class from the 1890s to elect a girl its president, one wonders what to make of these stock figures. Some prophecies, those written by girls, may well have been engaging in fictive wish fulfillment. But others, written by boys, also include such characters. Clearly, whether individual students favored or opposed women's rights (and writers took a range of positions), they acknowledged them. One could argue, in fact, that the competitive experience of the coeducational classroom had made women's suffrage something of a foregone conclusion.

Active Citizenship

Women's rights talk, though contentious, fed a growing sense of generational solidarity. Although usually prophecies drew from a conventional roster of vocations, as the end of the century approached, they sometimes took flight above and away from them, scrambled genders, and devised humorous and arcane fates for classmates. Together, they suggested a sense of moment, a sense that this generation of American high school students had global and even cosmic reach.

Individual accomplishment was only one focus of class prophecy. Claims for greatness were also made on behalf of a generational cohort. In the same article which imagined that the class of 1895 might produce a future president of the United States, a student acknowledged that there would be many of humbler fate. To those students the reporter was reassuring:

> *If you cannot be professor*
> *In the halls of Harvard fair,*

If you cannot teach the students all the new things in the air,
You at least can join the seniors,
And be one of that fine crew
Who with earnest zeal and ardor
Hope the red will beat the blue.[22]

Not truly egalitarian (there were clearly graduates of lesser and greater accomplishment), nonetheless this collective spirit briefly embraced a common cohort. Salem High's class of 1895 proclaimed a collective identity which was at the heart of a generational identity of "new girls" and new youth at the turn of the century.

By the 1890s high school culture had come into its own. The historian Reed Ueda argues that high schools had accumulated a sufficient number of students to support complex peer groups for the first time. This peer culture united around a shared identity forged in the coeducational high school, and included boys and girls alike. It was based in part on equal hard work. (One prophecy imagined a "sanitarium for high school graduates who have become run down from too much work," an institute now "so full that they will have to build an annex.")[23] In some ways it was an individualistic culture. Class prophecies testified to the uniqueness of each personality, based on features of temperament and history. It was certainly competitive, between individuals, but also between the sexes, as the gender sparring in each newspaper suggested.

What that sparring also suggested, though, was that it was a common culture. Although the term *young lady* never completely disappeared, increasingly "girls" shared school culture with "boys" in theoretical equality. Girls with boys followed out the trajectory of their classroom competition and, as the class prophecies indicate, increasingly imagined vocations for themselves. These vocations were not simply jobs but the pursuit of work that they "liked," an avenue for finding fulfillment. Writing in the *Oak, Lily, and Ivy* in 1893, Annie Gates described the "practically unlimited" range of choices now available to young women and indicated she would be looking for a "life-work." She noted, optimistically, "It is encouraging to know that in independent lines of business there is no discrimination between the sexes as to remuneration." Her optimism was a reflection of the egalitarian high school she knew and not an accurate reflection of the work world she would be entering, of course. In fact, women could expect to earn only a fraction of what men made in the 1890s, ranging from a high of nearly 60 percent of a male wage in sales to a low of just over a quarter of a male wage in professional occupations, especially the teaching profession.[24] Nearly a century before the passage of the Equal Pay Act and the Civil Rights Act of the 1960s, Gates's naïveté is a compelling tribute to the expectations of fair play bred by the Victorian high school.

Going Home, Going Out to Work

Class prophecies, of course, were imaginative—projections composed by students still in school to suggest what the consequences of shared educational experience might be. What did girls actually do after leaving high school? In the short term, many of them went home and occupied themselves with new home chores, learning domesticity and enacting eligibility. This pattern was especially prevalent at midcentury and continued to characterize the lives of members of a middle- and upper-middle-class elite into the twentieth century. By the 1880s and 1890s, though, alumni surveys suggest, more and more girls as well as boys made good on at least one component of their high school prophecy and went out to work.

Tracking girls through their life courses is usually difficult, given the ease of losing them upon marriage when their surnames changed. The movement west in the nineteenth century, too, makes it difficult to use the public record to determine what happened to ordinary people. School spirit and pride at Milford High School, though, left an extraordinary document compiled by the Graduates' Association in 1926. Beginning with questionnaires, which they sent out to recalcitrant respondents three and four times, the Graduates' Association compiled a directory of all graduates of Milford since 1862. The directory includes further education, marital status, work life, number of children, and place of residence. It almost always lists date of marriage as well, and appears to be virtually complete. (Comparison with several lists of graduates in graduation programs, for instance, shows that these fledgling social scientists were unusually thorough in their acquisition of "longitudinal" data for nearly an entire student population.) For those who resisted all their efforts, or who had already died, they secured the information "as accurately as possible, from outsiders," and so labeled such entries. *Statistics of the Graduates of the Milford High School, 1862–1926,* provides a rare and unusual profile of a number of generations in one working-class, increasingly immigrant community.[25]

Milford's high school had a high proportion of girls and also undoubtedly an unusually high expectation that those girls would work after graduation. This expectation seems to have been borne out from the first graduating classes during the Civil War until the turn of the century. The Civil War, of course, was a national emergency which raised questions about any boy's ability to survive and any girl's ability to count on a conventional marital destiny. Whether prompted by that kind of thinking, the early generations of female graduates taught school in high numbers. Sixty-two percent of the graduates from the 1860s and 1870s worked at some point in their postgraduate years, virtually all of them as teachers in the local schools.[26] Whatever the reputation of teaching initially as a desirable destiny, clearly many families and their daughters considered it an appropriate sequence to the years invested in sending girls to high school.

Few girls from these early years appear to have made teaching what we would think of as a career. Indeed, like the pattern of "helping" in rural America earlier in the century, teaching in local schools was often an activity for a stage of life before marriage. Most high school graduates, those who taught and those who didn't, eventually married, even in this generation which had incurred heavy Civil War losses. More than two-thirds of Milford High School girls from the 1860s and 1870s married. This contrasts significantly with the statistics on female college graduates from the late century, half or more of whom stayed unmarried.[27]

If high school graduates eventually married, they often married late, a significant number of years following graduation. Graduates of the 1860s and 1870s tended to marry seven to eight years after high school graduation. Whether helping a natal family, saving for a dowry, waiting for an appropriate mate in a market of scarcity, or simply enjoying the choice of whether to marry, young women with high school educations married later than their cohort.

As might be expected for women marrying later, high school graduates were likely to have fewer children than the national norm. Even taking later age at marriage into consideration, the statistics reveal strikingly small families throughout the last forty years of the century. The average number of children reported in the 1926 figures for female graduates of these decades was 2.4. Contrast this with an average of about 3.7 for all married women from these decades. Over the course of the nineteenth century, as many historians have noted, a demographic revolution was in progress in the United States, as women began to gain control of their fertility; the average number of births in each woman's lifetime declined from a peak of more than seven in 1800 to 3.56 in 1900.[28] As in the developing world today, the education of women was a critical component in this decline, borne out by the especially low fertility of this cohort of high school–educated women. Not yet New Women in the 1860s and 1870s (though some would identify themselves as such in the latter decades), women who had been to high school took control over their lives in ways which set them at the vanguard of women of their generation.

If high school graduates did eventually marry, though, the delay before they did, sometimes extending to twenty years and more, meant that many of them lived substantial portions of their lives as single women, often teaching school in the early decades of their work lives. The 1860s and 1870s showed the beginnings of a trend which intensified in the 1880s and 1890s as new occupations in offices and shops opened for women in Milford. If 62 percent of high school graduates from the 1860s and 1870s worked, 69 percent of Milford graduates in the 1880s and 1890s worked for a time. By those decades, though, a minority of those graduates from the industrial town of Milford even started out their work lives as teachers, instead taking up work in what would be called the pink-collar sector some hundred years later. Milford graduates worked as bookkeepers and clerks in the offices of Milford's straw factories and its big manufactory, the Draper Company. A smattering worked as librarians, social workers, and nurses.

The *Oak, Lily, and Ivy,* the Milford student newspaper, helps to contextualize these statistics. Particularly revealing is a report written by a member of the class of 1884 eleven years later, reporting on the doings of his classmates. His was the class that had considered itself the "banner class" of Milford High School, comprising thirty graduates, an equal number of boys and girls, with such fellow feeling that "a certain young lady" proposed that a marriage of the fifteen couples was in order. By 1895 six female classmates had married (though not one of them to a classmate, it would appear). Four were teaching, one "sojourning" in Europe. The female class poet was dead. Of the others, the correspondent observed that "4 misses and 1 man" were "all living in Milford, doing their duty, all making hosts of friends." Long-term, high school education opened up possibilities of self-support for women as teachers and decreased the incentive to marry. It did not remove the notion of "duty" for women or men. High school experience opened an ongoing social world; classmates were not just keeping old friendships but making new ones. A report on the next year's class of twenty-two girls and eighteen boys a year out suggested less immediate variety. The 1886 editors of the *Oak, Lily, and Ivy* observed about the class of 1885: "If our information is correct, all but two of the 40 are engaged in regular work, and these two are only waiting for an opening in the particular line of work which they wish to enter."[29] The statistics suggested that a number of graduates were working. Beyond that, though, the commentator added an insight about what that work meant: high school graduates had vocational goals. They were willing to wait for openings in "particular" lines of work they had chosen.

The Milford statistics thus suggest a complex statistical portrait of the life courses of female high school graduates in this community. Most went out to work for a time, initially as schoolteachers and then in a range of different occupations opening for women. Of those who worked, two-thirds eventually married, often a number of years after graduating from high school.[30] A few went on for further education. If the population were broken into ninths, it would produce these rough proportions: four-ninths worked for a number of years and then married; two-ninths worked and didn't marry; two-ninths didn't work and married. Yet another ninth neither worked nor married, many of those "at home," filling the helping role of daughter or aunt (the traditional spinster's role within a family economy), or invalided.[31]

Perhaps the most significant evolution over those decades came in the decline in the category of those women who worked and eventually married, with a 10-point spread opening from the early to the later decades. In the 1860s and 1870s, 70 percent of all women who worked eventually married. By the 1880s and 1890s, though, that number declined to 60 percent. It seems likely that more working women were beginning to feel that marriage was an option rather than a necessity.[32] This figure is matched by a slight increase in the evidence of lifetime workers in the Milford survey. Though less complete than other measures, the Milford data show a rise from 12 percent to 18 percent of women who ended up working not just as a stage in their lives but as a life commitment, whether voluntary or not.

This evidence supports the idea that high school—or secondary education in general—gradually contributed to new approaches to women's work, such that it might be considered "life work" and be worth waiting for. It allowed some women to choose not to marry at all. It allowed others to postpone marriage and to contemplate other possibilities for their lives. And it undoubtedly also provided new substance to the lives of girls "doing their duty" for whom the identity of New Woman meant a reframing of ostensibly traditional choices. But if high schools helped to create the social environment for the creation of new life patterns for women, it fell to polemicists and journalists to create the vocabulary to name it.

Making and Combating an Image

The New Woman was not at first a social reality at all but an image—constructed in popular culture in the 1890s by magazine writers and illustrators on both sides of the Atlantic. The term came to crystallize a flurry of debate about women's lives, but it also popularized and thereby promoted a cultural icon that embodied those changes, providing a convenient catchphrase for writers, advocates, publicists, and ordinary people. Illustrators and advertisers joined in the construction of the New Woman, who was as often a style or a way of dress as she was a fully developed life history.

The phenomenon, and the debate over it, was trans-Atlantic, and it significantly emerged in 1894 as a debate about girls' rights rather than women's. Unlike the earlier and largely negative depiction of the "Girl of the Period" in the 1860s, the discussion about the rights of girls in the 1890s was often understanding. As with the earlier debate, the discussion originated in Britain. Titling her critique "The Revolt of the Daughters," B. A. Crackanthorpe, a barrister's wife and a mother of sons, noted the increasing resistance of daughters of the middle class to their prescribed role in life. Sympathetically, she advanced their claims to selfhood—to the "right to be an individual as well as a daughter." She explained, "They are young. They are vital. The springs of life, the thirst to taste its joys run very strong in their veins. They desire ardently to try things on their own account."[33]

An actual British daughter was more concrete. Kathleen Cuffe depicted herself as speaking for the ordinary girl in the elite mainstream, not the college girl or the artist but "the average more or less unemployed, tea-drinking, lawn-tennis playing, ball-going damsel, whose desire for greater emancipation does not run in the same lines as those of the independent shop-girl, or of the young woman with a mission." Yet her plea was just as ardent. "The so-called revolting maiden only asks for a small amount of liberty." Cuffe explained: "What she wants, first of all, is the abolition of chaperons on all possible occasions. . . . She considers it hard that she cannot walk the length of two or three—even five or six—streets to visit a friend, without having first provided herself with an unhappy maid or attendant of some description. . . . A young married woman does not wear her wedding ring in her nose or other prominent spot to assure the passer-by of her social status . . . yet she can walk through the streets alone. . . . Why cannot the girl?"[34] Claiming that girls married just so they could get out of the house alone, Cuffe argued that freedom in public space, freedom in the streets, was at the essence of girls' demands for destinies of their own.

When the debate emerged in the American press, however, its contours changed. As one British commentator noted, the battle for girls' freedom in the streets had been won in the United States. ("An American girl travelling is *not* looked at askance.") Girls had largely gained their freedom to move. The question the *North American Review* took up at nearly the same time had to do with the women these girls became. The British novelist Sarah Grand led off with an article in March 1894 entitled "The New Aspect of the Woman Question," in which she described a new kind of woman, neither subordinate wife nor prostitute, who had been "sitting apart in silent contemplation all these years, thinking and thinking, until at last she . . . proclaimed for herself what was wrong with Home-is-the-Woman's Sphere." This woman had come to understand her oppression at the hands of righteous man and was coming to envisage a world in which women would be "stronger and wiser," with "practical good sense."[35] Grand's article, in fact, coined no new terminology, advancing familiar themes from decades of discussion of "the woman question."

Her respondent did. The British "sensation" novelist Louise de la Ramée wrote in rebuttal in a later issue of *North American Review*. She titled her piece "The New Woman" and capitalized the term throughout. "Ouida," as she signed her piece, ridiculed Grand's argument and characterized the New Woman as a humorless and graceless women's rights advocate. ("Why cannot this orator learn to gesticulate and learn to dress, instead of clamoring for a franchise?") The New Woman's major sin, however, was that despite the richness of her private life, "she wants to be admitted into public life," a role which included political participation and higher education. Ouida abhorred both possibilities, arguing that "the publicity of a college must be odious to a young girl of refined and delicate feeling." Far worse than either the domestic drudge or the fast woman, Ouida argued, was this New Woman, "with her fierce vanity, her undigested knowledge, her over-weening estimate of her own value and her fatal want of all sense of the ridiculous."[36] Ouida's critique typified early commentary on the subject. In fact, the New Woman was most successful with the public when she was not a woman at all but instead still a girl.

Charles Dana Gibson's subjects were not originally New Women but stylish "girls," and they gained enormous iconographic power as bold, resourceful figures of American beauty. Published in the humor magazine *Life* and the mainstream genteel press beginning in the late 1880s and early 1890s, Gibson's girls became bold New Women and an American prototype only in his 1896 collection *Pictures of People*. The beautiful and haughty Gibson Girl appeared as a judge, general, diplomat, ambassador, football player, and minister, and she was independent and confident. The image was sufficiently resonant that writers were drawn to the subject. The literary realist Frank Norris, who made his reputation by writing about the small corruptions of daily life, allowed himself to participate in this admiration in a review of Gibson's book.

He compared Gibson's subjects with more conventional images of domestic womanhood, which he found "a little superficial." He preferred "another girl who is very beautiful and stylish and all that who smiles just as readily but who is capable of the graver, sterner note as well. She is Mr. Gibson's American girl. She has lived an eventful life. When I first knew her she was (very gently) repudiating foreign noblemen. . . . Of late she has been going about in the costume of a general, or a diplomat, or a minister of the gospel . . . just as charming and as irresistible as ever in spite of—or perhaps because of— her change of raiment." She was "very tall and a little slim. . . . Tall enough in fact to look down on most men, . . . not at all the kind of girl you would choose to quarrel with." Norris praised "her dignity and imposing carriage" and her "seriousness." His perspective was clear: he was interested in her attractions. He found her "costumes" of general or diplomat to be beguiling, her "eventful life" intriguing and her strength appealing. When it came down to it, "somehow you feel that she is a 'man's woman' and would stand by a fellow and back him up if things should happen." His contrast of Gibson's girl with the frivolous domestic girl was clear. He concluded about Gibson's girl, "I would like to put her to the test—if I were the man." Strong "girls" were attractive, and on those aesthetic and erotic grounds, Norris approved.[37]

In fact, though, if a "girl" had been politely rebuffing foreign noblemen or if she had served as diplomat, general, or minister, she was surely no longer in her teens, and therefore not a girl at all. As Norris's review demonstrated, defining and classifying young American females—whether girls or young ladies—was an endlessly engaging project at the turn of the century, as witnessed by another piece on the subject that appeared in *Atlantic Monthly* in 1900. Entitled "The Steel-Engraving Lady and the Gibson Girl," Caroline Ticknor's contrast differed from Norris's in several particulars. Her "Steel-Engraving Lady" was a lovely but extinct type, sitting dreamily in her parlor next to an idle embroidery hoop in "an air of quiet repose." Onto this placid scene the Gibson Girl strode, wearing mannish shoes, suntanned. In contrast with Norris's, Ticknor's Gibson Girl was defined by her attitudes rather than her looks. She announced herself prepared to enter a profession, determined to "make the most of her Heaven-given talents." Ticknor's girl proclaimed: "We're not a shy, retiring, uncomplaining generation. We're up to date and up to scuff, and every one of us is self-supporting." Although Ticknor deemed one character a "lady" and the other a "girl," it is clear that age was not the characteristic that distinguished them. The Gibson Girl actually claimed New Woman status by stating: "You see the motto 'Heaven helps her who helps herself' suits the 'new woman.'" Gibson's "girl" is in fact a New Woman, just

10.2 Gibson Girl, 1896. The figure shown in this detail from *An Ambassador's Ball in the Days to Come* was both an ambassador and a "girl," bringing new meaning to the latter term. Reprinted from Charles Dana Gibson, *Pictures of People* (New York: Russell, 1896).

as the New Woman is often portrayed as a "girl." In contrast with Norris, as well, Ticknor was not concerned with whether the Gibson Girl was attractive to men: "Whether *he* likes it or not makes little difference; *he* is no longer the one whose pleasure is to be consulted. The question now is not 'what does man like? but 'What does woman prefer?' This is the keynote of modern thought."[38] This indeed was the key to the turn-of-the-century transformation in women's roles. What defined them was their declaration of independence from the traditional woman's sphere, and their commitment to individuality and freedom. But it was the Gibson Girl who brought allure and cachet to the New Woman.

This cultural power did not translate into direct political power. As the scholar Martha Banta points out (and Frank Norris indirectly suggested), the various costumes worn by the Gibson Girl did not thereby create woman ambassadors or generals: "The girl who went cycling might not raise a finger to urge the vote for women, but her *image* as the type of the American Girl became part of the process that altered social perceptions and formed new conceptions of what it was possible for females to do and to be." Banta quotes a near-contemporary of Charles Dana Gibson, Fairfax Davis Downey: "The Goddess of the wheel, as Gibson and many another artist now drew her, was . . . a pretty American girl speeding joyously along on a bicycle. On that simple machine she rode like a winged victory, women's rights perched on the handlebars and cramping modes and manners strewn on her track."[39] Downey's words in 1936 suggest nicely the way the creation of the cultural type of the Gibson Girl provided validation for turn-of-the-century girls who might have started by going cycling and playing basketball but ended by taking their claims to their own preferences into adult womanhood.

Critics of the Gibson Girl and the New Woman at the time had some ideas about what might make girls susceptible to these new ideals. Marie de la Ramée, whose blast "The New Woman" in 1894 helped set off the debate, in part blamed American coeducation. The problem was "everything which tends to obliterate the contrast of the sexes, like your mixture of boys and girls in your American common schools." Her attack on the egalitarian education of boys and girls in American schools went directly to a source of turn-of-the-century cultural change. This analysis was supplemented ten years later by another extensive critique of new American girlhood which touched on the impact of single-sex women's college education. G. Stanley Hall was a sharp critic of the autonomy of girls, and he blamed women's colleges for their misguided instruction in this regard. "I insist that the cardinal defect in the woman's college is that it is based upon the assumption, implied and often expressed . . . that girls should primarily be trained to independence and self-support, and that matrimony and motherhood, if it come, will take care of itself, or, as some even urge, is thus best provided for." Hall's suggestion that education helped to produce New Women was confirmed by L. T. Meade, a British writer of popular fiction. Meade wrote about the girls' school experience in a series of essays for the British *Strand* magazine in 1895 and made the connection explicit: "Girls, so trained, must surely be the New Women for whom we long."[40] If illustrators and novelists like Strand crystallized the image, schoolgirls helped to make it possible.

The social reality of single-sex and especially coeducational schooling provided part of the audience for the literary and commercial image of the Gibson Girl. Schoolgirls recognized themselves in the "Big American Girl," to whom Gibson dedicated *Pictures of People,* and in turn illustrators drew on such new figures and attitudes as former schoolgirls brought to the public sphere. Indeed, one could argue that the new associations which Gibson Girls brought to the idea of the New Woman derived from meanings mediated through the identity of the schoolgirl.

"Girl": The Evolution of a Term

The term *girl* had traditionally referred to both age and status. A girl who was not a prepubescent child was faintly sexualized, a servant, or a social inferior. (The secondary dictionary meanings from midcentury all have these connotations, including "maid servant," "lady-love," and "prostitute.") The language needed to change to enable Charles Dana Gibson to be painting "girls" instead of "young ladies." Initially, school facilitated the use of the diminutive *girl* to refer to respectable females after puberty. The midcentury protests of the Agassiz School student Nellie Browne about the loss of her status as a schoolgirl centered around this terminology of self. There was only one way for her to stave off womanhood, which was as a schoolgirl. (The term *young lady* already gave too much away to adulthood.) "But I intend to be a school-girl, for certainly two years if not longer," she insisted, as she left school and considered the alternative. Nellie Browne's resistances suggest the dynamics by which later generations of women might be tempted to consider themselves girls for much of their lives. "I will be called a school-girl, if other people won't call me one, I will call my-self one."[41] By the end of the century, the prefix *school* was no longer necessary to describe postpubertal youth. Coeducation helped to establish parallel terms for male and female students.

In the early century, it was difficult to find such parallel terms for students. Male students were occasionally "gentlemen," but often the terms were *young ladies* and *boys.* An example of the endemic asymmetry of polite language emerged in the Bridgton Academy catalog of 1833, which listed its students by sex: "ladies" and "males." When Eliza Lynn Linton titled her critique "The Girl of the Period" in 1868, she did so advisedly. The title of the piece, as well as its contents, impugned the virtue and propriety of the "girls" it featured.[42]

Gradually, though, the term *girl* moved into polite usage, and the modifier *school* dropped off. In the 1880s and beyond, student journalists sought parallelism, referring to themselves as boys and girls. Such parallelism was important in suggesting shared culture. Thus a columnist for the Concord *Volunteer* mused on the formation of a Young Ladies' Literary Union, "We hope that, if it should be organized, it will be given another name. How would the boys like to belong to a 'Young Gentlemen's Christian Association?' How would they like their Lyceum to be dubbed the 'Young Gentlemen's Lyceum'?" The columnist explained that the term *young lady* was offensive because it was associated with domestic propriety: "It is too suggestive of her 'favorite stitch,' 'The Maiden's Prayer,' or 'Home, Sweet, Home.'" The columnist concluded: "The prefix 'young ladies,' in this connection does not suit the young new woman." Despite the association between New Women and youth, the language which emerged to describe the reality of high school students was not "women" and "men" but "girls" and "boys." A *Volunteer* column from the next year acknowledged as much when it spoofed *Ladies' Home Journal*'s famous column for girls in a feature "Side Talks with Girls and Boys."[43] When Ruth Ashmore's column first appeared in 1890, *Ladies' Home Journal* editor Edward Bok had made a statement with his decision to direct the column to "girls," a modern way of referring to teenage females. By the late century, it was coming to be standard usage. Unlike a young lady, a girl was a boy's peer, for whom the honorifics of the language of "ladyhood," even if coupled with the modifier "young," were inappropriate.

Sally Mitchell, in her insightful study of British girls, *The New Girl*, suggests that a new evaluation of the meaning of work helped to construct modern girlhood. As all girls increasingly expected to go out to work, Mitchell argues, the term *girl* lost its meaning as a mark of class status, instead denoting exclusively an "age class." I would contend, though, that the meaning of girlhood was evolving simultaneously within schools. It was initially secondary schooling that created the new contrary category *schoolgirl*. (As Mitchell puts it, a schoolgirl "is not a child; a 'schoolgirl,' in Victorian usage, is probably over eleven.'") A schoolgirl had passed puberty but had preserved her innocence, individuality, and class status. She had freedom in the city streets, yet was not of the streets. She was a peer and equal of boys, not a refined creature of the parlor. It was perhaps not until the 1920s and beyond that all women aspired to be such girls. But by the 1880s and 1890s, when Charles Gibson began his painting, to be an American girl was a desired and desirable status, in part created by the institution of school. The historian Joseph Kett observed that teenage middle-class Victorian females were "the first adolescents," the first youths granted a special status free from adult work and responsibilities.[44] They were also the first modern girls.

New Girls, New Women

"New girls," many of them former schoolgirls, constituted a large and significant cohort, larger than that of those who might qualify as New Women under some contemporary academic definitions. If polemicists and journalists first constructed the term New Woman, it has been reconstituted in a specific and narrower context by contemporary historians, who have made this suggestive cultural category into a concrete social cohort. Identifying New Women as college graduates, the historians Carroll Smith-Rosenberg, Sara Evans, and most recently Sarah Deutsch suggest the radical challenge such women made to gender relations. Smith-Rosenberg defines the New Woman as "single, highly educated, economically autonomous. The New Woman constituted a revolutionary demographic and political phenomenon. Eschewing marriage, she fought for professional visibility, espoused innovative, often radical, economic and social reforms, and wielded real political power." The presence of New Women on the scene may in part be charted by rising ages of marriage and increasing rates of singleness, which were the highest they had ever been. It may also be charted in the steady decline in the number of children born over the late part of the century. (The decline in the birth rate, especially among the native born, triggered national debates about possible "race suicide.") In conjunction with the rising rate of divorce, it was increasingly clear that some middle-class women could envision a degree of independence their mothers could not have. Yet this narrow definition of New Women, confined as it is to unmarried, college, and professional women, does not do justice to the breadth of the debate over sex roles at the turn of the century and to the depth of the change which was affecting American women. Work experience and especially secondary school attendance could predispose young women to identify with Gibson's independent girl. The historian Lynn Gordon has argued the conservative impact of this "new girl" as portrayed in Charles Dana Gibson's portraits. In particular she suggests that the tendency to conflate the college woman of the new century with Gibson's portrait of the attractive, sportive, independent girl represented a way of bleaching the substance from the social activism and single livelihoods of many of the members of the first generation of college graduates. Rather than eviscerating the strength of the New Woman, though, the Gibson Girl was the popular culture's vehicle for redeeming her.[45] One type of the New

Woman was indeed educated and autonomous, as historians have argued, but the New Woman was something more, too. The New Woman who rejected the model of the self-sacrificing Victorian woman carried her claim to a self of her own into a broad variety of life destinies and family patterns.

In studying African-American political culture in Jim Crow North Carolina, the historian Glenda Gilmore suggests the role of coeducation in promoting a particular kind of new womanhood. Gilmore notes that coeducational normal schools for blacks in 1877 contributed to uniquely egalitarian gender relations and public lives for women among an educated elite. The result of black women's experience with coeducation was that black women did not remain single but formed "industrious" partnerships with their spouses. White women were several decades behind black women in their access both to coeducation and to progressive ideas in the South, where Gilmore concludes, educated African-American women "had been New Women since 1877."[46] If African-American graduates of coeducational normal schools became New Women in the 1870s, the same is true for graduates of coeducational high schools in the North. The experience of coeducation had lasting impact on girls' self-conceptions. Lacking the self-conscious racial solidarity Gilmore describes, nonetheless, schoolgirls in the North felt allied with their male classmates in a "civic partnership" which transformed marriage as well as the trajectories of girls' lives.

The measure of the emergence of New Women lies as much in culture as in social reality. In *American Moderns,* the historian Christine Stansell suggests the ways that images might interact with experience, conflating New Woman with Gibson Girl. "What one read shaped how one lived. One could learn about the New Woman from novels and magazine fiction and admire her elegant image—slim, shirtwaisted, fine-featured, hair piled high—in the proliferating illustrations that accompanied them. The New Woman inspired a stream of Anglo-American writing. . . . In fiction, New Womanhood turned upon a desire for experience." Stansell suggests that like the Gibson Girl, the type of the New Woman "took on independent weight and plausibility, announcing a wide spectrum of respectable femininity."[47] The social contours of the New Woman are well captured by many of the statistics made possible through the Milford survey. The cultural manifestations emerge more dramatically in life stories begun in high school. For many the evidence consists in shards. Let me sketch some examples:

♦ Cassie Upson attended school and had her knuckles rapped in rural Charlemont, Massachusetts, where she lived with her aunts. She moved to immigrant Milwaukee to live with her father and stepmother in the 1860s and cruised the city with abandon, keeping a lively diary often written during school itself, detailing her uninhibited reading and socializing. Unfortunately, she ended her diary at the age of sixteen, but she continued on to a lively public life, attending seminary and normal school, graduating in 1872. Like many of the Milford graduates, she began her work life teaching school, going on to write for the *Springfield* (Illinois) *Republican*. She married her editor in 1874. As Kate Upson Wells, she wrote for the mainstream genteel press, mothered three sons, edited the periodical *Good Cheer*, participated in suffrage work, and lectured on the Chautauqua circuit. Although she lived too early to adopt the name New Woman, it would be hard to distinguish many of her traits from those who might.

◆ Growing up motherless in the post–Civil War South, as a lonely boarding-school girl Mary Thomas was anxious about her future, imagining herself at different times a teacher of calisthenics and of music as she worried about her father's lack of resources. She appears to have been lucky in the marriage lottery, however, marrying a successful lawyer. She mothered a large family. Probably assisted by substantial household help, she gathered a group of friends together in her Athens, Georgia, parlor in 1891, to found a garden club, said to have been the nation's first. Her biographer reports that she became known as the "iris lady," and that she loved flowers "not only for their beauty but also for the outlet they provided for her creative spirit."[48]

◆ Mary Elizabeth Morrissey, who called herself "Lizzie" in her teens, came home after she graduated from Girls' High School in 1876 and learned to sweep. She also learned how to look for work as a teacher, however, and within several years had secured a job teaching in East Boston primary schools. She taught in a number of primary schools for much of her life, continuing to live in an extended family consisting of her mother, grandparents, and uncle. Whether out of patriotic loyalty or for a break from teaching or for enhanced wages, Mary Elizabeth Morrissey (or Elizabeth Mary Morrissey, as she had become) enlisted in the armed services during World War I at the age of fifty-four to help run the trolley system. She earned the rank of corporal in motor transport as one of the war's woman workers. In 1932 city directories still listed her as a teacher at the age of sixty-nine. Did Lizzie Morrissey define herself as a New Woman? It is unlikely that one as concerned with propriety as she was in her youth would have elected that identity in the 1890s when she was in her thirties. Yet her willingness to sign on as an earlier war's "Rosie the Riveter" suggests a spirit both patriotic and experimental, a flexibility in her maturity.

♦ Margaret Tileston lingered at home for a number of years, taking classes at Miss Hall's Kindergarten School, reading aloud to family members, leading a life of routine and small event. At the age of twenty-five in 1892 she finally made good on her collegiate plans and entered the Harvard Annex (which became Radcliffe in 1894). As a student in her mid-twenties, she was not alone among early Radcliffe students. When she graduated at the age of twenty-eight in 1895, she was a year younger than the average age of graduation from Radcliffe in the 1890s.[49] Certainly there is every evidence that Tileston aimed to do the conventional thing and marry at an appropriate age. But when she failed in that endeavor, she had clear alternatives set in place while a stellar student at Salem High School in the 1880s. After a sojourn in Europe, she took a teaching job in Philadelphia, where in 1899, at the age of thirty-one, she met and married a medical researcher and teacher, mothering three children. She continued to write her daily diary until her early death from pneumonia in 1912.

♦ Ethelwyn Blake graduated from Milford High School in 1889. She worked on the student newspaper her senior year, commending cooking and sewing instruction for boys as well as girls: "Those boys who intend going away to school will find it very convenient to know how to sew on a button or mend a tear."[50] After graduating from high school, she became Milford's librarian and president of the Quinshipaug Woman's Club.

♦ Daughters of a clergyman, sisters Louise and Myra Lamprey both went to Concord (New Hampshire) High School in the 1890s. Elmira Lamprey (as she was known while in high school) edited the student paper, the *Volunteer,* and wrote a trenchant column attacking gushing schoolgirl language, urging her classmates to "put 'pretty' and 'lovely' in a drawer until you can learn to do without them." In this sensitivity to language, she was perhaps in part inspired by her elder sister, also a graduate of Concord High and of Mount Holyoke, who was in the process of launching a career in journalism in Washington, D.C. By 1898 Louise, going temporarily under the more fashionable pen name of Lunette, was living back at home, though contributing editorials to Washington papers. In 1905 the sisters moved to New York, where Louise was described in a Concord newspaper article as a "well-known magazine writer" who had "gained a high place in the professional life of the American metropolis." Myra apparently had a music studio and pupils on Fifth Avenue, and the sisters were said to be inhabiting "handsomely furnished apartments."[51] Both sisters, as witnessed by their professional vocation and their flair for self-creation, were undoubtedly New Women.

- Luella Ballou too might qualify. As a high school editor of the *Oak, Lily, and Ivy,* Lulu Ballou urged her classmates to "let there be no limit" to their ambition, and to "pack their bags" for the great excursion which was to be their lives. She herself went off to Comer's Business College in Boston. From there she headed for New York, where she was a stenographer and secretary for the New York manager of the library bureau before marrying a "wool merchant" eleven years after graduating from Milford High School. (She had three children.)[52]

- The Catholic hierarchy was highly critical of the figure of the New Woman and her challenge to the family, so it is unlikely that Mary McDermott, who was kept from giving the valedictory for the class of 1892 by her Milford parish priest, would have adopted that term for herself. Mary McDermott served a lifetime in the Milford elementary schools, first as a teacher and then as a principal, retiring in the early 1940s. Upon her retirement, Mary McDermott returned to her newspaper roots, writing a number of poems which appeared in local papers under her full three names. Mary Honor McDermott wrote occasional poetry, in memory of the wartime dead and in honor of the centennial of St. Mary's parish, but she also published a more ambitious poem, a meditation on the emotion jealousy. ("She looks askance with measuring eye / And checks her neighbors' goods and wealth; / Turns inward thoughts upon her own, / Appraising both with cunning stealth.")[53] She gave a lifetime of service, but in the end, too, dared to call attention to herself as a literary figure.

- Graduating the same year as Mary McDermott, Ida Mabel Lancraft shopped, flirted, and kept an irreverent and arch diary in Fair Haven, Connecticut, in the 1880s. A prototypical "new girl," she graduated from Hillhouse High School, and after attending Wellesley College for two years, dropped out permanently in January 1896. (Lancraft was never a serious scholar, but the record does not indicate the reasons for her departure.) She nonetheless maintained lifetime ties with her original Wellesley class, writing regularly for alumnae publications. The voice of these alumnae reports is unmistakable: the writing style she developed as a teenager lasted a lifetime. These self-reports describe a career as a newspaper correspondent: in 1907 she was "editing a special section in a local Sunday newspaper, and doing correspondence work for a New York and a Boston daily"; in 1909 she demurred about her success, noting she was still seeking "a niche in the literary corner of the Hall of Fame." During World War I, she published profiles of servicemen; "Real concern for the comfort of the boys 'Over There' and a sincere wish not to add to their troubles has kept me from knitting sox," she reported.[54]

Mabel Lancraft had been an irreverent and free-spirited high school girl in the 1880s and early 1890s and was in many ways a New Woman, as her journalistic career, self-dramatization, and significant singlehood might suggest. Yet in 1913, when Wellesley asked her class, "Do You Desire Equal Franchise?" Mabel Lancraft was listed in the "No" column. (In this she joined a minority of 31, with 49 in favor, and 26 "indifferent.") One scarcely knows what to make of Lancraft's opposition to suffrage, except to wonder what associations Lancraft might have had with suffragism—certainly an issue for a woman of a certain age still open to matrimony. Mabel Lancraft was working as a secretary in her father's oyster business in 1914. (Her newspaper work was probably on commission and did not pay her a living wage.) She had clearly not chosen against marriage, reporting in 1909 only, "Nothing doing as yet." That changed when a Yale Ph.D. student eighteen years her junior began boarding next to Lancraft Brothers Oysters. The two were married in 1917, when Ida Lancraft was forty-four, and she spent the remainder of her life as a professor's wife.[55]

◆ Sarah Woodward had no compunctions about the franchise. As editor of the Concord *Volunteer* in 1900, she had urged the girls in her class to teach themselves how to snowshoe. Perhaps following the example of her mother, who graduated from Concord High School in 1875, Sarah Woodward was a suffragist and a participant in athletic culture, attending Wellesley, where she rowed crew her first year and played basketball for four years, serving as president of the athletic association. She continued her studies at Columbia, where she was active in student government, and assembled a diverse portfolio as a progressive teacher in subsequent years.[56] College education encouraged a career as a New Woman that had been well launched while she was still in high school.

The list could go on and on. I offer here a personal example: my grandmother, Edna Elizabeth Hill, who grew up in the small village of North Bridgton, Maine. The daughter of the local livery man, a student at the local academy in her rural community, she wrote for the school newspaper, the *Stranger*, serving under a male editor in chief. A school picture shows her in a four-in-hand tie in 1896, and a class profile notes her interest in "anything progressive." In her last year of academy, she was a self-defined New Woman.[57] Unable to go to college as she had hoped because her mother became ill,

10.3 Interested in "anything progressive," 1896. Attending Bridgton Academy in the village of North Bridgton, Maine, Edna Elizabeth Hill, back row, second from right, found a lifetime identity as a New Woman. Courtesy of Bridgton Academy.

she stayed home to fulfill the traditional daughter's role and worked as the town postmistress. In her later life as the wife of her academy sweetheart in a New Hampshire college town, she never forgot the persona forged at the age of nineteen. Edna Hill Hunter played tennis, ran her own dress business for a time, raised two children, and acted in local dramatic productions. She founded a woman's walking club, and sang a strong alto in the church choir. She liked to dance. As her grandchildren, we all knew her through that cherished lifelong identity. My grandmother became a New Woman not from collegiate experience but, probably as much as anything, from her exhilarating experience at Bridgton Academy.

The psychologist Judith Harris has taught us that we need to take seriously the role of peers in setting foundational identity at the age when many students graduated from high school, the age of eighteen or twenty. (When asked how old she was turning, Harris's own grandmother, stricken with Alzheimer's, reverted to the age above other ages, responding "Twenty?")[58] In rural communities and cities around the country, there were surely many women like my grandmother—women who had discovered significant identities in schools and academies as New Women who carried that identity into diverse adulthoods. Such ordinary women, many of them former schoolgirls, joined with their generation's professionals to swell the support for a new gender system at the century's cusp, a movement historians of women know as "the first wave."

Individuality and Personality

The debate over the New Woman was really a debate within a debate. The emergence of New Women represented an important evolution within the liberal and individualist culture of the nineteenth century. As the market expanded into most corners of American life, middle-class American women had functioned as a significant check on its excesses, instead allying their claims to power with their role as representatives of a corporate familial culture of caring and self-sacrifice. Apostles of woman's sphere had argued that true women set aside thoughts of self in deference to the needs of other family members. When middle-class girls joined their brothers in asserting claims to self—and worse yet when adults supported their right to do so—traditionalist critics cried out.

They took aim at the language which today has become the way we talk about ourselves. A story in *The Youth's Companion* in 1880 suggested the pejorative connotation attaching to such words as *individual,* especially when attached to women. (The punch line: "I thought you never could call such a nice lady as that an 'individual.'") More broadly suspect was the term *personality.* As the historian Richard Fox and others have pointed out, by midcentury a debate had arisen over whether and how much "personality" a person should have in contrast to the stalwart values of sturdy character. As Fox put it, "The character ideal stressed self-sacrifice and self-control as the keys to moral development: individuals were subordinated to a higher *law.* The personality ideal, by contrast, preached the development of a higher *self:* the dynamic self became its own higher law." If individuality was suspect as a goal for girls, "personality," with its connotations of self-display, was just what girls were being schooled to avoid throughout much of the nineteenth century. In her "Side Talks with Girls," the reliable Ruth Ashmore raised the question with her readers. In a column entitled "Did You Ever Think, My Dear" she queried girls on this very question. Did you ever think, she asked, "that personalities are not always interesting and very often offensive?"[59] For much of the previous century, advisers had been of one mind.

Yet by the turn of the century, such language as Ashmore's was in decline among those prescribing destinies for American schoolgirls. Advisers from the liberal and reform communities had for several decades been urging American girls to take themselves seriously and bring their gifts to the world. Christian reformers like the Rev. Francis E. Clark and Frances Willard were among the voices in the 1880s arguing for a sense of self-reliance among girls. Clark, the founder and guiding spirit of the popular evangelical youth organization Christian Endeavor, published an article in the *Ladies' Home Journal* which substantially challenged Ruth Ashmore's message. Clark observed that the young woman of 1886 "always seems to be afraid of her own individuality." Cautioning that he did not mean to encourage anything "odd and bizarre or pert and perverse," he urged on his reader her God-given right to "be yourself." Worth more than a "right to shave and sing bass," he wrote, was "your right to *be self-reliant, and in the best sense of the term, independent.*" Clark saw his counsel to self-sufficiency as in no way a challenge to his admonitions to follow the Lord. His enemy, he felt, was not girl's independence but the shallowness of her domestic life. In 1888 Willard, the inspired leader of the Women's Christian Temperance Union, imperiously admonished American girls to action: "Yes, the world wants the best thing; *your best,* and she will smite you stealthily if you do not hand over your gift." She modeled her book for girls, entitled *How to Win,* on a book for boys, and urged them to forsake "reverie" to take "resolute aim" beyond the household to apply their special gifts to the world at large.[60] The discourse of self-reliance confirmed girls' rights and responsibilities to consider themselves as individuals.

Even those in the women's rights community reflected a new attitude toward the female self. Elizabeth Cady Stanton, most known for her demands for women's political rights, urged her sex to self-reliance in an extraordinary existential oration, which she delivered to the U.S. House of Representatives Committee on the Judiciary in January 1892. Arguing the ultimate "solitude of self" she protested the common myth that women could rest in semidependent complacency: "As an individual, she must rely on herself. No matter how much women prefer to lean, to be protected and supported, nor how much men desire to have them do so, they must make the voyage of life alone, and for safety in an emergency, they must know something of the laws of navigation." Stanton gave this address upon her resignation as president of the major suffrage organization in the country, the National American Woman Suffrage Association, and it was published in the feminist *Woman's Journal.* The *Woman's Journal* was initially the creature of Lucy Stone and Henry Blackwell. By 1892, though, the editorship had devolved upon their daughter, the irrepressible Alice Blackwell, whose own efforts to learn the laws of navigation made her a proof-text of Stanton's words. But Blackwell was not alone in appreciating Stanton's wisdom. The House Committee on the Judiciary itself reprinted ten thousand copies of Stanton's address for distribution throughout the country.[61]

When Eva Lovett wrote her advice book *The Making of a Girl* in 1902, conventional opinion advocated self-determination rather than self-suppression. In a chapter entitled "Standards," Lovett encouraged girls to set their own: "The only important thing to that girl, is, that she should do what she is satisfied is the right thing to do." She might suffer for her decision, "but that is what she should do—the thing that she knows to be right." Another book from this era, Eleanor Ames's *Where Are You?* (1897), adopted the language of the mind-cure movement in its urging of girls to "a larger liberty." Like Lovett and Willard, Ames resisted girls' confinement to domestic duties, observing that previously "The furniture of the house has been of far more importance than any knowledge of self." Instead of locating girls within domestic walls, she hoped to give them "knowledge of our location in the universe." Whether engaged in volunteer work for a religious or social cause, or embarked on a new woman's profession, the girl was increasingly counseled to set goals and try to meet them, to avoid "drift."[62]

The words of advisers provide an accessible way of charting changes in ideas of the female self over the late century. The documents of girls themselves provide striking evidence of how that change actually occurred. Whatever middle-class parents' expectations for the school training of their daughters, school attendance involved girls in a complex of cultures which challenged domestic subordination. When girls left school to take up a place in the parlor as family possession in the 1860s, 1870s, and beyond, they discovered themselves unfit for it. They adapted or rebelled in varying ways. Some developed depression. Yet there were many others who were able to hold some of that adolescent identity in abeyance for use at some later time. Girls like Margaret Tileston, who followed a rigorous high school course and graduated in triumph, may have settled into a "stupid" routine for a time, but when that failed to produce the conventional expectation of an appropriate marriage, they had alternative experience, drawn from their varied school days, to return to.

In the latter decades of the nineteenth century, some girls who graduated from high school and went home reemerged sooner rather than later. By the

1890s girl graduates in diverse communities took up teaching or one of the new respectable employments increasingly available to middle-class young women before marriage. Indeed, one of the ways that the cohort of schoolgirls of the 1860s and 1870s might have reflected its own postgraduation malaise was in its later acquiescence in the paid work of its daughters.

Culture did not change overnight, of course, and domestic admonitions still packed enormous power, even in the twentieth century. Yet the ambition for refinement which had encouraged parents to send girls to school decades before had opened an array of unexpected consequences. The competitive meritocracy of the classroom, with seats arranged hierarchically, presented a harsh but telling counterpoint to the gentle nurturance of idealized domesticity. The membership in a corporate senior class conveyed a surprising foreshadowing of political equality. Visits to bake shops and soda fountains challenged a service-oriented domestic culture with a nascent consumerism based on indulging rather than suppressing desire. And the walking parties of friends filling the city streets meant that domestic modesty would yield ground to light-hearted and public display.

For Victorian girls, the licensing of desire and display was revolutionary. Victorian rectitude had exacted a heavy tribute from middle-class Victorian girls. Girls trying to be good and protect their nerves had learned that they needed to censor or repress joy itself, whether in each other, as did Lucy Breckinridge, or in their studies, as had Fredrica Ballard. School peer culture contributed to the changing of that culture and the legitimizing of joy, whether in friends, work, or the streets themselves.

Guardians of Victorianism assessed the costs. G. Stanley Hall's stage-defining work entitled *Adolescence,* published in 1904, provided a name for a worry that had characterized much of the late nineteenth century. From Elizabeth Blackwell's midcentury concerns about early precocity, to the debates about the "Girl of the Period," myriad advisers had worried about the consequences of this new popular culture for the nation's daughters. Hall saw girls' attention to their looks, and their "activity of mind and body" as indicative of their "individuality," and worried that it would diminish the "altruism," the selflessness, necessary for "home and posterity."[63] His analysis was correct: trained in self-culture and defined by school spirit, girls increasingly resisted a generic femininity which would confine them to home and define them by family service. Writing just after the turn of the century, Hall wrote as a late Victorian, hoping to protect a mystified, albeit sexualized, femininity from the many dangers of the modern world. But he was too late to rescue the increasing numbers of middle-class girls who went to school. Well before the turn of the century, the cultures of school and peers propelled these girls of the middle class into the streets, into popular culture, and into a consciousness of an augmented individuality which took them well beyond their mothers' houses.

Notes

Introduction

1. Florence C. Peck, Florence C. Peck diaries, 11 Nov. 1901, Manuscripts and Archives Division (New York: New York Public Library; Astor, Lenox and Tilden Foundations).

2. Today, a rich critical literature suggests the ways in which Jo March provided an alternative identity for intellectual girls within the context of Victorian domesticity. Barbara Sicherman, "Reading *Little Women:* The Many Lives of a Text," in *U.S. History as Women's History: New Feminist Essays,* ed. Linda K. Kerber, Alice Kessler-Harris, and Kathryn Kish Sklar (Chapel Hill: University of North Carolina Press, 1995), 264, for instance, argues that generations of readers, up to the present, "reading individualistically," have seen "Jo as an intellectual and a writer, the liberated woman they sought to become." Such readings are to some degree ahistorical, projecting contemporary delight on capers which caused Jo herself (and, evidence suggests, Alcott as well), real Victorian guilt and dismay. As Anne Scott MacLeod, "The *Caddie Woodlawn* Syndrome: American Girlhood in the Nineteenth Century," in *A Century of Childhood,* ed. Mary Lynn Heininger et al. (Rochester, N.Y.: Strong Museum, 1984), 108–9, argues, though, "Generations of girls knew as did Jo that adolescence was the beginning of limitations and restraints that would last the rest of their lives." On another Alcott heroine, Jill of *Jack and Jill,* MacLeod notes: "Alcott tells the story with a certain realism. She never minimizes the hardness of the lessons for a spirited girl."

3. Mary P. Ryan, *Cradle of the Middle Class: The Family in Oneida County, New York, 1790–1865* (Cambridge: Cambridge University Press, 1981), 193–94; for a critical perspective on the Victorian family, see Joan Jacobs Brumberg, *Fasting Girls: The Emergence of Anorexia Nervosa as a Modern Disease* (Cambridge: Harvard University Press, 1988).

For a discussion of similar themes in Britain, see Elaine Showalter, *The Female Malady: Women, Madness, and English Culture, 1830–1980* (New York: Pantheon, 1985).

4. Nancy Armstrong, *Desire and Domestic Fiction: A Political History of the Novel* (New York: Oxford University Press, 1987).

5. Ari Joel Perlmann, "Education and the Social Structure of an American City: Social Origins and Education Attainments in Providence, R.I., 1880–1925," Ph.D. diss. (Cambridge: Harvard University, 1980), 278. The book derived from this dissertation, Joel Perlmann, *Ethnic Differences: Schooling and Social Structure Among the Irish, Italians, Jews, and Blacks in an American City, 1880–1935,* Interdisciplinary Perspectives on Modern History (Cambridge: Cambridge University Press, 1988), omits much material contained in his exhaustive dissertation.

6. Henry James, "The Speech of American Women," *Harper's Bazar* 41, no. 2 (1906–7): 17.

7. Joseph Kett, *Rites of Passage: Adolescence in America, 1790 to the Present* (New York: Basic, 1978), 137.

8. The term came into usage with the two-volume tome by Granville Stanley Hall, *Adolescence: Its Psychology and Its Relations to Physiology, Anthropology, Sociology, Sex, Crime, Religion, and Education.* (New York: D. Appleton, 1904).

9. Albert Browne to daughter Nellie, 28 Jan. 1859, MC 232, Schlesinger Library (Cambridge: Radcliffe Institute, Harvard University).

10. Elliott West and Paula Evans Petrik, *Small Worlds: Children and Adolescents in America, 1850–1950* (Lawrence: University Press of Kansas, 1992), 4.

11. See Evelyn Brooks Higginbotham, *Righteous Discontent: The Women's Movement in the Black Baptist Church, 1880–1920* (Cambridge: Harvard University Press, 1993), 188, for the introduction of the term "politics of respectability." "From the perspective of the Baptist women and others who espoused the importance of 'manners and morals,' the concept of respectability signified self-esteem, racial pride, and something more." Ida B. Wells-Barnett, *Crusade for Justice: The Autobiography of Ida B. Wells,* ed. Alfreda M. Duster (Chicago: University of Chicago Press, 1970), 21; (Mary) Elizabeth Morrissey, diary, 21 Mar., 18 Jul. 1876 (Boston: Boston Public Library).

1. Daughters' Lives and the Work of the Middle-Class Home

1. Jeanne Boydston, *Home and Work: Housework, Wages, and the Ideology of Labor in the Early Republic* (New York: Oxford University Press, 1990).

2. Faye E. Dudden, *Serving Women: Household Service in Nineteenth-Century America* (Middletown, Conn.: Wesleyan University Press, 1983), 10.

3. Catharine Esther Beecher, *A Treatise on Domestic Economy, for the Use of Young Ladies at Home, and at School.* (Boston: T. H. Webb, 1842), 27–28, 267, 345, 362. Beecher's *Treatise* reveals that she retained some ambivalence on this subject, however, because as she elaborated detailed directions for the chores of housework, she envisioned domestics taking instruction on the upkeep of the parlor, making beds, and doing dishes.

4. Hasia R. Diner, *Erin's Daughters in America: Irish Immigrant Women in the Nineteenth Century* (Baltimore: Johns Hopkins University Press, 1983), 32. Diner has documented the growth of a new cult of celibacy among Irish youth as families grew reluctant to subdivide barely adequate bits of bog among several sons. Superfluous daughters in massive numbers ventured overseas, where home habits of domestic service predisposed them to fill the growing need in American homes. Women accounted for 52.9 percent of Irish immigrants, with very few of them children. (Only 5 percent of Irish immigrants, compared with 28 percent of Jewish immigrants, were children.) Between 1850 and 1887 more than 66 percent of all immigrants were between the ages of fifteen and thirty-five. For the last statistic, see Carol S. Lasser, "Mistress, Maid, and Market: The Transformation of Domestic Service in New England, 1790–1870," Ph.D. diss. (Cambridge: Harvard University, 1981), 243.

5. Catharine Esther Beecher and Harriet Beecher Stowe, *The American Woman's Home; or, Principles of Domestic Science, Being a Guide to the Formation and Maintenance of Economical, Healthful, Beautiful, and Christian Homes.* (New York: J. B. Ford, 1869), 13.

6. Ibid., 3, 308–9.

7. Ibid., 309, 317.

8. Ibid., 318.

9. Joel Myerson and Daniel Shealy, eds., *Journals of Louisa May Alcott* (Boston: Little, Brown, 1989), 16–17, 65; Joel Myerson and Daniel Shealy, eds., *Selected Letters of Louisa May Alcott* (Boston: Little, Brown, 1987), xx.

10. Myerson and Shealy, *Journals of Louisa May Alcott,* 166.

11. Alcott's heroine Cristie Devon agrees to work only "if I need not do it with a shiftless Irish girl to drive me distracted by pretending to help." Louisa May Alcott, *Work: A Story of Experience* (New York: Arno, 1977), 245.

12. Margaret Harding Tileston [Edsall], diary, 24 Nov. 1878, MC 354, Schlesinger Library (Cambridge: Radcliffe Institute, Harvard University).

13. Dudden, *Serving Women,* 1. "In general, the higher proportion of native-born among servants in cities or states, the lower the ratio of servants per thousand families." David M. Katzman, *Seven Days a Week: Women and Domestic Service in Industrializing America* (New York: Oxford University Press, 1978), 63–64. For the rates of hiring, see Daniel E. Sutherland, *Americans and Their Servants: Domestic Service in the United States from 1800 to 1920* (Baton Rouge: Louisiana State University Press, 1981), 59–61, 66.

14. David Katzman sees as early as 1880 a downturn in the hiring of domestic servants in all areas of the country except for the West. Katzman, *Seven Days a Week,* 55–56.

15. Ruth Schwartz Cowan, *More Work for Mother: The Ironies of Household Technology from the Open Hearth to the Microwave* (New York: Basic, 1983), 121, for instance, estimates that "prior to industrialization" as many as one-half of the nation's households included resident domestic servants, many of them "helpers" in farm production, and that "during the nineteenth century, the relative number of households employing full-time servants probably fell." Also see Lasser, "Mistress, Maid, and Market," 283. On

the share of household income spent on servants, see Sutherland, *Americans and Their Servants,* 14.

16. Christine Stansell, *City of Women: Sex and Class in New York, 1789–1860* (New York: Knopf, 1986), 156; Beecher and Stowe, *The American Woman's Home,* 319; Alice Cone Perry, *A Valley Family,* ed. Clinton C. Gardner and Loren Cone-Coleman (Norwich, Vt., 1988), 32. Perry noted in her memoir, written in 1957, that her grandmother Almira Morris took good care of her help, tending them in sickness—a paternalist model rather than one based simply on market relations.

17. Boydston, *Home and Work,* 79.

18. Boydston, *Home and Work,* 83; Marlene Deahl Merrill, ed., *Growing Up in Boston's Gilded Age: The Journal of Alice Stone Blackwell, 1872–1874* (New Haven: Yale University Press, 1990), 233, 185.

19. Beecher and Stowe, *The American Woman's Home,* 314; Louisa May Alcott, *Eight Cousins; or, The Aunt-Hill* (Boston: Little, Brown, 1874), 93; Louisa May Alcott, *An Old-Fashioned Girl* (Boston: Roberts Brothers, 1870), 164–65.

20. Mary Ashton Rice Livermore, *What Shall We Do with Our Daughters? Superfluous Women, and Other Lectures* (Boston: Lee and Shepard, 1883); Marion Harland [Mary Virginia Terhune], *Eve's Daughters; or, Common Sense for Maid, Wife, and Mother* (New York: J. R. Anderson and H. S. Allen, 1882), 105. Black mothers may well have taught different lessons. Ida Wells-Barnett wrote that in her African-American home the "job" of her and her siblings "was to go to school and to learn all we could." Rather than spurning housework, however, her mother insisted that her children learn both lessons: "She taught us to do the work of the home—each had a regular task besides schoolwork." Wells knew that this education set her apart from many other girls of the time: "I often compare her work in training her children to that of other women who had not her handicaps." Ida B. Wells-Barnett, *Crusade for Justice: The Autobiography of Ida B. Wells,* ed. Alfreda M. Duster (Chicago: University of Chicago Press, 1970), 9.

21. Beecher and Stowe, *The American Woman's Home,* 317; Agnes Hamilton, diary, 28 Jun. 1866, MC 278, M-24, Hamilton family papers, Schlesinger Library (Cambridge: Radcliffe Institute, Harvard University).

22. May Mackintosh, "An Ideal Education of Girls," *Education* 6, no. 8 (1886): 647–51.

23. Helen P. Kennedy, M.D., "Effect of High School Work upon Girls During Adolescence," *Pedagogical Seminary* 3, no. 3 (June 1896): 478.

24. E. Prentiss, *Stepping Heavenward.* (New York: A. D. F. Randolph, 1869), 75; William M. Thayer, *The Poor Girl and True Woman; or, Elements of Woman's Success, Drawn from the Life of Mary Lyon and Others: A Book for Girls* (Boston: Gould and Lincoln, 1859), 266.

25. Emily Marshall Eliot [Morison], diary, 10 Oct. 1869, 13 Aug. 1871, A/M861, Emily Marshall Eliot Morison papers, 1874–1883, Schlesinger Library (Radcliffe Institute, Harvard University); Martha Josephine Moore, diary, vol. 2, no. 631, 4 May 1863, Frank Liddell Richardson papers, Southern Historical Collection (Chapel Hill: Wilson

Library, University of North Carolina); Mary D. Robertson, ed., *Lucy Breckinridge of Grove Hill: The Journal of a Virginia Girl, 1862–1864* (Kent, Ohio: Kent State University Press, 1979), 170.

26. Harland, *Eve's Daughters,* 324–36; George Stewart Stokes, *Agnes Repplier: Lady of Letters* (Philadelphia: University of Pennsylvania Press, 1949), 14; Prentiss, *Stepping Heavenward,* 75.

27. [Edsall], diary, 13, 14 Jul. 1885; "Annie Burnham Cooper Diary," in *Private Pages: Diaries of American Women 1830s–1970s,* ed. Penelope Franklin (New York: Ballantine, 1986), 147.

28. Jessie Baldwin to Annie Ware Winsor, 20 Aug. 1884, MC 322, papers of Annie Ware Winsor Allen, 1884–1950, Schlesinger Library (Cambridge: Radcliffe Institute, Harvard University); Jessie Wendover, diary, 25 Apr. 1887, Ac. 2383, MC 463, J. Wendover papers, Special Collections and University Archives (New Brunswick, N.J.: Rutgers University Libraries); Florence C. Peck, Florence C. Peck diaries, 1898–1903, Manuscripts and Archives Division (New York: New York Public Library; Astor, Lenox and Tilden Foundations).

29. For instance, see the diary of seventeen-year-old Catherine Hardenburgh, who seemed to have responsibility for managing the household in the absence of her mother. Catherine Hardenburgh, diary, Ac. 552, Hardenburgh family papers, Special Collections and University Archives (New Brunswick, N.J.: Rutgers University Libraries).

30. Gates's story for a high school student newspaper ended with the youthful protagonist in tears, a classic tale of girlish incompetence in the kitchen repeated throughout Victorian domestic literature. Annie C. Gates, "My First Experience in Cooking," *Oak, Lily, and Ivy,* October 1891; Mary Bartine, diary, 9 Mar. 1897, Ac. 2702, Gaston family papers, Special Collections and University Archives (New Brunswick, N.J.: Rutgers University Libraries); Eleanor Hooper to Annie Ware Winsor, 16 Nov. 1880, MC 322, papers of Annie Ware Winsor Allen, 1884–1950, Schlesinger Library (Cambridge: Radcliffe Institute, Harvard University); "Annie Burnham Cooper Diary," 149.

31. Hamilton, diary, 29 Jul. 1886, MC 278, M-24; Fredrica Louisa Ballard Westervelt, *A Victorian Childhood* (Privately printed), 96; Emma E., "Our Post-Office Box," *Harper's Young People* 6, no. 290 (1885): 287.

32. Boydston, *Home and Work,* 51.

33. Harland, *Eve's Daughters,* 327; Frances Willard, *How to Win: A Book for Girls* (1888), 31.

34. Annie Ware Winsor [Allen], "Country Doctor: Frederick Winsor, 1829–1889," 30–31; Annie Ware Winsor [Allen] to mother, Ann Ware Winsor, summer 1883, both MC 322, papers of Annie Ware Winsor Allen, 1884–1950, Schlesinger Library (Cambridge: Radcliffe Institute, Harvard University).

35. Annie Ware Winsor [Allen], journal, 13 Jan. 1884; Frederick Winsor to daughter Annie Ware Winsor [Allen], 18 Oct. 1885, both MC 322, papers of Annie Ware Winsor Allen, 1884–1950, Schlesinger Library (Cambridge: Radcliffe Institute, Harvard University).

36. Mary Thomas [Lumpkin], diary, 7 Jul. 1873, Joseph Henry Lumpkin papers, Hargrett Rare Book and Manuscript Library (Athens: University of Georgia); "Our Post-Office Box," *Harper's Young People,* 4 March 1884, 287; "The Letter-Box," *St. Nicholas* 5 (July 1878): 637.

37. Harland, *Eve's Daughters,* 72.

38. [Edsall], diary, 22 Apr., 10, 29 May, 11 Jun. 1878, 22 Feb., 22 May, 29 Jun. 1881, 16 Jul. 1886.

39. Anna Kohler, "Children's Sense of Money," *Studies in Education* 1 (March 1897): 323–31; Wendover, diary, passim.

40. Agnes Garrison, diary, Garrison family papers, Sophia Smith Collection (Northampton, Mass.: Smith College); *Sixteenth Annual Report of the Bureau of Statistics of Labor* (Boston: Wright and Potter, 1885), 185; Florence C., "Our Post-Office Box," *Harper's Young People* 6, no. 310 (1885): 767; Marian Nichols, diary, 23 Aug. 1884, 20 Jan. 1885, A-170, papers of the Nichols-Shurtleff family, 1780–1953, Schlesinger Library (Cambridge: Radcliffe Institute, Harvard University); Anne Firor Scott, Introduction to Jane Addams, *Democracy and Social Ethics,* ed. Scott (Cambridge: Harvard University Press, 1964), x.

41. [Edsall], diary, 23 Sep., 29 Oct., 11, 12 Dec. 1882.

42. [Edsall], diary, 5, 8 Dec. 1885.

43. [Edsall], diary, 17 Feb., 21 Apr. 1887.

44. Robert D. Clark, "Ada Harris, Teenager: Oswego County, New York, 1873," *New York History* 66 (January 1985): 29, 32–33.

45. Myra Etta Dolloff, diary, 9 Feb. 1877, Dolloff family papers (Concord, N.H.: New Hampshire Historical Society); Kate Upson [Clark], diary, 6 Jun. 1864, 20, 21 Jul., 21 Aug. 1865; Kate Upson Clark, "My Reminiscences," all Kate Upson Clark papers, 1851–1935, Sophia Smith Collection (Northampton, Mass.: Smith College).

46. Lydia Maria (Francis) Child, *The Frugal Housewife, Dedicated to Those Who Are Not Ashamed of Economy* (Boston: Carter, Hendee, and Babcock, 1831), 94; Washington Gladden, "A Talk with Girls and Their Mothers," *St. Nicholas* 7 (May 1880): 521.

47. Harland, *Eve's Daughters,* 323.

48. (Mary) Elizabeth Morrissey, diary, 18, 21 Mar., 18 Jul. 1876 (Boston: Boston Public Library).

49. Dorothy M. Johnson, "A Short Moral Essay for Boys and Girls: Or How to Get Rich in a Frontier Town," *Montana* 24, no. 1 (1974): 27–29.

2. Writing and Self-Culture

This chapter is adapted from a previous article, "Inscribing the Self in the Heart of the Family: Diaries and Girlhood in Late-Victorian America," *American Quarterly* (March 1992). Used with permission.

1. William M. Thayer, *The Poor Girl and True Woman; or, Elements of Woman's Success, Drawn from the Life of Mary Lyon and Others: A Book for Girls* (Boston: Gould and Lincoln, 1859), 21.

2. One study comments on the failure of adult diarists to comment on reading, surprising given the omnipresence of books. Louise L. Stevenson, *The Victorian Homefront: American Thought and Culture, 1860–1880* (New York: Twayne, 1991), 24. If true (and my evidence calls that into question), the same was certainly not true for girl writers, for whom reading was often a keenly lived experience, which provided the substance of written reflection.

3. Heloise Edwina Hersey, *To Girls: A Budget of Letters* (Boston: Small, Maynard, 1901); Margaret Harding Tileston [Edsall], diary, 27 Feb. 1881, 15 Aug., 5 Oct. 1887, MC 354, Schlesinger Library (Cambridge: Radcliffe Institute, Harvard University); Kate Upson [Clark], diary, 14 Jul. 1864, Kate Upson Clark papers, 1851–1935, Sophia Smith Collection (Northampton, Mass.: Smith College).

4. Hannah Davis, diary, 20 Oct. 1851 (Columbus: Ohio Historical Society).

5. "The Letter-Box," *St. Nicholas* 1 (March 1874): 308. Mark Twain, *Adventures of Huckleberry Finn* (New York: Norton, 1962), 84–85; thanks to Dan Heaton for this reference. For an example of florid poetry see Robert D. Clark, "Ada Harris, Teenager: Oswego County, New York, 1873," *New York History* 66 (January 1985): 34.

6. For this phrase, see Karen Lystra, *Searching the Heart: Women, Men, and Romantic Love in Nineteenth-Century America* (New York: Oxford University Press, 1989), 12.

7. Richard Rabinowitz, *The Spiritual Self in Everyday Life: The Transformation of Personal Religious Experience in Nineteenth-Century New England* (Boston: Northeastern University Press, 1989), 39, 164, 257. Foucault stresses the role of authority in shaping self-scrutiny: "The obligation to confess is now relayed through so many different points, is so deeply ingrained in us, that we no longer perceive it as the effect of a power that constrains us." Michel Foucault, *The History of Sexuality*, vol. 1, *Introduction*, trans. Robert Hurley (New York: Pantheon, 1978), 60.

8. Agnes Repplier, "The Deathless Diary," *Atlantic Monthly* 79 (May 1897): 475, 642; Agnes Repplier, *In Our Convent Days* (Boston: Houghton, Mifflin, 1906), 23; Ellen K. Rothman, *Hands and Hearts: A History of Courtship in America* (New York: Basic Books, 1984), 9; Peter Gay, *The Bourgeois Experience, Victoria to Freud*, vol. 1, *Education of the Senses* (New York: Oxford University Press, 1984), 448. Both Gay and Rothman concur that diary writing was more common among women than among men.

9. W. S. Jerome, "How to Keep a Journal," *St. Nicholas* 5 (October 1878): 789.

10. Testimonials to the importance of handwriting include Emily Marshall Eliot [Morison], diary, 20 Aug., 10 Oct., 3, 14 Dec. 1869, 15 Nov. 1870, A/M861, Emily Marshall Eliot Morison papers, 1874–1883, Schlesinger Library (Cambridge: Radcliffe Institute, Harvard University); [Edsall], diary, 7 Jun. 1878, 13 Dec. 1882; [Clark], diary, 6 Jun. 1862. Testimonials to less stress: [Clark], diary, 19 Jul. 1864; Elizabeth Ellery Dana, diary, 18 Dec. 1864, A-85, Dana family papers, 1822–1956, Schlesinger Library (Cambridge: Radcliffe Institute, Harvard University).

11. Jerome, "How to Keep a Journal," 790–91.

12. Foucault's second volume locates the original "techniques of the self" in Greco-Roman culture, "as those intentional and voluntary actions by which men not only set

themselves rules of conduct, but also seek to transform themselves." Michel Foucault, *The History of Sexuality,* vol. 2, *The Use of Pleasure,* trans. Robert Hurley (New York: Pantheon, 1985), 10–11. The conflict between romanticism and moralism, especially in adults' relations with youth, is apparent in the historiography of Victorianism. Thus Gay celebrates the nineteenth century as "the golden age of the diary" and argues that self-reflective diaries "became almost obligatory companions to a class endowed with a modicum of leisure." At the same time, he notes that parents would "open children's letters, superintend their reading, chaperon their visitors, inspect their underwear." Gay asserts, "If parents exacted truthfulness from their children, this all too often served as a screen for the brutal assertion of adult power, as an arrogant, and at time prurient, invasion of young lives." Gay, *Bourgeois Experience,* 1: 446–448. Unlike the romantic explorations of some Victorian adults, girls' diaries in theory did not permit uninhibited freedom but rather were designed for internalizing adult dicta.

13. Margaret H. Eckerson, "Jottings Versus Doings," *St. Nicholas* 6 (February 1879): 282.

14. Kate Gannett Wells, "She Couldn't: A Story for Big Girls," *St. Nicholas* 6 (May 1879): 462–468. Dora's self-soothing through eating is interesting here in terms of work on the association between eating disorders and female identity. See especially Joan Jacobs Brumberg, *Fasting Girls: The Emergence of Anorexia Nervosa as a Modern Disease* (Cambridge: Harvard University Press, 1988).

15. David D. Hall notes the imprecations of seventeenth-century moralists who warned, "Let not your Children read these vain Books, profane Ballads, and filthy songs. Throw away all fond and amorous Romances, and fabulous Histories of Giants . . . for these fill the Heads of Children with vain, silly and idle imaginations." David Hall, "The Uses of Literacy in New England," in *Printing and Society in Early America,* ed. William Leonard Joyce (Worcester: American Antiquarian Society, 1983), 17.

16. Ann Fabian, *The Unvarnished Truth: Personal Narratives in Nineteenth-Century America* (Berkeley: University of California Press, 2000); Susan Miller, *Assuming the Positions: Cultural Pedagogy and the Politics of Commonplace Writing* (Pittsburgh: University of Pittsburgh Press, 1998), 13.

17. Trumbull quoted in Rothman, *Hands and Hearts,* 8.

18. One farmer's daughter who relished the book was Victoria Lodge, who read Prentiss at the age of sixteen in 1874. She reported, "I want to be good and do good but I almost always end there. I read Stepping Heavenward to day and in it I read that just so far as we obey God just so far we love him. . . . I wish I could stop speaking sharply to mother. It is disrespectful and wrong. Must stop now and study my lesson." Quoted in Harvey J. Graff, *Conflicting Paths: Growing up in America* (Cambridge: Harvard University Press, 1995), 223. For other testimonials, Georgia Mercer [Boit], diary, 23 Jul. 1871, A 99, Cabot family papers, Schlesinger Libraray (Cambridge: Radcliffe Institute, Harvard University); Agnes Hamilton, quoted in Barbara Sicherman, "Sense and Sensibility: A Case Study of Women's Reading in Late-Victorian America," in *Reading in*

America: Literature and Social History, ed. Cathy N. Davidson (Baltimore: Johns Hopkins University Press, 1989), 207.

19. E. Prentiss, *Stepping Heavenward* (New York: A. D. F. Randolph, 1869), 7, 75.

20. On "writing it oneself," see Ola Winslow, biography of Elizabeth Prentiss in *Notable American Women* (Cambridge: Harvard University Press, 1971), 96; [Boit], diary, 23 Jul. 1871.

21. Mary Boit [Cabot], diary, 3 Dec. 1890, 30 Aug. 1891, A 99, Cabot family papers, Schlesinger Libraray (Cambridge: Radcliffe Institute, Harvard University).

22. Charlotte Norris, diary, 1886, Sophia Smith Collection (Northampton, Mass.: Smith College); Marian Nichols, diary, 27 Jan. 1892, A-170, papers of the Nichols-Shurtleff family, 1780–1953, Schlesinger Library (Cambridge: Radcliffe Institute, Harvard University). An early focus of the debate between prescription and behavior was on expression of sexuality. See Carl Deglar, "What Ought to Be and What Was: Women's Sexuality in the Nineteenth Century," *American Historical Review* 79 (December 1974): 1479–90; Gay, *Bourgeois Experience,* vol. 1; Lystra, *Searching the Heart.*

23. Diary of Alice James, as quoted in Jean Strouse, *Alice James: A Biography* (Boston: Houghton Mifflin, 1980), 87; Henry James quoted in Jean Strouse, "Private Strife: Some Social Consequences of the Anatomical Distinction Between the Sexes," in *Women and Higher Education in American History,* ed. John Mack Faragher, Florence Howe (New York: Norton, 1988), 11.

24. Agnes Hamilton, diary, 7 Jan. 1884, 10 Aug., 12 Dec. 1886, 31 Jul. 1887, MC 278, M-24, Hamilton family papers, Schlesinger Library (Cambridge: Radcliffe Institute, Harvard University).

25. Hamilton, diary, 1 Jan. 1888.

26. In A. A. Brill, trans. and ed., "The History of the Psychoanalytic Movement," in *The Basic Writings of Sigmund Freud* (New York: Modern Library, 1938), 933, Freud himself attributes the origins of psychoanalysis to Josef Breuer's work with hysteria. Elaine Showalter, *The Female Malady: Women, Madness, and English Culture, 1830–1980* (New York: Pantheon, 1985), 155, champions the role of the patient Bertha Pappenheim [Anna O.]: "Anna O., in fact, was the inventor of the 'talking cure' of psychoanalysis, Breuer's partner in a remarkably shared and egalitarian therapeutic exchange." Brumberg, *Fasting Girls,* 138, suggests that Victorian girls lacked "voice" and resorted to appetite as one way of "speaking." "Since emotional freedom was not a common prerogative of the Victorian adolescent girl, it seems reasonable to assert that unhappiness was likely to be expressed in nonverbal forms of behavior." However, like therapy, the diary represented one solution to the problem of emotional restraint that Brumberg sees embodied in food refusal.

27. This term is introduced and explored in Katherine Dalsimer, *Female Adolescence: Psychoanalytic Reflections on Literature* (New Haven: Yale University Press, 1986). Nancy Chodorow, *The Reproduction of Mothering: Psychoanalysis and the Sociology of Gender* (Berkeley: University of California Press, 1978), 130, notes that adolescents "replay"

early maternal separation, and that this conflict is more intense for girls, for whom maternal identification is less completely disrupted in early childhood.

28. [Edsall], diary, 4, 7, 11 Jan. 1882; Helen Marcia Hart, diary, 9 Oct. 1862, A/H325, Schlesinger Library (Cambridge: Radcliffe Institute, Harvard University).

29. [Cabot], diary, 10, 11 Aug. 1891.

30. Mary Thomas [Lumpkin], diary, 1 Jul. 1873, Joseph Henry Lumpkin papers, Hargrett Rare Book and Manuscript Library (Athens: University of Georgia); Rothman, *Hands and Hearts,* 224.

31. Harriet Burton [Laidlaw], diary, M-133, 20 Apr. 1887, 1 Jan., 27 Jul., 23 Sep. 1888, 29 Feb. [*sic*] 1890, Harriet Burton Laidlaw papers, 1851–1958, Schlesinger Library (Cambridge: Radcliffe Institute, Harvard University). See also correspondence between fifteen-year-olds Eleanor Hooper and Annie Winsor: "Perhaps but few girls have experienced this longing so soon as we, for as a rule, womanhood comes before such feelings can grow while we are but girls in our first teens. . . . There are few girls with such mature, intense natures as we have. In truth, as far as I can find out, we have the thoughts and feelings of women with the few years and inexperience of little more than children." Eleanor Hooper to Annie Ware Winsor, 7 Sep. 1880, MC 322, papers of Annie Ware Winsor Allen, 1884–1950, Schlesinger Library (Cambridge: Radcliffe Institute, Harvard University,).

32. Charlotte Perkins Gilman, *Charlotte Perkins Gilman Reader: "The Yellow Wallpaper" and Other Fiction,* ed. Ann J. Lane (New York: Pantheon, 1980), 7.

33. [Laidlaw], diary, 29 Feb. [*sic*], 10 Mar., n.d., 1890.

34. Charlotte Perkins Gilman, *The Diaries of Charlotte Perkins Gilman,* ed. Denise D. Knight (Charlottesville: University Press of Virginia, 1994), 98. Writing was clearly one of the strategies which helped Charlotte Perkins Gilman negotiate her difficult life. It was a device of self-management as much as self-indulgence. At the age of twenty-one, she inscribed her New Year's resolutions for 1882, so similar in kind to those kept by other young female diarists: "I have on my mind this year three cares. (So far.)
1. Others first.
2. *Correct and necessary* speech only.
3. Don't waste a minute."
She combined these messages with another resolution. "Furthermore, I wish to form the habit of *writing* as much I can." Gilman was looking to curtail her speech, perhaps as indulgent and exhibitionist. When Gilman "broke down" in 1887 following her marriage and the birth of her daughter, she gave up her diary as part of the "cure" she would experience at the hands of S. Weir Mitchell. Gilman, *Diaries,* 384.

35. Judith P. Salzman, "Save the World, Save Myself: Responses to Problematic Attachment," in *Making Connections: The Relational Worlds of Adolescent Girls at Emma Willard School,* ed. Carol Gilligan, Nona Lyons, and Trudy J. Hanmer (Cambridge: Harvard University Press, 1990), 111, asserts the significance of attachment to adolescent development. The historian Mary Kelley has suggested that women's autobiographies

often represented "an alternative tradition" in which identity is constructed "in relation to others" rather than as a journey toward autonomy. Mary Kelley, Introduction to *The Power of Her Sympathy: The Autobiography and Journal of Catharine Maria Sedgwick,* ed. Mary Kelley (Boston: Massachusetts Historical Society, 1993), 5.

3. Reading and the Development of Taste

1. William J. Gilmore, *Reading Becomes a Necessity of Life: Material and Cultural Life in Rural New England, 1780–1835* (Knoxville: University of Tennessee Press, 1989), 318. Joel Perlmann and Dennis Shirley, "When Were New England Women Literate," *William and Mary Quarterly,* January 1991, 50–67, contend that many New England women were literate in the colonial era, challenging the standard theory that women were educated in the aftermath of the American Revolution in order to supply "republican mothers" for the new nation. Perlmann and Shirley's argument finds support in David Hall's suggestion that in the colonial era, rates of reading were far higher than suggested by the ability to write, the previous way of calculating literacy. As Hall puts it, "those who were able to read in some degree comprise the vast majority of white colonists, and the print market was potentially very broad." David Hall, "The Uses of Literacy in New England," in *Printing and Society in Early America,* ed. William Leonard Joyce (Worcester, Mass.: American Antiquarian Society, 1983). See also Carl F. Kaestle, "Literacy and Diversity: Themes from a Social History of the American Reading Public," *History of Education Quarterly* 28, no. 4 (Winter 1988): 525.

2. Ronald J. Zboray, "Antebellum Reading and the Ironies of Technological Innovation," in *Reading in America: Literature and Social History,* ed. Cathy N. Davidson (Baltimore: Johns Hopkins University Press, 1989), 190–91.

3. Frank Luther Mott, *A History of American Magazines* (Cambridge: Harvard University Press, 1938).

4. Kate Upson [Clark], diary, 11 May, 9 Aug. 1862, Kate Upson Clark papers, 1851–1935, Sophia Smith Collection (Northampton, Mass.: Smith College).

5. Lois Wells, diary, 10 Apr. 1886, MC-39, Schlesinger Library (Cambridge: Radcliffe Institute, Harvard University); Dee Garrison, *Apostles of Culture: The Public Librarian and American Society, 1876–1920* (New York: Macmillan Information, 1979), 174.

6. Anne M. Boylan, *Sunday School: The Formation of an American Institution, 1790–1880* (New Haven: Yale University Press, 1988), 50; Ida B. Wells-Barnett, *Crusade for Justice: The Autobiography of Ida B. Wells,* ed. Alfreda M. Duster (Chicago: University of Chicago Press, 1970), 21; [Clark], diary, 25 Jan., 15, 17 May 1863.

7. John Tomsich, *A Genteel Endeavor: American Culture and Politics in the Gilded Age* (Stanford: Stanford University Press, 1971), 122.

8. Elizabeth Oakes Smith, "Girls," *Potter's American Monthly* 14, no. 101 (May 1880): 372; Grace Rossman Boone, "The Use of Myths with Children," *Education* 25, no. 5 (January 1905): 303–10.

9. Keddie was published in Boston under the pseudonym Sarah Tytler in 1866, her

advice fashioned as the monologue of a dear aunt advising her niece, in Sarah Tytler, *Sweet Counsel: A Book for Girls* (Boston: Roberts Brothers, 1866), 50; Smith, "Girls," 372. Also see Harriet E. Paine, *Chats with Girls on Self-Culture* (New York: Dodd, Mead, 1891), 107–8.

10. Paine, *Chats with Girls on Self-Culture,* 107–8.

11. On "mire," Smith, "Girls," 372; *St. Nicholas* 7 (May 1880): 523. Other periodicals as well made this point. "Her Town Experience," *Youth's Companion* 57, no. 27 (3 July 1884): 266–67, depicted a city cousin who reads novels on the sly, talks in slang, indulges in illicit escapades and ends in disgrace after running off with a roué who deserts her. An even more pointed attack entitled "What Dime Novels Did," *Youth's Companion* 49, no. 41 (12 October 1876): 334, assaulted the dangerous effects of cheap reading on boys. In this case the hero reads novels during his spare time working at his father's store and is inspired by them to run away; the result again is ruin and disgrace, with a moral: "Keep poisoned reading out of the home."

12. Garrison, *Apostles of Culture,* 74.

13. Louisa May Alcott, *An Old-Fashioned Girl* (Boston: Roberts Brothers, 1870), 22–24; (Mary) Elizabeth Morrissey, diary, 7 Jan. 1876 (Boston: Boston Public Library).

14. Andrew Blake, *Reading Victorian Fiction: The Cultural Context and Ideological Content of the Nineteenth-Century Novel* [Macmillan Studies in Victorian Literature] (Basingstoke, Hampshire: Macmillan, 1989), 72; Elizabeth Gaskell, *The Letters of Mrs. Gaskell,* ed. J. A. U. Shapple and Arthur Pollard (Cambridge: Harvard University Press, 1967), 221.

15. Sarah Browne, diary, 23 Oct. 1858, 28 Oct. 1859, MC 232, Schlesinger Library (Cambridge: Radcliffe Institute, Harvard University).

16. Helen Marcia Hart, diary, 31 Jan. 1864, A/H325, Schlesinger Library (Cambridge: Radcliffe Institute, Harvard University); Mary A. Hill, *Charlotte Perkins Gilman: The Making of a Radical Feminist, 1860–1896* (Philadelphia: Temple University Press, 1980), 27; Agnes Hamilton, diary, 3 Aug. 1884, MC 278, M-24, Hamilton family papers, Schlesinger Library (Cambridge: Radcliffe Institute, Harvard University).

17. Marlene Deahl Merrill, ed., *Growing Up in Boston's Gilded Age: The Journal of Alice Stone Blackwell, 1872–1874* (New Haven: Yale University Press, 1990), 39.

18. W. L. Jacquith, "The Guardians of the Public Taste," *Education* 11, no. 3 (1890); Paine, *Chats with Girls on Self-Culture,* 104; Edith E. W. Gregg, ed., *The Letters of Ellen Tucker Emerson* (Kent, Ohio: Kent State University Press, 1982), 62.

19. Hamilton, diary, [27 Dec.] 1883, 1 Jan. 1884, 25 Mar. 1886.

20. Margaret Harding Tileston [Edsall], diary, 16 Feb., 24 Mar. 1883, 12 Mar. 1886, MC 354, Schlesinger Library (Cambridge: Radcliffe Institute, Harvard University).

21. Smith, "Girls," 367, 372.

22. Frank Luther Mott, *A History of American Magazines* (Cambridge: Harvard University Press, 1938), 2: 359.

23. Merrill, *Journal of Alice Blackwell,* 33, 67, 99, 105, 125.

24. "The Letter-Box," *St. Nicholas* 2 (November 1874): 672; 3 (July 1876): 466.

25. Nancy Mitford, *Savage Beauty: The Life of Edna St. Vincent Millay* (New York: Random House, 2001), 6; "The Letter-Box," *St. Nicholas* 2 (Nov. 1874): 57.

26. "The Letter-Box," *St. Nicholas* 2 (July 1875): 588; 2 (July 1875): 588; Cathy N. Davidson, Introduction to *Revolution and the Word: The Rise of the Novel in America,* ed. Davidson (New York: Oxford University Press, 1986), 3–14.

27. Dodge quoted in Mott, *A History of American Magazines,* 3: 501; "The Letter-Box," *St. Nicholas* (December 1876): 150; 6 (May 1879): 492.

28. Mary D. Robertson, ed., *Lucy Breckinridge of Grove Hill: The Journal of a Virginia Girl, 1862–1864* (Kent, Ohio: Kent State University Press, 1979), 95; "Our Post-Office Box," *Harper's Young People* 5 (12 February 1884): 238; Mary Boit [Cabot], diary, 12, 31 Aug. 1891, A 99, Cabot family papers, Schlesinger Libraray (Cambridge: Radcliffe Institute, Harvard University).

29. Mary Thomas [Lumpkin], diary, 5 Jul. 1873, Joseph Henry Lumpkin papers, Hargrett Rare Book and Manuscript Library (Athens: University of Georgia).

30. Browne, diary, 17 Oct. 1859; Jessie Wendover, diary, 11 Aug. 1885, 12–13 May 1886, Ac. 2383, MC463, J. Wendover papers, Special Collections and University Archives (New Brunswick, N.J.: Rutgers University Libraries).

31. Joan Shelley Rubin, "Listen, My Children: Modes and Functions of Poetry Reading in American Schools, 1880–1950," in *Moral Problems in American Life: New Perspectives on Cultural History,* ed. Karen Halttunen and Lewis Perry (Ithaca, N.Y.: Cornell University Press, 1998), 266, 268, considers the significance of this pedagogical practice, mentioning a succession of volumes issued by different editors from the 1870s into the twentieth century.

32. [Edsall,] diary, 29 Jul. 1884, 15 Jul. 1886.

33. [Edsall], diary, 22 Feb., 26 Jul. 1882. Tileston here quotes the poet Harriet Winslow Sewall (1819–1889).

34. [Edsall], diary, 8 Mar., 25 May, 31 Jul. 1883; Joel Myerson and Daniel Shealy, ed., *Journals of Louisa May Alcott* (Boston: Little, Brown, 1989), 58. Rubin, "Listen, My Children," 267, analogizes reciting poetry with saying prayers for late-century Victorians, especially for readers undergoing their own crises of faith. "To stand before a hushed class and speak edifying lines on Sunday and do the same thing on Monday could make both experiences seem forms of devotion."

35. Maria Grey and Emily Shirreff, "Thoughts on Self-Culture Addressed to Women," in Helsinger, Sheets, and Veeder, *Woman Question,* 3: 27; Paine, *Chats with Girls on Self-Culture,* 49, 111; Elizabeth Barrett Browning, "Aurora Leigh," in Helsinger, Sheets, and Veeder, *Woman Question,* 3: 38.

36. Quoted in Nancy Armstrong, *Desire and Domestic Fiction: A Political History of the Novel* (New York: Oxford University Press, 1987), 221.

37. [Cabot], diary, 1 Jul. 1891; Hamilton, diary, 26 Jan. 1890.

38. Susan Leaphart, ed., "Frieda and Belle Fligelman: A Frontier-City Girlhood in the 1890s," *Montana Episodes* 32, no. 3 (1982): 89; Gregg, *Letters of Ellen Tucker Emerson,* 140; Hamilton, diary, "Friday after Christmas" [n.d.].

39. [Edsall], diary, 17 Jul. 1885; Eleanor Hooper to Annie Ware Winsor, 14 Apr. 1883, MC 322, papers of Annie Ware Winsor Allen, 1884–1950, Schlesinger Library (Cambridge: Radcliffe Institute, Harvard University); [Clark], diary, 31 Dec. 1865.

40. Martha Josephine Moore, diary, vol. 2, 4 Apr. 1863, #631, Frank Liddell Richardson papers, Southern Historical Collection (Chapel Hill: University of North Carolina Library); [Edsall], diary, 21 May 1881, 20 Apr. 1884; 5 May 1887.

41. Mary Custis deButts, ed., *Growing Up in the 1850s: The Journal of Agnes Lee* (Chapel Hill: University of North Carolina Press, 1984), 40; Robertson, *Lucy Breckinridge,* 76; [Edsall], diary, 26, 28 Dec. 1885.

42. [Edsall], diary, 12 Aug. 1884; Robertson, *Lucy Breckinridge,* 136; Merrill, *Journal of Alice Blackwell,* 175; Hamilton, diary, 2 Jan. 1890. Louise Stevenson suggests that probably "little reading took place in bedrooms at night," based on images of bedrooms, few of which had reading lamps. The secretive nature of late-night reading in girls' accounts suggests that it likely did take place in bedrooms, perhaps with carried light. Louise L. Stevenson, *The Victorian Homefront: American Thought and Culture, 1860–1880* (New York: Twayne, 1991), 24.

43. "The Letter-Box," *St. Nicholas* 3 (March 1876): 340.

44. "Sensation Novels," in *Nineteenth-Century Literature Criticism,* ed. Laurie Lanzen Harris (Detroit: Gale Research, 1981), 174; Emily Marshall Eliot [Morison], diary, 14 Aug. 1868, A/M861, Emily Marshall Eliot Morison papers, 1874–1883, Schlesinger Library (Cambridge: Radcliffe Institute, Harvard University), describes reading Collins's *Armadale,* originally published serially in *Cornhill Magazine* in the 1860s. In Robertson, *Lucy Breckinridge,* 150, Breckinridge calls *Woman in White* "interesting." [Clark], diary, 11 May 1862, 12, 14 Aug. 1863.

45. Merrill, *Journal of Alice Blackwell,* 30, 33, 34, 145, 213, 233, 235.

46. Dodge quoted in Mott, *A History of American Magazines,* 3: 501. By 1906, a librarian lamented, *Westward Ho* was no longer being read, nor were Dickens and Scott. Survey conducted by Lutie E. Stearns, "The Problem of the Girl," Conference of Librarians, Narragansett Pier, R.I., June 29–July 6, 1906, *Library Journal* (1906): 103, 105; "The Letter-Box," *St. Nicholas* 2 (April 1875): 388; 3 (May 1876): 469; Wells-Barnett, *Crusade for Justice,* 21.

47. Margaret Oliphant, "Tigresses in Novels," in Helsinger, Sheets, and Veeder, *Woman Question,* 3: 275; deButts, *Journal of Agnes Lee,* 64.

48. Judith Fetterley, *The Resisting Reader: A Feminist Approach to American Fiction* (Bloomington: Indiana University Press, 1978), xii, xx; Merrill, *Journal of Alice Blackwell,* 166; Frances Willard, *How to Win: A Book for Girls* (1888), 29.

49. Caroline Kirkland, "Novels and Novelists," in Helsinger, Sheets, and Veeder, *Woman Question,* 3: 61.

50. Peter Gay, *The Bourgeois Experience, Victoria to Freud,* vol. 2, *The Tender Passion* (New York: Oxford University Press, 1986), 165; Hamilton quoted in Barbara Sicherman, "Sense and Sensibility: A Case Study of Women's Reading in Late-Victorian America," in *Reading in America: Literature and Social History,* ed. Cathy N. Davidson (Balti-

more: Johns Hopkins University Press, 1989), 209; Robertson, *Lucy Breckinridge,* 122, 137.

51. Gay, *Bourgeois Experience,* 2: 164. Gay suggests, 2: 121, that reading unleashes fantasies which are analogous to child's play. In healthy adults and children, those fantasies provide pleasure and enjoyment but do not influence the reader's relation to reality. Sigmund Freud, "Creative Writers and Day-Dreaming," in *The Standard Edition of the Complete Psychological Works of Sigmund Freud,* trans. and ed. James Strachey (London: Hogarth, 1959), 9: 143–58, writes "In spite of all the emotion with which he cathects his world of play, the child distinguishes it quite well from reality." The result of reading can be "a liberation of tensions in our minds. It may even be that not a little of this effect is due to the writer's enabling us thenceforward to enjoy our own day-dreams without self-reproach or shame." As elaborated by Freud's editor Strachey, absorbed reading represents "simultaneous self-absorption and self-abnegation," or a pleasure "akin to that of the 'oral' (pre-Oedipal) phase." Strachey quoted in Sara van den Berg, "Reading Dora Reading: Freud's 'Fragment of an Analysis of a Case of Hysteria,'" *Literature and Psychology* 32, no. 3 (1986): 28; Gay and Freud concur that the result of reading can be pleasurable without being transformative.

Contemporary reader-response theorists grant greater transformative power to both text and reader and to the interaction between the two. Norman Holland, "The Miller's Wife and the Professors: Questions About the Transactive Theory of Reading," *New Literary History* 17 (Spring 1986): 423–47, for instance, describes "the text, the interpersonal situation, or the rules for reading, as all interacting with a self in a feedback . . . *in which the self is the active, creative element.*" Marshall W. Alcorn and Mark Bracher, "Literature, Psychoanalysis, and the Re-Formation of the Self: A New Direction for Reader-Response Theory," *PMLA* 100 (May 1985): 324–54, integrate psychoanalytic perspectives with those of reader-response proponents. They suggest that "what is sometimes called wish *fulfillment* in novels and plays can . . . more plausibly be described as wish *formulation* or the definition of desires which would constitute an alteration or accommodation of the reader's identity theme." They go on to suggest the transformative possibilities of literature as akin to analysis itself: "The process of reading and discussing literatures is similar in a number of crucial ways to the process of psychoanalysis, which is specifically designed to mobilize and alter the internalized structure of the self."

52. Here, Gay's analysis departs from Freud. The implication of Freud, "Creative Writers and Day-Dreaming," 153, is that excessive investment in fantasies can be the basis for hysteria or psychosis. "If phantasies become over-luxuriant and over-powerful, the conditions are laid for an onset of neurosis or psychosis."

53. Blake, *Reading Victorian Fiction,* 62.

54. [Elizabeth Rigby], "'Vanity Fair'—and 'Jane Eyre,'" in Harris, *Nineteenth-Century Literature Criticism,* 3: 45; William Dean Howells, "Heroines of Nineteenth-Century Fiction," in Harris, *Nineteenth-Century Literature Criticism,* 3: 60; Willard, *How to Win,* 102. Mary Kelley, "'Vindicating the Equality of Female Intellect': Women and Authority in the Early Republic," *Prospects* 17 (1992): 5, notes that mature women

remained guilt-ridden over their fascination with novels, with one noting of her reading of Samuel Richardson's *Pamela*, "I am conscious it was wrong." In their monitoring of their daughter's reading, they may well have been applying standards they had difficulty following themselves.

55. Michael Warner, *The Letters of the Republic: Publication and the Public Sphere in Eighteenth-Century America* (Cambridge: Harvard University Press, 1990), 19.

56. [Morison], diary, 27 Aug. 1871; [Cabot], diary, 17 Jun. 1891; Kate Upson [Clark], diary, 16, 26 Nov. 1863; 8, 9, 13 Jan., 5 Feb., 4 Jun. 1864, Kate Upson Clark papers, 1851–1935, Sophia Smith Collection (Northampton, Mass.: Smith College).

57. "The Letter-Box," *St. Nicholas* 3 (January 1876): 205; [Cabot], diary, 17 Apr. 1892; [Edsall], diary, 27 Jan. 1883.

58. Merrill, *Journal of Alice Blackwell*, 214–15.

59. Merrill, *Journal of Alice Blackwell*, 67.

60. Robertson, *Lucy Breckinridge*, 25.

61. Jane Addams, *Twenty Years at Hull House* (New York: Macmillan, 1910), 73.

62. Walt Whitman, "Democratic Vistas," in *Prose Works 1892*, ed. Floyd Stovall (New York: New York University Press, 1964), 424–25.

4. Houses, Families, Rooms of One's Own

1. Jane Addams, "Filial Relations," in *Democracy and Social Ethics* (Cambridge: Harvard University Press, 1964), 82–83; William James, *The Principles of Psychology* (New York: Henry Holt, 1890), 1: 294.

2. "A Further Notion or Two About Domestic Bliss," *Appleton's Journal of Popular Literature, Science, and Art* 3 (March 19, 1870): 328–29.

3. Ari Joel Perlmann, "Education and the Social Structure of an American City: Social Origins and Education Attainments in Providence, R.I., 1880–1925," Ph.D. diss. (Cambridge: Harvard University, 1980), 284.

4. Charlotte Perkins Gilman, *The Home, Its Work and Influence* (New York: McClure, Phillips, 1903), 255.

5. For a full exploration of this topic, see Karen Lystra, *Searching the Heart: Women, Men, and Romantic Love in Nineteenth-Century America* (New York: Oxford University Press, 1989).

6. Colleen McDannell, *The Christian Home in Victorian America, 1840–1900* (Bloomington: Indiana University Press, 1986), 26; Elizabeth Ellery Dana, diary, 1 Jan. 1865, A-85, Dana family papers, 1822–1956, Schlesinger Library (Cambridge: Radcliffe Institute, Harvard University). Norbert Elias, *The Civilizing Process* (New York: Urizen, 1978), 17, sees the back rooms of the Victorian house as the embodiment of an increasing distance between "the behavioral and emotional standards of adults and children."

7. Steven Mintz, *A Prison of Expectations: The Family in Victorian Culture* (New York: New York University Press, 1983), 35; Clifford Edward Clark, *The American Family Home, 1800–1960* (Chapel Hill: University of North Carolina Press, 1986), 40, notes that books of architectural plans promoted the goal of separate bedrooms for each child.

Mrs. [Amelia] Opie, *Madeline's Journal,* Works of Mrs. Opie in Twelve Volumes (Boston: S. G. Goodrich, 1827).

8. Penelope Franklin, ed., Annie Burnham Cooper diary, 8 Jan. 1885, in *Private Pages: Diaries of American Women, 1830s-1970s* (New York: Ballantine, 1986), 152.

9. Joel Myerson and Daniel Shealy, eds., *Journals of Louisa May Alcott* (Boston: Little, Brown, 1989), 59; Joel Myerson and Daniel Shealy, eds., *Selected Letters of Louisa May Alcott* (Boston: Little, Brown, 1987), 6.

10. Elizabeth Collins Cromley, "A History of American Beds and Bedrooms, 1890–1930," in *American Home Life, 1880-1930: A Social History of Spaces and Services,* ed. Jessica H. Foy and Thomas J. Schlereth (Knoxville: University of Tennessee Press, 1992), 126, notes that home decorating books often suggested separate bedrooms "when the children had grown to preadolescence, had become boys and girls." Marion Harland [Mary Virginia Terhune], *Eve's Daughters; or, Common Sense for Maid, Wife, and Mother* (New York: J. R. Anderson and H. S. Allen, 1882), 71.

11. Myerson and Shealy, *Journals of Louisa May Alcott,* 63.

12. Peter N. Stearns, "Girl, Boys, and Emotions: Redefinitions and Historical Change," *Journal of American History* 80, no. 1 (June 1993): 37; Joel Pfister and Nancy Schnog, eds., *Inventing the Psychological: Toward a Cultural History of Emotional Life in America* (New Haven: Yale University Press, 1997), 8. See also Carol Zisowitz Stearns and Peter N. Stearns, *Anger: The Struggle for Emotional Control in America's History* (Chicago: University of Chicago Press, 1986); Carol Zisowitz Stearns and Peter N. Stearns, eds., *Emotion and Social Change: Toward a New Psychohistory* (New York: Holmes and Meier, 1988); Linda W. Rosenzweig, *Another Self: Middle-Class American Women and Their Friends in the Twentieth Century* (New York: New York University Press, 1999).

13. Marlene Deahl Merrill, ed., *Growing Up in Boston's Gilded Age: The Journal of Alice Stone Blackwell, 1872-1874* (New Haven: Yale University Press, 1990), 123, 150; Vivian C. Hopkins, ed., "Diary of an Iowa Farm Girl: Josephine Edith Brown, 1892–1901," *Annals of Iowa* 42, no. 2 (1973): 1 Jan. 1894.

14. Richard Rabinowitz, *The Spiritual Self in Everyday Life: The Transformation of Personal Religious Experience in Nineteenth-Century New England* (Boston: Northeastern University Press, 1989), 104; Jeanne Boydston, *Home and Work: Housework, Wages, and the Ideology of Labor in the Early Republic* (New York: Oxford University Press, 1990), 110.

15. Harriet E. Paine, *Chats with Girls on Self-Culture* (New York: Dodd, Mead, 1891), 163. Ruth Ashmore, "Side Talks with Girls," *Ladies' Home Journal,* August 1894, 16 [hereafter STG]. I refer to Ruth Ashmore, rather than Isabel Mallon, who wrote most of the columns, throughout this manuscript. "Ruth Ashmore" appears to have been nearly an institution, and may or may not have accurately reflected Mallon's perspective. Myerson and Shealy, *Journals of Louisa May Alcott,* 63.

16. Agnes Hamilton, diary, 7 Jan. 1884, MC 278, M-24, Hamilton family papers, Schlesinger Library (Cambridge: Radcliffe Institute, Harvard University); (Mary) Eliza-

beth Morrissey, diary, 30 Apr. 1876 (Boston: Boston Public Library); Charlotte Perkins Gilman, *The Diaries of Charlotte Perkins Gilman*, ed. Denise D. Knight (Charlottesville: University Press of Virginia, 1994), 98; Mary Boit [Cabot], diary, 2 Aug. 1888, A 99, Cabot family papers, Schlesinger Libraray (Cambridge: Radcliffe Institute, Harvard University); Mary D. Robertson, ed., *Lucy Breckinridge of Grove Hill: The Journal of a Virginia Girl, 1862–1864* (Kent, Ohio: Kent State University Press, 1979), 101; Jean Strouse, *Alice James: A Biography* (Boston: Houghton Mifflin, 1980), 87.

17. Nancy Schnog, "Changing Emotions: Moods and the Nineteenth-Century American Woman Writer," in Pfister and Schnog, *Inventing the Psychological*, 90–91, notes the centrality of "cheerfulness" to the enactment of domesticity among grown women. She suggests that Harriet Beecher Stowe and Catharine Beecher's *American Woman's Home* (1869), a promoter of this idea, works from "a premise akin to modern-day behaviorism," suggesting that the " 'habitual' performance of this role will facilitate a woman's successful adjustment to the stance of cheerfulness." Mrs. Burton Kingsland, "Daughter at Sixteen," *Ladies' Home Journal*, March 1894, 4; Ashmore, STG "(The Sunshiny Girl)," May 1895, 20.

18. "A Pleasant Girl," *Youth's Companion* 53 (May 6, 1880).

19. Rabinowitz, *Spiritual Self in Everyday Life*, xxix; Ann Ware Winsor to daughter Annie Ware Winsor, 11 May 1885, MC 322, papers of Annie Ware Winsor Allen, 1884–1950, Schlesinger Library (Cambridge: Radcliffe Institute, Harvard University).

20. For a discussion of how this concern permeated Victorian society and culture see Karen Halttunen, *Confidence Men and Painted Women: A Study of Middle-Class Culture in America, 1830–1870*, Yale Historical Publications (New Haven: Yale University Press, 1982); Paine, *Chats with Girls on Self-Culture*, 182; Annie Ware Winsor [Allen] to mother, Ann Ware Winsor, 19 Feb. 1885, MC 322, papers of Annie Ware Winsor Allen, 1884–1950, Schlesinger Library (Cambridge: Radcliffe Institute, Harvard University).

21. Anna Stevens, diary, insert, privately owned (1895).

22. Margaret Harding Tileston [Edsall], diary, 6 Feb. 1884, MC 354, Schlesinger Library (Cambridge: Radcliffe Institute, Harvard University). For a discussion of hysteria, see Nancy Armstrong, *Desire and Domestic Fiction: A Political History of the Novel* (New York: Oxford University Press, 1987), 94–95; for *anorexia nervosa*, see Joan Jacobs Brumberg, *Fasting Girls: The Emergence of Anorexia Nervosa as a Modern Disease* (Cambridge: Harvard University Press, 1988).

23. See Brumberg, *Fasting Girls*. For a discussion of similar themes in Britain, see *Elaine Showalter, The Female Malady: Women, Madness, and English Culture, 1830–1980* (New York: Pantheon, 1985). Mary P. Ryan, *Cradle of the Middle Class: The Family in Oneida County, New York, 1790–1865* (Cambridge: Cambridge University Press, 1981), 193–94, argues, "The Victorian daughter enjoyed a privileged position in a feminine universe where with relatively little trauma and at an easy pace, she learned her adult gender role from her mother."

24. Ryan, *Cradle of the Middle Class*, 193–94, makes this observation. Nancy Chodo-

row, *The Reproduction of Mothering: Psychoanalysis and the Sociology of Gender* (Berkeley: University of California Press, 1978).

25. Ida Mabel Lancraft, diary, New Haven Colony Historical Society (New Haven, Conn.); Agnes Garrison, diary, 27 Apr. 1881, Sophia Smith Collection (Northampton, Mass.: Smith College); Robertson, *Lucy Breckinridge*, 25.

26. Patricia Ann Meyer Spacks, *The Female Imagination* (New York: Knopf, distributed by Random House, 1975), 150. Florence Nightingale is quoted in Carolyn G. Heilbrun, *Writing a Woman's Life* (New York: Norton, 1988), 118.

27. Mary Custis deButts, ed., *Growing Up in the 1850s: The Journal of Agnes Lee* (Chapel Hill: University of North Carolina Press, 1984), 82, 94.

28. That Woolf changed her mind is revealed in her delicate and affectionate portraits of maternal figures in *To the Lighthouse* and *Mrs. Dalloway.*

29. Elaine Showalter, *A Literature of Their Own: British Women Novelists from Brontë to Lessing* (Princeton: Princeton University Press, 1999), 61; [Cabot], diary, 30 Aug. 1891; Mary Thomas [Lumpkin], diary, 16, 29 Jun., 5 Jul. 1873, Joseph Henry Lumpkin papers, Hargrett Rare Book and Manuscript Library (Athens: University of Georgia). Katherine Dalsimer, *Female Adolescence: Psychoanalytic Reflections on Literature* (New Haven: Yale University Press, 1986), 124, suggests that parental loss complicates the process of adolescent development by blocking normal separation impulses. Instead, the mourning adolescent seeks to sustain rather than to attenuate the maternal bond. Margo Culley, ed., "Helen Ward Brandreth," in *A Day at a Time: The Diary Literature of American Women from 1764 to the Present* (New York: Feminist Press at the City University of New York, 1985), 2 Jan. 1876.

30. Jane P. Tompkins, *Sensational Designs: The Cultural Work of American Fiction, 1790–1860* (New York: Oxford University Press, 1985), 164; [Cabot], diary, 25, 30 Aug. 1891.

31. Myerson and Shealy, *Journals of Louisa May Alcott*, 55. Schnog, "Changing Emotions," 96–99, sees Alcott's 1864 novel *Moods* as representing an acceptance of the naturalness of such moods in girls, at the same time as they must be eradicated for successful womanhood.

32. "No Secrets from Mother," *Youth's Companion* 49 (July 13, 1876): 229. Elias, *Civilizing Process*, 182–90. David H. Flaherty, *Privacy in Colonial New England* (Charlottesville: University Press of Virginia, 1972), 56, writes of colonial New England, "The prevailing theory of family government, while beneficial for the maintenance of good order in a Puritan society, was inimical to personal privacy. It charged the head of the household with the duty of surveillance over the behavior of everyone, of ruling the home with an iron hand and all-seeing eye."

33. Robertson, *Lucy Breckinridge*, 61.

34. Robertson, *Lucy Breckinridge*, 96, 99.

35. Merrill, *Journal of Alice Blackwell*, 25.

36. Merrill, *Journal of Alice Blackwell*, 25, 73; Ashmore, STG, February 1895, 26.

37. Annie Ware Winsor [Allen], diary inscription, 1884; Ann Ware Winsor to Daughter, Jeannie Winsor, Dec. 1889; Ann Ware Winsor to Daughter, Annie Ware Winsor [Allen], 28 Sep. 1885, all MC 322, papers of Annie Ware Winsor Allen, 1884–1950, Schlesinger Library (Cambridge: Radcliffe Institute, Harvard University).

38. [Allen] to mother, Ann Ware Winsor, 7 Aug. 1886.

39. Mary Winsor to sister, Annie Ware Winsor [Allen], 7 Aug. 1879, 29 Jun. 1883; Annie Ware Winsor [Allen] to sister, Elizabeth Winsor, 12 Sep. 1885; [Allen] to Mother, Ann Ware Winsor, 7 Aug. 1886.

40. Annie Ware Winsor [Allen], journal, MC 322, papers of Annie Ware Winsor Allen, 1884–1950, Schlesinger Library (Cambridge: Radcliffe Institute, Harvard University), n.d. 1881, 20 Jul., 7 Oct., 25 Feb. 1882.

41. [Allen], journal, 30 Jun., 7 Oct. 1882, 15 Apr., 3, 10 Jun., 13 Dec. 1883.

42. [Allen], journal, 19 Jul., 1 Aug. 1882, 2 Aug. 1883, 24 Mar. 1885.

43. [Allen], Journal, May 1885, [n.d. 1885?]. Kate Gannett Wells, "She Couldn't: A Story for Big Girls," *St. Nicholas* 6 (May 1879): 462–67.

44. Linda W. Rosenzweig, *The Anchor of My Life: Middle-Class American Mothers and Daughters, 1880–1920,* History of Emotion Series (New York: New York University Press, 1993), has argued the importance of the mother-daughter bond even to turn-of-the-century New Women. In this she follows on a number of earlier works suggesting the significance of mother-daughter bonds to nineteenth-century female identity. See Carroll Smith-Rosenberg, *Disorderly Conduct: Visions of Gender in Victorian America* (New York: Knopf, 1985), especially the essays "The Female World of Love and Ritual" and "Hearing Women's Words"; see also Ryan, *Cradle of the Middle Class.*

45. Emily Marshall Eliot [Morison], 1857–1925, diary, 14 Feb. 1869, 14 Feb. 1871, A/M861, Emily Marshall Eliot Morison papers, 1874–1883, Schlesinger Library (Cambridge: Radcliffe Institute, Harvard University); Lois Wells, diary, 10 Apr. 1886, MC-39, Schlesinger Library (Cambridge: Radcliffe Institute, Harvard University).

46. DeButts, *Journal of Agnes Lee,* 124. May Mackintosh, "An Ideal Education of Girls," *Education* 6, no. 8 (1886): 647–51. When Margaret Tileston changed her course at the young ladies' finishing school she attended after graduation from high school, it was her father she admitted as the ultimate authority. [Edsall], diary, 12 Oct. 1885.

47. Kathryn Kish Sklar, *Catharine Beecher: A Study in American Domesticity* (New Haven: Yale University Press, 1973); deButts, *Journal of Agnes Lee,* 138; [Edsall], diary, 15 May 1878; Albert Browne to daughter Nellie, MC 232, Schlesinger Library (Cambridge: Radcliffe Institute, Harvard University), 28 Jan. 1859.

48. Culley, "Eliza Frances Andrews," 137, 157.

49. Alice Browne to Albert Browne, n.d. Oct., 4 Dec. 1863; Eddie Browne to Albert Browne, 23 Oct. 1863; Nellie Browne to Albert Browne, 6 Nov. 1863, all MC 232, Schlesinger Library (Cambridge: Radcliffe Institute, Harvard University).

50. Rev. Charles H. Parkhurst, "The Father's Domestic Headship," *Ladies' Home Journal,* November 1895, 15.

51. Addams remembered of her father: "I centered upon him all that careful imita-

tion which a girl ordinarily gives to her mother's ways and habits." Jane Addams, *Twenty Years at Hull House* (New York: Signet Classic, 1961), 25. Away at a girls' seminary, Mary Thomas used her diary to obsess over her need for her father—who appears to have been out of touch with his daughter, as she waited to be picked up to return home. Her father provided Mary Thomas with her own social compass in her efforts to chart an appropriate relationship with young men. Mary Thomas [Lumpkin], diary, 5 Jul. 1873, Joseph Henry Lumpkin papers, Hargrett Rare Book and Manuscript Library (Athens: University of Georgia).

52. Albert Browne to daughter Nellie, 28 Jan. 1859.

53. Harland, *Eve's Daughters,* 58. Barbara Sicherman, "Reading *Little Women:* The Many Lives of a Text," in *U.S. History as Women's History: New Feminist Essays,* ed. Linda K. Kerber, Alice Kessler-Harris, and Kathryn Kish Sklar (Chapel Hill: University of North Carolina Press, 1995), 255.

54. Following the death of her one brother, Cady's father had lamented to her, "Oh, my daughter, would that you were a boy." Stanton reported: "All that day and far into the night I pondered the problem of boyhood. I thought that the chief thing to be done in order to equal boys was to be learned and courageous. So I decided to study Greek and learn to manage a horse." Cady's study of Greek paid off with an award, which she brought proudly to her father. Her memory, designed to explain and justify her later life, recounted the experience this way: "Then, while I stood looking and waiting for him to say something which would show that he recognized the equality of the daughter with the son, he kissed me on the forehead and exclaimed, with a sigh, 'Ah, you should have been a boy!' My joy was turned to ashes." Theodore Stanton and Harriot Stanton Blatch, *Elizabeth Cady Stanton, As Revealed in Her Letters Diary and Reminiscences* (New York: Harper, 1922), 23–25. Harland, *Eve's Daughters,* 58.

55. Louisa May Alcott, *An Old-Fashioned Girl* (Boston: Roberts, 1870), 41, 45, 57.

56. Edward Bok, "The Daughter in the Home: As a Help to Her Parents and to Herself," *Ladies' Home Journal,* September 1894, 14; Ashmore, STG, April 1894, 34; Abba Goold Woolson, *Woman in American Society* (Boston: Roberts, 1873), 39; Kingsland, "Daughter at Sixteen."

57. [Morison], diary, 8 Jun., 14, 16 Dec. 1869, 28 Sep., 1, 7 Oct. 1870, 18 Feb., 14, 26 Jul., 9 Aug., 1871; [Cabot], diary, 24 Sep. 1888.

58. Franklin, "Annie Burnham Cooper Diary," 162.

59. Frederick Winsor to daughter Annie Ware Winsor [Allen], MC 322, papers of Annie Ware Winsor Allen, 1884–1950, Schlesinger Library (Cambridge: Radcliffe Institute, Harvard University), 8 Jul., 3 Sep. 1888; Harland, *Eve's Daughters,* 125.

60. Leonore Davidoff and Catherine Hall, *Family Fortunes: Men and Women of the English Middle Class, 1780–1850* (London: Hutchinson, 1987), 356.

61. [Cabot], diary, 24 Oct. 1896. Robert Boit, Mary's father and Edward's brother, shared his daughter's concern about her uncle and his family, considering his engagement a misfortune. Several months before Mary ventured to Europe, he noted about his nieces, "Of course they are still in mourning for their mother and three sadder looking

girls I have seldom seen . . . especially Isa who seemed most affected by her mother's death, and was also the special and intimate friend of Florence Little with whom their father fell in love so shortly after their mother's death." Robert A. Boit, diary, Robert A. Boit papers (Boston: Massachusetts Historical Society), 14 Jun. 1896.

62. Peter Gay, *The Bourgeois Experience, Victoria to Freud,* vol. 1, *Education of the Senses* (New York: Oxford University Press, 1984), 102, notes that "for the prosperous especially, the father was the bringer of pleasure, the liberator from rules, and the maker of holidays."

63. Hope Ledyard, "The Most Thoroughly Educated Young Lady in Miss Neal's School," *St. Nicholas* 6 (November 1878): 28–29.

64. Lancraft, diary, 16 Sep. 1889. [Morison], diary, 10 Oct. 1870.

65. [Cabot], diary, 22, 27 Jun. 1891.

66. [Cabot], diary, 17 Jun. 1891. Bold italic indicates double underlining; underscored bold italic indicates triple underlining.

67. [Cabot], diary, 30 Jun. 1891.

68. Diana K. Appelbaum, *The Glorious Fourth: An American History* (New York: Facts on File, 1989), 81; [Cabot], diary, 4, 5 Jul. 1891.

69. Merrill, *Journal of Alice Blackwell,* 218. Respectable opinion disapproved of abortion, even as it remained common practice among the middle classes. "Madame Restelle" was in fact Ann Trow Lohman, a former seamstress who ran a successful mail-order business, advertising her pills and services in newspapers and in circulars on the eastern seaboard. A novel from the 1840s depicted her in terms similar to Blackwell's. "Do you see that lady . . . the one smiling in such a sweet motherly way . . . one of the prettiest and most amiable in the room. . . . I have watched her tonight and have seen more than one cheek turn pale as death as she passed smilingly around the room." Thomas Low Nichols, *The Lady in Black,* quoted in Janet Farrell Brodie, *Contraception and Abortion in 19th-Century America* (Ithaca, N.Y.: Cornell University Press, 1994), 228–30.

5. Interiors

1. Elizabeth Blackwell, *The Laws of Life, with Special Reference to the Physical Education of Girls* (New York: Putnam, 1852), 139.

2. Helen P. Kennedy, M.D., "Effect of High School Work upon Girls During Adolescence," *Pedagogical Seminary* 3, no. 3 (June 1896): 470. The best nineteenth-century data come from Norway. Information from Oslo Maternity Hospital suggests that the median age for menarche in Norway was higher by about a half year than the American, but that the rate of decline was similar, with a rapid fall from 1860 to 1890, a leveling off until 1920, and then another marked decline, stabilizing after 1960 at just over thirteen in Norway. See Phyllis B. Evelyth and James M. Tanner, *Worldwide Variation in Human Growth* (Cambridge: Cambridge University Press, 1990), 170.

3. Blackwell, *Laws of Life,* 28; Kennedy, "Effect of High School Work."

4. Thomas Laqueur, *Making Sex: Body and Gender from the Greeks to Freud* (Cambridge: Harvard University Press, 1990).

5. Norbert Elias, *The Civilizing Process* (New York: Urizen, 1978).

6. Tilt quoted in Elaine Showalter, *The Female Malady: Women, Madness, and English Culture, 1830–1980* (New York: Pantheon, 1985), 56; Kennedy, "Effect of High School Work," 472; Joan Jacobs Brumberg, "'Something Happens to Girls': Menarche and the Emergence of the Modern American Hygienic Imperative," *Journal of the History of Sexuality* 4 (1993): 107. In a recent book, Joan Jacobs Brumberg, *The Body Project: An Intimate History of American Girls* (New York: Vintage, 1998), 43, suggests that this silence cuts across ethnic and racial divides, with Jewish and African American mothers no more eager to discuss "the facts of life" than Victorian mothers.

7. Robert D. Clark, "Ada Harris, Teenager: Oswego County, New York, 1873," *New York History* 66 (January 1985): 29–47; Mabel Barbee Lee, *Cripple Creek Days* (Garden City, N.Y.: Doubleday, 1958), 32.

8. Elias, *Civilizing Process,* 182.

9. Marion Harland [Mary Virginia Terhune], *Eve's Daughters; or, Common Sense for Maid, Wife, and Mother.* (New York: J. R. Anderson and H. S. Allen, 1882), 5, 76, 86.

10. Harland, *Eve's Daughters,* 88.

11. Annie Ware Winsor [Allen], "Country Doctor: Frederick Winsor, 1829–1889," MC 322, papers of Annie Ware Winsor Allen, 1884–1950, Schlesinger Library (Cambridge: Radcliffe Institute, Harvard University), 15–16. In response to a reader's query, "Marion Sprague" wrote: "The virginal delicacy of a girl's very nature, the instinctive shrinking that is part of our own rightful inheritance as women make the subject sacred and apart as it can never be for boys and men. It certainly does not seem right to speak graphically and explicitly to any girl. . . . On the other hand, I think a girl should rightly know, from the time she enters her teens, that children, like flowers and all young things, spring from the union of a life-giving essence with a seed of the race. In human beings, as in all creatures, the male possesses the essence of life, the female the seed. And when through the organs of sex the essence passes to the seed a child is brought into the beginning of its being." Marian Sprague [Annie Ware Winsor (Allen)], "Letter to Mrs. Eickhoff," *Ladies' Home Journal,* October 1907, 29.

12. Frederick Winsor to daughter Annie Ware Winsor, 21 Jul. [1883?], 28 Jul. 1884; Annie Ware Winsor [Allen] to father, Frederick Winsor, 26 Jul. 1884, MC 322, papers of Annie Ware Winsor Allen, 1884–1950, Schlesinger Library (Cambridge: Radcliffe Institute, Harvard University).

13. Sally Dana to mother, 11 Dec. 1857, A-85, Dana family papers, 1822–1956, Schlesinger Library (Cambridge: Radcliffe Institute, Harvard University); John L. Rury, *Education and Women's Work: Female Schooling and the Division of Labor in Urban America, 1870–1930,* SUNY Series on Women and Work (Albany: State University of New York Press, 1991), 33; Charles Ledyard Norton, "The Badminton Fairies," *Harper's Young People* 6, no. 298 (1885): 579–80; Granville Stanley Hall, *Adolescence: Its Psychology and Its Relations to Physiology, Anthropology, Sociology, Sex, Crime, Religion, and Education* (New York: D. Appleton, 1904), 1: 511, 2: 574.

14. Mrs. J. Walter Spooner, "Baby Maud's Book" (Concord: New Hampshire Historical Society).

15. Catherine Hardenburgh, diary, 8 Jun., 21 Nov. 1869, 22 Apr., 24 May 1870, Ac. 552, Hardenburgh family papers, Special Collections and University Archives (New Brunswick, N.J.: Rutgers University Libraries).

16. Margaret Harding Tileston [Edsall], diary, 10, 11 Aug. 1883, 26 Oct. 1885, 17 Nov. 1886, 25 Feb. 1887, MC 354, Schlesinger Library (Cambridge: Radcliffe Institute, Harvard University). For a debate on this subject see Thomas Buckley and Alma Gottlieb, "Introduction: A Critical Appraisal of Theories of Menstrual Symbolism," in *Blood Magic: The Anthropology of Menstruation* (Berkeley: University of California Press, 1988), and Sally Price, "The Curse's Blessing," *Frontiers* 14, no. 2 (1992).

17. Kennedy, "Effect of High School Work," 473, 478.

18. Yonge quoted in Mary Elliott, "When Girls Will Be Boys: 'Bad' Endings and Subversive Middles in Nineteenth-Century Tomboy Narratives and Twentieth-Century Pulp Novels," *Legacy: A Journal of American Women Writers* 15, no. 1 (1998): 92–97.

19. Mary Boit [Cabot], diary, 13, 14 Dec. 1888, 3 Dec. 1890, A 99, Cabot family papers, Schlesinger Libraray (Cambridge: Radcliffe Institute, Harvard University). Margaret Tileston, however, hung a Christmas stocking for Santa Claus until the age of nineteen, noting the Christmas of 1884, "For the first time I didn't hang up my stocking." [Edsall], diary, 24 Dec. 1886.

20. Isabel A. Mallon, "Dressing a Growing Girl," *Ladies' Home Journal,* August 1893, 21; Emma Hooper, "A Schoolgirl's Outfit," *Ladies' Home Journal,* September 1894, 26; Ruth Ashmore, "Side Talks with Girls," *Ladies' Home Journal,* February 1895, 26 [hereafter STG].

21. Ashmore, STG, April 1891, August 1894, February, March 1895.

22. [Edsall], diary, 31 Aug. 1881, 1 Jan., 4 Feb. 1882, 26 Jul. 1885; Agnes Garrison, diary, 29 Jan. 1881, Sophia Smith Collection (Northampton, Mass.: Smith College). For bustles, see Bellamy Partridge, *Big Family* (New York: McGraw-Hill, 1941), 241–42.

23. For Alcott insight see Anne Scott MacLeod, "The *Caddie Woodlawn* Syndrome: American Girlhood in the Nineteenth Century," in *A Century of Childhood,* ed. Mary Lynn Heininger et al. (Rochester, N.Y.: Strong Museum, 1984), 111. For Newberry see Harvey J. Graff, *Conflicting Paths: Growing up in America* (Cambridge: Harvard University Press, 1995), 256. For Willard see Sharon O'Brien, "Tomboyism and Adolescent Conflict: Three Nineteenth-Century Case Studies," in *Woman's Being, Woman's Place: Female Identity and Vocation in American History,* ed. Mary Kelley (Boston: G. K. Hall, 1979), 357. Emily M. Eliot, "Journal of the XIX Year of My Life," 14 Feb. 1876, HUG(FP) 33.6, Samuel Eliot Morison papers, Harvard University Archives (Cambridge: Pusey Library).

24. For Willard see O'Brien, "Tomboyism and Adolescent Conflict," 359. Julia Butler, diary, 29 Jun. 1890, Ac. 1919, Frances E. Butler papers, Special Collections and University Archives (New Brunswick, N.J.: Rutgers University Libraries); Mary D. Robert-

son, ed., *Lucy Breckinridge of Grove Hill: The Journal of a Virginia Girl, 1862–1864* (Kent, Ohio: Kent State University Press, 1979), 146; [Edsall], diary, 1 Nov. 1885.

25. Penelope Franklin, ed., "Annie Burnham Cooper Diary," in *Private Pages: Diaries of American Women, 1830s-1970s* (New York: Ballantine, 1986), 147, 150.

26. Elizabeth W. Coffin, *A Girl's Life in Germantown* (Boston: Sherman, French, 1916), 63.

27. Mary Custis deButts, ed., *Growing Up in the 1850s: The Journal of Agnes Lee* (Chapel Hill: University of North Carolina Press, 1984), 78.

28. Emma Hidden, diary, 14 Feb. 1860 (Concord: New Hampshire Historical Society).

29. Sally Dana to father, 24 Jan. [1858?], A-85, Dana family papers, 1822-1956, Schlesinger Library (Cambridge: Radcliffe Institute, Harvard University).

30. Dana to father, 9 Jan. 1858.

31. DeButts, *Journal of Agnes Lee,* 95–96; Dana to father, 9 Jan. 1858. Sometimes family groups converted together. See Vivian C. Hopkins, ed., "Diary of an Iowa Farm Girl: Josephine Edith Brown, 1892–1901," *Annals of Iowa* 42, no. 2 (1973): 23 Jun. 1895; Lois Wells, diary, 21 Mar. [n.d.], MC-39, Schlesinger Library (Cambridge: Radcliffe Institute, Harvard University); Sally Dean to father, 9 Jan. 1858.

32. Franklin, "Annie Burnham Cooper Diary," 149, 151.

33. Franklin, "Annie Burnham Cooper Diary," 152.

34. Ernest M. Lander, Jr., "A Confederate Girl Visits Pennsylvania, July–September 1863," *Western Pennsylvania Historical Magazine* 49, no. 3 (1966): 198–99.

35. Lander, "Confederate Girl," 203.

36. Marlene Deahl Merrill, ed., *Growing Up in Boston's Gilded Age: The Journal of Alice Stone Blackwell, 1872–1874* (New Haven: Yale University Press, 1990), 68–70, 90, 103.

37. Merrill, *Journal of Alice Blackwell,* 73, 74, 143, 146, 148, 160–61, 168.

38. Merrill, *Journal of Alice Blackwell,* 168.

39. Ella Lyman [Cabot], "Scraps of Thoughts and Feelings," A-139, Ella Lyman Cabot papers, 1855–1934, Schlesinger Library (Cambridge: Radcliffe Institute, Harvard University), 85–86.

40. Ann Ware Winsor to daughter Annie Ware Winsor [Allen], 11 May 1885, MC 322, papers of Annie Ware Winsor Allen, 1884–1950, Schlesinger Library (Cambridge: Radcliffe Institute, Harvard University), 15–16.

41. Ashmore, STG, *Ladies' Home Journal,* March 1893, 14.

42. Ellen Regal, diary, 20 Apr. 1857, Michigan Historical Collections (Ann Arbor: Bentley Historical Library). Regal reported that she "attended family worship. Read memorized in the Bible, also attended to secret divotion."

43. [Edsall], diary, 20 Jan. 1878, 12, 13 May 1882. Going to church alone: 7 Aug. 1881, 10 Feb., 23 Mar., 18, 25 May 1884. Uncle Henry's church: 4 Jul. 1884.

44. [Edsall], diary, 15 Jan., 12, 13 May, between 5 and 6 Jun. 1882. Fénelon was a

"quietist," practicing a form of religious mysticism eventually condemned as heretical by Popes Innocent XI and XII.

45. [Edsall], diary, 12, 18 Jun. 1882, 4 Feb., 2, 14 Dec. 1883, 11, 28 Apr., 12 Oct. 1884. Several days after promising to "be good and to love God," Tileston referred to "fresh resolves, especially on Papa's account" (8 Feb. 1883).

46. Kate Upson [Clark], diary, 18 Apr., 11 May 1866, Kate Upson Clark papers, 1851–1935, Sophia Smith Collection (Northampton, Mass.: Smith College).

47. Joel Myerson and Daniel Shealy, ed., *Journals of Louisa May Alcott* (Boston: Little, Brown, 1989), 61. Cassie Upson's end-of-the-year statement in 1865 marked as one of her year's trials "the galling concessions I have been forced to make to nearly everyone." She announced that "I will try to do away with this odious self-esteem and put modesty and humility in its stead." Kate Upson [Clark], diary, 31 Dec. 1865.

48. The Centers for Disease Control in 1995 suggested that adolescent suicide has been an increasing problem recently, rising especially dramatically in the age 10–14 group. The rate in that age group increased 86 percent among white boys and 233 percent among white girls—the latter statistic rising from what was once a significantly lower rate of successful suicides among girls. The availability of guns has been blamed for the recent rise in successful attempts among all groups. *New York Times,* April 21, 1995. We would do well to remember that adolescent suicide today—as well as the anorexic self-starving of girls—often takes place among high achievers who can mix gaiety and laughter with a fundamental sense of hopelessness and despair.

49. "Crocus," " 'Nothing to Do,' " *St. Nicholas,* December 1876, 59; Louisa May Alcott, *An Old-Fashioned Girl* (Boston: Roberts, 1870), 164–65.

50. Charlotte Perkins Gilman, *The Home, Its Work and Influence* (New York: McClure, Phillips, 1903), 257–58.

51. Anne Firor Scott, Introduction to Jane Addams, *Democracy and Social Ethics,* ed. Scott (Cambridge: Harvard University Press, 1964), 213.

52. [Edsall], diary, 22 Dec. 1882.

53. [Edsall], diary, 8 Jan. 1883; Ralph Greenson, "On Boredom," *Journal of the American Psychoanalytic Association* 1 (1953): 7–21.

54. Ida Mabel Lancraft, diary, 10, 25 Sep. 1889, 16 Jan. 1890 (New Haven: New Haven Colony Historical Society); Greenson, "On Boredom."

55. Janet Mendelsohn, "The View from Step Number 16: Girls from Emma Willard School Talk About Themselves and Their Futures," in *Making Connections: The Relational Worlds of Adolescent Girls at Emma Willard School,* ed. Carol Gilligan, Nona Lyons, and Trudy J. Hanmer (Cambridge: Harvard University Press, 1990), 241. Mendolsohn argues that girls today at one elite girls' school differ from girls of the past in their sense of active agency. "There is . . . an astonishing absence of passivity in the Emma Willard girls' responses. . . . There is no sign of the kind of interlude of passivity described by Erikson (1968) [*Identity: Youth and Crisis*]. Whereas these girls do tend to perceive development as occurring within a context of relationship, their ongoing relationships with friends, with family, and teachers form the crucible in which identity is forged. There

is no hint of holding identity in abeyance, no suggestion that one has the option of waiting to be defined by an intimate relationship with a future husband." Mendelsohn also notes the active agency in the language of the future: "I am still deciding how I am going to be." She writes: "Contrast this with the single response that is clearly passive: 'I often wonder what's going to happen to me.'" Says Mendelsohn, "It seems clear, then, that these girls do not see themselves as needing to be rescued from the responsibility of making choices about the future."

"What is it that gives rise in other girls and women to the need to abdicate responsibility for choice? Gilligan, in her book *In a Different Voice* (1982) says: 'To the extent that women perceive themselves as having no choice they correspondingly excuse themselves from the responsibility that decision entails.'" Jane P. Tompkins, *Sensational Designs: The Cultural Work of American Fiction, 1790–1860* (New York: Oxford University Press, 1985), 172.

56. Robertson, *Lucy Breckinridge,* 17.

57. Robertson, *Lucy Breckinridge,* 22; Sigmund Freud, "Creative Writers and Day-Dreaming," in *The Standard Edition of the Complete Psychological Works of Sigmund Freud,* trans. and ed. James Strachey (London: Hogarth, 1959), 9: 147.

58. Robertson, *Lucy Breckinridge,* 124.

59. (Mary) Elizabeth Morrissey, diary, 25 Jul. 1876 (Boston: Boston Public Library).

60. Morrissey, diary, 6 Jan., 17 Apr., 27 May, 9, 19 Sep. 1876.

61. MacLeod, "The *Caddie Woodlawn* Syndrome," 114; F. M. Edselas, "What Shall We Do with Our Girls?" *Catholic World* 61, no. 364 (July 1895): 540.

62. Freud, "Creative Writers and Day-Dreaming," 148.

63. Josef Breuer and Sigmund Freud, *Studies of Hysteria,* in *The Standard Edition of the Complete Psychological Works of Sigmund Freud,* trans. and ed. James Strachey (London: Hogarth, 1955), 2: 41–42.

64. Elaine Showalter, *The Female Malady: Women, Madness, and English Culture, 1830–1980* (New York: Pantheon, 1985), 62–64; Carolyn G. Heilbrun, *Writing a Woman's Life* (New York: Norton, 1988), 130; Sally Hunter, "Annotated Bibliography on the Socialization of Adolescent Women" (Chapel Hill, North Carolina, 1974).

65. Jane Addams, *The Spirit of Youth and the City Streets* (Urbana: University of Illinois Press, 1972), 77.

66. DeButts, *Journal of Agnes Lee,* 78.

67. DeButts, *Journal of Agnes Lee,* 78.

68. Nancy Armstrong, *Desire and Domestic Fiction: A Political History of the Novel* (New York: Oxford University Press, 1987), 212.

69. Franklin, "Annie Burnham Cooper Diary," 163.

6. Competitive Practices

1. John L. Rury, *Education and Women's Work: Female Schooling and the Division of Labor in Urban America, 1870–1930,* SUNY Series on Women and Work (Albany: State University of New York Press, 1991), 17, 64.

2. Ari Joel Perlmann, "Education and the Social Structure of an American City: Social Origins and Education Attainments in Providence, R.I., 1880–1925," Ph. D. diss. (Cambridge: Harvard University, 1980), 38, 278, 280. The statistics on high school attendance can be misleading. Educational historians conclude that most teenage girls and boys in school in the nineteenth century were not going to secondary school at all but instead were those big boys and girls who sat in the back of country schoolrooms terrorizing youthful teachers. Some historians see that pattern continuing well into the twentieth century, even after the relative popularization of the high school. The pattern of grammar school attendance even for teenagers persisted in Providence in 1880, according to Perlmann. In that year nearly half of all 14–16-year-old boys had been in school in the past year but only about 10 percent of all teenage boys were in secondary schools. This left some 35 percent of all of Providence's teenage boys whose school attendance had been in elementary or grammar school classrooms, the obvious first stop for immigrant and working-class youths. Perlmann does not provide this statistic for girls, but we can imagine that many more teenage girls than attended high school had some exposure to elementary schooling. As a city in the Northeast, Providence could be expected to have had a higher proportion of youths in school of any kind, and particularly of youths in secondary schools, than in other parts of the country. The educational historian John Rury has estimated that in 1870 only 2 percent of American teenagers went to secondary school, a figure which rose to 5 percent in 1900. Rury, *Education and Women's Work,* 17. Parental information on students at Girls' High School in Boston in the 1890s suggests increasing representation from a wide swath of the middle class. Daughters of butchers, blacksmiths, lamplighters, and junk dealers joined the daughters of businessmen and ministers at this all-girls' school which trained many teachers. A significant number of daughters of single mothers also attended Girls' High School. Records of Girls' High School (Boston: Dearborn Middle School Library, 1860–1900).

3. Reed Ueda, *Avenues to Adulthood: The Origins of the High School and Social Mobility in an American Suburb* (Cambridge: Cambridge University Press, 1987), 104, makes this point in his study of Somerville High School: "Since a working-class daughter could earn only half what an employed son could earn due to the lower wage scale of female workers, the cost of her 'finishing,' in income forgone for the family due to school attendance, was much smaller. To parents concerned about status, an educated daughter who brought prestige to the family and enhanced her marriageability was well worth such a cost."

4. Richard L. Bushman, *The Refinement of America: Persons, Houses, Cities* (New York: Knopf, 1992), 81.

5. Eliza Southgate Bowne, *A Girl's Life Eighty Years Ago: Selections from the Letters of Eliza Southgate Bowne* (New York: Scribner, 1888), 17 Oct. 1797; Rachel Mordecai, "Log of Educating a Younger Sister," VHS Mss 1: M9924a: 44–45 (Richmond: Virginia Historical Society, 1860–1920), 17. Thanks to Susan Miller for Mordecai reference.

6. M. A. Denison, "Aunt Jenny's Niece," *Youth's Companion* 41, no. 51 (17 December 1868): 202.

7. Catherine E. Kelly, *In the New England Fashion: Reshaping Women's Lives in the Nineteenth-Century* (Ithaca, N.Y.: Cornell University Press, 1999), 41; Rury, *Education and Women's Work*, 21.

8. Susan B. Carter and Mark Prus, "The Labor Market and the American High School Girl, 1890–1928," *Journal of Economic History* 42, no. 1 (March 1982): 166; Benjamin Andrews, "The Public School System of Chicago," *Education* 20, no. 4 (December 1899): 201–7.

9. Jason Whitman, *The Young Lady's Aid to Usefulness and Happiness* (Portland, Maine: S. H. Colesworthy, 1845); Anna L. White, *Kate Callender; or, School-Girls of '54, and the Women of to-Day* (Boston: self-published, 1870), 19; Mary Thomas [Lumpkin], diary, 28 Jun. 1873, Joseph Henry Lumpkin papers, Hargrett Rare Book and Manuscript Library (Athens: University of Georgia).

10. Rury's evidence demonstrates that the feminization of high schools was most pronounced in the West before the feminization of the teaching force and the opening of other white-collar job opportunities for women there. Nonetheless, even as Rury argues that nineteenth-century high schools did not primarily prepare girls for a vocation, he acknowledges that if it did, that vocation was teaching. Rury, *Education and Women's Work*, 64; Victoria Bissell Brown, "Golden Girls: Female Socialization in Los Angeles, 1880 to 1910," Ph.D. diss. (University of California, San Diego, 1985), 306, makes the point that high schools received an "extra share" of girls from the middle and lower-middle classes. Kelly, *In the New England Fashion*, 73.

11. Mary J. Oates, "Catholic Female Academies on the Frontier," *U.S. Catholic Historian* 12, no. 4 (Fall 1994): 121, 126–27; Carol K. Coburn and Martha Smith, *Spirited Lives: How Nuns Shaped Catholic Culture and American Life, 1836–1920* (Chapel Hill: University of North Carolina Press, 1999), 170.

12. Ueda, *Avenues to Adulthood*, 40; Lucy R. Woods, *History of the Girls' High School of Boston, 1852–1902.* ([Boston], 1904), 1; Edward August Krug, *The Shaping of the American High School* (Madison: University of Wisconsin Press, 1969), 5. Also important in the growth of high schools in Massachusetts was a state law which proclaimed the rights of Massachusetts youths to a high school education.

13. William J. Reese, *The Origins of the American High School* (New Haven: Yale University Press, 1995), 34. Krug, *Shaping of the American High School*, 6, cites federal statistics from the commissioner of education's *Report for the Year 1884–1885*, which estimates that only 10 percent of students at academies were college bound. Krug quotes James Angell's *Reminiscences* about the rural academy he attended in Maine in 1912. Angell recalled that even then only a small number of his fellow students were preparing themselves for college: "I joined them in their classes with no such purpose distinctly formed. I also took nearly all the scientific instruction which was given, and given as well as it could be without laboratories or much apparatus. Many of the students were men in years. They were diligent students. Some of them were awkward and rustic in manners, but they were thoroughly earnest and gave a good tone to the school."

14. Brown, "Golden Girls," 267.

15. Elizabeth Ellery Dana, diary, 28 Feb. 1860, A-85, Dana family papers, 1822–1956, Schlesinger Library (Cambridge: Radcliffe Institute, Harvard University); Margaret Harding Tileston [Edsall], diary, 6 Feb. 1882, MC 354, Schlesinger Library (Cambridge: Radcliffe Institute, Harvard University).

16. Julia Sloane Spalding, "Reminiscences of My Schooldays, 1853–58," Notes taken by Mary J. Oates, Sisters of Charity of Nazareth (Louisville, Kentucky, 1900). Many thanks to Mary J. Oates for sharing the fruits of her research in the Sisters of Charity Archives. Mary Anne Murphy, "Reminiscences of Civil-War Days at Nazareth Academy," Sisters of Charity of Nazareth Archives (Louisville, Kentucky, 1894).

17. Sister Wilfrida Hogan, "'My Reminiscences,'" Written to Sister Lucida Savage, copied by Sister Helen Angela, 11 January 1949, Archives (St. Paul, Minn.: Sisters of St. Joseph of Carondelet, 1920–21), 1: 3; Edith E. W. Gregg, ed., *The Letters of Ellen Tucker Emerson* (Kent, Ohio: Kent State University Press, 1982), 52–53; Dana, diary, 13, 18, 22 Nov. 1858. Etta Luella Call attended St. Mary's from her Iowa home in the 1880s. Suzanne L. Bunkers, *Diaries of Girls and Women: A Midwestern American Sampler* (Madison: University of Wisconsin Press, 2001), 75.

18. Agnes Repplier, *In Our Convent Days* (Boston: Houghton, Mifflin, 1906), 36.

19. Marion Harland [Mary Virginia Terhune], *Eve's Daughters; or, Common Sense for Maid, Wife, and Mother* (New York: J. R. Anderson and H. S. Allen, 1882), 143; Emily Edwards, *Stones, Bells, Lighted Candles: Personal Memories of the Old Ursuline Academy in San Antonio at the Turn of the Century* (San Antonio: Daughters of the Republic of Texas Library, 1981); Josephine Tilton, diary, 16 May 1881, Archives, Friends Historical Library (Swarthmore, Penn.: Swarthmore College); Dana, diary, 26 Feb. 1860.

20. Nora Nellis, ed., "Daughter of the Valley: The 1840s Letters of Maria Nellis," unpublished, 13 Dec. 1842.

21. Carroll Smith-Rosenberg, "The Female World of Love and Ritual," in *Disorderly Conduct: Visions of Gender in Victorian America* (New York: Knopf, 1985).

22. The Oxford English Dictionary notes that the term *crush* was of American derivation, and cites an early usage in I. M. Rittenhouse's *Maud* (1884). "Wintie is weeping because her crush is gone." Dana, diary, 12 Nov. 1858.

23. Sally Dana to mother, 13 Nov. 1857, A-85, Dana family papers, 1822–1956, Schlesinger Library (Cambridge: Radcliffe Institute, Harvard University). Elizabeth Dana noted her conflict with one girl who wanted "to change the day she walks with me, and wont tell me why," and then invited a third to their afternoon walk, a violation of the rules. During that same period, yet another friend forgot her walking date and went skating instead. Dana, diary, 6, 15, 27 Feb. 1860.

24. Glenda Elizabeth Gilmore, *Gender and Jim Crow: Women and the Politics of White Supremacy in North Carolina, 1896–1920* (Chapel Hill: University of North Carolina Press, 1996), 10; Roberta Fitzgerald, composition book, Scotia Seminary, Concord, North Carolina, Folder 305, African-American Women's History Collection, Schlesinger Library (Cambridge: Radcliffe Institute, Harvard University, 1902).

25. Agnes Hamilton, diary, 1, 9 Nov. 1886, MC 278, M-24, Hamilton family papers, Schlesinger Library (Cambridge: Radcliffe Institute, Harvard University, 1886–87).

26. Hamilton, diary, 16 Nov. 1886.

27. Hamilton, diary, 27 Nov., 5 Dec. 1886.

28. Hamilton, diary, 27 Oct. 1887, 7 Feb. 1888. Later, Hamilton crossed out the "not much" in her complaint about her social life, clearly an afterthought about her discontent.

29. Mary Custis deButts, ed., *Growing Up in the 1850s: The Journal of Agnes Lee* (Chapel Hill: University of North Carolina Press, 1984), 83.

30. DeButts, *Journal of Agnes Lee,* 82–3.

31. Dana, diary, 27 Jan. 1869.

32. "Side Talks with Girls," *Ladies' Home Journal,* January 1890, 10 [hereafter STG]. For one description of the evolving stigmatizing of intense female friendships, see Carroll Smith-Rosenberg, "The New Woman as Androgyne: Social Disorder and Gender Crisis, 1870–1936," in *Disorderly Conduct.*

33. Emma Plimpton, "Wild Becky," *St. Nicholas* 6 (December 1878): 74.

34. Gregg, *Letters of Ellen Tucker Emerson,* 82, 116, 181; Edwards, *Stones, Bells, Lighted Candles,* 27; Hogan, "'My Reminiscences,'" 2: 1.

35. Nellis, "Daughter of the Valley," 5 Jan., 17 Mar. 1843.

36. Edwards, *Stones, Bells, Lighted Candles,* 9, 39. Emily Edwards remembers the efforts of one "big girl" who had been put in the convent against her will, who "spent days trying to escape," unable to climb the high wall or the even higher palisades." See also Coburn and Smith, *Spirited Lives,* 169; George Stewart Stokes, *Agnes Repplier: Lady of Letters* (Philadelphia: University of Pennsylvania Press, 1949), 20; Repplier, *In Our Convent Days,* 16.

37. [Edsall], diary, 24 Jan. 1881, 2 Jan. 1882.

38. [Edsall], diary, 7, 11, 15, 16, 20, 26, 30 Jan., 21 Apr. 1882.

39. [Edsall], diary, 1, 10 May, 17, 22 Jun. 1882.

40. [Edsall], diary, 13 Jul., 9 Oct. 1882, 14 Mar. 1885, 19 Mar. 1886.

41. [Edsall], diary, 18 Jun. 1882.

42. Dana, diary, 4 Nov. 1858.

43. Hogan, "'My Reminiscences,'" 1: 2; Coburn and Smith, *Spirited Lives,* 80.

44. Linda K. Kerber, "'Why Should Girls Be Learn'd and Wise?' Two Centuries of Higher Education for Women as Seen Through the Unfinished Work of Alice Mary Baldwin," in *Women and Higher Education in American History,* ed. John Mack Faragher and Florence Howe (New York: Norton, 1988), 35, concurs that the curriculum of girls' seminaries "was, of course, not often rigorous." Nancy Green, "Female Education and School Competition: 1820–1850," *History of Education Quarterly* 18, no. 2 (1978): 133, 135, 137, notes that the debate over emulation subsided in the 1850s and conjectures that as girls moved into teaching, the need for standards and intellectual mastery even in the teaching of girls seemed more acute. My evidence suggests, though, that

female seminaries sustained their tradition of muting academic competition at least into the 1880s, in sharp contrast with both public high schools and academies and convent schools, which continued to conduct semipublic examinations with visiting dignitaries and present awards to their distinguished students. Hogan, "'My Reminiscences,'" 1: 1a, for instance, remembers the stress of being examined by "many intellectuals," including Bishop John Ireland himself, in St. Joseph's Academy in St. Paul in the 1870s.

45. Examinations too seemed to be intermittent. Agnes Lee had been at Staunton Female Academy for seven months before she took her first test. DeButts, *Journal of Agnes Lee,* 77; Hamilton, essay in back of diary, 1886; Dana, diary, 13 Nov. 1858. Lily Dana noted, "Mrs. Richards says my hair looks awfully and that I must either curl it tie it up have a round comb or put it in a net because being short it flies around so. Informed me that she supposed my mother let me do everything." Sally Dana to mother, 11 Dec. 1857.

46. Ralph Rusk, ed., *The Letters of Ralph Waldo Emerson* (New York: Columbia University Press, 1939), 157, 372, 407; Gregg, *Letters of Ellen Tucker Emerson,* 4 Dec. 1853.

47. Mary Kelley, "'Vindicating the Equality of Female Intellect': Women and Authority in the Early Republic," *Prospects* 17 (1992): 16, 18. Anne Firor Scott, "The Ever Widening Circle: The Diffusion of Feminist Values from the Troy Female Seminary, 1822–1872," *History of Education Quarterly* 19, no. 1 (1979): 3–25, suggests Willard's protofeminist influence on her students, despite her sometimes conservative rhetoric. Frederick Rudolph, "Emma Willard," in *Notable American Women* (Cambridge: Harvard University Press).

48. Gregg, *Letters of Ellen Tucker Emerson,* 163; Sara Annie Burstall, *The Education of Girls in the United States* (London: Swan Sonnenschein Macmillan, 1894), 75.

49. Emily M. Eliot, "'Journal of the XIX Year of My Life,'" HUG(FP) 33.6, Samuel Eliot Morison papers, Harvard University Archives (Cambridge: Pusey Library), 14 Feb. 1876.

50. Robert A. Boit, diary, 31 Dec. 1891, Robert Apthorp Boit diaries (Boston: Massachusetts Historical Society).

51. Boit, diary, 31 Dec. 1891; [Edsall], diary, 8, 25 Aug. 1881.

52. Caroline M. Burrough, "Girls and Their Training," *Ladies' Repository,* December 1841, 372; Shirley Blotnick Moskow, *Emma's World: An Intimate Look at Lives Touched by the Civil War Era* (Far Hills, N.J.: New Horizon, 1990), 9.

53. The importance of a liberal education was early acknowledged by female students, as embodied in the graduation essay of Priscilla Mason, class salutatorian of Philadelphia's Young Ladies' Academy in 1793. Mason noted that men had "early seized the sceptre and the sword," as well as denying women "the advantage of a liberal education." Kelley, "'Vindicating the Equality of Female Intellect,'" 13.

54. Gilmore, *Gender and Jim Crow,* 26.

55. The embarrassment of recitation might result from other matters as well. Correspondence between two friends in 1861 reveals some resistance from two girl students to reciting with boys, or before a male teacher. Writing from Illinois to a friend in Mas-

sachusetts, Mary Sargent reported, "You say you dislike to recite Physiology to a man. We used to have to recite with a whole lot of boys that made bad out of everything to a lady teacher. But we made such a fuss that Mr. Newman took the boys and we recite separate. . . . I never saw such a man as Mr. Newman is when we wanted to recite separate from the boys. He 'brought the matter before the school' and said 'some folks tried to make bad out of everthin.'" Moskow, *Emma's World*, 64; Nikola Baumbarten, "Education and Democracy in Frontier St. Louis: The Society of the Sacred Heart," *History of Education Quarterly* 34 (Summer 1994): 181.

56. Theodore Stanton and Harriot Stanton Blatch, *Elizabeth Cady Stanton, As Revealed in Her Letters Diary and Reminiscences* (New York: Harper, 1922), 25. The Rev. J. M'D. Mathews encouraged girls' schooling, but warned, "The girl who applies with diligence to the study of algebra or geometry, for the sake of obtaining a gold medal, or for the reputation of being the best scholar in the class, will be in danger of being influenced by the wrong motives all her life." J. M'D. Mathews, *Letters to School Girls* (Cincinnati: Swormstedt and Pie, for the Methodist Episcopal Church, 1853), 24. The educational historians John Rury, Elisabeth Hansot, and David Tyack concur about the strength and significance of this finding, seeing the public high school as the least unequal among the unequal institutions of the nineteenth-century world. Rury, *Education and Women's Work*, 12, argues that "the years extending from about 1870 to 1900 may have marked the first general period of gender equality in the history of American secondary education. In one important American institution, it appears, gender was *not* a critical factor." David B. Tyack and Elisabeth Hansot, *Learning Together: A History of Coeducation in American Schools* (New Haven: Yale University Press, 1990). Victoria Bissell Brown, "The Fear of Feminization: Los Angeles High Schools in the Progressive Era," *Feminist Studies* 16, no. 3 (1990): 511, raises a significant dissent here: "It may be that in the actual classroom setting, girls and boys faced similar demands and rewards. However, girls and boys were not always in the same classrooms; did not bring the same attitudes, goals, and expectations with them to their classrooms; and did not experience school only in the classroom. If Hansot and Tyack's argument is that gender has been less salient in the schools than in the home or workplace, then the argument here is that the attempt to separate the effects of these institutions imposes a theoretical artifice that flattens historical reality, for home and work were ever-present influences in the schools."

I would argue to the contrary. Home and work were certainly in the minds of educators, parents, and teachers. However, for students, they paled in the face of the vibrant community of peers in school. The historical reality I hope to capture here is precisely that full and surprising reality of the Victorian high school as it represented a challenge to the gendered worlds of both home and work.

57. Milford High School graduation programs, Milford Room (Milford, Mass.: Milford Public Library). Rural Bridgton Academy in North Bridgton, Maine, graduated slightly more boys than girls in the last twenty years of the twentieth century, but girls took 57 percent of the honors. These statistics were compiled from "Record Book," "Pro-

gram for 1895 Reunion," and "Alumni Directory" (1916) from the archives of Bridgton Academy.

58. *Oak, Lily, and Ivy,* June 1887.

59. Almyra Hubbard, journal, 5 Apr., 10 May 1859, Hosmer-Hubbard diaries, Joint Collection, University of Missouri–Western Historical Manuscript Collection (Columbia: Columbia and State Historical Society of Missouri Manuscripts); *Oak, Lily, and Ivy,* June 1890.

60. Annie Roberts Godfrey, diary (privately owned), 7 Feb. 1865; *High School Advance,* December 1894.

61. Kate Upson [Clark], diary, 16 May 1862, 18 Mar. 1863, 22 Jul., 3 Nov. 1864, 11 Apr. 1866, Kate Upson Clark papers, 1851–1935, Sophia Smith Collection (Northampton, Mass.: Smith College).

62. Bunkers, *Diaries of Girls and Women,* 147; Mary Boit [Cabot], diary, 9, 13, 27, Sep. 1891, A 99, Cabot family papers, Schlesinger Libraray (Cambridge: Radcliffe Institute, Harvard University); Boit, diary, 28 Nov. 1889.

63. Jessie Wendover, diary, Dec. 1884, Ac. 2383, MC463, J. Wendover papers, Special Collections and University Archives (New Brunswick, N.J.: Rutgers University Libraries).

64. Rury, *Education and Women's Work,* 43.

65. [Edsall], diary, 21 Dec. 1882, 5 Jan., 10 Apr. 1883.

66. [Edsall], diary, 30 Jun. 1883.

67. [Edsall], diary, 22, 28 Nov., 5 Dec. 1883.

68. [Edsall], diary, 5 Sep. 1883, 11 Feb. 1884.

69. [Edsall], diary, 5 Sep. 1883, 7 Apr., 15 May 1884.

70. [Edsall], diary, 3 Jul., 12 Sep. 1884, 5 Mar., 10 Apr. 1885.

71. [Edsall], diary, 22 Oct., 8 Dec. 1884, 13, 15 Jan. 1885.

72. [Edsall], diary, 11 Feb. 1884; Anna J. Cooper, *A Voice from the South,* Schomburg Library of Nineteenth-Century Black Women Writers (New York: Oxford University Press, 1988), 76; Gilmore, *Gender and Jim Crow,* 39.

73. Katherine (Graves) Busbey, *Home Life in America* (New York: Macmillan, 1910), 80.

74. Evidence of the costs of this practice emerged earlier in the century when educators were describing the deleterious effects of competition especially on girl students. R. Putnam, for instance, who taught at Salem High School, in 1849 reported on his own revision of his pedagogical practices as a response to their ill effects on his female students. The practice of reassigning seats according to performance meant that "scarcely a recitation was heard from which some scholar did not return to her seat shedding tears, sobbing, pouting, or giving other indications that all was not peaceful within. After hesitating and deliberating for months," Green reports, he gave up the practice, arranged seats alphabetically and reported "on the happy results, a more 'healthful moral aliment.'" Green, "Female Education and School Competition," 133.

75. Wendover, diary, 29 Sep. 1886.

76. Dana, diary, 14 Jul. 1862; Wendover, diary, 10 Jun. 1887.

77. Louisa May Alcott, *Eight Cousins; or, The Aunt-Hill* (Boston: Little, Brown, 1874), 123; Godfrey, diary, 8, 29 Jan. 1866; Rusk, *Letters of Ralph Waldo Emerson,* 379; Dana, diary, 24 Jul. 1862; Eleanor Hooper to Annie Ware Winsor, Sep. 1878, MC 322, papers of Annie Ware Winsor Allen, 1884–1950, Schlesinger Library (Cambridge: Radcliffe Institute, Harvard University).

78. Annie Ware Winsor [Allen] to mother, 17 Oct. 1886, Ann Ware Winsor, MC 322, papers of Annie Ware Winsor Allen, 1884–1950, Schlesinger Library (Cambridge: Radcliffe Institute, Harvard University). The historian of technology Ronald Zboray has described the dimensions of ocular problems in antebellum America as formidable. Ronald J. Zboray, "Antebellum Reading and the Ironies of Technological Innovation," in *Reading in America: Literature and Social History,* ed. Cathy N. Davidson (Baltimore: Johns Hopkins University Press, 1989), 194–95.

79. Kieff, "Mrs. Headache," *St. Nicholas* 2 (June 1875): 479; "Headaches: Causes and Cures," *Ladies' Home Journal,* August 1896, 22.

80. Martha Josephine Moore, diary, v. 2, 20 Apr. 1863, #631, Frank Liddell Richardson papers, Southern Historical Collection (Chapel Hill: University of North Carolina, Wilson Library); see also 6 Apr. 1863.

81. Georgia Mercer [Boit], diary, 23 Aug. 1871, A 99, Cabot family papers, Schlesinger Libraray (Cambridge: Radcliffe Institute, Harvard University).

82. Elizabeth Blackwell, *The Laws of Life, with Special Reference to the Physical Education of Girls* (New York: George P. Putnam, 1852), 168; Eva Kellogg, "Needs in American Education," *Education* 5, no. 2 (November 1884): 187–99; John D. Philbrick, "Overwork in Schools," *Education* 6, no. 4 (February 1886): 330–34. M. Carey Thomas, who went on to found Bryn Mawr College, remembered the impact on her cohort of college woman of "that gloomy little specter, Dr. Edward H. Clarke's *Sex in Education,*" a treatise which cautioned that excessive study would lead to the degeneration of a young woman's reproductive system. M. Carey Thomas, "Present Tendencies in Women's College and University Education," *Publications of the Association of Collegiate Alumnae* (1908): 49.

83. Harland, *Eve's Daughters,* 170; Granville Stanley Hall, *Adolescence: Its Psychology and Its Relations to Physiology, Anthropology, Sociology, Sex, Crime, Religion, and Education* (New York: D. Appleton, 1904), 2: 574. "Again and again, on explaining some English custom, we were told that it could not be adopted because it would involve too great a strain on the health of girls or teachers." Burstall, *Education of Girls,* 55.

84. Anne Scott MacLeod, "The *Caddie Woodlawn* Syndrome: American Girlhood in the Nineteenth Century," in *A Century of Childhood,* ed. Mary Lynn Heininger et al. (Rochester, N.Y.: Strong Museum, 1984), 111; Hall, *Adolescence,* 1: 505. Hall's and Clark's views did not reign unchallenged. Mary Ashton Rice Livermore, *What Shall We Do with Our Daughters? Superfluous Women, and Other Lectures* (Boston: Lee and Shepard, 1883), 23, for instance, suggested that nurture, not nature, was responsible for the invalidism of young women: "Many of our girls are made the victims of disease and weakness for

life through the evils of the dress they wear from birth. The causes of their invalidism are sought in hard study, co-education, too much exercise, or lack of rest and quiet in certain period when nature demands it. All the while the medical attendant is silent concerning the 'glove-fitting,' steel-clasped corset, the heavy, dragging skirts, the bands engirding the body, and the pinching, distorting boot."

85. Dana, letter to mother, 11 Dec. 1857.

86. Agnes Garrison, diary, 13 Aug. 1882, Garrison family papers, Sophia Smith Collection (Northampton, Mass.: Smith College); "Precocious Girls," *Youth's Companion* 56, no. 29 (19 July 1883): 294; also Martha T. Freeman, "Her Four Boy Cousins," *Youth's Companion* 56, no. 46 (15 November 1883): 472; Garrison, diary, 1 Nov. 1882; Marian Nichols, diary, 2 Oct. 1884, A-170, papers of the Nichols-Shurtleff family, 1780–1953, Schlesinger Library (Cambridge: Radcliffe Institute, Harvard University).

87. Wendover, diary, 7 Jun. 1881, 5 May, 24 Aug. 1883.

88. Wendover, diary, 5 Sep. 1884, 6 Apr. 1886.

89. Wendover, diary, 10, 12 Nov. 1886. For girls who wanted to remain in school, it was important to conceal any signs of sickness. In the 1850s one girl wrote to a friend that she hadn't been feeling well for some time: "I have not said anything about it to mother nor any of the rest of the folks because I am afraid she will not let me go to school for the school is a mile from our house and therefore it makes me very tired to walk which I have to do." Elvira, Palmer Depot, Mass. to Emma Barbour, Cambridge, Mass., Nov. 5, 1854. Moskow, *Emma's World,* 11; Wendover, diary, 13 Dec. 1886, 19 Apr. 1887.

90. Wendover, diary, 17 Feb., 12 Apr., 28 Jun. 1887, 23 Feb., 1 Mar., 8 Jun. 1888.

91. Wendover, diary, 4 Dec. 1888.

92. Ueda, *Avenues to Adulthood,* 90.

93. Fredrica Louisa Ballard Westervelt, *A Victorian Childhood* (privately printed), 4, 105.

94. Research in Baltimore and New York in the 1920s produced the diphtheria estimates, reported in Iain R. B. Hardy and Sieghart Dittmann, "Current Situation and Control Strategies for Resurgence of Diphtheria in Newly Independent States," *Lancet* 347, no. 9017 (1996): 1739. Westervelt, *A Victorian Childhood,* 113, 121. As Ueda's evidence suggests, stories of girls who left off studying because of health worries abound. Julia Newberry had in 1869 expressed to her diary the desire to "be somebody," but after she left school because of sickness, she was forbidden from returning under doctor's orders. "It is so horrid for I like it so much." Quoted in Harvey J. Graff, *Conflicting Paths: Growing Up in America* (Cambridge: Harvard University Press, 1995), 256. Godfrey, who had left school for a few weeks because of worries about her eyes, announced on her return that she had to "leave off Vergil this term on account of my eyes. Am very sorry to do it"; diary, 6 Mar. 1866.

95. Westervelt, *A Victorian Childhood,* 167.

96. Westervelt, *A Victorian Childhood,* 167, 190.

97. Jean Strouse, "Private Strife: Some Social Consequences of the Anatomical Dis-

tinction Between the Sexes," in *Women and Higher Education in American History*, ed. John Mack Faragher and Florence Howe (New York: Norton, 1988), 4.

7. High School Culture

1. Dennis Laurie, "Amateur Newspapers," *Collectible Newspapers: Official Journal of the National Collectible Newspapers Association* 5, no. 2 (April 1988).

2. Reed Ueda, *Avenues to Adulthood: The Origins of the High School and Social Mobility in an American Suburb* (Cambridge: Cambridge University Press, 1987), 125.

3. "The Letter-Box," *St. Nicholas* 5 (October 1878): 830; Jessie Wendover, diary, 16 Jan. 1885, 28 Jun. 1888, Ac. 2383, MC463, J. Wendover papers, Special Collections and University Archives (New Brunswick, N.J.: Rutgers University Libraries); Ernest N. Stevens, *A Brief History of Bridgton Academy, 1808–1957* (Privately printed, 1958).

4. Sara Annie Burstall, *The Education of Girls in the United States* (London: Swan, 1894), 163–64; *Radiator,* April 1896; Edith E. W. Gregg, *The Letters of Ellen Tucker Emerson* (Kent, Ohio: Kent State University Press, 1982), 163, 178. Wendover, diary, 23 Sep. 1885; Margaret Harding Tileston [Edsall], diary, 13 Apr. 1883, MC 354, Schlesinger Library (Cambridge: Radcliffe Institute, Harvard University).

5. *Sagamore,* March 1896, 144.

6. *High School Offering,* February 15, 1861. *High School News* 1, no. 5 (May 1879).

7. "High School Notes," *Granite Echo* 5, no. 6 (December 1881); *Comet,* October 15, 1883. Although this correspondent somewhat misstated the case in Concord, girls' academic and literary accomplishments were considered to reflect badly on their male classmates.

8. *Comet,* March 22, 1884.

9. *Volunteer* 1, no. 3 (October 1, 1887).

10. Victoria Bissell Brown, "The Fear of Feminization: Los Angeles High Schools in the Progressive Era," *Feminist Studies* 16, no. 3 (1990): 508. *Volunteer,* November 1897.

11. *Comet,* October 15, 1883.

12. *Comet,* February 20, 1884; *Volunteer,* December 1887.

13. The Concord High School *Comet* ceased publication in in May of 1884, and for three years, Concord High School had no student newspaper. Its replacement, the Concord High School *Volunteer* appeared in October 1887, reporting on the proposal for a girls' debating society in *Volunteer,* December 1, 25, 1887.

14. *Volunteer,* February 25, 1888.

15. *Volunteer,* February 25, 1888.

16. *Volunteer,* February 25, April 28, May 28, 1888.

17. *Volunteer,* November 23, 1888; Stevens, *Brief History,* 71.

18. For mention of joint activities, see *Volunteer,* November 23, 1888, January 4, February 1, April 5, 1889. On amendment, *Volunteer,* February 8, 1896. On inaction, *Volunteer,* April 6, 1896.

19. On not debating with girls, *Volunteer,* January 3, 1897. On dissolving debate society, *Volunteer,* March 1897. The debate team did have a new lease, for a city news-

paper story in 1900 announced a reprise of the debate between Concord and Manchester, an all-boys affair. The paper reported a lackluster event, however, "the hall not being more than a quarter filled," with "but little interest manifested in the discussion, unless it was by participants." *Concord Evening Monitor,* June 2, 1890; *Volunteer,* February 25, 1888.

20. *Sagamore,* April 1895, January 1896.

21. *High School Advance,* May 1897; Brown, "Fear of Feminization," 508.

22. *Volunteer,* March 1897.

23. *Comet,* March 22, 1884; *Oak, Lily, and Ivy,* October 1891, January 1894, January 1895.

24. *Volunteer,* March 1896; *Oak, Lily, and Ivy,* March 1897, January 1898.

25. *Oak, Lily, and Ivy,* March 1890, February 1892.

26. *Volunteer,* May 31, 1889; Sara Annie Burstall, *The Education of Girls in the United States* (London: Swan Sonnenschein Macmillan, 1894), 159.

27. Stevens, *Brief History,* 86; *Volunteer,* June 22, 1888; *Oak, Lily, and Ivy,* May 1895.

28. *Oak, Lily, and Ivy,* December 1898, April 1899.

29. *Oak, Lily, and Ivy,* April 1898.

30. *Oak, Lily, and Ivy,* April, November 1898.

31. *Oak, Lily, and Ivy,* April 1898.

32. *Oak, Lily, and Ivy,* December 1889, March 1890.

33. *High School Advance,* October, November 1892.

34. *Volunteer,* March, May, December 1898.

35. *Volunteer,* May, June 1898.

36. *Volunteer,* November 1898.

37. *High School Advance,* September 1898.

38. *Oak, Lily, and Ivy,* June, November 1898.

39. *Oak, Lily, and Ivy,* March 1899; *Volunteer,* January 1899. The paper had been advocating a girls' drill team since 1888.

40. *High School Mite,* April, May, June 1880.

41. *Amateur Sportsman,* July 1880.

42. In one issue the editors described their paper as a "Monthly Journal Devoted to Embryo Journalism" and contrasted it with "the FLASHY N.Y. boys' papers." *Granite Echo,* April 1881. In another issue they described it as "A Monthly Journal Devoted to the Interests of Boys and Girls of the Present Generation," as well as a representative of the "Noble Work" of amateur journalism. *Granite Echo,* February 15, 1882. In the next issue, they refined their definition yet again, describing the publication as a "Monthly Journal, Devoted to the Promotion of Pure Literature [in Opposition to the Blood and Thunder Stories in the N.Y. Flash Papers], to Educational Jottings, and the Interests of Boys and Girls of the Rising Generation." *Granite Echo,* March 15, 1882.

43. *Granite Echo,* November 1880, May 1881, May, June 1882.

44. *Comet,* November 1, 1882.

45. *Comet,* January 21, March 22, 1884.

46. *Volunteer,* November 23, 1888.

47. *Bombshell* 1, no. 1 (1889); the copy in the Concord Public Library is listed as "from Mrs. Gesen" (1959).

48. *Volunteer,* April 5, 1889.

49. *Volunteer,* January, April 1897.

50. *Volunteer,* February 1898.

51. *Volunteer,* February 1898.

52. *Volunteer,* Graduation Issue 1898.

53. Laurel Thatcher Ulrich, *A Midwife's Tale: The Life of Martha Ballard, Based on Her Diary, 1785–1812* (New York: Knopf, 1990), 75.

54. *Volunteer,* April 1899.

55. *Volunteer,* December 1899. This description recalls one from earlier in the century, "Football as It Appears to School Girls," in the Holyoke, Massachusetts, *High School Monthly,* November 1878. In the rush that follows kickoff, the anonymous author reports, "boys from both sides mingle, and this seems to be a good time to knock over small boys or to wreak vengeance on an enemy."

56. *Volunteer,* December 1899, March 1900.

57. *Volunteer,* May, June 1896.

58. *Oak, Lily, and Ivy,* November 1884.

59. African-American student bodies may have been ahead of the times in this respect. Glenda Gilmore notes the strength of female leadership at coeducational AME-Zion Livingstone College, Salisbury, North Carolina, where two women and one man founded the campus newspaper, the *Living Stone,* in 1890. Glenda Elizabeth Gilmore, *Gender and Jim Crow: Women and the Politics of White Supremacy in North Carolina, 1896–1920* (Chapel Hill: University of North Carolina Press, 1996), 42.

60. *Oak, Lily, and Ivy,* Nov. 1885, June 1886, March, June 1887.

61. *Oak, Lily, and Ivy,* March 1889, September 1891, Nov. 1885.

62. *Oak, Lily, and Ivy,* May 1887.

63. *Oak, Lily, and Ivy,* January, October 1887, December 1889, October, November 1892.

64. *Oak, Lily, and Ivy,* April, December 1893, October 1887.

65. A recent history of the impact of Catholic sisterhoods on American culture observes another such linguistic "normalization." Although by 1910 the Sisters of the Community of St. Joseph had been teaching boys for decades, their republished teaching manual retains the use of the normative female student. Such examples, of course, are noteworthy because rare. Carol K. Coburn and Martha Smith, *Spirited Lives: How Nuns Shaped Catholic Culture and American Life, 1836–1920* (Chapel Hill: University of North Carolina Press, 1999), 139; *Oak, Lily, and Ivy,* April 1886.

66. *Oak, Lily, and Ivy,* March 1888.

67. *Oak, Lily, and Ivy,* January 1891.

68. *Oak, Lily, and Ivy,* September 1890.

69. *Oak, Lily, and Ivy,* February 1892.

70. See Florence Howe, *Myths of Coeducation* (Bloomington: Indiana University Press, 1984), x–xi. One can argue that second-wave skepticism about coeducational high schools was in part incurred by a significant backlash against girls' domination of the nineteenth-century high school. Victoria Bissell Brown demonstrates the deleterious impact on girls of the twentieth-century campaign to solve the "boy problem"—the tendency of boys to drop out of secondary school—which had the effect of marginalizing girls in an institution that they had once dominated. Victoria Bissell Brown, "Golden Girls: Female Socialization in Los Angeles, 1880 to 1910," Ph.D. diss. (San Diego: University of California, 1985); Brown, "The Fear of Feminization."

A negative view of coeducational higher education occurs in several articles published in a volume to celebrate women's education at Mount Holyoke College. Both Rosalind Rosenberg and Joyce Antler document some of the hardships young women experienced in coeducational colleges and universities. Antler's biographical study of Lucy Sprague Mitchell contains a description of Sprague's shame-ridden journey to the Harvard Library, chaperoned by her knitting grandmother. Rosenberg notes that male students at Wesleyan beat any men seen talking to female students, barred women from the yearbook, and excluded them from membership in student organizations. Nonetheless, Rosenberg acknowledges the importance of coeducation. "Conditioned from childhood to doubt her own intelligence, the woman admitted to a male institution had the pleasure of discovering that she could match or surpass the achievements of male students." Rosalind Rosenberg, "The Limits of Access: The History of Coeducation in America," in *Women and Higher Education in American History,* ed. John Mack Faragher and Florence Howe (New York: Norton, 1988), 114. Joyce Antler, "The Educational Biography of Lucy Sprague Mitchell: A Case Study in the History of Women's Higher Education," in Faragher and Howe, *Women and Higher Education,* 50, is slower to acknowledge the contributions of coeducation, suggesting a kind of false consciousness among female students who identified with their male classmates. "Unfortunately the constraints that Harvard imposed on women students led them to identify with the standards of the superior lot—Harvard men—in the way that less privileged groups often internalize the morality of those with greatest power."

In demonstrating the failings of coeducational higher education, Rosenberg notes that gender practices in colleges were better than those in society at large. Like the college students Rosenberg studies, high school graduates too "walked through to lives women never had experienced before." Rosenberg, "Women and Higher Education," 121.

8. Friendship, Fun, and the City Streets

1. Carolyn Steedman, *Strange Dislocations: Childhood and the Idea of Human Interiority, 1780–1930* (London: Virago, 1995), 117, makes this argument about Henry Mayhew's famous 1850 interview with "the little watercress girl," a London street peddler. The eight-year-old child denied her status as a child because she saw herself as a worker instead, Steedman suggests. The little watercress girl told Mayhew, "I ain't a child, and I

shan't be a woman till I'm twenty, but I'm past eight, I am." Steedman concludes that a child's job description does not include being a worker. "Our Post-Office Box," *Harper's Young People,* 19 February 1884, 255.

2. Joel Myerson and Daniel Shealy, eds., *Journals of Louisa May Alcott* (Boston: Little, Brown, 1989), 45; Joel Myerson and Daniel Shealy, eds., *Selected Letters of Louisa May Alcott* (Boston: Little, Brown, 1987), 3.

3. Emily Marshall Eliot [Morison], diary, 6 Mar., 12 May, 19 Aug. 1868, 17 Mar., 8, 13, 24 Apr., 7, 26, 31 May 1869, A/M861, Emily Marshall Eliot Morison papers, 1874–1883, Schlesinger Library (Cambridge: Radcliffe Institute, Harvard University). For withdrawal of women, see Mary P. Ryan, *Cradle of the Middle Class: The Family in Oneida County, New York, 1790–1865* (Cambridge: Cambridge University Press, 1981), 148; Christine Stansell, *City of Women: Sex and Class in New York, 1789–1860* (New York: Knopf, 1986), 194.

4. *Ladies' Home Journal,* December 1897, 41; Ellen LeGarde, "Out-Door Sports for Girls," *Ladies' Home Journal,* June 1890. One dissenter was Elizabeth Blackwell, *The Laws of Life, with Special Reference to the Physical Education of Girls* (New York: George P. Putnam, 1852), 130. Blackwell advocated calisthenics over the boarding school practice of a group promenade. "What is there attractive or invigorating in a walk through our streets? Can there be a more melancholy spectacle than a boarding-school of girls, taking their afternoon walk?"

5. Granville Stanley Hall, *Adolescence: Its Psychology and Its Relations to Physiology, Anthropology, Sociology, Sex, Crime, Religion, and Education.* (New York: D. Appleton, 1904), 2: 572.

6. Sarah Browne, diary, 15 Oct. 1859, MC 232, Schlesinger Library (Cambridge: Radcliffe Institute, Harvard University).

7. Margaret Harding Tileston [Edsall], diary 23 Jan. 1882, 18 Sep., 3 Oct., 3 Dec. 1883, 1 Feb., 1 May, 18 Jul. 1884, MC 354, Schlesinger Library (Cambridge: Radcliffe Institute, Harvard University).

8. Marlene Deahl Merrill, ed., *Growing Up in Boston's Gilded Age: The Journal of Alice Stone Blackwell, 1872–1874* (New Haven: Yale University Press, 1990), 55, 169; Agnes Hamilton, diary, 23 Aug., 4 Dec. 1887, MC 278, M-24, Hamilton family papers, Schlesinger Library (Cambridge: Radcliffe Institute, Harvard University); Annie Ware Winsor [Allen], diaries, 15 Oct. 1884, MC 322, papers of Annie Ware Winsor Allen, 1884–1950, Schlesinger Library (Cambridge: Radcliffe Institute, Harvard University).

9. Jessie Wendover, diary, 23 Sep., 7 Oct. 1887, Ac. 2383, MC463, J. Wendover papers, Special Collections and University Archives (New Brunswick, N.J.: Rutgers University Libraries); Vivian C. Hopkins, ed., "Diary of an Iowa Farm Girl: Josephine Edith Brown, 1892–1901," *Annals of Iowa* 42, no. 2 (1973): 128; Rowena Cooke, diary, 12 Sep. 1873, Ohio Historical Society (Columbus, Ohio), described waving her handkerchief while her friend waved her umbrella at "the boys" down the street. "Went to school in the daytime had a pretty gay time coming home especially."

10. [Edsall], diary, 19 Apr., 15 Oct. 1883, 7 Feb., 18, 22 Mar., 15, 26 Apr., 1 Jul. 1884.

For examples of the use of "walking up and down" to describe girls' walks, see Mary Boit [Cabot], diary, 1 Jul. 1888, A 99, Cabot family papers, Schlesinger Library (Cambridge: Radcliffe Institute, Harvard University); [Morison], diary, 4 Apr., 9 May 1869.

11. U.S. Federal Writers' Project, "Girlhood Life in Portland, 1860–1876," Oral history of Etta Crawford, Portland, Oregon, Works Progress Administration Records, Oregon Historical Society (Portland).

12. Kate Upson [Clark], diary, 20 Aug. 1863, Kate Upson Clark papers, 1851–1935, Sophia Smith Collection (Northampton, Mass.: Smith College); Wendover, diary, 26 Nov. 1885.

13. [Allen], MC 322, 19 Jan. 1885; Edith E. W. Gregg, ed., *The Letters of Ellen Tucker Emerson* (Kent, Ohio: Kent State University Press, 1982), 258.

14. [Clark], diary, 30 Apr. 1866. The *Freeman* (Kingston, N.Y.) is quoted in *Comet,* November 15, 1883. The writer attempted to finesse the real question, however, suggesting that a girl leaving church was "accompanied probably by parents or friends," thus not having to choose between walking alone and receiving unappealing accompaniment.

15. *The Oak, Lily, and Ivy,* September 1888; Elizabeth Ellery Dana, diary, 10 Jul. 1862, A-85, Dana family papers, 1822–1956, Schlesinger Library (Cambridge: Radcliffe Institute, Harvard University); Beth Bailey, *From Front Porch to Back Seat: Courtship in Twentieth-Century America* (Baltimore: Johns Hopkins University Press, 1988).

16. Merrill, *Journal of Alice Blackwell,* 85–86; (Mary) Elizabeth Morrissey, diary, 17 Jul. 1876 (Boston: Boston Public Library).

17. Ida Mabel Lancraft, diary, 14 Jul., 25 Aug. 1887 (New Haven: New Haven Colony Historical Society).

18. Lancraft, diary, 19 Jan. 1890; Charlotte Perkins [Gilman], journal, v. 8, 177, Schlesinger Library (Cambridge: Radcliffe Institute, Harvard University), 8 Jan., 3 Feb., 25 Mar., 24 Aug. 1879.

19. [Gilman], journal, 11 Jan., 29 Mar. 1879; Sarah Deutsch, *Women and the City: Gender, Space, and Power in Boston, 1870–1940* (New York: Oxford University Press, 2000), 83.

20. Sarah Browne, diary, 20 Oct. 1859; Sarah Ellen Browne to mother, [Jun. 1857?], MC232, Schlesinger Library (Cambridge: Radcliffe Institute, Harvard University).

21. Merrill, *Journal of Alice Blackwell,* 188; Lancraft, diary, 10 Aug. 1889.

22. [Edsall], diary, 22 Jun. 1881, 4 Feb., 3 Apr. 1882, 6 Oct. 1884, 24 Sep. 1885.

23. [Edsall], diary, 20 Feb. 1886; Dana, diary, 24 Jul. 1862.

24. [Clark], diary, 28 Apr., 4 Sep., 24 Oct., 5 Nov., 12 Dec. 1863, 27 Apr. 1864; [Edsall], diary, 11 May 1885.

25. [Morison], diary, 18 Apr. 1871; [Edsall], diary, 3 Jan. 1885; Wendover, diary, 27 Nov. 1885, 12 Oct. 1887.

26. Lancraft, diary, 23 Sep. 1889.

27. Wendover, diary, 25 Jun. 1885, 3 Dec. 1887, 6 Apr. 1888. For more on Christmas shopping, [Edsall], diary, 22 Dec. 1883; Anna Stevens, diary, insert, 19, 24 Dec.

1895, privately owned; Wendover, diary, 30 Nov. 1888. Anna Stevens, who lived in a Maine mill town, was not a regular shopper. Nonetheless, on Christmas Eve 1895 she announced, "No school. . . . Went about the different stores all day, most with different ones."

28. Wendover, diary, 3, 5 Mar. 1885, 31 Jul. 1886.

29. Elaine S. Abelson, *When Ladies Go A-Thieving: Middle-Class Shoplifters in the Victorian Department Store* (New York: Oxford University Press, 1989), 57; Wendover, diary, 26 Nov. 1887. Wendover's negative judgment on Macy's window gives extra credibility to her rave review of the Cyclorama of the Battle of Gettysburg she saw the next year: "It is *very* well done; the perspective is perfect, and the scenery seems to stretch away before one till it is lost in the dim distance." Wendover, diary, 22 Apr. 1888.

30. [Clark], diary, 26 Aug., 3 Oct. 1863.

31. Stevens, diary, 18 Mar., 20, 21 Apr., 27 Jun., 17 Jul., 28 Aug. 1895.

32. [Clark], diary, 11 May 1865. Lois Wells reported on one trip "to the market" with a friend which proved "an exciting time": "I lost my handkerchief—Lillie lost a pair of mitts and worst of all let a gentleman embrace her on the street." Lois Wells, diary, 17 Jul. 1887, MC-39, Schlesinger Library (Cambridge: Radcliffe Institute, Harvard University). Here Wells appears to blame her friend for what today would be considered an act of harassment.

33. Wendover, diary 22 Jun. 1886; Marian Nichols, diary, 13 Feb. 1884, A-170, papers of the Nichols-Shurtleff family, 1780–1953, Schlesinger Library (Cambridge: Radcliffe Institute, Harvard University); [Clark], diary, 17 Oct. 1865.

34. Victoria Bissell Brown, "Golden Girls: Female Socialization in Los Angeles, 1880 to 1910," Ph.D. diss. (San Diego: University of California, 1985), 215.

35. Sam Bass Warner, *Streetcar Suburbs: The Process of Growth in Boston, 1870–1900* (Cambridge: Harvard University Press, 1962), 58; Merrill, *Journal of Alice Stone Blackwell,* 40, 43, 148, 162–63.

36. Alexis de Tocqueville, *Democracy in America,* trans. Henry Reeve (New York: Random House, 1981), 484–85.

37. Eliza Lynn Linton, "Girl of the Period," in *The Woman Question: Society and Literature in Britain and America, 1837–1883,* ed. and comp. Elizabeth K. Helsinger, Robin Ann Sheets, and William R. Veeder (Chicago: University of Chicago Press, 1989), 109–13.

38. Henry James, "Modern Women," in Helsinger, Sheets, and Veeder, *Woman Question,* 1: 120–22.

39. James, "Modern Women," 121–22.

40. Louisa May Alcott, *An Old-Fashioned Girl* (Boston: Roberts, 1870), 4.

41. Alcott, *An Old-Fashioned Girl,* 10, 13, 38, 48.

42. Alcott, *An Old-Fashioned Girl,* 19–20, 42.

43. Washington Gladden, "A Talk with Girls and Their Mothers," *St. Nicholas* 7 (May 1880): 524.; Marion Harland [Mary Virginia Terhune], *Eve's Daughters; or, Com-*

mon Sense for Maid, Wife, and Mother (New York: J. R. Anderson and H. S. Allen, 1882), 65.

44. Alcott, *An Old-Fashioned Girl*, 11, 41, 45.

45. Gladden, "A Talk with Girls and Their Mothers," 524.

46. "Why Girls Disappear," *Ladies' Home Journal*, January 1884.

47. Mrs. J. G. Fraser, "Our Lost Girls: A Mother Sadly Regrets That She Can Not Have the Training of Her Daughter," *Ladies' Home Journal*, November 1889.

48. Dio Lewis, *Our Girls* (New York: Harper, 1871).

49. Kate Tannatt Woods, "Manners in Public," *Ladies' Home Journal*, June 1890, 10.

50. Henry James, "The Speech of American Women," *Harper's Bazar* 41, no. 2 (1906–7): 17.

51. James, "Speech of American Women," 18; Jean Strouse, "Private Strife: Some Social Consequences of the Anatomical Distinction Between the Sexes," in *Women and Higher Education in American History,* ed. John Mack Faragher and Florence Howe (New York: Norton, 1988), 11.

52. James, *Speech and Manners of American Women,* 15, 31.

53. "Why Girls Disappear"; "Flirting Girls," *Ladies' Home Journal*, April 1885.

54. Ruth Ashmore, "Side Talks with Girls," *Ladies' Home Journal*, January 1890, 10 [hereafter STG]. In fact, the first two columns were written by *Journal* editor Edward Bok himself, as he sought a regular columnist. Edward William Bok, *The Americanization of Edward Bok: The Autobiography of a Dutch Boy Fifty Years After.* (New York: Scribner's, 1920), 171; "A Well-Known Writer Succumbs to Pneumonia, Following Grip," *New York Times,* December 28, 1898.

55. STG, January 1890, 10; February 1890, 10; March 1890, 10; July 1891, 12.

56. STG, February 1890, 10; January 1891, 12; January 1892; April 1894, 35; June 1894, 27; July 1895, 29; February 1896, 35. For cosmetics, chewing gum, and eating, STG, October 1894, 29; March 1895, 33; February 1897, 31; May 1898, 31.

57. STG, February 1892, 16; June 1894, 27; March 1896, 18. On rumors, STG, July 1894, 31; January 1895, 29. Margaret E. Sangster, "My Girls," *Ladies' Home Journal,* December 1899, 38; Edith Lawrence, "The Gossip of a New York Girl," *Ladies' Home Journal,* May 1899, 15.

58. Edward William Bok, *The Americanization of Edward Bok: The Autobiography of a Dutch Boy Fifty Years After* (New York: Scribner, 1920), 169.

59. "The Letter-Box," *St. Nicholas* 2 (August 1875): 650; Ethel Sturges [Dummer], "Street Scenes," compositions, A-127, M-55, Ethel Sturges Dummer papers, 1766–1962, Schlesinger Library (Cambridge: Radcliffe Institute, Harvard University). Sturges later worked as a philanthropist in the progressive era.

60. The 1860 census indicates that Lizzie had an infant brother, but by the time of her diary, he had left home. Morrissey, diary, 20, 22, 26 Feb. 1876.

61. Morrissey, diary, 16, 24, 25, 31 Aug., 3, 4 Sep. 1876.

62. Morrissey, diary, 21 Jul., 12, 20, 21 Oct. 1876.

63. Morrissey, diary, 5 Jan., 3 Oct., 11 Nov. 1876.

64. Henry Adams, *The Education of Henry Adams: An Autobiography* (Boston: Houghton Mifflin, 1918), 7–8.

65. Richard L. Bushman, *The Refinement of America: Persons, Houses, Cities* (New York: Knopf, 1992), 404, notes that "gentility was particularly useful in securing one's identity along the lower boundary of the middle class, where people were emerging from a cruder traditional culture and were uneasy about the validity of their refinement." Evelyn Brooks Higginbotham, *Righteous Discontent: The Women's Movement in the Black Baptist Church, 1880–1920* (Cambridge: Harvard University Press, 1993), 1–3, refers to a "politics of respectability" at the turn of the century.

66. Bok, *Americanization of Edward Bok,* 170.

67. [Allen], diaries, 27 Oct. 1884; Hamilton, diary, 31 Mar. 1886; [Edsall], diary, 20 Feb. 1885. In Alcott's *Old-Fashioned Girl,* Polly goes with her fashionable friends to "one of the new spectacles which have lately become the rage, . . . dazzling, exciting, and demoralizing the spectator by every allurement French ingenuity can invent, and American prodigality execute." Once there, however, she discovered that the fairyland she was witnessing (perhaps early vaudeville) was illusion, "for the lovely phantoms sang negro melodies, talked slang, and were a disgrace to the good old-fashioned elves whom she knew and loved so well." Her conclusion: "I didn't think it was proper." Alcott, *An Old-Fashioned Girl,* 15, 17. For a discussion of the respectability of theater, see John F. Kasson, *Rudeness and Civility: Manners in Nineteenth-Century Urban America* (New York: Hill and Wang, 1990), 231.

68. [Edsall], diary, 7, 8 Apr. 1885; Emily M. Eliot, "Journal of a Boston Girl of 18 Years," HUG(FP) 33.6, Samuel Eliot Morison papers, Harvard University Archives (Cambridge: Pusey Library), 27 Nov., 6, 11, 12, 30 Dec. 1875.

69. Morrissey, diary, 10, 11 Aug. 1876.

70. Mary Bartine, "Our Jolly S.F.J.," poem inserted in 1897 diary, Ac. 2702, Gaston family papers, Special Collections and University Archives (New Brunswick, N.J.: Rutgers University Libraries).

71. As a venue for individual accountability, a diary might counter the shared esprit of a group of friends. Bartine, diary, 24 Feb. 1897.

72. Florence C. Peck, diaries, 22 Jan., 20 Apr. 1898, Manuscripts and Archives Division (New York: New York Public Library. Astor, Lenox, and Tilden Foundations). She focused her comment on Becca Middleton Samson's "A Devotee and a Darling" on the style of the diary entries. For development of the relation between attending the symphony and class, see Kasson, *Rudeness and Civility.*

73. Peck, diaries, 17, 19, 27 Aug., 11 Nov. 1901.

74. Lancraft, diary, 8 Aug. 1889, 24 Jan. 1890.

75. Lancraft, diary, 26 Dec. 1889.

76. Alcott, *Old-Fashioned Girl,* 250; Peck, diaries, 11 Dec. 1898. Earlier that year Peck and two friends stopped on Main Street, and one of them bought some flowers, which they divided up, put on, and "looked very spruce." Peck, diaries, 22 Mar. 1898.

77. Rudyard Kipling, "The American Girl," *Ladies' Home Journal,* October 1899, 5.

78. Jane Addams, *The Spirit of Youth and the City Streets* (Urbana: University of Illinois Press, 1972), 8–9; Carolyn G. Heilbrun, *Writing a Woman's Life* (New York: Norton, 1988), 17.

79. Hall, *Adolescence,* 589.

9. Commencement

1. Victoria Bissell Brown, "Golden Girls: Female Socialization in Los Angeles, 1880 to 1910," Ph.D. (San Diego: University of California, 1985), 265, notes that between 1890 and 1910 girls represented 57 percent of those in high school but 63 percent of high school graduates.

2. Frances Abbott, "The Song of the Graduation Gown," (Concord) *Union Paper* (1875).

3. Rev. R. W. Bailey, *Patriarch or Family Library Magazine,* 1 (1841); Ann Ferguson, "Woman's Moral Voice: Superior, Inferior, or Just Different?" in *Women and Higher Education in American History,* ed. John Mack Faragher and Florence Howe (New York: Norton, 1988), 187.

4. Elizabeth Ellery Dana, diary, 11 Jul. 1862, A-85, Dana family papers, 1822–1956, Schlesinger Library (Cambridge: Radcliffe Institute, Harvard University).

5. Barbara Myerhoff, "Rites of Passage: Process and Paradox," in *Celebration: Studies in Festivity and Ritual,* ed. Victor Turner (Washington, D.C.: Smithsonian Institution Press, 1982), 130.

6. Lois Wells, diary, 14 Jun. 1888, MC-39, Schlesinger Library (Cambridge: Radcliffe Institute, Harvard University).

7. "Girls and Literary Calisthenics," *Ladies' Home Journal,* May 1896, 14; Myerhoff, "Rites of Passage," 112.

8. "Girls and Literary Calisthenics," 14.

9. Florence C. Peck, diaries, 11, 28 Jun. 1901, Manuscripts and Archives Division (New York: New York Public Library, Astor, Lenox, and Tilden Foundations).

10. Harriet E. Paine, *Chats with Girls on Self-Culture* (New York: Dodd, Mead, 1891), 1.

11. Margaret Harding Tileston [Edsall], diary, 2, 6, 13, 19, 27 Mar., 16 Apr. 1885, MC 354, Schlesinger Library (Cambridge: Radcliffe Institute, Harvard University).

12. [Edsall], diary, 24, 28, 30 Apr. 1885.

13. [Edsall], diary, 9 May, 20, 21 Jun. 1885.

14. [Edsall], diary, 21 Jun. 1885.

15. [Edsall], diary, 24 Jun. 1885.

16. [Edsall], diary, 23 Jun. 1885.

17. [Edsall], diary, 27 Mar., 14 Apr. 1885.

18. [Edsall], diary, 27 Jun. 1885.

19. [Edsall], diary, 1 Jul. 1885.

20. [Edsall], diary, 1, 2 Jul. 1885.

21. [Edsall], diary, 3 Jul. 1885.

22. Edith E. W. Gregg, *The Letters of Ellen Tucker Emerson* (Kent, Ohio: Kent State University Press, 1982), 189.

23. Dana, diary, 12, 16 Jul. 1862.

24. Dana, diary, 11, 12 Jul. 1862.

25. Dana, diary, 16 Jul. 1862.

26. Sarah Rice, *He Included Me: The Autobiography of Sarah Rice,* ed. Louise Westling (Athens: University of Georgia Press, 1989), 67.

27. Adin Ballou, *History of the Town of Milford, Worcester County, Massachusetts, from Its First Settlement to 1881* (Boston: Franklin, 1882), 256; Annie Roberts Godfrey, diary (privately owned), 16 Mar. 1865; *Oak, Lily, and Ivy,* March 1892.

28. *Oak, Lily, and Ivy,* May 1886, June 1889, June 1895.

29. *Milford Gazette,* June 20, 1890; Ernest N. Stevens, *A Brief History of Bridgton Academy, 1808–1957* (Privately printed, 1958), 78; *Oak, Lily, and Ivy,* June 1890.

30. *Oak, Lily, and Ivy,* June 1890. *Comet,* November 15, 1883, noted, "There are always some in a class who wish to appear in rich attire on such an occasion, and these are generally stubborn and will not yield to a more reasonable arrangement, consequently the others, not willing to be inferior in appearance to their classmates, will often spend more in dress than they can really afford." Emily M. Eliot, "Red Letter Days for the Summer of 1875," HUG(FP) 33.6, Samuel Eliot Morison papers, Harvard University Archives (Cambridge: Pusey Library), 30 Jun. 1875; *Oak, Lily, and Ivy,* April 1886, June 1888.

31. *Oak, Lily, and Ivy,* June, September 1890; *Milford Daily News,* June 16, 19, 1891.

32. *Oak, Lily, and Ivy,* September 1891; "The High School Graduation Matter," *Milford Gazette,* June 24, 1892.

33. Many thanks to the generosity of the Milford historian Paul Curran for bringing this event to my attention and sharing his research with me. "The High School Graduation Matter," *Milford Gazette,* June 24, 1892.

34. "Meeting at the School Board," *Milford Gazette,* June 24, 1892; *Milford Daily News,* June 24, 1892.

35. Paul Curran has discovered that a Catholic priest, the Rev. James T. Canavan, had given the high school graduation address ten years earlier. "The High School Graduation Matter."

36. *The Oak, Lily, and Ivy,* June 1886; Dana, diary, 21 Jul. 1862; (Mary) Elizabeth Morrissey, diary, 30 Jun. 1876 (Boston: Boston Public Library); Peck, diaries, 8, 9, 16, 18 Jul., 11 Aug. 1901.

37. Sarah Ellen Browne to mother, Jun. 1859; Sarah Browne, diary, 27 Jun., 27 Oct 1859, both MC 232, Schlesinger Library (Cambridge: Radcliffe Institute, Harvard University); Gregg, *Letters of Ellen Tucker Emerson,* 189.

38. Morrissey, diary, 18 Sep. 1876; Peck, diaries, 12 Jul. 1901.

39. Mary Custis deButts, ed., *Growing Up in the 1850s: The Journal of Agnes Lee* (Chapel Hill: University of North Carolina Press, 1984), 103, 129.

40. Albert Browne to daughter Nellie, 28 Jan. 1859, MC 232, Schlesinger Library (Cambridge: Radcliffe Institute, Harvard University); Sarah Ellen Browne, to father, Albert, 30 Jan., 21 May, 14 Jun. 1859.

41. Shirley Blotnick Moskow, *Emma's World: An Intimate Look at Lives Touched by the Civil War Era* (Far Hills, N.J.: New Horizon, 1990), 2 Aug. 1860; Georgia Mercer [Boit], diary, 12 Apr. 1871, A 99, Cabot family papers, Schlesinger Library (Cambridge: Radcliffe Institute, Harvard University); Peck, diaries, 10 Jun. 1901.

42. Ada E. Hazell, "True Relationship of Mother and Daughter," *Ladies' Home Journal*, October 1888; Rosamond Elfeth, "Our Girls—After School Days," *Ladies' Home Journal*, October 1888, 5.

43. Ruth Ashmore, "Side Talks with Girls (The Elder Sister in the Home)," *Ladies' Home Journal*, April 1894, 7 [hereafter STG].

44. Sarah Browne, diary, 9 Jul. 1859.

45. Cynthia Griffin Wolff, *Emily Dickinson* (New York: Knopf, 1986), 77; Emily Dickinson, *The Letters of Emily Dickinson*, ed. Thomas H. Johnson (Cambridge, Mass.: Belknap, 1986), 13, 82.

46. Dickinson, *Letters*, 84.

47. Wolff, *Emily Dickinson*, 100–101; Anna L. White, *Kate Callender; or, School-Girls of '54, and the Women of To-Day* (Boston: self-published, 1870), 94.

48. Ashmore, STG, April 1894, 35; September 1890, 10; Granville Stanley Hall, *Adolescence: Its Psychology and Its Relations to Physiology, Anthropology, Sociology, Sex, Crime, Religion, and Education* (New York: D. Appleton, 1904), 582.

49. Hall, *Adolescence*, 621.

50. White, *Kate Callender*, 9.

51. Charlotte Perkins [Gilman], "Literary and Artistic Vurks of the Princess Charlotte," Schlesinger Library (Cambridge: Radcliffe Institute, Harvard University, 1870–71).

52. [Edsall], diary, 15 Nov 1884; Mary Boit [Cabot], diary, 20 Jun. 1891, A 99, Cabot family papers, Schlesinger Libraray (Cambridge: Radcliffe Institute, Harvard University), fortune pasted under 26 Oct. 1888 but accompanies Aug. 1891 entries.

53. Mary D. Robertson, ed., *Lucy Breckinridge of Grove Hill: The Journal of a Virginia Girl, 1862–1864* (Kent, Ohio: Kent State University Press, 1979), 167; Mary Winsor to sister, Annie Ware Winsor [Allen], 22 Aug. 1882, MC 322, papers of Annie Ware Winsor Allen, 1884–1950, Schlesinger Library (Cambridge: Radcliffe Institute, Harvard University); Ella Lyman [Cabot], diary, 25 Jan. 1885, A-139, Ella Lyman Cabot papers, 1855–1934, Schlesinger Library (Cambridge: Radcliffe Institute, Harvard University); Karen Lystra, *Searching the Heart: Women, Men, and Romantic Love in Nineteenth-Century America* (New York: Oxford University Press, 1989), 258.

54. Lystra, *Searching the Heart*, 59.

55. Marlene Deahl Merrill, ed., *Growing Up in Boston's Gilded Age: The Journal of Alice Stone Blackwell, 1872–1874* (New Haven: Yale University Press, 1990), 178.

56. Dana, diary, 4 Aug. 1862.

57. Gregg, *Letters of Ellen Tucker Emerson*, 182, 211, 269; Charles Strickland, *Victorian Domesticity: Families in the Life and Art of Louisa May Alcott* (University: University of Alabama Press, 1985), 54.

58. Robertson, *Lucy Breckinridge*, 55, 167. Lystra, *Searching the Heart*, 182–83, argues that the postponement of a wedding was part of the ritual of testing to which women subjected men in order to guarantee the quality of the love.

59. *Ladies' Home Journal*, November 1896, 11; Ashmore, STG, November 1894, 18; [Edsall], diary, 5 Apr. 1886.

60. Robertson, *Lucy Breckinridge*, 22; Margo Culley, ed., "Helen Ward Brandreth," in *A Day at a Time: The Diary Literature of American Women from 1764 to the Present* (New York: Feminist Press at the City University of New York, 1985), 13; [Boit], diary, 22 Jun. 1871.

61. Robertson, *Lucy Breckinridge*, 31, 55.

62. Lystra, *Searching the Heart*, 192.

63. Abba Goold Woolson, *Woman in American Society* (Boston: Roberts, 1873), 31.

64. Lystra, *Searching the Heart*, 158–59, 164, notes that "by the 1830s at least" men and women came to an agreement first and only then sought parental blessing. "The indirect manipulation of associational networks . . . was all that remained of parental control in the mate-selection process" in the midcentury and beyond.

65. Robert A. Boit, diary, 8 Dec 1894, 14 Jan. 1900, Robert Apthorp Boit diaries (Boston: Massachusetts Historical Society); Maureen E. Montgomery, "Female Rituals and the Politics of the New York Marriage Market in the Late Nineteenth Century," *Journal of Family History* 23, no. 1 (January 1998): 53.

66. Sarah Ellen Browne to mother, 9 Jan. 1859; Sarah Browne, diary, 22 Sep. 1859.

67. Susan Coolidge, "A Coming Out," *Ladies' Home Journal*, October 1889, 4.

68. Emily Marshall Eliot [Morison], diary, 1871, drawings at end of journal "Done by Nellie Eldredge at Miss Foote's," 8, 9, 11, 12, 13 Jan. 1878, A/M861, Emily Marshall Eliot Morison papers, 1874–1883, Schlesinger Library (Cambridge: Radcliffe Institute, Harvard University).

69. Woolson, *Woman in American Society*, 26; Edith Wharton, *A Backward Glance* (New York: D. Appleton-Century, 1934), 78.

70. *Comet*, January 21, 1884. Huybertie Pruyn Manlin quoted her own diary in a later memoir used by Montgomery, "Female Rituals," 52.

71. Elizabeth W. Coffin, *A Girl's Life in Germantown* (Boston: Sherman, French, 1916), 65.

72. Boit, diary, 5 Sep. 1896, 7 Jan. 1900.

73. Fredrica Louisa Ballard Westervelt, *A Victorian Childhood* (privately printed), 217; Charlotte Perkins Gilman, *The Diaries of Charlotte Perkins Gilman*, ed. Denise D. Knight (Charlottesville: University Press of Virginia, 1994), 360.

74. Leonore Davidoff, *The Best Circles: Society, Etiquette, and the Season* (London: Croom Helm, 1973), 17. Davidoff's study has no equivalent for the United States.

75. Ella Lyman [Cabot], diary, 25 Jan. 1885; Christine Ladd [Franklin], diary, 23

Jul. 1866, Special Collections (Poughkeepsie, N.Y.: Vassar College Library). Ladd noted that her grandmother had offered this objection to her desire to attend Vassar College.

76. Elizabeth Fisher Nichols to Rose Nichols, 14 Dec. 1893, A-170, papers of the Nichols-Shurtleff family, 1780–1953, Schlesinger Library (Cambridge: Radcliffe Institute, Harvard University).

77. Myerhoff, "Rites of Passage," 118.

78. [Edsall], diary, 14 Dec. 1883, 17 Oct. 1884.

79. [Edsall], diary, 22 Nov. 1884, 12 Jan., 25, 26 Feb. 1885.

80. [Edsall], diary, 7, 13 Jun., 31 Aug. 1884.

81. [Edsall], diary, 2 Jul. 1885.

82. [Edsall], diary, 29 Aug., 23 Sep., 26 Dec. 1885.

83. [Edsall], diary, 12 Oct., 23 Nov. 1885, 8, 10, 22 Mar. 1886.

84. [Edsall], diary, 19 Nov., 14 Dec. 1885, 19, 25 Jan., 20 May 1887.

85. [Edsall], diary, 28 Nov. 1884, 17 Jan., 26 Jul., 3, 23 Sep. 1886.

86. [Edsall], diary, 5 Sep., 26 Oct., 7, 30 Nov., 4, 11, 12 Dec. 1886, 1, 15 Jan. 1887.

87. [Edsall], diary, 21 Feb., 6 Mar. 1887.

88. [Edsall], diary, 27, 30 Sep., 19 Oct., 5, 12, 13, 25 Nov. 1887.

89. [Edsall], diary, 6 Apr., 30 Jan. 1885, 9 Mar. 1887; James Hain Friswell, *The Gentle Life: Essays in the Formation of Character* (London: Sampson, Low, Son, and Marston, 1866), 21, 57.

90. [Edsall], diary, 12 Jan. 1884.

91. [Edsall], diary, 17 May, 15, 28 Jul. 1885, 19, 23 Jan., 10 Jul., 7 Aug. 1886; Maureen E. Montgomery, "Female Rituals and the Politics of the New York Marriage Market in the Late Nineteenth Century," *Journal of Family History* 23, no. 1 (January 1998): 51.

92. [Edsall], diary, 6 Feb., 1 Nov. 1887.

93. [Edsall], diary, 6 Jun. 1887.

94. Ethel Spencer, *The Spencers of Amberson Avenue: A Turn-of-the-Century Memoir,* ed. Michael P. Weber and Peter N. Stearns (Pittsburgh: University of Pittsburgh Press, 1983), 84; Agnes Hamilton, diary, 26 Jan. 1890, MC 278, M-24, Hamilton family papers, Schlesinger Library (Cambridge: Radcliffe Institute, Harvard University, 1886–87).

95. Josef Breuer and Sigmund Freud, *Studies of Hysteria,* in *The Standard Edition of the Complete Psychological Works of Sigmund Freud,* trans. and ed. James Strachey (London: Hogarth, 1955), 2: 22.

96. Alice James, *The Diary of Alice James,* ed. Leon Edel (New York: Dodd, Mead, 1964), 66, 149, 151, 223. For a good discussion of Freud and Breuer's treatment of Bertha Pappenheim (Anna O.), see Elaine Showalter, *The Female Malady: Women, Madness, and English Culture, 1830–1980* (New York: Pantheon, 1985), 155. Other historians, too, have noted the impact of colliding roles in producing hysteria. Carroll Smith-Rosenberg, for instance, suggests that hysteria probably arose when the "fragile, sensitive, and dependent child" encountered the demanding responsibilities of the adulthood. Carroll Smith-Rosenberg, "The Hysterical Woman: Sex Roles and Role Conflict

in Nineteenth-Century America," in *Disorderly Conduct: Visions of Gender in Victorian America* (New York: Knopf, 1985); Steven Mintz and Susan Kellogg, *Domestic Revolutions: A Social History of American Family Life* (New York: Free Press/Collier/Macmillan, 1988), 63, suggest that the conflict lay between "woman's preparation for self-fulfillment and her role as the family's key nurturing figure."

97. DeButts, *Journal of Agnes Lee,* 103; Sarah Ellen Browne to mother, 14 Jun. 1859.

98. Woolson, *Woman in American Society,* 1.

99. The similarities in the iconography are striking. Maureen Montgomery notes that "coming-out rituals necessitated display to draw attention to the young woman's change in status" coded visually. "The requisite white gown, signifying her virginity in the traditional manner, marked the debutante out from the rest of the women present." Floral bouquets "signifying purity and innocence" also characterized both graduations and social debuts. Montgomery, "Female Rituals," 54.

100. Catherine E. Kelly, *In the New England Fashion: Reshaping Women's Lives in the Nineteenth-Century* (Ithaca, N.Y.: Cornell University Press, 1999), 81, argues that girls in rural New England also said final good-byes to school friends, despite the sometimes small distances that would separate them, as they moved on to a different stage in their lives.

10. New Girls, New Women

1. Ari Joel Perlmann, "Education and the Social Structure of an American City: Social Origins and Education Attainments in Providence, R.I., 1880–1925," Ph.D. diss. (Cambridge: Harvard University, 1980), 454.

2. Lucy C. Lillie, "Rolf House," *Harper's Young People* 6, no. 278 (1885): 262–64; Louisa May Alcott, *An Old-Fashioned Girl* (Boston: Roberts, 1870), 168–69.

3. On Boston, see Thomas Dublin, *Transforming Women's Work: New England Lives in the Industrial Revolution* (Ithaca, N.Y.: Cornell University Press, 1994), 23, 156. Married black women were ten times more likely to work than married women in either other group. Claudia Dale Goldin, *Understanding the Gender Gap: An Economic History of American Women* (New York: Oxford University Press, 1990), 119.

4. Ruth Ashmore, "Side Talks with Girls," *Ladies' Home Journal,* March, September 1890 [hereafter STG].

5. "Woman's Sphere," *Ladies' Home Journal,* November 1886; "The Girl Who Loves to Sing," *Ladies' Home Journal,* December 1891; Ashmore, STG, August 1885.

6. Joanne J. Meyerowitz, *Women Adrift: Independent Wage Earners in Chicago, 1880–1930,* Women in Culture and Society. (Chicago: University of Chicago Press, 1988), 6; Ashmore, STG, January 1897.

7. "Another gown": Ashmore, STG, March 1890; for more on selfless service see Ashmore, STG, February 1891, March 1892, December 1897, February 1898.

8. Thomas Dublin, *Transforming Women's Work: New England Lives in the Industrial Revolution* (Ithaca, N.Y.: Cornell University Press, 1994), 232; Goldin, *Understanding the Gender Gap,* 53, concurs that "young workers who lived at home in the late nine-

teenth century gave their earnings to their families, while those who boarded generally retained all." She concludes: "Young working daughters living with their parents . . . gained very little from their employment. Although there is only scant evidence concerning the material treatment of these workers within the home, social reformers of the day were probably correct in viewing their plight as they viewed child labor."

9. Reed Ueda, *Avenues to Adulthood: The Origins of the High School and Social Mobility in an American Suburb* (Cambridge: Cambridge University Press, 1987), 159; Goldin, *Understanding the Gender Gap*, 144.

10. Mary Custis deButts, ed., *Growing Up in the 1850s: The Journal of Agnes Lee* (Chapel Hill: University of North Carolina Press, 1984), 61; Newberry quoted in Harvey J. Graff, *Conflicting Paths: Growing Up in America* (Cambridge: Harvard University Press, 1995), 256.

11. Harriet E. Paine, *Chats with Girls on Self-Culture* (New York: Dodd, Mead, 1891), 75; Eleanor Hooper to Annie Ware Winsor, 19 May 1881, MC322, papers of Annie Ware Winsor Allen, 1884–1950, Schlesinger Library (Cambridge: Radcliffe Archives, Harvard University).

12. Mary Thomas [Lumpkin], diary, 27 Jun. 1873, Joseph Henry Lumpkin papers, Hargrett Rare Book and Manuscript Library (Athens: University of Georgia).

13. Florence C. Peck, diaries, 22 Feb., 29 Jul. 1901, Manuscripts and Archives Division (New York: New York Public Library, Astor, Lenox, and Tilden Foundations).

14. Barbara Sicherman, "Sense and Sensibility: A Case Study of Women's Reading in Late-Victorian America," in *Reading in America: Literature and Social History*, ed. Cathy N. Davidson (Baltimore: Johns Hopkins University Press, 1989), 212; Will S. Monroe, "Vocational Interests of Children," *Education* 18, no. 5 (1898): 259–64.

15. "Colloquy—Our Class Meeting, 1885," *North Granville Quarterly*, July 1866.

16. "Colloquy."

17. *Oak, Lily, and Ivy*, June 1886, March 1891.

18. Glenda Elizabeth Gilmore, *Gender and Jim Crow: Women and the Politics of White Supremacy in North Carolina, 1896–1920* (Chapel Hill: University of North Carolina Press, 1996), 42, cites the *Living-Stone*, June 1891. A female debater asked for gentle courtesies from men, "the attentive glance, the quiet cordial bow, and the sweet disposition." A male student sought similar qualities in women, hoping for "a modest, sweet-tempered girl—one you can depend on."

19. "Prophecies," *Oak, Lily, and Ivy*, June 1892.

20. The *Advance* also predicted more conventional women's lots for the girls of the class of 1891—artist, missionary, society belle, "matron in Old Ladies' Home," "governess for the president's children," and, more creatively "dog exhibitor." Boys might be president of Harvard, president of the Farmer's Alliance, explorer of the North Pole. "Prophecies," *High School Advance*, June 1891; "Prophecy," *Volunteer*, October 26, 1888.

21. "Prophecies," *High School Advance*, June 3, 1896, June 1897, June 1898; "Prophecy," *Oak, Lily, and Ivy*, June 1893.

22. "Thoughts," *High School Advance*, June 1895.

23. Reed Ueda, *Avenues to Adulthood: The Origins of the High School and Social Mobility in an American Suburb* (Cambridge: Cambridge University Press, 1987), 150; "Prophecies," *High School Advance,* May–June 1899.

24. *Oak, Lily, and Ivy,* April 1893. Goldin, *Understanding the Gender Gap,* 64. Goldin's statistics suggest that the highest-paid sectors for women were the clerical and sales sectors, with annual wages averaging $456–59 for women, compared with $677–943 for men. Women professionals averaged $366 annually, compared with an average male professional wage of $1,391. This low ratio suggests, of course, the evolution of teaching, along with librarianship and nursing, as underpaid "women's professions," as well as the tendency to underpay women for doing the same work as men.

25. *Statistics of the Graduates of the Milford High School, 1862–1926* (Milford, Mass.: Graduates' Association, Milford High School, 1926). Contrast the effort of the Milford High School Graduates' Association with that of the Somerville High School alumni association in 1902. For the directory celebrating Somerville's fiftieth anniversary, its alumni could find only a small and unrepresentative sample of the female graduates as a result of the problems of tracking women after marriage. Ueda, *Avenues to Adulthood,* 169.

26. Richard M. Bernard and Maris Vinovskis, "The Female School Teacher in Antebellum Massachusetts," *Journal of Social History* 20 (Spring 1977): 333.

27. The proportion of college graduates who remained single is a matter of debate among historians. Barbara Sicherman notes that "most historians claim that 60 (or even 70) percent of late-nineteenth-century alumnae never married." She suggests, however, that such a conclusion derives from a survey which predated the eventual marriage of some graduates, instead suggesting that by fifteen years following graduation, 51 percent of college alumnae had married. Barbara Sicherman, "College and Careers," 140–41.

28. It is possible, of course, that the 1926 Milford numbers reflect living children, not children born, which would account in part for this low number. Comparison with earlier figures for one class printed in the student newspaper, though, revealed in every case fewer children in the earlier statistics than emerged in the 1926 data among a still fertile population. Nancy Woloch, *Women and the American Experience: A Concise History* (New York: McGraw-Hill, 1996), 70; *Oak, Lily, and Ivy,* June 1895; Peter R. Uhlenberg, "A Study of Cohort Life Cycles: Cohorts of Native Born Massachusetts Women, 1830–1920," *Population Studies* [Great Britain] 23, no. 3 (1969): 413.

29. *Oak, Lily, and Ivy,* June 1895, June 1886.

30. This contrasts significantly with the rates of marriage for graduates of all-female Mount Holyoke who had worked; fewer than a third of that cohort who had worked ever married. Barbara Sicherman, "College and Careers: Historical Perspectives on the Lives and Work Patterns of Women College Graduates," in *Women and Higher Education in American History,* ed. John Mack Faragher and Florence Howe (New York: Norton, 1988), 140.

31. From the first Milford classes graduating during the Civil War until the end of the century, there is only slight drift in the statistical portrait of the graduate woman's

life course. The percentages of graduates who worked shifted from 62 percent in the 1860s and 1870s to 69 percent in the 1880s and 1890s; those who eventually married decreased from 68 percent in the 1860s and 1870s to 63 percent in the 1880s and 1890s. The size of graduates' families remained constant, with an average of 2.4 children for all decades.

32. Uhlenberg, "A Study of Cohort Life Cycles," 411, suggests another influence—the increasing percentage of second-generation daughters among the native-born population. This cohort was more likely than those of native-born parents never to marry, a pattern especially common among the Irish.

33. Linda W. Rosenzweig, *The Anchor of My Life: Middle-Class American Mothers and Daughters, 1880–1920,* History of Emotion Series (New York: New York University Press, 1993), 137, drew my attention to this British debate. B. A. Crackanthorpe, "The Revolt of the Daughters," *Nineteenth Century* 35 (January 1894): 24, 26; Alys Pearsal Smith, "A Reply from the Daughters," *Nineteenth Century* 35 (March 1894): 443.

34. Kathleen Cuffe, "A Reply from the Daughters," *Nineteenth Century* 35 (March 1894): 438–39.

35. M. E. Haweis, "Daughters and Mothers," *Nineteenth Century* 35 (March 1894): 435; Sarah Grand, "The New Aspect of the Woman Question," *North American Review* 158, no. 448 (March 1894): 270–76.

36. Ouida [Louise de la Ramée], "The New Woman," *North American Review* 158, no. 450 (May 1894): 610–19.

37. Frank Norris, "A Question of Ideals: The American Girl of 1896 as Seen by Wenzel and by Gibson," in *The Literary Criticism of Frank Norris,* ed. Donald Pizer (New York: Russell and Russell, 1976), 167.

38. Caroline Ticknor, "The Steel-Engraving Lady and the Gibson Girl," *Atlantic Monthly,* July 1901, 105–8.

39. Martha Banta, *Imaging American Women: Idea and Ideals in Cultural History* (New York: Columbia University Press, 1987), 88.

40. Ouida, "New Woman"; Granville Stanley Hall, *Adolescence: Its Psychology and Its Relations to Physiology, Anthropology, Sociology, Sex, Crime, Religion, and Education* (New York: D. Appleton 1904), 632. Meade is quoted in Sally Mitchell, *The New Girl: Girls' Culture in England, 1880–1915* (New York: Columbia University Press, 1995), 22.

41. Sarah Ellen Browne to mother, 21 May 1859, MC 232, Schlesinger Library (Cambridge: Radcliffe Institute, Harvard University).

42. Ernest N. Stevens, *A Brief History of Bridgton Academy, 1808–1957* (privately printed, 1958), 38. One might argue that Henry James's decision to share Linton's vocabulary in his retort represented linguistic innovation. When he defended American young women as "very pretty and, on the whole, very fresh-looking girls," he at first shaved off Linton's invidiousness; when he titled the piece, however, he referred to modern "women," and not girls. Henry James, "Modern Women," in *The Woman Question: Society and Literature in Britain and America, 1837–1883,* ed. and comp. Elizabeth K. Helsinger, Robin Ann Sheets, and William R. Veeder (Chicago: University of Chicago

Press, 1989). Louisa May Alcott, of course, qualified the term when she used it as the title for her 1872 novel *Old-Fashioned Girl.*

43. For example, see the *Granite Echo,* of Concord, New Hampshire, which advertised itself as "Devoted to the Interests of Boys and Girls of the Present Generation." *Granite Echo,* February 15, 1882. *Volunteer,* November 1895; "Side Talks with Girls and Boys," *Volunteer,* January 1896, 14.

44. Mitchell, *New Girl,* 23, 43; Joseph F. Kett, *Rites of Passage: Adolescence in America, 1790 to the Present* (New York: Basic, 1977), 137.

45. Carroll Smith-Rosenberg, "The New Woman as Androgyne: Social Disorder and Gender Crisis, 1870–1936," in *Disorderly Conduct: Visions of Gender in Victorian America* (New York: Knopf, 1985), 245; Sara M. Evans, *Born for Liberty: A History of Women in America* (New York: Free PressPress/CollierPress/Macmillan, 1989), 147, too emphasizes the genesis of New Womanhood in college education, noting that nearly half of all college women never married. "For a few years or for a lifetime these independent career women began to create a new life-style. Barred from traditional male fields, they moved into growing female professions such as teaching and nursing." In a recent book about women in public Boston, Sarah Deutsch, too, uses the term to refer to single, professional women, describing settlement house workers as "those for whom the term 'New Women' was invented." Sarah Deutsch, *Women and the City: Gender, Space, and Power in Boston, 1870–1940* (New York: Oxford University Press, 2000), 104. Lynn D. Gordon, "The Gibson Girl Goes to College: Popular Culture and Women's Higher Education in the Progressive Era, 1890–1920," *American Quarterly* 39 (1976): 211.

46. Glenda Elizabeth Gilmore, *Gender and Jim Crow: Women and the Politics of White Supremacy in North Carolina, 1896–1920* (Chapel Hill: University of North Carolina Press, 1996), 18, 31, 37.

47. Christine Stansell, *American Moderns: Bohemian New York and the Creation of a New Century* (New York: Metropolitan, 2000), 28, 29.

48. Beth Abney, "Mary Bryan Thomas ['Mamie'] Lumpkin," in *Dictionary of Georgia Biography,* ed. Kenneth Coleman and Charles Stephen Gurr (Athens: University of Georgia Press), 2: 644.

49. Sicherman, "Women and Higher Education," 141. Sicherman points out that the high correlation between celibacy and college attendance may have been misinterpreted in the past. Perhaps it was not college which led to celibacy, but women's single lives which encouraged them to attend college. Margaret Tileston's story supports that notion.

50. *Oak, Lily, and Ivy,* March 1889. Although this editorial is not signed, the copy in the Milford Room, Milford Public Library, has initials inked in indicating authorship.

51. *Concord Evening Monitor,* March 21, 1910. An article documenting Myra Lamprey's collapse in Madison Park contains this background information.

52. *Statistics of the Graduates of the Milford High School, 1862–1926* (Milford, Mass.: Graduates' Association, Milford High School, 1926), 68.

53. Thanks again to Paul Curran for bringing these materials to my attention. Mary Honor McDermott, "Gelosia," *Milford* (Massachusetts) *Daily News,* April 15, 1948.

54. Forty years after graduation Lancraft offered to do her best to welcome visiting classmates "even if the mayor and the civic band happen to be otherwise engaged." "Class of 1896 Yearbook," no. 24 (1937); "Ninety-Six Annual," March 1907; "Ninety-Six Biennial," December 1918, all Wellesley College Archives, Wellesley, Mass.

55. "Services Slated on Monday for Mrs. M. R. Thorpe," *New Haven Evening Register,* July 26, 1958. Clearly Mabel Lancraft was embarrassed about this discrepancy in age, for her birth date in her obituary is ten years later than her actual birth date. There is some ambiguity, too, about the date of her marriage to Malcolm R. Thorpe, who went on to be a paleontologist at Yale. Although the newspaper and a biographical entry on Thorpe concur on the 1917 date, city directories suggest that as late as 1919 the two were still unmarried, boarding separately. "Class of 1896 Yearbook," "Ninety-Six Biennial," Wellesley College Archives, Wellesley, Mass., 1909. Thanks to Lisa Cody for this work in the New Haven City Directories.

56. Henry Harrison Metcalf and Frances M. Abbott, *One Thousand New Hampshire Notables* (Concord, N.H.: Rumford, 1919), 87.

57. *Stranger,* June 1896.

58. Judith Rich Harris, *The Nurture Assumption: Why Children Turn Out the Way They Do* (New York: Free Press, 1998), 288.

59. "An Individual," *Youth's Companion* 53, no. 1 (January 1, 1880); Richard Wightman Fox, "The Culture of Liberal Protestant Progressivism, 1875–1925," *Journal of Interdisciplinary History* 23, no. 3 (Winter 1993): 639–60; Ashmore, STG, March 1891.

60. Rev. F. E. Clark, "A Young Woman's Rights," *Ladies' Home Journal,* November 1886; Frances Willard, *How to Win: A Book for Girls* (1888) 26–27, 33.

61. Elizabeth Cady Stanton, "The Solitude of Self," *Woman's Journal,* January 23, 1892; Elisabeth Griffith, *In Her Own Right: The Life of Elizabeth Cady Stanton* (New York: Oxford University Press, 1984), 203–4.

62. Eva Lovett, *The Making of a Girl* (New York: Taylor, 1902), 232–33; Eleanor Kirk [Eleanor Ames], *Where You Are: Talks with Girls* (1897), introduction; Sallie Joy White, "Letters to American Girls," in *American Women's Legal Status,* comp. and ed. George James Bayles (New York: Collier, 1905).

63. Hall, *Adolescence,* 589.

Bibliography

Manuscript Sources

[Allen], Annie Ware Winsor. Diaries. MC 322, papers of Annie Ware Winsor Allen, 1884–1950. Schlesinger Library. Cambridge: Radcliffe Institute, Harvard University.

Bartine, Mary. Diary. Ac. 2702. Gaston family papers. Special Collections and University Archives. New Brunswick, N.J.: Rutgers University Libraries.

[Boit], Georgia Mercer. Diary. A 99. Cabot family papers. Schlesinger Library. Cambridge: Radcliffe Institute, Harvard University.

Boit, Robert. Robert Apthorp Boit diaries. Boston: Massachusetts Historical Society.

Bosworth, Louise. Papers. 85-M71. Schlesinger Library. Cambridge: Radcliffe Institute, Harvard University.

Browne, Albert. Letters to daughter Nellie. MC 232. Schlesinger Library. Cambridge: Radcliffe Institute, Harvard University.

Browne, Eddie. Letters to father, Albert Browne. MC 232. Schlesinger Library. Cambridge: Radcliffe Institute, Harvard University.

Browne, Sarah. Diary. MC 232. Schlesinger Library. Cambridge: Radcliffe Institute, Harvard University.

Browne, Sarah Ellen [Nellie]. Letters to mother, Sarah, and father, Albert. MC 232. Schlesinger Library. Cambridge: Radcliffe Institute, Harvard University.

[Cabot], Ella Lyman. Diary. A-139, Ella Lyman Cabot papers, 1855–1934. Schlesinger Library. Cambridge: Radcliffe Institute, Harvard University.

———. "Scraps of Thoughts and Feelings." A-139, Ella Lyman Cabot papers, 1855–1934. Schlesinger Library. Cambridge: Radcliffe Institute, Harvard University.

[Cabot], Mary Boit. Diary. A 99, Cabot family papers. Schlesinger Library. Cambridge: Radcliffe Institute, Harvard University.

[Clark], Kate Upson. Diary. Kate Upson Clark papers, 1851–1935. Sophia Smith Collection. Northampton, Mass.: Smith College.

———. *My Reminiscences*. Kate Upson Clark papers, 1851–1935. Sophia Smith Collection. Northampton, Mass.: Smith College.

Cooke, Rowena. Diary. Columbus: Ohio Historical Society.

Crawford, Etta. "Girlhood Life in Portland, 1860–1876." Federal Writers' Project. Oral history. Works Progress Administration Records. Portland: Oregon Historical Society.

Dana, Elizabeth Ellery. Diaries. A-85, Dana family papers, 1822–1956. Schlesinger Library. Cambridge: Radcliffe Institute, Harvard University.

Dana, Sally. Letters to father, Richard Henry, Jr. A-85, Dana family papers, 1822–1956. Schlesinger Library. Cambridge: Radcliffe Institute, Harvard University.

———. Letters to mother, Sarah Watson. A-85, Dana family papers, 1822–1956. Schlesinger Library. Cambridge: Radcliffe Institute, Harvard University.

Dolloff, Myra Etta. Diary. Dolloff family papers. Tuck Library. Concord: New Hampshire Historical Society.

[Dummer], Ethel Sturges. "Street Scenes." Compositions. A-127, M-55, Ethel Sturges Dummer papers, 1766–1962. Schlesinger Library. Cambridge: Radcliffe Institute, Harvard University, 1883.

[Edsall], Margaret Harding Tileston. Diaries. MC 354. Schlesinger Library. Cambridge: Radcliffe Institute, Harvard University, 1878–1912.

Eliot, Emily Marshall. Journals. Samuel Eliot Morison papers. HUG(FP) 33.6. University Archives. Cambridge: Pusey Library, Harvard University.

[Franklin], Christine Ladd. Diary. Special Collections. Poughkeepsie, N.Y.: Vassar College Library.

Garrison, Agnes. Diary. Sophia Smith Collection. Northampton, Mass.: Smith College.

[Gilman], Charlotte Perkins. "Literary and Artistic Vurks of the Princess Charlotte." Schlesinger Library. Cambridge: Radcliffe Institute, Harvard University, 1870–71.

———. Journal. V. 8, 177. Schlesinger Library. Cambridge: Radcliffe Institute, Harvard University.

Godfrey, Annie Roberts. Diary. Courtesy of Jeanne Godfrey Stephenson.

Hamilton, Agnes. Diary. MC 278, M-24. Hamilton family papers. Schlesinger Library. Cambridge: Radcliffe Institute, Harvard University, 1886–87.

Hogan, Sister Wilfrida. "My Reminiscences." Written to Sister Lucida Savage, copied by Sister Helen Angela, January 11, 1949. Archives. St. Paul, Minn.: Sisters of St. Joseph of Carondelet, 1920–21.

Hooper, Eleanor. Letters to Annie Ware Winsor. MC 322, papers of Annie Ware Winsor Allen, 1884–1950. Schlesinger Library. Cambridge: Radcliffe Archives, Harvard University.

Hubbard, Almyra. Journal. Hosmer-Hubbard diaries. Joint Collection, University of Missouri–Western Historical Manuscript Collection. Columbia: Columbia and State Historical Society of Missouri Manuscripts.

[Laidlaw], Harriet Burton. Diary. M-133, Harriet Burton Laidlaw papers, 1851–1958. Schlesinger Library. Cambridge: Radcliffe Institute, Harvard University.

Lancraft, Ida Mabel. Diary. New Haven: New Haven Colony Historical Society.

[Lumpkin], Mary Thomas. Diary. Joseph Henry Lumpkin papers. Hargrett Rare Book and Manuscript Library. Athens: University of Georgia.

Marietta, Sister. "Reminiscences of School Days During War Years." Louisville, Ky.: Sisters of Charity of Nazareth Archives. 1894.

Moore, Martha Josephine. Diary, v. 2, no. 631. Frank Liddell Richardson papers. Southern Historical Collection. Chapel Hill: University of North Carolina Library.

Mordecai, Rachel. "Log of Educating a Younger Sister." VHS mss. 1, M9924a: 44–45. Richmond: Virginia Historical Society, 1816–1820.

[Morison], Emily Marshall Eliot. Diaries. A/M861, Emily Marshall Eliot Morison papers, 1874–1883. Schlesinger Library. Cambridge: Radcliffe Institute, Harvard University.

Morrissey, Elizabeth Mary. Diary. Rare Books Department. Boston: Boston Public Library.

Nichols, Elizabeth Fisher. Letters to Rose Nichols. A-170, papers of the Nichols-Shurtleff Family, 1780–1953. Schlesinger Library. Cambridge: Radcliffe Institute, Harvard University.

Nichols, Marian. Diary. A-170, papers of the Nichols-Shurtleff family, 1780–1953. Schlesinger Library. Cambridge: Radcliffe Institute, Harvard University.

Nichols, Rose. Letters to mother. A-170, papers of the Nichols-Shurtleff family, 1780–1953. Schlesinger Library. Cambridge: Radcliffe Institute, Harvard University.

Peck, Florence. Florence C. Peck diaries, 1898–1903. Manuscripts and Archives Division. New York: New York Public Library.

Regal, Ellen. Diary. Michigan Historical Collections. Ann Arbor: Bentley Historical Library.

Skinner, Mrs. J. Walter. "Baby Maud's Book." Tuck Library. Concord: New Hampshire Historical Society.

Stevens, Anna. Diary. Insert. Privately owned, 1895.

Tilton, Josephine. Diary. Archives. Friends Historical Library. Swarthmore, Penn.: Swarthmore College.

Wells, Lois. Diary. MC-39. Schlesinger Library. Cambridge: Radcliffe Institute, Harvard University.

Wendover, Jessie. Diaries. Ac. 2383, MC463. Special Collections and University Archives. New Brunswick, N.J.: Rutgers University Libraries.

Winsor, Ann Ware. Letters to daughter, Annie Winsor. MC 322, papers of Annie Ware Winsor Allen, 1884–1950. Schlesinger Library. Cambridge: Radcliffe Archives, Harvard University.

Winsor, Frederick. Letters to daughter, Annie Ware Winsor [Allen]. MC 322, papers of Annie Ware Winsor Allen, 1884–1950. Schlesinger Library. Cambridge: Radcliffe Archives, Harvard University.

Winsor, Mary. Letters to sister, Annie Ware Winsor [Allen]. MC 322, papers of Annie Ware Winsor Allen, 1884–1950. Schlesinger Library. Radcliffe Archives, Harvard University.

Newspapers

Amateur Sportsman. Concord, N.H. Concord Public Library.
Bombshell. Concord, N.H. Concord Public Library.
Comet. Concord, N.H.: Concord High School. Concord Public Library.
Concord Evening Monitor. Concord, N.H. Concord Public Library.
Granite Echo. Concord, N.H. Concord Public Library.
High School Advance. Salem, Mass.: Salem High School. Essex Institute, Salem.
High School Mite. Concord, N.H. Concord Public Library.
High School Monthly. Holyoke, Mass.: Holyoke High School. American Antiquarian Society, Worcester, Mass. (Hereafter AAS.)
High School News. Great Falls, N.H.: Great Falls High School. AAS.
High School Offering. Winchester, Mass.: Winchester High School. Winchester City Archives.
High School Recorder. Winchester, Mass.: Winchester High School. Winchester City Archives.
Milford Daily News. Milford, Mass. Milford Public Library.
Milford Gazette. Milford, Mass. Milford Public Library.
North Granville Quarterly. North Granville, N.Y.: North Granville Ladies' Seminary. AAS.
Oak, Lily, and Ivy. Milford, Mass.: Milford High School. Milford Public Library.
Radiator. Somerville, Mass.: Somerville High School. Somerville Public Library.
Sagamore. Brookline, Mass.: Brookline High School. Brookline Public Library.
Stranger. North Bridgton, Maine: Bridgton Academy. Bridgton Academy Archives.
Union Paper. Concord, N.H.: Concord High School. Concord Public Library.
Volunteer. Concord, N.H.: Concord High School. Concord Public Library.

Index

Page numbers in italics denote illustrations.

Proletarianization of domestic labor, 16

Prostitutes: in domestic service, 27; distinguished from "girl of the period," 291

Providence, R. I. school attendance. *See* School enrollment

Puberty. *See* Health; Menarche

Public space, 4; girls' freedom in, 280–82; sense of danger in, 282–83. *See also* Freedom, girls'

Rabinowitz, Richard, 98, 100

Reading, *66, 77, 81;* addiction to novels, 82, 86; advice literature on, 60–61; attachment to literary figures, 70; cautions against sensational fiction, 61, 65, 418n11; as constructing ideology, 84; encouragement of competing selves, 88; family circles, 62–64; fascination with novels causing shame, 85, 421–22n56; of history praiseworthy, 71; parental oversight, 64–68, 413–14n12; as personal community, 68–70, 86; as plastic medium, 71; as "playful regression," 84; producing self grounded in taste, 91; as quest for the beautiful, 74–75; responses to male heroes, 80–82; scholarly interpretations of, 84, 421n52; as secret life, 75–76; as support in conflicts with parents, 87–88; time spent in, 39; trans-Atlantic culture of, 60

Recitation, 193, 199, 438n55. *See also* Competition; Exhibitions, public

Refinement, quest for: encouraged education of daughters, 12, 170–71, *187*

Religious quest, 145; challenged by moralists, 152; contributing to romantic self, 149, 152, *153;* culminating in professing faith, 148; emotional protocols, 98, 100. *See also*

Confirmation, religious; Conversion experience

Repplier, Agnes, 23, 178, 189

"Reproduction of mothering," 103

"Republican motherhood," 20

Resolutions, recorded in diaries, 48–50, 97, 98, 416n34

Restelle, Madam, 428

Rites of passage, 140, 317, 341, 357, 367. *See also* Coming out; Graduation, high school

Room of one's own, 95–98, 422n7, 423n10

Rothman, Ellen, 53

Rousseau, Jean-Jacques: *Confessions,* 43

Rury, John, 173, 206

Ryan, Mary, 3

St. Nicholas, 26, 41, 44, 45, 58, *77, 81, 122, 187;* history of, 68; Mary Mapes Dodge's prospectus for, 80; role in fostering youth culture, 69, passim

Salem High School: coeducation in, 206–9; graduation of Class of *1885,* 321–26

—*Advance:* support for military drill, 239–40; woman's rights prophecies, 381, 382

Sanborn School, 225

Sargent, John Singer: "The Daughters of Edward D. Boit," *124*

School enrollment, 170; and family status, 171; low "opportunity cost" for girls, 28; in Providence, R.I., 4, 94, 223, 369, 434n2; ratio of girls to boys, 254

Schools. *See* Academies; Coeducation; Common schools; Convent schools; Girls' schools; High schools

"School skills," 203

"School spirit": centered around boys' sports, 253